A HISTORY OF ECONOMIC IDEAS

A HISTORY OF ECONOMIC IDEAS

BY

EDMUND WHITTAKER

LONGMANS, GREEN AND CO.

NEW YORK · LONDON · TORONTO

LONGMANS, GREEN AND CO., INC.
55 FIFTH AVENUE, NEW YORK 3

LONGMANS, GREEN AND CO. LTD.
6 & 7 CLIFFORD STREET, LONDON W. 1

LONGMANS, GREEN AND CO.
215 VICTORIA STREET, TORONTO 1

WHITTAKER

A HISTORY OF ECONOMIC IDEAS

First edition June 1940
Reprinted August 1943
November 1946, October 1947
June 1950

PRINTED IN THE UNITED STATES OF AMERICA

To

Kitty, Roger, Margaret, and Felicity
in inadequate apology
for a lengthy period of seclusion
with a typewriter

PREFACE

There are two lines of approach to the history of economic thought, which may be called chronological and ideological respectively. In the former, teacher and students work together along the broad path of historical evolution, considering the various writers and schools of thought as they occur one after the other in historical sequence. This method has some merit, in that the ideas of a period can be looked upon as a whole and related to their environment. On the other hand, it has the disadvantage that every period possesses a variety of ideas, often conflicting with one another and only understandable in the light of their own development. A course of study founded on the principle of tracing the evolution of ideas helps to meet this situation. This plan has the further advantage that most students, who join classes in the history of economic thought, do so to get the background that is necessary to understand contemporary theories. Past ideas on wealth or value, related to the environment in which they were propounded and to the theories that are significant at the present time, are of interest to twentieth century students of these subjects, rather than the ideas of Adam Smith or the British Classical School *per se*. Probably the majority of teachers compromise in some way between the chronological and the ideological lines of approach ; but experimentation has convinced the writer that it is desirable that there should be more emphasis on the evolution of leading ideas, and less on particular schools and individuals, than is provided by most of the textbooks available in the field. The work here offered bears the imprint of this belief.

Some sections of the book go beyond what are often regarded as the limits of economics. Certain economists, notably members of the German Historical School and the American Institutionalists, have taken the view that society can be understood only as a whole, from which follows the conclusion that it must be studied as a whole. Without going so far as to adopt this attitude, it is apparent that students of economics should have some acquaintance with thought in allied fields, such as ethics, political science, and psychology. How can men's actions be examined intelligently if the objectives that lie behind them are unknown ? As an instance, economists of the Classical and Neo-Classical Schools, accepting the maximization of individual wealth as a social objective, have criticized the theories of the medieval Canonists, the Mercantilists of the sixteenth and seventeenth centuries, and the economic nationalists of more recent times. The criticism has been in large measure inapplicable. The Canonists did not aim at the maximization of individual wealth but at the attainment of God's kingdom, and it was logical enough for them to advise men to give away wealth rather than to seek it. The professed objective of the Mercantilists — like that of the later economic nationalists—was a State good which was quite different from individual riches, so their arguments were not disproved when it was shown that Mercantilism did not make individuals rich. In view of such facts, economists must take the trouble to ascertain something of human objectives. A science of means to attain objectives (as economics is defined by one of its leading exponents) is apt to be unintelligible unless the ends themselves are recognized.

The economist must have some acquaintance with men's reactions to their wants, in the form of willingness to strive for their attainment, that is, he must know something of human incentives. Wage theory, especially, is bound up closely with this problem. In the division of studies that is now common, consideration of ends or objectives is regarded as being within the province of ethics, that of incentives as part of psychology. If only for the practical reason that an intimate knowledge of all phases of human affairs cannot be compressed within the compass of a single mind, the specialist can hope for no more than a working knowledge of such subjects as bear upon his specialty. All that is aimed at, in the excursions taken in this book outside what is usually regarded as the field of economics, is the provision of this minimum of knowledge without which the economist cannot understand his own subject properly. The teacher of economics may reject the claim that economics should be made a science of life but he owes it to his students to present material that will enable them to link up economics with other phases of life.

A generation or two ago, when it seemed that economic individualism, almost unalloyed, had come to stay, there was little more than an antiquarian interest in the ideas of mercantile times, the middle ages, and the ancient world. It seemed optional, therefore, at what stage the historian of thought began his study. But the prominent role played by authoritarian control and the attention paid to such concepts as reasonable value in our own day give practical significance to the old ideas. Even primitive life is found interesting by contemporary investigators of economic incentives. Although at some points the treatment is necessarily sketchy, an endeavor is made to describe the evolution of ideas from the beginning to the present, giving attention to certain developments that have significance in the world in which we live. This was impossible when some of the older texts on the history of economic thought were written. As the ideas and interests of men change, so does the spirit with which they look back upon the thought of their predecessors.

Some comment is necessary on the choice of material. It has been the experience of the author and of most other teachers with whom the matter has been discussed that English-speaking students make little use of works printed in foreign languages. To encourage those who study this book to read more fully the historic works discussed in it, these have been selected as far as possible so as to be available in English, either at first hand or in translations. This explains some of the choices made, such as the emphasis placed on Jevons, as compared with Menger and Walras. As the book is intended for English-speaking students, no apology is needed for devoting special attention to ideas of importance to them.

The reader is advised to examine the summaries, given at the end of the various chapters, before perusing the more detailed material that appears in the chapters themselves. It is strongly recommended, also, that as far as time permits the more important writers treated should be studied directly. It is not enough to discover from others what was said by such authorities as Plato and Ricardo. In this book quotations have been given freely for the purpose of allowing the leaders of economic thought to tell their own stories, but some reference should be made to the original works. The footnotes are intended as guides for this purpose. Some of the more useful collateral readings are listed in the bibliography that appears at the end of the volume.

In studying the originals, the reader should bear in mind the conditions of the times in which they appeared. For those who come to economics without having made a preliminary study of social history, the first chapter of the book will help to provide the necessary background. More is furnished in later sections, as need arises. It cannot be overemphasized that ideas and environment react upon each other. What men think is explained by what they do, and *vice versa.* Moreover, the works of leading writers do not always represent the popular thought of the times in which they appear. Written opinions may be "beyond their time," forecasting what the masses of people think later, or, on the other hand, they may defend lost causes. Writers and men of action are often different personages and, even when they are not, what is written may not coincide with what is done. For instance, commonly wealth was spoken of in unfavorable terms in medieval literature. Men were counseled to seek salvation rather than riches; yet historical records present evidence that numerous steps were taken away from this straight and narrow path. The fact must be faced, too, that many early writers were practical philosophers, concerned with offering advice on human conduct more than with describing the social system in which they lived. Advice cannot be expected to coincide with conduct, since, if the latter were all that observers desired, there would be no reason for offering advice. Both writings and actions must be examined, therefore, if thought is to be understood. The robber baron in his castle and Saint Thomas Aquinas in his cloister were contemporaries and each in his way was typical of the times, yet the gap between their viewpoints was immense.

Critics will discover numerous sins of omission. The intention has been, not to mention every individual who has contributed something of importance, but to select by criteria of usefulness and accessibility a sufficient number of writings to illustrate the principal developments of thought. A broad picture has been aimed at, rather than an attempt made to pursue economic theory into all its multitudinous ramifications. There has been no endeavor to follow the precedent set by Procrustes, who is said to have performed surgical operations on his visitors to fit them into a standard-sized bed, racking them out or chopping off their feet as the case might require. As a result, the chapters and sections are of somewhat unequal length. It is hoped, however, that the sub-divisions are adequate to prevent this from being a defect in teaching. The length of treatment is not always proportionate to the importance of the matter considered, but it has been thought preferable to incur the risk of criticism on this score rather than to make the discussion unnecessarily lengthy or illucidly condensed. With its shortcomings, the book is offered in the hope that it may prove of service to teachers and students in its field.

Grateful acknowledgments are made of assistance received from Dr. E. L. Bogart, Editor of Longmans' Economics Series, in his editorial capacity and otherwise; to Dr. M. H. Hunter, Head of the Department of Economics in the University of Illinois, who read portions of the material; to Dr. Simon Litman, Professor of Economics in the University of Illinois, who read the entire manuscript; to Dr. D. P. Locklin, Associate Professor of Economics in the University of Illinois, who read the section of Chapter IX dealing with regulated prices; and to Dr. Glenn R. Morrow, Professor of Philosophy in the University of Pennsylvania, who read the first four chapters. All made valuable suggestions, many of which have been incorporated in the book.

Appreciation is expressed to the publishers who permitted the quotation of passages from works of which they hold the copyrights and whose names are indicated in footnotes. Without their co-operation, it would have been impossible to complete the book on the lines selected.

Much is due to co-workers in three continents, but the main indebtedness is to the stream of students who have provided the raw material for experiments in teaching methods and whose share in class discussions and many helpful comments have contributed greatly to what this book contains.

E. W.

CONTENTS

A HISTORY OF ECONOMIC IDEAS

CHAPTER I

SOCIAL EVOLUTION AND SOCIAL THOUGHT

INTRODUCTION

If economic thought is to be understood, it must be related to its environment. One great teacher advanced the theory that the progress of human ideas governs the evolution of social institutions. Another maintained the opposite principle, that thought is itself explained by the social — and especially the economic — environment. Without supporting either of these rather extreme statements, we may say that there is an obvious connection between ideas and the conditions under which men live. Throughout this book the relationship between the two is emphasized. Thoughts, too, evolve together. What men think about economic affairs is influenced by their ideas on ethics and politics. This chapter is intended to furnish a background of social history and social thought into which the more detailed studies that succeed it can be fitted.

Theories of Social Development

An immense amount of information is available on the evolution of human society, yet serious difficulties attend historical study. As inquiries are carried back into the past, evidence becomes scantier and less reliable. On the other hand, where information is plentiful, often difficulty is experienced in reducing it to something which can be comprehended. Men cannot assimilate an infinite quantity of detail, and university students and teachers are no exception to this rule. As a result, there is pressure to reduce history to broad outlines. Besides serving this pedagogical purpose, generalizations — if regarded as tentative — are useful in the early stages of historical research, forming pathways into unexplored material. But interpretations vary and different aspects of social development are emphasized, so that a remarkable diversity of historical outlines has appeared.

One of the best-known summaries of social history is that of Friedrich List (1789–1846), a German economist, whose writings are discussed later in this book. In his *Das nationale System der politischen Oekonomie* (Stuttgart 1841),[1] List spoke of five stages of development, through which "As respects their economy, nations have to pass." These were (1) a barbarian or hunting stage, which characterized primitive society, (2) pastoral civilization of the type described in the early books of the Bible, (3) self-sufficing agriculture, such as prevailed over much

[1] Translated by S. S. Lloyd, as *The National System of Political Economy*, London 1885, reprinted 1922.

of Europe down to modern times and existed among the early settlers in America, (4) agriculture, along with manufactures for local consumption, as in Germany and the eastern United States a century ago, and (5) agriculture, together with manufactures for world trade, that is, the condition of Britain in List's time and of the United States of America in the twentieth century. Another German economist, Bruno Hildebrand (1812–1878), in *Die Nationalökonomie der Gegenwart und Zukunft* (Frankfort 1848), emphasized forms of exchange. He distinguished three stages, characterized by barter, money, and credit, respectively. L. H. Morgan (1818–1881), an American lawyer, who devoted considerable attention to the study of the customs of the North American Indians, in his book, *Ancient Society* (New York 1877), described a series of periods based on cultural advances. Such developments as the beginning of articulate speech, the use of fire, the inventions of the bow and arrow and of pottery, the domestication of animals, the smelting of iron, and the discovery of the phonetic alphabet, marked his stages. The German economist, Karl Bücher (1847–1930), in *Die Entstehung der Volkswirtschaft* (Tübingen 1893),[2] built up a series of stages round the economic unit, that is, the social group knit together by economic relationships. First came the independent *domestic economy*, which was individualistic at the beginning, next the *town economy*, typical of the middle ages, and finally the *national economy* of modern times.

The general attitude that was responsible for these theories receives attention in Chapter XVI, where the scope and method of economic study are discussed. For the present, it is sufficient to say that the compression of history into a simple series of stages is useful pedagogically but is open to the objection that, if it is taken too literally, it gives an unreal picture of social change—unreal because the complexities that characterize the actual course of human evolution are obscured. Social history is much less simple than some of the architects of stage-systems have appeared to imply. Developments that have assumed great importance in one area have been omitted elsewhere. Thus, under the influence of white settlers, the pastoral Bantu people of parts of southern Africa have jumped in a generation or two from primitive barbarianism into modern industrial capitalism. Again, at times, the movement has appeared retrogressive, as when the highly developed civilization of the Roman Empire gave place to the barbarian kingdoms of the middle ages. As was pointed out by the English legal historian, F. W. Maitland (1850–1906),

> Even had our anthropologists at their command materials that would justify them in prescribing a normal programme for the human race and in decreeing that every independent portion of mankind must, if it is to move at all, move

[2] Translated by S. M. Wickett, as *Industrial Evolution*, New York 1901.

through one fated series of stages which may be designated as Stage *A*, Stage *B*, Stage *C* and so forth, we still should have to face the fact that the rapidly progressive groups have been just those which have not been independent, which have not worked out their own salvation, but have appropriated alien ideas and have thus been enabled, for anything that we can tell, to leap from Stage *A* to Stage *X* without passing through any intermediate stages. Our Anglo-Saxon ancestors did not arrive at the alphabet, or at the Nicene Creed, by traversing a long series of 'stages'; they leapt to the one and to the other.[3]

Cause and Effect in Social Evolution

At the beginning of the chapter mention was made of a conflict of views on the relationship between human thought and the social environment. The theories referred to were those advanced by G. W. F. Hegel (1770–1831) and Karl Marx (1818–1883), respectively. Hegel was the leading German teacher of philosophy of his generation and one of the outstanding thinkers of all time. He regarded evolution as progress towards an ideal. Thought advanced by the logical process of thesis, antithesis, and synthesis, he said. An argument was presented (the thesis). It was criticized and opposed (the antithesis). From the argument and criticism, together, there emerged a synthesis, which in turn might form the basis of a new thesis. Thus were human ideas advanced towards their goal in the absolute or final truth. Hegel believed that the course of history was a reflection of the advancement of the mind towards finality. Changes in art and religion, for example, were but outward manifestations of the continued progress of inner knowledge. From the development of ideas came the changing facts of human life:

> the History of the World, with all the changing scenes which its annals present, is this process of development and the realization of Spirit. . .[4]

> history is the embodiment of spirit in the form of events. . .[5]

Hegel developed this idea in a series of works and his views have had great influence, both directly and indirectly.

After Hegel, Marx offered the inevitable criticism. Marx had intended to engage in university teaching, but soon developed radical views, which in the Germany of his days made academic work impracticable, so he became a political journalist, was exiled, and finally emerged as one of the leading socialists of the nineteenth century. In his *Misère de la philosophie* (Brussels 1847)[6] and later writings, Marx challenged

[3] *Domesday Book and Beyond*, Cambridge 1897, reprinted 1921, p. 345. Quoted by permission of the Cambridge University Press.

[4] Hegel's *Lectures on the Philosophy of History*, translated by J. Sibree, London 1858, p. 477. Quoted by permission of G. Bell & Sons, Ltd. The lectures were first published in Berlin in 1837.

[5] Hegel's *Philosophy of Right*, translated by S. W. Dyde, London 1896, p. 343. Quoted by permission of G. Bell & Sons, Ltd. First published in Berlin in 1821.

[6] Translated by H. Quelch as *Poverty of Philosophy*, Chicago 1910.

the Hegelian theory of social evolution. Instead, he offered a materialistic interpretation of history. Social institutions were not a reflection of changes in the human mind, Marx argued. Thoughts were explained by facts, not the opposite way round. Marx's own statement of the difference in *Das Kapital*[7] is worth quoting:

My dialectic method is not only different from the Hegelian, but is its direct opposite. To Hegel, the life-process of the human brain, *i.e.*, the process of thinking, which, under the name of "the Idea," he even transforms into an independent subject, is the demiurgos [*i.e.*, creator] of the real world, and the real world is only the external, phenomenal form of "the Idea." With me, on the contrary, the ideal [idea] is nothing else than the material world reflected by the human mind, and translated into forms of thought.[8]

On the subject of the materialistic interpretation of history, Marx's friend and collaborator, Friedrich Engels (1820–1895), wrote as follows in *Herrn Eugen Dührings Umwälzung der Wissenschaft* (Leipzig 1878, 5th edition, Stuttgart 1904):

The materialist conception of history starts from the principle that production, and with production the exchange of its products, is the basis of every social order; that in every society which has appeared in history the distribution of the products, and with it the division of society into classes or estates, is determined by what is produced and how it is produced, and how the product is exchanged. According to this conception, the ultimate causes of all social changes and political revolutions are to be sought, not in the minds of men, in their increasing insight into eternal truth and justice, but in changes in the mode of production and exchange; they are to be sought not in the *philosophy* but in the *economics* of the epoch concerned. The growing realisation that existing social institutions are irrational and unjust, that reason has become nonsense and good deeds a scourge, is only a sign that changes have been taking place quietly in the methods of production and forms of exchange with which the social order, adapted to previous economic conditions, is no longer in accord. This also involves that the means through which the abuses that have been revealed can be got rid of must likewise be present, in more or less developed form, in the altered conditions of production. These means are not to be *invented* by the mind, but *discovered* by means of the mind in the existing facts of production.[9]

[7] This work appeared in three volumes, the first in 1867 during the lifetime of its author. Vols. 2 and 3 were edited by Engels from the manuscript of Marx and published in 1885 and 1894, respectively. All three have been translated under the title *Capital* – vol. 1 by S. Moore and E. Aveling (2 vols., London 1886) and by E. and C. Paul (London 1928), vols. 2 and 3 by E. Untermann (2 vols., Chicago 1909).

[8] *Capital*, vol. 1 (Moore and Aveling translation). The passage appears in the author's preface to the 2nd ed. Quoted by permission of George Allen & Unwin Ltd. The word "creator" has been inserted in explanation, square brackets being used to indicate insertions in passages quoted throughout this book.

[9] Translated by E. Burns as *Herr Eugen Dühring's Revolution in Science (Anti-Dühring)*, New York n. d., p. 300. Quoted by permission of International Publishers Co., Inc., and Lawrence and Wishart Ltd.

From this viewpoint, evolution resembled a logical process. Institutions that had come out of the past (the thesis) reacted with the altered environment they met in the present (the antithesis), giving rise (as a synthesis) to a new social structure. This, in its turn, became the starting point for further development, until finality was reached. Hegel's ideal, or final truth, in political affairs was an autocratic monarchy on the Prussian model, and this was one of the reasons why his views were accepted so readily by the German officialdom of his day. Marx's ideal, on the other hand, was a classless and communist State. Marx admitted that in some cases—as in early societies—changes might be caused by natural phenomena, such as soil exhaustion. But he thought that the method of economic production was the major factor in more complex societies. When the form of production changed, existing social arrangements were out-moded and the class that was in a position to gain by removing them became revolutionary, aiming at the acquisition of political power for the purpose of bringing about the change. It was true that revolutionary groups used catchwords—such as the *liberty, equality, and fraternity,* of the French Revolution—but, according to Marx, this was merely a disguise and did not alter the essentially economic character of the revolt. Viewed in this light, the whole of history was a record of class struggles, which, in the opinion of Marx, would cease only when the proletarians, in a final battle with the capitalists, seized the reins of power and established a classless State.

Two objections can be raised against the theories of both Hegel and Marx. (1) It must be said that the concept of history as a relentless movement toward a definite point (*e.g.*, the Hegelian or the Marxian ideal State) has been abandoned by modern historians and social theorists. Many of the latter regard social progress as something resembling the biological evolution described by Darwin. According to this view, ideas and social arrangements are inherited from the past. They are molded in the light of the environment of the present. The forms and thoughts that survive, or arise from, this molding process represent the heritage which passes on to the future. What that future will be, no man can tell. (2) The principle of one-sided causal relationship between thoughts and facts is questionable. Few people doubt that there is a close association between social structure and the ideas of men, but correlations prove nothing respecting causal relationships. Investigation may bring to light a virtually complete coincidence in the occurrence of two factors, yet nothing can be concluded as to which is cause and which effect. Each may be a cause, to some extent. Both, indeed, may result from the operation of some other factor. This is an elementary principle of logic. It is accepted in statistics and has equal applicability to historical research. Against a purely economic interpretation of history, it must be pointed out that individuals do not pursue only economic ends. Why, then, should it be postulated that classes do so? Even if it be true that men and women of today are motivated mainly by economic incentives, can it be assumed that this was true of the past and will be so in the future? Marx was not alone in formulating the concept that history is influenced by material factors. The English historian, H. T. Buckle (1821–1862), put forward what was essentially the same idea, in his *History of Civilisation in England* (2 vols., London 1857–1861). Undoubtedly, Marx and Buckle did a good deal to teach historians the importance of giving attention to the physical and economic environment,[10] but to imply that this is the only consideration of significance is now accepted as mistaken. History is regarded as a complex of economic and other factors. Thus, it is not thought that the development of American civilization can be interpreted purely in terms of the cultural heritage that came to this country in ships. Nor is it to be explained solely by the environment of North America. Both these factors—and others—have contributed to the result.

This brief criticism of some of the most influential theories of social history should provide the skepticism which is a necessary part of the equipment of the scientific inquirer. The remainder of the chapter claims to do no more than give an account of those broad outlines of social history on which there is a measure of agreement, except where, as in the prehistoric period, conflicting explanations have been important enough to warrant attention.

Primitive Life

A serious impediment to the study of life and thought in the beginnings of human evolution is the paucity of direct evidence. In the absence of contemporary written accounts, something can be done with such materials as broken tools and kitchen utensils found in domestic refuse heaps left behind by the inhabitants of long ago, pictures scratched on rock surfaces, and even the traditions that have come down to later periods. Fortunately, however, these data have been supplemented by the study of primitive peoples existing at the present time, in regions relatively unaffected by civilization. Much of the older material of this latter type has been derived from the observations of explorers, missionaries, and settlers—people for the most part untrained in the social sciences and likely to misinterpret what they saw. But in recent years a number of more reliable studies have been made. The accounts of the Ceylon Veddas by C. G. and B. Z. Seligman,[11] of the inhabitants of the Andaman Islands in the Indian Ocean by A. R. Brown,[12] and of the Tro-

[10] See Chapter XVI, however, for references to earlier writers who dealt with this point, notably Montesquieu.

[11] C. G. and B. Z. Seligman, *The Veddas,* Cambridge 1911.

[12] A. R. Brown, *The Andaman Islanders,* Cambridge 1922.

briand Islanders of the Melanesian Archipelago in the western Pacific by B. Malinowski,[13] are outstanding examples.

It should be borne in mind, however, that results obtained from the study of twentieth century savages possess only limited validity when used to interpret the distant past of the European peoples. It is one matter to discover what existing primitive folk think and do, and quite another to conclude that the ancestors of the white people of present-day Europe and America behaved similarly. If the idea of a standard pattern of social history—based on sets of stages like those of Morgan and Bücher—could be accepted, little hesitation need be felt in projecting the results of the study of such people as the Andaman Islanders into prehistoric European society. But, as has been mentioned, the stage idea has to be regarded with skepticism. This is not to say that research among twentieth century savages is valueless for the purpose of arriving at an understanding of the distant past of Europe. On the contrary, it may be very suggestive, but care is required in using it.

The Theory of Primitive Individualism

One of the commonest views concerning primitive life has been that its basis was individualistic. Some of the philosophers of ancient Greece and Rome, as well as the *social contract* theorists of later times, accepted this view. It was surmised that early men and women lived solitary lives, for the most part. They associated with one another from time to time, it was thought, when powerful animals had to be attacked or the promptings of sex urged male and female to unite; but such attachments were temporary and isolation was the general rule. Independence meant weakness and strife, however, so that life was hazardous. With the passage of time men sought an escape from this precarious existence, by agreeing to combine in a permanent association or society. The famous poem, *De rerum natura* (On the nature of things), by the Roman, Lucretius (c. 98–55 B.C.), illustrates this view. Describing the course of social evolution in the fourth book of the poem, Lucretius remarked, in regard to men in the early, non-social, period:

> Not yet did they know how to work things with fire, nor to use skins and to clothe themselves in the strippings of beasts; but they dwelt in the woods and forests and mountain caves, and hid their rough bodies in the underwoods when they had to escape the beating of wind and rain. They could not look to the common good, they knew not how to govern their intercourse by custom and law. Whatever prize fortune gave to each, that he carried off, every man taught to live and be strong for himself at his own will.[14]

[13] B. Malinowski, *Argonauts of the Western Pacific,* London 1922, reprinted 1932.

[14] *De rerum natura,* translated by W. H. D. Rouse, London 1924, 3rd ed. 1937, pp. 407-409. Quoted by permission of the Harvard University Press, and William Heinemann, Ltd. Lucretius observed, somewhat cynically, that, notwithstanding the hard-

The human race was continued, Lucretius said, not by any system of continuous marriage, but by promiscuous sex contacts. Thomas Hobbes (1588–1679), English political philosopher and a leading advocate of the social contract theory, gave a similar description of early life. Hobbes said that primitive men lived in a state of war with each other, every man's hand being against his fellow, and security non-existent. Civilization was impossible under such conditions:

> there is no place for industry; because the fruit thereof is uncertain: and consequently no culture of the earth; no navigation, nor use of the commodities that may be imported by sea; no commodious building; no instruments of moving, and removing, such things as require much force; no knowledge of the face of the earth; no account of time; no arts; no letters; no society; and which is worst of all, continual fear, and danger of violent death; and the life of man, solitary, poor, nasty, brutish, and short.[15]

As late as the close of the nineteenth century, the general theory that the first stage of human evolution was solitary found support from Karl Bücher, who declared in his book on economic evolution,

> Let us strike out of the life of the Bushman or of the Veddah the use of fire, and bow and arrow, and nothing remains but a life made up of the individual search for food. Each individual has to rely entirely upon himself for his sustenance. Naked and unarmed he roams with his fellows, like certain species of wild animals, through a limited stretch of territory, and uses his feet for holding and climbing as dexterously as he uses his hands. All, male and female, devour raw what they catch with their hands or dig out of the ground with their nails: smaller animals, roots, and fruits. Now they unite into little bands or larger herds; now they separate again, according to the richness of the pasturage or hunting-ground. But these unions do not develop into communities, nor do they lighten the existence of the individual. . . . As every child must have his name, we will call this the *stage of individual search for food.*[16]

Recent research among primitive people, however, challenges this view. Not independence but social attachments are emphasized. Thus,

---

ships of their lives, primitive men had a hold on life which was as secure as that of their successors in his own time. True, early men ran the risk of being torn to pieces by animals, which he described in harrowing terms, but they had compensations:

> one day did not send to destruction many thousands of men in the battlefield, then ships and mariners were not dashed on the rocks by the turbulent billows of the sea. . . The wicked art of navigation then lay hidden and obscure. In those days again, it was lack of food that drove fainting bodies to death; now contrariwise it is the abundance that overwhelms them. In those days men often unwittingly poured poison for themselves, now more skilfully taught they give poison to others. *Ibid.*, pp. 411-413.

[15] Thomas Hobbes, *Leviathan,* 1651, in *The English Works of Thomas Hobbes,* ed. W. Molesworth, 11 vols., vol. 3, London 1839, p. 113.

[16] *Industrial Evolution*, pp. 26-27. Quoted by permission of Henry Holt and Company, Inc.

Malinowski, who has given the matter considerable attention, concludes a description of the task of canoe-building on the Trobriand Islands with the following remarks:

We saw also that the work of felling, of scooping, of decorating, would in some cases be performed by various men, or it might be performed by one only. Certainly the minute tasks of lashing, caulking and painting, as well as sail-making, were done by communal labour as opposed to individual. And all these different tasks were directed towards one aim: the providing the chief or headman with the title of ownership of a canoe, and his whole community with its use.

It is clear that this differentiation of tasks, co-ordinated to a general purpose, requires a well developed social apparatus to back it up, and that, on the other hand, this social mechanism must be associated and permeated with economic elements. There must be a chief, regarded as representative of a group; he must have certain formal rights and privileges, and a certain amount of authority, and also he must dispose of part of the wealth of the community. There must also be a man or men with knowledge sufficient to direct and co-ordinate the technical operations. All this is obvious. But it must be clearly set forth that the real force which binds all the people and ties them down in their tasks is obedience to custom, to tradition.

Every man knows what is expected from him, in virtue of his position, and he does it, whether it means the obtaining of a privilege, the performance of a task, or the acquiescence in a *status quo*. He knows that it always has been thus, and thus it is all around him, and thus it always must remain. The chief's authority, his privileges, the customary give and take which exist between him and the community, all that is merely, so to speak, the mechanism through which the force of tradition acts. For there is no organised physical means by which those in authority could enforce their will in a case like this. Order is kept by direct force of everybody's adhesion to custom, rules and laws, by the same psychological influences which in our society prevent a man of the world doing something which is not "the right thing." The expression "might is right" would certainly not apply to Trobriand society. "Tradition is right, and what is right *has* might" – this rather is the rule governing the social forces in Boyowa, and I dare say in almost all native communities at this stage of culture.[17]

Malinowski mentions that communal labor is employed, not only in canoe-building, but in the construction of living-huts and storehouses, in the transportation of goods, especially at harvest, in fishing, gardening, etc., with social custom always the motivating factor. Much the same situation is referred to by Firth, in his work on the economic system of the Maori.[18] Even the Andaman Islanders, commonly regarded as among the most primitive races extant, are similarly described. According to A. R. Brown, the men of the Andamans hunt in parties of two to

[17] *Argonauts of the Western Pacific*, pp. 158-159. Quoted by permission of George Routledge & Sons Ltd. and E. P. Dutton & Co., Inc.

[18] R. Firth, *Primitive Economics of the New Zealand Maori*, London 1929.

five, while the women collect vegetable foods and firewood. In some instances, families join in erecting large huts. Canoes are made by a number of men who work together. As to the initiation ceremonies which accompany accession to the adult state in the Andaman Islands, as elsewhere among primitive people, Brown expressed the following view :

the growing boy or girl is made to feel very strongly the importance of conforming to the customs of the community to which he belongs, thus having implanted in his mind what is certainly one of the most powerful of the sentiments that regulate conduct in the Andamans.[19]

These are not the passing observations of untrained travelers, but the findings of scientists who spent long periods among the people they describe. If their judgments are correct, the savage of the present time acts, not independently and on the basis of a personal decision or habit, but as part of a group and in a manner which conforms with the traditions of the group. The general tenor of the conclusions reached by other recent investigators is on similar lines. Bücher's theory and the opinions of recent students of primitive life can be reconciled, if it be assumed either (1) that the early European savages were different from the tropical natives of the twentieth century or (2) that Bücher referred to an earlier period of human development, before anything in the nature of society was established. But it must be recognized that no reliable instance of a race of men living in isolation, as Bücher described, has been vouched for at any time. The examples Bücher used to support his argument were drawn from the very people — such as Melanesian Islanders, Veddas, and African Bushmen — regarding whom later researchers have come to a very different conclusion. The *not proven* verdict of Scottish law is the most favorable one that can be given to the theory of primitive individualism. Aristotle's assertion that "man is by nature a political animal" (he meant a social animal) is in better accord with the evidence, at least so far as the *political* — as distinct from the *by nature* — portion of the statement is concerned.

Man's distant past has to be interpreted, however, in the light of the fact that his demarcation from the rest of the animal world has been a gradual process. From this it follows that a thorough study of the problem involves consideration of the existence of social life among the lower animals. Communities of ants and bees testify to the extent to which this is carried. Then there would have to be inquiry as to how this state of affairs was reached, with a view to forming conclusions on the subject of how far animals were social when man's ancestors parted company with their kin on the road to a higher estate. Such speculation, interesting though it may became, is not within the province of the historian of economic thought.

[19] *The Andaman Islanders,* p. 278. Quoted by permission of the Cambridge University Press.

Theories of the Establishment of Society and the State

If it were believed that primitive men lived independently, obviously some explanation was called for on the subject of how societies came to be formed, since throughout history social life has been the rule. Controversies about political authority, and social institutions generally, have led men to inquire as to their origin and their early forms. Thus there appeared several theories on the emergence of continuing human association, that is, on the formation of societies and of the political or government units which are called States.

The social contract. Outstanding in this connection has been the theory of the *social contract* or *compact.* This assumed that primitive men, hitherto individualistic, sought escape from the strife and uncertainty of independent life by agreeing with each other to live together in peace. In the association thus established, individual rights were recognized and the use of force within the particular society was excluded. This theory is to be found in a rudimentary form in the writings of various early Greek and Roman philosophers, including the Athenian teachers Plato (c. 428–c. 348 B.C.) and Epicurus (341–270 B.C.), as well as the Roman statesman, Cicero (106–43 B.C.). Lucretius, who was a follower of Epicurus, may be quoted on this subject. After describing the independent life of the early savages, he proceeded to say that

> when they had got them huts and skins, and fire, and woman mated with man was appropriated to one, (and the laws of wedlock) became known, and they saw offspring born of them, then first the human race began to grow soft.[20]

The result was that

> neighbours began eagerly to join friendship amongst themselves to do no hurt and suffer no violence, and asked protection for their children and womankind, signifying by voice and gesture with stammering tongue that it was right for all to pity the weak.[21]

Complete accord was not produced in this way, yet

> a good part, nay the most kept the covenant unblemished, or else the race of mankind would have been even then wholly destroyed. . .[22]

It will be noticed that here Lucretius depicted family organization as something preceding the establishment of a wider society, but this is not essential to a social contract theory, because either individuals or family heads could enter into such a contract. The fundamental point was that men, who hitherto had been independent, agreed to surrender their independence and associate themselves in a society.

[20] *De rerum natura,* p. 413. [21] *Ibid.* [22] *Ibid.*

Like some other ideas of Cicero, through Augustine (354–430), a bishop of the Catholic Church, the social contract theory became a part of medieval thought, but not until the Reformation and afterwards did it come to be of any great practical significance. Hobbes's statement of it will serve to illustrate the form the theory took in the seventeenth century. Having given an account of the perils of primitive independence, Hobbes said that men found escape in submitting themselves to a common power or ruler:

The only way to erect such a common power, as may be able to defend them from the invasion of foreigners, and the injuries of one another, and thereby to secure them in such sort, as that by their own industry, and by the fruits of the earth, they may nourish themselves and live contentedly; is, to confer all their power and strength upon one man, or upon one assembly of men, that may reduce all their wills, by plurality of voices, unto one will: which is as much as to say, to appoint one man, or assembly of men, to bear their person; and every one to own, and acknowledge himself to be author of whatsoever he that so beareth their person, shall act, or cause to be acted, in those things which concern the common peace and safety; and therein to submit their wills, every one to his own will, and their judgments, to his judgment. This is more than consent, or concord; it is a real unity of them all, in one and the same person, made by covenant of every man with every man, in such manner, as if every man shall say to every man, *I authorise and give up my right of governing myself, to this man, or to this assembly of men, on this condition, that thou give up thy right to him, and authorize all his actions in like manner.* This done, the multitude so united in one person, is called a COMMONWEALTH, in Latin CIVITAS. This is the generation of that great LEVIATHAN, or rather, to speak more reverently, of that *mortal god,* to which we owe under the *immortal God,* our peace and defence.[23]

Although, as is shown later in this chapter, the social contract theory was useful in emphasizing the rights of men, as history it is without substantiation. Individuals may contract themselves into societies that already exist, as when an immigrant enters the country of his choice and, later, makes application for citizenship. Groups have been formed for such purposes as land settlement, on a basis somewhat similar to the social contract, but there is no evidence of an original contract entered into by free individuals, hitherto living independently in the territory which the future society is to occupy. In the political writings of the last century and more, the social contract has been unimportant.

The family. Some of the philosophers of the ancient world, seeking the origin of Greek society, attributed it to the primitive family. Thus, Plato made one of the characters in his *Dialogues* inquire:

And were not such states composed of men who had been dispersed in single habitations and families by the poverty which attended the devastations; and

[23] *Leviathan,* pp. 157-158.

did not the eldest then rule among them, because with them government originated in the authority of a father and a mother, whom, like a flock of birds, they followed, forming one troop under the patriarchal rule and sovereignty of their parents, which of all sovereignties is the most just?[24]

Plato also offered an economic explanation of the origin of society, namely the advantages attending division of labor, referred to in Chapter VIII.

Aristotle (384–322 B.C.), pupil of Plato and, like the older philosopher, head of a famous school in Athens, also looked to the family for the origin of the larger social group:

The family is the association established by nature for the supply of men's everyday wants. . . But when several families are united, and the association aims at something more than the supply of daily needs, the first society to be formed is the village. And the most natural form of the village appears to be that of a colony from the family, composed of the children and grandchildren, who are said to be 'suckled with the same milk'. And this is the reason why Hellenic states were originally governed by kings; because the Hellenes were under royal rule before they came together, as the barbarians still are. Every family is ruled by the eldest, and therefore in the colonies of the family the kingly form of government prevailed because they were of the same blood. As Homer says: 'Each one gives law to his children and to his wives.'[25]

Both Plato and Aristotle had in mind the large or patriarchal family, described below, which appears to have existed in Greece in the Homeric period, about 1200 B.C., and which they thought evolved from a smaller primitive family more like that familiar to modern Americans. The theory that the community or society originated in the family and was characterized by descent from a common ancestor has been of lasting influence. For example, it was used in England during the political controversy of the seventeenth century to support the "divine right of kings" theory against the advocates of popular sovereignty. Granting an earlier stage of primitive individualism, the family theory appears sensible enough as an explanation of the origin of society, but, in view of what has been said earlier in this chapter, this cannot be granted. It must be admitted, however, that the patriarchal theory, in the hands of its most notable exponent, the English historian Sir Henry J. S. Maine

[24] *Laws,* in *The Dialogues of Plato,* translated by B. Jowett, 3rd ed., 5 vols., vol. 5, Oxford 1892, p. 60. Quoted by permission of the Jowett Trustees and the Oxford University Press. Plato wrote in the form of dialogues between characters who were real people. This practice has been variously interpreted but it is now accepted that Plato used it merely as a technique, putting his own words into the mouths of his characters. However, when attributing views to important figures (among whom Socrates was outstanding), undoubtedly he had regard to the opinions of the originals.

[25] *The Works of Aristotle,* ed. W. D. Ross, vol. 10, *Politica,* translated by B. Jowett, Oxford 1921, 1252b. Quoted by permission of the Oxford University Press.

(1822–1888), was not so much a theory of *social origin* as of *social evolution*. However society was formed in the first instance, Maine believed that patriarchal organization was characteristic of an early stage of human society:

> The conclusion, then, which is suggested by the evidence is, not that all early societies were formed by descent from the same ancestor, but that all of them which had any permanence and solidity either were so descended or assumed that they were. An indefinite number of causes may have shattered the primitive groups, but wherever their ingredients recombined, it was on the model or principle of an association of kindred.[26]

Maine's early research was done on ancient Roman law but later his conclusions were reinforced by evidence drawn from regions as far afield as Ireland and India. As a theory of evolution, Maine's suffers from the objection that has been laid against other such theories. It may be true that the patriarchal system obtained in the early stages of society over an extensive area around the Mediterranean Sea and reaching northward and eastward from there, but this does not justify the sweeping assertion that Maine made in the passage quoted.

The horde. Alternative to the family, the horde or band has been suggested as the earliest form of continuing social group. The names of L. H. Morgan, mentioned already, and of the Scottish lawyer-ethnologist J. F. McLennan (1827–1881) are associated with this idea. In their opinion, the family did not appear in an atomistic human existence but was itself the product of lengthy social evolution. Starting from the promiscuous intercourse which he believed to be the first stage of human sex-relationship, Morgan considered the next step to be one in which there was group intermarriage of brothers and sisters. Later, there came a stage in which group marriage existed under conditions which prevented the intermarriage of near relatives. Later still, there was pair marriage without exclusive cohabitation, etc. Morgan mentioned sixteen stages in all, of which the patriarchal family occupied the thirteenth position. In Morgan's view, this was a relatively late step in social evolution: the beginning was in the first aggregation of men and women into companies or hordes. The theory has had a certain influence. Engels gave it a whole-hearted acceptance and made it the basis of his *Der Ursprung der Familie, des Privateigenthums und des Staats* (Zurich 1884).[27] Through this book the horde theory was introduced to a wide range of socialist readers. Like the patriarchal explanation, the horde theory appears reasonable on the assumption of primitive in-

[26] *Ancient Law*, London 1861, new edition with notes by Sir F. Pollock, London 1906, reprinted 1920, p. 139. Quoted by permission of John Murray, and Henry Holt and Company, Inc.

[27] Translated by E. Untermann as *The Origin of the Family, Private Property and the State*, Chicago 1902.

dividualism. It has been criticized severely, however, by a leading contemporary anthropologist, E. A. Westermarck (1862–1939), a Finn by birth, who, from 1907, taught in the University of London. In his book, *The History of Human Marriage* (1889, 5th edition, 3 vols., London 1921), Westermarck examined the evidence in favor of primitive promiscuity and, arguing that it was susceptible of other interpretations, rejected the theory completely as an explanation of the origin of marriage. The problem is largely one of the evaluation of evidence and it would be out of place here to pursue it farther.

Ancient Mediterranean Civilization

Primitive conditions persisted down to very dissimilar dates in different parts of the world. The Homeric poems show the Greek tribes emerging from savagery about twelve centuries before the birth of Christ. The British and the Germans of the Rhine country were in a similar position at the time of Caesar's campaigns in the first century B.C. Large sections of the African continent, as well as the islands of the Indian and Pacific Oceans, are still peopled by savages.

European civilization began in the eastern Mediterranean area but there were advanced cultures in Egypt and the Mesopotamian valleys long before any part of Europe passed beyond the primitive state.

Patriarchal Society

Historians reach back to a patriarchal civilization in the countries bordering the Mediterranean Sea. Pastoral nomads were scattered thinly over large tracts of land, with the patriarchal family as the dominant social unit. This family was different from that familiar to twentieth century Americans and Europeans. It was larger, more flexible, and longer lasting. Not merely husband and wife, with their young children, were included. There were more distant relatives, as well as bondmen or serfs (who worked in return for maintenance and protection), and a few slaves. Children remained in the family group when they married, subject to the authority of the family head or patriarch. Outsiders came in by adoption, while family members could be transferred to other families by the same process. When the patriarch died, he was succeeded by the eldest surviving male with full rights (*i.e.*, was not a bondman or slave). The group was characterized by descent from a common ancestor, because of the fiction that adopted members became possessed of the common blood. In such a family the patriarch exercised considerable power. He had the right of punishment, even to death. He could alter the status of family members by arranging for their marriage or divorce, transferring them to other families or accepting similar transfers into his own family by the adoption process. His was the decision regarding such economic problems as how long the group was to stay on one pasturage and where its next dwelling place would be. The patriarch's powers, however, were not his personal possession. He was the personification of the family and exercised rights on its behalf, just as is supposed to be the case with the modern king or dictator.

It is easy to understand that, when nomads settled down on the banks of rivers and similar sites, the patriarchs of the mobile families might become village chiefs or minor kings in the settled communities. This furnishes an explanation of the priest-kings of early Egypt, from whom it was but a step to the Pharaohs. The stronger Pharaohs—combining in their persons the spiritual and temporal powers—were masters of Egypt and ruled their country, economically as well as politically, in a manner unparalleled until the appearance of the totalitarian States of recent years. The tradition of subjection of the individual to the family group appears to explain also his subordination to the State in classical Greece.

The Greek City-States

Pastoral culture remained important for a long time over vast stretches of country, but quite early agriculture appeared and towns began to develop in favorable spots. Fertile valleys attracted settlers. Agricultural and industrial specialization furnished the economic basis of close settlement and cultural advancement. But wealthy villages and cities offered a standing temptation to neighboring tribes of nomads, which accounts for many of the struggles of early history. As compared with the area comprising the delta and valley of the Nile in Egypt, the natural units of Greece were small, because the country was cut up by mountains, through which communication was difficult. This goes far to explain the appearance of the small city-States of ancient Greece.

In some of these cities culture was carried to a high level, not on the basis of social uniformity, but on that of class differentiation. Sparta had a remarkable social system. A small class of citizens—the Spartiates, who were descendants of the original conquerors—formed a military autocracy. Each Spartiate had for his support an area of land, with laboring helots or serfs, the land being inalienable and inherited from eldest son to eldest son. His time was spent in physical exercises—if not in actual fighting—or, as he became older, in government. So efficient was the Spartan military system that, not only was the Spartiate minority able to keep in subjection a much larger number of helots, but the city dominated Greece for many centuries. Even in Athens, whose political system is revered by many present-day admirers of democratic institutions, there was no equality but a society that resembled in some respects that of the southern part of North America before the Civil War. In the great age of the Greek cities there were many slaves—war, crime, and debt, operating to maintain or increase their numbers. The slave class performed not merely the manual work but tasks requiring a high degree of technical skill. Outside the citizen group but personally free were numerous foreigners living in the city and engaged largely in commercial pursuits. A considerable number of the citizens possessed both wealth and leisure, a circumstance which goes far to explain the cultural development of Athens.

The Athenians did not live for the State so much as did the Spartans and the early Egyptians. Private enterprise and individual rights were of greater importance. Greece was moving away from centralized authority toward a more individualistic social system and Athens was a leader in this movement. Yet even in Athens individual rights had to yield precedence to the needs of the State, as is shown in Chapter IV.

The Empires of Alexander and of Rome

After the glorious age of the Greek cities came the Alexandrian Empire. The city-State organization gave place to a far-flung dominion, the conquest of Philip of Macedonia (382–336 B.C.) and his son Alexander the Great (356–323 B.C.). Under Alexander the State was no longer a parochial affair, small enough to be everyone's business, like a New England settlement in the early days of American history. It extended over the Balkan Peninsula, Egypt, and a large area of Asia. Before Alexander's time foreigners had been coming into Greece from Asia Minor and elsewhere. During the Imperial period the influx grew considerably. Alexander's policy was to foster racial assimilation, and he set a personal example by taking two additional wives from the Persian royal house, and arranged a mass marriage of his followers with Asiatic women. Southwestern Asia and Egypt began to be permeated by Greeks and Greek culture, while Greece itself became more cosmopolitan. Barriers within the State were broken down, leaving a mass of individual citizens confronting a central power that was absolute but remote. This model was followed later by the builders of many States. Alexander's empire soon broke up but its characteristic features were continued in the successor States and from there diffused westward to the rising Roman power.

The position of Rome in the height of its power was in many respects similar to that of Greece during and after the Alexandrian Empire. Class differentiation was marked. In the early Republican period, much of Italy appears to have been in the hands of peasants. The conquests struck a heavy blow at these small cultivators, because they opened up cheap sources of grain supply abroad. In addition, they made available a considerable supply of slave labor. The captured territories largely passed into the occupancy of members of the upper or patrician class, immense estates being worked by slaves. But, as time went on, the landed men, who had consolidated their possession of the former public land, began to substitute for slaves the *coloni,* who were ancestors of the medieval serfs. As the Roman power grew, government became centralized, under the Republic as well as in the later Imperial period. The central authority was responsible for the Empire as a whole, with the security of the frontiers and internal peace as the official objectives. For a considerable time there was not only a State religion but a divine emperor, a situation that cannot be regarded as conducive to individualism in thought. As in Athens, private enterprise was relied upon in production but authoritarian interference in the distribution of wealth was not absent. As also was the case in Greece, political expansion had replaced sectionalism by a more cosmopolitan viewpoint. Under the Empire, large numbers of foreigners entered government service, including many Greeks, to whose business capacity much of the success of the Imperial financial administration has been attributed. The armies were recruited largely in the provinces and non-Romans rose to positions of eminence. Stilicho (d. 408), for example, father-in-law of the Emperor Honorius and defender of Rome against the Goth leader Alaric, was a Vandal. Marcus Aurelius (Emperor 161–180) was of Spanish descent, his father having been raised to patrician rank by an earlier ruler.

The cosmopolitanism of Greece during the decline of the city-States, and that of Rome at a later date, furnished a favorable environment for the political philosophy of the Stoics. *Stoicism* received its name from the Stoa, a porch on the market-place of Athens where, from the close of the fourth century B.C., its founder, Zeno, taught. Like Antisthenes (c. 444–c. 365 B.C.), who established the earlier school of Cynics, from whose doctrines Stoicism seems to have been developed, Zeno was a foreigner. He came to Greece from Cyprus and many of his pupils were drawn from the non-privileged groups of aliens and poor. The Stoics opposed the imposition of barriers between men, so that the school was attractive to persons of this type. In the Stoic view, Greek and foreigner, man and woman, freeman and bondman, were alike members of a world family and subject to an all-embracing natural law. Equality and fraternity, not privilege and separation, were emphasized. The Stoics thought that men were by nature free and had natural rights which were not to be subordinated in a political State. The conception of natural law was not new with the Stoics. Both Plato and Aristotle had mentioned it[28] and the idea goes back beyond them to the Sophists of

[28] Aristotle's definitions are worth quoting:

> By the two kinds of law I mean particular law and universal law. Particular law is that which each community lays down and applies to its own members: this is partly written and partly unwritten. Universal law is the law of nature. For there really is, as every one to some extent divines, a natural justice and injustice that is binding on all men, even on those who have no association or covenant with each other.

The Works of Aristotle, vol. 11, *Rhetorica,* translated by W. R. Roberts, Oxford 1924, 1373b. Quoted by permission of the Oxford University Press.

the fifth century B.C. But it was in Roman thought that natural law first attained real significance. In Rome a natural law was regarded as paralleling, and to some extent conditioning, man-made laws. It represented the common law of all humanity, being based upon the needs and instincts of mankind. Before this natural law, all men were equal and possessed personal rights which could not be abrogated. It is true that Roman lawyers did not maintain that the natural law overrode the civil law, as was done in the middle ages, but they regarded it as an underlying and idealistic principle. From Rome was derived the natural law concept of western Europe, which passed through the middle ages to modern times.

Social Conflict in the Ancient World

Notwithstanding the existence of a centralized political authority, whose power was supposed to be exercised on behalf of the State as a whole — indeed, perhaps to some extent because of this centralization — the ancient world experienced many social conflicts. Governor and governed, citizen and non-citizen, large landowner and small peasant, taxfarmer and taxpayer, freeman and slave, rich and poor, all were part of the State but they represented divergent viewpoints. The reforms of Solon in Athens at the beginning of the sixth century B.C. were an attempt to resolve a clash between debtor and creditor classes. The so-called *social war* of Rome in the second century before Christ, in which the brothers Tiberius and Gaius Gracchus were leaders on the popular or "have-nots" side, was another instance. The position was that ancient society, like its modern counterpart, was composed of groups whose interests were apt to conflict. It was all very well for the government to declare what purported to be the State's viewpoint when controversy arose, but in fact it was often possible for a contending party, by scheming or force, to get its particular interest adopted as the State's interest. Groups did not scruple to seize the State power for the purpose of securing their own ends, as was shown in the Roman social war. On the other hand, when the governing power was in strong hands, at least internal peace was preserved. The State's fiat on a disputed question might be obtained in undesirable ways but, once promulgated, it had to be accepted. The centralized government of Rome had this advantage over the feudal system which was to follow.

The Middle Ages

After the centralized State of the Romans came feudal decentralization. The economic order was changing, as specialization and exchange became less important, and estates were commonly organized as subsistence entities, with little need for external commerce. The political decline of Rome was a gradual process. The advance of the frontier into regions peopled by wild tribes and the incursion of others from outside the Empire meant that there came to be large numbers of barbarians living under the sway of Rome, many of them being used in the Imperial military service to resist the onslaught of groups who were still less civilized. Even the dissolution of the Empire was not followed immediately by absolute independence on the part of its barbarian successors, since at first the Teuton ruler of Italy professed allegiance to the eastern Emperor at Constantinople or Byzantium, whose State was the product of a division that had taken place in the Roman Empire in the fourth century A.D. and was to endure a thousand years after its western counterpart had disappeared. So it happened that the new society of western Europe represented in some degree a Roman-barbarian fusion, though the contributions made by the two elements varied greatly in different localities and are still a subject of debate among historians.[29]

Feudalism

During the period of Imperial decadence, the central power waned until it was little more than nominal, virtually disappearing over large areas. This was the condition that is commonly considered to have given rise to feudalism. Finding the Roman authority incapable of protecting their persons and property, men are said to have pledged or *commended* themselves to local dignitaries, such as tribal leaders or Imperial officials. Such a relationship had its counterpart in the patron-client arrangement of ancient Rome. The men so pledged (vassals or retainers) agreed to render military or other service to their lords, receiving in return legal and military protection as well as economic security. If they had land, they surrendered this to the lords, obtaining it back subject to the obligations mentioned. Landless men promised service in return for maintenance in the lord's castle or from grants of land allotted to them for the purpose. The military class of knights was in this group. Small farmers (some, no doubt, hitherto free tenants, or even landowners, and others bondmen or slaves on large estates) became serfs. They were bound to the soil and rendered labor service in cultivating the lord's farm and in transporting its produce to the castles where it was consumed by his retainers. In return, they received land for their support as well as personal protection. The need for protection was

[29] This is exemplified by the controversy which has taken place on the origin of the medieval village community, or manor. Two schools of thought have developed, emphasizing respectively the Roman and Teuton contributions. With respect to England, a summary of the arguments is given by E. Lipson in *The Economic History of England,* vol. 1, 7th ed., London 1937, Chap. 1, and a more extended treatment by P. Vinogradoff in *The Growth of the Manor,* London 1905. For the Continent, see A. Dopsch, *The Economic and Social Foundations of European Civilization,* abridged by E. Patzelt and translated by M. G. Beard and N. Marshall, London and New York 1937. The argument of Dopsch is that the Teutons gradually seeped into the Roman Empire, acquiring its culture and continuing this when the Empire disappeared.

only one of the factors that appear to have been behind the emergence of this situation. Taxation and debts seem to have caused some men to lose their property and even their freedom to those to whom payments must be made. But probably seizure and fear of this were often responsible, that is, men became vassals or bondmen not because they wanted a lord to protect them against others, but because they were too weak to defend themselves against their lords-to-be.

In reaching conclusions respecting the rise of the feudal system, four points should be borne in mind. First, the change was a gradual one, and legal ideas of later years—such as commendation—probably did not reflect fully what took place earlier. Second, the whole development was closely related to the decline of exchange and the growth in significance of self-sufficing estates. Third, bondage and slavery existed on a large scale on the estates of the Roman period, as well as in the cities. Last, the barbarian tribes that spread westward and southward over the Roman dominions were composed originally of pastoral nomads, organized for economic and military purposes under petty chiefs and more important kings, in some respects not unlike the inhabitants of Homeric Greece. When such a people settled down among a conquered race, feudalism was a not unnatural result. No doubt some of the tribal leaders became lords of serfs in the conquered dominions in due course, ruling over old followers and former foes alike—perhaps to a large extent the descendants of the former were freemen and those of the latter serfs. Other lords were probably ex-Romans, who swore allegiance to a victorious barbarian ruler exactly as Abyssinian chiefs did to King Victor Emmanuel of Italy in the 1930's. Be that as it may, the legal and fiscal organization of the Roman Empire fell into decay. Feudal vassals and serfs looked to their lords for justice and the functions of Imperial courts of justice disappeared. Taxation was no longer needed for the maintenance of military forces, because armies became feudal levies, raised at the command of the king or baron from those whose duty it was to supply him with fighting men.

The accompanying diagram will serve to make clear the nature of the feudal system in its simplest form, the arrows showing the direction of the several obligations. Thus a knight fought at his lord's command (represented by an arrow from knight to lord), in return for maintenance in the castle (represented by an arrow in the reverse direction).

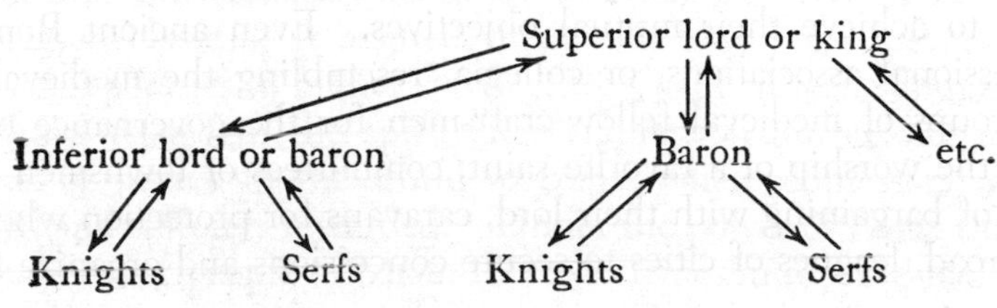

appeal, not merely in Judea and other outlying portions of the Empire, but even in Rome itself. Apart from this factor of class conflict, the permeation of Roman thought by Stoic conceptions had helped to prepare the ground for the new belief. The result was far-reaching. Like the leaven in Christ's parable, Christianity acted as a ferment among the people of Rome and other parts of the Empire. Its adherents had to face many difficulties. They were exhorted to forsake riches, place, and power, if these came their way, or at least to use them for the benefit of others. Some were crucified or thrown to the lions for the amusement and edification of the Roman populace. Yet the religion spread until, in 313, by the Edict of Milan, the Emperor Constantine granted it official toleration throughout the Empire. Subsequent extensions of the Christian privileges helped the new faith to its ultimate triumph. When the Roman Empire disappeared, Christianity had been accepted by many of the barbarians who fell heir to the western dominions and gradually it became the accepted religion of the entire European continent.

The Church as an Advisory and Regulatory Body

The general purport of Christ's teaching was to emphasize the equality of men. All were subjects of the same master—God. But Christ and his disciples offered guidance to believers in their practical conduct; and later there arose, in the Catholic Church, a great organization which claimed descent from Christ through the Apostle Peter and took upon itself the care of human affairs. The Church was international, so that medieval thought possessed a high degree of unity. Priests did not confine themselves to matters of doctrine, but offered counsel on the morality of everyday conduct in all walks of life, such as what occupations were suitable to Christian men and women, what prices and wages should be paid, whether interest should be demanded on loans, what kind of food should be eaten and what clothes might be worn, how marriage should be regarded, etc. The ethics of various lines of conduct were argued by theologians and the solutions they formulated became precepts, through local priests, for the people at large. A prominent example of a comprehensive treatise, composed by a leading churchman for the guidance of Christian men and women, through their priests, was the *Instructor* or *Tutor* of Clement of Alexandria (c. 150–c. 215). Apparently a Greek and a convert to Christianity, Clement taught at Alexandria, Egypt, in a time when the influence of the religion was growing and the meaning of its doctrines was widely canvassed. Under such conditions the need for practical interpretation was great. In Chapter II we consider the example for which Clement is most famous and to which he devoted an entire treatise—the Christian attitude to riches—but his *Instructor* dealt with a very wide range of practical problems. A few quotations will illustrate the type of advice it contained. On eating, the believer was told,

totally irrational, futile, and not human is it for those that are of the earth, fattening themselves like cattle. . .[30]

On sleep,

We must therefore sleep so as to be easily awakened. For it is said, "Let your loins be girt about, and your lamps burning; and ye yourselves like to men that watch for their lord. . .[31]

This refers to the early Christian belief in the imminence of Christ's return. On "How to conduct ourselves at feasts," the reader was informed,

Let revelry keep away from our rational entertainments, and foolish vigils, too, that revel in intemperance.[32]

Women were not to "smear their faces with the ensnaring devices of wily cunning,"[33] (*i.e.* paint) and were warned against display generally:

love of display is not for a lady, but a courtesan. Such women care little for keeping at home with their husbands; but loosing their husbands' purse-strings, they spend its supplies on their lusts, that they may have many witnesses of their seemingly fair appearance. . . As you might expect, they become lazy in housekeeping, sitting like painted things to be looked at. . . But what passes beyond the bounds of absurdity, is that they have invented mirrors for this artificial shape of theirs, as if it were some excellent work or masterpiece.[34]

As for men,

for one who is a man to comb himself and shave himself with a razor, for the sake of fine effect, to arrange his hair at the looking-glass . . . how womanly![35]

With regard to wearing apparel,

for those who are white and unstained within, it is most suitable to use white and simple garments.[36]

And, in conclusion,

Such are a few injunctions out of many, for the sake of example, which the Instructor, running over the divine Scriptures, sets before His children; by which, so to speak, vice is cut up by the roots, and iniquity is circumscribed.[37]

[30] *Ante-Nicene Christian Library*, ed. A. Robertson and J. Donaldson, 24 vols., Edinburgh 1868–1872, vol. 4, p. 192. Quoted by permission of T. & T. Clark.

[31] *Ibid.*, p. 241. Even the softness of the bed was considered.

[32] *Ibid.*, p. 215.

[33] *Ibid.*, p. 319.

[34] *Ibid.*, pp. 277-281.

[35] *Ibid.*, pp. 285-286.

[36] *Ibid.*, p. 259.

[37] *Ibid.*, pp. 339-340.

On the subject of guides to human conduct, the work of Thomas Aquinas (c. 1225–1274) must be mentioned. Aquinas was an outstanding theologian of the latter part of the middle ages, teaching in Paris, Rome, and other educational centers, and his *Summa theologica* (1265 onwards) was one of the most influential works of this nature. The practice of publishing such treatises, however, did not cease with the end of the middle ages. The *Christian Directory* (London 1673), of Richard Baxter (1615–1691), leading Nonconformist preacher of his time in England, was of this type; while an example is to be found in current use, in the volume entitled *Christian Practice* (London 1925), the second part of the "discipline" of the English Society of Friends. All such works appeared because general ethical principles required interpretation to meet the complex and ever-changing conditions of practical life, an interpretation which the uninformed individual had difficulty in making.

It should be emphasized that religious advice was not to be lightly disregarded in the middle ages, or, indeed, afterwards. Conformity with the rules made by the Church was enforced by spiritual and temporal sanctions, and in many cases these were extremely effective. Believers who regarded their lives on earth as a temporary condition, to be followed by an eternity which lay in the Church's keeping, were brought and kept to the straight path by fears of incurring severe penalties in the world beyond death. Condemnation to everlasting fire was a sanction before which most of the civil punishments, familiar to the present generation, pale into insignificance. In earthly life religious measures could be very effective, in view of the widespread allegiance given to the Church. Excommunication (*i.e.*, deprivation of the church sacrament) was an effective weapon even against kings, and the disobedient were penalized in their business dealings as well as in social intercourse. Moreover, as time passed, religious sanctions were reinforced by civil penalties, laws being promulgated by the various Christian rulers for the purpose of enforcing standards of conduct which received their approval. Punishments were often extremely heavy, torture, loss of limbs, or even death being ordered for what would now be regarded as comparatively trivial offenses.

As was to be expected, the nature of the penalties depended on that of the sins which had been committed. Like others similarly placed, church dignitaries were more apt to think in terms of severe punishment when their authority was questioned than when some human frailty had been displayed.

Ample evidence exists, however, to prove that the ascetic counsels of Church teachers were not always accepted. Often they were meant to be ideals towards which men should strive, rather than standards they were expected to reach. To a large extent they were practiced as examples and as means of personal salvation by groups of monks or nuns and individual priests, but the frequency of exhortations and legal enactments on usury, for instance, shows that practical conduct fell short of the standards set by the Church. Priests and even church bodies themselves were not free from blame, as is shown in Chapter II. But it must be admitted that discrepancies between the precepts of idealists and the everyday actions of practical people were not confined to the middle ages.

The Evolution of Religious Teachings

The teachings of the Church were adjusted constantly to meet alterations in the environment. In the early days, there was no pretense at building up a continuing policy respecting worldly affairs. The Saviour was expected to return at any moment, so that "watch and pray" seemed sensible enough advice in the circumstances. Gradually, however, it became apparent that Christ's return might be long delayed and that the Church must formulate a policy suited to the worldly activities which were necessary to men during the waiting period. There was pressure to give the Christian doctrines a construction which would not antagonize temporal authorities or new believers, the writings of Clement of Alexander on the subject of wealth, referred to in Chapter II, being a good example. The pacifist program of Christ's *Sermon on the Mount* gave way to open acceptance of military service. It is probably true to say that, had the Christian leaders shown an entirely uncompromising policy upon such matters, the rise of the religion to official toleration and ultimate acceptance would have been impeded, if not prevented altogether. Instead, the advance to general acceptance was accompanied by modification of the earlier teachings. This is not to say that principles were abandoned; of their nature, this was impossible. They were the revealed word of Christ and, since His life on earth was closed, must remain the final truths of Christianity. The interpretations that were put upon Christ's teachings changed, not merely in the early period but throughout the history of the Catholic Church. The environment was changing continually and the problems with which religious teachers were confronted altered accordingly. The Church endeavored to give counsel of such a nature that individuals would be able to apply it in their workaday lives. The result was a flexibility of religious interpretation to which the strength and lasting nature of the influence of the Roman Church are largely attributable.

The Problem of Authority

A matter of continuing controversy was the relative positions of spiritual and temporal powers. Christ himself had faced this problem and offered a solution :

Render to Cæsar the things that are Cæsar's, and to God the things that are God's.[38]

This, of course, raised the further question as to exactly which things were to be regarded as belonging to Cæsar and which to God. Marcus Aurelius, the Stoic Emperor of Rome, is credited with opposing the Christians, and at a later date Maximinus (Emperor 235–238), Decius (Emperor 249–251), and Valerianus (Emperor 253–258), waged open warfare on the Church. Undoubtedly one of the reasons for this official opposition to Christianity was the realization of those in authority that the believer's loyalty to his religion might conflict with his loyalty to the State. It seems that fear of disaffection in the army, where the influence of Christianity was growing, had much to do with the persecutions of the third century. In these circumstances, it was quite logical for the government to endeavor to crush the new faith, in order that the State might be left in undivided possession of the allegiance of men. With the Christianization of the State, from the fourth century onwards, the problem changed. No longer was it one of ultimate authority; there was general agreement that this rested with God. The earthly manifestations of authority were the subject of dispute.

The various possibilities can be represented in diagrammatic form, the arrows showing the direction in which authority was conferred:

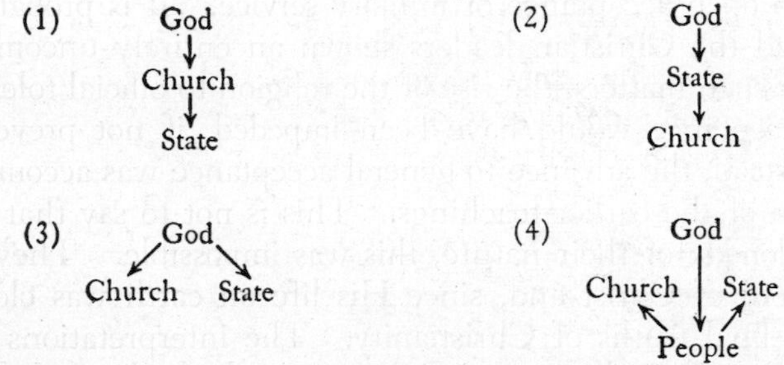

Was authority conferred by God upon the Church, which delegated the temporal portion to the State (Diagram 1)? This was the view of Church extremists, such as John of Salisbury (c. 1115–1180), an Englishman who became Bishop of Chartres, France, and had some part in the dispute between King Henry II and the religious authorities respecting the position of the Church in England. The Church received two swords from God, it was argued, representing the spiritual and the temporal powers, respectively. The former was retained in its own hands, but the latter was entrusted to the State, because the religious body was forbidden by divine law to use temporal power. Thus the State became a Church instrument, distinguished only by its possession of a special field

[38] *Mark* 12, v. 17.

and an organization of its own. A second possibility was that the State was the recipient of divine authority, and that the Church owed its position to the State (Diagram 2). A third was that both Church and State were divine creations, each with its proper sphere. They were parallel bodies, operating in the provinces of spiritual and temporal affairs respectively, and neither was superior to the other (Diagram 3). Finally, authority might be deposited by God with the people, who created both Church and State to achieve their ends, in the world of the spirit, on the one hand, and in earthly matters, on the other (Diagram 4). It was this fourth arrangement that was most prominent in the arguments of those who took the side of State power. John Duns Scotus (1266–1308), famous Scottish-born teacher of Paris and Cologne and outstanding opponent of Thomas Aquinas, took this line, as did Marsilius of Padua (c. 1270–c. 1342), who upheld Louis, Duke of Bavaria and Holy Roman Emperor, in his quarrel with the Pope. Such arguments as those of Scotus and Marsilius were important in the light of the later doctrine of popular sovereignty. But, though the idea of popular sovereignty was useful in supporting the State against the Church, if it were admitted, it followed that the State was no more supreme than was the Church itself. In other words, as was argued later by Spinoza and Gierke in their different ways, the rights of man were indefeasible and the State, like the Church, had to be regarded as merely one of man's instruments.

Even Thomas Aquinas, most influential of all the scholastic philosophers, was prepared to admit that the people had a right to disobey their ruler when his commands were not in accordance with divine law:

It is written (Acts v. 29): *We ought to obey God rather than men.* Now sometimes the things commanded by a superior are against God. Therefore superiors are not to be obeyed in all things. . . *if the emperor commands one thing and God another, you must disregard the former and obey God.*[39]

It followed that revolt against an unjust or tyrannical government was permissible:

A tyrannical government is not just, because it is directed, not to the common good, but to the private good of the ruler, as the Philosopher [*i.e.*, Aristotle] states. . . Consequently there is no sedition in disturbing a government of this kind, unless indeed the tyrant's rule be disturbed so inordinately, that his subjects suffer greater harm from the consequent disturbance than from the tyrant's government.[40]

Obviously, if State laws or royal commands were to be examined in the light of God's will, and civil disobedience were to be regarded as justifiable

[39] *Summa theologica*, translated by the Fathers of the English Dominican Province, 22 vols., London 1911–1925. Pt. II, Second Pt., Q. 104, Art. 5. Quoted by permission of Burns Oates and Washbourne Ltd.

[40] *Ibid.*, Pt. II, Second Pt., Q. 42, Art. 2.

if the two did not conform, it was very important to know whose interpretation of the will of God was to be accepted, that of the individual or that of the organized Church. John of Salisbury had supported the people's right to revolt but what he appeared to have in mind was a revolt to establish Church authority against a usurping king, not the assertion of individual freedom of thought with respect to the rules of both Church and State.

The dispute proceeded with varying arguments and fortunes throughout the entire middle ages. Now one side triumphed, now another. Popes crowned kings, and temporal monarchs raised their nominees to the Holy See. Alexander III, who was Pope during the period 1159–1181, humbled King Henry II of England over the murder of Thomas Becket, Archbishop of Canterbury (1118–1170), which resulted from a dispute between Archbishop and King principally concerning the relative jurisdictions of Church and State. The same Pope defeated Frederick I (c. 1123–1190), Holy Roman Emperor. On the other hand, at different times the papacy was subjected to the temporal power in both France and Germany. On the whole, it can be said that the Church was more successful in the contest than might have been expected, having regard to the fact that physical force was largely in the hands of its antagonists, because it exercised a strong moral leadership and was both international and lasting, whereas the power of its opponents was commonly local and temporary. Kings placed their ecclesiastical friends in positions of importance, as was the case with Becket, only to find that in office they deserted the cause that they had been appointed to support. Not until there was a major breach within the Church itself was its dominance imperiled.

Social Justice

As between man and man, medieval opinion accepted that the rules of justice were to apply, not those of force or of the higgling of the market. For the equalitarian outlook of early Christianity, there was substituted in the middle ages the idea of a hierarchy of social classes, every individual being contented in his allotted position, and justice being done so long as he got what was appropriate to his situation. This conception is discussed in some detail in later chapters, especially in connection with the writings of Aquinas, and its importance cannot be overemphasized.

The Reformation and the Rise of the Modern State

As has been noticed, leading features of the middle ages were the feudal system of decentralized government and the international unity of thought consequent on the dominant position of the Roman Catholic Church. The next period witnessed a change in both these respects, and the modern nation, at once more centralized and more independent, was the result.

The Break-up of Feudalism

Like many other great changes, the transition from feudalism to centralized government was a gradual one. It is easy to understand that, in a period of strife between contending barons, one of them might come to the front and claim royal rights over the area subjected to his power, an influential marriage, perhaps, or an ecclesiastical blessing, helping in the process. In some countries, the strength of the barons was dissipated in warfare, as was the case in the English Wars of the Roses (1455–1485) and the religious struggles accompanying the Reformation in France. The cities were growing in importance. Many of them had bought themselves out of the feudal system – a circumstance for which the heavy cost of the Crusades was partly responsible – while, in combats between king and barons, the larger cities, such as London, often sided with the monarch and put resources in men and money at his disposal. An influence of some significance was the change in the art of war which out-moded the feudal host – the typical military force of medieval times – and led to its replacement by hired soldiers directly in the service of the king. The feudal army was at best unreliable. Many of the men composing it had duties connected with their daily livelihood, which they did not care to neglect for an indefinite period, even if it were possible to do so. Being only short-term occasional fighters, they were unskillful. At times they acted against the interest of the king, because they came at the call of their lord and served under his command even when he was in revolt against the royal authority. As time passed by, experience made it clear that specialist long-service soldiers represented a greatly superior fighting force. In Italy, where the change first made its appearance, the earliest specialist soldiers were the mercenary *condottieri*, who fought in bands for whoever was willing to pay them. The fifteenth century saw the heyday of this development in Italy. Afterwards this form of army tended to be replaced by the national force, whose members were not open to the risk of going over to the enemy if he offered a higher salary. Mercenary bands equipped themselves but had to be paid. National armies required food, except when this could be raised from the country in which they were campaigning. The soldiers also had to be equipped and paid some wages. The effect was to give a new importance to national taxation and to destroy both the military and the fiscal functions of feudalism. On the land a parallel change took place. The feudal lords began to commute for money payments many of the labor dues on their estates, and to rent out to farmers the land that had supported their bands of retainers. A *service and subsistence economy* gave place to a *money economy*, and feudalism, though continuing as a legal system of landholding, became less and less a system of government.

The accession of Henry VII to the English crown in 1485, following the Wars of the Roses, is commonly taken as signifying the inauguration of the new order in Britain but it should be borne in mind that the change was a gradual one. It is true that this king sat rather uncertainly on his throne, but his son, Henry VIII (King 1509–1547), and the later Tudors, especially Elizabeth (Queen 1558–1603), exercised a power that was as near despotism as anything in British history. The pacification of France under Henry IV (King 1589–1610) can be compared with that of England under Henry VII, and the reign of Louis XIV (King 1643–1715) with Elizabeth's England. The centralized Prussian State dates from the rule of the Great Elector (Frederick William) in 1640–1688. Spain developed on similar lines during the sixteenth century, except that the possession by her king of the crown of the Holy Roman Empire kept that country in the forefront of international politics. The strength of the royal power in Spain in this period was demonstrated by the manner in which the king was able, against the wishes of the nobles, to keep that country at war for the purpose of furthering his non-Spanish interests.

The Decline of Church Authority

An evolution was taking place in the realm of thought, paralleling that in practical affairs. From the end of the eleventh century the Crusades had fostered in western Europe an acquaintance with the learning of the Eastern or Byzantine Empire, whose capital was Constantinople. Greek scholars from Constantinople had carried to the Moslems of Asia Minor the knowledge that had been elaborated upon the foundations laid by Aristotle and other early Greek philosophers. From there the resulting *Arabian philosophy* was spread through the Mohammedan world, so that Cordova, in Moorish Spain, and Palermo, in Saracen Sicily, were educational centers surpassing the cities of Christian Europe. It was from Spain, as well as through the Crusades to Constantinople and beyond, that Aristotelean ideas permeated into the Christian west. The universities of Oxford and Paris, established in the twelfth century, furnished the means whereby the new knowledge was disseminated. Grossteste (c. 1175–1253), Bishop of Lincoln, the English-born teacher Alexander of Hales (c. 1175–1245), and more especially Albertus Magnus of Cologne (c. 1206–1280) and his pupil Thomas Aquinas, were influential in combining Aristotelian thought with the teachings of the early Fathers. But the wider experience resulting from the Crusades, and the writings of such men as the Spanish philosopher Averroes (1126–1198), had the effect that medieval scholasticism or religious philosophy was undermined and thought became more skeptical. Men were taught to think things out for themselves, instead of accepting the authoritative interpretations that had satisfied them in the past. The succeeding centuries witnessed a great expansion in human knowledge. Such ideas as those of Copernicus (1473–1543), Kepler (1571–1630), and Galileo (1564–1642), in the natural sciences, and of Descartes (1596–1650), Spinoza (1632–1677), and Hobbes in general and social philosophy, could not have developed in the medieval period, dominated as it was by religious dogma. Even when the new doctrines appeared, some of them had to face considerable difficulties. Galileo, for example, an Italian and one of the most notable figures in the history of astronomy, received ecclesiastical censure and had to retract his teachings under a threat of torture by the Inquisition. In Holland, Descartes became embroiled on the same point as Galileo—acceptance of the Copernican theory that the earth revolves round the sun—and, learning of Galileo's troubles, endeavored to avoid opposition by modifying his own statements. It was not merely Catholic teachers who objected to the new philosophy, since Descartes's greatest quarrel was with the Protestant rector of the University of Utrecht.

The Church had difficulties of its own. In Italy it seemed to have degenerated into the position of a temporal dukedom, more concerned with local politics than with the spiritual keeping of the world. The increasing tendency of people to think for themselves led to severe criticism of many church practices. The result was shown in a long series of world councils on church affairs and finally in the events that gave rise to the Protestant Reformation.

The Protestant Reformation

The Reformation represented an uprising of individualism in religious interpretation. As was pointed out in an earlier section, during the middle ages the Church exercised the function of interpreting the will of God to individual believers. Interpretation had to proceed in the minds of men before being translated into the official opinions of the organized Church. Considerable freedom of discussion was allowed but, on fundamental points, views might be judged heretical if they appeared to the authorities to be too radical for the Church to accept. Then they must be retracted or their authors became liable to punishment. In the later period this was very severe, heretics often being burned at the stake.

It would be out of place to consider the immediate reasons for the Protestant Reformation but the general nature of the dispute that gave rise to it is important. The issue was the right of the individual teacher to his own interpretation of the Gospels. Martin Luther (1483–1546), a German monk and professor in the University of Wittenberg, questioned the sale of indulgences, or remissions of punishment for sins, and during the resulting controversy proceeded to draw up a positive program for the Church. The Pope issued a *bull*, or statement, that declared

Luther's views heretical. Instead of retracting, as he might have done, Luther burned the bull publicly (1520) and thereby raised the standard of revolt. Northern Europe was fruitful soil for such a movement. There was general dissatisfaction with the Church. It had immense possessions—estimated at one fifth to one third of the total property, in respect of which claims for exemption from public burdens were made. Papal assertions of supremacy over kings and princes caused annoyance. Luther's program was more palatable to these temporal magnates. The Reform leader made provision for a national church and, in the maneuvers that succeeded his revolt and established a league of Protestant princes, showed himself willing to concede a dominant position to the political authorities. At the diet or parliament of the Holy Roman Empire, held at Speyer in 1529, some of the princes and representatives of cities made a solemn protest against a vote that refused freedom of conscience, an action that gave the movement its name *Protestantism.* In the struggles that followed, the new faith spread over northern Europe, while Catholicism retained its hold on the southern countries. In some localities, as in France, Germany, and the Low Countries, only long and bloody wars decided the issue. In others, like Spain and Italy in the south, and Scandinavia and England in the north, there was little upheaval. As a result in the north there appeared a number of churches that were in effect national and were dominated by the State to a much greater extent than had been the case with the Catholic Church, while in the south the Catholic Church continued in its old position.

There had been disputes within the Church before, and even major breaks, but none that proved so fundamental or lasting as this. On the surface, little change took place in the relation of religion to social life. As was to be expected, in view of the current low level of education among the common people, the new churches continued to a large extent the old function of interpreting Christ's teachings to the individual. But there was no longer any finality about the interpretation. The precedent of successful revolt had been set. Once an important group had left the Church and established itself independently, others followed suit, not merely breaking away from the Catholic Church, but from the various Reformed bodies themselves. A wide range of Protestant sects came into existence. On the one hand were the Lutherans, who appeared to segregate spiritual affairs into a world apart, leaving the State virtually unchallenged in the secular sphere. Diametrically opposed to this position were the Quakers, who, giving to each individual a right to free interpretation of the Gospels, applied religion to the world and sought to re-make society into a Kingdom of Christ on earth. The Calvinists occupied an intermediate position. They resembled the Quakers in refusing to recognize State supremacy in worldly matters, but set up a more formal organization than did the Quakers and made the government a tool with which to Christianize the State, where, as in Geneva, they were powerful enough for this purpose.

A significant factor was that the international unity of the Church was destroyed. No longer did all Christian kings look to Rome. The Reformed churches were organized broadly on national lines. The King of England, for example, dealt with the Church of England and undoubtedly found it more approachable than was the Holy See. In such circumstances, serious disputes between Church and State were less frequent. The Catholic Church became much less important as an international force. The effect of the change was that the medieval international law (which was largely church law) was gone, leaving a new basis of international accord to be discovered.

The Theoretical Groundwork of the New System

A series of important writings laid the theoretical foundation of the new system.

The right to revolt against established authority. The principle of individual natural right was appealed to against both the Catholic Church and unpopular monarchs. This was the basis of the *Vindiciae contra tyrannos* (1579),[41] of French Huguenot authorship, and of the *De jure regni apud Scotos* (1579) of the Scottish reformer George Buchanan (1506–1582). Already it had been argued by Marsilius of Padua that the Church was merely an instrument employed by sovereign people in achieving their spiritual objectives. Where Marsilius used this idea to support the State against the claims of Church authority, it was now utilized to further the cause of the Reformation. It was said that those who had made the Church, namely the people, could unmake or change it. If the postulate of popular sovereignty were admitted, the Reformers' conclusion followed as a matter of course.

The political advantages of strong centralized government. A group of notable men wrote in support of strong central government. First may be mentioned Niccolò Machiavelli (1469–1527), who was a public official in Florence, Italy, while that city was independent. Machiavelli had carried out various missions for his government in a troubled time, and thus had the opportunity to observe the methods used by Cesare Borgia (1476–1507), the clever but unscrupulous son of Pope Alexander VI. Through war and intrigue, Borgia had amassed a considerable

[41] This work purported to be written by one Stephanus Junius Brutus, and issued in Edinburgh, Scotland. Actually it was published in Basle, Switzerland, and its authorship is in doubt, both Hubert Languet (1518–1581) and Philippe de Mornay (1549–1623) having been credited with the work. Languet was the son of a French official, being converted to Protestantism and later in the employment of the Protestant Elector of Saxony. Mornay belonged to a French aristocratic family which embraced the Reformation. He occupied an important position under Henry of Navarre, King of France, until that monarch abjured the Protestant faith.

dukedom and Machiavelli appears to have conceived an admiration for his daring methods. At all events, Borgia was the model of *Il principe* (*The Prince*),[42] written by Machiavelli in 1513, and the entire book was an argument for the concentration of power in the person of a ruler. Machiavelli compared feudalism, such as existed in France in his time, with absolute monarchy, like that of Turkey, which was then a major power in Europe. Where the French king was surrounded by a number of hereditary nobles, each acknowledged and loved by subjects or retainers of his own to such an extent that the king could challenge him only at his peril, Machiavelli pointed out that the Turkish system was centralized. Government was in the hands of royal officials, who had no special claim to the allegiance of the people but were appointed by the ruler and could be removed at his pleasure. As a result, the Turks were a united and powerful people, Machiavelli said, whereas France was torn by dissension. Machiavelli spoke as though any methods that secured strong centralized government were justifiable, but the common belief that he supported the unlimited exercise of sovereign power by the king or prince is incorrect. In *The Prince* it is clearly recognized that a ruler must consider the feelings of his subjects if his rule is to continue. For example, according to Machiavelli, Louis XI of France (King 1461–1483), having conquered extensive territory in Italy, lost it again because he neglected this point.

Similar in general argument, though much more comprehensive in its scope, was the *Six livres de la république* (1576)[43] of Jean Bodin (1530–1596). Bodin was a French lawyer who became interested in political philosophy and served as a member of the states-general, an advisory body representative of clergy, nobles, and commons. Of the three forms of government, democratic, aristocratic, and monarchial, Bodin thought that the last was the best:

> For if many wise and skilfull pilots hinder one another in striving to governe the helme; even so will many lords do, every one seeking to governe the Commonwealle, be they never so wise and vertuous.[44]

This was another way of stating the truth expressed in the proverb: "too many cooks spoil the broth." Not divine right, according to Bodin, but the need of man in the way of good government, was made the justification of absolute government.

Self-interest as the basis of social organization. Thomas Hobbes was still more emphatic on this point. Hobbes was born in England and acted as tutor in a noble family, traveling on the Continent and meeting

[42] There are numerous translations of this book. A good one is that by N. H. Thomson, 3rd ed., Oxford 1913.

[43] Translated by R. Knolles as *The Six Books of a Common-weale,* London 1606.

[44] Page 718 of the translation.

such men as Galileo and Spinoza. Like the Epicureans of ancient Greece and Rome, he based the social contract, which established society, upon men's self-interest. In his *Leviathan or The Matter, Form and Power of a Commonwealth, Ecclesiastical and Civil* (1651), he declared,

The final cause, end, or design of men, who naturally love liberty, and dominion over others, in the introduction of that restraint upon themselves, in which we see them live in commonwealths, is the foresight of their own preservation, and of a more contented life thereby; that is to say, of getting themselves out from that miserable condition of war, which is necessarily consequent . . . to the natural passions of men, when there is no visible power to keep them in awe, and tie them by fear of punishment to the performance of their covenants. . .[45]

Hobbes's viewpoint represented a reaction to the Renaissance. Freedom, he thought—and it must be remembered that he lived during the troubled seventeenth century—had led to anarchy, from which escape lay only in authority. The prince or ruler described in the *Leviathan* was absolute. In entering into the social contract, Hobbes asserted, individuals had signed away their liberties to the sovereign and they could not get them back again. It was left to Locke to resurrect the arguments of Marsilius and the *Vindiciae contra tyrannos* in favor of the indefeasible sovereignty of the common man.

The Dutch political philosopher, Hugo Grotius (1583–1645), in his *De jure belli ac pacis* (1625),[46] applied the same principle of self-interest to international comity. As long as the doctrines of the Catholic Church were everywhere accepted, these formed the basis of international law. The Reformation had swept away this foundation and Grotius sought for something to put in its place. In a world of sovereign States, or supreme powers "whose Acts are not subject to the power of another,"[47] could there be no law between nations, except that of struggle and the survival of the fittest? Grotius refused to accept this. The law of nature forbade it, he thought. Men had lifted themselves up into society and self-interest would not permit them to fall down again:

it was common profit, I grant, that occasioned the Civil Law: For that very Consociation or Subjection (whereof we have spoken) was first instituted for some utility: yea, and they that prescribe Laws unto others, either do, or should propose something of profit even therein. But as the Municipal Laws of every City do mainly regard the benefit of that City, even so among all, or at least the most Cities, there may, nay certainly are, some Laws by common consent agreed on, which respect the benefit not of those particular Cities, but of all in general. And this that we call the Law of Nations. . .

[45] *Leviathan*, p. 153.

[46] Translated by W. Evats as *The Most Excellent Hugo Grotius His Three Books Treating of the Rights of War & Peace*, London 1682.

[47] p. 37 of the translation.

For as by his own Confession, That Citizen is no Fool who observes the Civil Laws of the City he lives in, although he (for the reverence he bears unto those Laws) omits some things that would be profitable to himself : So neither is that a foolish people who have not so great an esteem for their own private gain, as for it, to trample upon the Laws Common to all, or to most Nations : There being the same reason for both. For as he that for his present profit, shall violate the Laws of the Countrey he lives in, doth as much as in him lies, but destroy that, which should perpetually defend both him and his, in whatsoever he hath or shall acquire ; so also a people in violating the Laws of Nature and Nations, do but pull down those Bulwarks, that should thenceforth secure their own peace and safety.[48]

According to Grotius, as to Hobbes, men found that it did not pay to fight continually against each other, so they associated themselves into States. In the passage just quoted, Grotius argued that the principle of self-interest, which kept order within States, led States to keep peace with each other. Grotius wrote in Holland where a long struggle for political and religious freedom had built up traditions of liberty and equality. He visualized a situation in which the sovereign power reposed, not in an *absolute monarch* – such as Hobbes, with his English background, had in mind – but in a *people*. Grotius thought that, in making the social contract, every person had equal power. The society constituted by the contract was democratic and "the major part" (*i.e.*, the majority) had "the power of the whole."[49] Notwithstanding this political disagreement, however, Hobbes and Grotius were alike in offering a general theory of society based on individual self-interest.

Economic Theories and Policies

The rise of the modern nation-State was reflected in economic thought and policy, what is commonly known as *Mercantilism* being the result.[50] The principle of ordered social relationships was inherited from the middle ages but it was given a new locus and an altered direction. Governments applied themselves to the destruction of medieval particularism. For the separate policies of Church, barons, gilds, municipalities, etc., there was substituted a centralized control aimed at the glorification of the State. The unity of the State, its power, its wealth, its self-sufficiency, were the prominent objectives. Politicians and pamphleteering traders busied themselves in suggesting all manner of schemes for the furtherance of these aims. Thus arose the considerable body of Mercantilist literature. Its diversification has impressed some subsequent

[48] *Ibid.*, pp. vii-viii.

[49] *Ibid.*, p. 113.

[50] Like many other words in economics, *Mercantilism* is used differently by various writers. Some employ it to denote the whole body of State economic policy which developed in western Europe during the sixteenth and seventeenth centuries, and here this definition is followed. Other authorities, however, give the word a narrower meaning, employing it to describe a particular type of monetary and trade policy.

students to such an extent as to cause them to deny that there was a Mercantilist system at all, but in the light of the circumstances in which the literature appeared can anything but complexity be expected? Germany, for example, had a special problem of disunity, which in some measure continued down to the present. The country was divided into independent States of different sizes and cities which possessed varying degrees of self-government. As it was not yet welded into a nation, it was natural that unifying policies received attention by German kings. On the other hand, in England, which was already unified in a large degree by 1500, national unity was less of a problem.

As might be expected, in Mercantilist literature often private and group objectives were made to masquerade as those of the nation, as when Mun and Child wrote to justify, on national grounds, the particular form of trade that was conducted by the British East India Company, with which they were connected. Even kings were not above identifying with the State good their personal interests, such as rights of succession, claims to other dominions, or even private wealth; and, in view of the great amount of power they possessed in this period, commonly this could be done without serious challenge from their subjects. Now that central governments had armies and civil servants to pay, fiscal needs were apt to loom large in State policy, as they do at present. Some of the chief aspects of this many-sided development receive attention in later chapters.

Modern Times

Despotism, State control of the economic activities of men, production methods that were not greatly in advance of those of the ancient world — these characteristics of the mercantile period were shortly to suffer eclipse. Centralized government remained but even this meant less, with the emergence of the individual as a social force. Such are the changes that must now be described.

Individualism and Laissez Faire

The internal regulatory policy of the English Mercantilists was not very successful. There was no adequate civil service and the administration of laws was left largely in the hands of part-time local officials, drawn mainly from the landed classes and often unsympathetic to the legislation that they were expected to enforce. The central government could chide or punish the local officials if the failings of the latter were too great to be overlooked and at times it did so strenuously. But the powerful position of the landed gentry in parliament after the fall of Stuart absolutism caused measures obnoxious to this class to sink into disuse, as appears to have been the case with the labor legislation of Elizabeth.

As early as the sixteenth century, while the system of industrial control that had been carried over from the middle ages was still important in the towns, manufactures began to move to the unregulated countryside. This fact, indeed, was one of the reasons behind national legislation. Factories appeared, supplanting the earlier system of domestic or workshop production. Stimulated by the opening up of new markets overseas at a time when industry on the continent of Europe was hampered by a series of wars, British industries advanced rapidly. A number of important inventions assisted the process. British ships, protected by a powerful navy, traded to all parts of the world. The British people became specialists, drawing raw materials from abroad and paying for them in manufactured goods and commercial services. Even agriculture shared in the general national prosperity. Improvements in materials and farming methods succeeded one another. The remaining open fields were enclosed for arable cultivation, as the needs of a growing population along with war-time price levels stimulated grain production. In France and on the Continent generally, industrial development proceeded more slowly. The broad belt of mineralized territory, that stretches from northeastern France and Belgium in a southeasterly direction to the foot of the Carpathian Mountains, was the battleground of Europe. Gild and feudal restrictions remained important on the Continent for a longer period than in England. A certain amount of encouragement was given to French industry by the Napoleonic Wars, which reduced the importation by France of British goods, but not until later did Continental manufactures begin a real advance. Through the second half of the nineteenth century they developed apace, and by its end were in a position to challenge the dominance of the English factories.

The results of this industrial revolution, in the areas affected by it—that is, Britain and northwestern and central Europe—were that self-sufficing agriculture declined or disappeared and farming became commercialized, while manufacturing industry and inter-local trade expanded by leaps and bounds. The urban worker, who in earlier times commonly owned his tools and simple machines, became a laborer simply, his place of work as well as the machinery on which he was employed being the property of the industrial capitalist. Even before the modern system of stockholding arose, businesses grew in size, through the plowing back of profits and also by amalgamation. Once joint-stock finance developed, it became possible for enterprises to be built on a scale undreamed of in previous times. "Bigger and bigger" seemed to have become the rule in industrial organization.

The economic regulations that had been inherited from the Mercantilist period appeared merely to impede the advance of business and in England they were removed. Thus government lost much of its ancient function of social regulation. Legislators were told that the country was best governed that was governed least, since private people were more capable of managing their business affairs than were interfering politicians. Chapter III describes this change in some detail.

British legislators applied to the colonies, which were not yet self-governing, the system that had come into popularity in the mother country. In internal policy, the new United States of America pursued a similar course. As a result, so far as it can be said that *laissez faire* was the rule at any time and place, the English-speaking world in the middle of the nineteenth century was in this position. On the continent of Europe, the alteration was slower and less complete. A movement had been made toward economic freedom in France at the close of the third quarter of the eighteenth century, under the influence of the school of *économistes* or Physiocrats. The term *laissez faire,* indeed, is commonly attributed to a member of this group, Gournay (1712–1759). Translated literally, it means *let to do,* that is, leave alone, signifying that the government should leave individuals alone in their economic activities. But, as is shown in Chapter III, the Physiocratic influence was short-lived. Though many of the internal restrictions associated with the gilds and feudal system disappeared in the Revolutionary and Napoleonic Wars period, not until after the middle of the nineteenth century was a significant move made toward freedom of international trade. In other parts of Europe the shackles of feudalism were removed at various dates, the Prussian agrarian reforms of 1807–1821 and the Russian emancipation in 1861 being noteworthy incidents.

The Downfall of Autocracy

The Stuart kings of England in the early half of the seventeenth century claimed to rule by divine right but the elected parliament demanded controlling powers. In the revolution of 1688 the dispute was finally settled in favor of the parliamentary claim, William and Mary coming from Holland as constitutional monarchs at the request of influential Britishers and jointly assuming the crown as constitutional monarchs. For a long time the limited nature of the franchise meant that the landowners dominated the legislature but the Reform Acts of 1832 and 1867 gave a good deal of political power to the rising industrial and commercial groups in the towns. In France royal absolutism lasted until toward the end of the eighteenth century, to disappear in blood in the Revolution. The effect of this latter was to place political control in the possession of the middle classes — town artisans and rural peasants — and resulted in a position not unlike that reached in England later. Elsewhere in Europe, though they were less pronounced, changes were in the same general direction.

The political revolutions of England and France had their associated philosophies, not unlike those that had accompanied earlier challenges to established authority. In England Sir Robert Filmer (d. 1653) was prominent on the Stuart side, writing to defend the divine right of kings. God, said Filmer, gave the first man, Adam, authority over his children. By inheritance, the divinely-conferred authority had descended through the ancient patriarchs to the kings of later times. Filmer's chief work, *Patriarcha: or, the Natural Power of Kings* (London 1680), was not published until after its author's death and its appearance coincided with the controversy that led to the revolution of 1688. As social history, as much was to be said, if not more, in favor of Filmer's ideas as for the social contract theory of the opposition; but critics of the King's conduct refused to accept Filmer's theory as a justification of royal rights. Chief among these was John Locke (1632–1704). Locke was the son of a landowner who had seen service in the parliamentary army during the Civil War. Having taught at Oxford, he became a friend of and secretary to the first Earl of Shaftesbury, an active opponent of the King. After spending a period in exile on the Continent, Locke returned to England in the train of the new King, William III, and received a minor government appointment. He now applied himself to writing a theoretical justification of the revolution. In *Two Treatises of Government* (London 1690), Locke countered Filmer's assertion of a patriarchal descent of divine authority by saying that power was not inherited by the eldest son any more than by the other children. God gave authority to all men. Government went back, Locke said, not to the divine appointment of a patriarch, but to the social contract, entered into by free men for purposes of protection. The natural rights of individuals, liberty (which included freedom of speech and of meeting), equality, and property, were antecedent to this contract and could not be destroyed by any action of the ruler, who owed his own appointment to the contract. If the king transgressed these natural rights, the people might rescind the contract, depose him, and select another monarch—which was precisely what they had done in England in 1688, according to Locke's interpretation.

The French philosopher, Jean Jacques Rousseau (1712–1778), took up a similar position. But France in the eighteenth century was different from the England of 1690. Locke wrote to justify an accomplished fact. The Stuart King, James II, had broken the social contract and had been deposed. France still had a despotic ruler, who claimed authority by divine right, and his administration was very unpopular with his subjects. Rousseau's assertions of liberty and equality, and the right of men to abrogate the social contract, which in England in 1690 were supports to the reigning government of William and Mary, in France provided a philosophical basis for the rising tide of revolution. Rousseau, too, was more radical than Locke in his attitude to property. Where Locke had made property a natural right, Rousseau regarded it as a usurpation of natural rights and so paved the way for some of the socialist criticism that arose later.

The Philosophers and the Nature of the Social Objective

Under the autocratic system of government, nominally at all events, it was for the king to say what constituted the common or social good. Some writers have maintained that real power is in the hands of a relatively small group or class of people under all forms of political organization (including democracy) and that this is true even of dictatorships or despotic monarchies.[51] Whether or not such a view is accepted, it is clear that tyrannical rulers have listened to advice from those surrounding them. If they wished to maintain their positions, they have had some regard for the opinions of influential followers, if not for those of a wider circle. On the surface, however, under a despotism, decisions rest with the ruler himself. When not justified frankly by force, in the period that has been studied this situation was based on a claim of divine authority (*e.g.*, by Filmer) or on a non-rescindable social contract (Hobbes).

John Locke. Locke put the social good in the people's hands. The good of England, according to Locke, was the sum of the separate goods or objectives of the individuals who were associated together to form the English nation. As to what constituted good, Locke was prepared to accept the individual's own interpretation. Whatever the men who composed society wanted, by that fact became the social good.[52] Locke recognized that all the people could not in practice be collected together to express an opinion on some disputed point. Even if this were possible, unanimity was too much to expect. To meet these difficulties, he said that the *will or aim of the majority* as expressed through the legislature should be accepted as the good of all. On this theory modern democracy has its foundations. In economics, the doctrines of Locke and his followers made it possible for the Classical economists to identify the satisfaction of individual wants with the common or social good.

Rousseau and Hegel. On the continent of Europe Rousseau and Hegel attempted to set up a different conception of society. The social contract described by Grotius and Locke was cold-blooded and materialistic. Rational men sacrificed their freedom to satisfy their desire for security, because they considered that they gained more than they lost by such a change. If, on the basis of a subsequent calculation of pleasures and pains, they so thought fit, they might withdraw from the particular society with which they had been associated (at least, according to Grotius) and migrate elsewhere. If the terms of the contract were infringed, they might rescind it. Moreover, the society was atomistic. Beyond the individuals in it, it amounted to nothing. It had no objective, spirit, or ideal, other than the sum of the separate objectives of the

[51] This theory is discussed later in Chapter I.

[52] See Chapter II for a fuller discussion of this point.

individuals who composed it. It was an aggregation of individuals, and nothing more. With that propensity to seek for the inner spirit which lay behind the surface, which characterized the Romantic movement [53] generally, Rousseau and Hegel attempted to build up an organic theory of society. Just as a human being was something more than a mere aggregation of living cells, because these cells were specialized so as to make up an interdependent whole, with a personality and a purpose transcending those of its component parts, so, argued these philosophers, did society transcend the individuals who made it up. It possessed a personality and a will that were something more than the mere summations of their separate personalities and wills.

Locke's conception of a social objective, made up by adding together individual objectives, Rousseau called a *volonté de tous,* or *will of all.* But when people associated together to form a society, Rousseau believed that they subordinated their several personalities in a new and greater personality, possessing a will of its own, the *volonté générale* or *general will:*

> The body politic, therefore, is also a moral being possessed of a will; and this general will, which tends always to the preservation and welfare of the whole and of every part, and is the source of the laws, constitutes for all the members of the State, in their relations to one another and to it, the rule of what is just or unjust. . .[54]

The idea of State dominance over the individual in the State was not new with Rousseau. It was significant in the ancient world, being well exemplified in the writings of Plato, and became important again after the end of the middle ages. Rousseau and Hegel attempted to give it an ethical and psychological basis. The general will, according to Rousseau, considered only the common interest and took no account of the special interests or concerns of individuals. On the other hand, the will of all was no more than the sum of these separate concerns. It cannot be said that Rousseau was very successful in explaining the difference between

[53] *Romanticism* may be described broadly as a revolt against materialism, affecting the entire front of thought and culture. J. W. von Goethe (1749–1832), J. C. F. von Schiller (1759–1805), and the brothers August (1767–1845) and Friedrich (1772–1829) von Schlegel, in literature, F. W. G. von Schelling (1775–1854) and J. G. Fichte (1762–1814) in general philosophy, and W. R. Wagner (1813–1883) in music, were German representatives of the movement. The poet, William Wordsworth (1770–1850), and the historian and essayist, Thomas Carlyle (1795–1881), may be grouped with them in Britain. Among Americans, R. W. Emerson (1803–1882) showed the influence of Romantic ideas. But the name is variously used and definitions overlap. Many would contrast philosophical *positivism* — which contents itself with the data of experience — with metaphysical speculation and with cultural Romanticism.

[54] Rousseau, *A Discourse on Political Economy* (published as *Sur l'économie politique,* 1758), printed in *The Social Contract and Other Essays* (Everyman's Library), London and New York 1913, reprinted 1935, p. 253. Quoted by permission of J. M. Dent & Sons, Ltd. and E. P. Dutton & Co., Inc.

influence public opinion, some modern governments that claim to be democratic can be considered to be not without a taint of tyranny, on Spinoza's definition.

Associations Other than the State

Individuals have been variously grouped at all times. The family has been a social unit from the earliest period for which records exist. Business partnerships are very old; so, too, are religious bodies and clubs of different types. Even in classical antiquity, there were organizations of craftsmen, forecasting the gilds of the middle ages. Trading companies, modeled on the gilds, anticipated the stock corporation, which dominates modern industry and trade. Some of these organizations—for example, the family and the Catholic Church—have played parts in society which have been at least as significant as that of any State. A little thought will demonstrate the importance of such associations in social life, even in the twentieth century. Undoubtedly, a very large number of men and women would place the interests of their families above those of the State, where the two appeared to be in conflict. From time to time, the Catholic Church and some other religious bodies still challenge State authority. Certain socialist organizations are international and their members work for what they accept as their common purpose within the various countries in which they reside.

History has provided numerous examples of strife between the State and voluntary associations, especially in the case of religious bodies, but modern law recognizes only associations that have been created by the State power and are, therefore, subordinate to this power. Such associations are given legal rights, becoming "collective persons," and possessing powers of holding property, etc., similar to those of individuals. Unless collective personality—with its attendant rights and duties—has been conferred upon it by State action, an association has no legal existence. This represents a logical conclusion from the doctrine of sovereignty advanced by Bodin and Hobbes. The State which was set up in the original contract of Hobbes was made master of society for all time.

The Hegelians gave recognition to associations within the State but were at pains to assert the subservience of these to the State power. They thought that in the latter there was manifested the supreme will of the society and that lesser associations were subordinated to this will. The German legal historian, Otto von Gierke (1844–1921), in his *Das deutsche Genossenschaftsrecht* (4 vols., Berlin 1868–1913),[59] with a wealth of illustration from early writings, advanced the thesis that the "natural right" of the individual to associate with other individuals—

[59] Two portions of this work have been translated: (1) by F. W. Maitland, as *Political Theories of the Middle Age*, Cambridge 1900, and (2) by E. Barker as *Natural Law and the Theory of Society 1500 to 1800*, 2 vols., Cambridge 1934.

The German philosopher, Friedrich von Schlegel, spoke favorably of the Indian caste system and even referred to the Christian ideal as sanctioning a division of the classes, with the duty laid upon those who were favorably placed to assist "those on whom the accident of birth, as the world speaks, or as we should prefer to say, a higher and a divine Providence, has laid all the hardships of life. . ."[62]

The idea that men are unequal and that society is (or should be) controlled by the individuals or groups who possess the position or quality of leadership has been developed by certain writers. The doctrine of class government, formulated by Marx, is an example. In modern society, according to Marx, the capitalist class was in the controlling position. The French philosopher and historian of religion, Ernest Renan (1823–1892), the German philosopher, Friedrich Wilhelm Nietzsche (1844–1900), and the Italians, Gaetano Mosca (1858–1941) and Vilfredo Pareto (1848–1923), adopted a different approach. Not economic conditions, as Marx had argued, but human qualities, were in their opinion the important factors in social control.

Renan's outlook was Romantic. He was impatient with the prevailing emphasis on "greatest happiness" and standard of material comfort. The aim of the individual, he thought, should not be to become happy or rich but to express or realize himself. The democratic form of government served to support the utilitarian ideals. Renan favored instead some form of aristocratic government or control by an élite, whose members did not seek their own gain but rather the realization and advancement of society. In place of a legislature elected on the basis of a democratic franchise, he proposed an assembly appointed by groups or corporations. The similarity of Renan's system and the ideals of Fascist Italy is evident and Mussolini identified Renan as one of his sources of inspiration. Further, Nietzsche, Mosca, and Pareto also were influenced by Renan's ideas.

Nietzsche formulated an evolutionary theory of ethics, such as was stated less consistently by the English philosophers, Herbert Spencer (1820–1903) and Sir Leslie Stephen (1832–1904). Carried to its logical conclusion, this involved the rejection of absolute systems of morals, like Christianity, substituting the principle that right is whatever conduces to social survival. It was the Darwinian law of survival of the fittest applied to ethics. Hegel had said that ideals such as right were connected with human types. Nietzsche associated the downtrodden Hebrew race with ideals of humility and submission. More vigorous races should have other ideals, like courage, he said. "The root of all evil" was that the slave morality of modesty, chastity, selflessness, and absolute obedience should have triumphed. Dominating natures were thus condemned

[62] *The Philosophy of Life,* translated by A. J. W. Morrison, London 1847, p. 313.

(1) to hypocrisy, (2) to qualms of conscience, — creative natures regarded themselves as rebels against God, uncertain and hemmed in by eternal values. . . . In this respect the concept, *"all men are equal before God,"* does an extraordinary amount of harm; actions and attitudes of mind were forbidden which belonged to the prerogative of the strong alone, just as if they were in themselves unworthy of man. All the tendencies of strong men were brought into disrepute by the fact that the defensive weapons of the most weak (even of those who were weakest towards themselves) were established as a standard of valuation.[63]

But, "A daring and ruling race" was building itself up —

the future "lords of the earth" — a new, vast aristocracy based upon the most severe self-discipline, in which the will of philosophical men of power and artist-tyrants will be stamped upon thousands of years: a higher species of men which, thanks to their preponderance of will, knowledge, riches, and influence, will avail themselves of democratic Europe as the most suitable and supple instrument they can have for taking the fate of the earth into their own hands, and working as artists upon man himself.[64]

Nietzsche appears to have had in mind not merely the dominance of the Teuton race but that of a ruling class of Teutons. However, his general idea was of wider significance and it is possible that more than one of the modern dictatorial regimes have looked upon themselves as fulfilling his prophecy.

The Italian political philosopher, Mosca, in his *Teorica dei governi e governo parlamentare* (1884) and *Elementi di scienza politica* (1896),[65] integrated the idea of a ruling class into general political theory. Partly as the result of studying Taine's inquiry into French political conditions under the pre-Revolutionary monarchy, Mosca advanced the theory that whatever be the form of government — autocracy, oligarchy, or democracy — States tended to be controlled by relatively narrow groups, composed of the persons whose abilities and circumstances enabled them to influence events. Majority rule, he thought, must lead to anarchism, followed in turn by totalitarianism. Government was best, in his opinion, where a ruling class was recruited from the most suitable individuals within the State, unimpeded by caste barriers.

Pareto — at once an economist and a social philosopher of first rank — spoke of the existence of a cyclical movement or circulation with respect to the ruling class. Men of cunning and of force, he said, alternate in possessing themselves of the reins of government. Men obtain power by the use of forceful methods but, with the passage of time, they are edged

[63] *The Complete Works of Friedrich Nietzsche,* ed. O. Levy, 18 vols., London 1909-1913, vol. 15, *The Will to Power,* 2, reprinted 1924, pp. 309-311. Quoted by permission of George Allen & Unwin Ltd. and The Macmillan Company.

[64] *Ibid.,* pp. 365-366.

[65] The latter of these works has been translated by H. D. Kahn as *The Ruling Class,* ed. A. Livingston, N. Y. 1939.

out by individuals who are skilled in intrigue, such as scheming politicians and clever enterprisers. Carried far enough, the resulting government itself becomes unstable and falls a prey to more courageous and forceful men. Though indicated in earlier writings, Pareto's theory was most fully expressed in his *Trattato di sociologia generale* (2 vols., Florence 1916; 2nd ed., 3 vols. 1923).[66] A quotation from this work will illustrate the idea :

Suppose a certain country has a governing class, *A,* that assimilates the best elements, as regards intelligence, in the whole population. In that case the subject class, *B,* is largely stripped of such elements and can have little or no hope of ever overcoming the class *A* so long as it is a battle of wits. . . But . . . In the majority of cases people who rely on their wits are or become less fitted to use violence, and *vice versa.* So concentration in the class *A* of the individuals most adept at chicanery leads to a concentration in class *B* of the individuals most adept at violence; and if that process is long continued, the equilibrium tends to become unstable, because the *A's* are long in cunning but short in the courage to use force and in the force itself; whereas the *B's* have the force and the courage to use it, but are short in the skill required for exploiting these advantages. But if they chance to find leaders who have the skill — and history shows that such leadership is usually supplied by dissatisfied *A's* — they have all they need for driving the *A's* from power. Of just that development history affords countless examples from remotest times all the way down to the present.[67]

Pareto thought that a revolution, in general terms, was beneficial to a society, and he speculated how history might have been written differently. Had the victims of the French Revolution not been "spineless humanitarians," instead of being destroyed, they might have been the ones to do the destroying, he said. According to Pareto, the western world, at the time he wrote, was ripe for such a revolution as was described in the passage quoted above :

The prosperity of our modern countries is due to freedom — be it only a limited freedom — of economic and social activity. . . Now crystallization is setting in, precisely as happened in the case of Rome. It is desired by the public and in many cases seems to increase prosperity. . . As regards the exploiters there is, to be sure, a great difference between our present condition and the situation under the Roman Empire, where the Imperial authority fixed the tax to be paid by the well-to-do. But the difference is much smaller as regards the victims, for after all it matters little to them whether their money goes to fatten the henchmen of an Emperor or the henchmen of a demogogic plutocrat. In point of fact, the legions of Alexander Severus, who was so liberal in paying his soldiers, cost much less money than it costs to

[66] Translated by A. Bongiorno and A. Livingston as *The Mind and Society,* ed. A. Livingston, London and New York, 1935.

[67] Vol. 4 of the translation, p. 1531. Quoted by permission of Harcourt, Brace and Company, Inc., and Jonathan Cape Ltd.

buy votes [for a modern political party]. . . In a word, we are very apparently moving along a curve such as Roman society traversed in its day after the founding of the Empire. . . History does not repeat itself. Unless one chooses to believe in some "yellow peril" there is little likelihood that the next period of prosperity that is to come will originate in another Barbarian invasion. There would be more plausibility in the guess that it will come from some internal revolution which will transfer power to individuals who are . . . able and willing to use force.[68]

Not unnaturally, many people have seen in Pareto's statement a prophecy of the Fascist and Nazi Revolutions of post-war Europe.

It would be out of place here to enter into a long discussion of these theories. Obviously, it is true to say that a considerable degree of social leadership is exercised by individuals and small groups, even in a democracy. On the other hand, time and time again history has shown that political power rests upon some measure of consent on the part of those over whom it is wielded. Even dictators have to keep their subjects in good humor, or at all events prevent their getting into very bad humor. To some extent these subjects can be molded at the will of their ruler, so that the latter is enabled, in the words of Nietzsche, to work as an artist upon man himself. To what degree men's minds can be altered by propaganda and coercion remains to be seen. It must be remembered that the latter may go to considerable lengths, making it difficult for objectors to earn a livelihood, or even to live at all. But it has yet to be demonstrated that governments can change their subjects indefinitely. Leadership is not the same as unlimited control.

The Decline of Individualism

The last fifty years have witnessed a pronounced tendency for the western world to move away from individualism and *laissez faire* toward State regulation in some form or other. This development is traced in later chapters. Briefly, it can be said that individual liberty was attended by evils. Certain commodities or services that society wanted, such as elementary education—very necessary in democratic countries—and health services, were not provided by private enterprise. Desires that seemed socially objectionable, like those for injurious drugs, were gratified. Children, and even adults in weak economic positions, could not protect themselves from exploitation. Powerful monopolies came into existence, enriching their owners at the expense of the consumer. Hence, governments stepped in to control the actions of individual producers, on the one hand, and to supplement these with government production, on the other. The war of 1914–1918, and the depression that began at the end of 1929, gave great impetus to this development, even in those countries—such as Britain and the United States of America—that re-

[68] *Ibid.*, pp. 1861–1864.

main largely individualistic. Public control predominates in the so-called authoritarian or totalitarian States, of which Germany, Italy, and Russia, are outstanding examples. The whole development has been accompanied by an emphasis on economic self-sufficiency which possesses a certain resemblance to the Mercantilism of earlier times.

The idea of Locke, that men's *desires* and their *good* coincide, has not been abandoned altogether. What has happened in the democratic countries is that Locke's provision for settling conflicts between individual desires by legislative action has been extended over a widening field. As for the things that one set of individuals wants, and another does not, the tendency has been increasingly to settle the matter by votes, the will of the majority prevailing. The justification for this interference by one group with the freedom of another has been that, in a complex society, few of men's actions leave their fellows entirely unaffected. If a narrow group were permitted to satisfy its craving for cocaine or brothels, for example, or its carelessness about sanitation, not only does the indulgent group suffer but repercussions arise that affect other members of society.

Theoretical argument on the subject of the place of government in business has followed the lines laid down by earlier philosophers. Some writers have approached the problem from the angle of individual utility. They have asked how far government action increases individual wealth or individual happiness. Henry Sidgwick (1838–1900) and F. Y. Edgeworth (1845–1926), teachers at Cambridge and Oxford respectively, and the Austrian, Friedrich von Wieser (1851–1926), took up this position, with which a large number of economists in the English-speaking countries have been associated. On the other hand, the German, W. M. Wundt (1832–1920), to some extent the Englishman, T. H. Green, mentioned earlier in the chapter, and others, found their inspiration in the Hegelian conception of a common good, to which individual benefits were subordinate. From both these viewpoints, there appeared to be no difficulty in giving some support to the movement toward increased government regulation of social life, though an astonishing variation was revealed in the lengths to which individual writers were prepared to go. Later chapters give some account of this development.

Where society is going, no man can say. There are those who look upon the growth of State control in such countries as America, where private capitalism is still important, as part of an inevitable march towards State socialism or authoritarianism.[69] Others speak of the development as being like the swing of a pendulum, which proceeds so far and then is reversed. Certainly, the intensity of regulation in the war years of 1914–1918 was followed by a decline in interventionism when peace was restored, and the same has been true in the United States after

[69] See *The Road to Serfdom,* F. A. von Hayek, University of Chicago Press, Chicago, 1944.

World War II, though these may be minor movements superimposed on a bigger trend. Will authoritarianism spread over the world? Will it recede where it is now important? Will the world continue in two camps or will the camps converge? Only change itself is sure. Alterations may be gradual and evolutionary, or sudden and revolutionary. The difference appears marked at close quarters but many of the revolutions of history, regarded in perspective, themselves fall into their background as part of an evolutionary movement and become symptomatic rather than causal. Probably few authorities would care to assert that France now is materially different from what it would have been if there had been no French Revolution, or the United States of America without the Civil War. Will the same be true of Germany, Italy, and the Soviet Union? Only time can answer this question.

Summary of Chapter

There have been numerous attempts to summarize and simplify social history by depicting it as a series of stages, but it must be recognized that the course of human evolution has been too complex to be portrayed adequately in this way. Recent research suggests that the older theory that primitive man lived an individual and solitary existence is unfounded. All evidence points to social life, even in the most rudimentary cultures.

Ancient Egypt can be described as an authoritarian State, but Greek and Roman civilization moved in the direction of individualism. Commerce and industry developed. Then came a thousand years of feudalism – the middle ages. During the medieval period, the Church wielded great influence. Possessed of a certain similarity to the older Stoic philosophy, in its beginnings Christianity represented a withdrawal from the affairs of the world. As time passed by, however, an organized Church came into existence and received official recognition, giving counsel on all manner of human relationships.

The Reformation destroyed the international unity of the Church and, in those countries where it was successful, religious organization became associated with the national States. This was the period when Mercantilism was important.

In the seventeenth century and afterwards, despotism gave place to democracy in some countries, and authoritarian control of the social system to individualism. The foundations of modern economics were laid. Yet the new ideas were not accepted without criticism. Antagonism arose among the Romantics, the Hegelians, and the socialists. Individualism was attacked from the standpoints to which it owed its earlier support. Even in countries where *laissez faire* had received wide acceptance, such as Britain and the United States of America, recent years have witnessed a growing emphasis on State control of economic life.

E. A. Westermarck has argued[5] that primitive people differ in their willingness to work, on account of the environment in which they live. Where economic conditions are easy, so that nature, with little assistance on the part of man, calls into existence an ample supply of food and other necessities of life, the inhabitants are indolent; whereas more severe conditions are favorable to industry. In support of this view, Westermarck gave numerous comparisons: energetic New Zealand Maori were contrasted with slothful Tongan Islanders, Greenlanders with North American Indians, etc. The opinion that men's character can be explained in terms of environment is an old one. It was suggested in Bodin's *Six livres de la république*, referred to in Chapter I. Bodin's compatriot, the political philosopher Montesquieu (1689–1755), in his *De l'esprit des lois* (2 vols., Geneva 1748),[6] compared northern and southern Europeans in respect of their willingness to work:

In Europe, there is a kind of balance between the southern and northern nations. The first have every convenience of life, and few of its wants: the last have many wants, and few conveniences. To one, nature has given much, and demands but little; to the other, she has given but little, and demands a great deal. The equilibrium is maintained by the laziness of the southern nations, and by the industry and activity which she has given to those in the north.[7]

Montesquieu attributed the difference to climate, but Westermarck rejected this explanation on the basis of further comparisons. For example, the people of Egypt and other countries "which yield their produce almost spontaneously," were described by him as indolent; while those of the mountains of Syria, whose climate was similar but whose economic conditions were more difficult, were reported to be energetic. Whatever be the reason, even in the twentieth century men and women are by no means alike in their attitudes toward the acquisition of wealth. Confronted by the alternatives of working longer or more intensively in order to expand consumption, and of consuming less but enjoying increased leisure, some people prefer that the balance rest in one position while others place it elsewhere. The author recalls a conversation on this subject with an Irish peasant, who remarked: "I have sons in London and New York, each earning as much in a day as I get in a week, but I have time to look at the sun and talk to my neighbor, which is more than they can say. I do not believe that they are any happier than I am." Undoubtedly, there is a remarkable contrast between the bustling life of the world's greatest cities and the placid existence of some parts of rural Ireland.

[5] See *The Origin and Development of the Moral Ideas,* 2nd ed., 2 vols., London 1912-1917, vol. 2, Chap. 36.

[6] Translated by T. Nugent as *The Spirit of Laws,* 2 vols., London 1773.

[7] Vol. 2 of the translation, pp. 25-26.

Incentives in Primitive Life

Numerous books on primitive life describe the activities of the men and women of native tribes when not occupied by labor. War-making, social intercourse in various forms, such as dancing, speech-making, the pursuance of love affairs, and the observation of religious practices, have their places; though from time to time one of these may assume such significance as to crowd out the remainder, as during a tribal war. Primitive people, like the rest of mankind, appear to appreciate the desirability of "killing two birds with one stone." Essential tasks of labor, like planting seeds, are often associated with magical practices. Work is undertaken by groups, with rest intervals in which news and banter are exchanged, so that laborious tasks become social events and the pleasure of company reinforces the economic stimulus. Feasting may precede or follow the launching of a canoe, or the in-gathering of the harvest, as was the case with the threshings and barn-raisings of pioneer America. Monotonous pieces of labor are accompanied often by rhythmic movements, songs and chants, by the squads performing them. Thus, it is a usual sight in any South African town, where negro labor is employed, to observe a line of ten or a dozen laborers engaged in road repair or constructional work, striking their picks in unison to time beats made by their leader, or a similar gang making movements that approach a dance while they lift a heavy log to its destination.[8]

Interesting studies of economic incentives among primitive people are to be found in the works of Malinowski and Firth.[9] The former authority, from experience gained in the Trobriand Islands of the western Pacific, roundly condemns the view that the primitive native is lazy and points out on the contrary that he works well if an appropriate stimulus is present:

> First of all, it is important to realise that a Kiriwinian is capable of working well, efficiently and in a continuous manner. But he must work under an effective incentive: he must be prompted by some duty imposed by tribal standards, or he must be lured by ambitions and values also dictated by custom and tradition. Gain, such as is often the stimulus for work in more civilised communities, never acts as an impulse to work under the original native conditions. It succeeds very badly, therefore, when a white man tries to use this incentive to make a native work.
>
> This is the reason why the traditional view of the lazy and indolent native is not only a constant refrain of the average white settler, but finds its way into good books of travel, and even serious ethnographic records. With us, labour is, or was till fairly recently, a commodity sold as any other, in the open market. A man accustomed to think in terms of current economic

[8] K. Bücher considered this subject at length in his *Arbeit und Rhythmus* (1896) but no English translation is available.

[9] *Argonauts of the Western Pacific* and *Primitive Economics of the New Zealand Maori.*

theory will naturally apply the conceptions of supply and demand to labour, and he applies them therefore to native labour. The untrained person does the same, though in less sophisticated terms, and as they see that the native will not work well for the white man, even if tempted by considerable payment and treated fairly well, they conclude that his capacity for labour is very small. This error is due to the same cause which lies at the bottom of all our misconceptions about people of different cultures. If you remove a man from his social milieu, you *eo ipso* deprive him of almost all his stimuli to moral steadfastness and economic efficiency and even of interest in life. If then you measure him by moral, legal or economic standards, also essentially foreign to him, you cannot but obtain a caricature in your estimate.[10]

Firth's study of the New Zealand Maori draws the same conclusion.

Civilization and the Growth of Wants

It is evident to all observers that many of the primitive people who still exist are changing rapidly under the influence of European civilization. This is seen with the African negroes in areas that have been opened up by the white man. The native begins to appreciate and want the goods he notices in the possession of the European or for sale at trading stores in native communities. He passes from colored beads and anklet wire to blankets, bicycles, and radio sets, as his desires multiply and change in their nature. Pressure from womenfolk, who rival each other in the possession of personal finery or articles of domestic utility, assists the process of what may be called *education in wants*. Primed, perhaps, by a small loan from a labor recruiting agent, the native leaves his tribal land to go to a city or mine to work for wages. In some instances, indeed, he goes unwillingly under pressure from his elders, who are to benefit from the proceeding. But once in the city or mining compound, he comes further under the attraction of new goods and changed ways of living. After his first contract has expired and he has had a short holiday, he goes again and again to engage in labor. In some instances, finally all regular relations with his tribe are broken and he becomes a detribalized urban native, dependent wholly on wages for his livelihood.[11] In Africa, this tendency was at work quite early:

It appears however that every year [about 1850] there was an increase in the number of natives seeking work, as an understanding of the value of money spread amongst them.[12]

Firth refers to a similar development in New Zealand and concludes, The practical inference seems fairly clear, that if we can succeed in raising the standard of comfort of the Maori by inducing him to conceive new wants

[10] *Argonauts,* pp. 156-157.

[11] The process is well described by G. St. J. Orde Browne in *The African Labourer,* Oxford, 1933.

[12] Axelson, *op. cit.,* p. 64.

from among the attractive budget offered him by civilization, then an increase in the quantity and regularity of his labour will follow.[13]

The fact is that the native is becoming *civilized* and his wants more expansible. If the primitive people who have remained to become the subject matter of modern investigations are to be taken as in any degree representative of the forebears of present-day Europeans and Americans, the rapid advance of the natives is highly interesting to the student of economic evolution, because it compresses within a short period developments which have taken many centuries in Europe.

The Ancient World

Wealth and Human Industry

Coming between primitive barbarism and the hardly more civilized middle ages, ancient culture exhibited certain features that are characteristic of modern times. Among these was the important position occupied by personal gain-seeking activities. This was a gradual development. Homeric Greece and early Italy possessed economies that were to a large extent self-sufficing and it was only later that specialization and trade arose. From what little is know of them, it seems possible that these early societies may have been similar, in their attitude towards wealth and gain, to those of the primitive negroes and Pacific islanders referred to in the preceding section. This, however, can be no more than surmise.

Plato and Aristotle. By the time of Plato, the Greeks had outgrown this primitive simplicity of tastes, if it had ever existed among them, for that teacher lamented,

> the class of men is small – they must have been rarely gifted by nature, and trained by education, – who, when assailed by wants and desires, are able to hold out and observe moderation, and when they might make a great deal of money are sober in their wishes, and prefer a moderate to a large gain. But the mass of mankind are the very opposite : their desires are unbounded, and when they might gain in moderation they prefer gains without limit. . .[14]

Aristotle also commented on this selfish propensity of men :

> the avarice of mankind is insatiable.[15]

By *avarice,* Aristotle had in mind not merely a greed for money. He believed that men were not so foolish as to confuse money with riches or wealth :

> how can that be wealth of which a man may have a great abundance and yet perish with hunger, like Midas in the fable, whose insatiable prayer turned

[13] *Primitive Economics of the New Zealand Maori*, p. 187. Quoted by permission of George Routledge & Sons Ltd. and E. P. Dutton & Co., Inc.

[14] *The Dialogues of Plato*, vol. 5, *Laws*, p. 305.

[15] *The Works of Aristotle*, vol. 10, *Politica*, 1267a.

everything that was set before him into gold? Hence men seek after a better notion of riches and of the art of getting wealth than the mere acquisition of coin, and they are right.[16]

Aristotle evidently considered that the men of his time were rational beings, who thought things out and pursued courses of action indicated by their reasoning as being beneficial to them; but also that they were subject to unreasoning appetites. Moreover, moral considerations sometimes inhibited the desires that were based on reason or appetite:

even when the mind does command and thought bids us pursue or avoid something, sometimes no movement is produced; we act in accordance with desire, as in the case of moral weakness. . . Lastly, appetite too is incompetent to account fully for movement; for those who successfully resist temptation have appetite and desire and yet follow mind and refuse to enact that for which they have appetite.[17]

All of this might stand for sound psychology today. Aristotle seemed to think that most men pursued their own happiness, but he recognized that happiness possessed varying meanings for different individuals:

To judge from the lives that men lead, most men, and men of the most vulgar type, seem (not without some ground) to identify the good, or happiness, with pleasure; which is the reason why they love the life of enjoyment. . . A consideration of the prominent types of life shows that people of superior refinement and of active disposition identify happiness with honour. . . Third comes the contemplative life. . . the activity of philosophic wisdom is admittedly the pleasantest of virtuous activities. . .[18]

Like Plato and other classical philosophers, Aristotle gave considerable attention to the ethical side of human conduct—the question of what men *should* seek, as distinct from the psychological problem of what they *do* seek—and he attempted to evaluate wants with a view to deciding which were more praiseworthy or better than others. Plato had distinguished between (1) *divine goods*—wisdom, temperance, justice, and courage, and (2) *lesser* or *human goods*—health, beauty, strength, and wealth. This gave the order of preference, wealth, in Plato's estimation, being the least commendable.[19] Aristotle followed with three classes: (1) goods that were *in the soul,* of which he mentioned three, wisdom, virtue, and pleasure, (2) goods *in the body,* for instance, health and beauty, and (3) *outside* or external goods, such as wealth, office, and honor. Goods in the soul were the highest category, and included happiness, but this was defined as "doing well and living well" and as "living

[16] *Ibid.,* 1257b.

[17] *The Works of Aristotle,* vol. 3, *De anima,* translated by J. A. Smith, Oxford 1931, 433a. Quoted by permission of the Oxford University Press.

[18] *Ibid.,* vol. 9, *Ethica Nicomachea,* translated by W. D. Ross, Oxford 1925, 1095b-1096a and 1177a. Quoted by permission of the Oxford University Press.

[19] *The Dialogues of Plato,* vol. 5, *Laws,* pp. 8-9.

in accordance with the virtues,"[20] so obviously it did not mean the enjoyment of luxuries, especially since wealth was included among external goods. Both philosophers made further comments on this subject.

Thus Plato said:

> The citizen must indeed be happy and good, and the legislator will seek to make him so; but very rich and very good at the same time he cannot be, not, at least, in the sense in which the many speak of riches. For they mean by 'the rich' the few who have the most valuable possessions, although the owner of them may quite well be a rogue. And if this is true, I can never assent to the doctrine that the rich man will be happy—he must be good as well as rich. And good in a high degree, and rich in a high degree at the same time, he cannot be. Some one will ask, why not? And we shall answer,—Because acquisitions which come from sources which are just and unjust indifferently, are more than double those which come from just sources only; and the sums which are expended neither honourably nor disgracefully, are only half as great as those which are expended honourably and on honourable purposes. Thus, if the one acquires double and spends half, the other who is in the opposite case and is a good man cannot possibly be wealthier than he. . . Our statement, then, is true, that the very rich are not good, and, if they are not good, they are not happy.[21]

Aristotle:

> we reply. . . happiness, whether consisting in pleasure or virtue, or both, is more often found with those that are most highly cultivated in their mind and in their character, and have only a moderate share of external goods, than among those who possess external goods to a useless extent but are deficient in higher qualities. . . all things useful are of such a nature that where there is too much of them they must either do harm, or at any rate be of no use, to their possessors, every good of the soul, the greater it is, is also of greater use. . .[22]

In this last statement Aristotle appears to have had in mind something of the nature of the modern conception of diminishing utility, which, according to his way of thinking, applied to external goods but not to goods of the soul. At least, he thought that the usefulness of goods of the soul did not fall to zero when their quantity was augmented, as, he argued, was the case with external goods. Wealth was placed in a subordinate position. Aristotle granted that a certain amount of it was desirable, as when, for example, in considering the best size of the State, he expressed the opinion that its area should be large enough in relation to the population to enable the citizens to live liberally.[23] Wealth was useful only as a *means*, however, not as an *end*:

[20] *The Works of Aristotle*, vol. 9, *Magna moralia*, translated by St. George Stock, Oxford 1915, 1184b. Quoted by permission of the Oxford University Press.

[21] *The Dialogues of Plato*, vol. 5, *Laws*, pp. 125-126.

[22] *The Works of Aristotle*, vol. 10, *Politica*, 1323b.

[23] See Chapter VII.

The life of money-making is one undertaken under compulsion, and wealth is evidently not the good we are seeking; for it is merely useful and for the sake of something else.[24]

Plato (or Socrates, for Plato purported to quote the older teacher) raised an economic objection to the possession of great wealth on the one hand, and the existence of poverty on the other. Either, he said, injured the productivity of the individual concerned:

S. (*Socrates*) : There seem to be two causes of the deterioration of the arts.
A. (*Adeimantus*) : What are they?
S. : Wealth, I said, and poverty.
A. : How do they act?
S. : The process is as follows: When a potter becomes rich, will he, think you, any longer take the same pains with his art?
A. : Certainly not.
S. : He will grow more and more indolent and careless?
A. : Very true.
S. : And the result will be that he becomes a worse potter?
A. : Yes; he greatly deteriorates.
S. : But, on the other hand, if he has no money, and cannot provide himself with tools or instruments, he will not work equally well himself, nor will he teach his sons or apprentices to work equally well.
A. : Certainly not.
S. : Then, under the influence either of poverty or of wealth, workmen and their work are equally liable to degenerate?
A. : That is evident.
S. : Here, then, is a discovery of new evils, I said, against which the guardians will have to watch, or they will creep into the city unobserved.
A. : What evils?
S. : Wealth, I said, and poverty; the one is the parent of luxury and indolence, and the other of meanness and viciousness, and both of discontent.[25]

Plato also mentioned a political argument against riches. Opposing the view that a poor nation might fare badly in war against one which was better off, Plato said that the former would possess hardy warriors and the latter an array of ineffective rich men.[26] This brings out a feature that cropped up constantly in the classical writings—a feeling in favor of military preparedness, which was significant in the Greek cities and influenced the outlook of the philosophers towards the various occupations as well as towards the accumulation of wealth.

[24] *The Works of Aristotle,* vol. 9, *Ethica Nicomachea,* 1096a. Aristotle's reference to "the good we are seeking" was to the ultimate or final good.

[25] *The Dialogues of Plato,* vol. 3, *Republic,* pp. 109-110. Quoted by permission of the Oxford University Press.

[26] Thus:

> And do you not suppose, Adeimantus, that a single boxer who was perfect in his art would easily be a match for two stout and well-to-do gentlemen who were not boxers? *Ibid.,* p. 110.

The Epicureans. Approaching the problem of how people should live, an important group of Greek thinkers set up happiness as a criterion. They said that men should seek happiness. This was the viewpoint of Aristippus of Cyrene (c. 435–356 B.C.) and his followers, the Cyrenaics, who took their name from Cyrene, the Greek colony in northern Africa where Aristippus was born and where, later, he taught. The great Athenian teacher Socrates (c. 470–399 B.C.), whose pupil Aristippus had been, appears to have given a place to happiness as both an ethical and a psychological principle. He thought that men *should* and *did* seek happiness. Thus, Plato described Socrates as saying,

I am rather disposed to say that things are good in as far as they are pleasant, if they have no consequences of another sort, and in as far as they are painful they are bad.[27]

And yet, perhaps, this is one of those ridiculous questions which I am afraid to ask, and which ought not to be asked by a sensible man : for what human being is there who does not desire happiness?[28]

Aristippus developed this line of thought, which has been called *hedonism*. The Cyrenaic philosophy gave rise to *Epicureanism,* which reîeived its name from Epicurus, who founded a school in Athens about 306 B.C. According to the Epicureans, pleasure was the ultimate good, such things as wealth and knowledge being merely instrumental. Already something of this approach has been noticed in the writings of Aristotle. The works of Epicurus are available only in fragmentary form but are sufficiently informative to make clear their author's point of view. Thus,

we call pleasure the beginning and end of the blessed life. For we recognize pleasure as the first good innate in us, and from pleasure we begin every act of choice and avoidance, and to pleasure we return again, using the feeling as the standard by which we judge every good.[29]

Here, as in the statements which Plato attributed to Socrates, the two aspects of hedonism are clearly defined. "From pleasure we begin every act" is an assertion of hedonism as a psychological principle : it says that people do in fact pursue pleasure as their objective. "Using the feeling as a standard by which we judge every good" sets up hedonism as a principle of ethics and makes pleasure the criterion of worth or goodness. Throughout the course of hedonistic thought, these two principles have been prominent.

But pleasure, according to Epicurus, was not entirely a matter of maximizing consumers' goods. Infinity of desires was recognized :

[27] *The Dialogues of Plato,* vol. 1, *Protagoras,* p. 175. Quoted by permission of the Oxford University Press.

[28] *Ibid., Euthydemus,* p. 213.

[29] *Epicurus : The Extant Remains,* translated by C. Bailey, Oxford 1926, p. 87. Quoted by permission of the Oxford University Press.

The wealth demanded by nature is both limited and easily procured; that demanded by idle imaginings stretches on to infinity.[30]

In this passage, a distinction was drawn between the demand for necessities, which, according to Epicurus, was satisfied easily, and that for luxuries, which was insatiable. Epicurus admitted that the demand for necessities of life must be satisfied:

The flesh cries out to be saved from hunger, thirst and cold.[31]

But given the attainment of this minimum standard of consumption, happiness could be secured without the possession of luxuries:

if a man possess this safety [from hunger, thirst and cold] and hope to possess it, he might rival even Zeus in happiness.[32]

Nothing satisfies the man who is not satisfied with a little.[33]

Many men when they have acquired riches have not found the escape from their ills but only a change to greater ills.[34]

By means of occupations worthy of a beast abundance of riches is heaped up, but a miserable life results.[35]

If you wish to make Pythocles rich, do not give him more money, but diminish his desire.[36]

A free life cannot acquire many possessions, because this is not easy to do without servility to mobs or monarchs, yet it possesses all things in unfailing abundance; and if by chance it obtains many possessions, it is easy to distribute them so as to win the gratitude of neighbours.[37]

This, obviously, differs considerably from the gluttony or voluptuousness with which the name Epicurean is commonly associated. There is no mere search for bodily gratifications but temperance and tranquillity.

The Stoics. Like the earlier Cynics, the Stoics did not look upon pleasure or wealth with favor. Their attitude was one of indifference toward the material world and toward such things as riches and power. Instead, they emphasized the right living which would flow from a disciplined mind. Probably their outlook on the subject of wealth is best depicted in the *Discourses* of Epictetus (born c. 60 B.C.). Epictetus was a remarkable character. The son of a slave woman and for many years a slave himself, lame and of poor health, he was taught by the Stoic, Musonius Rufus, and, becoming free, himself engaged in teaching. In the *Discourses,* which were prepared by one of his pupils, he asked, of "those who fear want,"

[30] *Ibid.*, p. 99. [32] *Ibid.* [34] *Ibid.*
[31] *Ibid.*, p. 111. [33] *Ibid.*, p. 137. [35] *Ibid.*
[36] *Ibid.*, p. 127.
[37] *Ibid.*, p. 117. This statement reflects the insecurity of the period in which Epicurus taught but it is not without general significance.

Aren't you ashamed to be more cowardly and ignoble than a runaway slave? How do they, when they run off, leave their masters? in what estates or slaves do they put their confidence? Don't they steal just a little bit to last them for the first few days, and then afterwards drift along over land or sea, contriving one scheme after another to keep themselves fed? And what runaway slave ever died of hunger? But you tremble, and lie awake at night, for fear the necessities of life will fail you.[38]

Even if death should come on account of hunger,

How many times have you boasted that, as far as death at least was concerned, you are in a fairly good state? – Yes, but my family too will starve. – What then? Their starvation does not lead to some other end than yours, does it? Have they not also much the same descent thereto, and the same world below? Are you not willing, then, to look with courage sufficient to face every necessity and want, at that place to which the wealthiest needs must go, and those who have held the highest offices, and very kings and tyrants? Only you will descend hungry, if it so happen, and they bursting with indigestion and drunkenness.[39]

Some of the implications of this attitude will be discussed later, in connection with the thought of the early Christians, whose attitude toward wealth was very similar.

The Ancient Attitude Toward Trade and Industry

The position of the classical philosophers in relation to trade and industry was in conformity with their opinions on the subject of wealth. Agriculture was looked upon as a more desirable occupation than manufactures and commerce. Thus, the *Œconomica* of the Aristotelian *corpus* stated:

Now in the course of nature the art of agriculture is prior, and next come those arts which extract the products of the earth, mining and the like. Agriculture ranks first because of its justice; for it does not take anything away from men, either with their consent, as do retail trading and the mercenary arts, or against their will, as do the warlike arts. Further, agriculture is natural; for by nature all derive their sustenance from their mother, and so men derive it from the earth. In addition to this it also conduces greatly to bravery; for it does not make men's bodies unserviceable, as do the illiberal arts, but it renders them able to lead an open-air life and work hard; furthermore it makes them adventurous against the foe, for husbandmen are the only citizens whose property lies outside the fortifications.[40]

[38] *Epictetus: The Discourses as Reported by Arrian,* translated by W. A. Oldfather, 2 vols., London and N. Y. 1926–1928, vol. 2, p. 227. Quoted by permission of the Harvard University Press and William Heinemann, Ltd.

[39] *Ibid.*, pp. 227-229.

[40] *The Works of Aristotle,* vol. 10, *Oeconomica,* translated by E. S. Forster, Oxford 1920, 1343a-1343b. Quoted by permission of the Oxford University Press. The first book of *Œconomica,* from which the passage is taken, is considered to be the work of a pupil or disciple of Aristotle.

Military preparedness was one reason for the favor bestowed upon agriculture, as the writer of *Œconomica* indicated. Probably another factor was the distaste felt by philosophers like Plato and Aristotle for the commercial spirit which was developing rapidly in the Athens of their time.

Plato spoke very harshly of trade. Having made the statement, quoted above, respecting the tendency of the mass of men to pursue gain without limit, he drew the conclusion that retail trade was objectionable, as it encouraged this propensity:

all that relates to retail trade, and merchandise, and the keeping of taverns, is denounced and numbered among dishonourable things.[41]

The remedy he proposed was that,

In the first place, they must have as few retailers as possible; and in the second place, they must assign the occupation to that class of men whose corruption will be the least injury to the state; and in the third place, they must devise some way whereby the followers of these occupations themselves will not readily fall into habits of unbridled shamelessness and meanness.[42]

To give effect to his second suggestion, Plato proposed that retailers should be strangers, not citizens, and under the third heading his suggestion was that the guardians should regulate the rate of profit, a point which receives attention in Chapter IX.

Aristotle was equally definite in his condemnation of retail trade:

There are two sorts of wealth-getting, as I have said; one is a part of household management, the other is retail trade: the former necessary and honourable, while that which consists in exchange is justly censured; for it is unnatural, and a mode by which men gain from one another.[43]

After this, the condemnation of usury, which receives consideration in Chapter XI, was but a short step.

The Extent to Which the Philosophers' Ideas Represented Contemporary Opinion

Enough has been said to make it evident that the criticisms of wealth set forth by the classical philosophers did not represent, even in the minds of their authors, the views of the rank and file of the people. Undoubtedly, it was the method of pursuing wealth that caused the opposition of the philosophers. It must be remembered that the latter corresponded to the college professors of today and, in the then-existing situation of Greece, their students were largely the sons of comparatively rich men. The philosophers mixed with people who were the leaders of their communities and who did not take part in manual labor, which was rele-

[41] *The Dialogues of Plato,* vol. 5, *Laws,* p. 305.
[42] *Ibid.,* p. 306.
[43] *The Works of Aristotle,* vol. 10, *Politica,* 1258a-1258b.

gated to slaves. It is quite common, even in the twentieth century, for individuals of the professional class to express a distaste for wealth-seeking. Later writers have questioned whether increases in wealth above the amount necessary for subsistence are attended by corresponding accessions to happiness. But it must be realized that individuals are variously placed in this respect. It may appear sensible enough for a man with an income adequate to cover his needs not to want more, but a neighbor living in poverty may be excused for a different feeling. The hopelessness of the position of the poor man may produce in his breast the grim satisfaction that was a feature of Stoic philosophy. No doubt there were some among the poorer classes of Greece and Rome who were real Stoics, contented with their lot. Very likely, however, the great body of poor people were reasonably well satisfied, not because they accepted the Stoic philosophy but because they did not trouble themselves overmuch about a situation that, if they thought about it at all, must have appeared impossible to change.

Whatever the philosophers thought of this development, certainly industry and trade were becoming more important in the Greece in which they wrote, while the Roman Empire in the days of its greatness was highly commercialized. State officials did not hesitate to use their stations to enrich themselves. People of position acquired landed estates, but the profits of tax-farming, of industrial and commercial enterprises, and even of money-lending were not neglected. In the later Imperial days, especially, a love of luxury was widespread. For the poor, bread and circuses, not readings from Stoic philosophy, formed the standard prescription.

Christian Thought

Material Wealth

The teaching of the Gospels. There is considerable general similarity between the Christian doctrines and those of the Stoics, already described. Some of the Gospel statements on the subject of wealth are open to more than one interpretation but in the main it is clear that Christ's attitude toward material gain was not favorable. His listeners were urged to address themselves to the furtherance of spiritual welfare and leave earthly things to take care of themselves:

> No man can serve two masters: for either he will hate the one and love the other; or else he will hold to the one, and despise the other. Ye cannot serve God and mammon. Therefore I say unto you, Take no thought for your life, what ye shall eat, or what ye shall drink; nor yet for your body, what ye shall put on. Is not the life more than meat, and the body than raiment? Behold the fowls of the air: for they sow not, neither do they reap, nor gather into barns; yet your heavenly Father feedeth them. Are ye not much better than they? . . . Consider the lilies of the field, how they grow; they

toil not, neither do they spin : And yet I say unto you, That even Solomon in all his glory was not arrayed like one of these. Wherefore, if God so clothe the grass of the field, which to day is, and to morrow is cast into the oven, shall he not much more clothe you, O ye of little faith? Therefore take no thought, saying, What shall we eat? or, What shall we drink? or, Wherewithal shall we be clothed ? . . . for your heavenly Father knoweth that ye have need of all these things. But seek ye first the kingdom of God, and his righteousness; and all these things shall be added unto you. Take therefore no thought for the morrow : for the morrow shall take thought of the things for itself.[44]

Here is an attitude of indifference to wealth : God would provide for the Christian's requirements and the believer need not trouble himself about the matter. But the subject was not allowed to rest here. The Gospels recounted the experience of a rich man who asked Christ's advice on the question of salvation. He was informed that this was impossible so long as he retained possession of his wealth and was counseled to give this away to the poor :

And when he [*i.e.,* Jesus] was gone forth into the way, there came one running, and kneeled to him, and asked him, Good Master, what shall I do that I may inherit eternal life? And Jesus said unto him. . . Thou knowest the commandments, Do not commit adultery, Do not kill, Do not steal, Do not bear false witness, Defraud not, Honour thy father and mother. And he answered and said unto him, Master, all these have I observed from my youth. Then Jesus beholding him loved him, and said unto him, One thing thou lackest : go thy way, sell whatsoever thou hast, and give to the poor, and thou shalt have treasure in heaven : and come, take up the cross, and follow me. And he was sad at that saying, and went away grieved : for he had great possessions. And Jesus looked round about, and saith unto his disciples, How hardly shall they that have riches enter into the kingdom of God! And the disciples were astonished at his words. But Jesus answereth again, and saith unto them, Children, how hard it is for them that trust in riches to enter into the kingdom of God! It is easier for a camel to go through the eye of a needle, than for a rich man to enter into the kingdom of God![45]

Here, Christ seemed to oppose the possession of wealth; but his argument did not assume an absence of feelings of self-interest on the part of his listeners. Rather their presence was postulated. Personal salvation was promised as a prize for good behavior. Considering the short period of earthly existence, compared with the infinity of life after death, this was a case in which future goods were decidedly more valuable than present goods.

The first *Epistle of Paul to Timothy* dwelled on the temptations to which the possessor of wealth was subjected :

[44] *Matthew,* 6, vv. 24-34.
[45] *Mark,* 10, vv. 17-24.

And having food and raiment let us therewith be content. But they that will be rich fall into temptation and a snare, and into many foolish and hurtful lusts, which drown men in destruction and perdition. For the love of money is the root of all evil. . .[46]

The *Epistle of James* was even more radical in its criticism of riches. Wealth was to be regarded not merely as something which ran its owner into risks, and should be given away as a condition of achieving salvation. It was evidence of wrong-doing and condemned its holder in the eyes of the Lord:

Go to now, ye rich men, weep and howl for your miseries that shall come upon you. Your riches are corrupted, and your garments are motheaten. Your gold and silver is cankered; and the rust of them shall be a witness against you, and shall eat your flesh as it were fire. Ye have heaped treasure together for the last days. Behold, the hire of the labourers who have reaped down your fields, which is of you kept back by fraud, crieth: and the cries of them which have reaped are entered into the ears of the Lord of sabaoth.[47]

The writings of the early Fathers. As the influence of the Christian religion extended, a marked difference in thought developed with respect to wealth. In the case of members of the lower classes of society, from whom many of the early converts were drawn, no sacrifice was involved by reason of the rejection of wealth and power. It was otherwise when individuals of the upper groups accepted the Christian faith and, even in the early days, some of these linked themselves with the Church. The spread of the religion gave increased significance to this aspect.

Clement of Alexandria, in his work, *Who is the Rich Man that Shall be Saved?* affirmed that the unfavorable comments of Jesus and his Apostles on riches were aimed at greed and the love of power rather than at wealth in itself. Clement taught in what was then one of the richest cities of the western world and it is probable that from time to time wealthy men sought admittance into the Christian Church. An attitude of "sell whatsoever thou hast, and give to the poor" would have kept many of them away. Clement studied the Gospel account of Christ's conversation with the rich man and offered a different solution:

What then was it which persuaded him [*i.e.*, the rich man, after his discussion with Jesus] to flight, and made him depart from the Master, from the entreaty, the hope, the life, previously pursued with ardour?—"Sell thy possessions." And what is this? He does not, as some conceive offhand, bid him throw away the substance he possessed, and abandon his property; but bids him banish from his soul his notions about wealth, his excitement and morbid feeling about it, the anxieties, which are the thorns of existence,

[46] *Timothy*, I, 6, vv. 8-10.

[47] *James*, 5, vv. 1-4. It is considered very doubtful, however, whether the *Epistle of James* is of Apostolic origin.

which choke the seed of life. For it is no great or desirable thing to be destitute of wealth, if without a special object,—not except on account of life. For thus those who have nothing at all, but are destitute, and beggars for their daily bread, the poor dispersed on the streets, who know not God and God's righteousness, simply on account of their extreme want and destitution of subsistence, and lack even of the smallest things, were most blessed and most dear to God, and sole possessors of everlasting life. . . He [*i.e.*, Jesus] bids Zaccheus and Matthew, the rich tax-gatherers, entertain Him hospitably. And He does not bid them part with their property, but, applying the just and removing the unjust judgment, He subjoins, "To-day salvation has come to this house . . ." (Luke v. 29, xix. 5.) He so praises the use of property as to enjoin, along with this addition, the giving of a share of it, to give drink to the thirsty, bread to the hungry, to take the houseless in, and clothe the naked. But if it is not possible to supply those needs without substance, and He bids people abandon their substance, what else would the Lord be doing than exhorting to give and not to give the same things . . . ? which were the most irrational of all things.

Riches, then, which benefit also our neighbours, are not to be thrown away. . . For he who holds possessions, and gold, and silver, and houses, as the gifts of God; and ministers from them to the God who gives them for the salvation of men; and knows that he possesses them more for the sake of the brethren than his own; and is superior to the possession of them, not the slave of the things he possesses; and does not carry them about in his soul, nor bind and circumscribe his life within them, but is ever labouring at some good and divine work, even should he be necessarily some time or other deprived of them, is able with cheerful mind to bear their removal equally with their abundance. This is he who is blessed by the Lord, and called poor in spirit, a meet heir of the kingdom of heaven, not one who could not live rich.[48]

So, according to Clement, the rich man, who did not allow himself to be the slave of his riches but used them in a Christian manner, could obtain salvation. Lactantius (c. 260–c. 340), who taught in France a century later, took up the same position. Discussing benevolence, he admitted that people might raise objections to charity that was so extensive as to leave them poor:

Some will perhaps say: If I shall do all these things, I shall have no possessions. For what if a great number of men shall be in want, shall suffer cold, shall be taken captive, shall die, since one who acts thus must deprive himself of his property even in a single day, shall I throw away the estate acquired by my own labour or by that of my ancestors, so that after this I myself must live by the pity of others?[49]

Arguing the point from the angle of self-interest, Lactantius replied that the loss would not be so great as might at first appear:

[48] *Ante-Nicene Christian Library*, vol. 22, Pt. 2, pp. 193-197.
[49] *Ibid.*, vol. 21, *The Divine Institutes*, p. 386.

Why do you so pusillanimously fear poverty, which even your philosophers praise, and bear witness that nothing is safer and nothing more calm than this? That which you fear is a haven against anxieties. Do you not know to how many dangers, to how many accidents, you are exposed with these evil resources? These will treat you well if they shall pass without your bloodshed. But you walk about laden with booty, and you bear spoils which may excite the minds even of your own relatives. Why, then, do you hesitate to lay that out well which perhaps a single robbery will snatch away from you, or a proscription suddenly arising, or the plundering of an enemy? Why do you fear to make a frail and perishable good everlasting, or to entrust your treasures to God as their preserver, in which case you need not fear thief or robber, nor rust, nor tyrant? He who is rich towards God can never be poor.[50]

In case this did not convince, Lactantius added that benevolence need not be pushed so far as to reduce the giver to poverty. More moderate giving—confined to what hitherto had been spent on luxuries—would suffice:

If you are not adequate to the performance of great works alone, cultivate justice with all your power, in such a manner, however, that you may excel others in work as much as you excel them in riches. And do not think that you are advised to lessen or exhaust your property; but that which you would have expended on superfluities, turn to better uses. Devote to the ransoming of captives that from which you purchase beasts; maintain the poor with that from which you feed wild beasts; bury the innocent dead with that from which you provide men for the sword.[51]

Thus, according to Lactantius, half a loaf was better than no bread and rich men who wished to continue to live comfortably need not be frightened away from the Christian Church.

Teachers like Cyprian (c. 200–258) and Chrysostom (c. 345–407), however, took the opposite view. Both these men were high dignitaries of the Church, being Bishops of Carthage and Constantinople respectively, and they exercised powerful influence on contemporary thought. For them, arguments such as those of Clement had no appeal. Thus, Cyprian declared,

He [*i.e.*, Jesus] teaches us that riches are not only to be condemned, but that they are also full of peril; that in them is the root of seducing evils. . . the Lord tells us that he becomes perfect and complete who sells all his goods, and distributes them for the use of the poor, and so lays up for himself treasure in heaven. He says that that man is able to follow Him . . . who, free from hindrance . . . is involved in no entanglements of worldly estate, but at large and free himself, accompanies his possessions, which before have been sent to God.[52]

[50] *Ibid.*, pp. 386-387.
[51] *Ibid.*, p. 387. The men provided "for the sword" were gladiators.
[52] *Ibid.*, vol. 8, *On the Lord's Prayer*, p. 412.

This is an entirely different interpretation from Clement's of the rich man incident. Both Cyprian and Chrysostom matched their words with deeds, devoting their considerable wealth to the service of the poor.

Luxurious living was condemned by the early Fathers. Even Clement, though not prepared to shut out of the Church rich men who used their wealth properly, did not look upon luxury with any favor :

We must, then, cast away the multitude of vessels, silver and gold drinking cups, and the crowd of domestics. . . A fair provision for the journey to heaven is theirs who bear frugality with chaste gravity. . . But that which is superfluous, what they call ornaments and the furniture of the rich, is a burden, not an ornament to the body. He who climbs to the heavens by force, must carry with him the fair staff of beneficence, and attain to the true rest by communicating to those who are in distress. For the Scripture avouches, "that the true riches of the soul are a man's ransom," that is, if he is rich, he will be saved by distributing it.[53]

Tertullian (c. 155–c. 222), a Carthaginian and one of the great writers of the early Church, devoted an entire treatise to women's dress, which was evidently in those days, as well as now, one of the principal ways in which love of luxury was displayed. Tertullian lamented that people were apt to value things not for their usefulness but for their rarity.[54] They ought to be content with what God had made plentiful among them, he said, not run after foreign luxuries :

For, as some particular things distributed by God over certain individual lands, and some one particular tract of sea, are mutually foreign one to the other, they are reciprocally either neglected or desired : (desired) among foreigners, as being rarities; neglected (rightly), if anywhere, among their own compatriots, because in *them* there is no such fervid longing for a glory which, among its own home-folk, is frigid. But, however, the rareness and outlandishness which arise out of that distribution of possessions which God has ordered as He willed, ever finding favour in the eyes of strangers, excites, from the simple fact of *not* having what God has made native to other places, the concupiscence of *having* it. . . concupiscence becomes proportionably greater as it has set a higher value upon the thing which it has eagerly desired. From the smallest caskets is produced an ample patrimony. On a single thread is suspended a million of sesterces. One delicate neck carries about it forests and islands. The slender lobes of the ears exhaust a fortune; and the left hand, with its every finger, sports a several money-bag. Such is the strength of ambition — (equal) to bearing on one small body, and that a woman's, the product of so copious wealth.[55]

Tertullian wanted the women to whom his remarks were addressed to be under no misapprehension :

[53] *Ibid.*, vol. 4, *The Instructor,* p. 302.
[54] See Chapter IX.
[55] *Ante-Nicene Christian Library,* vol. 11, *On Female Dress,* pp. 313-314.

> These suggestions are not made to you, of course, to be developed into an entire crudity and wildness of appearance; nor are we seeking to persuade you of the good of squalor and slovenliness; but of the limit and norm and just measure of cultivation of the person.[56]

But

> There must be no overstepping of that line to which simple and sufficient refinements limit their desires — that line which is pleasing to God.[57]

All excess in dress and personal adornment (including cosmetics) should be avoided. Incidentally, Tertullian remarked that what he had to say applied to men also, who, even in his days, seemed to have failings of their own, such as looking into mirrors and even dyeing gray hair!

Thomas Aquinas. The great theologian of the thirteenth century, Aquinas, went into the subject of wealth in some detail. Aquinas sought to establish principles which would be workable in the daily lives of ordinary people. Instead of asking men to obey God and abjure the world, he endeavored to interpret the will of God in a manner that would be of practical service in the world. An asceticism that was unworkable, on the one hand, and the self-seeking spirit that was only too common in worldly affairs, on the other, were alike rejected. In his *Summa theologica,* Aquinas considered innumerable problems of conduct and belief. His method was to pose a question and answer it, then examine the objections to his answer. Among the problems with which he dealt was almsgiving. Having asked, "Whether one ought to give alms out of what one needs," he offered the solution that the needs of the individual depended on his social station and that it would be unreasonable to expect a man to give so much to others that his accustomed standard of living was imperiled:

> a thing is said to be necessary, if a man cannot without it live in keeping with his social station, as regards either himself or those of whom he has charge. The *necessary* considered thus is not an invariable quantity, for one might add much more to a man's property, and yet not go beyond what he needs in this way, or one might take much from him, and he would still have sufficient for the decencies of life in keeping with his own position. Accordingly it is good to give alms of this kind of *necessary*; and it is a matter not of precept but of counsel. Yet it would be inordinate to deprive oneself of one's own, in order to give to others to such an extent that the residue would be insufficient for one to live in keeping with one's station and the ordinary occurrences of life: for no man ought to live unbecomingly.[58]

Three exceptions, however, Aquinas admitted to this rule. (1) A man who entered the Church had to give up his possessions. (2) Assistance should be given when it could be recovered easily, if need be. (3) When

[56] *Ibid.*, p. 320.
[57] *Ibid.*
[58] *Summa theologica,* Pt. 2, Second Pt., Q. 32, Art. 6.

"in the presence of extreme indigence in an individual, or great need on the part of the common weal," the customary requirements of one's station should not be permitted to stand in the way of almsgiving, for "in such cases it would seem praiseworthy to forego the requirements of one's station, in order to provide for a greater need." So charity remained a Christian duty, yet it did not mean a carefree disposal of wealth, but, save in exceptional circumstances, only such donations as his surplus over accustomed wants would permit. This was in accordance with Aquinas's conception of distributive justice.[59] In his opinion, people had a right to incomes proportioned to their station in life and should recognize this when deciding how much to give to others. The ordered social hierarchy of the middle ages was not a travesty of Christian justice, according to Aquinas, but in conformity with it. Probably it is true to say that many people still accept Aquinas's criterion as to the length to which charity should be carried.

By way of contrast, a statement made by Cyprian a thousand years before the time of Aquinas may be quoted:

If you dread and fear, lest, if you begin to act thus abundantly [*i.e.*, give generously], your patrimony being exhausted with your liberal dealing, you may perchance be reduced to poverty; be of good courage in this respect, be free from care: that cannot be exhausted whence the service of Christ is supplied, whence the heavenly work is celebrated. Neither do I vouch for this on my own authority; but I promise it on the faith of the holy Scriptures, and on the authority of the divine promise. The Holy Spirit speaks by Solomon, and says, "He that giveth unto the poor shall never lack, but he that turneth away his eye shall be in great poverty;" showing that the merciful and those who do good works cannot want, but rather that the sparing and barren hereafter come to want.[60]

Religious charity. The belief in charity as a Christian duty was largely responsible for the form taken by poor relief before the Reformation. Mention should be made of the Franciscan order, for its emphasis on charity. Founded in Italy by St. Francis of Assisi (c. 1182–1226), the order spread rapidly as a body of mendicant priests who took their commission from the Gospels:

And as ye go, preach, saying, The kingdom of heaven is at hand. Heal the sick, cleanse the lepers, raise the dead, cast out devils: freely ye have received, freely give. Provide neither gold, nor silver, nor brass in your purses, Nor scrip for your journey, neither two coats, neither shoes, nor yet staves: for the workman is worthy of his meat.[61]

As the order grew in importance, it established hospitals and undertook public works, taking part, also, in the organization of the *montes pietatis*,

[59] See Chapter IX.

[60] *Ante-Nicene Christian Library*, vol. 13, *On Works and Alms*, p. 7.

[61] *Matthew*, 10, vv. 7-10.

or poor people's loan institutions. In general, the Church exhorted individuals to give to the poor. Religious bodies provided food and lodging to all comers. Parish churches raised funds for the purpose of poor relief by gifts and sales of food and ale, which correspond to the church bazaars or sales of the present day. The fact that assistance was given to applicants, often without question as to the intensity of their need, undoubtedly encouraged mendicancy. Some church leaders, for example Basil, who lived in the fourth century, drew attention to the necessity for careful investigation of claims and discrimination between greedy beggars and deserving poor : the gift of alms to the latter was looked upon as a Christian duty but, to the former, merely waste. In practice, however, adequate consideration of individual cases often must have been impracticable and there is plenty of evidence that religious charity was abused. But notwithstanding its shortcomings, the system furnished something which was socially necessary and its disappearance raised problems in those countries which embraced the Reformation and where the church property which previously had met the expense entailed by almsgiving was seized for other purposes.

Trade and Industry

In most ancient countries labor was held in some disdain. The *Old Testament* appears to give expression to this view in God's command to Adam : "In the sweat of thy face shalt thou eat bread. . . ."[62] Traditionally, pastoral peoples have scorned manual labor. This attitude, which was noticed in the literature of early Greece and Rome, was carried into later periods through the continuance of serfdom and slavery. Even in modern times societies can be found in which the ordinary tasks of labor are left to individuals who are considered to be racially or socially inferior to the general body of citizens, with the result that manual work as such is thought by the latter to be demeaning. The South of this country in the slavery period, and to some extent since slavery was abolished, provides an example, as does the Union of South Africa at the present time.

Much of the appeal possessed by early Christianity, for the lowly classes from whom many of its adherents were drawn, lay in its insistence on the equality of men and the dignity of human labor. Joseph was a carpenter; Peter, Andrew, James, and John were fishermen. The disciples were told to preach and earn their living as they did so. They, themselves, taught in similar fashion :

> Let him that stole steal no more : but rather let him labour, working with his hands the thing which is good, that he may have to give to him that needeth.[63]

[62] *Genesis,* 3, v. 19.
[63] *Ephesians,* 4, v. 28.

And that ye study to be quiet, and to do your own business, and to work with your own hands, as we commanded you.[64]

Neither did we eat any man's bread for nought; but wrought with labour and travail night and day, that we might not be chargeable to any of you.[65]

A vocation could be pursued without loss of self-respect:

I therefore . . . beseech you that ye walk worthy of the vocation wherewith ye are called.[66]

Callings were examined as to their compatibility with the Christian ethic, and the believer was exhorted to refrain from following those that were not approved. As a result, adherents were debarred from entering some of the most important professions available to citizens of the time, such as those associated with building and maintaining the heathen temples in the period before Christianity itself became the State religion. The advice given by Tertullian in this connection may be quoted:

For it matters not whether you erect or equip: if you have embellished his temple [*i.e.*, the heathen's temple], or altar, or niche, if you have pressed out gold-leaf, or have wrought his insignia, or even his house: work of that kind, which confers not *shape*, but *authority*, is more important. If the necessity of maintenance is urged so much, the arts have other species withal to afford means of livelihood, without outstepping the path of discipline. . .[67]

Tertullian proceeded to point out that plasterers, painters, and masons could make their living in other branches of their crafts as well as in working on tasks connected with the heathen religion. From the beginning, however, some disposition to compromise on such matters was evident, for which Christ himself, in his "Render to Cæsar the things that are Cæsar's" had opened the way. At no period did Christianity formally set itself in a position of antagonism to the political system, so that always it was possible for anyone to argue that particular practices, pertaining to the temporal power, should be tolerated. With the passage of time this tendency became more pronounced, particularly after the reign of Constantine in the early part of the fourth century, when Christianity was recognized by the State. Christians were permitted to engage in official life generally and even in military service.

The question of what occupations were appropriate to the follower of Christ, however, continued to arouse interest. In the early thirteenth century Alexander of Hales gave attention to the subject of trade in his *Universae theologiae summa*. Trade was not evil in itself, Alexander thought. It was permissible when undertaken in an honest manner to supply fellow-men with the goods they needed, but it was wrong when

[64] *Thessalonians*, I, 4, v. 11. [65] *Thessalonians*, II, 3, v. 8. [66] *Ephesians*. 4, v. 1.
[67] *Ante-Nicene Christian Library*, vol. 11, *On Idolatry*, p. 150.

it involved sinful actions, such as extortion or usury, or when it was carried on by priests or on Sundays. Duns Scotus and Richard of Middleton (c. 1249–c. 1306), whose price doctrine is examined in Chapter IX, both regarded trade as legitimate, given the proper conditions.

Yet the attitude was one of tolerance, rather than of favor. It was thought that trade was apt to lead to sinful greed for gain and that those whose duty it was to set an example to others should abstain from it. Aquinas, for example, opposed trade as an occupation for priests, in the following language :

Clerics should abstain not only from things that are evil in themselves, but even from those that have an appearance of evil. This happens in trading, both because it is directed to worldly gain, which clerics should despise, and because trading is open to so many vices, since *a merchant is hardly free from sins of the lips* (Ecclus. xxvi. 28). There is another reason, because trading engages the mind too much with worldly cares, and consequently withdraws it from spiritual cares ; wherefore the Apostle says (2 Tim. ii. 4) : *No man being a soldier to God entangleth himself with secular business.*[68]

According to some, the problem of the Christian's choice of occupation took on an extended significance after the Reformation.

Practical Acceptance of Christian Precepts in the Middle Ages

There is considerable evidence that the ascetic views of Christian teachers did not find complete acceptance, at least outside some of the religious orders. They were set forth as ideals toward which men should strive, and practiced as examples and means of personal salvation by groups of monks and individual priests, but it can be assumed that exhortations on the subject would have been neither so frequent nor so emphatic had there not been many people whose practices fell short of those favored by the Christian leaders.

Examination of medieval city and national ordinances reveals that the civil authorities were by no means blind to the usefulness of wealth. Some important writers have even declared that medieval public policy aimed at securing a plenitude of commodities, and this view receives consideration later. Whatever its truth, however, it should be realized that the evidence on which it is based was drawn largely from the period of transition to modern times, rather than from the earlier centuries to which much of the material in this chapter must be related. During the medieval period consumption was regulated by sumptuary laws. But these were not a new development. They had appeared as early as the time of Solon in Greece and at various dates in ancient Rome. Further, they were continued into modern times, with Mercantilist objectives. Luxury was regarded as objectionable in itself, but especially so when it offended against prevailing standards respecting class distinctions.

[68] *Summa theologica,* Pt. 2, Second Pt., Q. 77, Art. 4.

Thus, in 1363, the government of Edward III in England told its subjects what clothes were permissible for knights worth four hundred marks, what for those with two hundred marks, what for handicraftsmen, etc. Such un-Christian practices as charging excessive prices for commodities and exacting usury on loans were forbidden, but the constant complaints and repetitions of laws aimed against such wickedness show that the measures taken were ineffectual. Priests and even the organized Church itself were not above blame. Thus, it was said of George of Cappadocia, Bishop of Alexandria, who lived in the fourth century, that he speculated in grain, cornered the salt trade, and formed a company to monopolize the funeral business of Alexandria.[69] By gift and bequest the Church as a corporate organization acquired vast possessions. In many of the buildings that were erected for religious purposes, the simplicity of the early Christian period gave place to elaborate and expensive ornamentation. Churchmen lived comfortably, rather than denied themselves to give alms to the poor. To some it seemed that the Church had embraced the worldly wickedness which it professed to oppose. This was the feeling of the English Lollards, followers of John Wycliffe (c. 1320–1384), who received the name "poor priests" because of their acceptance of the early Christian dictum of poverty. The Church was very tenacious of its property rights, the conclusion of Pollock and Maitland, historians of English law, being of interest in this connection:

> Now there is plenty of evidence that of all landlords the religious houses were the most severe—not the most oppressive, but the most tenacious of their rights; they were bent on the maintenance of pure villein tenure and personal villeinage. The immortal but soulless corporation with her wealth of accurate records would yield no inch, would enfranchise no serf, would enfranchise no tenement. In practice the secular lord was more humane, because he was more human, because he was careless, because he wanted ready money, because he would die.[70]

It is not surprising, therefore, that, when peasants revolted or city apprentices rioted, the local abbey and the bishop's palace were as frequently the object of attack as was the residence of the lay lord. Considerable discrepancy between the precepts of idealists and the ordinary actions of practical people is revealed. An interesting combination of religious ethics and worldly wisdom is to be found in the advice of Walter of Henley, who appears to have been a lord's bailiff in England early in the thirteenth century:

[69] See J. W. Thompson, *Economic and Social History of the Middle Ages,* New York 1928, Chap. 2. This chapter contains much information on the seamy side of Christian life in the medieval period.

[70] F. Pollock and F. W. Maitland, *The History of English Law before the Time of Edward I,* 2nd ed., Cambridge and Boston 1909, vol. 1, pp. 378-379. Quoted by permission of the Cambridge University Press and Little, Brown and Company.

The wealth that God lends you keep and spend prudently. In outlays and expenses you must know four things. The one is, when you ought to give, how, to whom, and how much. The first is, that you give before you are obliged to, for how much more shall two shillings be worth beforehand than ten when one is forced to give. The second is, if you must give or spend, do it with good will, and it shall be reckoned double to you, and if you give grudgingly you shall lose as much as you put out. The third is, give to him who can help and hurt you. The fourth is, how much you ought to give, neither more nor less than according to the person, and according as the business is small or great that you have to do with him. Have regard to the poor, not to have praise of the world, but to have praise of God, who finds you all.[71]

Clearly, the black side of medieval life can be overemphasized. If it could be said that many churchmen were corrupt, it was equally true that the lives of others were sources of inspiration to all around them. Further, if the Church had defects, at least these were recognized and reform, when it came, did so from within.

The Protestant Reformation and the Rise of Capitalism

To a certain extent the Reformation may be looked upon as a return toward the austerity of the early Christian Church, yet it has been credited with being responsible for the rise of modern capitalism, notably by the German sociologist and social historian Max Weber (1864–1920). How is this paradox to be explained?

In the first place, Weber argued in his famous essay *Die protestantische Ethik und der Geist des Kapitalismus* (in *Archiv für Sozialwissenschaft und Sozialpolitik,* 1904–1905)[72] that the Reformation effected a fundamental alteration in the attitude of the Christian teachers to labor. As has been noticed, the old position was that labor was necessary and honorable but morally largely a matter of indifference, providing that its nature was in keeping with the Christian spirit. Subject to this condition, the believer should live righteously in whatever calling he found himself. Luther's standpoint was not greatly different, but Weber said that the Geneva Reformer, John Calvin (1509–1564), and the English Nonconformists and Puritans raised the vocation into the position of a Christian duty. They believed labor to be a service that the individual owed to his fellows. It provided for his maintenance and possibly furnished a surplus that could, and should, be used in caring for the sick or old, or employed in some other manner for the general benefit. Labor was also a discipline, in their view. The industrious man had the calm conscience which befitted a Christian and the mere fact of his continual

[71] *Walter of Henley's Husbandry,* ed. E. Lamond, London and N. Y. 1890, pp. 5-7, Longmans.

[72] The second edition of this work has been translated by T. Parsons as *The Protestant Ethic and the Spirit of Capitalism,* London 1930.

labor preserved him from many worldly temptations. If there were no idle hands, the devil would find little work to do. He who did not work, it was argued, was both failing to shoulder his share of society's burden and laying himself open to temptation.

Richard Baxter's *A Christian Directory: Or a Summ of Practical Theologie, and Cases of Conscience* (London 1673) illustrates this outlook. Baxter's teachings and writings were very influential in seventeenth century England and his *Christian Directory,* like the *Instructor* of Clement of Alexandria, was intended to guide Christian men and women in the practical affairs of their daily lives. Among the subjects discussed was labor. Pointing out "how necessary a life of labour is," Baxter added,

> The *publick welfare,* or the good of many, is to be valued above our own. Every man therefore is bound to do all the good he can to others, especially for the Church and Commonwealth : And this is not done by *Idleness,* but by *Labour!*[73]

He asked, *"What Labour is it that is necessary?"* and answered that the Christian should perform

> Some labour that shall employ the faculties of the soul, and body, and be profitable (as far as may be) to others and our selves.[74]

This was so, because

> *Labour* and *diligence* do keep the mind upon a *lawful employment,* and therefore keep out many *dangerous temptations,* and keep the *thoughts* from *vanity* and *sin*. . .[75]

The possession of riches, far from avoiding the necessity to labor, made this more important :

> *Will not Riches excuse one from Labouring in a Calling? Answ.* No : but rather bind them to it the more : For he that hath most *wages* from God, should do most work.[76]

In view of the importance thus attached to labor, Baxter said that it was very desirable that the Christian man should follow a regular calling. Defining a calling as "a *stated ordinary course of labour,*" he continued :

> This is very needful for these Reasons. 1. Out of a *Calling* a mans *labours* are but *occasional,* or *unconstant,* and so more time is spent in *idleness* than in *labour*. 2. A man is best skilled in that which he is used to. 3. And he will be best *provided* for it, with instruments and necessaries. 4. Therefore he doth it *better* than he could do an other work, and so wrongeth not others, but attaineth more the ends of his labour. 5. And he doth it *more easily;* when a man *unused,* and *unskilled,* and *unfurnished,* toyleth himself much in doing little. 6. And he will do his work more *orderly,* when another is in

[73] *Christian Directory,* p. 448.
[74] *Ibid.,* p. 447.
[75] *Ibid.,* p. 449.
[76] *Ibid.,* p. 448.

continual confusion, and his business knoweth not its time and place, but one part contradicts another. Therefore some *certain Calling* or Trade of life is best for every man.[77]

In other words, Baxter gave a number of reasons why the specialization of labor increased its productive efficiency.

Baxter's next problem was that of choice of calling. Some employments were better than others from the standpoint of public good, which, along with the service of God, had to be borne in mind :

The first and principal thing to be intended in the choice of a Trade or Calling for your selves or children, is the service of God, and the publick good: And therefore (cæteris paribus) *that Calling which most conduceth to the publick good is to be preferred.* The Callings most useful to the *publick good,* are the *Magistrates,* the *Pastors* and *Teachers* of the *Church,* Schoolmasters, Physicions, Lawyers, &c. Husbandmen, (Plowmen, Grasiers, and Shepheards) : and next to them are Marriners, Clothiers, Booksellers, Taylors, and such other that are employed about things most necessary to mankind : And some Callings are employed about matters of so little use (as Tobacco-sellers, Lace-sellers, Feather-makers, Periwig-makers, and many more such) that he that may choose better, should be loth to take up with one of these, though possibly in it self it may be lawful. It is a great satisfaction to an honest mind, to spend his life in doing the greatest *good* he can ; and a prison and constant calamity to be tyed to spend ones life in doing little good at all to others, though he should grow rich by it himself.[78]

Riches were not to be preferred to the advantage of the soul, Baxter said :

When two Callings equally conduce to the publick good, and one of them hath the advantage of riches, and the other is more advantageous to your souls, the latter must be preferred: And next to the publick good, the souls advantage must guide your choice. . .[79]

By the soul's advantage, Baxter meant personal salvation, or entry into Heaven. As an example of the difference between employments in this respect, he contrasted divinity and law, to the disadvantage of the latter. Bodily health must be remembered, also; but provided that the public good, the soul's advantage, and the requirements of bodily health were all served, pecuniary advantage need not be disregarded. Indeed, in a sense, to seek it was a duty :

It is lawful and meet to look at the commodity [*i.e.,* pecuniary advantage] *of your Calling in the third place,* (that is, *after the publick good, and after your personal good of soul and bodily health.*) Though it is said, Prov. 23.4. *Labour not to be rich*: the meaning is, that you make not Riches your chief end : Riches for our fleshy ends must not ultimately be intended or sought. But in subordination to higher things they may : That is, you may labour in that manner as tendeth most to your success and lawful gain : You are bound

[77] *Ibid.,* p. 449. [78] *Ibid.* [79] *Ibid.*

to improve all your Masters Talents : But then your *end* must be, that you may be the better provided to do God service, and may do the more good with what you have. If God shew you a way in which you may lawfully get more than in another way, (without wrong to your soul, or to any other) if you refuse this, and choose the less gainful way, you cross one of the ends of your Calling, and you refuse to be Gods Steward, and to accept his gifts, and use them for him when he requireth it : You may labour to be *Rich for God,* though not for the *flesh* and sin.[80]

In a later section of the book, Baxter returned to this point, asking the question,

Is it a duty to desire and endeavour to get, and prosper, and grow rich by our labours; when *Solomon* saith, *Labour not to be rich?* Prov. 23.4.

He answered,

It is a sin to desire Riches as worldlings and sensualists do, for the provision and maintenance of fleshy lusts, and pride : But it is no sin, but a duty, to labour not only for labour sake, formally resting in the act done, but for that honest increase and provision, which is the end of our labour; And therefore to choose a gainful calling rather than another, that we may be able to do good, and relieve the poor. Eph. 4.28. *Let him labour, working with his hands the thing that is good, that he have to give to him that needeth.*[81]

Obviously an outlook which thus identified Christian duty with the more gainful way was favorable to the growth of capitalistic enterprise.

Along with advocacy of labor in a godly calling, went a campaign against luxurious consumption. As has been seen in earlier sections, this was not new with the Reformation, but Calvinism gave it extended significance. The practices of the Puritans in Europe and America were the result—simple speech, plain clothes, and homely food. Needless consumption was classed as wickedness. As the point was put by George Fox (1624–1691), founder of the Society of Friends or Quakers,

why will you followe Envie, malice drunkennesse, and foolish pleasures : Knowe yee not in your Conscience That all theise are evill and sinne, and such as act such thinges shall never enter into ye kingdome of god. . .[82]

Baxter also attacked high living :

Understand well the Aggravations of this sin of Prodigality: viz. 1. It is a wasting of that which is none of our own, and a robbing God of the use or service due to him in the improvement of his gifts. They are his, and not ours, and according to his pleasure only must be used. 2. It is a robbing the poor of that which the common Lord of the world, hath appointed for them in his Law : And they will have their Action in Heaven against the prodigal.

[80] *Ibid.*, p. 450.

[81] *Ibid.*, Pt. IV, pp. 146-147. (This Part is paged separately.)

[82] *The Journal of George Fox*, ed. N. Penney, Cambridge 1911, vol. 1, p. 100. Quoted by permission of the Cambridge University Press.

3. It is an inhumane vice, to waste that upon pleasures, pride and needless things, which so many distressed persons stand in need of. 4. It is an injury to the Common-wealth, which is weakened by the wasteful. And the covetous themselves (that are not oppressors) are much better members of public societies than the prodigal. 5. It feedeth a life of other vice and wickedness. It is a spending Gods gifts to feed those lusts which he abhorreth. 6. It usually engageth many others in Trades and labours which are unprofitable [*i.e.*, to the soul], that they may serve the lusts of these sensual prodigals. 7. And in the conclusion it prepareth a sad account, for these wretches when they must answer at the Bar of God, how they have used all his gifts and talents.[83]

Baxter's statement under the fourth heading, to the effect that the covetous were better members of society than the prodigals, indicated the length to which he was prepared to go in criticizing luxury. That great classic of English Puritanism, *The Pilgrim's Progress* of John Bunyan (1628–1688), recounts the story of a Christian's passage through a world of temptation into the haven of salvation. Among other experiences, Christian, as Bunyan's character was named, in his travels was shown a man who was once "a fair and flourishing Professor" but was now shut up in an iron cage. The following dialogue took place:

Christian: For what did you bring your self into this Condition?
Man: For the Lusts, Pleasures, and Profits of this World; in the enjoyment of which, I did then promise my self much Delight: but now every one of those things also bite me, and gnaw me like a burning Worm.[84]

Somewhat needlessly, in view of the awful condition in which the man found himself, Christian's guide admonished him to "Let this Man's Misery be remembered by thee, and be an everlasting Caution to thee."

Thus, those who would be saved were warned against the lusts of the world. They had to live simply. Working hard in commerce or industry, while living inexpensively, necessarily they accumulated wealth. Indiscriminate almsgiving was not encouraged. Baxter, indeed, in the 1678 edition of his *Christian Directory*, spoke of poverty as "a just and merciful chastisement of God to cure the sin" of idleness. As a result, savings were plowed back into business enterprises, especially as the Calvinist wing of the Reform movement reversed the age-old condemnation of trade. Hence, according to Weber, the development in the Protestant areas of northern Europe. Such a view was not new with Weber. As early as the 1670's, the observant Sir William Petty (1623–1687), British writer on economic statistics, had connected flourishing trade with religious nonconformity:

[83] *The Christian Directory*, Pt. IV, p. 147.

[84] *Grace Abounding and The Pilgrim's Progress*, ed. J. Brown, Cambridge 1907, p. 166. Quoted by permission of the Cambridge University Press.

it is to be observed that Trade doth not (as some think) best flourish under Popular Governments, but rather that Trade is most vigorously carried on, in every State and Government, by the Heterodox part of the same, and such as profess Opinions different from what are publickly established. . .[85]

Hegel, in his *Geschichte der Philosophie* (2nd edition, 1840),[86] forecast Weber's thesis:

Art and industry receive through this principle [*i.e.*, Protestantism] new activity, since now their activity is justified.[87]

But it was left to Weber to put forward the theory on a substantial basis. It has received wide acceptance. Moreover, economic historians have noticed that it was not merely the case that capitalism developed in Protestant *countries*. The association seemed also *personal*, for many of the pioneering industrial enterprises were developed by Puritan families. This was true especially of the English iron and steel industry.[88]

It is always dangerous, however, to isolate two factors, as Weber has done (in this instance, the attitude toward wealth and the emergence of modern capitalism), and, finding that there is some correlation between them, to conclude that one is cause and the other effect. The causal relationship may be the other way round. The growing commercial spirit in northern Europe might have helped to bring about the success of the Reformation in this area. Other factors were at work, besides Protestantism, making for the rise of modern industry there. The fact that the northern European countries faced the Atlantic Ocean gave them a front place in commercial development, once ocean-borne traffic became important. Turkish expansion in the eastern Mediterranean helped to send mariners round the southern end of the African continent. Columbus, searching for a new way to India by the western sea, discovered America. The Atlantic Ocean came to assume the place in trade formerly held by the Mediterranean. Inevitably, northern Europe benefited from the change. This was particularly true of England, because the English Channel saved her from the danger of disturbance from war. Britain also had coal in large quantities, together with some iron. Many of the European countries had little coal, particularly in the Catholic south. The cool climate of the north has been considered by some authorities to be more favorable to industry than the warmth of the Med-

[85] *The Economic Writings of Sir William Petty*, ed. C. H. Hull, 2 vols., Cambridge 1899, vol. 1, p. 263. Quoted by permission of the Cambridge University Press. The passage occurs in the posthumous *Political Arithmetic*, London 1690. The original was probably written in 1671.

[86] Translated as *Lectures on the History of Philosophy* by E. S. Haldane and F. H. Simson, 3 vols., London 1892–1896. The lectures were delivered 1805–1830.

[87] *Ibid.*, vol. 3, p. 148. Quoted by permission of George Routledge & Sons and Kegan Paul, Trench, Trubner & Co. Ltd.

[88] See T. S. Ashton, *Iron and Steel in the Industrial Revolution*, Manchester 1924, Chap. 9.

iterranean area. The relative insignificance of gild control in England at the time, as compared with some Continental countries, especially France, has been credited with some influence. Protestantism, political and military security, climate, geographical factors, natural resources, and social organization, were jumbled together as possible causes, and it is beyond the wit of man to decide how far any one of them was responsible for the development of capitalism in northern Europe. It is in place to point out that Belgium, which is to a considerable extent Catholic but possesses large mineral deposits, has become more industrialized than its Protestant but mineral-poor neighbor, Holland.

Weber's theory has been assailed from another angle. The German economist, Werner Sombart (1863–1941), has pointed out that theological doctrines favorable to the development of capitalism were not confined to the Reformers. As has been mentioned earlier in this chapter, the great teachers of the early Catholic Church actively discouraged luxurious living. This sentiment had not altogether disappeared at the time of the Reformation. Comments encouraging to industrious activity were not wanting in Catholic literature. The same was true of Jewish writings. Sombart, indeed, believed that the Jews and the Catholic Church played an important part in the emergence of capitalism (not merely from the side of ideology but from the practical standpoint, especially through the large-scale financial operations and machinery for which papal and royal finance were responsible).[89]

H. M. Robertson, of the University of Cape Town, in his *Aspects of the Rise of Economic Individualism: A Criticism of Max Weber and His School* (Cambridge 1933) has followed somewhat the same line. Robertson gave numerous quotations from the works of pre-Reformation Catholics and post-Reformation Protestants to demonstrate that their attitudes on the subjects of wealth, industry, and commerce were not dissimilar. He pointed out that the Roman Catholic order of Jesuits (the *Society of Jesus*), established in Italy in 1539 and the spearhead of the anti-Reformation movement in the Catholic Church, went very far in favoring commercial activities. From the Jesuit side, however, Robertson's statements have been controverted[90] and the matter remains in dispute. If a comparison be made between the *Summa theologica* of Thomas Aquinas, or, still more, the writings of the early Fathers on the one hand, and Baxter's *Christian Directory* on the other, a conclusion favorable to the Weber thesis appears not unreasonable. Yet even Baxter did not justify gain-seeking as such and, moreover, like the Calvinists on the continent of Europe, may perhaps be but the product of his environ-

[89] Sombart's views may be studied conveniently in his book, *The Quintessence of Capitalism,* translated and edited by M. Epstein, London 1915, chaps. 17-21.

[90] See J. Brodrick, *The Economic Morals of the Jesuits: An Answer to Dr. H. M. Robertson,* Oxford 1934. The author is a Jesuit priest.

ment among energetic and commercially-minded northerners as compared with the more easy-going south. Further, it must be remembered that, by the time modern industry appeared, even Catholic thought had moved in a direction that gave greater countenance to commerce than did that of earlier times. It might be questioned whether, in the absence of the Protestant Reformation, the evolution of thought and of practice would have been basically different. Summing up these various factors, probably the most that can be said is that Protestantism helped the contemporary movement in the direction of commercialism and industrialism, which is a long way from concluding that the religious factor was the primary one in motivating the change.

Mercantilism

As was pointed out in Chapter I, the sixteenth and seventeenth centuries witnessed a pronounced shift in men's ideas. The State came to the front and riches were viewed in a new light. In the middle ages wealth, when properly used, was regarded as merely incidental to the service of God. If not so used, it was considered objectionable. Even under the new order, thought was far from being secularized : Baxter's work furnishes an example of the continued influence of Christian ideas, if one were needed. But the State's interests received more attention. Baxter himself, in defining the "publick welfare" which he thought men should value above their own, placed the "Commonwealth" or State along with the Church. In these circumstances, wealth was no longer something of indifference or disdain. As it had its part to play in the service of the State, its production and accumulation began to be considered by writers and politicians.

The Nature of Wealth

Largely because of certain statements made by Adam Smith (1723–1790), it has been widely believed that the economic writers of this period identified wealth with money or treasure. In Chapter XIV it is shown that passages can be selected from Mercantilist treatises to lend support to this view. Yet it is apparent that certain of the Mercantilists, notwithstanding the attention they gave to money, were not oblivious to the fact that wealth was something different from currency or specie. Thus, Thomas Mun—one of the most prominent of Mercantilist writers and, moreover, one whom Adam Smith mentioned in connection with Mercantilist thought—in *A Discourse of Trade, From England unto the East-Indies* (London 1621), stated very definitely that wealth consisted of the things necessary to life :

And first therefore, all men doe know, that the riches or sufficiencie of every Kingdome, State, or Common-wealth, consisteth in the possession of those things, which are needfull for a civill life.

This sufficiency is of two sorts: the one is naturall, and proceedeth of the Territorie it selfe: the other is artificiall, and dependeth on the industry of the Inhabitants.

The Realme of *England* (praised be God) is happily possessed of them both: as first, having great plentie of naturall riches, both in the Sea for Fish, & on the Land for Wooll, Cattle, Corne, Lead, Tin, Iron, and many other things for food, Rayment & Munition; insomuch, that upon strickt tearmes of need, this land may live without the help of any other Nation.[91]

It was precisely what Mun here asserted that "all men doe know" that his critics, in later years, accused Mun himself of not knowing. The political philosopher, Thomas Hobbes, in his *Leviathan,* spoke of wealth as "materials conducing to life." Charles Davenant (1656–1714), English Mercantilist writer, in his *Discourses on the Publick Revenues, and on the Trade of England* (2 vols., London 1698), declared:

Gold and silver are indeed the measure of trade, but the spring and original of it in all nations, is the natural or artificial product of the country; that is to say, what their land, or what their labour and industry produces.

And this is so true, that a nation may be supposed, by some accident, quite without the species of money, and yet, if the people are numerous, industrious, versed in traffic, skilled in sea affairs, and if they have good ports, and a soil fertile in variety of commodities, such a people will have trade and gather wealth, and they shall quickly get among them a plenty of gold and silver; so that the real and effective riches of a country is its native product. . . Gold and silver are so far from being . . . "the only things that deserve the name of treasure, or the riches of a nation," that in truth, money is at bottom no more than the counters with which men, in their dealings, have been accustomed to reckon; for, suppose the Hollanders should lend to some foreign state, upon jewels, or the pledge of cautionary towns, ⅔ds of all their species, would they cease upon so doing, to be a wealthy people? most certainly not, and such security put into their hands, will be real and true riches.[92]

Finally, Nicholas Barbon (c. 1640–1698), a London business man who had an interest in economics and was opposed to Mercantilist trade policy, in *A Discourse of Trade* (London 1690),[93] stated:

The Native Staple of each Country is the Riches of the Country, and is perpetual, and never to be consumed; Beasts of the Earth, Fowls of the Air, and Fishes of the Sea, Naturally Increase: There is Every Year a New Spring and Autumn, which produceth a New Stock of Plants and Fruits. And the Minerals of the Earth are Unexhaustable; and if the Natural Stock be Infinite, the Artificial Stock that is made of the Natural, must be Infinite, as

[91] Reprinted by The Facsimile Text Society (Columbia University Press), N. Y. 1930; pp. 49-50 of the reprint.

[92] *The Political and Commercial Works of that celebrated writer Charles D'Avenant, Ll.D.*, ed. C. Whitworth, 5 vols., London 1771, vol. 1, pp. 354-355.

[93] Reprinted Baltimore 1905.

Woollen and Linnen Cloth, Calicoes, and wrought Silk, which are made of Flax, Wool, Cotton, and Raw Silks.[94]

The Mercantilists professed to be concerned about the good of the State, and wealth was examined in this light. Medieval ideas on the subject of luxury were taken over, because vain trifles, which the teachers of the middle ages had regarded as wicked in the eyes of God, now seemed objectionable from the standpoint of the State. Perhaps they conduced to the pleasure of individuals but they added nothing to the resources of the State. Indeed, since commonly they had to be imported at great expense, it was thought that they diminished the State's fund of wealth. On the other hand, goods of obvious usefulness—such as plain food, serviceable clothes, and even money itself—were looked upon as desirable. Money might not be useful directly to individuals but, if it were beneficial to the State—as it was from the Mercantilist viewpoint—it was sensible enough that it should be accumulated. How the Mercantilists thought that money could serve State objectives is shown in Chapter XIV.

This general attitude may be exemplified by a passage from *A Discourse of the Common Weal of this Realm of England,* first printed in 1581 and attributed to the English statesman, John Hales (d. 1571):[95]

And now they [*i.e.,* the foreigners] let us have nothinge frome theim, (but onelye) for oure commodities, as woll, felles, talow, butter, chese, tinne, and lead; and wheare before time they weare wount to bringe us for the same ether good gold or silver, or els as necessarie commodities againe, now they send us other trifles, as I spacke of before; as glasses, gally pottes, tennis balles, papers, gyrdelles, browches, owches, buttons, dialles, or such like wares that standes them in no charge or use. . .[96]

The composition of the two lists is interesting. Wool, fells (skins), and tallow were regarded as useful commodities, tennis balls and girdles were not.

The sixteenth century saw the enactment of some measures that displayed a curious mixture of religious and practical motives. For example, an English act of 1549 ordered abstinence from meat on Fridays, Saturdays, and during Lent,

considering that due and godly abstinence is a means to virtue and to subdue men's bodies to their soul and spirit, and considering also specially that fishers, and men using the trade of living by fishing in the sea, may thereby the rather

[94] pp. 10-11 of the reprint. Quoted by permission of The Johns Hopkins Press.

[95] In addition to Hales, Hugh Latimer (c. 1490–1555), English bishop and Protestant martyr, has been given some credit in respect of this work.

[96] Reprinted, ed. E. Lamond, Cambridge 1893, re-issued 1929; p. 78 of the 1929 issue. Quoted by permission of the Cambridge University Press.

be set to work, and that by eating of fish much flesh shall be saved and increased.[97]

Again—and this time with a care for the woolen industry—in 1571 parliament commanded everyone above six years of age "except ladies and gentlemen" (*i.e.*, the upper classes) to wear woolen garments on Sundays and holidays.

The Heckscher Thesis

In recent years a Swedish economist, Eli F. Heckscher (1879–), has advanced the theory that the predominant feature of Mercantilist thought was a reversal of the attitude of men to goods.[98] Following the British statesman and philosopher, Francis Bacon, Lord Verulam and St. Albans (1561–1626), and the pioneer economic historian of England, William Cunningham (1849–1919), Heckscher has argued that medieval economic policy was aimed at *plenty*. Before the emergence of a complex *money economy*, when people were self-sufficing or exchanged their products directly among one another, Heckscher said that men could not fail to perceive that their interest lay in possessing as large a supply as possible of useful goods. Evidence was submitted of the existence of this point of view, in the form of ordinances restricting imports and exports, Heckscher's data showing that, in various European countries about the fourteenth century, measures directed against exports were commoner than those whose object was to limit imports. Gradually, his argument ran, with the rise of a money economy and the interposition of the money medium between human wants and their satisfaction, men's ideas altered. What Heckscher called a *fear of goods*, that is, a fear of foreign goods, replaced the older favorable attitude toward these. It came to be felt that the earlier method of securing plenty by encouraging importation was short-sighted. It might bring about a temporary plenitude, it was true, but as a long-term program only the development of home industry would suffice. So protective measures were enacted, not merely against foreign luxuries but of a more general nature.

This theory merits some examination. In the first place, it can be said that, in so far as it is possible to identify a characteristic medieval viewpoint on wealth, it was that of the Christian Church, that riches should be subordinated to the saving of the soul. Any idea of promoting the acquisition of goods beyond sufficiency to sustain life on its accustomed standard was foreign to this attitude. Heckscher's data on the subject do

[97] *Statutes*, quoted by E. Lipson, *The Economic History of England*, vol. 3, London 1931, p. 118. Reproduced by permission of A. & C. Black Ltd. and The Macmillan Company.

[98] See *Mercantilism*, translated by M. Shapiro, 2 vols., London 1935. The work was first published in Swedish in 1931.

not refer to the medieval period proper but to its close, when secular thought was asserting itself. Earlier in this chapter, it has been shown that self-interest displayed itself during the middle ages. Obviously there has been no uniformity of interest in any period. Man is at once a producer and a consumer and has interests in both these respects. For example, a specialist maker of cloth produces more than he consumes of this commodity, so that in relation to cloth his interest is that of a producer. His concern with other goods is that of a consumer. The point was made clearly in *A Discourse of the Common Weal of this Realm of England*. The *Discourse* gives an account of a discussion between a capper (*i.e.*, cap-maker) and a husbandman (or farmer) on the subject of a proposal to prohibit the export of corn whenever the price rose above a certain figure, but to allow export when the price fell below the designated level. The capper expressed his opinion as follows:

> Thoughe this . . . doth please youe well that be husbandmen, yet it pleaseth us that be artificers nothinge at all, which must bie both bread corne and mault for oure penny.[99]

In other words, the capper pointed out that what was very satisfactory to the corn grower was injurious to consumers of corn. This situation has been true of tariff measures at all times. Practically every one of them has assisted some people (the producers of the protected commodity) at the expense of others (its consumers). For Heckscher's thesis to be acceptable, a reason must be found why the interests of people *as consumers* should have been allowed to dominate those *as producers* in the later middle ages, while the reverse situation came into existence during the mercantile period.

In recent years it has become obvious that producer interests are more vocal than those of consumers, so that numerous laws have been passed to promote the prosperity of the former at the expense of the latter. For instance, in this country, a tariff wall has been erected against foreign clothes and a measure passed for the purpose of reducing the acreage under cotton, with little obvious regard to the net effect of the entire body of such legislation upon the American people as consumers. Heckscher's argument, in effect, is that this situation was applicable to the mercantile period but did not go back to the middle ages. It might be asked, were the regulatory authorities of medieval times (gilds, municipal corporations, the officials of feudal lords, and such royal administrations as then existed) less amenable to the blandishments of interested producers and merchants than were the State organizations that were important in the mercantile period? Historians of the gilds have given innumerable instances of the manner in which these bodies defended the interests of their members as producers and endeavored to influence in

[99] *Op. cit.*, p. 57.

their favor the actions of municipal and even national governments. Were the export restrictions, to which Heckscher referred, in the same category as the assizes of bread and ale, that is, intended to shield the consumer against the machinations of these enemies? Probably so, to a considerable extent. Certainly, medieval opinion favored the ordering of social relationships in a manner that took into account the interests of all the parties concerned.

As for the mercantile period itself, if we consider only the long series of protectionist measures which appeared during that time, it appears plain enough that the interests of producers were dominant. Yet the national governments did not abdicate entirely the old governmental function of endeavoring to give justice to all. The English Statute of Monopolies of 1624, one of whose main objects was the limitation of producer monopolies in the interests of the consuming public, is evidence to the contrary. Cunningham's judgment of the policy of William Cecil, Lord Burghley (1520–1598), the leading English Mercantilist statesman, was that he aimed,

> not as the Spaniards did, at obtaining a treasure, but at procuring a supply of useful commodities.[100]

This is entirely different from Heckscher's conclusion. Plainly, it is all a matter of balance, of the emphasis to be given to this or that feature of a complex social organization, and the historical evidence is far from being completely satisfactory.

The Modern World

The Return of Hedonism

Happiness as an incentive from Hobbes to Bentham. In Chapter I, it was noticed that some of the outstanding philosophers of the seventeenth century attributed to men's propensity to seek their own benefit a crucial role in political affairs. Hobbes found in this trait the reason for the establishment of society, Grotius the way that the several nations managed to live at peace with one another.

According to Hobbes, men's selfish desires did not stop with their escape from anarchy into political society. It was contrary to human nature for people to be satisfied at all. Their desires were unending. Human happiness lay not in the attainment of some definite objective but in perpetual progress from one new satisfaction to another:

> there is no such *finis ultimus*, utmost aim, nor *summum bonum*, greatest good, as is spoken of in the books of the old moral philosophers. Nor can a man

[100] W. Cunningham, *The Growth of English Industry and Commerce in Modern Times: The Mercantile System* (vol. 2 of Cunningham's complete work), 4th ed., Cambridge 1907, pp. 61-62, marginal note. Quoted by permission of the Cambridge University Press.

any more live, whose desires are at an end, than he, whose senses and imagination are at a stand. Felicity is a continual progress of the desire, from one object to another; the attaining of the former, being still but the way to the latter.[101]

Hobbes proceeded to list the forms which the ever-expanding human desires might assume:

in the first place, I put for a general inclination of all mankind, a perpetual and restless desire of power after power, that ceaseth only in death. . . Competition of riches, honour, command, or other power. . . Desire of ease, and sensual delight. . . Fear of death, and wounds. . . Desire of knowledge, and arts of peace. . . Desire of praise. . . Desire of fame after death. . .[102]

Thus, there emerged in the writings of Hobbes the modern idea of civilized man, with desires that are insatiable. Barbon spoke in much the same language:

The Wants of the Mind are infinite, Man naturally Aspires, and as his Mind is elevated, his Senses grow more refined, and more capable of Delight; his Desires are inlarged, and his Wants increase with his Wishes, which is for every thing that is rare, can gratifie his Senses, adorn his Body, and promote the Ease, Pleasure, and Pomp of Life.[103]

Locke asserted that men's desire for ease or pleasure was the mainspring of human action:

Pleasure and pain, and that which causes them, good and evil, are the hinges on which our passions turn. . . The uneasiness a man finds in himself upon the absence of any thing, whose present enjoyment carries the idea of delight with it, is that we call desire; which is greater or less, as that uneasiness is more or less vehement.[104]

This uneasiness or desire was what stimulated men to work:

the chief, if not only spur to human industry and action, is uneasiness.[105]

Next should be mentioned the philosophers, Francis Hutcheson (1694–1746, teacher of Adam Smith and his predecessor in the chair of moral philosophy at the University of Glasgow, David Hume (1711–1776), who was a close friend of Smith, and Jeremy Bentham (1748–1832), who had great influence on the later members of the British Classical School of economists (Smith's followers). The views of these writers on the subject of incentive were similar to those of Locke; they thought that pleasures and pains explained men's desires and aversions and so motivated human conduct. Thus, Hutcheson said:

[101] *The English Works of Thomas Hobbes,* vol. 3, *Leviathan,* p. 85.

[102] *Ibid.,* pp. 85-87.

[103] *A Discourse of Trade,* p. 14.

[104] *An Essay Concerning Human Understanding,* in *The Works of John Locke,* 10th ed., 10 vols., London 1801, vol. 1, pp. 216-217.

[105] *Ibid.,* p. 217.

as soon as any sense, opinion, or reasoning, represents an object or event as immediately good or pleasant, or as the means of future pleasure, or of security from evil, either for ourselves or any person about whom we are sollicitous, there arises immediately a new motion of the soul, distinct from all sensation, perception, or judgment, a *desire* of that object or event. And upon perception or opinion of an object or event as the occasion of pain or misery, or the loss of good, arises a contrary motion called *aversion;* on all occasions of this sort, these primary motions of the will naturally arise without any previous choice or command, and are the general springs of action in every rational agent.[106]

Hume:

The great end of all human industry, is the attainment of happiness. For this were arts invented, sciences cultivated, laws ordained, and societies modelled, by the most profound wisdom of patriots and legislators. Even the lonely savage, who lies exposed to the inclemency of the elements, and the fury of wild beasts, forgets not, for a moment, this grand object of his being. Ignorant as he is of every art of life, he keeps still in view the end of all those arts, and eagerly seeks for felicity amidst that darkness with which he is environed.[107]

Every thing in the world is purchased by labour; and our passions are the only causes of labour.[108]

Bentham:

Nature has placed mankind under the governance of two sovereign masters, *pain* and *pleasure.* It is for them alone to point out what we ought to do, as well as to determine what we shall do. On the one hand the standard of right and wrong, on the other the chain of causes and effects, are fastened to their throne. They govern us in all we do, in all we say, in all we think: every effort we can make to throw off their subjection, will serve but to demonstrate and confirm it.[109]

Bentham here stated happiness as a psychological principle and an ethical criterion. It was an incentive to action: as Bentham put it, it governed what men "shall do." It was also a standard of conduct, determining what men "ought to do." This dualism was noticed in the writings of Epicurus and has been characteristic of hedonistic thought, but the major interest of the present section is in the psychological side — the problem of human incentive — and the ethical aspect must be passed over. The French philosopher C. A. Helvétius (1715–1771) took up the hedonist position, a fact of some importance because his

[106] *A System of Moral Philosophy*, 2 vols., London 1755, vol. 1, p. 7.

[107] *Essays and Treatises on Several Subjects*, 2 vols., London 1772, vol. 1, *The Stoic*, p. 149.

[108] *Ibid.*, vol. 1, *Of Commerce*, p. 271.

[109] *The Works of Jeremy Bentham*, ed. J. Bowring, 11 vols., London 1838–1843, vol. 1, *An Introduction to the Principles of Morals and Legislation*, p. 1.

writings gave the French school of Physiocrats an ideological background generally similar to that in which Adam Smith wrote in Britain. Helvétius, however, was influenced by Montesquieu's belief that men were affected by their surroundings, so he argued that what constituted pleasure and pain varied according to circumstances, and thus avoided some of the finality of Bentham's judgments.

But, as is shown in Chapter III, some of the philosophers did not believe selfishness to be the only motive. In England the third Earl of Shaftesbury (1671–1713), in writings collected under the title *Characteristicks of Men, Manners, Opinions, Times* (3 vols., London 1711), recognized benevolence, that is, desire for the happiness of others, as well as selfishness, as a human incentive. Hutcheson spoke of "two calm determinations of the will," self-love and benevolence, apparently regarding the two as equally important:

It is well known, that *general Benevolence* alone, is not a Motive strong enough to *Industry,* to bear *Labour* and *Toil,* and many other Difficultys which we are averse to from *Self-love.* For the strengthening therefore our Motives to *Industry,* we have the strongest Attractions of *Blood,* of *Friendship,* of *Gratitude,* and the additional Motives of *Honour,* and even of external *Interest. Self-Love* is really as necessary to the *Good* of the *Whole,* as *Benevolence. . .*[110]

Hume compared the savage and the "polished citizen," who sought their selfish advantage, with the "man of virtue," who

governs his appetites, subdues his passions, and has learned, from reason, to set a just value on every pursuit and enjoyment.[111]

The "just value," according to Hume, as to Bentham later, was that which would maximize social happiness, bringing in the happiness of others as well as that of the individual himself.

Bentham did not attach such importance to benevolence as had Shaftesbury, Hutcheson, and Hume, returning more nearly to the position of Hobbes and Locke. To Bentham, it is true, selfishness was not the only motive, but he said that it was the chief one:

In the general tenor of life, in every human breast, self-regarding interest is predominant over all other interests put together. More shortly thus, — Self-regard is predominant, — or thus, — Self-preference has place everywhere. . . By the principle of self-preference, understand that propensity in human nature, by which, on the occasion of every act he exercises, every human being is led to pursue that line of conduct which, according to his view of the case, taken by him at the moment, will be in the highest degree contributory to his

[110] *An Inquiry into the Original of our Ideas of Beauty and Virtue: II, Concerning Moral Good and Evil,* London 1738, pp. 284-285.

[111] *Essays and Treatises on Several Subjects,* vol. 1, *The Stoic,* p. 149.

> own greatest happiness, whatsoever be the effect of it, in relation to the happiness of other similar beings, any or all of them taken together.[112]

This view is significant, as Bentham was one of the outstanding philosophers of his day and his writings were influential in furnishing the ethical and psychological background of British Classical economics in the early part of the nineteenth century.

Locke, Shaftesbury, and Hutcheson on the relation of wealth to happiness. If individual happiness were and should be an aim of human endeavor, as was believed by the hedonist philosophers, it was only to be expected that questions would be asked concerning the relationship between wealth and happiness. Did accessions of wealth minister to the happiness and therefore to the good of the person concerned?

In *An Essay Concerning Human Understanding,* Locke laid down the general principle that the judgment of the individual concerned must be accepted on the problem of what promoted his happiness. The things that a man wanted must be assumed to minister to his happiness, at least in regard to the present:

> as to present happiness and misery, when that alone comes into consideration, and the consequences are quite removed, a man never chooses amiss; he knows what best pleases him, and that he actually prefers. Things in their present enjoyment are what they seem; the apparent and real good are, in this case, always the same.[113]

Locke made certain qualifications to the general rule. It applied only to present wants and not to comparisons of present and future:

> when we compare present pleasure or pain with future . . . we often make wrong judgments of them, taking our measures of them in different positions of distance. Objects, near our view, are apt to be thought greater than those of a larger size, that are more remote: and so it is with pleasures and pains; the present is apt to carry it, and those at a distance have the disadvantage in the comparison. Thus most men, like spendthrift heirs, are apt to judge a little in hand better than a great deal to come. . .[114]

This opinion was at least as old as Aristotle, as is indicated by the following passage from *De anima*:

> a pleasant object which is just at hand presents itself as both pleasant and good, without condition in either case, because of want of foresight into what is farther away in time. . .[115]

Further, Locke admitted that, when the ultimate consequences of an action were taken into account, what seemed more pleasurable at first

[112] *The Works of Jeremy Bentham,* vol. 9, *The Constitutional Code,* p. 5.
[113] *The Works of John Locke,* vol. 1, p. 258.
[114] *Ibid.,* p. 261.
[115] *The Works of Aristotle,* vol. 3, 433b.

thought might appear less preferable. Neglecting these complications, however, said Locke, "we should undoubtedly never err in our choice of good; we should always infallibly prefer the best."[116] This is an important point. According to Locke, men's wants indicated the directions in which their happiness lay. Since society, in Locke's opinion, was merely the sum total of the individuals composing it, it followed that the maximum satisfaction of wants coincided with the greatest happiness.

In the matter of choice between present and future satisfactions, some comment appears to be necessary. Locke did not seem to appreciate the inconsistency of his position. If he assumed arbitrarily—as he did—that men knew best what conduced to their happiness, why did he assert that their assessment of the relative importance of present and future wants was incorrect? Locke—and Aristotle—might have considered the future to be relatively more significant than did the rank and file of men, but why should it be postulated that the judgment of Locke and Aristotle was sound, rather than that of the rank and file? To no men is it given to forecast the future accurately. Many writers have assumed, since the time of Locke, that individuals take too short a view and that it is an economic function of government to institute remedial measures, for the purpose of protecting the interests of future generations. The statement of the German, Wundt, on this subject, which is quoted in Chapter III, is an illustration. Perhaps this attitude is correct. It may be that the State should intervene to prevent individuals from exploiting natural resources so wastefully that little is left for future generations, or to prevent personal decisions respecting marriage and the bearing of children from eliminating the problems of future generations altogether, but Locke said nothing whatever on this question. He merely asserted that men misjudged the needs of the future and left it at that.

Shaftesbury and Hutcheson, however, did not limit the possibility of mistakes to choices between present and future satisfactions. They thought that even in their present preferences men might want things that brought them no real happiness. Wealth was a case in point. Both Shaftesbury and Hutcheson doubted whether wealth necessarily conferred happiness on its possessor. Thus, in *An Inquiry Concerning Virtue, or Merit,* drafted when its author was about twenty years of age and published in the *Characteristicks,* Shaftesbury said:

> How far a COVETING or AVARITIOUS TEMPER is miserable, needs not, surely, be explain'd. Who knows not how small a Portion of worldly Matters is sufficient for a Man's single Use and Convenience; and how much his Occasions and Wants might be contracted and reduc'd, if a just Frugality were study'd, and Temperance and a natural Life came once to be pursu'd with half that Application, Industry and Art, which is bestow'd on Sumptuousness and Luxury? Now if Temperance be in reality so advantageous,

116 *The Works of John Locke,* vol. 1, p. 259.

and the Practice as well as the Consequences of it so pleasing and happy, as has been before express'd; there is little need, on the other side, to mention any thing of the Miserys attending those covetous and eager Desires after things which have no Bounds or Rule. . .[117]

Here is something very different from Hobbes's view that felicity or happiness consisted in "continual progress of the desire". Not happiness but misery was what Shaftesbury indicated in this situation. The statements in Hutcheson's *An Essay on the Nature and Conduct of the Passions and Affections* (London 1728) were comparable :

The *Pleasures* of *Wealth* or *Power,* are proportioned to the Gratifications of the *Desires* or *Senses,* which the Agent intends to gratify by them : So that . . . Wealth and Power give greater Happiness to the *Virtuous,* than to those who consult only *Luxury* or external *Splendor.* If these Desires are grown *enthusiastic* and *habitual,* without regard to any other end than *Possession,* they are an endless Source of Vexation, without any real *Enjoyment;* a perpetual *Craving,* without *Nourishment* or *Digestion.* . .[118]

Concerning the Desires of *Wealth* and *Power* . . . from considering the small Addition commonly made to the *Happiness* of the Possessor, by the greatest Degrees of them, and the *Uncertainty* of their Continuance; if we have obtained any share of them, let us examine their *true Use,* and what is the best Enjoyment of them. . . What moral *Pleasures,* what Delights of *Humanity,* what *Gratitude* from Persons obliged, what *Honour,* may a wise Man of a generous Temper purchase with them ? How foolish is the Conduct of heaping up Wealth for *Posterity,* when smaller Degrees might make them equally happy ! when great *Prospects* of this kind are the strongest *Temptations* to them, to indulge *Sloth, Luxury, Debauchery, Indolence, Pride,* and *Contempt* of their Fellow-Creatures; and to banish some noble Dispositions, *Humility, Compassion, Industry, Hardiness of Temper and Courage,* the Offspring of the sober rigid Dame *Poverty.*[119]

Obviously, here Hutcheson introduced an ethical element. A critic could answer that debauchery or pride might not be "moral pleasures" but to some people they appear pleasurable, nevertheless. Hutcheson's reference to the small additions made to happiness by the greatest degrees of wealth savors of the principle of diminishing utility and was based, no doubt, on some appreciation of this principle on his part. On the other hand, the statement he made in the second passage, to the effect that smaller degrees of wealth make men *equally happy,* is inconsistent with the concept (such as is popular nowadays) of a utility curve that falls off gradually. Hutcheson's estimation of the relation between wealth and happiness, however, is perhaps less important in itself than for its connection with the views of Adam Smith. As has been noted,

[117] *Characteristicks,* 3 vols., n.p. (London) 1732, vol. 2, pp. 155-156.
[118] Edition of 1730, p. 154.
[119] *Ibid.,* pp. 193-194.

Hutcheson was Smith's teacher and predecessor in the University of Glasgow, and there seems little question that Hutcheson's comments on this subject contained the germ of Smith's thought.

Quesnay and Smith. The philosophy of Locke, Hutcheson, Hume, Helvétius, and later Bentham, had great influence on contemporary thought. The leading French economist of the middle of the eighteenth century, head of the school of *économistes* or Physiocrats, François Quesnay (1694–1774), spoke of human incentives in language reminiscent of Locke and Hume:

> Need alone is the father of industry. . .[120]

Quesnay's definition of economics was in full accord with this philosophy:

> *to obtain the greatest possible amount of pleasure, with the least possible expense, is the perfection of economic conduct.*[121]

In the bible of British economics, Smith's *An Inquiry into the Nature and Causes of the Wealth of Nations,* the position was much the same. Perusal of Smith's writings as a whole, however, shows that he did not accept it as a fact that people's actions were dictated wholly by their desire for happiness or for the pleasure they got from ordinary consumption.

In *The Theory of Moral Sentiments* (London 1759), which appeared after its author had been teaching moral philosophy at Glasgow for a number of years, Smith argued that men's actions were influenced by their desire for the approbation of others. He went into greater detail than had Hutcheson in emphasizing that wealth and happiness were not necessarily coincident. Enough, declared Smith, was as good as a feast:

> What can be added to the happiness of the man who is in health, who is out of debt, and has a clear conscience? To one in this situation, all accessions of fortune may properly be said to be superfluous. .[122]

There must be enough, however:

> though little can be added to this state, much may be taken from it. Though between this condition and the highest pitch of human prosperity, the interval is but a trifle; between it and the lowest depth of misery the distance is immense and prodigious. Adversity, on this account, necessarily depresses the mind of the sufferer much more below its natural state, than prosperity can elevate him above it.[123]

[120] *Œuvres économiques et philosophiques de F. Quesnay,* ed. A. Oncken, Paris 1888, p. 391, translated. The words appeared in the *Réponse au mémoire de M. H.* (1766).

[121] *Ibid.,* p. 535, translated. The passage is from *Sur les travaux des artisans,* second dialogue (1766).

[122] *The Theory of Moral Sentiments,* 7th ed., 2 vols., London 1792, vol. 1, p. 107.

[123] *Ibid.,* p. 108.

In a sense, this accords with more modern views concerning diminishing utility. When a man has but little of the world's goods, increments of uniform size mean more to him that when he is richer. But Smith spoke as though utility or happiness did not increase at all, or increased only to a negligible extent, beyond the level that secured health, freedom from debt, and a calm conscience. Thus it would appear that had the author of the *Moral Sentiments* drawn a utility graph representing "wealth in general" (*i.e.*, all commodities) this would have had some such form as the figure below.

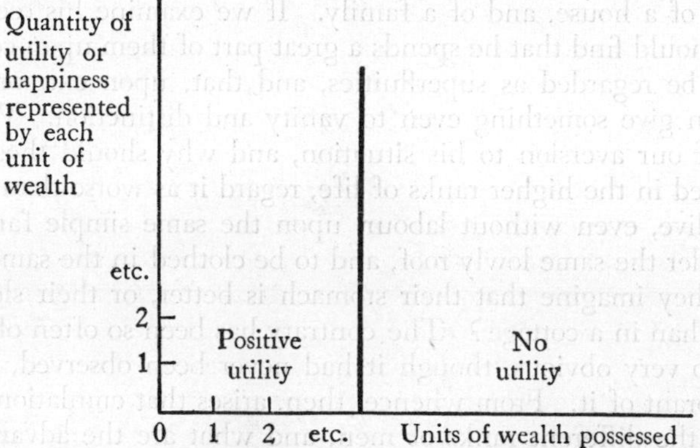

Elsewhere, Smith discussed the uselessness of riches :

in the languor of disease and the weariness of old age, the pleasures of the vain and empty distinctions of greatness disappear. To one, in this situation, they are no longer capable of recommending those toilsome pursuits in which they had formerly engaged him. In his heart he curses ambition, and vainly regrets the ease and the indolence of youth, pleasures which are fled for ever, and which he has foolishly sacrificed for what, when he has got it, can afford him no real satisfaction. In this miserable aspect does greatness appear to every man when reduced either by spleen or disease to observe with attention his own situation, and to consider what it is that is really wanting to his happiness. Power and riches appear then to be, what they are, enormous and operose machines contrived to produce a few trifling conveniences to the body. . . They are immense fabrics, which it requires the labour of a life to raise, which threaten every moment to overwhelm the person that dwells in them, and which while they stand, though they may save him from some smaller inconveniences, can protect him from none of the severer inclemencies of the season. They keep off the summer shower, not the winter storm, but leave him always as much, and sometimes more exposed than before, to anxiety, to fear, and to sorrow; to diseases, to danger, and to death.[124]

In what constitutes the real happiness of human life, they [*i.e.*, the poor] are in no respect inferior to those who would seem so much above them. In ease of body and peace of mind, all the different ranks of life are nearly upon a

[124] *Ibid.*, pp. 461-462.

level, and the beggar, who suns himself by the side of the highway, possesses that security which kings are fighting for.[125]

Why, then, did men strive so hard for wealth and greatness? Smith's answer was that they wanted these because of their effect on the minds of others:

For to what purpose is all the toil and bustle of this world? what is the end of avarice and ambition, of the pursuit of wealth, of power, and prehem-inence? Is it to supply the necessities of nature? The wages of the meanest labourer can supply them. We see that they afford him food and clothing, the comfort of a house, and of a family. If we examine his œconomy with rigour, we should find that he spends a great part of them upon conveniences, which may be regarded as superfluities, and that, upon extraordinary occa-sions, he can give something even to vanity and distinction. What then is the cause of our aversion to his situation, and why should those who have been educated in the higher ranks of life, regard it as worse than death, to be reduced to live, even without labour, upon the same simple fare with him, to dwell under the same lowly roof, and to be clothed in the same humble at-tire? Do they imagine that their stomach is better, or their sleep sounder, in a palace than in a cottage? The contrary has been so often observed, and, indeed, is so very obvious, though it had never been observed, that there is nobody ignorant of it. From whence, then, arises that emulation which runs through all the different ranks of men, and what are the advantages which we propose by that great purpose of human life which we call bettering our condition? . . . It is the vanity, not the ease, or the pleasure, which interests us. But vanity is always founded upon the belief of our being the object of attention and approbation. The rich man glories in his riches, because he feels that they naturally draw upon him the attention of the world. . . At the thought of this, his heart seems to swell and dilate itself within him, and he is fonder of his wealth, upon this account, than for all the other advantages it procures him. The poor man, on the contrary, is ashamed of his pov-erty. . . The poor man goes out and comes in unheeded, and when in the midst of a crowd is in the same obscurity as if shut up in his own hovel. . . The man of rank and distinction, on the contrary, is observed by all the world. Everybody is eager to look at him, and to conceive, at least by sympathy, that joy and exultation with which his circumstances naturally inspire him. His actions are the objects of the public care. . . It is this, which, notwithstand-ing the restraint it imposes, notwithstanding the loss of liberty with which it is attended, renders greatness the object of envy, and compensates, in the opinion of mankind, all that toil, all that anxiety, all those mortifications which must be undergone in the pursuit of it; and what is of yet more con-sequence, all that leisure, all that ease, all that careless security, which are forfeited for ever by the acquisition.[126]

Smith, it may be observed, was not a disillusioned old man, when *The Theory of Moral Sentiments* was published, but only thirty-six years of age.

[125] *Ibid.*, p. 467.

[126] *Ibid.*, pp. 120-125.

He did not approve the prevailing "disposition to admire the rich and great," speaking of it as a "corruption of our moral sentiments"[127] and describing it in caustic terms:

It is from our disposition to admire, and consequently to imitate, the rich and the great, that they are enabled to set, or to lead, what is called the fashion. Their dress is the fashionable dress; the language of their conversation, the fashionable style; their air and deportment, the fashionable behaviour. Even their vices and follies are fashionable; and the greater part of men are proud to imitate and resemble them in the very qualities which dishonour and degrade them. Vain men often give themselves airs of a fashionable profligacy, which, in their hearts, they do not approve of, and of which, perhaps, they are really not guilty. They desire to be praised for what they themselves do not think praise-worthy, and are ashamed of unfashionable virtues which they sometimes practise in secret, and for which they have secretly some degree of real veneration.[128]

Apparently, Smith had much the same idea as was developed so strikingly by Veblen in his *The Theory of the Leisure Class* (New York 1899).

Although, according to Smith, the "real satisfaction which all these things are capable of affording" must "always appear in the highest degree contemptible and trifling,"[129] men were so made that they rarely viewed it in this abstract and philosophical light. In their ordinary moments, therefore,

The pleasures of wealth and greatness . . . strike the imagination as something grand and beautiful and noble, of which the attainment is well worth all the toil and anxiety which we are so apt to bestow upon it.[130]

In Smith's opinion, "it is well that nature imposes upon us in this manner," because

It is this deception which rouses and keeps in continual motion the industry of mankind. It is this which first prompted them to cultivate the ground, to build houses, to found cities and commonwealths, and to invent and improve all the sciences and arts, which ennoble and embellish human life; which have entirely changed the whole face of the globe, have turned the rude forests of nature into agreeable and fertile plains, and have made the trackless and barren ocean a new fund of subsistence, and the great road of communication to the different nations of the earth.[131]

That is to say, Smith's theory of economic incentive, as given in the *Moral Sentiments,* was to the effect that men's desire to receive the attention and admiration of their fellows caused them to exert themselves, though it brought them no real happiness.

At first sight it appears that Smith here was inconsistent, speaking as

[127] *Ibid.*, p. 146.
[128] *Ibid.*, pp. 153-154.
[129] *Ibid.*, p. 463.
[130] *Ibid.*, p. 464.
[131] *Ibid.*, p. 464-465.

though industry and wealth were advantageous, whereas previously he had taken a different view. This was not the case. Smith believed that Providence had so arranged matters that the very delusions to which individuals were subjected, which caused them to seek wealth in the mistaken view that it would be of benefit to them, operated so as to serve society as a whole. Consideration of this aspect of Smith's theories, however, is deferred to Chapter III.

Taken alone, *An Inquiry into the Nature and Causes of the Wealth of Nations,* published sixteen years after *The Theory of Moral Sentiments,* reads quite differently from the earlier book. In the *Wealth of Nations,* Smith accepted it as a fact that men pursued gain and spoke of this as though it were a matter of common sense, not a delusion on their part:

In all countries where there is tolerable security, every man of common understanding will endeavour to employ whatever stock he can command, in procuring either present enjoyment or future profit.[132]

The consideration of his own private profit, is the sole motive which determines the owner of any capital to employ it either in agriculture, in manufactures, or in some particular branch of the wholesale or retail trade.[133]

Every individual is continually exerting himself to find out the most advantageous employment for whatever capital he can command. It is his own advantage, indeed, and not that of society which he has in view.[134]

All this is closer to the *economic man,* whom Smith's critics have alleged that he invented, than anything in the *Moral Sentiments.* Moreover, when discussing education in the later work, Smith did not disguise his contempt for ascetic or self-denying philosophy as it had been taught in Europe in earlier times.[135]

How is the difference between the two books to be interpreted? In the closing paragraph of the *Moral Sentiments,* its author mentioned his plans for further writing. There, it was indicated that Smith intended to discuss the general principles of law and government, "justice," along with "police, revenue, and arms" being mentioned specifically. There have since been discovered (and printed as *Lectures on Justice, Police, Revenue and Arms,* edited by E. Cannan, Oxford 1896) notes on lectures delivered by Smith at Glasgow University during the *Moral Sentiments* period. These show substantially the same viewpoint as is taken in the *Wealth of Nations,* which excludes the possibility that Smith changed his mind between the appearance of the two books.

The extracts from the *Moral Sentiments,* quoted above, make it clear

[132] *Wealth of Nations,* Bk. 2, Chap. 1. In view of the fact that variously-paged editions of Smith's book are in common use, this form of reference appears desirable. For the same reason, it is employed in the case of Karl Marx's *Capital,* vol. 1, and J. S. Mill's *Principles of Political Economy.*

[133] *Ibid.,* Bk. 2, Chap. 5.

[134] *Ibid.,* Bk. 4, Chap. 2.

[135] See *Ibid.,* Bk. 5, Chap. 1, Pt. 3, Art. 2.

that Smith emphasized selfishness, even in the earlier work. Further, in speaking of it his tone was not always one of disapproval. Certainly, he objected to self-interest that went beyond the bounds of justice, but within its own sphere he seemed to regard it as a commendable incentive.

The point of difference was that, in the *Moral Sentiments,* Smith appeared to look upon men's propensity to seek their own ends as mistaken (bringing them no real happiness), which was incompatible with the "every man of common understanding" terminology of the *Wealth of Nations.* It must be admitted that consistency was not one of Smith's literary virtues, but the matter at issue seems too important for a sensible man, such as Smith undoubtedly was, not to have thought it out. It was a problem of psychology. Did wealth confer happiness upon its possessor or did it not? In the *Moral Sentiments,* Smith granted that it did up to a point, but beyond this he said, as had Hutcheson before him, that increased wealth did not add to human happiness. When he spoke in the *Wealth of Nations* about men seeking their own advantage, did he or did he not believe that this so-called advantage was illusory? The *Wealth of Nations* was a book on economics, not psychology, so perhaps Smith thought that the matter had been dealt with sufficiently in his earlier book and could be omitted from the later publication. If so, however, at least he might have inserted a footnote or other guide to encourage those readers of his economics book to make themselves familiar with the contents of its predecessor. Because, if the author of the *Wealth of Nations* really accepted that beyond a certain point wealth had no utility, much of what was in that book could have appeared to him to be of no service to mankind. It may be answered that Smith's reference to the fact that the rich used their wealth to maintain others, discussed in Chapter III, offered a social justification for wealth-seeking. But it must be remembered that Smith had said already[136] that the wages of the "meanest labourer" were adequate to secure the necessities of life, which alone were able to confer happiness. If Smith were still of this opinion when he wrote the *Wealth of Nations,* then what he did in penning the later treatise was to minister to a demand that he thought was mistaken.

Though, as is shown in the concluding chapter of this book, the *Wealth of Nations* was not the first work to follow this line, it can be said that it effectively set the precedent of divorcing the study of men's search for wealth from moral or ethical considerations. *Wealth, if at all, for the service of God* said the religious teachers of earlier times. *Wealth for the good of the State* was the attitude taken by Mercantilist writers. *Wealth because it conferred happiness on its possessor* represented the standpoint of Locke. *Wealth merely because men wanted it, with no questions asked about why they did so* was the field of study delimited

[136] *The Theory of Moral Sentiments,* vol. 1, p. 120. The passage containing these words is quoted on p. 104.

in the *Wealth of Nations.* Perhaps Smith felt more able to adopt this approach, since he had asked the questions already. But after receiving such a disconcerting answer as had Smith, budding economists of weaker fiber might have been excused for taking up some other study. Bentham was to reach a different conclusion.

Bentham, diminishing utility, and greatest happiness. In the meantime, individual happiness or *utility* was being developed as the foundation of an ethical theory. Hutcheson, Hume, and Bentham, elaborated what became known as the *greatest happiness principle* or *principle of utility,* as the essential idea of a body of philosophy known as *utilitarianism.* According to these philosophers, the ultimate good of man was happiness. Further, society was

a fictitious *body,* composed of the individual persons who are considered as constituting as it were its *members.*[137]

—which, as was noticed in Chapter I, represented the view of Locke. From these two assumptions, it followed that the best social system was that which maximized individual happiness. On this subject, Hutcheson said:

we are led by *our moral Sense* of *Virtue* to judge thus; that in *equal Degrees* of Happiness, expected to proceed from the Action, the *Virtue* is in proportion to the *Number* of Persons to whom the Happiness shall extend (and here the *Dignity* or *moral Importance* of Persons, may compensate Numbers) and in equal *Numbers,* the *Virtue* is as the *Quantity* of the Happiness, or natural Good; or that the *Virtue* is in a *compound Ratio* of the *Quantity* of Good, and the *Number* of Enjoyers. In the same manner, the *moral Evil,* or *Vice,* is as the Degree of Misery, and *Number* of Sufferers; so that *That Action* is *best,* which procures the *greatest Happiness* for the *greatest Numbers;* and *that worst,* which, in *like manner,* occasions *Misery.*[138]

And Bentham:

An action then may be said to be conformable to the principle of utility, or, for shortness sake, to utility (meaning with respect to the community at large), when the tendency it has to augment the happiness of the community is greater than any it has to diminish it.[139]

Bentham developed this idea in great detail, devoting himself especially to the reformation of the legal system; but in his writings he dealt with all manner of topics, for instance, private property and the distribution of wealth, always asking the question of how the happiness or utility enjoyed by individual members of society could be maximized.

137 *The Works of Jeremy Bentham,* vol. 1, *An Introduction to the Principles of Morals and Legislation,* p. 2.

138 *An Inquiry into the Original of our Ideas on Beauty and Virtue,* II, pp. 180-181.

139 *An Introduction to the Principles of Morals and Legislation,* p. 2.

Bentham's views on the relation of wealth to human happiness were of great importance. Not merely did they anticipate the formal statement of the principle of diminishing utility which appeared in economic writings at a later date, but they colored economic thought on the distribution of wealth, through such utilitarians as John Stuart Mill and Henry Sidgwick, who were economists of high standing in England as well as authorities on ethics and politics.

In his *Principles of the Civil Code,* Bentham used the term *moral pathology* to describe "knowledge of the feelings, affections, and passions, and their effects upon happiness"; and spoke of a *moral thermometer* as being required to "exhibit every degree of happiness and suffering" for the guidance of the legislator.[140] Attempting to estimate the effect of wealth on happiness, he laid down the following propositions:

1. *Each portion of wealth is connected with a corresponding portion of happiness.*
2. *Of two individuals, possessed of unequal fortunes, he who possesses the greatest wealth will possess the greatest happiness.*
3. *The excess of happiness on the part of the most wealthy will not be so great as the excess of his wealth.*
4. *For the same reason, the greater the disproportion between the two masses of wealth, the less the probability that there exists an equally great disproportion between the masses of happiness.*
5. *The more nearly the actual proportion approaches to equality, the greater will be the total mass of happiness.*[141]

Bentham qualified his statement, however, by stating that he connected wealth not with happiness, strictly speaking, but with opportunity to cause happiness, and the "efficacy of any cause of happiness is always precarious." Again, discussing the subject in *The Constitutional Code,* he stated the same idea somewhat more fully:

The usefulness of the benefit of equality stands, then, upon these positions:—
1. The quantity of *happiness* possessed by a man, is not as the quantity of *property* possessed by the same man.
2. The greater the quantity of the matter of property [*i.e.,* wealth] a man is already in possession of, the less is the quantity of happiness he receives by the addition of another quantity of the matter of property, to a given amount.
3. The addition made by property to happiness goes on increasing in such a ratio, that, in the case of two individuals—he who has *least,* having, at all times, a quantity of the matter of property sufficient for a subsistence, while he who has *most,* possesses it in a quantity as great as any individual ever had, or ever can have; it is a question scarce capable of solution, whether the one who has the greatest quantity of the matter of property,

[140] *The Works of Jeremy Bentham,* vol. 1, p. 304.
[141] *Ibid.,* p. 305.

> has twice the quantity of happiness which he has whose quantity of the means of happiness, in that shape, is the least.
>
> If this ratio, of two to one, be regarded as too small a ratio, substitute to it the ratio of 3 to 1, the ratio of 4 to 1, and so on, till you are satisfied you have fixed upon the proper ratio : still, the truth of the practical conclusion will not be affected.[142]

That is to say, Bentham regarded it as a fact that the happiness or utility represented by increments of wealth diminished as the quantity of wealth possessed was increased, but he recognized that it was impossible to ascertain the rate of such diminution. In other words, in Bentham's opinion, the relationship between wealth and happiness was not a straight line so drawn that x units of wealth represented x units of happiness; nor was the connection of such a nature that above a certain level of wealth x units of wealth represented *zero* units of happiness (as Smith appeared to imply, in his *Moral Sentiments*). It was in the form of a curve of the type indicated below : x units of wealth represented y units of happiness, y increasing but at a diminishing rate as x increased.

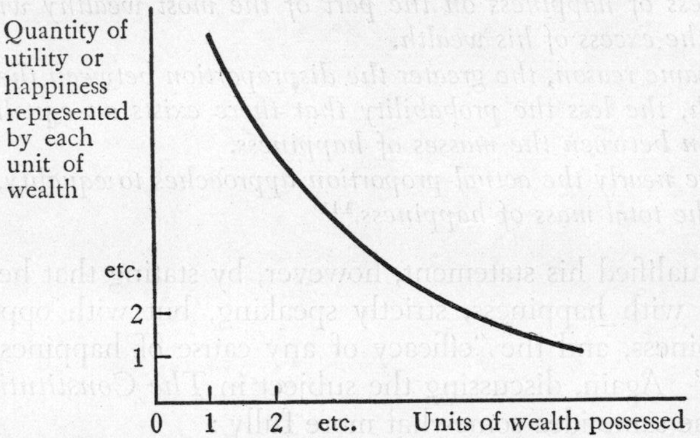

It was left to later writers to draw curves on this basis, though for particular commodities, rather than for wealth as a whole.[143]

Bentham's theory rehabilitated the search for wealth from the amoral, if not immoral, position in which Smith's *Moral Sentiments* had seemed to place it. Such a search was no longer to be regarded as a stupid proceeding of the rank and file of men, explained by the fact that they

[142] *Ibid.*, vol. 9, p. 18.

[143] See Chapter IX. In the form in which Bentham's statement was made, it did not obviously refer to a curve that was concave from above, such as is shown in the diagram and was beloved by later writers on this subject. But he spoke as though a rich man, who might have possessed a hundred times as much wealth as his poor neighbor, would have only a few times as much happiness as the latter. Further, though under the second head of his *Constitutional Code* passage he introduced the qualification "to a given amount," he did not say specifically (like Smith) that the later increments of a rich man's wealth were productive of no happiness at all. These circumstances point to a curve of the nature indicated.

thought—mistakenly—that an increase in the quantity of the wealth they possessed would add to their happiness. According to Bentham, additions to wealth *would* increase happiness, *but* would do so in a diminishing ratio. Thus there was provided a principle that furnished at once a psychological and an ethical basis for economic study and wealth-seeking activity; a psychological basis, because it was accepted that there was a positive relationship between wealth and happiness (more wealth meant more happiness); an ethical justification, because it was granted that increased happiness was desirable. Orthodox economics has been erected on these foundations.

Because of this, it becomes necessary to criticize the Benthamite theory. First it should be pointed out that there is no known means of measuring happiness, except in an empirical manner, such as is employed when an individual expresses his preferences. A person may realize that he prefers a glass of milk to a cup of coffee, in a particular situation, but exactly *how much* more happiness he gets from the milk he cannot state with any certainty. In any scheme of social action—for example, the imposition of a tax to finance certain public expenditure—gains and losses on the part of individuals have to be set against each other. *A* may both gain and lose: *B* also may gain and lose. On consideration, *A* decides that his gain more than counterbalances his loss. *B* reaches the opposite conclusion: his loss is in excess. Society is composed of such *A's* and *B's*. How is the greatest good to be determined? Hutcheson offered two methods. First, he said, numbers should be counted. "Degrees" (*i.e.*, quantities) of happiness being equal, the happiness of the greater number should prevail (though he suggested that quality or importance of the different people might be taken into account). Obviously, if numbers only be considered, it may happen that the losses suffered by less numerous *B's* represent a greater quantity of happiness than do the gains of the more common *A's*. Under the second method, the quantities of happiness gained and lost are weighed against each other, irrespective of the numbers of people affected. With this procedure, the fewer *B's* (if their losses are heavy enough) may more than offset the more numerous *A's*. Bentham did not make clear which of the two tests he thought should be applied. Clearly, the criteria of *greatest happiness* and *happiness of the greatest numbers* are entirely different, and cases can arise when the use of one will give a particular result, while the employment of the other will yield the opposite decision. Provided that individuals recognize and select the things that confer happiness upon them, the determination of the *happiness of the greatest numbers* in a society can be ascertained by the simple process of counting these preferences. But in the absence of a mechanism for measuring the quantity of happiness conferred on different individuals, *greatest happiness* is incalculable. On the other hand, subject to the same conditions of recognition and selection of the things that yield him happiness, when confronted by a given range of choices, an individual can maximize *his* happiness, as the English economist W. S. Jevons (1835–1882) was to argue at a later date.

Another difficulty of the Benthamite system is that happiness has various meanings, or rather that individuals react differently to the same things. "One man's meat is another's poison." As that great philosopher of Victorian England, Herbert Spencer, put the point,

> no fact is more palpable than that the standard of happiness is infinitely variable. In all ages — amongst every people — by each class — do we find different notions of it entertained. To the wandering gypsy a home is tiresome; whilst a Swiss is miserable without one. Progress is necessary to the well-being of the Anglo-Saxons; on the other hand the Esquimaux are content in their squalid poverty, have no latent wants, and are still what they were in the days of Tacitus. An Irishman delights in a row; a Chinese in pageantry and ceremonies; and the usually apathetic Javan gets vociferously enthusiastic over a cock-fight. The heaven of the Hebrew is "a city of gold and precious stones, with a supernatural abundance of corn and wine;" that of the Turk — a harem peopled by houris; that of the American Indian — a "happy hunting ground;" in the Norse paradise there were to be daily battles with magical healing of wounds; whilst the Australian hopes that after death he shall "jump up a white fellow, and have plenty of sixpences" . . . Nor has greater unanimity been shown amongst ourselves. To a miserly Elwes the hoarding of money was the only enjoyment of life; but Day, the philanthropic author of "Sandford and Merton," could find no pleasurable employment save in its distribution. Rural quietude, books, and a friend, are the wants of the poet; a tuft-hunter longs rather for a large circle of titled acquaintance, a box at the Opera, and the freedom of Almack's. The ambitions of the tradesman and the artist are anything but alike; and could we compare the air castles of the ploughman and the philosopher, we should find them of widely-different orders of architecture. . . The members of each community disagree upon the question. Neither, if we compare the wishes of the gluttonous school-boy with those of the earth-scorning transcendentalist into whom he may afterwards grow, do we find any constancy in the individual. So we may say, not only that every epoch and every people has its peculiar conceptions of happiness, but that no two men have like conceptions; and further, that in each man the conception is not the same at any two periods of life.[144]

Spencer went on to ask on what grounds it was maintained that everyone had an equal claim to happiness. The admission of such a principle he said, would confer the same right on the lazy and criminal as on the industrious and virtuous, that is, it would contain no sanction for good conduct. This was a point to which Bentham had devoted considerable attention and his views are referred to in Chapter IV. It is enough to say

[144] *Social Statics*, London 1851, pp. 3-5. Quoted by permission of the D. Appleton-Century Company, Inc.

here that Bentham agreed that, if all were granted an equal title to happiness, irrespective of their behavior, there would be no inducement to behave well. In terms of wealth, if everyone were given an equal share of wealth, regardless of what the different individuals produced, there would be no incentive to industry and efficiency. But Spencer's comment on the fact that happiness has widely different meanings raises the problem of whether all of these are to be treated alike or whether some kinds of happiness should be preferred over others.

Aristotle recognized the existence of different types of happiness and ranged them in order of merit, as was seen earlier in this chapter. Grappling with the same problem, certain nineteenth century utilitarians expressed the opinion that some kinds of happiness, or the happiness of some individuals, should take precedence over others. Francis Hutcheson's comment on the subject has been noticed in an earlier section. James Mill (1773–1836), in his *Elements of Political Economy* (London 1821) considered a proposal to increase the sum paid in wages by levying an income tax for the purpose and decided against it on the ground that it would reduce social happiness. He accepted that the middle class was the most important in this connection and thought that anything that prejudiced its position would reduce social happiness:

It is also, in a peculiar manner, the business of those whose object it is to ascertain the means of raising human happiness to its greatest height, to consider, what is that class of men by whom the greatest happiness is enjoyed. It will not probably be disputed, that they who are raised above solicitude for the means of subsistence and respectability, without being exposed to the vices and follies of great riches, the men of middling fortunes, the men to whom society is generally indebted for its greatest improvements, are, indeed, the men, who, having their time at their own disposal, freed from the necessity of manual labour, subject to no man's authority, and engaged in the most delightful occupations, obtain, as a class, the greatest sum of human enjoyment. For the happiness, therefore, as well as the ornament of our nature, it is peculiarly desirable that a class of this description should form as large a proportion of each community as possible.[145]

James Mill's son, John Stuart Mill (1806–1873), recognized the difficulty and maintained that it was "quite compatible with the principle of utility" to admit that "some *kinds* of pleasure are more desirable and more valuable than others."[146] He proceeded:

It is better to be a human being dissatisfied than a pig satisfied; better to be Socrates dissatisfied than a fool satisfied. And if the fool, or the pig, is of a different opinion, it is because they only know their own side of the question.[147]

[145] *Elements of Political Economy*, p. 49.
[146] *Utilitarianism*, London 1863, 8th ed., London 1882, p. 11.
[147] *Ibid.*, p. 14.

Obviously, it was an assertion, and nothing more, for James Mill to say that the middle classes were more capable of pleasure than the remaining groups of society, or that their pleasures were higher in some manner. The same is true of his son's statement, respecting the human being and Socrates. Of course, man has triumphed over the lower animals and is not in the habit of studying their feelings, so John Stuart Mill has ample precedent for his disregard of the pig, but could not members of the upper classes of society say the same thing, to a certain extent, about their social inferiors? Even the comparison between the fool and Socrates represented nothing more than Mill's opinion. Another observer might have thought that the man, who—to Mill—was a fool, was by no means devoid of sense, while, recalling the circumstances of Socrates's death,[148] might have considered that philosopher rather foolish. This would have made the comparison of persons yield the opposite result. Obviously, neither of the Mills had any scientific means of judging such cases.[149]

An important point is that ideas as to what constitutes happiness—in fact, ideals generally—can be modified. As was pointed out in Chapter I, it is within the power of a resolute State administration, by propaganda and other means, to influence the minds of the individuals under its rule. Taught to want what their government intends them to get, the probability is that they will be satisfied. Who really doubts that, after a generation or two of authoritarian government, the "greatest happiness" of the Russian people may be found in Soviet Communism, that of the Germans and Italians in their statist systems had these lasted. The same is true, in a way, under private capitalism. Unwittingly, or as the result of carefully-laid schemes of advertising, people's tastes are modified. Strings of bones or teeth—wealth to the savage of a few generations ago—become objects of contempt to his civilized descendant. Parlor ornaments and family Bibles, the cherished possessions of our own grandparents, repose under layers of dust in the attics of the twentieth century. Mass production conduces to human satisfaction, in part at least because human tastes have been altered to suit. If men's happiness be not an independent factor—and, under these conditions, obviously it is not—how can it be said that happiness is an ultimate standard? Wealth, that is, the mass of things that satisfy human wants, thus is seen to be, not a thing absolute and unchanging, but something whose nature alters with the evolving wants which it satisfies. And the evolution of wants is not a mere matter of expansion, incorporating new wants along with the

[148] Socrates was charged with impiety and, by rash conduct of his own defense, led the court to impose the death penalty. Refusing an opportunity to escape, he met his death.

[149] The relativity of ethical standards has been discussed by the writer, in regard to economic questions, in an article entitled *Some Fundamental Questions on Economic Planning, South African Journal of Economics,* Johannesburg 1935.

older ones, as Hobbes suggested, but involves fundamental alterations as old wants disappear and new ones arise in their place.

Senior. Smith's successors in the so-called British Classical School of economists, T. R. Malthus (1766–1834), David Ricardo (1772–1823), N. W. Senior (1790–1864), and to a certain extent the two Mills in their economic writings, with J. B. Say (1767–1832) in France, and a number of lesser lights, followed the lead he had given in the *Wealth of Nations.* Regarding such questions as the relationship of wants to happiness and the relative merits of different forms of happiness as being outside the purview of economics, they concentrated on studying the means of satisfying wants. That men endeavored to satisfy their wants as fully as possible was regarded as axiomatic. Thus Senior, in laying down the basic assumptions of political economy, declared that the first was

That every man desires to obtain additional Wealth with as little sacrifice as possible.[150]

In developing this proposition, Senior admitted that no man wished for an infinite quantity of everything:

What we mean to state is, that no person feels his whole wants to be adequately supplied: that every person has some unsatisfied desires which he believes that additional wealth would gratify. The nature and the urgency of each individual's wants are as various as the differences in individual character. Some may wish for power, others for distinction, and others for leisure; some require bodily, and others mental amusement; some are anxious to produce important advantage to the public; and there are few, perhaps there are none, who, if it could be done with a wish, would not benefit their acquaintances and friends. Money seems to be the only object for which the desire is universal; and it is so, because money is abstract wealth. Its possessor may satisfy at will his ambition, or vanity, or indolence, his public spirit or his private benevolence; may multiply the means of obtaining bodily pleasure, or of avoiding bodily evil, or the still more expensive amusements of the mind. Any one of these pursuits would exhaust the largest fortune within the limits of individual acquisition; and, as all men would engage in some of them, and many in all, the desire for wealth must be insatiable, though the modes in which different individuals would employ it are infinitely diversified.

An equal diversity exists in the amount and the kind of sacrifices which different individuals, or even the same individual, will encounter in the pursuit of wealth. And not only is the same sacrifice more severe to one than to another, as some will not give up ease or leisure for study, others good air and a country life, and others recreation and society, but the absolute desire for wealth on the one hand, and the absolute will to encounter toils or priva-

[150] *Political Economy,* London 1850, p. 26. This work was published as part of the *Encyclopædia Metropolitana* which first appeared in 1845.

tions in its pursuit on the other, are stronger in some men than in others. These differences form some of the principal distinctions in individual and national character. . . The inhabitants of Holland and of Great Britain, and of the countries that have derived their institutions from Great Britain, the nations which up to the present time have best enjoyed those advantages, have up to the present time been the most ardent and the most successful in the pursuit of opulence. But even the Indians of Mexico, though their indolence makes them submit to poverty under which an Englishman would feel life a burden, would willingly be rich if it cost them no trouble.[151]

This, of course, is Hobbes's principle of the insatiability of human desires. Senior did not rule out the benevolent motive but he excluded passivity. All men wanted wealth, he said, if only to give it away. Yet, notwithstanding the theoretical position assumed in his work on *Political Economy,* Senior's other writings, notably the letter on the Irish poor law referred to in Chapter XVI, made it clear that he was not himself afraid to express the view that maximum wealth did not coincide with greatest happiness or social welfare.

John Stuart Mill. The younger Mill, in *A System of Logic, Ratiocinative and Inductive* (2 vols., London 1843), entered into a discussion of human motives. Though, as has been noticed, Mill accepted utilitarianism as an ethical principle, he had moved far enough away from Bentham to be able to assail what he called the "interest-philosophy of the Bentham school," that is, the assumption that "men's actions are always determined by their interest [self-interest]."[152] Discussing "The Logic of the Moral Sciences" in this work, Mill considered the case of kings or rulers:

It is not true that the actions even of average rulers are wholly, or anything approaching to wholly, determined by their personal interest, or even by their own opinion of their personal interest. I do not speak of the influence of a sense of duty, or feelings of philanthropy, motives never to be mainly relied upon, though (except in countries or during periods of great moral debasement) they influence almost all rulers in some degree, and some rulers in a very great degree. But I insist only on what is true of all rulers, viz. that the character and course of their actions is largely influenced (independently of personal calculation) by the habitual sentiments and feelings, the general modes of thinking and acting which prevail throughout the community of which they are members; as well as by the feelings, habits, and modes of thought which characterize the particular class in that community to which they themselves belong. And no one will understand or be able to decypher their system of conduct, who does not take all these things into account. They are also much influenced by the maxims and traditions which have descended to them from other rulers, their predecessors; which maxims

[151] *Ibid.*, pp. 27-28.

[152] *A System of Logic,* 4th ed., London 1861, vol. 2, p. 471.

and traditions have been known to retain an ascendency during long periods, even in opposition to the private interests of the rulers for the time being.[153]

Thus, not merely self-interest, but habit and tradition were identified as motivating factors in human conduct. The private interest of the rulers, Mill admitted to be an important force, but it was quite insufficient to account for their actions as a whole. Mill's stand on the subject was important, having regard to the fact that he was recognized as at once the leading economist and political philosopher in England at the time. His book on economics, the *Principles of Political Economy with Some of their Applications to Social Philosophy* (2 vols., London 1848) was the outstanding textbook on the subject in its generation and for years afterwards, and his work on logic occupied a comparable position.

Jevons. The English economist, W. S. Jevons, in formulating the principles of what is commonly called the *Marginal* or *Neo-Classical* School of economics ("Neo-Classical," on account of its resemblance to the "Classical" School of Smith and his successors as far as the younger Mill), went back to Benthamism. Jevons announced in the preface of his *The Theory of Political Economy* (London 1871):

In this work I have attempted to treat Economy as a Calculus of Pleasure and Pain, and have sketched out, almost irrespective of previous opinions, the form which the science, as it seems to me, must ultimately take. I have long thought that as it deals throughout with quantities, it must be a mathematical science in matter if not in language. I have endeavoured to arrive at accurate quantitative notions concerning Utility, Value, Labour, Capital, etc., and I have often been surprised to find how clearly some of the most difficult notions, especially that most puzzling of notions *Value,* admit of mathematical analysis and expression. The Theory of Economy thus treated presents a close analogy to the science of Statical Mechanics, and the Laws of Exchange are found to resemble the Laws of Equilibrium of a lever as determined by the principle of virtual velocities. The nature of Wealth and Value is explained by the consideration of indefinitely small amounts of pleasure and pain, just as the Theory of Statics is made to rest upon the equality of indefinitely small amounts of energy.[154]

In Jevons's theory, the pleasures or satisfactions of consuming wealth were balanced against the efforts or pains of producing it, and the working of the human mind in the economic sphere was represented as a matter of equilibrating the two. The object of the individual was to ensure that all efforts yielding a surplus of pleasure over pain were undertaken, but none whose pains did not receive adequate compensation. Jevons said that the same principle applied when commodities were exchanged

[153] *Ibid.,* vol. 2, p. 473.

[154] *The Theory of Political Economy,* Preface to 1st ed., reprinted in 4th ed., London 1911, pp. vi-vii. Quoted by permission of Macmillan & Co., Ltd. and The Macmillan Company.

against each other. An exchange that resulted in a surplus of pleasure over pain was carried through but not one where there was no such gain. Pleasure and pain (in other words, happiness), therefore, became the basis of economics. The theory receives more detailed examination in Chapter IX. But it must be noted here that Jevons, like the two Mills, felt it necessary to admit that there were different grades of happiness. Man's "mere physical pleasure or pain, necessarily arising from his bodily wants and susceptibilities," he put at the bottom. "The safety of a nation, the welfare of great populations" came higher up. In the highest rank were "motives of uprightness and honour."[155] Having mentioned this complexity and indulged himself in the luxury (for an economist!) of making an ethical judgment, by speaking of higher and lower ends, Jevons refused to weave these ideas into his thought and announced that economics treated only of the means of satisfying wants of the lowest kind:

> My present purpose is accomplished in pointing out this hierarchy of feeling, and assigning a proper place to the pleasures and pains with which the economist deals. It is the lowest rank of feelings which we here treat. The calculus of utility aims at supplying the ordinary wants of man at the least cost of labour. Each labourer, in the absence of other motives, is supposed to devote his energy to the accumulation of wealth.[156]

This limitation of Jevons's system — and, indeed, of the work of the Marginal Utility School generally, which Jevons and certain like-thinking contemporaries may be said to have established — has been a point of dispute between them and members of other schools of thought in recent years. Some German writers have wanted to include within the compass of economics such matters as the "safety of a nation"; just as others, like John Ruskin, have wished to incorporate what Jevons called "a higher calculus of moral right and wrong" (the "motives of uprightness and honour", etc.), which that economist expressly left out. These views receive examination in later sections of the present chapter.

The "Economical Calculus." From the Jevonsian system it was but a short step to the economics of F. Y. Edgeworth and Vilfredo Pareto.

In 1881, Edgeworth published his *Mathematical Psychics,* whose subtitle read significantly: *An Essay on the Application of Mathematics to the Moral Sciences.*[157] In this book, the author referred to the Utilitarian conception of maximizing happiness (the "Utilitarian Calculus") and carried this over — as Jevons had done before him — into economics. In economic affairs men shifted their positions, exchanging things already possessed for others capable of yielding to them a greater utility. The grand object of economic activity was to maximize utility, Edgeworth said. The appropriate method of representing the situation was the mathemati-

[155] *Ibid.*, p. 25. [156] *Ibid.*, pp. 26-27. [157] Reprinted, London 1932.

cal calculus, he thought, and, in this connection, he employed the term "Economical Calculus." Edgeworth used this method of approach in his later contributions to economic literature,[158] while on the continent of Europe Vilfredo Pareto followed a similar line in his *Cours d'économie politique* (2 vols., Lausanne 1896–1897) and *Manuale d'economia politica* (Milan 1906).[159] In these writings the economic man was depicted as engaged in a restless search for the maximum position—not maximum wealth, it is true, but maximum utility, the relationship between the two being grounded upon the Benthamite principle of diminishing utility. Since the approach to maximization was through exchange, the theory of value became, more than ever before, the central feature of economic doctrine. But this fact makes it appropriate to postpone further discussion of the matter to Chapter IX.

Scarcity and the Conflict Between Private and Public Wealth

Before examining further the Neo-Classical ideas on wealth, it is necessary to say something on another subject. Adam Smith spoke of wealth as being composed of commodities and services:

> Every man is rich or poor according to the degree in which he can afford to enjoy the necessaries, conveniences, and amusements of human life.[160]

Smith passed on at once to deal with exchange values and the tenor of his book left no doubt that what he regarded as the "Wealth of Nations" was the sum of the exchange values in the hands of individuals. This was true of the Classical School generally, descended from Smith; and a notable member of it, namely Senior, with the clarity which distinguished most of his work, stated the fact in terms that placed the Classical position beyond doubt. Senior defined wealth as

> all those things, and those things only, which are transferable, are limited in supply, and are directly or indirectly productive of pleasure or preventive of pain; or, to use an equivalent expression, which are susceptible of *exchange*; (using the word exchange to denote hiring as well as absolute purchase;) or, to use a third equivalent expression, which have *Value*. . .[161]

This definition of wealth opens up the problem of what is the relationship between exchange value—based on scarcity—and human welfare. Bentham and a long series of writers on economics who came after him elaborated the principle of diminishing utility, which stated that, as a commodity became less scarce, the usefulness of successive increments of equal size declined. But the question had another aspect. A commodity

[158] Collected in *Papers Relating to Political Economy*, 3 vols., London 1925.

[159] Pareto's economic works have not been translated into English but some account of his ideas on the subject here considered can be obtained from the early portion of *Value and Capital*, by J. R. Hicks, Oxford 1939.

[160] *Wealth of Nations*, Bk. 1, Chap. 5.

[161] *Political Economy*, p. 6.

that was not scarce was not classified as wealth or riches. One that was scarce in the first instance could be made more so, or one that was abundant could be made scarce, when the value of what was left might be pushed up sufficiently to more than counterbalance the diminution in quantity, thereby raising total value. This happened when — to use modern terminology — the demand was inelastic. The paradoxical conclusion was reached that total wealth, on the definition adopted by Smith and Senior, could be augmented by destroying useful commodities.

The weakness of this identification of wealth with exchange value was pointed out by James Maitland, eighth Earl of Lauderdale (1759–1839), a Scottish peer who had become interested in economics. In *An Inquiry into the Nature and Origin of Public Wealth, and into the Means and Causes of its Increase* (Edinburgh 1804), Lauderdale said:

National wealth has by all been considered merely as made up of the riches of individuals belonging to the community; the capital of a society has been regarded, in every respect, as the same with that of all the individuals who compose it * ; and the sum-total of the fortunes of individuals, has been conceived to convey an accurate description of the mass of national wealth. . .

It is, however, impossible to subscribe to the idea, that the sum-total of individual riches forms an accurate statement of public wealth. . .

It must, then, appear, that a commodity being useful or delightful to man, cannot alone give it value; that to obtain value, or to be qualified to constitute a portion of private riches, it must combine with that quality, the circumstance of existing in a certain degree of scarcity. Yet the common sense of mankind would revolt at a proposal for augmenting the wealth of a nation, by creating a scarcity of any commodity generally useful and necessary to man. For example, let us suppose a country possessing abundance of the necessaries and conveniences of life, and universally accommodated with the purest streams of water: — what opinion would be entertained of the understanding of a man, who, as the means of increasing the wealth of such a country, should propose to create a scarcity of water, the abundance of which was deservedly considered as one of the greatest blessings incident to the community? It is certain, however, that such a projector would, by this means, succeed in increasing the mass of individual riches; for to the water, which would still retain the quality of being useful and desirable, he would add the circumstance of existing in scarcity. . .

But further to illustrate this proposition, that the wealth of the nation, and the mass of individual riches, cannot be regarded as in every respect the same, let us for a moment suppose it possible to create as great an abundance of any species of food as there exists of water: what would be thought of the advice of a man, who should cautiously recommend, even at the moment of the pressure of scarcity, to beware of creating this boasted abundance? for, however flattering it might appear as a remedy for the immediate evil, it would inevitably diminish the wealth of the nation.[162]

[162] *Public Wealth*, pp. 40-45. The asterisk refers to a passage from Smith's *Wealth of Nations*.

The French mathematician and writer on economics, A. A. Cournot (1801–1877), in a book entitled *Recherches sur les principes mathématiques de la théorie des richesses* (Paris 1838)[163] brought out the same point. Cournot was developing a theory of exchange values and, in connection with his discussion on this subject, felt it necessary to admit that exchange values could be increased by scarcity:

It has sometimes happened that a publisher, having in store an unsalable stock of some work, useful and sought after by connoisseurs, but of which too many copies were originally printed in view of the class of readers for whom it was intended, has sacrificed and destroyed two-thirds of the number, expecting to derive more profit from the remainder than from the entire edition.

There is no doubt that there might be a book of which it would be easier to sell a thousand copies at sixty francs, than three thousand at twenty francs. Calculating in this way, the Dutch Company [*i.e.*, the Dutch East Indies Company] is said to have caused the destruction in the islands of the Sound of a part of the precious spices of which it had a monopoly. Here is a complete destruction of objects to which the word *wealth* is applied because they are both sought after, and not easily obtainable. Here is a miserly, selfish act, evidently opposed to the interests of society; and yet it is nevertheless evident that this sordid act, this actual destruction, is a real creation of *wealth* in the commercial sense of the word. The publisher's inventory will rightly show a greater value for his assets; and after the copies have left his hands, either wholly or in part, if each individual should draw up his inventory in commercial fashion, and if all these partial inventories could be collated to form a general inventory or balance sheet of the wealth in circulation, an increase would be found in the sum of these items of wealth.[164]

It must be remembered that Lauderdale wrote more than a century before the coffee-burning and cotton-plowing exploits of the 1930's. Had he been alive today, he might have thought the idea of increasing "wealth" by destroying useful commodities less preposterous, though possibly no less objectionable, than he did in 1804. To say that a country as a whole was *richer* after such a destruction was easy enough to Cournot, whose mind ran in mathematical channels and was concentrated on exchange values. But this meant that the word *riches* as used by Cournot, like the *wealth* of Adam Smith, was something other than was implied in popular usage. The matter, however, goes deeper than this. Whatever were the intentions of Smith and Senior on the subject, undoubtedly many readers interpreted their writings to mean that these men thought there was some sense in increasing wealth. The examples given by Lauderdale and Cournot demonstrated that, while this might be true for individuals, certainly it was not always so for societies. Yet an-

163 Translated by N. T. Bacon, as *Researches into the Mathematical Principles of the Theory of Wealth*, N. Y. 1897.

164 pp. 11-12 of the translation. Quoted by permission of The Macmillan Company.

other aspect of the problem must be considered. Lauderdale was thinking of the amount of wealth available for consumption by the entire society and it was correct to say that this was diminished when goods were made scarcer. The destroyers of spice or books, about whom Cournot wrote, like the advocates of coffee or cotton scarcity in recent years, were facing a problem of *distribution*. How might it be ensured that those who made livings by selling these commodities received higher incomes? One way was to make their products scarcer and, therefore, dearer in the market. Bearing in mind the principle of diminishing utility, it is *possible* that impoverished printers of books published for the purpose of sale to rich connoisseurs, might have gained more utility than the purchasing group lost by destruction of a portion of the books. In this case, utility was increased by a destruction of physical goods. But it is clear that the process was wasteful. Utility would have increased more if the surplus books had not been produced and the workers concerned had applied their efforts in some other field. It would have increased more, too, if the supernumerary books could have been disposed of in some useful manner, without reducing the price to the connoisseurs. So that Lauderdale's argument is as sensible in the last resort, as it appears at first sight.

MacLeod's Conception of Incorporeal or Intangible Wealth

H. D. MacLeod (1821–1902) took up a position that was, in a sense, diametrically opposed to that of Lauderdale. Lauderdale had criticized Smith for confining the name "wealth" to goods and services that possessed exchange value, excluding those that—though useful—had no value. MacLeod attacked the Classical economists for excluding from "wealth" valuable things that were not commodities or services. *Rights,* said MacLeod, were wealth just as much as were goods. MacLeod was a Scottish lawyer and bank director and, as such, was interested in credit and negotiable instruments, so that it was perhaps to be expected that he would take this view. In addition to a work on banking and an incomplete *Dictionary of Political Economy,* he wrote a general treatise on economics, of which successive editions bore the titles : *The Elements of Political Economy* (London 1858), *The Principles of Economic Philosophy* (2 vols., London 1872–1875) and *The Elements of Economics* (2 vols., London 1881–1886, re-issued 1899). The first of these stated his point of view as follows :

in all civilized societies there is property of enormous value, which is bought and sold, which has no present existence, which has only a *future* existence, and which is yet the subject of exchange. And this comprehends the whole theory of the *Present Value of Deferred Payments.*[165]

[165] p. 11. Longmans.

In *The Elements of Economics* he quoted with approval a definition of Roman law which ran,

Under the term WEALTH, not only ready money, but all things, both immovable and movable, both corporeal things as well as RIGHTS, are included.[166]

And another,

We are accustomed to buy and sell DEBTS, payable at a certain event, and on a certain day. For that is WEALTH which can be bought and sold.[167]

MacLeod argued that *rights,* like bonds or promissory notes, should be included under the heading of wealth, just as were tangible goods; and he used the term *incorporeal wealth* to designate such things. Obviously, the existence of rights is not devoid of significance in economics. With respect to the theory of capital, what men regard as their capital is to a large extent merely capitalized rights to future income, which MacLeod called "the present value of deferred payments." Again, the point is important in considering the distribution of wealth. A person may have too little to consume, because he is obligated to hand over to someone else much of what goes to him in the first instance. The same is true of social groups. A community or nation may have wealth in excess of the tangible goods within its boundaries, because of its ownership of property elsewhere. In former years the frontier communities of America were heavily in debt to the more settled areas and were therefore poorer, exactly as such countries as Argentina and Australia are in debt to Europe at present. For the world as a whole, however, such obligations cancel out. What MacLeod called incorporeal wealth was not wealth from the standpoint taken in this chapter, but obligations respecting the distribution of wealth, a matter to which attention is given in Chapter IV.

Müller and List

While British thought was developing along rational and individual lines, on the continent of Europe and especially in Germany events had taken a different turn. Romanticism had arisen as a movement affecting the broad front of culture, characterized by a search for the ideal or spirit beyond the substance which met men's gaze. What is marriage to a Romantic? Not a mere matter of bread and butter or animal instinct, obvious and calculable, but something that springs, as it were, from the spirit and in which the individuals concerned express themselves. So some writers have looked upon wealth. It is not a matter of rational calculation, ministering to selfishness. It is deeper, giving personal expression and serving the nation. The philosophy of Kant and his successors, which went beyond human experience in an attempt to discover

[166] Vol. 1, p. 40. Longmans. [167] *Ibid.*

the fundamentals of knowledge and purpose, and the nationalism that developed in Germany in the eighteenth and nineteenth centuries, furnished an environment in which such a vein of thought could thrive. It was inevitable that this movement should place its adherents in opposition to the principles of Smith and Bentham. Adam Müller (1779–1829) and Friedrich List best express the Romanticist viewpoint in economics. Müller spent some time as political tutor to one of the German princes and later entered the Austrian Imperial service. In 1810 he published *Die Elemente der Staatskunst* (Berlin), containing the substance of a course of lectures that he had given to a group of statesmen and diplomatists in Dresden. His leading idea was the logical correlative of the social theories of Rousseau and Hegel. Müller thought that the economy of a society or State was something more than the sum of the economies of the individuals composing the group. The State represented, as it were, the spirit of the whole. Unlike the individual, it was a continuing thing, Müller pointed out. The State did not die and so had to take a long view. Productive power, in this situation, was more important than wealth itself. Free trade might be all very well for England, which was already a coherent nation, but Müller believed that on the Continent it was necessary for governments to do something to build up national spirit and national consciousness. The systematic development of the nation's productive resources was important, and restrictions on international trade were favored from this standpoint. List's arguments were on these lines also. List was first a clerk in government service and later ministerial official, professor of economics, and member of the legislature in Württemberg. Meeting political difficulties, he spent a number of years in the United States of America and this helped to give direction to his opinions, especially in regard to the development of national industry. List looked upon society as an interwoven whole, not a set of parts that could be studied independently. He said that not merely material wealth but the whole of culture had to be taken into account, for proper understanding. List's outlook was nationalistic, as opposed to the individualism of Adam Smith. What List had in mind was not a maximization of individual riches, in accordance with the ideas of Smith and Bentham, leading to internationalism or cosmopolitanism because national trade barriers were not permitted to stand in the way of this maximization, but national wealth as part of a broader concept of national good. A plentiful supply of goods was important but national self-reliance — that is, national self-sufficiency, based on the nation's own territory and that of its colonial possessions — and continuity of the powers of the nation into the future were at least of equal significance. These latter, in List's opinion, were neglected in the system of Adam Smith. Hence, the German writer emphasized them in his own teaching. How

List's views on wealth were colored by this outlook is indicated by the following extract from *The National System of Political Economy*:

The errors and contradictions of the prevailing school [*i.e.*, that of Adam Smith] . . . can be easily corrected from the standpoint of *the theory of the productive powers.* Certainly those who fatten pigs or prepare pills are productive, but the instructors of youths and of adults, virtuosos, musicians, physicians, judges, and administrators, are productive in a much higher degree. The former *produce values of exchange,* and the latter *productive powers,* some by enabling the future generation to become producers, others by furthering the morality and religious character of the present generation, a third by ennobling and raising the powers of the human mind, a fourth by preserving the productive powers of his patients, a fifth by rendering human rights and justice secure, a sixth by constituting and protecting public security, a seventh by his art and by the enjoyment which it occasions fitting men the better to produce values of exchange. In the doctrine of mere values [*i.e.*, that of Smith's school], these *producers of the productive powers* can of course only be taken into consideration so far as their services are rewarded by values of exchange; and this manner of regarding their services may in some instances have its practical use. . . But whenever our consideration is given to the nation (as a whole and in its international relations) it is utterly insufficient, and leads to a series of narrow-minded and false views.

The prosperity of a nation is not, as Say believes, greater in the proportion in which it has amassed more wealth (*i.e.*, values of exchange), but in the proportion in which it has *developed its powers of production.* Although laws and public institutions do not produce immediate values, they nevertheless produce productive powers, and Say is mistaken if he maintains that nations have been enabled to become wealthy under all forms of government, and that by means of laws no wealth can be created.[168]

Thus List's position was in some respects similar to that of the Mercantilists. The concept of a State economy, as opposed to individual economy, and the correlative that wealth was to be regarded in terms of State objectives — both characteristic of Mercantilism — stand out clearly in the ideas of List.

Later Romanticist and Institutionalist Ideas

The relation of wealth to life. Some notable English-speaking writers, who have been influenced by the ideas of German Romanticism, have gone far to discredit orthodox economics on account of the emphasis on exchange values which List criticized. This is true of Thomas Carlyle, the leading interpreter of German Romanticism to Victorian England. What Carlyle thought of the struggle for wealth, as exemplified by the commercial system of his time, may be illustrated by a passage from *Past and Present* (London 1843):

[168] *Op. cit.*, pp. 116-117. Longmans. As is mentioned later, Say, referred to in this passage, was a follower of Adam Smith.

True, it must be owned, we for the present, with our Mammon-Gospel, have come to strange conclusions. We call it a Society; and go about professing openly the totalest separation, isolation. Our life is not a mutual helpfulness; but rather, cloaked under due laws-of-war, named 'fair competition' and so forth, it is a mutual hostility. We have profoundly forgotten everywhere that *Cash-payment* is not the sole relation of human beings; we think, nothing doubting, that *it* absolves and liquidates all engagements of man. 'My starving workers?' answers the rich mill-owner: 'Did not I hire them fairly in the market? Did I not pay them, to the last sixpence, the sum covenanted for? What have I to do with them more?—Verily Mammon-worship is a melancholy creed. When Cain, for his own behoof, had killed Abel, and was questioned, 'Where is thy brother?' he too made answer, 'Am I my brother's keeper?' Did I not pay my brother *his* wages, the thing he had merited from me?

O sumptuous Merchant-Prince, illustrious game-preserving Duke, is there no way of 'killing' thy brother but Cain's rude way! 'A good man by the very look of him, by his very presence with us as a fellow wayfarer in this Life-pilgrimage, *promises* so much': woe to him if he can forget all such promises, if he never know that they were given! To a deadened soul, seared with the brute Idolatry of Sense, to whom going to Hell is equivalent to not making money, all 'promises,' and moral duties, that cannot be pleaded for in Courts of Requests, address themselves in vain. Money he can be ordered to pay, but nothing more. I have not heard in all Past History, and expect not to hear in all Future History, of any Society anywhere under God's Heaven supporting itself on such philosophy.[169]

The writings of John Ruskin (1819–1900), in England, and H. D. Thoreau (1817–1862), in the United States of America, were imbued by the same spirit. Ruskin, who for a time taught fine art at Oxford, had an intense concern in social affairs and has been referred to as one of the greatest social teachers of his age. He applied his interest in art to social life and saw, or thought he saw, that the artistic side of human nature was being sacrificed for material wealth. And this was not true of art alone. According to Ruskin, people were so anxious to become rich that they were unable to live a full and rounded life. Thoreau, on the other hand, was deeply interested in nature and preferred to watch her ways and philosophize on them to joining in the popular rush for riches. He thought that men were wrong in sacrificing for gain the leisure which would enable them to think and to develop themselves:

A broad margin of leisure is as beautiful in a man's life as in a book. Haste makes waste no less in life than in housekeeping. . . What are threescore years and ten hurriedly and coarsely lived to moments of divine leisure, in which your life is coincident with the life of the universe. We live too fast

[169] *Centenary Edition of the Works of Thomas Carlyle,* 30 vols., London 1896-1899, vol. 10, pp. 146-147. Quoted by permission of Chapman & Hall, Ltd.

and coarsely, just as we eat too fast and do not know the true savor of our food.[170]

In his *Walden or, Life in the Woods* (1854), Thoreau told the story of a period spent in living simply, in a cottage of his own construction, near Concord, Massachusetts. There he lived his philosophy of life. The way to true living, he considered, was to restrict material wants to the simple things of life and this he proceeded to do. Food was required but he showed that it need not be expensive. Shelter was necessary but a rude hut would serve the purpose. People were mistaken in living in such expensive homes that a disproportionate part of their lives had to be spent in paying for them, for, he said,

the cost of a thing is the amount of what I will call life which is required to be exchanged for it, immediately or in the long run.[171]

Clothes must be worn, of course, but it was a bad social custom which made a man afraid to exhibit patches. The necessities of life met — and Thoreau believed that they could be supplied without undue labor — plus leisure to philosophize, summed up Thoreau's idea of social good, just as it had been that of the ancient Greek philosophers. Instead of this ideal, modern America was building up a false set of social standards:

We worship not the Graces . . . but Fashion. . . The head monkey in Paris puts on a traveller's cap, and all the monkeys in America do the same.[172]

Like Thoreau, Ruskin emphasized that *living*, not getting rich, should be the end of human endeavor. What mattered was not goods but life. This attitude was brought out in the essay entitled "Ad Valorem," in *Unto This Last* (first published in the London *Cornhill Magazine* in 1860):

I desire . . . to leave this one great fact clearly stated. THERE IS NO WEALTH BUT LIFE. Life, including all its powers of love, of joy, and of admiration. That country is the richest which nourishes the greatest number of noble and happy human beings; that man is richest who, having perfected the functions of his own life to the utmost, has also the widest helpful influence, both personal, and by means of his possessions, over the lives of others.[173]

There were two points involved in the Thoreau-Ruskin position. First it was assumed that what was important was the construction of a philosophy or science of life, and that wealth was merely subordinate to this. Second — though this was not indicated in the passage that has been

[170] *The Writings of Henry David Thoreau,* 11 vols., Boston 1894–1895, vol. 8, *Winter,* p. 45. Quoted by permission of Houghton Mifflin Company.

[171] *Ibid.*, vol. 2, *Walden*, p. 51.

[172] *Ibid.*, p. 42.

[173] *The Works of Ruskin,* ed. by E. T. Cook and A. Wedderburn, 39 vols., London 1903–1912, vol. 17, p. 105. Quoted by permission of George Allen & Unwin Ltd.

quoted from Ruskin's writings—both Thoreau and Ruskin believed that men were overemphasizing wealth in their philosophy of life and that life as a whole was suffering from this overemphasis. That is to say, Thoreau and Ruskin were tackling the problem to which Smith had given attention in *The Theory of Moral Sentiments.* Ruskin's belief that "there is no wealth but life," excluded any logical foundation for such a book as Smith's *Wealth of Nations.* In Ruskin's opinion, wealth could not be made a matter of independent study.

Men's desire for distinction. Comments on the subject of what lies behind men's wants have been common from early times. Plato and Aristotle arranged human wants in a hierarchy of merit, as has been noticed earlier in this chapter. Attacks on luxury were common in the medieval and mercantile periods, as also has been seen. Neither John Law (1671–1729), Scottish-born financier and writer on economic subjects, nor Adam Smith, was above comparing useful commodities and luxuries—water and diamonds being the articles they chose. This was done, not in what purported to be ethical treatises, but in books professedly dealing with economics. Law and Smith thought that water was useful and that diamonds were not. Obviously, they were not thinking of usefulness as synonymous with desiredness, since, as Law pointed out, diamonds had a value because the demand for them was intense, while water had no value because it was not scarce in relation to the demand. Twentieth century economists apply the principle of diminishing utility to such cases and reply to Law and Smith that what they were thinking of was the immense utility of the early increments of water which were necessary to support human life. None the less, the water-diamond comparison savored of an ethical judgment.

Nicholas Barbon thought it in place in his *Discourse of Trade* to discuss the manner in which men strove for distinction. They had done so, he pointed out, from the earliest times:

> There was never any part of Mankind so wild and barbarous, but they had Difference and Degree of Men amongst them, and invented some things to shew that Distinction. Those that Cloathed with Skins, wore the Skins of those Beasts that are most difficultly taken; thus *Hercules* wore a Lyons Skin; and the Ermins and Sable, are still Badges of Honour.[174]

The Irish churchman and philosopher, George Berkeley (1685–1753), Bishop of Cloyne, in *The Querist* (Dublin 1735–1737), among other things, asked,

> Whether claret be not often drunk rather for vanity than for health, or pleasure?[175]

[174] *A Discourse of Trade,* pp. 14-15.

[175] *The Works of George Berkeley,* ed. A. C. Fraser, 4 vols., Oxford 1901, vol. 4, p. 435. Quoted by permission of the Oxford University Press.

Francis Hutcheson commented on the same general subject, in *An Essay on the Nature and Conduct of the Passions and Affections*:

This Desire of *Distinction* has great Influence on the Pleasures and Pains of Mankind, and makes them chuse things for their very *Rarity, Difficulty,* or *Expence*; by a confused Imagination that they evidence *Generosity, Ability,* or a *finer Taste* than ordinary. . .[176]

Adam Smith's opinions, as expressed in the *Moral Sentiments,* have been described.

John Rae (1796–1872), a Scotsman who settled in North America, published a book on economics, *Statement of Some New Principles on the Subject of Political Economy* (Boston 1834),[177] which, though neglected at the time of its appearance, has since received considerable attention. Treating "Of the Nature and Effects of Luxury," Rae criticized severely the form that consumption often took. He spoke of Cleopatra's having caused a precious pearl to be dissolved, in order that she might consume it at a draught, and remarked,

There could be here no pleasure in the taste of the liquor, that must have been rather disagreeable; the gratification consisted in having drunk what no one else could afford to drink.[178]

He went on to say,

The things to which vanity seems most ready to apply itself are those to which the use or consumption is most apparent, and of which the effects are most difficult to discriminate. Articles of which the consumption is not conspicuous, are incapable of gratifying this passion.[179]

The American economist and sociologist, Thorstein Veblen, later popularized the term "conspicuous consumption." Rae quoted with approval the statement of an earlier writer:

All the ornaments which decorate the apartments of the rich, that gilt work, those sculptures which art and taste seem to have formed solely to delight the mind, are nothing but a sort of magical characters, presenting everywhere this inscription: *Admire the extent of my riches.*[180]

Possibly reflecting a Scotsman's reactions to the more extravagant standard of living of Americans compared with his own countryfolk, Rae commented on the luxuries he found in North America:

Something of the same genius may, I think, be observed in the expenditure of the North Americans. Their houses are frequently larger than they have

[176] *Op. cit.,* p. 12.

[177] Edited (and rearranged) by C. W. Mixter as *The Sociological Theory of Capital,* New York 1905.

[178] *Ibid.,* p. 246. Quoted by permission of Macmillan & Co., Ltd., and The Macmillan Company.

[179] *Ibid.,* p. 247.

[180] *Ibid.,* p. 253.

use for, so that part of them remains unoccupied. They are, also, often built with a greater regard to show than comfort. There is little substantial difference between a gold and silver watch, but that the former costs double of the latter. Gold watches are perhaps more common in North America, than in any other part of the world. It is pure vanity that leads to so general an adoption of this luxury, by classes who in England would not think of it. . .[181]

However, he admitted that

it is a vanity that fixes itself on something permanent. In the end, there is no cheaper way in which man can write, "I am rich, or at least, I am not absolutely poor," than to carry a gold watch. It is ready to meet all occasions, and all persons.[182]

No doubt, this appealed to Rae's Scottish mind.

John Ruskin's lecture on "Work" (1865), reprinted in *The Crown of Wild Olive* (London 1866), is interesting in this connection. It was an attack upon what its author regarded as objectionable social traits, made in the form of an intimate talk to working men. In it, Ruskin divided the people of England into "the classes who work and the classes who play" and inquired into the kind of games in which the playing classes engaged:

The first of all the English games is making money. That is an all-absorbing game; and we knock each other down oftener in playing at that, than at football, or any other roughest sport: and it is absolutely without purpose; no one who engages heartily in that game ever knows why. Ask a great money-maker what he wants to do with his money, – he never knows. He doesn't make it to do anything with it. He gets it only that he *may* get it. "What will you make of what you have got?" you ask. "Well I'll get more," he says. Just as, at cricket, you get more runs. There's no use in the runs, but to get more of them than other people is the game. . .

Our next great English games, however, hunting and shooting, are costly altogether; and how much we are fined for them annually in land, horses, gamekeepers, and game laws, and the resultant demoralization of ourselves, our children, and our retainers, I will not endeavour to count now; but note only that, except for exercise, this is not merely a useless game, but a deadly one, to all connected with it. . .

Then, next to the gentlemen's game of hunting, we must put the ladies' game of dressing. It is not the cheapest of games. . .

Then, there are other games. . . There's playing at literature, and playing at art; – very different, both, from working at literature, or working at art, but I've no time to speak of these. I pass to the greatest of all – the play of plays, the great gentleman's game, which ladies like them best to play at, – the game of War. It is entrancingly pleasant to the imagination; we dress for it, however, more finely than for any other sport; and go out to it, not merely in scarlet, as to hunt, but in scarlet and gold, and all manner of fine

[181] *Ibid.*, p. 261. [182] *Ibid.*

colours; of course we could fight better in grey, and without feathers; but all nations have agreed that it is good to be very well dressed at this play.[183] Then the bats and balls are very costly. . . A costly game!—not to speak of its consequences. . .[184]

Ruskin thought very little of the way in which men had utilized the benefits conferred on them by the increase of productive efficiency:

Before you got your power-looms, a woman could always make herself a chemise and petticoat of bright and pretty appearance. I have seen a Bavarian peasant-woman at church in Munich, looking a much grander creature, and more beautifully dressed, than any of the crossed and embroidered angels in Hess's high-art frescoes: (which happened to be just above her, so that I could look from one to the other). Well, here you are, in England, served by household demons, with five hundred fingers, at least, weaving, for one that used to weave in the day of Minerva. You ought to be able to show me five hundred dresses for one that used to be; tidiness ought to have become five hundred-fold tidier; tapestry should be increased into cinque-cento-fold iridescence of tapestry. Not only your peasant-girl ought to be lying on the sofa reading poetry, but she ought to have in her wardrobe five hundred petticoats instead of one.[185]

Thorstein Veblen (1857–1929) developed a line of thought that had some similarity to that of Ruskin. Unlike Ruskin, who was wealthy and held in high esteem, Veblen was a child of comparatively poor parents and, taking up university teaching as a profession, met with difficulties because of his unorthodox opinions. It may be that the somewhat bitter and cynical outlook he showed was partly a consequence of his experiences. In *The Theory of the Leisure Class* (New York 1899), described in its sub-title as "An Economic Study of Institutions," Veblen stated that public opinion maintained a distinction between the employments considered appropriate to the several classes of society. Men attempted to distinguish themselves in the eyes of others, he said, and this had characteristic results in the different periods of social evolution. Thus,

During that primitive phase of social development, when the community is still habitually peaceable, perhaps sedentary, and without a developed system of individual ownership, the efficiency of the individual can be shown chiefly and most consistently in some employment that goes to further the life of the group. What emulation of an economic kind there is between the members of such a group will be chiefly emulation in industrial serviceability. . .

When the community passes from peaceable savagery to a predatory phase

[183] Ruskin's reference was to the brightly colored military costumes of the nineteenth century.

[184] *The Works of John Ruskin*, vol. 18, pp. 405-408. Quoted by permission of George Allen & Unwin Ltd.

[185] *Ibid.*, vol. 27, *Fors Clavigera*, p. 89. Quoted by permission of George Allen & Unwin Ltd.

of life, the conditions of emulation change. The opportunity and the incentive to emulation increase greatly in scope and urgency. The activity of the men more and more takes on the character of exploit. . . Tangible evidence of prowess — trophies — find a place in men's habits of thought as an essential feature of the paraphernalia of life. . . As accepted at this cultural stage, the accredited, worthy form of self-assertion is contest; and useful articles or services obtained by seizure or compulsion, serve as a conventional evidence of successful contest. . . Labour acquires a character of irksomeness by virtue of the indignity imputed to it.[186]

Gradually, as industrial activity further displaces predatory activity in the community's everyday life and in men's habits of thought, accumulated property more and more replaces trophies of predatory exploit as the conventional exponent of prepotence and success. . . So soon as the possession of property becomes the basis of popular esteem, therefore, it becomes also a requisite to that complacency which we call self-respect.[187]

Abstention from labor, Veblen said,

is not only a honorific or meritorious act, but it presently comes to be a requisite of decency.[188]

Industry was tabooed to those who wished to be held in high esteem, Veblen asserted, leisure alone being a title to respect. Such leisure served its purpose only if it were conspicuous, that is, if it were plain for all men to see. Consumption was looked at from the same angle:

Unproductive consumption of goods is honourable, primarily as a mark of prowess and a perquisite of human dignity. . . When the quasi-peaceable stage of industry is reached, with its fundamental institution of chattel slavery, the general principle, more or less rigorously applied, is that the base, industrious class should consume only what may be necessary to their subsistence. In the nature of things, luxuries and the comforts of life belong to the leisure class. . . Drunkenness and the other pathological consequences of the free use of stimulants therefore tend in their turn to become honorific, as being a mark, at the second remove, of the superior status of those who are able to afford the indulgence. Infirmities induced by over-indulgence are among some peoples freely recognised as manly attributes. . . Conspicuous consumption of valuable goods is a means of reputability to the gentleman of leisure. As wealth accumulates on his hands, his own unaided effort will not avail to sufficiently put his opulence in evidence by this method. The aid of friends and competitors is therefore brought in by resorting to the giving of valuable presents and expensive feasts and entertainments.[189]

Other things, such as dress, were mentioned. Concerning dress, Veblen expressed the view that

We find things beautiful, as well as serviceable, somewhat in proportion as they are costly. With few and inconsequential exceptions, we all find a costly

[186] Reprint of 1912, pp. 16-17. Quoted by permission of The Viking Press, Inc.
[187] *Ibid.*, pp. 28-31. [188] *Ibid.*, p. 41. [189] *Ibid.*, pp. 69-75.

hand-wrought article of apparel much preferable, in point of beauty and of serviceability, to a less expensive imitation of it, however cleverly the spurious article may imitate the costly original; and what offends our sensibilities in the spurious article is not that it falls short in form or colour, or, indeed, in visual effect in any way. . . It loses caste æsthetically because it falls to a lower pecuniary grade.[190]

Especially was feminine wearing apparel the subject of Veblen's attack:

The dress of women goes even farther than that of men in the way of demonstrating the wearer's abstinence from productive employment. It needs no argument to enforce the generalisation that the more elegant styles of feminine bonnets go even farther towards making work impossible than does the man's high hat. The woman's shoe adds the so-called French heel to the evidence of enforced leisure afforded by its polish; because this high heel obviously makes any, even the simplest and most necessary manual work extremely difficult. . . The corset is, in economic theory, substantially a mutilation, undergone for the purpose of lowering the subject's vitality and rendering her permanently and obviously unfit for work. . . It may broadly be set down that the womanliness of woman's apparel resolves itself, in point of substantial fact, into the more effective hindrance to useful exertion offered by the garments peculiar to women. . . Obviously, if each garment is permitted to serve for but a brief term, and if none of last season's apparel is carried over and made further use of during the present season, the wasteful expenditure on dress is greatly increased.[191]

Much of this savors of the writings of Tertullian on the same subject seventeen hundred years before. Feminine fashions have changed somewhat since Veblen wrote, invalidating his statements on points of detail, though not his main argument. What Veblen called "Modern survivals of prowess" had their place in *The Theory of the Leisure Class.* In civilized societies, Veblen remarked, the fight or duel was confined to two groups, (1) military and naval officers, who were ordinarily members of the leisure class, and (2) low-class rowdies. Much of what was called "sport" was explained, he believed, not by a love of nature, but by the survival of the primitive exploit. The same was true of athletic games. The "modern woman" movement was attributed to a revolt by woman against her ornamental position:

She is petted, and is permitted, or even required, to consume largely and conspicuously. . . She is exempted, or debarred, from vulgarly useful employment. . . But the woman is endowed with her share . . . of the instinct of workmanship, to which futility of life or of expenditure is obnoxious.[192]

Finally, a gibe was made about higher education. It began as a byproduct of the "priestly vicarious leisure class," Veblen said, and even in his generation he commented that

there are such things in the usage of the learned community as the cap and

[190] *Ibid.*, p. 169. [191] *Ibid.*, pp. 171-173. [192] *Ibid.*, p. 358.

gown, matriculation, initiation, and graduation ceremonies, and the conferment of scholastic degrees, dignities, and prerogatives in a way which suggests some sort of scholarly apostolic succession.[193]

The new and poor communities of early America had little patience for such things but, Veblen declared, as colleges came to depend more on the wealthy leisured class, intellectual interest was thrown in the direction of classical and formal erudition rather than on the side of sciences bearing a relation to the industrial life of society.

Two features stand out in Veblen's argument. In the first place, the the theory was advanced that men's wants were not a matter of rational election, independent of institutional factors, but they were conditioned largely by social arrangements. Secondly, there was a vein of disapproval of the form that human desires seemed to take.

A long series of writers before Veblen had linked wants with the desire for distinction and few will question the reality of this view, though some may feel that Veblen has overemphasized it. Many families endeavor to "keep up with the Joneses," merely because they accept it as the thing to do, without asking themselves whether such a course brings them more happiness or a fuller life. As to whether such a mode of living gives satisfaction to those who follow it, no adequate answer can be given. Some people are so accustomed to this standard that they would be unhappy—for a time at least—if it were taken away. On the other hand, undoubtedly many observers of independent mind, as Smith, Ruskin, and Thoreau certainly were, would answer the question as it was answered in the writings of these men, and say that as long as the necessities of life are present it is very doubtful whether increased wealth is productive of greater happiness. Bentham made the matter one of mathematics. The more material wealth a man already possessed, the less the amount of happiness yielded by an additional increment. But obviously much depends on what one means by happiness. A new automobile may be bought because of the joys of country jaunts assured, or because of the pleasure derived from reflecting on the envy of the neighbors. Moralists, like Smith in *The Theory of Moral Sentiments,* are apt to rule out the latter kind of pleasure as unreal or immoral, and probably many people in their innermost minds will agree with them. But, at all events, it is a matter of morals, not of economics. Yet there is another aspect. Progress continually offers man a choice between a greater quantity of material wealth and an increased amount of leisure. Thoreau apparently believed that modern civilization was giving men more of the former and less of the latter than was desirable. That is to say, men were getting too many new things and insufficient opportunity to make use of what they already possessed. To give a twentieth century

[193] *Ibid.*, pp. 368-369.

example, they obtain new cars, but little time for pleasure drives and for developing other sides of their lives. Again, without a doubt, many thinking people will be found to accept this contention. Considerations of this sort are not matters that lie within the scope of economics as laid down in *The Wealth of Nations*. How wealth measures up with other human objectives, what is its part in life as a whole, were questions that Adam Smith discussed in his moral treatise. But no one will assert that they are not of immense significance in the construction of a philosophy of life, which, after all, was the problem to which Ruskin and Thoreau applied themselves. Practical statesmen have to look upon life as a whole. They must recognize that consumers sometimes are not competent to judge the commodities set before them, and that it is not always desirable that wants be satisfied. Hence, articles like milk are required to conform with certain minimum standards if their sale is permitted. The satisfaction of some demands is prohibited on moral grounds, such as when the sale of cocaine for other than medical purposes or the keeping of brothels is forbidden. Other demands are checked without being outlawed altogether, as when anti-liquor ministers of finance impose taxes on alcoholic beverages. The feelings aroused on both sides by such incidents as the burning of heretic literature by the Catholic Church centuries ago, or the modern counterpart of these holocausts in Nazi Germany, show how relative moral standards can be. There may be a ninety-nine per cent approval of a prohibition of the free sale of cocaine and one of only fifty-one per cent in the case of intoxicating liquor. The majority of the German people may approve the destruction of a book that in Russia receives general praise. But to enter into an extended consideration of the problem of ethical standards is outside the scope of this book.

Incentives. Fortunately, in view of the objections they had raised to wealth-seeking, some of the social critics whose writings have been mentioned thought that they could discern other motives for human industry. According to Carlyle, in *Past and Present,* work was a duty. Men recognized it as such and worked accordingly :

> The only happiness a brave man ever troubled himself with asking much about was, happiness enough to get his work done. Not 'I can't eat!' but 'I can't work!' that was the burden of all wise complaining among men. It is, after all, the one unhappiness of a man, That he cannot work; that he cannot get his destiny as a man fulfilled. Behold, the day is passing swiftly over, our life is passing swiftly over; and the night cometh, wherein no man can work.[194]

In *Sesame and Lilies* (London 1865), Ruskin commented on the interest men got from their work :

[194] *Op. cit.,* p. 156.

When men are rightly occupied, their amusement grows out of their work, as the colour-petals out of a fruitful flower. . .[195]

An "instinctive bias," spoken of as the sense or instinct of workmanship, in Veblen's opinion was chief "among those instinctive dispositions that conduce directly to the material well-being of the race,"[196] only the parental bent being able to dispute its primacy. Under the handicraft system of production in the middle ages, Veblen said that this instinct was not in conflict with the motive of selfishness, or "pecuniary self-help," because

the gilds were organised to maintain the craft's advantages in the market, as well as to regulate the quality of the output. . . Efficiency in the crafts came in this way presently to be counted very much as the modern "efficiency engineers" would count it, — proximately in terms of mechanical performance, ultimately in terms of price, and more particularly in terms of net gain.[197]

Under modern conditions, on the other hand, Veblen believed that the self-seeking nature of the business man was opposed to the ideal of workmanship:

If the "efficiency engineers" are to be credited, it is probably within the mark to say that the net aggregate gains from industry fall short of what they might be by some fifty per cent, owing to the trained inability of the business-men in control to appreciate and give effect to the visible technological requirements of the industries from which they draw their gains.[198]

Veblen wrote at a time when psychologists gave more importance to instincts as explanations of human conduct than is usual today, and especially was he strongly influenced by the work of the American psychologist and philosopher, William James (1842–1910). His "instinct of workmanship," however, is characteristic of a tendency among modern critics of capitalism to search for factors that may serve as incentives sufficiently strong to give the community the wealth it needs, in a society from which the stimulus of gain is absent. Just as one line of criticism of wealth-seeking led into ethics, therefore, so another leads into the field of psychology.

The Neo-Classical Reaction to Romanticist and Institutionalist Criticism

Rejection of hedonistic psychology. Faced with such criticism as that of Veblen, some members of the Neo-Classical or Marginal School of economists shifted their position from that which Jevons had occupied. If psychologists had come to believe that hedonistic motives — pleasure and pain working rationally on the human mind — were inadequate to

[195] *The Works of John Ruskin,* vol. 18, p. 97.

[196] *The Instinct of Workmanship and the State of the Industrial Arts,* N. Y. 1914, p. 25. Quoted by permission of The Viking Press, Inc.

[197] *Ibid.,* pp. 211-212.

[198] *Ibid.,* p. 193.

explain men's desires, then it no longer seemed sensible to interpret wants in these terms. Jevons's hedonism, therefore, was neglected or even abandoned altogether. His calculus of pleasures and pains was transformed into one of returns and costs as measured by the market. Instead of drawing curves that purported to show the gradual diminution in the pleasure or utility conferred by successive units of a commodity, say bread, and the pain or disutility resulting from the productive activity necessary to get it, as did Jevons, economists continued to draw the curves but declared that they represented *market facts,* rather than people's feelings. In this group must be placed the Cambridge teacher, Alfred Marshall (1842–1924), probably the most influential writer on economics in the English-speaking world in recent years, and more especially the American, H. J. Davenport (1861–1931) and the Swede, Gustav Cassel (1866–1945).

It was immaterial to these writers whether bread was wanted because its consumption gave pleasure or avoided pain, as Jevons believed, because of some individual habit or social custom, or because of mere impulse. It was for psychology to explain wants. This was where economics began. Such a position is exemplified by the following passage from *The Economics of Enterprise* (New York 1913) of H. J. Davenport:

> Hedonistic implications gratuitous. — But first it is to be said that in the notion of utility there is no necessary implication of any hedonistic theory of desire. Doubtless the word has hedonistic connotations — the more the pity — and might perhaps be better replaced by some other term, or even abandoned out of hand. The utility of an object need mean nothing more, and should be taken to mean nothing more, than one way of expressing the simple fact that the object is desired. Whether a desire or want traces back to instinct or to impulse or to experience, is an inquiry not as to the existence of the want but as to the genesis of the want. This is not especially the economist's task, nor is he especially equipped for its performance, nor is the promise of success especially alluring for him — or for any one else. It is enough for the economist that the desire exists, that the external thing attracts : thereby it is a *good* in the mere sense that it is desired ; one wants it. Thus there is no force in the assertion that instinct and impulse and spontaneity lie, in greater or less degree, back of desire. They certainly do ; but there is still the desire ; and only in this sense is there utility. And utility in this sense there clearly is. If the present wish to purchase is merely the expression of the habit, it is, nevertheless, a present wish. Doubtless one might — were the history of the case a pressing inquiry — ask how and why one got the habit ; why has it so long been the custom to wish ? We merely stop with the wish — hence *the utility.*[199]

Yet, notwithstanding their position on this matter, the general conclu-

[199] pp. 99-100. Quoted by permission of The Macmillan Company.

sions of economists of the group of which Davenport is a member remain singularly close to those of Bentham and Jevons. Thus Cassel in his *Theoretische Sozialökonomie* (Leipzig 1918),[200] declared that "the wants of civilized humanity as a whole are insatiable" and laid down the principle that the task of economics is

> to equate wants with the available means for their satisfaction in the way which is most advantageous.[201]

This looks like an edited version of the hedonistic concept of pleasure and pain being balanced rationally for the purpose of maximizing happiness. Marshall's use of such terms as "surplus enjoyment" in connection with his conception of *consumers' surplus* seems entirely Jevonsian.

Logically, in view of their rejection of psychological explanations of demand, it might have been expected that such men as Davenport and Cassel would disclaim them also on the side of production, thus meeting the argument of Veblen to the effect that instincts and not reasoned selfishness are the causes of human effort. Certainly, this was not true of Davenport, who, as will be seen in Chapter IX, based his theory of the supply of the factors of production on rational choice. Marshall gave considerable attention to the motives under which supplies of the productive factors were forthcoming and adhered in general to the view of Senior and J. S. Mill, that people work and save because the payments therefor are sufficient, in their minds, to compensate the efforts that working and saving entail. Even Cassel—who admitted that children (the labor supply of the future) were not born for economic reasons, and that a good deal of capital would be saved if no interest were paid—considered that grown men and women work in response to such stimuli as piece-wages and that the owners of capital selfishly balance the returns available from living on interest, on the one hand, and from consuming the capital itself, on the other. The Cambridge economist, J. M. (later Lord) Keynes (1883–1946), in *The General Theory of Employment Interest and Money* (London and New York 1936), has gone as far as any member of the Neo-Classical group in furnishing an institutional explanation of the supply of productive factors—in his case, the supply of capital—but this book is perhaps to be regarded as signalizing its author's revolt from Neo-Classical economics rather than as a portion of the body of Neo-Classical literature. Broadly, it must be agreed that the Neo-Classical economists have stood by the Classical ideas on the subject of production stimuli with more steadfastness than has been the case with their explanations of demand.

[200] Translated by S. L. Barron as *The Theory of Social Economy* (from 5th ed.), London and New York 1932.

[201] p. 5 of the translation. Quoted by permission of Ernest Benn Ltd. and Harcourt, Brace and Company, Inc.

Defense of Classical psychology. At least one contemporary economist has followed the opposite tack to that of Davenport and Cassel. Instead of abandoning the hedonistic theories of human conduct in response to the attack of such men as Veblen, the American, Z. C. Dickinson (1889–), in his *Economic Motives* (Cambridge, Mass., 1922), examined the question from the psychological side and reached a general conclusion favorable to hedonism, rather than the reverse. In recent years, as is well known, psychologists have come to believe that instinct is a much less important factor than was thought a generation or two ago, so that those economists who favor non-hedonistic explanations of human action emphasize such factors as habit and custom, rather than instinct. These, at all events, are in good standing among the psychologists, which is no longer true of instincts.

Perhaps one of the weakest features of the work of many modern economists is that they have referred to wants without always making clear the kind of things that they were assuming were wanted, and by whom they were desired. Their terminology has included the wants of individuals in the way of personal goods and services, but commonly has not covered the State's wants for power and prestige, nor, indeed, the wants of individuals and governments in the way of well-doing. Plainly, these wider classes of wants conflict with each other exactly as do narrower wants, such as those for radio sets and suits of clothes. It is certain that desires for social security and for the prestige of America may, if given expression, impinge on power to purchase automobiles just as does a love of concert music; yet Jevons formally excluded the first class of wants from economic study and many writers of the Neo-Classical group appear to have thought only of desires of the automobile and concert music type, that is, individual wants. Probably the English economist P. H. Wicksteed (1844–1927), whose work is referred to later in this book, went as far as any member of the Neo-Classical School in admitting the realities of this situation. Fuller discussion of this subject must be reserved to Chapter XVI.

Summary of Chapter

Men's attitude to wealth has shown great changes. Much of the behavior of primitive people is explained by the limited importance many of them attach to the acquisition of wealth. Ancient philosophers and Christian teachers of a later age were sharply critical of wealth-seeking. Yet it is difficult to believe that these views fully reflected the popular opinion of the times. The Mercantilists claimed to subordinate individual riches to what were thought to be the needs of the State — an attitude which has taken on new significance in our own time.

In the seventeenth century philosophers began to argue — as the Epicureans of the ancient world had done before them — that the greatest good, or ultimate aim of human endeavor, was happiness. Questions were asked about the relationship between wealth and happiness. The position taken up by Adam Smith, in his *Theory of Moral Sentiments*, was that beyond a certain point wealth did not confer happiness upon its possessor. "In ease of body and peace of mind," said Smith, "all the different ranks of life are nearly upon a level, and the beggar, who suns himself by the side of the highway, possesses that security which kings are fighting for." But Jeremy Bentham gave a different answer; he stated the principle of diminishing utility. The happiness conferred by wealth diminished as the quantity of wealth possessed increased, Bentham said. Thus was furnished a rational basis for modern economics.

Critics appeared, however. Lauderdale and others drew attention to the paradox that wealth as it had come to be defined by economists could be increased by the physical destruction of useful goods. Romanticist and Institutional writers insisted that the study of wealth must be integrated with that of life as a whole. Pleasure and pain theories declined in popularity among the psychologists and such factors as personal habits and social customs received emphasis as human incentives. So, for the most part, the later economists of the Neo-Classical School reacted by abandoning the psychological assumptions upon which their predecessors had grounded the science of economics.

CHAPTER III

ECONOMIC INDIVIDUALISM

The idea that, if left alone, men act so as to promote the general welfare was a cardinal point in the doctrines of the Classical and Neo-Classical Schools of economists, descended from Adam Smith. It was believed that the selfish attempts of individuals to add to their own riches increased the wealth at the disposal of the whole. The conclusion seemed obvious that governments should follow the policy of *laissez faire,* that is, should stand aside as much as possible in order that the beneficent principle of individual self-interest could operate. Though there was scattered criticism elsewhere, only among the Germans was there a persistent refusal to accept the Classical and Neo-Classical tenets, so that in English-speaking countries the history of economic thought in the nineteenth century centers round the development of these ideas.

The Motive of Self-Interest in Early Times

It has been mentioned already that private enterprise played an important part in early Greece and Rome. Even the ancient philosophers felt able to say something in favor of the system, the arguments used by Aristotle in attacking Plato's communist project being a famous example.

When compared with the extent of the recognition given to the spirit of commercialism in Rome, the middle ages showed a decided swing in the opposite direction. The village community operated according to rules, that were themselves based largely on custom. Common cultivation of the open fields, and the circumstance that the livestock of the entire community ran together on the pasturage, meant that improvements in tillage and breeds of livestock were either impossible or brought little benefit to those who introduced them. Urban industry was closely regulated. In fact, the whole medieval system was one of ordered relationships and except in royal and ecclesiastical service, or foreign trade (which was of limited importance), there was little opportunity for men to rise by their own efforts. Yet the motive of self-interest was constantly at work within the framework of medieval society. To a very considerable extent, indeed, the efficiency of the regulatory system depended upon it. What were penalties and rewards—whether operating in this world or the next—but appeals to self-interest?

The Mercantilism of the sixteenth century and afterwards similarly was characterized by regulation. The power of the State was used to induce or compel individuals to direct their activities along lines that were considered to serve State ends. As practical men, the Mercantilists admitted that if people were left to do as they pleased they would be likely to further their own interests and neglect those of the State. As a result, government interference was favored. But the basis of much Mercantilist legislation was an appeal to men's selfishness. The promotion of the State good was made a paying proposition. Penalties were imposed on actions which Mercantilist statesmen believed were inimical to the interests of the State : rewards were offered for good behavior. As an example of thought along these lines the *Discourse of the Common Weal of this Realm of England* may be quoted. One of the characters appearing in the *Discourse,* the doctor, discussed with another, the knight, the problem of enclosure of arable land, which at the time of the *Discourse* was causing considerable concern. The doctor argued in favor of using the selfishness of farmers and landowners to achieve the State objective of fostering corn growing instead of sheep grazing :

> everie man will seke wheare most advauntage is, and they see theire is most advantage in grasinge and breedinge then in husbandrie and tillage, by a great deale. And so long (as) it is so, the pasture shall (evere) encroche upon the tillage, for all the lawes that ever can be made to the contrarie.[1]

As a remedy for this situation, the doctor proposed :

> To make the proffitt of the plow to be as good, rate for rate, as the proffit of the graisiers and shepmasters [*i.e.,* owners of sheep].[2]

This might be done by restricting the export of wool, the doctor suggested, an export tax being levied on this commodity whenever it was exported "unwrought" (that is, not manufactured into cloth), while the export of corn was permitted without any such restriction. The doctor's plan was in keeping with Mercantilist policy generally. Home manufactures were encouraged by measures that appealed to the self-interest of those who operated them. Import duties or prohibitions rendered home manufacture more profitable than importation. People were not compelled to weave cloth or make glass. Instead, they were offered pecuniary inducements to engage in these activities. Even where compulsion was applied, it was accompanied by sanctions that depended on self-interest for their effectiveness.

The doctor in the *Discourse* stated this as a general principle :

> We must understand also that all thinges that should be done in a common wealth be not to be forced, or to be constrained by the streyght penalties of the law; but some so, and some other by allurement, and rewardes rather. For what law can compell men to be industrious in travell, and laboure of theire bodies, or studious to learne anie science or knowledge of the mynd? to these thinges they maie be well provoked, encouraged, and allured, yf they that be industrious and painfull be well Rewarded for theire paines, and be

[1] *Op. cit.,* p. 53. [2] *Ibid.*

suffered to taike gaines and wealth as reward of theire labours. And so likewise (they) that be learned, yf they be advaunced and honored accordinge to theire forwardnes in learninge, everie man will then studie ether to be industrious in bodely labour, or studious in thinges that pertaine to knowledge. Taike this reward from them, and goe abowt to compell them by lawes therto, what man will plowghe or digge the grounde, or exercise anie manuell occupation whearin is anie payne? Or who will adventure over sease for anie marchandize? or use anie facultie whearin anie perill or dainger should be, seinge his Rewarde shall be no more than his that sittethe still? But ye will percase answere me, that all theire Rewardes shall not be taiken awaie, but part of it. Yet then youe must graunte me, that as yf all these rewardes weare taken from them, all these faculties must nedes decay; so yf part of that rewarde be minished [*i.e.*, if the reward be diminished], the use of those faculties shall minishe withall, after the rate; and so they shalbe the lesse occupied, the lesse they be rewarded and estemed.[3]

When the doctor asked what men would "plowghe or digge the grounde," or "adventure over sease" for merchandise, if the gains resulting from such activities were taken from them, he had in view the principle that was to be so prominent in the writings of the advocates of *laissez faire* at a later date.

The Theoretical Basis of Laissez Faire

The Moralists

The philosophical environment was changing. In the middle ages it had not been considered decent or respectable to find merit in self-interest. This was something to be discouraged in order that salvation might be attained. But secularism had asserted itself with the Renaissance and later men like Hobbes and Grotius brought selfishness into the open as a ruling principle of social life.

Subsequent writers, however, did not yield to self-interest the significance it had been given by these philosophers. Opposing Hobbes, Shaftesbury argued that men were not entirely selfish. They were concerned with the good of others as well as their own; that is, they had a moral sense, apart from religious ideas and fear of legal penalties, which caused them to endeavor to benefit their fellows. An action was regarded by individuals as praiseworthy if it promoted the welfare of other members of the community. This feeling in men's breasts acted as a check on mere selfishness, Shaftesbury said. Hutcheson's views were similar. In his treatise, *Concerning Moral Good and Evil,* Hutcheson argued that men were so constituted that they approved actions on the part of others that were useful to the general body of mankind, even when they did not appear directly beneficial to themselves. It was true that such actions promoted their own good indirectly, since individuals

[3] *Ibid.*, pp. 57-58.

were themselves part of mankind and received their share of the general benefit. But men did not always realize this, Hutcheson commented, and so they gave the stamp of their approval without knowing that they themselves would gain from the actions approved. Intending only the benefit of others, therefore, they brought about their own good :

It is true, that the Actions which we approve, are useful to Mankind; but not always to the Approver. It would perhaps be useful to the *Whole*, that all Men agreed in performing such Actions; and then every one would have his Share of the *Advantage*: But this only proves, that *Reason* and *calm Reflection* may recommend to us, from *Self-Interest,* those Actions, which at first View our *moral Sense* determines us to admire, without considering this *Interest*. Nay, our *Sense* shall operate even where the *Advantage* to ourselves does not hold. We can approve the Justice of a Sentence against ourselves. . . It remains then, "That as the AUTHOR of *Nature* has determin'd us to receive, by our *external Senses,* pleasant or disagreeable Ideas of Objects, according as they are useful or hurtful to our Bodys; and to receive from *uniform Objects* the Pleasures of *Beauty* and *Harmony,* to excite us to the Pursuit of Knowledge, and to reward us for it . . . in the same manner he has given us a MORAL SENSE, to direct our Actions, and to give us still *nobler Pleasures*: so that while we are only intending the *Good* of others, we undesignedly promote our own greatest *private Good*."[4]

Thus, like Adam Smith later, Hutcheson believed that private and social good coincided. Smith, it is true, put the point the opposite way round. Where Hutcheson said that men sought the good of others and thereby benefited themselves, Smith argued that, intending only their own advantage, men promoted that of their fellows. But Hutcheson was Smith's teacher and there is little doubt that he was an important source of inspiration to the great economist.

Hume applied himself to the same problem. Benevolence, or attention to the good of others, he believed, received social approbation and led observers to be themselves benevolent :

It may be esteemed, perhaps, a superfluous task to prove, that the benevolent or softer affections are ESTIMABLE; and wherever they appear, engage the approbation, and good-will of mankind. The epithets *sociable, good-natured, humane, merciful, grateful, friendly, generous, beneficent,* or their equivalents, are known in all languages, and universally express the highest merit, which *human nature* is capable of attaining. . . no qualities are more entitled to the general good-will and approbation of mankind, than beneficence and humanity, friendship and gratitude, natural affection and public spirit, or whatever proceeds from a tender sympathy with others, and a generous concern for our kind and species. These, wherever they appear, seem to transfuse themselves, in a manner, into each beholder, and to call forth, in their

[4] *An Inquiry into the Original of our Ideas of Beauty and Virtue*: *II, Concerning Moral Good and Evil*, pp. 127-129.

own behalf, the same favourable and affectionate sentiments, which they exert on all around.[5]

People, therefore, strove to secure this social approval:

is not a monk and inquisitor enraged when we treat his order as useless or pernicious to mankind? The historian exults in displaying the benefit arising from his labours. The writer of romances alleviates or denies the bad consequences ascribed to his manner of composition.[6]

The result, Hume said, was to promote the social good:

The happiness of mankind, the order of society, the harmony of families, the mutual support of friends, are always considered as the result of their gentle dominion [*i.e.*, the dominion of the benevolent sentiments] over the breasts of men.[7]

In other words, if men were left alone they would consider the interests of others as well as of themselves and would, therefore, benefit the whole. This belief furnished a favorable background for the proposals that were soon forthcoming, to the effect that the government should leave individuals alone. Not merely Adam Smith and his fellow-economists, but anarchists like William Godwin, argued on these lines.

Perhaps the most famous of all the utilitarian philosophers, Jeremy Bentham, gave a much less important place to benevolence. He regarded men as being dominated by selfishness and looked to sanctions (*i.e.*, punishments and rewards) to check this selfish propensity of individuals and secure the social good:

whatsoever evil it is possible for man to do for the advancement of his own private and personal interest, (or what comes to the same thing, what to him appears such,) at the expense of the public interest, – that evil, sooner or later, he will do, unless by some means or other, intentional or otherwise, he be prevented from doing it.[8]

Thus, Bentham went back to the position of Hobbes in his assessment of men's motives and, quite logically, threw himself into a study of the sanctions whereby men's selfishness might be kept under proper control. But this was in the early part of the nineteenth century and it is necessary to examine the manner in which ideas on economics had evolved in the meantime.

British Economic Writers before 1776

Even in the seventeenth century pamphleteers began to assert that government regulation of commerce served no useful purpose. One of

[5] *Essays and Treatises on Several Subjects*, vol. 2, *An Enquiry Concerning the Principles of Morals*, sect. 2, pp. 239-241.
[6] *Ibid.*, p. 242. [7] *Ibid.*, p. 245.
[8] *The Works of Jeremy Bentham*, vol. 9, *The Constitutional Code*, p 192.

the first writers to take this line was Edward Misselden (flourished 1608–1654), who was associated with a leading trading company of the time. In *The Circle of Commerce: Or the Balance of Trade, in defence of Free Trade . . .* (London 1623), Misselden asked,

Is not gaine the end of trade? Is not the publique involved in the private, and the private in the publique? What else makes a Common-wealth, but the private-wealth, if I may so say, of the members thereof in the exercise of *Commerce* amongst themselves, and with foraine Nations?[9]

At the end of the century, Sir Dudley North (1641–1691), concluded a tract entitled *Discourses upon Trade; Principally directed to the Cases of the Interest Coynage Clipping Increase of Money* (London 1691) with the following declaration:

Thus we may labour to hedge in the Cuckow, but in vain; for no People ever yet grew rich by Policies; but it is Peace, Industry, and Freedom that brings Trade and Wealth, and nothing else.[10]

North was the younger son of an English peer and had engaged in trade ventures in the Near East before being appointed to a government office in London, where he is said to have managed the finances of King James II. The pamphlet was a general appeal for economic freedom and is interesting as coming from the pen of such a man. Its contemporary influence was slight but it was reprinted when *laissez faire* doctrines were at the height of their popularity in England. The sponsor of the reprint then regarded North's work as an anticipation of that of Adam Smith, praiseworthy on its own account but not comparable with the writings of that great master:

Such anticipations take something from the novelty, but nothing from the value of that portion of his [*i.e.*, Adam Smith's] immortal work in which these doctrines are developed. Truth had revealed herself partially and feebly in earlier writings [*i.e.*, in such writings as those of North]: *here* [in the *Wealth of Nations*] She shone forth in meridian splendour, illuminating the whole field of inquiry, and commanding universal homage.[11]

Charles Davenant took up a position between that of Sir Dudley North and the one occupied by the Mercantilists themselves. Davenant was a member of the British parliament, Commissioner of Excise and later Inspector-General of Exports and Imports, and his interest in trade matters led him to study the question of commercial restrictions. He granted the general premise of the Mercantilists, that the government

[9] p. 17.

[10] Reprinted Edinburgh 1822 and Baltimore 1907, p. 37 of the Baltimore reprint. Quoted by permission of The Johns Hopkins Press.

[11] p. vii of the 1822 reprint.

should supervise the economic activities of men, but recognized that such supervision might be injurious, by limiting what was beneficial (*i.e.*, commercial intercourse):

Trade is the general concern of this nation, but every distinct trade has a distinct interest. The wisdom of the legislative power consists, in keeping an even hand to promote all; and chiefly to encourage such trades as encrease the public stock, and add to the kingdom's wealth, considered as a collective body.

Trade is in its nature free, finds its own channel, and best directeth its own course: and all Laws to give it rules and directions, and to limit and circumscribe it, may serve the particular ends of private men, but are seldom advantageous to the public.

Governments, in relation to it, are to take a providential care of the whole, but generally to let 2d [*i.e.*, second] causes work their own way; and considering all the links and chains, by which they hang together, peradventure it may be affirmed, that, in the main, all traffics whatsoever are beneficial to a country.[12]

In one of the most-discussed books of its time, *The Fable of the Bees: Or, Private Vices, Publick Benefits* (London 1714),[13] Bernard de Mandeville (1670–1733) put forward the thesis that it was *vice* that made society active and prosperous. Mandeville was the son of a Dutch physician and himself took a medical degree. Later he went to England, where he wrote the *Fable*, primarily as a political or social satire. He argued that human desires or passions explained men's actions and were themselves accounted for by self-interest. Industry, therefore, was motivated by ambition, greed, and pride, which Mandeville called "vices." From what has been said already, it will be appreciated that it was but a short step from the ideas of Hobbes and Locke to those of Mandeville. The conclusions of the later writer were set forth in allegorical form, in the story of a hive of bees that remained prosperous so long as the bees were selfish but fell into poverty immeditely they mended their ways. If it were granted that riches were beneficial, it was open to anyone to draw the conclusion from Mandeville's *Fable* that the selfish attempts on the part of individuals to benefit themselves redounded to the benefit of all. This, of course, was the opposite of Francis Hutcheson's opinion that the benevolent actions of individuals operated so as to do good to themselves. A few extracts from Mandeville's work will illustrate his point of view.

[12] *An Essay on the East-India Trade* (London 1696), reprinted in *The Political and Commercial Works of . . . Charles D'Avenant*, vol. 1, pp. 98-99.

[13] First published in 1705, under the title of *The Grumbling Hive or Knaves Turn'd Honest.*

In the early (and wicked) state of the bees,

Vast Numbers throng'd the fruitful Hive;
Yet those vast Numbers made 'em thrive;
Millions endeavouring to supply
Each other's Lust and Vanity;
Whilst other Millions were employ'd,
To see their Handy-works destroy'd;
They furnish'd half the Universe;
Yet had more Work than Labourers. . .
And all those, that in Enmity,
With downright Working, cunningly
Convert to their own Use the Labour
Of their good Natur'd heedless Neighbour.
These were call'd Knaves, but bar the Name
The grave Industrious were the same:
All Trades and Places knew some Cheat,
No Calling was without Deceit.[14]

Of these deceits, Mandeville gave a number of examples, such as those lawyers, "of whose Art the Basis, Was raising Feuds and splitting Cases," physicians who "valu'd Fame and Wealth Above the drooping Patient's Health," and so on. He continued,

Thus every Part was full of Vice,
Yet the whole Mass a Paradise;
Flatter'd in Peace, and fear'd in Wars,
They were th' Esteem of Foreigners,
And lavish of their Wealth and Lives,
The Ballance of all other Hives,
Such were the Blessings of that State;
Their Crimes conspir'd to make them Great:
And Vertue, who from Politicks
Head [had] learn'd a Thousand Cunning Tricks,
Was, by their happy Influence,
Made Friends with Vice: And ever since
The worst of all the Multitude,
Did something for the Common Good.
This was the State's-Craft, that maintain'd
The Whole, of which each Part complain'd:
This, as in Musick Harmony,
Made Jarrings in the main agree. . .
The Root of Evil, Avarice,
That damn'd ill-natur'd Vice,
Was Slave to Prodigality,
That noble Sin; whilst Luxury
Employ'd a Million of the Poor,
And odious Pride a Million more:

[14] Second edition, London 1723, pp. 2-4.

Envy it self, and Vanity,
Were Ministers of Industry;
Their darling Folly, Fickleness
In Dyet, Furniture and Dress.
That strange ridic'lous Vice, was made
The very Wheel that turn'd the Trade. . .
Thus Vice nurs'd Ingenuity,
Which joyn'd with Time and Industry,
Had carry'd Life's Conveniencies,
It's real Pleasures, Comforts, Ease,
To such a Height, the very Poor
Liv'd better than the Rich before,
And nothing could be added more.[15]

But, suddenly, the bees were converted to honesty, whereupon "Oh ye Gods! What Consternation," and, in consequence,

As Pride and Luxury decrease,
So by degrees they leave the Seas.
Not Merchants now, but Companies
Remove whole Manufacturies.
All Arts and Crafts neglected lie;
Content, the Bane of Industry,
Makes 'em admire their homely Store,
And neither seek nor covet more.[16]

Numbers decreased, especially in consequence of attacks by enemies now that they were less rich and powerful, and finally the bees "flew into a hollow Tree, Blest with Content and Honesty."

Severely criticized by Hume and others, to whom the moral principles that the book seemed to support were objectionable, the *Fable* was known to Adam Smith and is generally believed to have exercised some influence on his ideas.

The French Physiocrats

Already, as is shown in Chapter VI, Hume had delivered a frontal attack upon Mercantilist trade policy. The French banker, Richard Cantillon (c. 1680–1734), demonstrated that, in the absence of government direction, production would regulate itself in a manner that was beneficial to society. If there were a scarcity of meat, then the high price of this commodity attracted farmers into its production. If meat were too plentiful, low prices stimulated a contraction in production.[17] The manuscript of Cantillon's book, entitled *Essai sur la nature du commerce en général* and not published until 1755 in London, was for a number of years in the possession of the Marquis de Mirabeau (1715–1789).

[15] *Ibid.*, pp. 9-11. [16] *Ibid.*, p. 21.
[17] Cantillon's theory is discussed in Chapter IX.

Mirabeau's work, *L'ami des hommes, ou traité de la population* (Avignon 1756), showed the influence of Cantillon's ideas, but François Quesnay was the founder and leader of the new school of Physiocrats. The son of a peasant, Quesnay had received a medical education and had risen to be court physician. While in this position—which left him time for study—Quesnay gave considerable attention to economics, writing articles in 1756 and 1757 on *Fermiers* and *Grains* for the great French *Encyclopédie,* which was being issued at that time. In 1758 Quesnay published his famous chart, the *Tableau économique,*[18] at Versailles. This purported to give a graphical account of the distribution of wealth in society. All wealth arose from the land, Quesnay believed; and agriculture alone of all branches of activity produced more than was necessary to maintain the persons engaged in it. The chart showed how this surplus was distributed.

It was a central feature of Physiocratic doctrine that there existed a natural law, which, in the absence of government interference, would ensure the good working of the economic system. As was shown in Chapter I, the conception of a natural law is very old; but the Physiocratic natural law differed from that of the ancient and medieval philosophers. Helvétius had done for France what Hutcheson and Hume accomplished in Britain, that is, developed and popularized hedonistic philosophy. The work of Helvétius had considerable influence on the Physiocrats, so that their natural law was closer to Adam Smith's conception of beneficent self-interest, derived from the same basic philosophy, than to the natural law of earlier times. Its essence was the idea that the propensity of individuals to seek their own ends would bring about the general good.

The Physiocratic theory of production and distribution, advanced in the *Tableau économique,* lent support to economic freedom. As has been mentioned, the theory postulated that the only surplus of income (surplus in the sense that it was unnecessary for the maintenance of those who received it) was in income obtained from the cultivation of land. This alone was available for purposes of taxation. According to the Physiocrats, if taxes were imposed on other income, they were merely shifted until they reached their final resting place on the rent of land. Such shifting was needlessly expensive and inconvenient. It could be avoided if taxes were concentrated upon rent: hence the Physiocratic proposal for an *impôt unique,* or single tax. It followed from this idea that most of the imposts upon which the Mercantilists had relied for regulation of the economic system should be removed, since they were not levied on the rent of land. The Physiocratic theory of exchange likewise supported the removal of trade restrictions. Commerce was seen

[18] A translation of the *Tableau économique* is given by A. E. Monroe in *Early Economic Thought, Cambridge* (Mass.) 1924, pp. 339-348.

as an exchange of superfluities, which was only impeded by artificial restrictions. On the other hand, the theory of a unique surplus led the Physiocrats, except Turgot, to justify government action to restrict interest on loans for commercial and industrial purposes, on the ground that these occupations were not productive of any surplus out of which interest could be paid.

In general, the influence of the school was decidedly in the direction of free trade. A. R. J. Turgot (1727–1781), a scholar of mark who had entered government service and become converted to Physiocratic doctrines, was given a high place in the royal financial administration. In this position, in 1774, he abolished the restrictions impeding movement of grain between the various provinces of France and shortly afterwards made a move to destroy the gild system. This triumph of liberalism was short-lived, however. Antagonism raised by Turgot's reforms and by the single-tax proposal, along with other factors, led to the minister's fall from power.

The Economic System of Adam Smith

Smith's *An Inquiry into the Nature and Causes of the Wealth of Nations* showed signs of Physiocratic influence. After studying under Hutcheson at the University of Glasgow and pursuing further his search for knowledge at Oxford, Smith taught in Glasgow for some years and then resigned to become tutor to a young Scottish nobleman. In this capacity, he spent some time in France during the period of Physiocratic ascendancy, but not until ten years afterwards did the *Wealth of Nations* make its appearance, much of the interval being spent on this book. Formerly it was believed that Physiocratic doctrine had a good deal to do with the ideas expressed in Smith's work, but the discovery of notes of his earlier Glasgow lectures showed that the basic lines of his thought were laid down before he came into contact with the Physiocrats. It is in the writings of Hutcheson and Hume, and, no doubt, in those of Mandeville, Cantillon, and Harris,[19] as well as in his own *Theory of Moral Sentiments,* that the derivation of Smith's liberalism is to be found.

In the *Moral Sentiments,* as was seen in Chapter II, Smith made it clear that he regarded the pursuit of wealth as the result of a delusion on the part of men. But in his view Providence, fortunately, had so arranged matters that this delusion served a useful purpose. The rich could not consume all they received and so were compelled to divide some of it with those who were poorer, thus bringing about the good of the whole society :

It is to no purpose, that the proud and unfeeling landlord views his extensive fields, and without a thought for the wants of his brethren, in imagination

[19] For the significance of Harris in this connection, see Chapter VI, p. 296.

consumes himself the whole harvest that grows upon them. The homely and vulgar proverb, that the eye is larger than the belly, never was more fully verified than with regard to him. The capacity of his stomach bears no proportion to the immensity of his desires, and will receive no more than that of the meanest peasant. The rest he is obliged to distribute among those, who prepare, in the nicest manner, that little which he himself makes use of, among those who fit up the palace in which this little is to be consumed, among those who provide and keep in order all the different baubles and trinklets, which are employed in the œconomy of greatness; all of whom thus derive from his luxury and caprice, that share of the necessaries of life, which they would in vain have expected from his humanity or his justice. The produce of the soil maintains at all times nearly that number of inhabitants which it is capable of maintaining. The rich only select from the heap what is most precious and agreeable. They consume little more than the poor, and in spite of their natural selfishness and rapacity, though they mean only their own conveniency, though the sole end which they propose from the labours of all the thousands whom they employ, be the gratification of their own vain and insatiable desires, they divide with the poor the produce of all their improvements. *They are led by an invisible hand to make nearly the same distribution of the necessaries of life, which would have been made, had the earth been divided into equal portions among all its inhabitants*; and thus, without intending it, without knowing it, advance the interest of the society, and afford means to the multiplication of the species. When Providence divided the earth among a few lordly masters, it neither forgot nor abandoned those who seemed to have been left out in the partition. These last too enjoy their share of all it produces.[20]

In the *Wealth of Nations*, Smith applied to economics this conception of a beneficent Providence, who had so arranged human affairs that individual and social objectives coincided. If men were left to themselves, he said, though seeking only their own gain, they would bring about the general benefit.

The beginning of the book was characteristic of the whole. The division or specialization of labor was the chief cause of increase in its productive power, Smith said.[21] In the second chapter a reason was assigned for this specialization. It was explained, not by human design, but by nature, by the hand of Providence:

The division of Labour, from which so many advantages are derived, is not originally the effect of any human wisdom which foresees and intends that general opulence to which it gives occasion. It is the necessary, though very slow and gradual, consequence of a certain propensity in human nature which has in view no such extensive utility; the propensity to truck, barter, and exchange one thing for another. Whether this propensity be one of those original principles in human nature, of which no further account can

[20] *The Theory of Moral Sentiments,* vol. 1, pp. 465-467. Italics ours.

[21] See Chapter VIII.

be given; or whether, as seems more probable, it be the necessary consequence of the faculties of reason and speech, it belongs not to our present subject to inquire. It is common to all men, and to be found in no other race of animals, which seem to know neither this nor any other species of contracts.[22]

This thread runs through the book. In the absence of interference, Smith believed that men would produce the articles for which society had greatest need. They would engage in the particular trade that was most economical to their nation. That great bugbear of the medieval and Mercantilist regulators—the supply of money—was nothing to worry about, because the supply of the precious metals would regulate itself better than any public authority could manage it. Even population kept itself right, because the demand for men regulated their production. In general, the individual, in directing his industry into what seemed to him to be the most profitable channels, having in mind only his own interest—without knowing it, indeed more effectively than if he intended it—served the public interest:

he intends only his own gain, and he is in this, as in many other cases, led by an invisible hand to promote an end which was no part of his intention. Nor is it always the worse for the society that it was no part of it. By pursuing his own interest he frequently promotes that of the society more effectually than when he really intends to promote it. I have never known much good done by those who affected to trade for the public good. It is an affectation, indeed, not very common among merchants, and very few words need be employed in dissuading them from it.[23]

Government restrictions were injurious, Smith thought, doing harm where they sought to do good. They prevented the free flow of capital and labor from less advantageous to more advantageous employments and they forced international trade into less economic channels. The solution was to be found in economic freedom:

It is thus that every system which endeavours, either by extraordinary encouragements, to draw towards a particular species of industry a greater share of the capital of the society than what would naturally go to it; or by extraordinary restraints, to force from a particular species of industry some share of the capital which would otherwise be employed in it; is in reality subversive of the great purpose which it means to promote. It retards, instead of accelerating, the progress of the society towards real wealth and greatness; and diminishes, instead of increasing, the real value of the annual produce of its land and labour. All systems either of preference or of restraint, therefore, being thus completely taken away, the obvious and simple system of natural liberty establishes itself of its own accord. Every man, as long as he does not violate the laws of justice, is left perfectly free to pursue his own interest his own way, and to bring both his industry and capital into competition with

[22] *Wealth of Nations*, Bk. 1, Chap. 2. [23] *Ibid.*, Bk. 4, Chap. 2.

those of any other man, or order of men. The sovereign is completely discharged from a duty, in the attempting to perform which he must always be exposed to innumerable delusions, and for the proper performance of which no human wisdom or knowledge could ever be sufficient; the duty of superintending the industry of private people, and of directing it towards the employments most suitable to the interest of the society.[24]

Thus, one of the most influential works ever written on economic subjects became a tract in favor of *laissez faire*.

A series of writers developed Smith's idea. Among the most prominent of these were David Ricardo, a London stockbroker who, having accumulated a fortune at an early age, retired to practical politics and theoretical economics; T. R. Malthus, clergyman and professor of political economy in the East India Company's training college; James Mill, who, after writing a history of India, obtained employment in the East India Company's London office and rose to be its chief; his son, John Stuart, who followed James as head of the East India Company's office; and Nassau Senior, who, after an early training in law, became an economics professor. J. B. Say, French business man and teacher of economics, popularized and expanded Smith's theories on the continent of Europe. That Say's views on State regulation of economic activities were as decided as those of Smith himself is shown by the following passage from his *Traité d'économie politique* (2 vols., Paris 1803):[25]

When authority throws itself in the way of this natural course of things, and says, the product you are about to create, that which yields the greatest profit, and is consequently the most in request, is by no means the most suitable to your circumstances, you must undertake some other, it evidently directs part of the productive energies of the nation towards an object of less desire, at the expense of another of more urgent desire.[26]

To Say, this situation appeared so ridiculous, that he ventured to forecast,

The day will come, sooner or later, when people will wonder at the necessity of taking all this trouble to expose the folly of a system [*i.e.*, the Mercantile System], so childish and absurd, and yet so often enforced at the point of the bayonet.[27]

As for the Mercantile System in England, C. R. Prinsep (1789–1864), translator of Say's work, declared in 1821 that

All thinking men have long since reprobated its continuance; and even those, who are commonly the last to listen to theoretical reasoning, merchants

[24] *Ibid.*, Bk. 4, Chap. 9. The reference to "real wealth and greatness" is interesting, in view of what was said in Chapter II, concerning Smith's attitude to wealth.

[25] Translated by C. R. Prinsep as *A Treatise on Political Economy; or the Production, Distribution, and Consumption of Wealth*, 2 vols., London 1821. A new American edition was published in Philadelphia 1841.

[26] p. 144 of the Philadelphia edition. [27] *Ibid.*, p. 159.

and manufacturers themselves, have joined in remonstrance and supplication, though hitherto without success.[28]

This situation was soon to be changed.

The Practical Success of Economic Liberalism

It is safe to say that no small amount of the practical success of the new doctrines was due to the economic and political environment in which they were put forward. Britain appeared to have everything to gain from a policy of free trade, especially the growing commercial and industrial classes. Even before 1800, *laissez faire* sentiments were running strongly. Thus, in 1795–1796, a debate took place in the British Parliament on the subject of a minimum wage bill. The younger Pitt, Prime Minister at the time and apparently a student of Smith's writings, quoted Classical economics against the supporters of the bill:

It is unnecessary to argue the general expediency of any legislative interference, as the principles have been perfectly recognised by the hon. gentleman himself. The most celebrated writers upon political economy, and the experience of those states where arts had flourished the most, bore ample testimony of their truth. They had only to enquire, therefore, whether the present case was strong enough for the exception, and whether the means proposed were suited to the object intended?[29]

A little later, in 1814, moving for leave to repeal the Statute of Apprentices of 1563 (which regulated wages and labor conditions and was a major piece of Mercantilist legislation) Sergeant Onslow claimed that

The reign of Queen Elizabeth [when the Statute was passed], though glorious, was not one in which sound principles of commerce were known. . . So little was political economy then understood that the idea never seemed to have occurred, that agriculture [to favor which, Onslow thought, was the object of the Statute] was best promoted by the prosperity of commerce and manufactures; and that restraints on them defeated the end they aimed at, and discouraged the very employment which they ought to promote.[30]

In 1820 Alexander Baring, on behalf of the London merchants, presented to parliament a petition which set forth the economic arguments for free trade. This was drawn up by Thomas Tooke, who in the following year helped to establish the Political Economy Club for the purpose of advancing the new ideas. The favorable impression created by this petition is said to have influenced William Huskisson in taking his stand in the low tariff camp. At all events, Huskisson appears to have been responsible for a proposal to relax the corn laws (regulating

[28] pp. 222-223 of the English issue of 1821.

[29] A. E. Bland, P. A. Brown, and R. H. Tawney, *English Economic History: Select Documents,* London 1914, reprinted 1937, p. 559. Quoted by permission of G. Bell & Sons, Ltd.

[30] *Ibid.*, pp. 581-582.

overseas traffic in grain[31]), made in 1821 by a committee of which he was a member, appointed to study the prevailing agricultural depression. Soon Huskisson was in the cabinet, and did a good deal to reduce the restrictions on trade. But—though modified—the corn laws remained on the statute book for another generations. The statement made by Sir Robert Peel, then Prime Minister, in a debate in 1846 on the abolition of these laws may be quoted:

> I want not to deprive those who, arguing *a priori,* without the benefit of experience, have come to the conclusion that protection is objectionable in principle—I want not to deprive them of any credit which is fairly their due. Reason, unaided by experience, brought conviction to their minds. My opinions have been modified by the experience of the last three years. I have had the means and opportunity of comparing the results of periods of abundance and low prices with periods of scarcity and high prices. I have carefully watched the effects of the one system, and of the other—first, of the policy we have been steadily pursuing for some years, viz., the removal of protection from domestic industry; and next, of the policy which the friends of protection recommend. I have also had an opportunity of marking from day to day the effect upon great social interests of freedom of trade and comparative abundance . . . and I am led to the conclusion that the main grounds of public policy on which protection has been defended are not tenable; at least, I cannot maintain them.[32]

The experience to which Peel referred was connected with the high food prices that attended years of dearth and especially with the Irish potato famine of 1845–1847, but obviously he regarded the results of the steps already taken in the direction of free trade as sufficient to encourage further moves along the same course. One after another, in England, the laws that had come down from Mercantilist times were swept away. The United States and the British dominions overseas—at least outside the special field of tariff policy in the case of the first-named—for the most part followed the British lead. On the continent of Europe, however, as was mentioned in Chapter I, reforms came more slowly and were less complete.

Pessimism and Optimism

But some of Smith's successors—Ricardo, Malthus, and John Stuart Mill, in England, and J. C. L. Simonde de Sismondi (1773–1842) on the Continent—were less optimistic than was Smith himself about the beneficent working of the economic system. Malthus had taught that if people were left alone they would reproduce at such a rate as to cause a constant pressure upon the means of subsistence, lead-

[31] In England, the word "corn" is used to describe what in America are called "small grains," *i.e.*, wheat, barley, oats, and rye.

[32] A. E. Bland, P. A. Brown, and R. H. Tawney, *English Economic History: Select Documents*, pp. 707-708.

ing to vice and misery among the lower classes.[33] The growth of population would intensify the demand for food, Malthus said, and this would raise rents, and result in the enrichment of the already well-off landowning group. Business crises made their appearance and distress was severe, especially during the price deflation that followed the conclusion of the Napoleonic Wars. In consequence, Malthus and Sismondi began to doubt the efficacy of the Classical principles. The latter writer, in his *De la richesse commerciale* (2 vols., Geneva 1803), had given support to *laissez faire;* but in a later work, *Nouveaux principes d'économie politique* (2 vols., Paris 1819), he came out in open revolt against this system.[34] Malthus remained in the orthodox camp but his theories, like those of Ricardo and John Stuart Mill, seemed no longer to possess the Smithian optimism. Instead, they revealed an outlook that a later commentator considered to justify terming economics *the dismal science.* It was left to the Frenchman, Frédéric Bastiat (1801–1850), and the American, H. C. Carey (1793–1879), to attempt a restoration of the old optimistic position.

Carey advocated the protection of home industry by means of import duties but Bastiat was an out-and-out supporter of *laissez faire.* He published a remarkable series of pamphlets, attacking government interference in economic affairs, of which the best-known, perhaps, is the petition of the candlemakers against the sun, quoted in Chapter VI. But Bastiat was not merely a pamphleteer. In the closing years of his life he wrote a general treatise on economics, significantly entitled *Harmonies économiques,*[35] of which the first volume was published in Paris in the year 1850. The central theme of this work was that economic principles operate to harmonize what, at first sight, seemed to be conflicting interests. The book began with a moving dedication *To the Youth of France,* in which the author admitted that the prevailing economic doctrines were pessimistic in nature. This, Bastiat asserted, was unjustified:

it is not true that the great providential laws urge on society to evil.[36]

In the book that followed, Bastiat attempted to demonstrate how, in the absence of government intervention, human actions would operate harmoniously for the good of all. Wealth would be distributed on the basis of service and unjust inequality would be avoided. The increase of population would be beneficial, Bastiat said, not harmful, as Malthus had alleged.

But Bastiat wrote at a time when economic freedom was losing some of

[33] See Chapter VII. [34] See Chapter XV.

[35] Translated by P. J. Stirling as *Harmonies of Political Economy,* 2 vols., London 1860 and Edinburgh 1870; 2nd ed., Edinburgh n. d.

[36] *Ibid.,* 2nd. ed., p. 40. Quoted by permission of Oliver & Boyd, Ltd.

its early popularity. Even J. E. Cairnes (1823–1875), in his economic philosophy a linear descendant of Smith and Ricardo and probably the most outstanding British Classical economist after the death of the younger Mill, criticized rather severely Bastiat's extreme statement of the *laissez faire* position.[37]

Laissez Faire in Declension

The Retreat of the Economists

Smith's exceptions. Adam Smith had allotted three main functions to the government, defense, justice, and certain public works:

According to the system of natural liberty, the sovereign has only three duties to attend to . . . first, the duty of protecting the society from the violence and invasion of other independent societies; secondly, the duty of protecting, as far as possible, every member of the society from the injustice or oppression of every other member of it, or the duty of establishing an exact administration of justice; and, thirdly, the duty of erecting and maintaining certain public works and certain public institutions, which it can never be for the interest of any individual, or small number of individuals, to erect and maintain; because the profit could never repay the expense to any individual, or small number of individuals, though it may frequently do much more than repay it to a great society.[38]

The last heading might have included a wide range of economic activities, but Smith restricted it to education for the common people and regarded the postal service as "perhaps the only mercantile project which has been successfully managed by . . . every sort of government."[39] On State trading generally, his comment was most unfavorable:

No two characters seem more inconsistent than those of trader and sovereign.[40]

A trader was a bad sovereign or ruler, said Smith, and *vice versa,* the British East India Company—which traded with and governed India—being the example that attracted his attention. Somewhat surprisingly, in view of the high praise that he had bestowed on the principle of division of labor at the beginning of his book, towards the end, when discussing education, he gave support to State action for the purpose of mitigating the evils of specialization:

In the progress of the division of labour, the employment of the far greater part of those who live by labour, that is, of the great body of the people, comes to be confined to a few very simple operations; frequently to one or

[37] In an article on Bastiat, which appeared in the *Fortnightly Review* 1870, and was reprinted in Cairnes's *Essays in Political Economy: Theoretical and Applied,* London 1873.

[38] *Wealth of Nations,* Bk. 4, Chap. 9.

[39] *Ibid.,* Bk. 5, Chap. 2, Pt. 1.

[40] *Ibid.*

two. But the understandings of the greater part of men are necessarily formed by their ordinary employments. The man whose whole life is spent in performing a few simple operations of which the effects too are, perhaps, always the same, or very nearly the same, has no occasion to exert his understanding, or to exercise his invention in finding out expedients for removing difficulties which never occur. He naturally loses, therefore, the habit of such exertion, and generally becomes as stupid and ignorant as it is possible for a human creature to become. The torpor of his mind renders him not only incapable of relishing or bearing a part in any rational conversation, but of conceiving any generous, noble, or tender sentiment, and consequently of forming any just judgment concerning many even of the ordinary duties of private life. Of the great and extensive interests of his country he is altogether incapable of judging; and unless very particular pains have been taken to render him otherwise, he is equally incapable of defending his country in war. The uniformity of his stationary life naturally corrupts the courage of his mind, and makes him regard with abhorrence the irregular, uncertain, and adventurous life of a soldier. It corrupts even the activity of his body; and renders him incapable of exerting his strength with vigour and perseverence, in any other employment than that to which he has been bred. His dexterity at his own particular trade seems, in this manner, to be acquired at the expense of his intellectual, social, and martial virtues. But in every improved and civilized society this is the state into which the labouring poor, that is, the great body of the people, must necessarily fall, unless government takes some pains to prevent it.[41]

Few writers have offered a more severe criticism of modern industrialism. Smith also supported laws fixing minimum rates of interest, a point on which Bentham assailed him with considerable vigor,[42] and even advocated progressive taxation.[43]

The utilitarians. The subsequent development of Classical and Neo-Classical views on the economic functions of government may be summarized by saying that there was a gradual widening of Smith's list of exceptions to *laissez faire.* The history of ideas respecting progressive taxation is outlined in Chapter IV: that of opinions on money and banking in Chapter XIV. Each of these fields was the scene of important breaches of *laissez faire* doctrines.

John Stuart Mill and Henry Sidgwick, both followers of Bentham, were outstanding for the attention they gave to the general principle of intervention. Respecting each form of government activity they put the question, *will this increase or decrease human happiness?* Both writers concluded that, in general, happiness was best promoted by leaving men to follow their own inclinations, rather than by government action.

[41] *Ibid.*, Bk. 5, Chap. 1, Pt. 3, Art. 2.
[42] See Chapter XI. [43] See Chapter IV.

According to Mill,

> To be prevented from doing what one is inclined to, or from acting according to one's own judgment of what is desirable, is not only always irksome, but always tends, *pro tanto,* to starve the development of some portion of the bodily or mental faculties, either sensitive or active; and unless the conscience of the individual goes freely with the legal restraint, it partakes, either in a great or in a small degree, of the degradation of slavery.[44]

A second objection to government action, Mill said, was

> that every increase of the functions devolving on the government is an increase of its power, both in the form of authority, and still more, in the indirect form of influence.[45]

A third rested on administrative difficulties:

> Every additional function undertaken by the government, is a fresh occupation imposed upon a body already overcharged with duties.[46]

Evidently, Mill did not believe that the principle of increasing returns was applicable to government activity. He admitted that this objection might be mitigated by better organization. But, even so,

> it would still remain true that in all the more advanced communities, the great majority of things are worse done by the intervention of government, than the individuals most interested in the matter would do them, or cause them to be done, if left to themselves.[47]

What Mill regarded as "one of the strongest of the reasons against the extension of government agency," however, was that it avoided the necessity for the spontaneous action of individuals, "their labour, contrivance, judgment, self-control." This was an essential part of man's education:

> A people among whom there is no habit of spontaneous action for a collective interest – who look habitually to their government to command or prompt them in all matters of joint concern – who expect to have everything done for them, except what can be made an affair of mere habit or routine – have their faculties only half developed; their education is defective in one of its most important branches.[48]

So that Mill's opposition to government action was not primarily economic.

On the other hand, he admitted that there was something to be said on the other side. The "proposition that the consumer is a competent judge of the commodity" – which went back to Locke and was basic to *laissez faire* doctrine – could be admitted "only with numerous abatements and exceptions":

[44] *Principles of Political Economy with Some of their Applications to Social Philosophy,* Bk. 5, Chap. 11, Sect. 2.

[45] *Ibid.,* Sect. 3. [46] *Ibid.,* Sect. 4. [47] *Ibid.,* Sect. 5. [48] *Ibid.*

He is generally the best judge (though even this is not true universally) of the material objects produced for his use. These are destined to supply some physical want, or gratify some taste or inclination, respecting which wants or inclinations there is no appeal from the person who feels them; or they are the means and appliances of some occupation, for the use of the persons engaged in it, who may be presumed to be judges of the things required in their own habitual employment. But there are other things, of the worth of which the demand of the market is by no means a test; things of which the utility does not consist in ministering to inclinations, nor in serving the daily uses of life, and the want of which is least felt where the need is greatest. This is peculiarly true of those things which are chiefly useful as tending to raise the character of human beings. The uncultivated cannot be competent judges of cultivation. Those who most need to be made wiser and better, usually desire it least, and if they desired it, would be incapable of finding the way to it by their own lights. It will continually happen, on the voluntary system, that, the end not being desired, the means will not be provided at all, or that, the persons requiring improvement having an imperfect or altogether erroneous conception of what they want, the supply called forth by the demand of the market will be anything but what is really required.[49]

In this connection, Mill justified the provision of education by the government. Even Adam Smith had admitted this particular case and it is now so widely accepted in practice as to arouse little interest. Mill's criterion was the Benthamite one of happiness, so presumably he considered that education would promote human happiness more than would the other commodities and services that had to be foregone in favor of education. In fact, to a large extent education has been treated as a distributional problem. Nature has so designed it that big incomes (out of which education can be paid for) and large families (where the need for education is great) do not go together, so the rich are taxed to pay for the education of the poor.

Mill's general conclusion on the functions of government was a compromise. *Laissez faire* was to be the rule, but it was to be subjected to "large exceptions," the onus of proof being on those who favored the exceptions. Mill himself admitted a rather long list, elementary education, colonization, hours of labor, the support of the poor, contracts in perpetuity, and inheritance being mentioned as subjects for government regulation, along with

> a variety of cases, in which important public services are to be performed, while yet there is no individual specially interested in performing them, nor would any adequate remuneration naturally or spontaneously attend their performance [such as a voyage of geographical or scientific exploration].[50]

The protection of infant industries, under suitable conditions, received special attention.[51]

[49] *Ibid.*, Sect. 8. [50] *Ibid.*, Sect. 15. [51] See Chapter VI.

Sidgwick's position and conclusions were similar to those of Mill, but the work of the later writer is of special interest because of the manner in which he linked economics formally with utilitarian ethics. Mill had done so, but less obviously, with the result that his exceptions to the broad rule of *laissez faire* had the appearance of being empirical. Sidgwick, on the other hand, made it clear that he supported any and every form of government intervention whose effect would be to increase human happiness. Like Mill, Sidgwick wrote widely, publishing important works on ethics and politics, as well as on economics. In *The Elements of Politics* (London 1891), he stated his fundamental position:

> I think, however, that we may . . . claim general – if not universal – assent for the principle that the true standard and criterion by which right legislation is to be distinguished from wrong is conduciveness to the general "good" or "welfare." And probably the great majority of persons would agree to interpret the "good" or "welfare" of the community to mean, in the last analysis, the happiness of the individual human beings who compose the community; provided that we take into account not only the human beings who are actually living but those who are to live hereafter. This, at any rate, is my own view. Accordingly, throughout this treatise I shall take the happiness of the persons affected as the ultimate end and standard of right and wrong in determining the functions and constitution of government.[52]

Sidgwick's inclusion of individuals "who are to live hereafter" raised a point of some significance in relation to population theory, but this must be left for consideration to Chapter VII. With reference to the opponents of utilitarianism, and especially to the Hegelians, he said,

> I hold that if this good [*i.e.*, the good of the State] is not chimerical and illusory, it must mean the happiness of *some* individual human beings: if not of those living now, at any rate of those who are to live hereafter. And I have tried in vain to obtain from any writer who rejects this view, any other definite conception of the "good of the State."[53]

Sidgwick devoted Book 3 of his work on economics, *The Principles of Political Economy* (London 1883), to what he called "The Art of Political Economy." The "Art," he said, consisted mainly in "what ought to be done by government to improve production and distribution, and to provide for government expenditure." Sidgwick agreed that the common assumption that *laissez faire* was socially beneficial contained "a very large element of truth."[54] As Mill had done before him, he admitted that there were "important qualifications and exceptions"[55] but – again

[52] pp. 34-35. Quoted by permission of Macmillan & Co., Ltd. and The Macmillan Company.

[53] *Ibid.*, p. 35.

[54] *The Principles of Political Economy*, London 1883, 3rd ed. 1901, p. 402. Quoted by permission of Macmillan & Co., Ltd. and The Macmillan Company.

[55] *Ibid.*, p. xix.

like Mill — considered that the onus of proof should be on those who advocated exceptions:

> I do not at all mean to imply that all government interference which is palpably and undeniably "paternal" ought therefore to be rejected without further inquiry. I consider that so uncompromising an adhesion to the principle "that men are the best guardians of their own welfare" is not rationally justified by the evidence on which the principle rests. I regard this principle as a rough induction from our ordinary experience of human life; as supported on an empirical basis sufficiently strong and wide to throw the *onus probandi* heavily on those who advocate any deviation from it, but in no way proved to be an even approximately universal truth.[56]

Sidgwick recognized that the application of the greatest happiness principle might mean a considerable extension of government activities:

> I see no reason to regard unqualified *laisser faire* as tending to realise the most economical production any more than the best possible distribution of wealth: and it seems to me quite possible that a considerable extension of the industrial functions of government might be on the whole advantageous, without any Utopian degree of moral or political improvement in human society. But at any rate to be successful such extension must, I think, be gradual; and the first experiments in this direction ought to be made in departments in which the defects of private enterprise, and the advantages of unitary administration, have been shewn to be greatest, — *e.g.*, in departments where there is a manifest tendency to the establishment of monopolies in the hands either of single individuals or of associations. And, moreover, it ought to be an object in any such extension to maintain as far as possible in the governmental organisation of industry an effective stimulus to individual exertion, and to allow scope for invention and improvement of methods.[57]

Such other economists of the period as J. E. Cairnes in Britain and F. A. Walker (1840–1897) in the United States supported the Mill-Sidgwick position. *Laissez faire* should be the general rule, they thought, but exceptions should be admitted whenever these seemed likely to add to human happiness.

The Neo-Classical School. For the most part the Neo-Classical economists built upon the superstructure laid by their predecessors, whose writings were studied in the last section. But there was one significant difference. As has been explained in Chapter II, an important group of the later school rejected the hedonistic approach of the earlier writers and endeavored to build up a theoretical system without it. This had repercussions in Neo-Classical ideas respecting government activity.

W. S. Jevons based his economics formally on hedonistic psychology

[56] *Elements of Politics*, p. 131.
[57] *The Principles of Political Economy*, p. 529.

but his treatment of the economic functions of government was pragmatic. Every case should be considered on its merits, he thought. The conclusion of his book on *The State in Relation to Labour* (London 1882) gave a statement of this position:

it is clear that there can be no royal road to legislation in such matters. We cannot expect to agree in our utilitarian estimates, at least without much debate. We must agree to differ, and though we are bound to argue fearlessly, it should be with the consciousness that there is room for wide and *bonâ fide* difference of opinion. We must consent to advance cautiously, step by step, feeling our way, adopting no foregone conclusions, trusting no single science, expecting no infallible guide. We must neither maximise the functions of government at the beck of quasi-military officials, nor minimise them according to the theories of the very best philosophers. We must learn to judge each case upon its merits, interpreting with painful care all experience which can be brought to bear upon the matter.[58]

Other writings of Jevons showed the same viewpoint, notably that on *The Coal Question* (London 1865), to which reference is made in Chapter VI.

The Austrian economists, Emil Sax (1845–1927) and his better-known contemporary Friedrich von Wieser, in line with their general theory, regarded the problem as one of value. It was accepted that the purpose of economic study was to discover how value could be maximized, and government was looked upon as a means to this end. In satisfying their wants, men had two alternatives. They could procure the necessary commodities or services themselves, without government action. Or the government could do the job for them. According to Sax and Wieser, whichever of these courses added more to value should be selected. Governments should take wealth from individuals, by taxation, only if it were believed that this wealth could be so used as to yield a greater gain, not necessarily to the individuals from whom it was taken but to the nation or people as a whole (that is, in the common Neo-Classical view, to the summation of the individuals who made up the nation). Wieser put the point in his *Der natürliche Werth* (Vienna 1889)[59] as follows:

If the state should claim too much, it diminishes value, by expending goods for purposes of state economy which would have a higher value if employed in private economy. If it claims too little, value is again diminished—as in this case also the entire importance of the goods is not realised.[60]

The same principle applied to government regulation of private industry and State operation of industrial enterprises. Undertakings, though

[58] p. 166.
[59] Translated by C. A. Malloch as *Natural Value*, London 1893, reprinted N. Y. 1930.
[60] p. 235 of the translation. Quoted by permission of G. E. Stechert & Co.

profitable to the individuals who owned them, should be restricted if they injured the whole society. Others, not profitable in private hands, might pay from the standpoint of the group:

Just as private economic interests, where they compete with each other, are ranked according to their relative importance, so the interests of private and of national economy are ranked in relation to each other. The more important aim takes precedence of the less important — this forms the theoretic basis on which the estimate of value is built. . . Very frequently it is the same goods that may be employed by either private or national economy; in the last resort, indeed, there is nothing but one fund out of which to provide for both, and only a few goods are from the first specifically reserved for one or the other sphere. A characteristic and common instance of the competition between the two interests occurs where an undertaking, which is profitable as a private business as shown by its calculable return in direct results, is maintained, from the side of national economy, to have an unfavourable, destructive, or undermining effect; that is to say, as regards results which are more remote and difficult to follow. Alongside of this we have the converse instance, that an undertaking which is unprofitable as a private business, and whose valuable returns do not cover the costs, may, from the point of view of national economy, be regarded as profitable. . . It might *e. g.* be disputed whether agriculture or the labouring classes ought to have public subsidy — *i.e.* support which might not be justified, from the point of view of private economy, by the value of the land products or the results of labour, but might be justified if one looked at the maintenance of the stability of the national economy and of the life of the people.[61]

Where Sidgwick had spoken of happiness, Wieser referred to wealth and value. But otherwise there is little difference between the two approaches. Even Wieser did not circumvent the difficulty that, once the valuation of the marketplace was left behind, decision became a matter of opinion. Take, for instance, the choice between present and future gratifications. Writers since the days of Aristotle have said that men tend to make insufficient allowance for future needs and this has often been given as a reason for State action. Yet any scientific comparison between present and future wants is impossible, if only for the reason that no one knows exactly how intense future needs will be.

The English economists, Alfred Marshall and A. C. Pigou, have followed a line possessing a broad similarity to that taken by Sax and Wieser. Marshall, whose interest in the subject of government activity was only incidental and arose from his general value theory, constructed curves that displayed how consumers' and producers' gains might be increased or diminished by government intervention. His conclusion showed the high expectations he held of the practical usefulness of this method and, also, his appreciation of its implications respecting *laissez faire*:

[61] *Ibid.*, pp. 229-230.

It is perhaps not unreasonable to hope that as time goes on, the statistics of consumption will be so organized as to afford demand schedules sufficiently trustworthy, to show in diagrams that will appeal to the eye, the quantities of consumers' surplus that will result from different courses of public and private action. By the study of these pictures the mind may be gradually trained to get juster notions of the relative magnitudes of the interests which the community has in various schemes of public and private enterprise; and sounder doctrines may replace those traditions of an earlier generation, which had perhaps a wholesome influence in their time, but which damped social enthusiasm by throwing suspicion on all projects for undertakings by the public on its own behalf which would not show a balance of direct pecuniary profit.[62]

Full understanding of Marshall's statement may have to await perusal of Chapter IX.

Marshall thought that he had discovered a means whereby comparisons could be made between benefits to the individuals composing society, accruing from private and government action respectively, or from alternative forms of government control. On the basis of such comparisons, decisions upon public policy could be made. This is exactly what Bentham had looked for, in the "moral thermometer," mentioned in Chapter II,[63] except that Marshall abandoned the use of words like pleasure, pain, and happiness, in favor of others—such as benefit—that he thought had fewer hedonistic implications.

Marshall's pupil and successor at Cambridge, A. C. Pigou (1877–), in *Wealth and Welfare* (London 1912) and more especially *The Economics of Welfare* (London 1920, 4th edition 1932), developed a well-rounded theory of government economic activity. Like Sidgwick, Pigou looked upon economics as something of an *art*. It was not merely descriptive but purposeful and its "main motive" was "to help social improvement."[64] What Pigou called *economic welfare* was to be maximized, this being defined as

that part of social welfare that can be brought directly or indirectly into relation with the measuring-rod of money.[65]

The relationship between "satisfactions and dissatisfactions," on the one hand, and money on the other, according to Pigou, was displayed "through desires and aversions."[66] Pigou granted that his "economic welfare" was not an accurate index of welfare as a whole but, of course,

[62] *Principles of Economics*, London 1890, 8th ed., London 1920, pp. 492-493. Quoted by permission of Macmillan & Co., Ltd. and The Macmillan Company.

[63] See p. 109.

[64] *The Economics of Welfare*, 4th ed., p. ix. Quoted by permission of Macmillan & Co., Ltd. and The Macmillan Company.

[65] *Ibid.*, p. 11.

[66] *Ibid.*, p. 23.

it was necessary for him to assume that there was a positive correlation between the two (*i.e.*, more economic welfare = more total welfare; less economic welfare = less total welfare) or there would be no sense in studying economic welfare alone.

Like the happiness which had been Sidgwick's criterion, Pigou's economic welfare was a function involving two components, *quantity* and *distribution*. In the first place, it was assumed that the amount of economic welfare, other things being equal, increased with the size of the *national dividend* or real income of the community:

> Provided that the dividend accruing to the poor is not diminished, increases in the aggregate national dividend of the community, unless they result from coercing people to work more than they wish to do, carry with them increases in economic welfare.[67]

The same applied to greater equality in distribution:

> Changes in the distribution of the national dividend in favour of the poor may be brought about in several ways, the most important of which is by a transference of purchasing power to them from richer persons. . . Except in very special circumstances such a transference must increase economic welfare.[68]

Pigou's general argument was that government action should be favored whenever it appeared likely that economic welfare would be increased, and abstained from in cases where the expectation was that welfare would be diminished. The main fields of modern government intervention were examined in detail in the light of this principle—the operation of industrial enterprises by public bodies, the control of monopoly, wage regulation, unemployment relief, and so forth, with sections which later grew into separate treatises on business cycles and public finance. Undoubtedly, Pigou's work represents one of the chief contributions that have been made to the theory of government intervention and its practical applications.

As such, it must stand or fall by the validity of the assumptions upon which it was based, that is, that individual utilities can be estimated and that the maximization of satisfactions to individuals is a major social objective. To economists who have been trained in the ideas of Smith, Jevons, Sidgwick, and Marshall, the approach of Pigou is very convincing, because its basic postulates are familiar to them. The criticisms have come from those who question the utilitarian assumptions, or rule them out of economic discussion on the ground that they are ethical or psychological but not the kind of thing on which economists can speak with any authority. This subject is discussed further in Chapter IV.

[67] *Ibid.*, p. x, summary of Pt. I, Chap. 7.
[68] *Ibid.*, p. xi, part of summary of Pt. I, Chap. 8.

The Hegelians and the Economic Functions of Government

In the preceding section it was seen that *laissez faire*—whose root in Classical economics rested substantially on the individualistic philosophy of utilitarianism—was in the course of time whittled down, if not destroyed altogether, by the application of the utilitarian theory on which it had been based. Individual happiness had seemed to call for economic freedom : now it appeared to demand the limitation of this freedom. But the writers whose inspiration has been in philosophy such as that of Hegel have never accepted individual happiness as their objective. To Fichte, Hegel, and their successors, the *group,* and especially the *State,* not the individual, was of supreme importance. From this it followed that some concept of a good of the State, or common good, not the greatest happiness of individuals, was the primary end.

Support of State action did not necessarily follow as a corollary of this position. If it were true, as the Hegelians seemed to suggest, that when individuals were associated in a society their individual wills or wants were subordinated to a common will or to common wants, then men could be left alone with the certainty that they would strive to attain the general good. This, to some extent, provided the justification of Marx's theories respecting the rise and progress of the future socialist State. As is shown in Chapter V, Marx visualized that the revolting proletarians would use the State mechanism for the purpose of liquidating the non-proletarian classes, after which the State would disappear. Obviously, only if the individuals, who lived in the future society to which Marx looked forward, were actuated by some kind of common or social will, or at least controlled their personal wills in a manner that enabled them to fit into society, would a community without political government be a practical proposition. The great influence which Hegel exercised over Marx, revealed in various directions, is here apparent.

In the present, however, as distinct from the problematical society of the future, the Hegelians have experienced no difficulty in using their conception of a common or national good to justify State intervention in economic affairs. In England, for example, T. H. Green was instrumental in giving philosophical support to the movement of the Liberal Party—long the advocate of *laissez faire*—in the direction of social reform during the latter part of the nineteenth century. It is interesting to note that, in considering what he called "The right of the State to promote morality," Green, in his *Lectures on the Principles of Political Obligation,* advocated much the same forms of government action as were included by Mill and Sidgwick in their lists of "qualifications and exceptions" to *laissez faire.* There were important differences (as, for example, in regard to property) but in general it seemed that Green's objectives—the development of personality and the realization of freedom

— in practice led to much the same results as did the greatest happiness principle favored by the followers of Bentham.

The statement of the function of the State by the German philosopher, Wundt, in his *Ethik* (Stuttgart 1886, 4th edition 1912),[69] is worth quoting:

> The State performs a pre-eminently moral function in thus seeking with a wise moderation and a due regard for the conditions of historical development to reform society, or, if necessary, to alter its whole constitution. It rescues social structures from the hazards of their mode of origin and adapts them to its own plans, which are guided by the moral purposes of the whole. Society as such lives in the present: but the State is absorbed in the problems of the future, and thus enlists the more transitory forces of social life in the service of enduring ends. It must therefore direct its attention chiefly to the support of all those bonds of association and union among individuals which tend to further a necessary division of labour and the participation of citizens in the general objects sought by the State. And it must seek to obviate all those forms of friction between social classes that operate to retard the moral functions of the whole.[70]

In other words, the State was to promote the common good. But this was not merely happiness. It was something more complex: perhaps, indeed, as Sidgwick said,[71] it was less comprehensible. Certainly, Wundt's standard is no nearer being calculable than that of Sidgwick and Pigou. The general will or common good, which, to men like Green and Wundt, justified reforms that now would be regarded as mildly liberal, may serve no less to support the changes introduced by Lenin or Hitler.

The Institutional Decline of Laissez Faire

In the meantime, government intervention in practical affairs has been growing. At no time was *laissez faire* carried to its logical conclusion. Even in England — where, of the great western countries, the policy was most complete — new forms of government activity were being born before decent burial had been given to the old. Major pieces of Mercantilist legislation, in the shape of the corn laws, the navigation acts, and the Statute of Apprentices, were still on the statute book when the East India Company dividends became subject to regulation, and the first factory act was passed in 1802, forecasting one of the most significant defeats of *laissez faire* doctrines. Working conditions in the newly-established textile factories were bad. Young children were employed for long days, with insufficient rest, inadequate supervision of

[69] Translated by E. B. Tichener and others, as *Ethics*, 3 vols., London and N. Y., 1897-1901.

[70] *Ibid.*, vol. 3, pp. 271-272. Quoted by permission of George Allen & Unwin, Ltd., and The Macmillan Company.

[71] See the second of the two passages quoted on p. 162.

living conditions which resulted in disease and immorality, and little regard for the provision of education. The fiction was that they were apprenticed to the textile manufacturing trade, just as their forebears had been apprenticed to crafts centuries before. Little skill was needed to operate the new machinery. Child labor would serve the purpose and those who lived through their infancy in the factories could not look forward to employment in their adult years, as in the older system of handicraft production. Many of the so-called apprentices were paupers, sent to the factories to relieve the public purse. The factory law of 1802 bore the explanatory title of *An act for the preservation of the health and morals of apprentices and others* . . . and it applied only to a narrow field. Later, women's labor was also regulated but it was a long time before it was recognized officially that adult men required State protection. At first, indeed, this was accepted only with reference to specially unhealthy or dangerous occupations, but ultimately the whole field of industry was covered and an efficient inspectorate built up, so that, unlike the earlier State regulatory system of the sixteenth and seventeenth centuries, the new one was effective.

Another early departure from *laissez faire* principles was in banking regulation, and especially in central banking, a circumstance for which the recurring crises of the nineteenth century were largely responsible. Railroads provided another example of government intervention in economic affairs. Private construction, coupled with a certain amount of government supervision, was the system followed in Britain, where railway development commenced. Regulatory provisions were inserted in railway charters from the beginning, but only toward the close of the century were rates controlled effectively. American regulation of railroad rates dates from the Granger legislation of the 1870's and that of other public utility enterprises from shortly afterwards. Some of the States of south Germany charted out a different path, their railroads being publicly owned from the start. Prussia began with the British system of private enterprise but under Bismarck entered upon a program of nationalization. In France competition was ruled out, in favor of a scheme whereby a few large enterprises parceled out the country between them—a system which was adopted in Britain in 1921 and has been suggested for the United States of America. The policy of State ownership has been followed by different countries in dealing with various public utilities. The postal service has been a government monopoly for most of its history. Roads, too, commonly have been regarded as a government affair. Indeed, usually they have been operated on communist principles, without any charge being levied on those who make use of them. The toll-pikes constructed in England and elsewhere, during the eighteenth and early nineteenth centuries, were public enterprises, not private concerns, and their disappearance with the rise of the railroad led to a reversion to the old communal system. Even Adam Smith regarded elementary education as a suitable function for government bodies. The provision of gas and electricity, though originally undertaken by private companies in many districts, afforded a growing field for municipal enterprise, as did the supply of water.

Wide disparities have developed between different countries in the ownership and management of public utilities. In the English-speaking countries, private enterprise has been dominant in the United States; in Canada, like Great Britain, both private and public undertakings have been important; in the British dominions of the southern hemisphere — Australia, New Zealand, and the Union of South Africa — public ownership has been usual. In France and Germany there have been interesting experiments in the way of mixed public and private concerns. Generally, it can be said that the trend has been in the direction of increased government participation in public utility undertakings, through either operation or control. In other industries government regulation has grown. The anti-trust acts of 1890 and 1914, the activities of the Federal Trade Commission, the far-reaching control of the war years, and the National Industrial Recovery Act of 1933, tell something of the story for the United States of America. The series might be repeated almost indefinitely for other aspects of economic life as well as for other countries, even those regarded as basically individualistic. In the totalitarian States individualism has been liquidated to an even greater extent. And, from all appearances, the end is not yet.

Economic Individualism on the Offensive Again

One result of this great spread of interventionism has been to place economic individualism, which for a hundred years has been on the defensive, in a position to attack once more. Government activity has reached a point where some economists — including Pigou, with respect particularly to unemployment measures — are asking whether harm is not being done. Thus, a leading authority on British unemployment, Sir William Beveridge (1879–), commented on the working of the unemployment insurance scheme in Great Britain in the following terms:

> once it is admitted in principle, that, either under the guise of insurance or in some other form, genuine unemployment can be relieved indefinitely by the simple device of giving money from a bottomless purse, prevention is only too likely to go by the board. The thoughts and time of Governments and Parliaments may be absorbed — as they have largely been absorbed during the past ten years — in successive extensions and variations of the relief scheme. The fear of causing unemployment may vanish from the minds of trade union negotiators and open the way to excessive rigidity of wages and so to the creation of unemployment. Industries practicing casual engagement or perpetual short time may settle down to batten on the taxation of

other industries or of the general public in place of reforming their ways. The immobilising influence of generous unemployment relief upon the recipient can be controlled by Labour Exchange machinery, simply and as completely as we choose. For its immobilising influence on the minds of Governments and leaders of industry the remedies needed are stronger and may be painful.[72]

Lionel Robbins (1898–), of the University of London, has attributed the severity of the depression after 1929 in a large degree to government intervention. In his book, *The Great Depression* (London 1934), Robbins asked and answered a significant question. What were the causal contributions made by private capitalism and State control?

is not the restoration of capitalism [which Robbins favored] the restoration of the causes of depression? If the analysis of this essay is correct, the answer is unequivocal. The conditions of recovery which have been stated do indeed involve the restoration of what has been called capitalism. But the slump was not due to these conditions. On the contrary, it was due to their negation. It was due to monetary mismanagement and State intervention operating in a *milieu* in which the essential strength of capitalism had already been sapped by war and by policy. Ever since the outbreak of war in 1914, the whole tendency of policy has been away from that system, which in spite of the persistence of feudal obstacles and the unprecedented multiplication of the people, produced that enormous increase of wealth per head which was characteristic of the period in which it was dominant. Whether that increase will be resumed, or whether, after perhaps some recovery, we shall be plunged anew into depression and the chaos of planning and restrictionism – that is the issue which depends on our willingness to reverse this tendency.[73]

Robbins's argument was that private enterprise operated through a system of automatic checks. When some commodity was produced in excess, its price declined and in due course the output was reduced. But governments intervened. When there was excess and prices fell, they stepped in with restriction policies, which maintained prices and effectively prevented any natural readjustment. What was needed, said Robbins, was not more government regulation, but less.

The Austrian economist, Ludwig von Mises (1881–), in *Die Gemeinewirtschaft* (1922, 2nd edition, Jena 1932),[74] has asserted that economic individualism is desirable because neither socialism nor the so-called *planning* has anything to offer by way of an alternative means of ensuring the economic utilization of productive resources. It is probably true to say that, on the economic side, Mises's work has fur-

[72] *Unemployment: A Problem of Industry* (1909–1930), London 1930, p. 294. Longmans. The author is now Lord Beveridge.

[73] p. 194. Quoted by permission of Macmillan & Co., Ltd., and The Macmillan Company.

[74] Translated by J. Kahane as *Socialism*, London and N. Y. 1936.

nished the most potent criticism of socialist tendencies in recent years, but detailed consideration of it must be deferred to Chapter IX. Robbins's writings have been in similar vein and, undoubtedly, have gained both inspiration and support from Mises.

A weak point of the arguments in favor of *laissez faire* is that competitive enterprise appears to be in some measure self-defeating in important fields of economic life. Monopolistic organizations have come into existence which themselves restrict or eliminate competition. This argument can be overdone, because conditions that are monopolistic in the short run may become competitive in the longer period. None the less, the problem is a real one. Until comparatively recently it was commonly felt that the government should interfere, whenever this was necessary to preserve or restore competition. Now this doctrine is less popular; and toleration of monopolies, coupled with some form of public regulation, receives greater favor. So completely have ideas and practices altered, that such books as Robbins's *The Great Depression* and Mises's *Socialism* read as though they have come from another world. So, perhaps, they have — the world of Dudley North and Adam Smith. Just as North's *Discourses upon Trade* and Smith's *Wealth of Nations* attacked the obvious defects of Mercantilist regulation, so do the writings of Robbins and Mises assail the interventionism of the twentieth century — which, indeed, has Mercantilist characteristics.

Summary of Chapter

The history of economics during the modern period can be summarized as the rise and decline of *laissez faire*. Even before 1700, certain writers believed that there was something to be said in favor of leaving men to follow their own inclinations. Early in the eighteenth century, moralists were arguing that men had benevolent motives, which directed their actions in accordance with the general well-being. Books began to appear that introduced something of the same viewpoint into economic affairs: men's selfishness, it was said, operated to increase the wealth at the disposal of society and thereby to promote the common good. Adam Smith expressed this view so strongly in his *Wealth of Nations* that what has been described as the bible of modern economics was regarded by many of its author's contemporaries as a polemic in favor of economic freedom. *Laissez faire,* as a theory, reached its high-water point in the works of the Frenchman, Bastiat.

But even Smith admitted that the government must exercise certain economic functions, and later writers gradually widened his list. Applying the utilitarian or greatest happiness criterion, men like John Stuart Mill and Henry Sidgwick justified extensive government interference in economic life. The followers of Hegel, possessed of a conception of

State dominance which the utilitarians rejected, moved even farther along the same road. Socialism became more influential. The result is seen in the world in which we live. Economists support a multitude of government activities and twentieth century counterparts of Adam Smith — men, who, like him, believe in *laissez faire* — are in a position to take the offensive again.

CHAPTER IV

PROPERTY AND THE DISTRIBUTION OF WEALTH

Ideas on property are fundamental to much economic discussion. Are the factors requisite for production held by some individuals to the exclusion of others? If so, in an economy based on price, this will have an important influence on the distribution of incomes. In favor of the system of private property, it has been claimed that the legal recognition of property rights encourages men to produce. The socialists have challenged property in land and capital, and urged that labor alone should confer a title to the produce of human endeavor. Throughout the entire course of history, there have been limitations of, or interference with, property. Property rights have been conditioned by the performance of specified duties. Charity, government assistance to the poor, and taxation of the rich, have existed at various times—perhaps, indeed, at all times. In arguments on the subject, often economic considerations have been subordinated to, or mingled with, those of ethics and of laws. *What is* and *what should be* have not always been separated in men's minds. In consequence, it is necessary to examine the discussion as a whole, though paying special attention to the economic aspect.

Property in the Early Period

Primitive Property

The view that primitive society was characterized by ownership of land in common has had a wide popularity. In a series of German works—of which the *Geschichte der Markenverfassung in Deutschland* (Erlangen 1856) by the legal historian G. L. von Maurer (1790–1872) perhaps is most worthy of mention here—the theory was advanced that the basis of early German agrarian society was the communal *mark*, or village in which land was owned in common. The medieval village community, described in Chapter I, was considered to have descended from this mark, which had become subject to a lord.

Other writers, notably Sir Henry Maine, have argued on similar lines with respect to primitive societies elsewhere. Maine strongly criticized the theories of the history of property that were current in the middle of the nineteenth century. Instead of individual rights of ownership being fully developed in early times, as these beliefs implied, Maine argued that private property developed gradually, as the rights of individuals were separated out of those of the social group. In the patriarchal family, which Maine thought was typical of an early stage of social history, the property rights that reposed in the family head were not his individual possession but were exercised by him on the family's behalf. The family did not die but continued in the persons of the heirs from generation to generation, and its property continued with it. In the ordinary case, inheritance presented no difficulty, since custom decreed who should succeed. If there were no natural heir, adoption remedied the deficiency. What passed from one generation to another was not the mere right to property but a set of obligations that were interlinked and included both rights and duties. *Custom* and *status* dominated early society, according to Maine, and the progress of law was from custom and status towards *contract*. Maine admitted that in no society was contract absent altogether. Within the early families, it was true that individuals had no independent rights of contract but one family could contract with another through the respective family heads. Individual contract was a later development, he said. Maine drew largely on Indian and Irish evidence, as well as that of Roman law, his conclusions being published in *Ancient Law* (London 1861), *Village Communities in East and West* (London 1871), *Lectures on the Early History of Institutions* (London 1875) and *Dissertations on Early Law and Custom* (London 1883). Maine's thesis accorded with the mark theory. His view, as given in *Ancient Law*, was that

> We have the strongest reason for thinking that property once belonged not to individuals nor even to isolated families, but to larger societies composed on the patriarchal model. . .[1]

The Belgian economist, E. L. V. de Laveleye (1822–1892), in *De la propriété et de ses formes primitives* (Paris 1874),[2] generalized from data relating to a large number of countries and reached the same conclusion. Communism, he said, not private property, was characteristic of primitive society. This view was attractive to the socialists and it was incorporated in Engels's book on *The Origin of the Family, Private Property and the State*. Engels asserted vigorously that the family arose out of primitive promiscuity and that private property developed from early communism. The State was the means by which the propertied classes preserved their so-called rights of ownership. This idea of the origin of property and of the State is to be found in the works of Locke and other social contract theorists, discussed below. But Locke and his fellows had no adequate evidence in support of their contention that early society was communistic. Maurer, Maine, and others, appeared to remedy this deficiency. So, with an acknowledgment to Maurer, the general features of the idea of primitive communism were incorporated in the later editions of the famous *Manifesto of the Communist Party (Communist Manifesto)*, first issued by Marx and Engels in 1848 and subsequently revised.

[1] Pollock's edition, p. 279.

[2] Translated by G. R. L. Marriott, as *Primitive Property*, London 1878.

The Maurer-Maine theories have been combatted by other writers. As has been mentioned, Westermarck has controverted the idea that marriage arose out of promiscuity. A French historian, N. D. Fustel de Coulanges (1830–1889), assailed Maurer's communal village theory, in his *Histoire des institutions politiques de l'ancienne France* (6 vols., Paris 1875–1892) and other works. Fustel de Coulanges sifted the evidence used by Maurer and showed that it need not bear the interpretation put upon it by the German author, reaching the conclusion that the communal mark theory was untenable.[3] An English historian, Frederic Seebohm (1833–1912), advanced an alternative explanation of the origin of the medieval village community to that of Maurer. Not the free mark of Maurer but the unfree Roman *villa* or plantation, according to Seebohm, was the beginning of the medieval village. Later and more exhaustive researches by B. H. Baden-Powell (1841–1901),[4] in one of the fields that had been explored by Maine, namely India (where both men spent some years in public service), did much to upset the earlier writer's conclusions respecting that country. In the light of Baden-Powell's studies, it seems clear that there was no "typical" Indian village community, at least of the type described by Maine.

Recent anthropological inquiries have added considerably to our knowledge of primitive forms of property. In many savage societies, private property in land, as it exists in England or America, is not to be found. Land is not regarded as an economic good but as a heritage in which all have certain rights. Once it has been allotted, however, usually to a family head, rights belong to the individual or family rather than to the entire group. This is well seen in polygamous societies, such as the African Ubena.[5] The produce raised by one wife is available to sustain her and her children, but not for the support of other wives and their dependents. True, the husband may dispose of the surplus produce in the market but if he does so he is expected to bring back a present for the wife whose labor has been responsible for the crop. Should one wife be unfortunate, on account of illness or crop failure, no objection is raised to assistance from her family, but the husband fares ill who utilizes the produce raised by a hardworking but perhaps plain wife, for the support of another who is pretty but lazy. Commonly in Africa it is accepted that once land has been allotted to a family, this has the right of continued possession; but, while a son may succeed his parent, there is not the right of unrestricted inheritance which elsewhere has led to great inequalities of wealth. Allotments are confined to what can be

[3] The same view has been taken by Dopsch. See this writer's *The Economic and Social Foundations of European Civilization*, where the literature on the subject is surveyed.

[4] See *The Indian Village Community*, London 1896.

[5] A. T. and G. M. Culwick give an account of the life of this tribe in their *Ubena of the Rivers*, London 1935.

tilled by the occupants and is needed for their support and, in the absence of a system of hiring laborers, larger areas are useless to their possessors. What each savage family has, therefore, is the right to a holding of standard size, not to a fractional plot or a large tract. Where inheritance is recognized, a son or other heir may pay his predecessor for the privilege of early entry. Even where there is an appearance of communal ownership, as is the case with the Trobriand Island canoes described by Malinowski and referred to in Chapter II, although the canoes are built and operated by co-operative labor the produce is not shared communally but is divided in a manner determined with great precision, in accordance with the several rights of the parties concerned. Within the family, savages recognize property rights that are ignored in civilized society. Thus, the American anthropologist, R. H. Lowie, in his *Primitive Society* (New York 1920), mentioned the example of a Crow Indian who bought from his mother the right to use a particular ceremonial paint. The fact that family ties are less stable in many primitive communities than is the case in modern Europe or America, leads to more attention in the former to the demarcation of *mine* and *thine,* as between husband and wife. The possibility of severance of the marital relationship makes it necessary for both parties to be clear as to the ownership of property. Cattle may be reserved as the wife's possession in order that the animals may be available for the maintenance of her family should the husband no longer serve in this capacity. In general, however, savage women are more self-supporting than is the case in advanced cultures. Thus it is seen that, while recent anthropological studies lend a certain amount of support to the hypothesis of primitive communism, the matter appears to be very much more complex than Maurer believed. If, in one direction, there is a good deal of communism, in another, namely the family, there is distinctly less than exists in present-day England and America.

The Ancient World

The nature of property rights. The main features of property in the patriarchal society which seems to have prevailed over much of the Mediterranean country in early times have been described already. The essential point is that rights were concentrated in the person of the family head, or patriarch, on behalf of the group.

This situation appears to have influenced the attitude toward property in the settled societies of the ancient world. In early Egypt, theoretically the land was owned by the Pharaoh in the name of the deity and private property in it was unknown (though in practice for a time something in the nature of feudalism existed, the land being administered by lords). In Greece it was accepted that private rights were subordinate to the interest of the State. The inferior status of women was to some extent explained by this fact. They were not merely their husbands' possessions but the State's instruments for the perpetuation of the race. Rights in land and goods were likewise limited by the needs of the State. Greek colonists were not granted unconditional ownership of the land they occupied but held possession subject to a residence obligation. If they left to return to the mother country, they had to furnish successors in the persons of sons or others. People of wealth were expected to make contributions for the maintenance of temples and other public purposes. Taxation proper, therefore, was levied on aliens and bondmen rather than on free citizens, and this remained generally true of the ancient world. When necessity arose, the State did not hesitate to interfere with property rights. Perhaps the most notable example of such interference in Greece was the legislation of Solon. Apparently for the purpose of maintaining the class of small property owners, mortgages were canceled and freedom restored to those who had lost it for non-payment of debts—an early instance of the debt-adjustment which was common in various countries during the depression of the 1930's.

In Rome the *patria potestas,* or right of the family-head over the family group, gave the parent extensive powers over the persons and possessions of his children and other dependents. Though he might permit ownership of goods by those who were subject to his authority, in law such goods were his alone, with the exception of any that had been earned by military service. As time passed by, however, the range of exceptions was extended and property rights became more diverse. Ownership could be secured by occupancy. Some things had never possessed an owner, such as wild animals or newly-discovered lands. Others were temporarily ownerless, as was the case with movables that had been abandoned or land left unoccupied. In either case, whoever took possession acquired ownership, though, as Maine remarked,

> The chances surely are that his right to possession would be exactly co-extensive with his power to keep it, and that he would be constantly liable to disturbance by the first comer who coveted the spot and thought himself strong enough to drive away the possessor.[6]

Things already owned, however, had to be conveyed properly. A distinction was drawn between *res mancipi* (land, slaves, and laboring cattle), where *mancipation* or formal transfer was necessary, and *res nec mancipi,* where simple delivery was enough to pass ownership. Maine regarded this difference as being due to the circumstance that the first of these types of property assumed importance at an earlier date, when all transfers took place in a formal or ceremonial manner. The source of the property was important. Thus, with respect to India, Maine said:

[6] *Ancient Law,* p. 266.

The inherited property of the father is shared by the children as soon as they are born; but according to the custom of most provinces, the acquisitions made by him during his lifetime are wholly his own, and can be transferred by him at pleasure.[7]

Whatever is concluded as to the property law of the preceding period, by the time of the Twelve Tables (about 450 B.C.) Roman property law had become largely individualistic. Thus it can be said that the evolution of property law in the ancient world was toward individualism. Private property, which in Egypt was non-existent at least in land and in early Greece was relatively unimportant, came to the front. Even in Rome, however, private property rights were not entirely unlimited. The social interest received recognition, as when public rights of way across private grounds were upheld and when it was forbidden to build as far as the boundary of a lot. The owner's rights over slaves were restricted. Lastly, income was redistributed to a certain extent by means of the fiscal system, a famous example being the corn law of Gracchus, which established the practice of subsidizing the food of the Roman populace at the cost of the provinces.

Plato and Aristotle. The outstanding contributions of classical literature to ideas on property are to be found in the discussions of Plato and Aristotle on communism. In connection with his scheme for an ideal State, put forward in the *Republic,* Plato suggested a system of communal property for the guardians or administrators of the State. This included wives and children, be it noted, as well as goods. The advantages of this arrangement, Plato remarked, were as follows:

Then now let us consider what will be their way of life [*i.e.,* that of the guardians], if they are to realize our idea of them. In the first place, none of them should have any property of his own beyond what is absolutely necessary; neither should they have a private house or store closed against any one who has a mind to enter; their provisions should be only such as are required by trained warriors, who are men of temperance and courage, they should agree to receive from the citizens a fixed rate of pay, enough to meet the expenses of the year and no more; and they will go to mess and live together like soldiers in a camp. . . But should they ever acquire homes or lands or moneys of their own, they will become housekeepers and husbandmen instead of guardians, enemies and tyrants instead of allies of the other citizens; hating and being hated, plotting and being plotted against, they will pass their whole life in much greater terror of internal than of external enemies, and the hour of ruin, both to themselves and to the rest of the State, will be at hand.[8]

Both the community of property and the community of families . . . tend to make them more truly guardians; they will not tear the city to pieces by

[7] *Ibid.,* p. 290.

[8] *The Dialogues of Plato,* vol. 3, p. 106.

differing about 'mine' and 'not mine;' each man dragging any acquisition which he has made into a separate house of his own, where he has a separate wife and children and private pleasures and pains; but all will be affected as far as may be by the same pleasures and pains because they are all of one opinion about what is near and dear to them, and therefore they all tend towards a common end. . . And as they have nothing but their persons which they can call their own, suits and complaints will have no existence among them; they will be delivered from all those quarrels of which money or children or relations are the occasion.[9]

Obviously, Plato's arguments were political, not economic. Private property was to be forbidden to public officials in order that corruption and dissension might be minimized. In his more practical *Laws,* Plato abandoned the communism of the *Republic,* substituting a form of peasant proprietorship. Thus, speaking of the establishment of a city, he said:

Let the citizens at once distribute their land and houses, and not till the land in common, since a community of goods goes beyond their proposed origin, and nurture, and education. But in making the distribution, let the several possessors feel that their particular lots also belong to the whole city. . .[10]

Inequality of property was permitted in the *Laws,* because people were themselves unequal:

for servants and masters never can be friends, nor good and bad, merely because they are declared to have equal privileges. For to unequals equals become unequal, if they are not harmonised by measure; and both by reason of equality, and by reason of inequality, cities are filled with seditions.[11]

However, Plato said that this inequality should be kept within limits:

Let the limit of poverty be the value of the lot; this ought to be preserved, and no ruler, nor any one else who aspires after a reputation for virtue, will allow the lot to be impaired in any case. This the legislator gives as a measure, and he will permit a man to acquire double or triple, or as much as four times the amount of this.[12]

Any wealth that the citizen possessed beyond this limit was to go to the State, a bonus being offered to informers. Evidently what Plato sought was some sort of compromise between the ideal of equality and the inequality which practical conditions seemed to necessitate.

To the communistic arguments of Plato's *Republic,* Aristotle replied with psychological and economic objections. In the opinion of the later philosopher, man's nature was such that he enjoyed the possession of property:

[9] *Ibid.,* p. 159.
[10] *Ibid.,* vol. 5, p. 122.
[11] *Ibid.,* p. 137.
[12] *Ibid.,* p. 127.

how immeasurably greater is the pleasure, when a man feels a thing to be his own. . .[13]

Moreover, if people did not share equally in toil as well as enjoyment,

those who labour much and get little will necessarily complain of those who labour little and receive or consume much.[14]

In addition,

there is another objection to the proposal [of Plato]. For that which is common to the greatest number has the least care bestowed upon it. Every one thinks chiefly of his own, hardly at all of the common interest; and only when he is himself concerned as an individual. For besides other considerations, everybody is more inclined to neglect the duty which he expects another to fulfil; as in families many attendants are often less useful than a few. Each citizen will have a thousand sons who will not be his sons individually, but anybody will be equally the son of anybody, and will therefore be neglected by all alike.[15]

The last sentence of this passage refers, of course, to Plato's scheme for community of wives and children. Thus, where Plato had rested his argument for equality on the needs of the State, against it Aristotle set the happiness of the individual and the stimulus of property to human industry.

As is pointed out in Chapter IX, Aristotle appeared to favor a system of pricing that rewarded people according to their station in life. Yet the philosopher was not an unqualified opponent of equalitarianism. He advocated the limitation of inheritances, "for in this way properties will be equalized, and more of the poor rise to competency."[16] Justifying this, he said:

It is a principle common to democracy, oligarchy, and every other form of government not to allow the disproportionate increase of any citizen, but to give moderate honour for a long time rather than great honour for a short time. For men are easily spoilt; not every one can bear prosperity. . . Especially should the laws provide against any one having too much power, whether derived from friends or money. . .[17]

Common meals, such as existed in Sparta, were to be provided free, because "it is not easy for the poor to contribute the requisite sum out of their private means, and to provide also for their household."[18] The expenses of worship, also, were to be a public charge, met by the allocation of a portion of the public land. Finally, Aristotle advocated a combination of private ownership and public use of property:

I do not think that property ought to be common, as some maintain, but

[13] *The Works of Aristotle,* vol. 10, *Politica,* 1263a.
[14] *Ibid.*
[15] *Ibid.,* 1261b-1262a.
[16] *Ibid.,* 1309a.
[17] *Ibid.,* 1308b.
[18] *Ibid.,* 1330a.

only that by friendly consent there should be a common use of it; and that no citizen should be in want of subsistence.[19]

Unfortunately, this point was not elucidated.

To twentieth century people it appears that Plato was a revolutionary and Aristotle more conservative. In the then-existing Greek situation, however, the opposite was the case. Greece had moved away from the socialistic system of patriarchal times toward something more individualistic, so that it was Plato who was a conservative and Aristotle a liberal, arguing in support of individualism.

Christianity and the Middle Ages

Equality among the early Christians. It is said very commonly that the early Christions practiced communism. This view finds support in the *Acts of the Apostles*:

And all that believed were together, and had all things common; And sold their possessions and goods, and parted them to all men, as every man had need.[20]

And the multitude of them that believed were of one heart and of one soul: neither said any of them that ought of the things which he possessed was his own; but they had all things common. . . Neither was there any among them that lacked: for as many of them as were possessors of lands or houses sold them, and brought the prices of the things that were sold, And laid them down at the apostles' feet: and distribution was made unto every man according as he had need.[21]

Following this statement, a comparison was made between the deeds of Joses or Barnabus, who disposed of his possessions in this manner, and of Ananias and Sapphira, who kept back a part of the price from Peter and the other apostles and were punished by God with death in consequence. Not unnaturally, "great fear came upon all the church, and upon as many as heard these things."[22]

Cyprian took at its face value this description of early Christian practices, saying:

Let us consider, beloved brethren, what the congregation of believers did in the time of the apostles, when at the first beginnings the mind flourished with greater virtues, when the faith of believers burned with a warmth of faith as yet new. Then they sold houses and farms, and gladly and liberally presented to the apostles the proceeds to be dispensed to the poor; selling and alienating their earthly estate, they transferred their lands thither where they might receive the fruits of an eternal possession, and there prepared homes where they might begin an eternal habitation. . . This is truly to become sons of God by spiritual birth; this is to imitate by the heavenly law the equity

[19] *Ibid.*, 1329b-1330a.

[20] *Acts*, 2, vv. 44-45.

[21] *Acts*, 4, vv. 32-35.

[22] *Acts*, 5, v. 11.

of God the Father. For whatever is of God is common in our use; nor is any one excluded from His benefits and His gifts, so as to prevent the whole human race from enjoying equally the divine goodness and liberality.[23]

In this statement, Cyprian seemed to be holding out communism as a counsel of perfection; but only a short time before him Tertullian had written as though it were still the usual practice among believers:

One in mind and soul, we do not hesitate to share our earthly goods with one another. All things are common among us but our wives.[24]

Yet, other passages in the writings of the early Fathers make it clear that private property was not abandoned altogether by professing Christians. Thus Tertullian told how the Church was supported and the manner in which its revenue was expended:

Though we have our treasure-chest, it is not made up of purchase-money, as of a religion that has its price. On the monthly collection day, if he likes, each puts in a small donation; but only if it be his pleasure, and only if he be able: for there is no compulsion; all is voluntary. These gifts are, as it were, piety's deposit fund. For they are not taken thence and spent on feasts, and drinking-bouts, and eating-houses, but to support and bury poor people, to supply the wants of boys and girls destitute of means and parents, and of old persons confined now to the house; such, too, as have suffered shipwreck; and if there happen to be any in the mines, or banished to the islands, or shut up in the prisons, for nothing but their fidelity to the cause of God's church, they become the nurslings of their confession.[25]

Cyprian, speaking of alms, said:

In which example of equality [or equity], he who, as a possessor in the earth, shares his returns and his fruits with the fraternity, while he is common and just in his gratuitous bounties, is an imitator of God the Father.[26]

Both of these statements obviously assumed that the Christians retained in their possession private wealth, out of which gifts to the Church were made.

Even in the early Christian period communism went further among the disciples or teachers than in the general body of believers, and this is more true of a later date. Persons who became members of religious orders gave up their property to the general body; but Godly charity, rather than communism, was what was expected of the rank and file of Christians. There was considerable variation in the manner in which the possessions acquired by religious orders were treated. In some cases, these organizations became wealthy in goods that were regarded as the common property of the body and were withheld from outsiders. In

[23] *Ante-Nicene Christian Library,* vol. 13, *On Works and Alms,* pp. 19-20.
[24] *Ibid.,* vol. 11, *Apology,* p. 120. [25] *Ibid.,* p. 119.
[26] *Ibid.,* vol. 13, *On Works and Alms,* p. 20.

others, gifts were made with great generosity and the religious societies themselves remained very poor.

Items of property remaining at the disposal of believers were not looked upon as their personal belongings entirely. The earth and all that was in it were the Lord's so that the ultimate dominion rested with God. At the most, it was the right of private use in the service of God that was accepted, rather than any personal utilization of possessions. As has been explained in connection with wealth generally, there came to be two views on the subject of property. Basil (c. 330–379, Bishop of Cæsarea in Palestine) and Ambrose (c. 340–397, Bishop of Milan) represented the radical standpoint that private property was un-Christian:

The rich who deem as their own property the common goods they have seized upon, are like to those who by going beforehand to the play prevent others from coming, and appropriate to themselves what is intended for the common use.[27]

Let no man call his own that which is common property. . .[28]

Augustine spoke as if the opposite view were the common one, and communistic practices exceptional:

The 'Apostolici' are those who with extreme arrogance have given themselves that name, because they do not admit into their communion persons who are married or possess anything of their own, such as both monks and clerics who in considerable number are to be found in the Catholic Church.[29]

Thomas Aquinas. The problem of whether it was just for the Christian man to possess property was still debated at the close of the middle ages. Thomas Aquinas considered conflicting arguments on the question of "Whether it is lawful for a man to possess a thing of his own" and gave his own opinion as follows:

I answer that, Two things are competent to man in respect of exterior things. One is the power to procure and dispense them, and in this regard it is lawful for man to possess property. Moreover this is necessary to human life for three reasons. First because every man is more careful to procure what is for himself alone than that which is common to many or to all: since each one would shirk the labour and leave to another that which concerns the community, as happens where there is a great number of servants. Secondly, because human affairs are conducted in more orderly fashion if each man is charged with taking care of some particular thing himself, whereas there would be confusion if everyone had to look after any one thing indeterminately. Thirdly, because a more peaceful state is ensured to man if each one is contented with his own. Hence it is to be observed that quarrels arise more frequently where there is no division of the things possessed.

[27] Basil, quoted by Aquinas, *Summa theologica,* Pt. 2, Second Pt., Q. 66, Art. 2.
[28] Ambrose, quoted *Ibid.* [29] *Ibid.*

The second thing that is competent to man with regard to external things is their use. In this respect man ought to possess external things, not as his own, but as common, so that, to wit, he is ready to communicate them to others in their need. Hence the Apostle says . . . *Charge the rich of this world . . . to give easily, to communicate to others,* etc.[30]

Here there appears, first, an economic argument in favor of individual possession of property. Aquinas said that production would be greater under a system of private property than under communism – a point that was mentioned by Aristotle, as has been noted. Next, two political reasons were put forward. Order and peace were preserved by private property – a view that was anticipated by Aristotle, also, though diametrically opposed to Plato's opinion. Lastly, it was pointed out that Aquinas was not justifying private property in any absolute form but rather private property limited by the condition that those who possessed it would communicate it "to others in their need." Basil's argument, quoted above, was admitted by Aquinas but qualified. According to the later teacher private property was unjust only if it were used in a manner that excluded or injured others:

A man would not act unlawfully if by going beforehand to the play he prepared the way for others: but he acts unlawfully if by so doing he hinders others from going. In like manner a rich man does not act unlawfully if he anticipates someone in taking possession of something which at first was common property, and gives others a share: but he sins if he excludes others indiscriminately from using it. Hence Basil says (*ibid.*): *Why are you rich while another is poor, unless it be that you may have the merit of a good stewardship, and he the reward of patience?* . . . When Ambrose says: *Let no man call his own that which is common,* he is speaking of ownership as regards use, wherefore he adds: *To spend more than enough is to take by violence.*[31]

Ownership by God, with individual usufruct, therefore, may be taken as characterizing the Christian position, but it must be understood that such usufruct did not mean usage by the individual for his own personal benefit, but utilization for the general good and for the glory of the Lord.

On the subject of the distribution of wealth, reference should be made to the section of Chapter IX in which the views of Aquinas are discussed. Not equality, but incomes that varied according to the social stations of the persons concerned, received the support of the great Dominican teacher.

The feudal system. The rise of feudalism was not coincident with that of Christianity. The new religion had permeated the Roman Empire before the decline of the Imperial power produced the conditions that were responsible for the appearance of the feudal system. In a cer-

[30] *Ibid.* [31] *Ibid.*

tain way, feudalism can be said to have carried property back to the position it had occupied in the earliest days of Mediterranean civilization. Individual property, which had been developed over a long period and had reached a high point in Rome in the days of its greatness, was destroyed.

Under the feudal system, private property in any absolute or individual form was unknown. Typically, an "owner" of land held it *of* someone else, that is to say, he possessed it by grant from a superior or lord, subject to the fulfillment of prescribed duties. The cultivator held the land he worked on the condition of rendering labor and other services to his lord. He had to work so many days per week or as called upon by his superior, on the estate of the latter, and he had to pay fines and fees of various kinds. His superior, in turn, held from the king and was obliged to render military service to him, as well as to pay taxes. As an example of the kind of duties a lord owed to his king, the *Rectitudines singularum personarum* (*i.e.*, duties of separate persons), an English document dated about 1000, may be quoted, although it antedates the final form of feudalism in England:

> The thegn's law is that he be worthy of his book-right, and that he do three things for his land, fyrdfare [military service], burhbote [repair of castles and town walls], and bridge-work [repair of bridges].[32]

In the lower strata the people themselves were not free but were in the position of serfs, personally bound to their lord and unable to leave his service. Their property was the lord's because they themselves were his. Accordingly, they could be tallaged or taxed at the lord's will, even to the full amount of the property in their possession. Obviously, if this were done, serfs engaged in agriculture or, as was sometimes the case, in industry and trade, were left with no inducement to produce efficiently. It was not until later, however, that writers pointed this out.

At the apex of the system was the king and only of him could there be said to be any absolute property in land. Even here, there were two important limitations. First, kings who professed Christianity were in the position of other Christians. They "held," as it were, from God himself and owed to Him the duty of using their property in accordance with His will and for the general good. This restriction was more serious than might be thought nowadays because the Church could, and did, bring pressure to bear upon kings who departed from religious precepts. On the other hand, often the Church itself was placed in a position of subordination, because bishops and other religious dignitaries held lands from kings on feudal terms, exactly like their lay contemporaries. The second limitation was the necessity imposed on kings to act in such a manner as not to antagonize unduly their subjects and

[32] A. E. Bland, P. A. Brown, and R. H. Tawney, *English Economic History: Select Documents*, p. 5.

others. The experience of the English King John (King 1199–1216) serves as an example of the fate that was likely to overtake any monarch who transgressed this rule.[33]

There seem to have been some men of property who stood outside the feudal system—who were so free that "they could go with their land whither they would,"[34] that is, they could break their attachments to one lord and take their allegiance—and their land—elsewhere. Manumission and the flight of serfs to the growing cities added to the number of free men. Inheritance was a major problem. Once it was recognized that a man's son had a right to inherit his land, an essential feature of the feudal system was destroyed, yet this right was conceded widely. There is evidence that serfs were permitted to possess chattels of their own and, on occasion, were allowed to use them to purchase their freedom. Obviously, there was no legal basis for this practice, because a serf could not employ for such a purpose goods that were in the eyes of the law the property of his lord. Fines in the form of payments of money or goods were commonly exacted by the superior when his rights were foregone. When a son succeeded his father in the possession of land that the superior (baron or king) had a legal right to bestow elsewhere, it appeared reasonable enough that the successor should pay for the privilege. But in a social system in which custom was a ruling factor, these fines tended to become fixed. In the course of time, the purchasing power of the fixed payments declined until, in many instances, they became negligible. This, in effect, is the history of copyhold tenure in England. The copyholder was the descendant of the medieval serf, and his title to land was contained in a *copy* of the manor roll that indicated the dues for which he was liable. As time passed and prices rose, especially during the great inflation of the sixteenth and seventeenth centuries, it became a matter of considerable importance to the parties concerned whether or not sons had the right to inherit their fathers' holdings subject to the payment of fixed fees or fines to their lords. Those copyholds that were in this position became virtually freeholds. But many cultivators were not on such land. Either they rented farms previously in the lords' possession, or were on peasant land where there was no fixed inheritance fine. The land they occupied came to belong to the lords, much of it being let out to farmers for cash rents. True, the lords remained liable for certain services to the king; but military service was replaced by taxes, that ultimately became an integral part of the tax system, and such governmental duties as court-holding passed into disuse with the extension of the functions of the central government. Formally, the old feudal system cannot be said to

[33] John's barons rose in rebellion, compelling him to sign a charter of rights. As a result, the forerunner of the present English parliament was set up.

[34] F. W. Maitland, *Domesday Book and Beyond,* p. 49.

have disappeared yet in Britain. It is still the case that a British "owner" of land "holds" it from the king, but this is no more than a vestige of the past system and, for practical purposes, the English freeholder is as free from duties as his American counterpart.

On the Continent the feudal system of landholding had a different history. In France, in the middle of the eighteenth century, onerous dues still remained payable by the peasants to their lords. Their abolition, in the early days of the Revolution, destroyed the feudal system of landholding and conferred proprietorship on many peasants. In central and eastern Europe feudalism lasted longer. Generally, however, it can be said that the system disappeared everywhere in either of the two ways that have been mentioned. Either (1) the descendants of the medieval serfs lost their status on the land, so that alteration of the relations of the lord to the king left the lord in the position of a landowner, or (2) abolition or commutation of the serf's duties to the lord converted the serf into a peasant proprietor.

The controversy respecting the relationship between Church and State, referred to in Chapter I, was reflected in theories of property rights. Thus the Italian jurist, Martinus (one of the famous "Four Doctors" of Bologna), about 1150, ascribed to the temporal ruler an absolute right of property, while on the Church side this was claimed for the Pope. Against the asserted rights of State and Church it was argued by Bulgarus, another of the "Four Doctors" and a contemporary of Martinus, that what stood above individual property rights was not ownership but *superiority*. In other words, land or goods were not *held* of a higher authority but *owned* by the man who possessed them, subject to some limitations imposed by the existence of the superiority. It was admitted that the superiority included the right of expropriation but only for "good cause" (*i.e.*, crime or public necessity), and not arbitrarily; and, as some jurists had it, the case of land taken because of public necessity was subject to payment of compensation. Obviously, this came very close to the legal theory of property as its exists in America and England at present.

Modern Times

The changes in the landholding system and in the Church were reflected in the emergence of new ideas on property rights.

Equalitarianism in the Sixteenth and Seventeenth Centuries

More and Bodin. One of the most famous protests against inequality was the *Utopia* of Sir Thomas More (1478–1535), published at Louvain in 1516 and translated into English in 1551. More was a high official of the English king but was out of sympathy with much that he saw around him. Greedy landlords were turning peasant cultivators from the soil and therefore from their means of livelihood, in order to make profits from sheep farming. There were many abuses in the Church. A willful and despotic monarch was surrounded by a court that was one of the most luxurious in Europe, though many of the people at whose cost it was maintained were extremely poor. More was both religious and courageous and ultimately lost his head for opposition to the King's policies. In *Utopia,* he sought escape to what he thought was a better civilization and, in doing so, uttered his protest against the existing one. *Utopia* is described in some detail in Chapter V and requires no long consideration here, it being sufficient to note that the Utopian economic system was based upon the communistic principle of equality in production and distribution.

Perhaps the most outstanding statement on the other side, made during the sixteenth century, was that of the French political philosopher, Jean Bodin. Recognizing More's work to be not merely an entertaining fantasy but a serious assault on private property, Bodin coupled it with similar ideas exemplified in the laws of Solon and the writings of Plato. The abolition of debts—such as had been undertaken by Solon in ancient Greece and transfered wealth from creditor to debtor classes—was discussed. Like modern insurance companies that advertise against currency inflation, Bodin pointed out that creditors were often poor and deserving, and that it was not for the general good that they should be despoiled:

> generall abolitions do most commonly hurt the poore, and ruine many, for the poore widowes, orphelins, and meaner sort having nothing but some little rent, are undone when this abolition of debts comes; whereas the usurers prevent it, and oftentimes gaine by it: as it happened when as *Solon* and *Agis* did publish an abolition of debts, for the usurers (having some intelligence thereof) borrowed money of all men, to defraud their creditors.[35]

Bodin said that, if debts were reduced, the hope of additional reductions or abolitions would encourage people to run further into debt and then to agitate for legislation in their favor. Thrift would be discouraged:

> the hope of these abolitions do incourage the prodigall to borrow at what rate soever, and when their credit is crackt, to joyne with the poore which are discontented and desperate, and to stir up seditions: whereas if the hope of these abolitions were not, every one would seek to governe his estate wisely, and to live in peace.[36]

Equality, indeed, according to Bodin, would be the ruin of human society:

> If it be unjust for the creditor to lose his goods, and the debtor to gaine that which is not his, how much more unjust is it to take land from the lawfull owners to enrich other men with their spoyles: for they that seeke to be freed

[35] *The Six Books of a Common Weale,* p. 570.
[36] *Ibid.*

from their debts, pretend the oppression of usurie, and the barren nature of silver . . . so as we may rightly say, that such a division of another mans goods, is a meere robberie under a shew of equalitie, and the ruine not only of a Commonweale, but of all human societie.[37]

Lastly, Bodin said that unless population or inheritances were controlled, even after equality had been attained, differences in the numbers of children in the various families would soon bring about inequality again.

But, notwithstanding this criticism of equality, Bodin was prepared to admit that there was something to be said against undue disparity in the wealth possessed by different individuals. Riches were not wholly beneficial. Poverty was a stimulus to useful activity. The "younger sons" of Sparta, he commented, who had nothing to advance them but their virtues, were those who became most famous.

Agrarian unrest and Gerrard Winstanley. Not unnaturally, the breaking of the peasant's hold on the soil, which has been described already, was accompanied by considerable dissatisfaction in the rural areas. In England the Pilgrimage of Grace (1536) and the Norfolk revolt led by Robert Ket or Kett (1549) were in part explained by this fact. These movements were suppressed, however, and for a time no serious uprisings took place, though the attempts of the English government to maintain the position of the peasant cultivators were not very effective. After the defeat of royal absolutism in the Civil War of the seventeenth century, agrarian unrest reappeared. The reforms introduced by the victorious parliamentary party, led by Oliver Cromwell, were insufficient to satisfy some of its adherents and discontent arose, even in the army itself, finding its expression in the *Leveller* movement of the 1640's and 50's. The name Leveller signified one of the objectives sought—the principle that everyone should be placed on a level, or made equal. Many of the Levellers appear to have desired only political equality but Gerrard Winstanley (born 1609?) and his followers, called Diggers, attacked private property. In 1649 the Diggers took possession of an area of untilled land close to London and began to cultivate it. In a pamphlet entitled *A Watchword to the City of London and the Army* (1649), Winstanley justified the action on two grounds. (1) In so far as the owners claimed possession of their land by divine right, it was replied that land was intended by God to be a "Common Treasury" and not the exclusive property of a few men. (2) If, on the other hand, the owners rested their claims on conquest, the answer was that the former conquerors had been defeated (when King Charles I was overthrown by the parliamentary forces) and their claims destroyed. Those who had shared in the new conquest should obtain possession of the land, Winstanley said:

[37] *Ibid.*

we justify our act of digging. . . First, *because the Earth was made by Almighty God to be a Common Treasury of Livelihood to the whole of mankind in all its branches, without respect of persons. . .* Secondly, because all sorts of people have lent assistance of purse and person to cast out the kingly order as being a burden that England groaned under. Therefore those from whom money and blood were received, ought to obtain freedom in the Land to themselves and posterity, by the Law of Contract between Parliament and People. But all sorts, poor as well as rich, Tenant as well as Land Lord, have paid taxes, free-quarter, excise, or adventured their lives to cast out the kingly office. Therefore all sorts of people ought to have freedom in this the Land of their Nativity, without respecting persons, now that kingly power is cast out by their joint assistance.[38]

In a later publication, *The Law of Freedom in a Platform: Or True Magistracy Restored* (1652), which has been compared[39] with More's *Utopia,* Winstanley made a more general plea for equality. The exclusive right of a few men to own the land being rejected, the conclusion was drawn that all incomes not gained as the result of personal labor represented exploitation:

But shall not one man be richer than another?

There is no need for that; for riches make men vainglorious, proud, and to oppress their brethren, and are the occasion of wars. No man can be rich but he must be rich either by his own labors, or by the labors of other men helping him. If a man have no help from his neighbors, he shall never gather an estate of hundreds and thousands a year. If other men help him to work, then are those riches his neighbor's as well as his; for they be the fruits of other men's labors as well as his own. But all rich men live at ease, feeding and clothing themselves by the labors of other men, not by their own, which is their shame and not their nobility; for it is a more blessed thing to give than to receive. But rich men receive all they have from the laborer's hand, and what they give, they give away other men's labors, not their own. Therefore they are not righteous actors in the Earth.[40]

Many socialists advanced this idea in later years. The parliamentary soldiers ejected Winstanley's Diggers, who, in accordance with their pacifist principles, offered no resistance. As a practical assault upon private property, therefore, the movement collapsed.

The Social Contract Theory

In earlier chapters it was mentioned that the period under consideration witnessed the emergence of a new social theory, or rather the resurrection and development of an old one, namely that of the social contract.

[38] Reprinted in *The Digger Movement in the Days of the Commonwealth,* by L. H. Berens, London 1906, p. 118. Quoted by permission of H. A. Berens and Simpkin, Marshall, Hamilton, Kent, & Co., Ltd.

[39] By Berens.

[40] *The Digger Movement in the Days of the Commonwealth,* p. 173.

Grotius, Hobbes, and Locke, in their several ways, made the evolution of property rights an integral part of the social contract theory. According to these philosophers, property rights were based upon the contract by which society itself was established.

In *De jure belli ac pacis,* Grotius gave what purported to be an account of the progress of society from its beginnings :

Almighty God, as soon as he had created the World, did immediately confer a Right generally to all mankind in things of this Inferiour Nature. And so again when he had renewed the world after the Flood. . . *All things at first* (saith *Justin*) *were promiscuously common and undivided to all, and as it were one intire Patrimony bequeathed unto all.* Whence it came to pass, that every man did catch whatsoever he would to his own use, and consume what could be consumed. And the free exercise of this Universal Right was then instead of Propriety [*i.e.,* property] : For whatsoever any man did thus catch unto himself, no man could take from him without injury. . . Which state of things might very well have lasted, had men either persisted in the same inoffensive simplicity, or could they have embraced each other with the same mutual endearments of charity.[41]

Goods, therefore, became possessed by individuals, but not yet land, and there was still plenty of this for all comers :

still among Neighbours there remained a Communion not of Cattle but of Pasturage ; for so large a proportion of ground (being but thinly peopled) might without any Inconvenience, sufficiently supply all their necessities. *To mark their own, and trench out others Land Was not yet Lawful.* (*Virgil, Georg.* I) [42]

Ultimately, however, even land passed into private possession :

at length, the numbers both of Men and Cattle encreasing, the Land also became sub-divided, not into Nations and Provinces as before, but into single Families. And whereas in dry and sandy regions, Springs though very necessary, yet were not able to supply a multitude ; Therefore did every man strive by taking the first possession of them to make them his own. All these things we may trace out of the Sacred story, whereunto we might add the concurrent Testimonies both of Philosophers and Poets, who have treated of the first state of things held in common, and of the subsequent distribution of them. . . From hence we learn the true cause why men departed from that Primitive Community of things, first of movables, and afterwards of immovables : Namely, because repining to be at Natures bare allowance, that is, to feed on Roots and Herbs, to make their habitations in Caves, to go naked, or clad with barks of Trees, or Skins of Beasts . . . they made choice of a more delicate kind of living, which would require industry, which every particular man was in every thing to use for himself. Now that the Fruits of the Earth could not be conveniently laid up or disposed of in common, will easily be granted ; First, by reason of the vast distance of the places inhabited, the one

[41] *Rights of War & Peace,* p. 78.

[42] *Ibid.,* p. 79.

from the other. And Secondly, because of the great defect of Love and Charity among men : By reason whereof, no due equality could be observed, either of Labour in their Acquisition, or of Temperance in their Consumption. And from hence we may further learn, for what causes things were reduced into Propriety : Not by the sole act of the Mind ; for no one man could possibly know what another would have to be his own, that he might forbear it. Besides, possible it is, that diverse men might be competitors for one and the same thing. But things became proper [*i.e.*, property] by compact or agreement, and that either express, or by partition ; or tacite, as by present occupancy : But as soon as experience had taught them the inconveniences of holding things in common, and yet before Division was first instituted, it is very probable, that they unanimously agreed, That what every man possest at that time should be his own.[43]

That is to say, men had taken goods and land into their individual possession and property rights in the things so possessed were recognized by mutual agreement. Grotius cited Cicero and it is obvious that the Epicurean theories respecting the origin of the State, to which reference has been made elsewhere, were the source of his inspiration.

In the social contract, as Hobbes explained it, men conferred upon their sovereign unlimited power, including the right to dispose of property :

Seventhly, is annexed to the sovereignty, the whole power of prescribing the rules, whereby every man may know, what goods he may enjoy, and what actions he may do, without being molested by any of his fellow-subjects ; and this is it men call *propriety* [*i.e.*, property]. For before constitution of sovereign power . . . all men had right to all things ; which necessarily causeth war : and therefore this propriety, being necessary to peace, and depending on sovereign power, is the act of that power, in order to the public peace. These rules of propriety, or *meum* and *tuum,* and of *good, evil, lawful,* and *unlawful* in the actions of subjects, are the civil laws. . .[44]

Property, therefore, which with Grotius rested upon *contract,* by the very fact of that contract was made by Hobbes to depend upon the *will of the sovereign* power. Hobbes said that the first law of the sovereign respecting property in land was to dispose of it in whatever manner he considered to be conducive to the common good :

the first law, is for division of the land itself : wherein the sovereign assigneth to every man a portion, according as he [*i.e.*, the sovereign], and not according as any subject, or any number of them, shall judge agreeable to equity, and the common good.[45]

Hobbes gave as an example the partition of England by William the Conqueror.

[43] *Ibid.*, pp. 79-80.
[44] *The English Works of Thomas Hobbes,* vol. 3, *Leviathan,* p. 165.
[45] *Ibid.*, p. 234.

As the sovereign was supreme, it followed that a subject had no right to exclude him from whatever property he (the subject) possessed:

the propriety which a subject hath in his lands, consisteth in a right to exclude all other subjects from the use of them; and not to exclude their sovereign, be it an assembly, or a monarch.[46]

Thus the sovereign might interfere with existing distribution if he thought fit, and the fact that such an action might conflict with the intentions of individuals when they entered into the original social contract did not preclude the exercise of this sovereign right. Title to compensation on dispossession by the sovereign did not arise. According to Hobbes, in the social contract men had transferred their resources to the sovereign and, whatever he did, it was beyond their power to interfere.

Grotius, on the other hand—though explicitly recognizing the right of *eminent domain,* that is, the right of the sovereign to take possession of the property of his subjects for public purposes—made it subject to the payment of compensation:

But here there usually ariseth another Question, namely, What Right Kings have over the Estates of private men. . . That the things belonging to Subjects are under the supereminent power of the Commonwealth, whereof they are a part we have already proved, so that that Commonwealth, or he that exercises the supreme power in it, hath a Right to make use thereof, either by even destroying them, or by alienating them, and that not only in a case of extreme necessity, which is even between private men justifyable; but when it extends even to the good of the publick, which is always to be preferred before any private mans, by the general consent of those who first entred into civil society: Which notwithstanding is so to be understood, that the whole Commonwealth is obliged to repair the damages, that shall befal any of her Subjects or Citizens, by reason of any such spoil or alienation, out of their publick stock, or by a publick contribution; whereunto even he who hath sustained the loss, shall (if need be) pay his proportion.[47]

Grotius admitted, also, the right of any individual who desired to leave the society (*i.e.,* leave his city or country and proceed elsewhere) to do this, provided that before he left he fulfilled any public obligations for which he was liable.

It was Locke, in England, who controverted the theory that the king was the fount of property rights. Immediately, he was attacking Filmer's divine ordination theory, not Hobbes's social contract explanation of royal rights. Locke's arguments, however, applied to both. In his essay, "Of Civil Government," in *Two Treatises of Government* (London 1690), in opposition to Filmer's statement that God had conferred upon kings the right to govern and to dispose of property, like Winstanley earlier in the century Locke asserted that God had given natural

[46] *Ibid.,* p. 235.

[47] *The Rights of War & Peace,* p. 545.

resources for the use of all men. Property rights, he said, wherever they existed, depended in the first instance upon labor :

God, who hath given the world to men in common, hath also given them reason to make use of it to the best advantage of life, and convenience. The earth, and all that is therein, is given to men for the support and comfort of their being. And though all the fruits it naturally produces, and beasts it feeds, belong to mankind in common, as they are produced by the spontaneous hand of nature; and no-body has originally a private dominion, exclusive of the rest of mankind, in any of them, as they are thus in their natural state; yet being given for the use of men, there must of necessity be a means to appropriate them some way or other, before they can be of any use, or at all beneficial to any particular man. The fruit, or venison, which nourishes the wild Indian, who knows no enclosure, and is still a tenant in common, must be his, and so his, i. e. a part of him, that another can no longer have any right to it, before it can do him any good for the support of his life.

Though the earth, and all inferiour creatures, be common to all men, yet every man has a property in his own person : this no-body has any right to but himself. The labour of his body, and the work of his hands, we may say, are properly his. *Whatsoever then he removes out of the state that nature hath provided, and left it in, he hath mixed his labour with, and joined to it something that is his own, and thereby makes it his property.* It being by him removed from the common state nature hath placed it in, it hath by this labour something annexed to it, that excludes the common right of other men. For this labour being the unquestionable property of the labourer, no man but he can have a right to what that is once joined to, *at least where there is enough, and as good, left in common for others.*[48]

This appears a doubtful justification, to say the least. It would be difficult nowadays to admit that a man's action in mixing his labor with something that previously was common property, conferred property rights on the laborer. If such a claim were granted, soon there would be no common property left. So, instead of permitting anyone to dig up and plant the public streets or parks, and thereby acquire title to them, modern governments instruct the police to stop such proceedings and even go so far as to levy damages against any individual who undertakes them. Locke, himself, in the portion italicized at the end of the passage quoted above, recognized that the validity of his argument might turn on whether there was "enough, and as good" of the common property left for others to use. Clearly, if the first comers mixed their labor with so much of the common property that there was not enough left to sustain those who came later, trouble was bound to arise. Locke thought that this difficulty was not serious at first. No man could claim a right to more than he could use, the philosopher said :

The same law of nature, that does by this means give us property, does also

[48] *The Works of John Locke,* vol. 5, pp. 353-354. Italics ours.

bound that property too. . . As much as any one can make use of to any advantage of life before it spoils, so much he may by his labour fix a property in : whatever is beyond this, is more than his share, and belongs to others. Nothing was made by God for man to spoil or destroy. . . The measure of property nature has well set by the extent of men's labour, and the conveniencies of life : no man's labour could subdue, or appropriate all ; nor could his enjoyment consume more than a small part ; so that it was impossible for any man, this way, to intrench upon the right of another, or acquire to himself a property, to the prejudice of his neighbour, who would still have room for as good, and as large a possession (after the other had taken out his) as before it was appropriated.[49]

Translated into the environment of early America, Locke believed that a man should be given title to as much land as he could cultivate and no more. The history of land settlement in this country, however, showed that an expanding population might take up possession of the land so quickly that there was soon no longer "enough, and as good" for others. Locke perceived that the course of settlement had the effect of making land scarce, whereupon, following Grotius, he brought in the social contract :

Thus at the beginning, Cain might take as much ground as he could till, and make it his own land, and yet leave enough to Abel's sheep to feed on ; a few acres would serve for both their possessions. But as families increased, and industry enlarged their stocks, their possessions enlarged with the need of them ; but yet it was commonly without any fixed property in the ground they made use of, till they incorporated, settled themselves together, and built cities ; and then, by consent, they came in time to set out the bounds of their distinct territories, and agree on limits between them and their neighbours ; and by laws within themselves settled the properties of those of the same society. . .[50]

And :

labour, in the beginning, gave a right of property, wherever any one was pleased to employ it upon what was common, which remained a long while the far greater part, and is yet more than mankind makes use of. Men, at first, for the most part, contented themselves with what unassisted nature offered to their necessities : and though afterwards, in some parts of the world, (where the increase of people and stock, with the use of money, had made land scarce, and so of some value) the several communities settled the bounds of their distinct territories, and by laws within themselves regulated the properties of the private men of their society, and so, by compact and agreement, settled the property which labour and industry began : and the leagues that have been made between several states and kingdoms, either expressly or tacitly disowning all claim and right to the land in the others possession, have, by common consent, given up their pretences to their nat-

[49] *Ibid.*, pp. 355-358.

[50] *Ibid.*, p. 360.

ural common right, which originally they had to those countries, and so have, by positive agreement, settled a property amongst themselves, in distinct parts and parcels of the earth. . .[51]

Locke went on to remark that, when he wrote (*i.e.*, in 1690), there still existed "great tracts of ground," whose inhabitants "not having joined with the rest of mankind, in the consent of the use of their common money," lay waste and, presumably, were available to future settlers to mix their labor with them and so make them their property.

The purport of Locke's argument was that property was a *natural right*. Its existence was a condition antecedent to the social contract. Property rights, therefore, became a condition of this contract, which was, indeed, entered into primarily for the purpose of protecting them. It followed that the sovereign could not abrogate property rights and any attempt on his part to do so would be a violation of the social contract, entitling his erstwhile subjects to revolt and depose him.

Now, of course, the social contract theory of the establishment of the state is no longer accepted, so that whatever justification it conferred on property rights has passed away. Locke's natural right argument was more fundamental but later writers had no difficulty in turning it against the titles of existing property owners. If man had a natural right to use his labor upon land and take possession of the resulting produce, how was it that those who happened to inherit the soil could prevent others from exercising this natural right? It was inevitable that those who arrived upon the scene after all the land was taken up, and so were unable to obtain property by mixing their labor with unoccupied land, yet were unfortunate enough to inherit none, would refuse to accept Locke's social contract justification of property rights, just as Winstanley's Diggers rejected the "divine right of kings" argument. This, in brief, was the position taken up by a long series of socialist writers.

Happiness and the Right to the Produce of Labor

Early in the eighteenth century, Francis Hutcheson based property on his greatest happiness principle. Property encouraged industry and so added to human happiness, he said:

The very subsistence therefore of our species, as well as all our agreeable conveniencies, require an universal laborious industry. Nature hath given to all men some ingenuity and active powers, and a disposition to exert them: and each man has not only selfish desires towards his own happiness and the means of it, but some tender generous affections in the several relations of life. We are all conscious of some such dispositions in ourselves, and justly conclude that others have the like. We know that these are the ordinary springs of the activity of mankind in employing their labour to cultivate the

[51] *Ibid.*, p. 364.

earth, or procure things useful in human life. We all feel a sense of liberty within us, a strong desire of acting according to our own inclinations, and to gratify our own affections, whether selfish, or generous : we have a deep resentment of any obstruction given to these natural desires and endeavours. . . and we must disapprove it as unkind and cruel, where no important publick interest requires it. . . From these strong feelings in our hearts we discover the right of property that each one has in the fruits of his own labour; that is, we must approve the securing them to him, where no publick interest requires the contrary; and must condemn as cruel, unsociable, and oppressive, all depriving men of the use and free disposal of what they have thus occupied and cultivated. . . Now nothing can so effectually excite men to constant patience and diligence in all sorts of useful industry, as the hopes of future wealth, ease, and pleasure to themselves, their offspring, and all who are dear to them, and some honour too to themselves on account of their ingenuity, and activity, and liberality. All these hopes are presented to men by securing to every one the fruits of his own labours, that he may enjoy them, or dispose of them as he pleases. If they are not thus secured, one has no other motive to labour than the general affection to his kind, which is commonly much weaker than the narrower affections to our friends and relations. . . Nay the most extensive affections could scarce engage a wise man to industry, if no property ensued upon it. He must see that universal diligence is necessary. Diligence will never be universal, unless men's own necessities, and the love of families and friends, excite them. Such as are capable of labour, and yet decline it, should find no support in the labours of others. If the goods procured, or improved by the industrious lye in common for the use of all, the worst of men have the generous and industrious for their slaves. The most benevolent temper must decline supporting the slothful in idleness, that their own necessities may force them to contribute their part for the publick good. Thus both the immediate feelings of our hearts, and the consideration of the general interest, suggest this law of nature, "that each one should have the free use and disposal of what he has acquired by his own labour;" and this is property, which may be defined, when it is unlimited, "a right to the fullest use of any goods, and to dispose of them as one pleases." [52]

The essence of this argument is as old as Aristotle, as has been seen.

Hutcheson saw that the conferment of a right to property in the produce of labor might lead to the accumulation of possessions, because this produce might exceed what was needed for current consumption. But he did not support property in all its forms. He refused to accept the mere occupancy of land as a title to ownership :

But as property is constituted to encourage and reward industry, it can never be so extended as to prevent or frustrate the diligence of mankind. No person or society therefore can by mere occupation acquire such a right in a vast tract of land quite beyond their power to cultivate, as shall exclude others who may want work, or sustenance for their numerous hands, from a share proportioned to the colonies they can send. Thus it would be vain for a private

[52] *A System of Moral Philosophy*, vol. 1, pp. 319-320.

man with his domesticks to claim a property, upon the circumstance of his having first discovered or arrived at it, in a country capable of maintaining ten thousand families, and requiring so many to cultivate it. Equally vain would it be in a nation of eight or ten millions of souls to claim, upon the like foundation, a property in a vast continent capable of maintaining three times that number. . . such capricious claims, beyond all possible use or conveniency of the claimants, must not keep large tracts of the earth desolate, and exclude nations too populous from obtaining for some of their people that use of the earth which *God* intended for mankind.[53]

Some may consider that this statement has a certain applicability to such a situation as that of Australia in the twentieth century.

In these writings Hutcheson had in mind the relation of production and distribution to happiness. Apparently forgetting for the moment his own doubts on the subject,[54] he assumed that, if more wealth were produced and if wealth were more evenly divided, human happiness would be increased. His justification of property was that it was favorable to production. He was prepared to limit proprietary rights under conditions where the "greatest happiness" criterion seemed to indicate that limitation was desirable. But Hutcheson said very little on distribution and so it was left to Godwin and Bentham to open up the distributional objection to property rights, from the utilitarian viewpoint.

The Attack on Private Property by Rousseau and the Socialists

In developing his property theory, Locke had come upon the labor explanation of value, described in Chapter IX. Asking why men's property in their labor had overbalanced community in land, so that the fact of mixing labor with land conferred ownership of the latter on him whose labor was so mixed, Locke stated the principle that labor accounted almost entirely for value. From this it followed that title to the produce followed the ownership of the labor, not that of the land. In other words, land was a free good, to use modern terminology.[55] Adam Smith, who was familiar with Locke's work, started his own theory from this point. Smith granted that Locke's statement was correct with respect to early society:

In that early and rude state of society which precedes both the accumulation of stock and the appropriation of land, the proportion between the quantities

[53] *Ibid.*, pp. 326-327.

[54] See Chapter II.

[55] A recent historian of early economic thought (M. Beer, *Early British Economics from the XIIIth to the middle of the XVIIIth century*) has attributed the origin of the notion that the produce of labor belongs rightfully to the laborer to the teachings of the medieval Catholics (especially those of Richard of Middleton), whose works Locke is said to have read. Certainly it is true that the religious teachers of the thirteenth century believed that prices and wages should represent labor-cost in a sense, and that surpluses above what was accounted for in this manner — such as scarcity profits and interest on capital — were sinful. But, as is shown in Chapters IX and XI, where the early ideas are discussed, this view appears to go back at least as far as Aristotle.

of labour necessary for acquiring different objects s
cumstance which can afford any rule for exchanging

If it cost twice the amount of labor to kill a beaver as
then one beaver would exchange for two deer. "In t
the whole produce of labour belongs to the labourer,"
such was no longer the case, once capital and land
property:

As soon as stock has accumulated in the hands of particular pers
them will naturally employ it in setting to work industrious pe
they will supply with materials and subsistence, in order to make a profit by the sale of their work, or by what their labour adds to the value of the materials. . . In this state of things, the whole produce of labour does not always belong to the labourer. He must in most cases share it with the owner of the stock which employs him. . .

As soon as the land of any country has all become private property, the landlords, like all other men, love to reap where they never sowed, and demand a rent even for its natural produce. The wood of the forest, the grass of the field, and all the natural fruits of the earth, which, when land was in common, cost the labourer only the trouble of gathering them, come even to him, to have an additional price fixed upon them. He [*i.e.*, the laborer] must then pay for the licence to gather them; and must give up to the landlord a portion of what his labour either collects or produces.[57]

What Smith evidently had in mind was that the scarcity of land that appeared as society progressed and population multiplied, together with the assistance that could be furnished to laborers by the capital that belonged to others, resulted in payments to the owners of land and capital. The effect was that the laborer no longer received the entire produce of his labor. That is to say, land and capital had not merely become property, they were valuable property: they had a price. This, then, was the economic aspect of the evolution of property, which had been described by Grotius and Locke. But there was no consideration of property, as an institution, in Smith's book, let alone a justification of it. His language, indeed, implied that he regarded property rights as unjust; but in the *Wealth of Nations* Smith's concern was not with the justice or injustice of the distribution of income but with how, in fact, distribution took place.

Rousseau. A generation before Smith wrote, Rousseau's memorable attack upon property had appeared in France. In his work, *Sur l'origine de l'inégalité parmi les hommes* (1755),[58] Rousseau declared:

The first man who, having enclosed a piece of ground, bethought himself of saying *This is mine,* and found people simple enough to believe him, was the

[56] *Wealth of Nations,* Bk. 1, Chap. 6. [57] *Ibid.*

[58] Translated as *A Discourse on the Origin of Inequality,* in *The Social Contract and Other Essays.*

nder of civil society. From how many crimes, wars and murders, how many horrors and misfortunes might not any one have saved mankind, by pulling up the stakes, or filling up the ditch, and crying to his fellows, "Beware of listening to this imposter; you are undone if you once forget that the fruits of the earth belong to us all, and the earth itself to nobody.[59]

Rousseau described a process of aggrandizement, in which to him who had was given more. When all land had become private property, one man could enrich himself only at the expense of others, acquiring dominion or slavery over his fellows, Rousseau said. Such a man used his old slaves to acquire new ones, and so became rich. Rousseau refused to accept the fact of possession, whether originating in occupation or in acquisition, as evidence of a right to possess:

> however speciously they [*i.e.*, the rich] might disguise their usurpations, they knew that they were founded on precarious and false titles; so that, if others took from them by force what they themselves had gained by force, they would have no reason to complain. Even those who had been enriched by their own industry, could hardly base their proprietorship on better claims. It was in vain to repeat, "I built this well; I gained this spot by my industry." Who gave you this standing, it might be answered, and what right have you to demand payment of us for doing what we never asked you to do? Do you not know that numbers of your fellow-creatures are starving, for want of what you have too much of? You ought to have had the express and universal consent of mankind, before appropriating more of the common subsistence than you needed for your own maintenance.[60]

The social contract, Rousseau said, was merely a trick of the propertied class to retain possession of what they had seized:

> Such was, or may well have been, the origin of society and law, which bound new fetters on the poor, and gave new powers to the rich; which irretrievably destroyed natural liberty, eternally fixed the law of property and inequality, converted clever usurpation into unalterable right, and, for the advantage of a few ambitious individuals, subjected all mankind to perpetual labour, slavery and wretchedness.[61]

Rousseau's ideas had great influence and undoubtedly were one of the sources of inspiration of socialist writings on the subject of property.

British writers of the late eighteenth century, especially William Godwin. The idea that property represented exploitation appeared in the works of several British reformers towards the end of the eighteenth century. *The Meridian Sun of Liberty: or the whole rights of man displayed and most accurately defined* (London 1796), by Thomas Spence (1750–1814), schoolmaster and later bookseller and radical agitator, is worth mentioning. Another example was *An Essay on the Right of Property*

[59] *Ibid.*, p. 207. [60] *Ibid.*, pp. 219-220. [61] *Ibid.*, p. 221.

in Land with respect to its foundation in the Law of Nature. Its present establishment by the Municipal Laws of Europe, and the regulations by which it might be rendered more beneficial to the lower ranks of Mankind (London 1782), by William Ogilvie (1736–1819), a professor in Aberdeen, Scotland. Both Spence and Ogilvie followed Winstanley and Rousseau in discussing only property in land and leaving industrial capital out of account, Spence's book being of interest as furnishing Godwin with some of his ideas.

More influential was *An Enquiry Concerning Political Justice and its Influence on General Virtue and Happiness* (2 vols., London 1793; 2nd ed., 2 vols., London and Philadelphia 1796),[62] by William Godwin (1756–1836), one of the leading British reformers. In this book, Godwin recognized the existence of "three degrees" of property. The first, he said, was justified on the side of consumption by the greatest happiness principle, the second by the laborer's right to the produce of his labor, the third by the laws of Europe as they stood:

> The first and simplest degree, is that of my permanent right in those things, the use of which being attributed to me, a greater sum of benefit or pleasure will result, than could have arisen from their being otherwise appropriated. It is of no consequence in this case how I came into possession of them, the only necessary conditions being, their superior usefulness to me, and that my title to them is such as is generally acquiesced in by the community in which I live.[63]

> The second degree of property is the empire to which every man is entitled over the produce of his own industry. . .[64]

> The third degree of property is that which occupies the most vigilant attention in the civilised states of Europe. It is a system, in whatever manner established, by which one man enters into the faculty of disposing of the produce of another man's industry.[65]

Godwin believed that the three "degrees" of property were in conflict. The second degree, he thought, was

> in a less rigorous sense fundamental than the first. It is in one point of view a sort of usurpation. It vests in me the preservation and dispensing of that, which in point of complete and absolute right belongs to you.[66]

Godwin's "complete and absolute right" was the Hutcheson-Bentham greatest happiness principle, or principle of utility. In stating that the second degree of property was a usurpation of the first, Godwin had in mind the circumstance that, if every man were given title to the produce of his industry, it might often happen that one individual received in-

[62] The second edition was entitled *An Enquiry Concerning Political Justice, and its Influence on Morals and Happiness,* and modified the first in some respects.

[63] 2nd ed., Philadelphia, vol. 2, p. 314.

[64] *Ibid.*, p. 315.

[65] *Ibid.*, p. 316.

[66] *Ibid.*, pp. 315-316.

come that was more useful to another. In other words, distribution of produce according to *work done* might conflict with distribution according to *needs.* It is evident that needs and productive capacities, or abilities, do not coincide. A man in the prime of his working life may produce heavily, yet his needs may be far less than those of an older individual, if dependents are taken into account. Godwin preferred needs to productive contributions as titles to the product : hence his statement. On the subject of the third degree of property, he commented :

> There is scarcely any species of wealth, expenditure or splendour existing in any civilised country, that is not in some way produced by the express manual labour and corporeal industry of the inhabitants of that country. The spontaneous productions of the earth are few, and contribute little to wealth, expenditure or splendour. Every man may calculate, in every glass of wine he drinks, and every ornament he annexes to his person, how many individuals have been condemned to slavery and sweat, incessant drudgery, unwholesome food, continual hardships, deplorable ignorance and brutal insensibility, that he may be supplied with these luxuries. It is a gross imposition that men are accustomed to put upon themselves, when they talk of the property bequeathed to them by their ancestors. The property is produced by the daily labour of men who are now in existence. All that their ancestors bequeathed to them, was a mouldy patent, which they shew as a title to extort from their neighbours what the labour of those neighbours has produced. It is clear therefore that the third species of property, is in direct contradiction to the second.[67]

Thus, Godwin followed Winstanley and Rousseau in viewing the legal rights of property as a usurpation of the more fundamental rights of man.

The worker's right to the whole produce. A series of writers developed the second of Godwin's rights of property, that is, the theory that the laborer was entitled to the produce of his labor. Adam Smith had admitted that property income (*i.e.*, payment for the use of land and capital) was a deduction from the produce of labor. Godwin and his socialist successors added an ethical element to Smith's statement. In the opinion of the socialists, payments for the use of property were not merely *deductions* from the produce of labor, they were *unjust deductions* from this produce. The socialists believed that the laborer had a right to the entire produce of his labor and that this right was defeated by the existence of property rights in the instruments and materials employed in the productive process.

In connection with this theory, there should be mentioned William Thompson (1783–1833), an Irish landowner who was influenced by Robert Owen and Jeremy Bentham, and resided with Bentham for a time. Thompson published several works on social reform, the most important being *An Inquiry into the Principles of the Distribution of*

[67] *Ibid.*, p. 316.

Wealth Most Conducive to Human Happiness; Applied to the Newly Proposed System of Voluntary Equality of Wealth (London 1824).

Thompson's criterion of social good was the Benthamite one of greatest happiness and there is much in his writings that suggests Bentham. But where Bentham, like Hutcheson, was content to say that property and therefore inequality were necessary to encourage production, Thompson went on to ask how much property and what extent of inequality were required for this purpose. The answer, he thought, was that the worker should have the right to enjoy the whole produce of his labor:

> *The strongest stimulus to production (and that which is necessary to the greatest production) that the nature of things will permit, is "security" in the* ENTIRE USE of the products of labor, to those who produce them.[68]

> no extent of knowledge on the part of the productive labourers, no profusion of motives tempting them to exertion, not even the acquisition of industrious habits, will induce them to persevere in the continued production of wealth, if they are not by some means protected, whether by their own strength or by co-operation, in the *use* of what their labor has produced. To continue voluntary labor, uncompelled, for the benefit of others, would be a proof of insanity; and has in fact, on a national scale, never occurred. It is a moral impossibility. In order to *continue* voluntary production at all — for it may be begun without reflection or by the way of experiment — the producer must derive the expected benefit from the thing produced.[69]

> The same reason that would justify the *taking away* one portion of the produce of labor *without the laborer's consent* . . . would justify the taking away any other portion; till in the end, no stimulus being left, no possible exertion, no production but in obedience to physical want or compulsion, would ensue.[70]

This was not to say that the capitalist had no right to share in the produce, according to Thompson's view. He had such a right but only in so far as this rested on labor in the first instance, or on "voluntary exchange." The machinery and other equipment that assisted labor in production had itself cost labor to make and it merited remuneration on this account. Further, the employer supervised the productive process, and supervision was but a form of labor. Thus, argued Thompson, the capitalist-employer should receive compensation on a labor basis. If he received anything more than this — and Thompson believed that he did — then the additional amount was unmerited. This aspect of Thompson's theories, which forecast the surplus-value idea of Karl Marx, receives some attention in Chapter IX.

But Thompson recognized acquisition by exchange as a title to property, as well as labor. In this connection he distinguished two forms of exchange. One was *forced exchange,* into which the worker was com-

[68] p. 35, section heading. [69] *Ibid.*, pp. 35-36. [70] *Ibid.*, p. 44.

pelled to enter because of his non-possession of the land and capital required for production. The other was *voluntary exchange,* that is, free interchange of the products of specialized laborers. The first represented exploitation of the worker but Thompson looked to the second for a remedy for the unsatisfactory position in which the worker found himself. One worker was to exchange his product for that of another, the ratio of exchange being that which was "just," namely that which represented the labor incorporated in the commodities concerned. Here, Thompson showed the influence of Owen, for, as is shown in Chapter IX, a scheme of this nature had been proposed by Owen.

Reference should be made, also, to John Gray (1799–1850?), another British social reformer, and author of *A Lecture on Human Happiness* (London 1825)[71] and *The Social System: A Treatise on the Principle of Exchange* (Edinburgh 1831). In the first of these works, Gray utilized figures from the *Treatise on the Population, Wealth, Power, and Resources of the British Empire* (London 1814), published by Patrick Colquhoun (1745–1820), British municipal administrator and writer on social problems. On the basis of Colquhoun's data, and assuming that labor alone was responsible for the produce and therefore that only the laboring class had a right to share in the national income, Gray estimated the extent to which the workers were exploited or robbed by the owners of property. The whole income of Britain was calculated to amount to nearly £54 (say $270) a year for each man, woman, and child of the "productive class." Of this, they received only about £11, or "but a small trifle more than ONE FIFTH OF THE PRODUCE OF THEIR OWN LABOUR ! ! !"[72] The remainder went to the propertied classes and other unproductive members of society. Gray went over the various groups of people in detail, to decide how far they were to be classed as productive. For instance, he classed half of the persons employed in the army and navy as unproductive. He refused to admit any justification for property rights other than labor:

> The foundation of all property is LABOUR, and there is no other just foundation for it. In the rudest ages of antiquity, a man who had killed an animal for food would look upon it as his property. Should another take it from him, it would be looked upon as an act of injustice, and the attempt to do it would instantly be resisted. But we need not go into ages past for examples, for in every society, labour is the *exclusive source* of property, consequently the *exclusive foundation* of it. If a man can, in any case, say truly "this is mine," surely it is, when the thing spoken of is the produce of the labour of his hands. Is a man's right hand his own? We deny that it is more so than the produce of the labour of it.

[71] Reprinted, London 1931.

[72] Reprint, p. 20. Quoted by permission of the London School of Economics and Political Science.

It being evident, then, that labour is the sole foundation of property, and that, in fact, all property is nothing more than accumulated labour; the question which seems to arise is, "Do the persons we are speaking of [*i.e.,* the propertied classes] consume the produce of other person's labour, or do they consume the produce of their own?" They consume the former; but they give an equivalent for it in the shape of money, which is itself accumulated labour, or the representative of it. But is that money theirs to give? is IT the produce of their labour, or of other people's? What equivalent do they give for IT? THEY GIVE NO EQUIVALENT FOR IT: and we will clearly show to those, whose minds are not influenced by long existing custom, that the independent classes of society, are solely dependent upon injustice for their daily bread. These persons obtain their incomes, for the most part, from the rent of land and interest of money. Let us examine these a little.

In the first place we deny, that, strictly speaking, any man can be a proprietor of land at all. The earth is the habitation, the natural inheritance of all mankind: of ages present and to come; a habitation belonging to no man in particular, but to every man; and one in which *all* have an *equal* right to dwell. Ask any land-owner what right he has to the land he possesses, and he will produce a collection of parchments, to prove, that from God knows when, the property he holds has been in the possession of his ancestors. But how came his ancestors by it? He answers by conquest, or by taking possession. But neither of these could make it their property. There are but three ways, in which it is possible to become rightly possessed of property. The first is by making it; the second by purchasing it; the third is by donation from another, whose property it was. Now as it is clear that neither our present land-owners, nor their ancestors did create the earth; and as it is as clear, that he who did create it, neither gave it to them in particular, nor sold it to them; it is impossible that they, or any men living, can be the proprietors of an inch of it. . .[73]

Asking what equivalent the landowner gave for that portion of its produce that he claimed to be his, Gray answered:

He gives NO EQUIVALENT WHATEVER, and there is NO JUSTICE WHATEVER in his possessing himself of it. It was exclusively produced by the labour of others, and it is EXCLUSIVELY THEIR PROPERTY. But the world says it is his! Yes! – What has made it so? *The power and custom of obtaining it!* In this, and in *this alone,* consists his title to it; and if this be admitted as a just foundation of property, is it not at once allowing that any thing is justice which happens to be law; and that, as to a natural foundation for property, there is *no such thing!*[74]

Gray admitted the right of property in improvements on the basis of "that quantity of labour which would be required to convert the land from the quality it was to the quality it now is."[75]

As to the right of the capitalist to receive a share of the produce, Gray told a little parable:

[73] *Ibid.,* pp. 34-35. [74] *Ibid.,* p. 36. [75] *Ibid.,* p. 37.

Suppose a number of men were to commence their operations apart from the rest of society, and that each had a store-room for the produce of his labour. Suppose one of these men, more fortunate than the rest, having filled his store-room quite full, were to say to his fellows, "Gentlemen, having an abundant stock of produce, I will work no more, I will not, however, consume any portion of it; but you, who have accumulated nothing, shall labour still, and I will consume the produce as fast as you create it." The others would, certainly, look upon this as a singular kind of proposition. Strange, however, as it may appear, society, as it is now constituted, not only proposes this, but is actually practising it to the extent of many millions annually. All persons deriving their incomes from the interest of money, are living upon *this kind* of justice.[76]

He added,

It may perhaps be said, that requiring interest for the use of money is only requiring the fulfilment of a contract, made by the consent of both parties; and therefore that it cannot be called an act of injustice. This is no answer to our argument. We are not talking about men being obliged to *fulfil* contracts after they have made them, but about the justice of the contracts themselves.[77]

The arguments of J. F. Bray (1809–1895) were similar. Bray was an American, who was taken as a boy to England and there joined in the socialist agitation which was widespread during the 1830's, afterwards returning to the United States. His published works, of which *Labour's Wrongs and Labour's Remedy; or, The Age of Might and the Age of Right* (Leeds 1839)[78] was the chief, belonged to the English period. A few extracts from *Labour's Wrongs* will illustrate Bray's point of view:

What are the working classes of every nation but beasts of burthen, without hearts and without souls, whose doom it is to labour and to die![79]

If taxes are to be levied, the workers must pay them – if a war be undertaken, they must go out to fight – if unjust laws be enacted, they must obey without murmuring – if they complain of tyranny, and dare to resist, they are slaughtered like wild beasts! The very marrow of their bones, and the life-blood of their children, is drunk up with excessive toil![80]

going to the origin of the thing, we shall find that every form of government, and every social and government wrong, owes its rise to the existing social system – *to the institution of property as it at present exists* – and that, therefore, if we would end our wrongs and our miseries at once and for ever, THE PRESENT ARRANGEMENTS OF SOCIETY MUST BE TOTALLY SUBVERTED, and supplanted by those more in accordance with the principles of justice and the rationality of man.[81]

[76] *Ibid.*, p. 38. [77] *Ibid.*, pp. 38-39. [78] Reprinted, London 1931.

[79] p. 15 of the reprint. Quoted by permission of the London School of Economics and Political Science.

[80] *Ibid.*, pp. 15-16. [81] *Ibid.*, p. 17.

> if three men be placed upon a desart island, and they each give an equal portion of labour for the common good, and receive an equal reward, the communion is *equally* beneficial to the three. But if one of the party, by force or fraud, obtain *double* allowance of produce for only *single* work, the union cannot longer be *equally* beneficial to all the three. If, again, the same man compel his fellows to give him double allowance of produce for *no labour whatever*, every shadow of equality and justice vanishes at once; and no law nor regulation can restore the equilibrium of right, unless it compel this receiver of an unearned share to give his labour for such share. . . In all civilised countries, as they are called, society is thus divided into idlers and producers — into those who obtain double allowance for doing nothing, and those who obtain only half-allowance for doing double work; and so long as this difference of position and inequality of condition is suffered to exist, inequality of rights and laws and enjoyments will also exist.[82]

> It is labour alone which bestows value. . . Every man has an undoubted right to all that his honest labour can procure him. When he thus appropriates the *fruits* of his labour, he commits no injustice upon any other human being; for he interferes with no other man's right of doing the same with the produce of *his* labour. But if any individual appropriate to himself the *field* on which all labour is exercised — if he attempt to set up a claim to any particular part of the earth — he clearly does that which is unjust, and contrary to the common equality of rights, *for he interferes with the equal right of every human being to appropriate that same particular spot.* Priority of possession gives no title whatever; nor can any duration of enjoyment establish a right, where no right did originally exist. From the very nature of the thing, and the position in which man stands with regard to his fellows, he never did, and never can, individually, possess any exclusive right to one single inch of land.[83]

It will be noticed that there was a direct appeal to ethics in the statements made by Gray and Bray, quoted above. According to these authors, it was *unjust* that land was in private possession and that the worker did not receive the entire product of his labor. Gray's standard of justice was to some extent that of Kant: it was unjust for one man to exercise his freedom in a manner that impinged upon the like freedom of others. But Thompson's argument was based in the first instance on an economic consideration. If the worker were not granted the right to enjoy the entire produce of his toil, Thompson said that production would suffer. Only then was an ethical judgment brought in. Because production was diminished, the *quantum* of human happiness was reduced, and this, on the utilitarian standard of ethics which Thompson accepted, was wrong.

Mention must be made of certain French writers. First there was F. N. Babeuf (1760–1797). Babeuf was of lowly origin and gave enthusiastic support to the Revolution when this broke out in France.

82 *Ibid.*, pp. 22-23.

83 *Ibid.*, pp. 33-34.

The Revolution brought about political equality but not the economic equality which Babeuf desired. Instead, the small-propertied bourgeois and peasant classes gained control. Babeuf, therefore, began to agitate in favor of community of property, intending this to be obtained by the suppression of inheritance. Finally, he was discovered to be plotting to overthrow the government and institute an equalitarian regime, with the result that he was seized and executed.

C. H. de Rouvroy, Comte de Saint-Simon (1760–1825), was of an entirely different type. Saint-Simon was ruined by the Revolution but appears to have restored his fortunes by speculation, at least temporarily, and spent the latter portion of his life in social writing and experimentation. He cannot be regarded as strictly a socialist, though some of his theories have exercised great influence on socialist thought. According to Saint-Simon, wages should be apportioned according to the productive contributions made by the various individuals—obviously a negation of equality, since productive capacities differed. He appears to have looked upon capital as involving some sacrifice on the part of its owners and, therefore, justifying remuneration. Industrial equality, he said,

consists in each obtaining from society benefits exactly proportioned to his social contribution, that is to say, to his actual capacity and the use he makes of the means at his disposal, among which . . . is included his capital.[84]

His follower, B. P. Enfantin (1796–1864), refused to follow Saint-Simon in this interpretation and took up the position that Thompson and other socialists occupied in Britain. Interest and rent, argued Enfantin, represented taxes paid by the workers to the propertied class to obtain from the latter the use of the instruments of production. Enfantin expected this situation to disappear, as public opinion became antagonistic to such an unjust arrangement and as laborers organized themselves to do without the services of the capitalist. The Saint-Simonians called upon the government to bring about the change:

The Saint-Simonians do not advocate community of goods, for such community would be a manifest violation of the first moral law, which they have always been anxious to uphold, and which demands that in future every one shall occupy a situation becoming his capacity and be paid according to his labour.

In view of this law they demand the abolition of all privileges of birth without a single exception, together with the complete extinction of the right of inheritance, which is to-day the greatest of all privileges and includes every other. The sole effect of this system is to leave the distribution of social advantages to a chance few who are able to lay some pretence to it, and to condemn the numerically superior class to deprivation, ignorance, and misery.

They ask that all the instruments of production, all lands and capital, the funds now divided among individual proprietors, should be pooled so as to

[84] *Du Système industriel*, Paris 1821, p. 206, footnote. Translated.

form one central social fund, which shall be employed by associations of persons hierarchically arranged so that each one's task shall be an expression of his capacity and his wealth a measure of his labour.

The Saint-Simonians are opposed to the institution of private property simply because it inculcates habits of idleness and fosters a practice of living upon the labour of others.[85]

In other words, as Thompson argued in England about the same time, the followers of Saint-Simon believed that private property did not encourage industry, as Hutcheson thought, but discouraged it, and that the solution was to give rewards that depended on the work done.

One of the best-known criticisms of private property came from the French anarchist, P. J. Proudhon (1809–1865), in a work bearing the challenging title, *Qu'est-ce que la propriété?* (*What is Property?*), and whose sub-title, translated into English, read *An Inquiry into the Principle of Right and of Government* (Paris 1840).[86]

Proudhon's idea of justice was equality of distribution. He believed that work conferred a title to income. But he went further: he thought that all work was alike in this respect. The laborer's claim to the whole produce of his labor—reflecting inequality in productive capacity—roused no sympathy in Proudhon's breast. Men were not themselves responsible for whatever capacities they possessed. Superior ability, in Proudhon's opinion, therefore, was no more just as a title to income than property of other kinds, that is, than land or capital:

Whatever be then the capacity of a man,—when this capacity is once created,—it does not belong to him. Like the material fashioned by an industrious hand, it had the power of *becoming*, and society has given it *being*. Shall the vase say to the potter, "I am that I am, and I owe you nothing"?[87]

That the strong have no right to encroach upon the labor of the weak, nor the shrewd to take advantage of the credulity of the simple. . .[88]

Every capacity for labor being, like every instrument of labor, an accumulated capital, and a collective property, inequality of wages and fortunes (on the ground of inequality of capacities) is, therefore, injustice and robbery.[89]

Like Rousseau and the English socialists, Proudhon refused to accept the argument of Locke, that mixing labor with land conferred upon the laborer a title to the land itself. Property of any kind, he said, was robbery:

If I were asked the following question: *What is slavery?* and I should answer

[85] Statement addressed to the President of the Chamber of Deputies and reprinted in the *Doctrine de Saint-Simon, Exposition,* Paris 1829, quoted by C. Gide and C. Rist in *A History of Economic Doctrines,* translated by R. Richards, London and Boston 1915, pp. 220-221. Reproduced by permission of D. C. Heath and Company, and George G. Harrap & Co., Ltd.

[86] Translated by R. B. Tucker, as *What is Property,* Princeton, Mass. 1876.

[87] Reprinted, N. Y. n. d., p. 144. [88] *Ibid.*, p. 147. [89] *Ibid.*, p. 286.

in a word, *It is murder,* my meaning would be understood at once. No extended argument would be required to show that the power to take from a man his thought, his will, his personality, is a power of life and death; and that to enslave a man is to kill him. Why, then, to this other question: *What is property?* may I not now likewise answer, It is *robbery,* without the certainty of being misunderstood; the second proposition being no other than a transformation of the first?[90]

Yet Proudhon's later writings, as is mentioned in the following section, showed some suggestion of a different view on property rights.

The ideas of outstanding German socialists were on lines similar to those developed in Britain and France. Karl Johann Rodbertus (1805–1875), a reforming landowner, and Karl Marx should be mentioned. Like Smith and the British socialists who were discussed in the preceding section, Rodbertus and Marx believed that landowners and capitalists were able to obtain shares of the social income because the factors of production in their possession were scarce. The usefulness of land and capital in production explained why laborers were willing to sacrifice a portion of the product in order to procure these factors. The fact that the law permitted private property in them made it possible for the owners to obtain this portion for themselves. As Rodbertus stated the matter,

positive law declares land and capital to be as much the property of individual persons, as the power to work is the property of the labourer. By this the workers, in order to produce at all, are forced to combine with the owners of land and capital, and to share with them the produce of labour. . .[91]

Engels set out the Marxist position, in his *Herr Eugen Dühring's Revolution in Science (Anti-Dühring),* thus:

In commodity production as it had developed in the Middle Ages, the question could never arise of who should be the owner of the product of labour. The individual producer had produced it, as a rule, from raw material which belonged to him and was often produced by himself, with his own instruments of labour, and by his own manual labour or that of his family. There was no need whatever for the product to be appropriated by him; it belonged to him as an absolute matter of course. His ownership of the product was therefore based *upon his own labour*. . . Then came the concentration of the means of production in large workshops and manufactories, their transformation into means of production that were in fact social. But the social means of production and the social product were treated as if they were still, as they had been before, the means of production and the products of individuals. Hitherto, the owner of the instruments of labour had appro-

[90] *Ibid.*, p. 11.

[91] *Zweiter sociale Brief,* Berlin 1850, quoted by A. Menger in *The Right to the Whole Produce of Labour,* translated by M. E. Tanner, London 1899, p. 85. Reproduced by permission of The Macmillan Company.

priated the product because it was as a rule his own product, the auxiliary labour of other persons being the exception; now, the owner of the instruments of production continued to appropriate the product, although it was no longer *his* product, but exclusively the product of *others' labour*.[92]

So the socialists proposed the abolition of private property, in which connection the words of the Marx-Engels *Communist Manifesto* of 1848 may be quoted:

You are horrified at our intending to do away with private property. But in your existing society, private property is already done away with for nine-tenths of the population; its existence for the few is solely due to its non-existence in the hands of those nine-tenths. You reproach us, therefore, with intending to do away with a form of property, the necessary condition for whose existence is, the non-existence of any property for the immense majority of society. In one word, you reproach us with intending to do away with your property. Precisely so; that is just what we intend.

From the moment when labour can no longer be converted into capital, money, or rent, into a social power capable of being monopolised, i.e., from the moment when individual property can no longer be transformed into bourgeois property, into capital, from that moment, you say, individuality vanishes. You must, therefore, confess that by "individual" you mean no other person than the bourgeois, than the middle-class owner of property. This person must, indeed, be swept out of the way, and made impossible. Communism deprives no man of the power to appropriate the products of society: all that it does is to deprive him of the power to subjugate the labour of others by means of such appropriation.[93]

To meet objections, from the standpoint of production, the *Manifesto* added,

It has been objected, that upon the abolition of private property all work will cease, and universal laziness will overtake us. According to this, bourgeois society ought long ago to have gone to the dogs through sheer idleness; for those of its members who work, acquire nothing, and those who acquire anything, do not work.[94]

Marx and Engels, it may be said, accepted the subsistence theory of wages, according to which the worker could not receive more than was sufficient to maintain him and to permit the reproduction of his kind.

Thus did the labor justification of property rights, advanced by Locke, recoil in boomerang fashion upon the propertied classes. To a large extent, the discussion was ethical rather than economic. The statement that "labor alone produces" is a pure assertion. The fact is that the

[92] *Op. cit.*, p. 303.

[93] *Manifesto of the Communist Party*, ed. F. Engels, London 1888. There are a number of editions of this work, that quoted being published by Charles H. Kerr & Company, Chicago 1915, pp. 34-35. Convenient editions are by Lawrence and Wishart Ltd. and International Publishers Co., Inc.

[94] *Ibid.*, p. 35.

product results from the co-operation of a number of factors. Not only labor but land and capital — natural materials and waiting, respectively — are necessary for bread to come into existence. To say that labor alone has produced the bread is no more correct than to say that land or capital has done so. What the socialists had in mind was, not that land and capital had no share in making the product, but that there was no justification for their owners receiving portions of the resulting income. In other words, the point at issue was not what had happened in production (that is, which factor had produced) but what should be done in distribution (how the product should be divided).

As stated in the passages quoted above from socialist writings, the question of whether the owners of land and capital should be allowed to receive payment for their use, and the more fundamental one of whether private property in these factors should be permitted at all, were grounded largely in ethics. But there were economic aspects, as was shown by various writers, including Thompson. Is a factor of production present in unlimited supply, or is it scarce? Only if scarce does the competitive system admit of payment being made to the owners of that factor. Not ownership, but scarcity, is what explains the payment. Ownership only accounts for the direction in which this payment goes, that is, who receives it. Even under a system where there is no such thing as private property, scarcities of productive factors are exceedingly probable. Indeed, they seem certain unless standards of consumption are revised sharply downwards. From this it follows that even a socialist economy will have to find some means of apportioning scarce factors over the various uses that are open to them. It may make a charge for capital and land, putting the revenue received from such a source into the public purse. Alternatively, some method of rationing may be applied. The only circumstance in which labor can receive the entire product is when the other factors cost nothing, that is to say, when they are obtainable free of charge.

But not all the socialists have made clear what form of distribution they favor. A number of them, as has been seen, spoke as though the laborer should receive the produce of his work, regardless of whether this was in conformity with his consumptive needs. On the other side stood Godwin and Proudhon, who refused to accept this solution and gave preeminence to needs. That the two are incompatible is evident.

The Property Theories of the German Philosophers

Private property a means of personal development. Where the socialists had regarded private property as a usurpation of personal rights and an offence against society as a whole, philosophers like Fichte and Hegel not merely tolerated it, they looked upon property as playing a vital part in social development. In this view, property was essential to the realization of individual personality and thus to the character of the State. In his power over things, including himself, that is, in his property rights, a man expressed himself and realized his freedom. As Hegel stated the point,

The reasonableness of property consists not in its satisfying our needs, but in its superseding and replacing the subjective phase of personality. It is in possession first of all that the person becomes rational. The first realization of my freedom in an external object is an imperfect one, it is true, but it is the only realization possible so long as the abstract personality has this first hand relation to its object.[95]

The German anarchist, Johann Kaspar Schmidt (1806–1856), who wrote under the pseudonym of Max Stirner, gave this aspect of property even greater emphasis. According to Stirner, the individual was not free if possession of property were denied to him. In his *Der Einzige und sein Eigentum* (Leipzig 1845),[96] Stirner said:

All attempts to enact rational laws about property have put out from the bay of *love* into a desolate sea of regulations. Even Socialism and Communism cannot be excepted from this. Every one is to be provided with adequate means, for which it is little to the point whether one socialistically finds them still in a personal property, or communistically draws them from the community of goods. The individual's mind in this remains the same; it remains a mind of dependence. The distributing *board of equity* lets me have only what the sense of equity, its *loving* care for all, prescribes. For me, the individual, there lies no less of a check in *collective wealth* than in that of *individual others*; neither that is mine, nor this: whether the wealth belongs to the collectivity, which confers part of it on me, or to individual possessors, is for me the same constraint, as I cannot decide about either of the two. On the contrary, Communism, by the abolition of all personal property, only presses me back still more into dependence on another, *viz.*, on the generality or collectivity; and, loudly as it always attacks the "State," what it intends is itself again a State, a *status*, a condition hindering my free movement, a sovereign power over me. Communism rightly revolts against the pressure that I experience from individual proprietors; but still more horrible is the might that it puts in the hands of the collectivity.[97]

The French anarchist, Proudhon, whose striking attack on private property was mentioned in the preceding section, in his later writings showed evidence of Stirner's viewpoint. The general positions of Proudhon and Stirner, on the one hand, and Hegel, on the other, were widely different. Stirner was not merely an anarchist, to whom government of any kind was anathema. He was an intense individualist. He thought that property allowed the individual to express himself and that the property rights

[95] Hegel's *Philosophy of Right*, pp. 48-49.
[96] Translated by S. T. Byington as *The Ego and His Own*, New York 1907.
[97] *Ibid.*, The Modern Library edition, N. Y. n. d., pp. 269-270.

of other individuals, as well as restrictions imposed by society as a whole (which Stirner termed the "collectivity"), were limitations on individual freedom. Hegel's point of view was diametrically opposed to this. The whole or the collectivity, not the individual, was what mattered to him. The freedom, that property permitted the individual to realize, was freedom within this collectivity. But the idea of property as an avenue of personal expression was common to both.

T. H. Green, who here, as elsewhere, showed Hegelian influence, expressed himself in much the same way as had his master:

The rationale of property . . . is that everyone should be secured by society in the power of getting and keeping the means of realising a will, which in possibility is a will directed to social good.[98]

Green went on to say that the possibility that the power may be misused did not affect the individual's claim to it, so long as the misuse did not interfere with the exercise of like power by other men. It followed that

It is not then a valid objection to the manner in which property is possessed among us, that its holders constantly use it in a way demoralising to themselves and others, any more than such misuse of any other liberties is an objection to securing men in their possession.[99]

Only when the possession of property by one man interfered with the like right of another, should it be got rid of, in Green's opinion. This was Kant's principle of moral conduct, applied to property. Carried to its extreme point, however, it would sanction the complete destruction of property rights, because in essence these are *rights to exclude others*. But this would defeat the objects of personal expression and realization of freedom, about which men like Hegel and Stirner spoke so highly.

Inequality. If property were a means of individual expression, and individuals were unequal, as Hegel thought,[100] it followed that properties should be unequal. Hegel, therefore, declared that

the assertion that the property of every man ought in justice to be equal to that of every other is false, since justice demands merely that every one should have property. Indeed, amongst persons variously endowed inequality must occur, and equality would be wrong.[101]

Green's statement was to the same effect:

Property, whether regarded as the appropriation of nature by men of different powers, or as the means required for the fulfilment of different social functions, *must* be unequal.[102]

[98] *Works of Thomas Hill Green,* vol. 2, *Principles of Political Obligation,* p. 526.
[99] *Ibid.* [100] See p. 51.
[101] Hegel's *Philosophy of Right,* p. 56.
[102] *Works of Thomas Hill Green,* vol. 2, p. xlii.

This was entirely different from the position taken by the socialists. Obviously, the relative merit of the two viewpoints turns on that of the assumptions upon which they are based, inherent equality and inequality respectively. Something is said on this subject in a later section of the chapter.

Property rights coupled with social duties. Another feature of what may be called the Romanticist viewpoint on property is the manner in which property rights and social duties have been linked together. Something in the nature of feudalism was what men like Fichte and Hegel contemplated with regard to property. An individual possessed property, it is true, but did so subject to certain social obligations. The owner of land was required to use it for the benefit of society, the business man to manage his enterprise for the good of all. Perhaps the *Grundlage des Naturrechts* (Leipzig and Jena 1796),[103] of J. G. Fichte, best illustrates this position :

As citizen of the state, the agriculturist must contribute towards the needs of the state. So far as we can see now, he will have to make these contributions from the products of his field. Until he makes this contribution, he has no property, because he has not fulfilled the agreement which makes it his property.[104]

All property is of a double nature ; it is either absolute, and hence not under the jurisdiction of the state, as money and valuables, etc., or relative, and immediately under the jurisdiction of the state, as real estate, houses, licences, etc. . . The legal end of the state in all the property conveyed to citizens is, that this property shall be properly used for the necessities of the state. Hence, the purchaser must agree to use it, and must be in a position to be able to use it ; for instance, if he purchases lands, he must be able to farm ; if a profession, he must understand it.[105]

Carlyle took the same attitude, in his comparison of the idleness of English landowners with the activity of the German Duke of Weimar, in *Past and Present.* Where English dukes were content to draw rent, Carlyle pointed out that the German administered his dukedom, improved the land, maintained an army and educational institutions, and kept at his court four illustrious men, Goethe, Herder, Schiller, and Wieland. The Duke was fulfilling the duties of ownership, according to Carlyle : the English nobles were neglecting them. This idea of property rights being conditioned by social duties has been in some measure characteristic of German thought, to the exclusion of the individualistic property theory of Locke, which has been accepted in Britain and America.

[103] Translated by A. E. Kroeger as *The Science of Rights,* London 1889.

[104] p. 299 of the translation. Quoted by permission of George Routledge & Sons Ltd. and Kegan Paul, Trench, Trubner & Co. Ltd.

[105] *Ibid.,* p. 339.

A feature of interest in Fichte's property theory was his recognition of property in occupations. Subject to the same condition of social good that was applied to other forms of property, he thought that individuals had a right to practice their callings. In default of an opportunity to do so, a right to maintenance arose:

A class of citizens exclusively entitled to prepare certain objects in a certain manner is called a profession. To leave all professions open at all times to all citizens, renders a property-compact impossible. The artist must be able to live by his work. . . The substance of the agreement which all others make with the artists is as follows: You promise us to furnish this sort of work in sufficient quantity and of excellent quality; we, on the other hand, agree to purchase it only from you. If the professions do not furnish excellent work, they lose the exclusive right granted to them in the compact. Hence, the examination of candidates for a profession is a matter of common interest. The government, or each profession in the name of the government, must calculate how many persons can live from each profession, and how many are necessary in each to satisfy the needs of the public. If all can not make their living, government has made a miscalculation, and must bear the consequences. Those who cannot sustain themselves from the profession must be assigned to other branches of business.[106]

Behind this was the legal ideology of the gild system, which had not altogether disappeared in Europe when Fichte wrote.

In these ideas, which have come down from the middle ages, there will be recognized much that is characteristic, not merely of Nazi Germany, but of other countries in our own time. Men who argue that everyone should own his house and garden have commonly behind this idea some conception of the realization of personality through property. Politicians who assert the right of the farmer and the industrial worker to protection in their means of livelihood, or social security, have in their minds — though perhaps in a hazy form — the principle that it is the duty of the State to maintain the condition of its members.

Utilitarian Views on the Distribution of Wealth

It is of interest to trace the development in modern times of the view that the general welfare demands interference with property rights and the distribution of wealth. As was seen in Chapter III, the hedonistic principle, which utilitarian philosophers and Classical economists had used to justify economic freedom, was later appealed to in support of a limitation of this freedom.

An early example, touching on private property, was the article on *Foundations,* contributed by the Physiocrat, Turgot, to the French *Encyclopédie.* Turgot pointed out that many foundations, or trust funds, intended as charities or memorials to the dead, were either badly designed

[106] *Ibid.,* pp. 312-313.

in the first instance or had lost much of their usefulness with altered circumstances. Society had not always the same needs and it was desirable that this fact should receive recognition in the abolition or redirection of old foundations. Public utility should be the criterion, Turgot said.

Bentham and the principle of diminishing utility. Jeremy Bentham's statement of the principle of diminishing utility has received attention in Chapter II. Having set forth the principle, Bentham pushed it to its logical conclusion by arguing that happiness was maximized by equality in the distribution of wealth:

> This conclusion is, that, so far as is consistent with security, the nearer to equality the distribution is, which the law makes of the matter of property among the members of the community, the greater is the happiness of the greatest number. . .[107]

But Bentham did not stop there. Having admitted that equality was desirable on distributional grounds, he proceeded to declare that it was "neither possible nor desirable" for other reasons. In the first place, even if equality were achieved, Bentham said that it would be destroyed within a day of its establishment. Secondly,

> the very design alone, accompanied with any assurance of its being about to be followed by the corresponding endeavour, perseveringly exercised, would suffice to destroy the whole of the value, and the greatest part of the substance, of the matter thus undertaken to be divided.[108]

> The Law does not say to a man, "*Work and I will reward you;*" but it says to him, "*Work,* and by stopping the hand that would take them from you, *I will ensure to you the fruits of your labour,* its natural *and sufficient reward, which, without me, you could not preserve.*"[109]

If people were faced with the certainty that they would be compelled to divide equally with others the produce of their labor, they would cease to work, Bentham declared:

> If I despair of enjoying the fruits of my labour, I shall only think of living from day to day: I shall not undertake labours which will only benefit my enemies. . . When security and equality are in opposition, there should be no hesitation: equality should give way. The first is the foundation of life—of subsistence—of abundance—of happiness; everything depends on it. . . In such a state of things [*i.e.*, with equality], prodigality would be wisdom, and none but the mad would be industrious.[110]

Thus, having granted the force of Godwin's assertion of a *subsistence*

[107] *The Works of Jeremy Bentham,* vol. 9, *The Constitutional Code,* p. 18.
[108] *Ibid.*
[109] *Ibid.,* vol. 1, *Principles of the Civil Code,* p. 308.
[110] *Ibid.,* pp. 310-312.

right to equality, Bentham abandoned it in favor of a right to the produce of labor, realizing that the latter meant inequality. That is, although he had himself advanced a stronger case against inequality, Bentham supported Hutcheson in justifying it.

To reconcile the divergence between the consumption and production interests of society (the former supporting equality and the latter inequality), Bentham advocated the regulation of inheritances:

Time is the only mediator between these contrary interests. Would you follow the counsels of equality without contravening those of security, wait for the natural period which puts an end to hopes and fears — the period of death. When property is vacated by the death of the proprietors, the law may intervene in the distribution to be made, either by limiting in certain respects the power of disposing of it by will, with the design of preventing too great an accumulation of property in the hands of a single person, or by making the right of succession subservient to the purposes of equality, in case the deceased should not leave a husband, or wife, or relations, in the direct line, and should not have made use of his power of disposing of it by will. It passes then to new possessors, whose expectations are not formed, and equality may produce good to all, without deceiving the expectations of any.[111]

Digression on early proposals for progressive taxation. The idea of levying taxes for the purpose of reducing inequality — which is what Bentham's proposal amounted to — was not new with this writer. Even Aristotle was prepared to interfere with distribution in an equalizing direction. In the second quarter of the eighteenth century, Montesquieu described progressive taxation as having existed in ancient Greece. He supported it on consumption grounds:

In the taxing of persons, it would be an unjust proportion to conform exactly to that of property. At Athens the people were divided into four classes. Those who drew five hundred measures of liquid or dry fruit from their estates, paid a talent to the public; those who drew three hundred measures, paid half a talent; those who had two hundred measures, paid ten minae [= one sixth of a talent, as a talent was equal to sixty minae]; those of the fourth class paid nothing at all. The tax was fair, though it was not proportionable: if it did not follow the measure of people's property, it followed that of their wants. It was judged that every man had an equal share of what was *necessary for nature;* that whatsoever was *necessary for nature,* ought not to be taxed; that to this succeeded the useful, which ought to be taxed, but less than the superfluous; and that the largeness of the taxes on what was superfluous, prevented superfluity.[112]

The principle that the necessities of life should be untaxed, that things useful though not strictly necessary should bear some taxation, with superfluities or luxuries taxed most of all, was a first approximation to

[111] *Ibid.,* p. 312.
[112] *The Spirit of Laws,* vol. 1, pp. 309-310.

the modern idea of progressive taxation. Montesquieu's *De l'esprit des lois,* in which the quoted statement appeared, was one of the most widely-read books of its period and, undoubtedly, gave the idea of progressive taxation wide currency.

Adam Smith, in stating his general principles of taxation, proposed that taxes should be levied on people

as nearly as possible, in proportion to their respective abilities; that is, in proportion to the revenue which they respectively enjoy under the protection of the state.[113]

A little later in his book, however, discussing taxes on the rent of houses, Smith appeared to advocate progressive taxation:

A tax upon house-rents, therefore, would in general fall heaviest upon the rich; and in this sort of inequality there would not, perhaps, be any thing very unreasonable. It is not very unreasonable that the rich should contribute to the public expense, not only in proportion to their revenue, but something more than in that proportion.[114]

In France J. B. Say declared that only progressive taxation could be regarded as equitable, from the standpoint of consumption:

how is the line to be drawn between necessaries and superfluities? In this discrimination, there is the greatest difficulty, for the terms, necessaries and superfluities, convey no determinate or absolute notion, but always have reference to the time, the place, the age, and the condition of the party; so that, were it laid down as a general rule, to tax none but superfluities, there would be no knowing where to begin and where to stop. All that we certainly know is, that the income of a person or a family may be so confined, as barely to suffice for existence; and may be augmented from that minimum upwards by imperceptible gradation, till it embrace every gratification of sense, of luxury, or of vanity; each successive gratification being one step further removed from the limits of strict necessity, till at last the extreme of frivolity and caprice is arrived at; so that, if it be desired to tax individual income, in such a manner as to press lighter, in proportion as that income approaches to the confines of bare necessity, taxation must not only be equitably proportioned, but must press on revenue with progressive gravity.

In fact, supposing taxation to be exactly proportionate to individual income, a tax of ten per cent, for instance, a family possessed of 300,000 *fr.* per annum would pay 30,000 *fr.* in taxes, leaving a clear residue of 270,000 *fr.* for the family expenditure. With such an expenditure, the family could not only live in abundance, but could still enjoy a vast number of gratifications by no means essential to happiness. Whereas another family, with an income of 300 *fr.*, reduced by taxation to 270 *fr.* per annum, would, with our present habits of life, and ways of thinking, be stinted in the bare necessaries of subsistence. Thus, a tax merely proportionate to individual income would be far

[113] *Wealth of Nations,* Bk. 5, Chap. 2, Pt. 2.
[114] *Ibid.,* Art. 1.

from equitable; and this is probably what Smith meant, by declaring it reasonable, that the rich man should contribute to the public expenses, not merely in proportion to the amount of his revenue, but even somewhat more. For my part, I have no hesitation in going further, and saying, that taxation cannot be equitable, unless its ratio is progressive.[115]

The question of taxing the poor was given attention by a number of writers, like Mun, Locke, and Davenant, as well as by the Physiocrats. As is shown in Chapter XII, it was a logical corollary of a subsistence theory of wages, that taxes on wages or on the necessities of life could not be borne by the laboring class but were passed on in the form of higher wages. The Physiocrats proposed to exempt from taxation all income other than the rent of land. Ricardo gave attention to the problem. Having regard to such factors as the cost of shifting the taxes, his conclusion was against taxing the poor. This meant, of course, a progressive system. But it must be borne in mind that those who accepted the subsistence theory of wages had to admit the practical impossibility of any other tax system, for the simple reason that—whether taxes were imposed on him in the first instance or not—the worker who lived at a subsistence level had no capacity to bear taxation and so passed on to others any that was levied on him.

Mill, Sidgwick, and Cairnes. English thought on the subjects of property and inequality in the middle of the nineteenth century was greatly influenced by the work of Bentham, and the treatment given to them by J. S. Mill and Sidgwick was obviously based on that of the earlier writer. Mill, however, departed from the precedent set by Bentham and the Classical economists of the early part of the century, by giving his ideas an evolutionary approach. Like his contemporary, Senior, Mill accepted that the production of wealth was determined by laws that were fundamental and beyond human control. But, he went on,

It is not so with the Distribution of Wealth. That is a matter of human institution solely. The things once there, mankind, individually or collectively, can do with them as they like. They can place them at the disposal of whomsoever they please, and on whatever terms. Further, in the social state, in every state except total solitude, any disposal whatever of them can only take place by the consent of society, or rather of those who dispose of its active force. Even what a person has produced by his individual toil, unaided by any one, he cannot keep, unless by the permission of society. Not only can society take it from him, but individuals could and would take it from him if society only remained passive; if it did not either interfere *en masse,* or employ and pay people for the purpose of preventing him from being disturbed in the possession. The distribution of wealth, therefore, depends

[115] *A Treatise on Political Economy,* Philadelphia 1841, pp. 454-455. It has been thought appropriate to give money figures in the original francs.

on the laws and customs of society. The rules by which it is determined, are what the opinions and feelings of the ruling portion of the community make them, and are very different in different ages and countries; and might be still more different, if mankind so chose.[116]

Bentham would have admitted, of course, that "the things once there" mankind "can do with them as they like," but his argument was that unless mankind disposed of the things in a manner that was satisfactory to those who had produced them, production would cease. Against the argument that collective ownership or equality of property would remove the stimulus to labor, Mill pointed out that in the society that existed in his time it was untrue to say that the wage-earner received an income that was proportioned to his productive activity:

From the Irish reaper or hodman to the chief justice or the minister of state, nearly all the work of society is remunerated by day wages or fixed salaries. A factory operative has less personal interest in his work than a member of a Communist association, since he is not, like him, working for a partnership of which he is himself a member.[117]

Mill agreed that there would be some difficulty in distributing the produce of labor in a collectivist system, since tasks and personal capacities varied; but he thought that such difficulties might not be insuperable. He proceeded to compare existing distribution with what was possible under communism, to the disadvantage of the former:

If, therefore, the choice were to be made between Communism with all its chances, and the present state of society with all its sufferings and injustices; if the institution of private property necessarily carried with it as a consequence, that the produce of labour should be apportioned as we now see it, almost in an inverse ratio to the labour—the largest portions to those who have never worked at all, the next largest to those whose work is almost nominal, and so on in a descending scale, the remuneration dwindling as the work grows harder and more disagreeable, until the most fatiguing and exhausting bodily labour cannot count with certainty on being able to earn even the necessaries of life; if this or Communism were the alternative, all the difficulties, great or small, of Communism would be as dust in the balance.[118]

But it was wrong, Mill felt, to compare communism as it might be—that is, *at its best*—with private property *as it existed in practice.* The comparison should be with individual property *as it could be made.* Mill said that the existing laws of property had made property out of things that never should have been property and created absolute property where only a qualified property right should exist. If laws were passed that, instead of exaggerating inequality, sought to promote a more equal

[116] *Principles of Political Economy*, Bk. 2, Chap. 1, Sect. 1.
[117] *Ibid.*, Bk. 2, Chap. 1, Sect. 3.
[118] *Ibid.*

distribution of wealth as far as this could be done without removing the stimulus to industry, he believed that it would be found that the institution of private property had no necessary connection with the evils commonly attributed to it.

Mill proceeded to formulate what he thought were better rules. He accepted that the economic justification of private property was that it guaranteed to individuals the enjoyment of the produce of their labor and, therefore, encouraged them to produce, thus increasing happiness. But, like Bentham, he drew the conclusion that *inheritance* was not so justified:

Private property, in every defence made of it, is supposed to mean, the guarantee to individuals of the fruits of their own labour and abstinence. The guarantee to them of the fruits of the labour and abstinence of others, transmitted to them without any merit or exertion of their own, is not the essence of the institution, but a mere incidental consequence, which, when it reaches a certain height, does not promote, but conflicts with, the ends which render private property legitimate.[119]

The only reasonable claims of children on their parents, Mill said, were "such education, and such appliances and means, as will enable them to start with a fair chance of achieving by their own exertions a successful life."[120] But the right of *bequest* (*i.e.*, to give by will, rather than to receive), he thought, was included in the right of private property, because ownership was not complete without the power to bestow upon others. Yet even bequest was a means to an end, not an end in itself, the end being human happiness. So Mill suggested that, while the individual should be allowed to retain the right to dispose of his whole property by will, the amount that he could hand to one person should be limited. Like Bodin, Mill was by no means blind to the possibility that inheritance might interfere with the productive activities of the inheritors. Discussing primogeniture, that is, the system whereby property is inherited by the eldest son to the exclusion of other members of the family, he mentioned that it had the advantage of avoiding any deterrent to the industry of the younger sons. Mill quoted Dr. Johnson's dictum that "it makes but one fool in a family" but remarked, somewhat sarcastically, that

If unearned riches are so pernicious to the character, one does not see why, in order to withold the poison from the junior members of a family, there should be no way but to unite all their separate potions, and administer them in the largest possible dose to one selected victim.[121]

On the general principle of progressive taxation, Mill expressed himself unfavorably:

[119] *Ibid.*

[120] *Ibid.*, Bk. 2, Chap. 2, Sect. 3.

[121] *Ibid.*, Bk. 5, Chap. 9, Sect. 2.

I am as desirous as any one, that means should be taken to diminish those inequalities, but not so as to relieve the prodigal at the expense of the prudent. To tax the larger incomes at a higher percentage than the smaller, is to lay a tax on industry and economy; to impose a penalty on people for having worked harder and saved more than their neighbours. It is not the fortunes which are earned, but those which are unearned, that it is for the public good to place under limitation. A just and wise legislation would abstain from holding out motives for dissipating rather than saving the earnings of honest exertion. Its impartiality between competitors would consist in endeavouring that they should all start fair, and not in hanging a weight upon the swift to diminish the distance between them and the slow.[122]

In his taxation proposals Mill had in mind that private property and inequality should be maintained for the purpose of serving as a stimulus to people to work and to save; but that exceptions should be made where property was acquired by inheritance and (as will be seen later) in the case of the rent of land. In other words, where, in Mill's opinion, the question of stimulus to produce did not come in, he thought that the distributional argument, based on the principle of diminishing utility, should be allowed to prevail. Following Ricardo, Mill was willing to exempt a minimum of subsistence from taxation, but probably this arose from his theory of wages as much as from considerations specially applicable to taxation.

Behind all his arguments, and explaining them, was Mill's acceptance of utilitarian ethics—the principle that greatest individual happiness should be the aim of legislation. This was made very clear in his work on *Utilitarianism*:

How many, again, and how irreconcileable, are the standards of justice to which reference is made in discussing the repartition of taxation. One opinion is, that payment to the State should be in numerical proportion to pecuniary means. Others think that justice dictates what they term graduated taxation; taking a higher percentage from those who have more to spare. In point of natural justice a strong case might be made for disregarding means altogether, and taking the same absolute sum (whenever it could be got) from every one: as the subscribers to a mess, or to a club, all pay the same sum for the same privileges, whether they can all equally afford it or not. Since the protection (it might be said) of law and government is afforded to, and is equally required by, all, there is no injustice in making all buy it at the same price. It is reckoned justice, not injustice, that a dealer should charge to all customers the same price for the same article, not a price varying according to their means of payment. This doctrine, as applied to taxation, finds no advocates, because it conflicts strongly with men's feelings of humanity and perceptions of social expediency; but the principle of justice which it invokes is as true and as binding as those which can be appealed to against it. Accordingly, it exerts a tacit influence on the line of defence

[122] *Ibid.*, Bk. 5, Chap. 2, Sect. 3.

employed for other modes of assessing taxation. People feel obliged to argue that the State does more for the rich than for the poor, as a justification for its taking more from them : though this is in reality not true, for the rich would be far better able to protect themselves, in the absence of law and government, than the poor, and indeed would probably be successful in converting the poor into their slaves. Others, again, so far defer to the same conception of justice, as to maintain that all should pay an equal capitation tax for the protection of their persons (these being of equal value to all) and an unequal tax for the protection of their property, which is unequal. To this others reply, that the all of one man is as valuable to him as the all of another. *From these confusions there is no other mode of extrication than the utilitarian.*[123]

Mill's statement amounts merely to an assertion that there existed no other standard of ethics than that which he himself accepted, namely utilitarianism, at least with regard to taxation, but it is of interest in giving his point of view.

Sidgwick included a rather full consideration of property and distribution in his *Principles of Political Economy,* as well as in his work on *Elements of Politics.* In the section of the first of these works that dealt with "The Art of Political Economy,"[124] a chapter was devoted to "Economic Distribution." It began with the postulate, based on the principle of diminishing utility, that

A more equal distribution of wealth tends *primâ facie* to increase happiness. . .[125]

This, of course, was what Bentham had said. Like Bentham, Sidgwick raised objections to equality from the standpoint of the stimulus to work and save. The need for such a stimulus, along with the danger that population would increase unduly under a communistic system, made it necessary to reject communism as a solution, he thought. As Mill had done before him, Sidgwick opposed progressive taxation :

I must admit that, in my opinion, such a tax would be justifiable from the point of view of distribution alone : but it is open to the practical objection that the progression if once admitted would be very difficult to limit, owing to the impossibility of establishing any definite quantitative comparison between the pecuniary sacrifices of the rich and those of the poor ; and, therefore, there would be a serious danger that the progression would be carried so far as to check accumulation or drive capital from the country, thus causing a loss to production which would more than outweigh the gain in equalisation of sacrifice.[126]

It must be admitted that Sidgwick was correct in saying that sacrifices could not be measured with accuracy. But he does not appear to have

[123] 8th ed., pp. 87-88. Italics ours.
[124] See Chapter III, p. 162.
[125] *Ibid.*, p. xxii.
[126] *Ibid.*, pp. 566-567.

realized that, if the practical difficulty of estimating sacrifices or happiness were considered to be a good reason for not trying to minimize sacrifices or maximize happiness, not merely progressive taxation but the entire edifice of utilitarianism fell to the ground.

Cairnes's general position approximated to that of Mill and Sidgwick. In *Some Leading Principles of Political Economy Newly Expounded* (London 1874), he said:

> If our present system of industry is to be justified, it must, according to my view, find its justification in quite another order of ideas than those of abstract right or natural law — namely, in the considerations of practical utility; and more specifically in the fact that it secures for the mass of mankind a greater amount of material and moral well-being, and provides more effectually for their progress in civilization, than any other plan that has been yet, or apparently can be, devised.[127]

Applying this utilitarian principle to the question of private property, Cairnes found a justification for property rights in their stimulus to saving:

> the storing up of the products of past industry for the purpose of sustaining and assisting present industry, can only be attained at the cost of certain sacrifices. . . These sacrifices may be regarded as trivial or severe; but, as a matter of fact, they will not be undergone without an adequate motive in the form of a compensating reward. Such a motive our present system of industry provides in the maintenance of private property and industrial freedom.[128]

Cairnes rejected two possible substitutes for private saving, "benevolence and public spirit," as inadequate. Obviously, he had not contemplated the possibility of five-year plans of public savings being carried through by authoritarian governments. Another weakness of Cairnes's theory was that he made no attempt to determine how much property and inequality were necessary to induce the savings that society wanted. Like Senior and John Stuart Mill before him, he assumed that abstinence was a sacrifice that must be remunerated, but made no attempt to explore the nature of the response of savings to alterations in the net remuneration from capital investment. The changes that have taken place in the opinion of economists on this subject since Cairnes wrote are outlined in Chapter XI.

The least aggregate sacrifice principle of taxation. Subsequent developments of thought on the subject of interference with distribution by way of taxation have followed two major lines, according as the effects on distribution or on production have been emphasized.

Bentham's distributional argument for progressive taxation has been

127 American edition, N. Y. 1874, p. 270.
128 *Ibid.*, p. 272.

carried to its logical conclusion in what has been called the principle of *least aggregate sacrifice*. If the Benthamite postulate be accepted, that the happiness conferred by uniform increments of wealth diminishes as the quantity of wealth possessed is increased, and if the further assumption be made, that increments of wealth affect the happiness of all people in the same manner, then it follows that taxation would reduce happiness least if it were concentrated on the richest people. This view has been put forward by T. N. Carver (1865–) in the United States of America and by F. Y. Edgeworth in England. As Edgeworth put it,

> The solution of this problem in the abstract is that the richer should be taxed for the benefit of the poorer up to the point at which complete equality of fortunes is attained.[129]

Carver's statement of the principle of least aggregate sacrifice appeared in an article entitled *The Ethical Basis of Distribution and its Application to Taxation,* published in the *Annals of the American Academy of Political and Social Science* in 1895, and Edgeworth's contribution was made shortly afterwards. What these articles questioned was whether progressive taxation as such was enough to meet the distributional objections to inequality of wealth. The answer was given that what was needed for this purpose was a 100 per cent tax on all incomes above a certain level, namely that at which incomes were equalized. As a practical proposal, this scheme is open to the objection, raised by the series of men whose writings have been studied, to all projects for economic equality, that is, that it would injure production. Both Carver and Edgeworth appreciated this fact and regarded the principle as a distributional ideal rather than as a workable tax formula.

But it is necessary to inquire into the soundness of an equalitarian standard based upon the greatest happiness principle. Like other theories, its validity rests upon that of the assumptions on which it is based. Has wealth the same capacity to confer happiness or utility upon different individuals? Bentham postulated, in general terms, that people had all the same capacity for happiness. Hegel, on the other hand, believed individuals to be naturally unequal. There is nothing in economics to indicate which of these assumptions is correct. The position was well stated by Robbins in a recent article:

> I began to feel that there were profound difficulties in a complete fusion between what Edgeworth called the economic and the hedonistic calculus. I am not clear how these doubts first suggested themselves; but I well remember how they were brought to a head by my reading somewhere—I think in the works of Sir Henry Maine—the story of how an Indian official had

129 *The Pure Theory of Taxation* (*Economic Journal,* London 1897), reprinted in *Papers Relating to Political Economy,* vol. 2, p. 103. Quoted by permission of Macmillan & Co., Ltd. and The Macmillan Company.

attempted to explain to a high-caste Brahmin the sanctions of the Benthamite system. "But that," said the Brahmin, "cannot possibly be right. I am ten times as capable of happiness as that untouchable over there." I had no sympathy with the Brahmin. But I could not escape the conviction that, if I chose to regard men as equally capable of satisfaction and he to regard them as differing according to a hierarchical schedule, the difference between us was not one which could be resolved by the same methods of demonstration as were available in other fields of social judgment.[130]

Pigou, in *The Economics of Welfare,* grappled with this problem, which, it will be remembered, caused the two Mills such difficulty—the evident truth that individuals are differently constituted. Where rich and poor were *of different races,* Pigou accepted that equalizing wealth might not increase economic welfare. Otherwise, he argued that, given time, all could be treated alike:

It must be conceded, of course, that, if the rich and the poor were two races with different mental constitutions, such that the rich were inherently capable of securing a greater amount of economic satisfaction from any given income than the poor, the possibility of increasing welfare by this type of change [*i.e.,* equalitarianism] would be seriously doubtful. Furthermore, even without any assumption about inherent racial difference, it may be maintained that a rich man, from the nature of his upbringing and training, is capable of obtaining considerably more satisfaction from a given income—say a thousand pounds—than a poor man would be. For, if anybody accustomed to a given standard of living suddenly finds his income enlarged, he is apt to dissipate the extra income in forms of exciting pleasure, which, when their indirect, as well as their direct, effects are taken into account, may even lead to a positive loss of satisfaction. To this argument, however, there is a sufficient answer. It is true that at any given moment the tastes and temperament of persons who have long been poor are more or less adjusted to their environment, and that a sudden and sharp rise of income is likely to be followed by a good deal of foolish expenditure which involves little or no addition to economic welfare. If, however, the higher income is maintained for any length of time, this phase will pass; whereas, if the increase is gradual or, still better, if it comes about in such a way as not to be directly perceived—through a fall in prices, for example—the period of foolishness need not occur at all.[131]

It may be doubted whether the case is so simple as this. Are "different mental constitutions" confined to different races? What is race? These are not questions which an economist can be expected to settle. Where does Pigou draw the line between "exciting pleasure" and "economic satisfaction"? Nowhere is the problem more complex than in America, where widely different races are aggregated together and, to a large extent, regarded as equal before the law. But is the case of Britain, where

[130] *Interpersonal Comparisons of Utility, Economic Journal,* 1938, p. 636.
[131] *The Economics of Welfare,* pp. 90-91.

Pigou wrote, much simpler? Enormous numbers of colored people live under the British flag and are governed from London. Most of them are extremely poor. Is the principle of increasing economic welfare by redistributing wealth to be extended to comprehend these individuals? If so, then "the white man's burden" may become a burden indeed. Unless his comment on race differences was intended to cover it, Pigou ignored this aspect. But, if colored people are excluded, on the Bentham-Sidgwick-Pigou argument—why so? Few who have lived among the colored races will deny that they are capable of learning how to spend increased incomes with wisdom, if the process of raising these incomes be made a gradual one, as Pigou advocated with respect to all the poor. Why, then, does he leave them out? In South Africa, during the depression after 1929, colored people were taxed, while white men with higher incomes (drawn, in some cases, from public relief) escaped taxation. Very few individuals, either colored or white, questioned this policy, because most South Africans are accustomed to making the Hegelian assumption that all men are *not* equal. Something of the same viewpoint is met with in the southern part of the United States.

Faced with the decision as to whether to work less and consume a smaller quantity, or labor more intensively to enjoy a higher standard of consumption, it is obvious that some individuals put the balance in one position and others prefer that it rest elsewhere. A white mountaineer in Tennessee, or a negro in Alabama or Africa, may like to laze in the sun, while a New Yorker works energetically to pay installments on a new automobile. Broadly, perhaps Pigou is right in assuming that such differences are largely racial. But are they entirely racial? It is a commonplace daily observation that they are not. One brother may leave his birthplace on the farm and spend his life in a struggle to advance in the world. Another may pass a placid existence on the home farm. Are such individuals to be fitted into a bed of Procrustes, a common standard—perhaps a compromise between the two, which suits neither of them exactly? This is the basic difficulty which the exponents of equalitarianism have to face.

Land and the Taxation of Economic Surpluses

As was noticed in earlier sections, writers on equalitarianism have recognized the importance of the effect of the redistribution of wealth upon its production. It is necessary now to consider proposals for redistribution, based on production.

The orthodox economic theory of Britain and America during the greater part of the nineteenth century postulated that wages and interest were necessary, in order that labor and abstinence might be forthcoming, but that rent was an unnecessary payment, because land would be available for productive purposes even though no rent were paid. An almost inevitable consequence of this belief was a challenge to the existence of income from the ownership of land. Land nationalization and single tax programs were the result.

John Stuart Mill. What appeared especially objectionable from the standpoint of society was not merely the existence of land rent as an economic surplus but the fact that, according to accepted economic theory from Ricardo onwards, this surplus tended to increase with the growth of population. The interest of the landlords seemed to be antagonistic to that of other members of society. As John Stuart Mill said,

If population advances more rapidly than agricultural improvement, either the labourers will submit to a reduction in the quantity or quality of their food, or if not, rent and money wages will progressively rise, and profits will fall.[132]

Although it was admitted that agricultural improvements mitigated the situation, Mill's belief was that this tendency would be insufficient to offset the influence of population growth, so that rents and land values would rise :

Agricultural improvement may thus be considered to be not so much a counterforce conflicting with increase of population, as a partial relaxation of the bonds which confine that increase.[133]

So that

The economical progress of a society constituted of landlords, capitalists, and labourers, tends to the progressive enrichment of the landlord class. . .[134]

Mill suggested that measures should be taken to obtain this "unearned increment" for social uses :

Before leaving the subject of Equality of Taxation, I must remark that there are cases in which exceptions may be made to it, consistently with that equal justice which is the groundwork of the rule. Suppose that there is a kind of income which constantly tends to increase, without any exertion or sacrifice on the part of the owners : those owners constituting a class in the community, whom the natural course of things progressively enriches, consistently with complete passiveness on their own part. In such a case it would be no violation of the principles on which private property is grounded, if the state should appropriate this increase of wealth, or part of it, as it arises. This would not properly be taking anything from anybody; it would merely be applying an accession of wealth, created by circumstances, to the benefit of society, instead of allowing it to become an unearned appendage to the riches of a particular class.[135]

Mill's proposal was to leave landowners in the possession of whatever

[132] *Principles of Political Economy,* Book 4, Chap. 3, Sect. 5.
[133] *Ibid.* [134] *Ibid.*
[135] *Ibid.,* Book 5, Chap. 2, Sect. 5.

value had accrued to a given date, taking by taxation any that arose subsequently. Obviously, the plan raised difficulties. Did not present values capitalize expected future developments? What about decrements in value? Should compensation be paid and on what basis? All these points provided material for subsequent discussion.

Herbert Spencer. About the same time, Herbert Spencer was writing in favor of land nationalization. Equity, argued Spencer, did not permit property in land:

For if *one* portion of the earth's surface may justly become the possession of an individual, and may be held by him for his sole use and benefit, as a thing to which he has an exclusive right, then *other* portions of the earth's surface may be so held; and eventually the *whole* of the earth's surface may be so held; and our planet may thus lapse altogether into private hands. Observe now the dilemma to which this leads. Supposing the entire habitable globe to be so enclosed, it follows that if the landowners have a valid right to its surface, all who are not landowners, have no right at all to its surface. Hence, such can exist on the earth by sufferance only. They are all trespassers. Save by the permission of the lords of the soil, they can have no room for the soles of their feet. Nay, should the others think fit to deny them a resting-place, these landless men might equitably be expelled from the earth altogether. . .

Passing from the consideration of the possible, to that of the actual, we find yet further reason to deny the rectitude of property in land. It can never be pretended that the existing titles to such property are legitimate. Should any one think so, let him look in the chronicles. Violence, fraud, the prerogative of force, the claims of superior cunning—these are the sources to which those titles may be traced. The original deeds were written with the sword, rather than with the pen: not lawyers, but soldiers, were the conveyancers: blows were the current coin given in payment; and for seals, blood was used in preference to wax. Could valid claims be thus constituted? Hardly. And if not, what becomes of the pretensions of all subsequent holders of estates so obtained? . . .

"But Time," say some, "is a great legaliser. Immemorial possession must be taken to constitute a legitimate claim. That which has been held from age to age as private property, and has been bought and sold as such, must now be considered as irrevocably belonging to individuals." To which proposition a willing assent shall be given when its propounders can assign it a definite meaning. To do this, however, they must find satisfactory answers to such questions as—How long does it take for what was originally a *wrong* to grow into a *right*?[136]

Spencer, like Rousseau, refused to recognize any right of the first comer to acquire ownership of the land on which he settled. To the man who crossed the Mississippi and took possession of what had been empty land hitherto, Spencer said:

[136] *Social Statics*, pp. 114-116.

Suppose now that in the course of your wanderings you come upon an empty house, which in spite of its dilapidated state takes your fancy; suppose that with the intention of making it your abode you expend much time and trouble in repairing it—that you paint and paper, and whitewash, and at considerable cost bring it into a habitable state. Suppose further, that on some fatal day a stranger is announced, who turns out to be the heir to whom this house has been bequeathed; and that this professed heir is prepared with all the necessary proofs of his identity: what becomes of your improvements? Do they give you a valid title to the house? Do they quash the title of the original claimant?" "No." "Neither then do your pioneering operations give you a valid title to this land. Neither do they quash the title of its original claimants—the human race. . ."[137]

All that Spencer was prepared to admit was that the landholder whose property was taken from him should receive compensation for his improvements:

This extra worth which your labour has imparted to it is fairly yours; and although you have, without leave, busied yourself in bettering what belongs to the community, yet no doubt the community will duly discharge your claim.[138]

Spencer's position, professedly based on ethical considerations, had an economic aspect in that in part it rested on the special importance of land to human life. Men needed land upon which to stand, to work, to live. They required it even in death, as a burial place. To recognize absolute private property in land, therefore, placed everyone but the landowners at the mercy of these privileged individuals. Scottish dukes would be justified in closing the glens to tourists, in denying sites to religious bodies of which they did not approve, even in clearing out the people themselves to make room for sheep-walks. The landowners would become, in a word, "the only legitimate rulers of a country."[139] Obviously, however, intensities of need are relative. Men's need for land, or air, or water, may be great, but there are times when their need for, say, a surgeon's skill, is no less intense. Industrial organization being as it is, coal and iron and plumbers' services are looked upon by many people as necessities, perhaps not greatly less so than land itself. Other items, undoubtedly less needed, are desirable conveniences. Anyone to whom society has granted a favorable position respecting the possession of these things may exercise exploitative power over the remainder of mankind. Thus, not land alone but the occupancy of any kind of monopolistic position becomes the subject of attack, a development that is touched upon toward the close of the present chapter and taken up again in Chapter IX.

Though retracted later in *The Principles of Ethics* (London 1879–

[137] *Ibid.*, p. 118. [138] *Ibid.*, p. 119. [139] *Ibid.*, p. 122

1893)[140] partly on the ground that it had now become impossible to say which property was the result of spoliation and which had been obtained in a more laudable manner, Spencer's views had considerable influence. For example, Tolstoy was affected by them, as is shown in the explanation of the attitude towards land ownership taken by his character, Prince Dmítry Nekhlyúdov, in the novel, *Resurrection*.

Henry George. In the meantime, in America, Henry George (1839–1897) had come forward with a striking proposal. Born in Pennsylvania, George resided in California during the period 1859–1880 and engaged in printing and journalistic work, afterwards moving to New York. Living in a time of rapidly rising land values, accompanied by poverty on the part of many, George thought that he saw taking place such a development as that which had been prophesied by Ricardo and Mill. A growing population was pushing up land values and enriching a few people, while the masses remained poor. Why not deal with the situation by taxation, he asked? Why not, indeed, concentrate all taxation on land rents, eliminating these entirely as a source of individual income?

The general idea was not altogether new. The French Physiocrats had proposed to raise all government revenue from a single tax on the rent of land. The English radical, Thomas Spence, had suggested that the community take possession of all land in private ownership, without paying compensation to the existing proprietors, renting it out and using the revenue so obtained to defray public expenditure. William Ogilvie, also, in connection with a scheme of land reform that he favored, advocated a tax on the rent of large holdings. Thomas Paine (1737–1809), a radical agitator in America, England, and France, in his *Agrarian Justice* (Paris 1797), inscribed "To the Legislature and the Executive Directory of the French Republic," advocated an inheritance tax for the purpose of raising money with which to compensate those who had been born after all land had become private property and who were not fortunate enough to inherit any. But it was Henry George who gave the plan of taxing land values its wide appeal in America. In his famous *Progress and Poverty* (San Francisco 1879),[141] George declared,

> So long as all the increased wealth which modern progress brings goes but to build up great fortunes, to increase luxury and make sharper the contrast between the House of Have and the House of Want, progress is not real and cannot be permanent. The reaction must come. The tower leans from its foundations, and every new story but hastens the final catastrophe. To educate men who must be condemned to poverty, is but to make them restive; to base on a state of most glaring social inequality political institutions

[140] See appendix B in vol. 2 of this work, entitled *The Land-Question*, pp. 440-444.

[141] The book was sub-titled: 'An inquiry into the cause of Industrial Depressions, and of Increase of Want with Increase of Wealth. The Remedy."

under which men are theoretically equal, is to stand a pyramid on its apex.[142]

In the course of the book, the idea that had been advanced by Ricardo and Mill was presented as follows:

Take now . . . some hard-headed business man, who has no theories, but knows how to make money. Say to him: "Here is a little village; in ten years it will be a great city—in ten years the railroad will have taken the place of the stage-coach, the electric light of the candle; it will abound with all the machinery and improvements that so enormously multiply the effective power of labor. Will, in ten years, interest be any higher?"

He will tell you, "No!"

"Will the wages of common labor be any higher; will it be easier for a man who has nothing but his labor to make an independent living?"

He will tell you, "No; the wages of common labor will not be any higher; on the contrary, all the chances are that they will be lower; it will not be easier for the mere laborer to make an independent living; the chances are that it will be harder."

"What, then, will be higher?"

"Rent; the value of land. Go, get yourself a piece of ground, and hold possession."

And if, under such circumstances, you take his advice, you need do nothing more. You may sit down and smoke your pipe; you may lie around like the lazzaroni of Naples or the leperos of Mexico; you may go up in a balloon, or down a hole in the ground; and without doing one stroke of work, without adding one iota to the wealth of the community, in ten years you will be rich! In the new city you may have a luxurious mansion; but among its public buildings will be an almshouse.[143]

George concluded:

We have traced the unequal distribution of wealth which is the curse and menace of modern civilization to the institution of private property in land. We have seen that as long as this institution exists no increase in productive power can permanently benefit the masses; but, on the contrary, must tend to still further depress their condition.[144]

Having examined other remedies, and found them wanting, George declared that

There is but one way to remove an evil—and that is, to remove its cause. Poverty deepens as wealth increases, and wages are forced down while productive power grows, because land, which is the source of all wealth and the field of all labor, is monopolized. To extirpate poverty, to make wages what justice commands they should be, the full earnings of the laborer, we must therefore substitute for the individual ownership of land a common

[142] 4th ed., N. Y. 1881, p. 9. Quoted by permission of the D. Appleton-Century Company, Inc.

[143] *Ibid.*, pp. 264-265.

[144] *Ibid.*, p. 295.

ownership. Nothing else will go to the cause of the evil — in nothing else is there the slightest hope.[145]

As to the details,

I do not propose either to purchase or to confiscate private property in land. The first would be unjust; the second, needless. Let the individuals who now hold it still retain, if they want to, possession of what they are pleased to call *their* land. Let them continue to call it *their* land. Let them buy and sell, and bequeath and devise it. We may safely leave them the shell, if we take the kernel. *It is not necessary to confiscate land; it is only necessary to confiscate rent.*[146]

This George proposed to do by his single tax. On this program its author campaigned for the mayor of New York in 1886, being defeated only by a combination of the two major parties against him. He engaged in lecture tours in America and elsewhere and societies were established to advance his doctrines. The plan seemed simple enough at first sight but a practical difficulty arose. How was the economic rent, which was — according to the Ricardian theory — surplus and undeserved, to be separated from the other ingredients covered by rent payments, such as those for supervision, upkeep, and recompense for past improvements? More serious, from the theoretical angle, was the question of why a tax should be imposed only on this particular surplus, if — as was widely admitted — comparable surpluses existed elsewhere, in wages and interest? The growing attention to these other surpluses, no less unnecessary and undeserved, destroyed the theoretical appeal of the George proposal.

In place of the single tax on land, therefore, there was advanced a plan to tax all surpluses, that is, all incomes that were not necessary to call into use the factors of production concerned.

J. A. Hobson. The Englishman, John A. Hobson (1858–1940), has been responsible for an important contribution to thought on this subject, developing his ideas in *The Industrial System, An Inquiry into Earned and Unearned Income* (London 1909) and *Taxation in The New State* (London 1919). Hobson used the word *costs* to denote those payments for labor and capital that were required to call forth the supplies of these factors, and the word *surpluses* for any incomes beyond costs that were received by the owners of the factors. In principle this division went back to Senior and J. S. Mill, the latter of whom used the term "Necessary Value" to mean what Hobson called costs. But Hobson divided surpluses into two categories, those needed to provide for *growth* and those not required for this purpose. The former he called productive surpluses, the latter, *unproductive.* Hobson declared that

[145] *Ibid.*
[146] *Ibid.*, p. 364.

there was nothing in the economic system to ensure that the costs of maintenance of the productive factors were covered, still less that growth was properly taken care of. But the unproductive surplus had no functions in this respect. It was the obvious source of public revenue, he said, and his proposal was to tax it wherever it appeared. Thus,

The doctrine of unproductive 'surplus' or 'unearned increment,' in the meaning here given to it, including all sorts of scarcity gains, is of supreme significance in public finance. For this 'surplus' . . . is the sole source of public revenue : it alone can 'bear' a tax, and its ability to bear it is absolute. Just as economic rent cannot shift a tax once placed or settled on it, so with every other unearned element of income. That tax cannot be shifted, because the existence of the unearned income not being an incentive to the application of the land, capital, or ability from which is is derived, the imposition of the tax will cause no withdrawal of the supply, and therefore no raising of the price. A tax placed on economic rent cannot be shifted because, so long as it leaves any rent untaken, it will still pay the landowner to keep his land in use, and so long as he does so, the total supply of available land remaining as before, the landowners cannot by raising rents shift the tax on the lessee. Similarly with a tax placed upon high interest or profits. . . In tracing the elaborate and multifarious ways in which such 'surplus' is super-imposed upon necessary expenses, wherever a factor of production is in a position of natural or contrived scarcity, we have indicated a 'fund' of a complex nature which is, in principle at any rate, amenable to the tax process on the same terms as economic rent.[147]

This, of course, was a logical development of the conception of costs, elaborated in the writings of Senior, John Stuart Mill, and Marshall, and described in Chapter IX. The idea has been used by a large number of writers and practical statesmen to justify progressive taxation but obviously it does so only in so far as unproductive surpluses tend to be present in the higher income brackets. In practice, there has been a certain amount of experiment along these lines, that is, taxes have been imposed and attempts made to observe their effects on the supply of the productive factors.[148]

As a basis of taxation the surplus principle is incomplete, as it omits to take the consumption standard into account. A portion of wages, for example, may be unnecessary from the production viewpoint, in the sense that the worker concerned is willing to labor without it, yet his total remuneration may be so low — even when this portion is included — that to levy taxes on him may be objectionable from the side of consumption. This brings the investigation back to the standard of need, set up by

[147] *The Industrial System*, 2nd ed., London 1910, pp. 227-228. Longmans.

[148] See *Report of the* [British] *Committee on National Debt and Taxation* (Colwyn Committee), Cmd. 2800, London 1927.

Godwin and the communists generally. Economists of the Marginal Utility School, through their emphasis on the principle of diminishing utility of consumers' goods, furnished an excellent argument for equalizing the distribution of wealth. In the field of taxation this has become a principle of "ability to pay" different from that met with in the writings of Hobson — ability, not from the standpoint of production, but from that of consumption. What, having regard to his consumption needs, should a man be required to pay in taxes? Thus there is offered a dual test of ability to bear taxation, depending on production and consumption respectively, and providing an economic criterion in place of the ethical standard of fairness relied upon by earlier writers in this field.

Government Supplements to Private Income

In a price economy, such as has existed in the western world during the last century, the incomes of individuals are drawn largely from the payments they receive for the services of the factors of production that they own. Men's incomes are composed of rent for their land, if they happen to possess any, interest on their capital, under the same condition, and wages for their labor, if they perform paid work, together with any profits they may make on their capital. Such a distribution of incomes is the result of the circumstances that the factors of production are in private ownership and their owners are given title to the proceeds of the sale of factor-services. In this chapter it has been pointed out that such property rights have been challenged from time to time and that extensive interference has taken place with the system of distribution based on them. The interference has taken two forms. In the first place, the property rights themselves have been limited or destroyed so that the relevant incomes have not arisen. In the second, incomes have been allowed to arise but the government has taken some of the high incomes in taxes and supplemented the low ones from the proceeds of taxation. The growth of progressive taxation of incomes and inheritances in recent years has been remarkable, while, especially since the depression of 1930 onwards, the poorest class has come to receive a considerable portion of its income by way of public relief. From those who have much, something is taken away; to those with little, income is given. Public work or money is given to the unemployed. Schooling is provided free by State authorities. Families too poor to afford decent gardens have municipal parks provided for their use. Government or city institutions in some countries furnish hospitalization service for those unable to afford it, etc.

In this situation, what is available for individuals to consume is not the earnings of the factors of production that they are able to sell, but something that may be represented by the following formula : $E + B - T = C$, where

$E =$ factor earnings (wages, interest, profits, and rent),
$B =$ benefits received otherwise (*e.g.*, unemployment relief),
$T =$ taxation, and
$C =$ income available for consumption.

A case could be made, indeed, for including savings as a deduction from income (like T in the formula) and withdrawals from savings as an addition (like B). This procedure seems especially applicable where social factors operate to make saving more or less compulsory. Thus, in some rural communities, custom requires that parents accumulate money to start their sons in farming careers. Likewise in time of war, and (as experience in the authoritarian countries of Europe has shown) even during peace, government propaganda and other pressure may be brought to bear on individuals to induce them to save. It is difficult to regard as available for current consumption the income that custom or patriotism decrees shall be saved.

The B and the T are very important, especially at the extremes of the social scale. Poor families may receive a large percentage, or even all, of their income from relief sources. The rich may pay away more than half of theirs in taxation.

It is misleading, therefore, to speak of distribution in terms of factor earnings, that is, of rent, wages, interest, and profits. The real distribution of social income is quite different and, in view of the size of the B's and T's of the formula, much more equal than the apparent distribution calculated merely from factor earnings.

Economic theorists have tackled the problem of public relief in the same manner that they have dealt with the comparable question of taxation. For example, the taxation principles elaborated in the works of such men as Sidgwick, Hobson, Edgeworth, and Carver have been applied to the problem of public benefits by writers whose general outlook is similar, like Pigou and Hugh Dalton (1887–) in England. There has been elaborated a conception of "ability to receive" public benefits, comparable to that of "ability to pay" taxation. Just as it was asked, how do taxes affect production and consumption, so it is inquired, what is likely to be the effect of public supplements to private income upon the production and consumption of the individuals concerned?

Other Recent Developments

The generalization can be made that there seems a growing tendency in most countries to subject individual property rights to social control. The land reforms of the various eastern European countries, from the Black Sea to the Baltic, at the close of the war of 1914–1918, are instances that come readily to mind. Their effect was to transfer considerable areas of agricultural land from the estates of large proprietors into the hands of peasant cultivators. But it must be remembered that feudal conditions persisted until recent years in those countries and also that the reforms were undertaken at a time when a widespread communist revolution seemed a serious danger, so that they received support from conservatives who, in more stable times, might have opposed them.

Even in the English-speaking countries, however, it is incorrect to regard property as unlimited. The doctrine of *eminent domain* has always been applied and has been given a rather wide interpretation. For example, large estates in private ownership have been taken over by the government and converted into smaller farms for sale or rent to other cultivators. This policy has been followed to some extent in Great Britain and is the basis of the "closer settlement" legislation of Australia and New Zealand.

Everywhere taxation and price regulation have limited individual property rights. In Britain, though there is no written constitution, the *De Keyser's Royal Hotel, Ltd. vs. The King,* and *France, Fenwick & Co., Ltd. vs. The King,* cases of 1920 and 1926 respectively, made it clear that the government has no right at common law to take the property of an individual for reasons of state without paying compensation. In the United States of America, the constitutional protection of private property has been responsible for the elaboration of legal principles of rate determination. The fifth and fourteenth amendments to the Federal Constitution provide that individuals are not to be deprived of life, liberty, or property, without due process of law, and these amendments have been invoked by aggrieved property owners to upset rate decisions made by regulatory bodies, in the fields of railroad transportation and other public utility services. This subject, however, must be relegated to Chapter IX for fuller treatment.

Summary of Chapter

Over a large part of human history, property has not been absolute and individual but bound up with social arrangements. Rights and duties have been interwoven. The trend in the ancient world was toward freeing property from social trammels, but the process was never completed and was reversed when the Roman Empire fell. Feudalism was a complex system in which property relations were a vital part. Not until the decline of royal absolutism in western Europe in the seventeenth and eighteenth centuries did property partake of its modern individualistic character. In more recent years there has been a pronounced swing in the opposite direction.

At different periods strong support has been given to equalitarian distribution and in the nineteenth century this received strength from utilitarian arguments. On the other hand, from the time of Aristotle, equality in distribution has been opposed on the ground that it would be a deterrent to human incentive.

The Romantics have emphasized the part played by property in the development of personality and in integrating the individual into society. The socialists have attacked private property because they have believed that it represented a denial of the right of the laborer to the whole produce of his labor. The "unearned increment" in land values, which has arisen with the growth of population, has been assailed and proposals have been made for its confiscation by the government. Recently, though, recognition has been given to the fact that this is only one form of income that is surplus or unearned in the sense that the factors of production would offer themselves for employment without it. The conception of taxing surpluses has been expanded to include all income that has this characteristic. This, and the principle of ability to pay from the consumption angle, have been incorporated into the modern theory and practice of taxation.

CHAPTER V

MOVEMENTS FOR SOCIAL REFORM

Unsatisfactory social conditions are a breeding ground for schemes of radical reform. Given that leaders are available, together with the possibility of either peaceful change or successful revolt, a movement for alteration may result. It is probably true that at no time in history has society been free from inequality and poverty—things which make men dissatisfied. The class war in Republican Rome, the English peasant revolt of the fourteenth century, the French Revolution at the end of the eighteenth century, the European political uprisings of 1848, and the revolutions of post-war Europe, are instances of serious challenges to existing social orders. The list could be extended almost indefinitely. But experience teaches that men can display a surprising amount of contentment even when they are very badly off, as was the case with the servile population of Europe in the middle ages.

Not all reformers have advocated social changes of a far-reaching nature. A writing-down of debts, a limitation of the lord's power to take possession of lands in the hands of the small cultivators, the removal of an objectionable tax, or a monetary change that would send prices up instead of permitting them to fall—such have been the measures for which agitators have striven. One of the most influential movements for social reform has come from those Christian churches that have sought to change the world as they found it into a Kingdom of Christ on earth, though personal salvation rather than the reformation of the world has been emphasized by many Christian bodies. Some of the economic implications of the Christian ideas are considered in the various chapters of this book, under the headings of Wealth, Value, and so on; and the secular movements like socialism and anarchism might have been treated in the same fashion had not convenience made a different arrangement seem preferable.

This chapter deals largely with *socialism,* so something should be said about the meaning of the word. As commonly used, the name has both broad and narrow meanings. Broadly, it is used to define a body of doctrines sharply critical of existing society. Private ownership of land and capital, and the resulting inequality, are attacked and proposals are made for substituting for the present society one where these characters are unimportant or absent altogether. Employed in this manner, the word embraces movements like *anarchism* (where individual freedom is emphasized and the functions of government are minimized) on the one hand and *authoritarianism* or *etatism* (in which the government is all-powerful) on the other. But the name socialism is used also sometimes to indicate a particular type of these doctrines, namely those advocating a system of public ownership of capital and natural resources, with government organization of production but distribution that depends on wages, as distinct from *communism,* in which distribution is on the basis of need. In practice, however, there is a good deal of laxity in the use of the words socialism and communism. The present economic system of Soviet Russia, which on the system of terminology given above is socialistic but not communistic, is often referred to under the latter name.

Early Socialist Ideas

One often sees in literature a number of early socialist projects grouped together and described as "Utopian" – the *Republic* of Plato, Sir Thomas More's *Utopia,* and other less famous schemes. Such imaginary communities have a certain similarity in that their authors described what they thought were ideal forms of social organization, without much regard to immediate practicabilities. But it must be realized that there was an immense variation in the circumstances in which these works appeared, so that grouping them together cannot be regarded as a scientific procedure.

Plato and Aristotle

Plato wrote where men were familiar with the idea of the State exercising far-reaching social functions. What he did, in the *Republic,* was to depict an authoritarian State, which differed in degree rather than in kind from the States that were or had been in existence. In conformity with Greek thought in his times, Plato visualized, not the classless State of many modern socialists, but one containing a hierarchy of classes, each with its allotted function in the social organization. The guardians were the highest class and were to be entrusted with the governance of the whole. These men, with power to command, Plato spoke of as men of gold. Below came the auxiliaries, or men of silver, who were to be the soldiers of the State. Next again, came husbandmen and craftsmen, called men of brass or iron. One of the duties of the guardians was to ascertain the capacity of each young child and decide upon its future accordingly, special care being given to the selection of the future guardians. Most children would probably remain in the same category as their parents, Plato thought, but the guardians were to promote suitable youngsters and degrade those whom they considered unworthy of the class from which they were born. The minds of the young were to be molded carefully :

S. (*Socrates*) : You know also that the beginning is the most important part of any work, especially in the case of a young and tender thing; for that is the time at which the character is being formed and the desired impression is more readily taken.

A. (*Adeimantus*) : Quite true.

S. And shall we just carelessly allow children to hear any casual tales which may be devised by casual persons, and to receive into their minds ideas for the most part the very opposite of those which we should wish them to have when they are grown up?

A. We cannot.

S. Then the first thing will be to establish a censorship of writers of fiction, and let the censors receive any tale of fiction which is good, and reject the bad; and we will desire mothers and nurses to tell their children the authorised ones only. Let them fashion the mind with such tales, even more fondly than they mould the body with their hands. . .[1]

It would appear that the architects of modern totalitarian States have studied Plato to some purpose, if accounts concerning the school books of Soviet Russia, for instance, are to be trusted. No doubt the Athenian philosopher, had he thought of it, would have set his guardians the task of conducting propaganda among adults in favor of the policies decided upon by these officials : at least such an action would have been in full accord with his general thought.

In Plato's State, education was to be directed to social ends. Boys were to be familiarized with warfare at an early age, in order that they might make good fighters when they reached maturity. Social planning, however, was not to begin with infancy. Even births were to be regulated, especially as regards the quality of the children (this subject is dealt with in Chapter VII). If need arose, apparently, truth might be sacrificed to the interest of the State, the guardians being allowed to tell lies for the public good—a Machiavellian attitude which perhaps even yet has not passed entirely out of favor. But, notwithstanding the great care that was to be taken in their selection and training, Plato did not expect his guardians to be entirely above reproach. To prevent their advantaging themselves at the expense of the State, he forbade them to possess either property in goods or families of their own. In other words, they were to have communism in goods and wives, a point treated in Chapter IV.

Plato recognized that the society of his *Republic* was an ideal and that it might not be capable of practical attainment. He thought of it as a perfect State, by means of which others might be judged. In his later work, the *Laws,* there was offered something that its author regarded as more practicable, though it was less socialistic.

The *Republic* had considerable influence on later socialist thought. The *Civitas solis* (City of the Sun), published in 1623 by the Italian philosopher, Tommaso Campanella (1568–1639), owed a good deal to Plato's work, though Campanella introduced a religious element. Sir

[1] *The Dialogues of Plato,* vol. 3, *Republic,* p. 59.

Thomas More, likewise, and other makers of Utopian societies, derived inspiration from the *Republic*.

In Chapter IV it was shown that Plato's attitude to property found little favor in the mind of Aristotle. But even the later philosopher, in his *Politics,* described a society that appears highly socialistic, according to modern standards. A certain amount of communism in distribution was visualized. Land in private ownership was to be so divided that every proprietor possessed some of that near to the frontier, to give all an interest in national defense. Like the State depicted in Plato's *Republic,* Aristotle's society was to be based on class differentiation. There were to be warriors and councilors, priests drawn from both of these classes, as well as a third group of husbandmen, craftsmen, and laborers. To this third category citizenship was to be denied. Following again the precedent set by Plato, Aristotle laid down careful rules for the training of the future citizens. Attention was to be paid to physical fitness and hardihood, with preparation for military service. The character of the young was to be molded in Platonic fashion :

> The Directors of Education, as they are termed, should be careful what tales or stories the children hear, for all such things are designed to prepare the way for the business of later life, and should be for the most part imitations of the occupations which they will hereafter pursue in earnest.[2]

The legislators were to consider who should marry and at what age, while numbers of children were to be regulated in the State's interest. From this it is clear that, in spite of his well-remembered attack on communism, Aristotle was prepared to go a long way towards what now would be regarded as socialism. Certainly, the theoretical position he maintained was extreme. Searching for a social objective, at the beginning of one of his ethical works, *Magna moralia,* he declared,

> First of all, then, we must see that every science and art has an end, and that too a good one; for no science or art exists for the sake of evil. Since then in all the arts the end is good, it is plain that the end of the best art will be the best good. But statecraft is the best art, so that the end of this will be the good.[3]

Even Hegel went no farther than this in making a forthright identification of ethics with the good of the State.

Socialist Thought in Later Centuries

Christianity and social revolt. Stoic thought contained an important socialist ingredient, in its emphasis on the equality and brotherhood of men. The same was true of Christianity. But the communism of the early Christian groups was perhaps less of an attempt to reform the world

[2] *The Works of Aristotle,* vol. 10, *Politica,* 1336a.

[3] *Ibid.,* vol. 9, 1182a.

than to escape from it, in preparation for entry into God's kingdom, and this has been true throughout the history of Christianity. On the other hand, some religious bodies have made a real attempt to communize the world. The Anabaptist movement in Germany in the sixteenth century may be mentioned. The Anabaptists can be described as being on the left wing of the Protestant Reformation. They criticized many of the practices of the older Catholic Church, receiving their name from their rejection of infant baptism. Individual judgment, with equality and community of goods, were the tenets of their faith. They rose in revolt in an endeavor to establish a new social order based on these principles but were defeated and their leaders executed.

More's Utopia. Contemporary with the Anabaptist movement, and to some extent explained by the same causes, was the *Utopia* of Sir Thomas More. In the guise of an anonymous explorer, who had visited the country in the course of his travels, More told of an island State whose government was democratic and whose ruler was elected for life, with lesser functionaries appointed for shorter terms. The inhabitants preferred meals in common to those partaken of individually:

> For thoughe no man be prohibited to dyne at home, yet no man doth it willynglye, because it is counted a pointe of small honestie. And also it were a follye to take the payne to dresse a badde dyner at home, when they maye be welcome to good and fyne fare so nyghe hande at the hall.[4]

The communistic family arrangements favored by Plato were not found in Utopia, though population received some attention. Thus, if the number of citizens in Utopia proper fell below the desired level, inhabitants were withdrawn from outer settlements. All healthy persons had to work:

> The chyefe and almoste the onelye offyce of the Syphograuntes [*i.e.*, administrative officials] ys to see and take hede that no man sytte ydle, but that everye one applye hys owne crafte wyth earneste delygence. . .[5]

Yet men did not have to labor like beasts. Six hours a day sufficed to complete all necessary work. Indeed, even this short period was more than enough, the author said, because Utopia did not contain large numbers of idlers, who in other countries included "almoost all women, which be the halfe of the hole numbre," to say nothing of priests, rich men, and beggars. As a result, proclamations had to be made from time to time, reducing hours of labor, because "the magistrates do not exercise their citizens againste theire willes in unneadfull laboures." The sick were supported without working, being nursed back to health if this were pos-

[4] *Sir Thomas More's Utopia,* ed. J. C. Collins, Oxford 1904, new impression 1927, p. 70. Quoted by permission of the Oxford University Press.

[5] *Ibid.*, p. 60.

sible, but persuaded to allow themselves to be put to death if affected by incurable and painful diseases. The volume of production does not appear to have been great. More spoke of the Utopians as having simple tastes. At work they wore leather garments that were said to last for seven years. A cloak hid this homely apparel when walks were taken abroad. Even these cloaks were all of one color, "the naturall colour of the wul." Equality was preserved by the treatment of all alike in production and consumption, allowing for differences in age and physique.

These features have been copied by numerous writers. *Looking Backward 2000–1887* (Boston 1888), by the American, Edward Bellamy (1850–1898), and *News from Nowhere* (London 1891), by William Morris (1834–1896), the English socialist, exercised great influence on socialist thought in the English-speaking countries at the end of the nineteenth century. *Economic Equality in the Co-operative Commonwealth* (London 1933), by the economist, H. S. Jevons (1875–), is a recent example of a work on Utopian lines. Indeed, so popular have Utopias become that another contemporary economist, who happens also to be a humorist of some standing, Stephen Leacock (1869–1944), recently wrote, poking fun at them by describing the experiences of an individual who woke up in Utopia, only to astonish the inhabitants of that community by showing them that he knew all about them from his previous reading. Notwithstanding its age and the multitude of imitators, however, More's work remains pre-eminent.

It is free from an important error into which some later Utopian writers have fallen. The society depicted by More was equalitarian. Its people had a greater quantity of this world's goods than the poor of the England with which its author was familiar, but they lived more simply than did More's richer contemporaries. The short period of daily labor required to maintain their society rested on two factors, (1) simplicity of wants, and (2) the fact that everyone worked. Probably the gain in the latter direction, from the adoption of an equalitarian system, would be less in fact than More implied, if only because it was untrue to assume that women (who, as More said, represented half of the total population) did not work in non-Utopian society. Much women's work, such as cooking food, washing dishes, repairing clothes, and caring for children, must continue in any form of social system, though some gain would arise by reason of mass production under a communistic plan. Undoubtedly, therefore, the simplification of wants requires attention in any project to lighten the labor performed by mankind. Yet many socialists have appeared to assume that merely reforming society in the manner they advocate will remove all need for economizing resources, human and otherwise, so that a level of output that is ample to meet all conceivable wants will be attainable with only short working days. The truth is that, unless for some reason scarcity can be abolished, any form of society must pay attention both to the level of output and to the disposal of resources. In any given state of technical knowledge, society can decide how far it will satisfy its wants. It can put forward a greater effort, in order that consumption may be carried to a higher point, or it can work less, being satisfied with a lower level of consumption. The benefits of improvements in production technique can be disposed of similarly. Output can be raised so as to satisfy new wants. Alternatively the existing wants can be met with a smaller expenditure of labor and other resources. Or men can divide their gain between the two. But no society can escape from the fact that consuming more and working less are things that are mutually exclusive. More's book gave some indication that he realized this circumstance but it has received less recognition than might have been expected in later socialist literature.

Winstanley and Bellers. The English political struggles of the seventeenth century were reflected in a certain amount of socialist ideology. Mention was made in Chapter IV of the Digger movement, inspired by Gerrard Winstanley. The *Law of Freedom in a Platform,* referred to in that chapter, depicted Winstanley's ideal society. How far it went in the direction of the communist principle of "distribution according to needs" is indicated by the passage which follows :

There shall be Storehouses in all places, both in the Country and in Cities, to which all the fruits of the Earth, and other works made by Tradesmen, shall be brought, and thence delivered out again to particular Families, and to every one as they want for their use ; or else to be transplanted by ships to other Lands to exchange for those things which our Land will not or does not afford. For all the labors of Husbandmen and Tradesmen within the Land, or by Navigation to or from other Lands, shall be upon the Common Stock. And as everyone works to advance the Common Stock, so everyone shall have a free use of any commodity in the Storehouse for his pleasure and comfortable livelihood, without buying or selling or restraint from any. Having food and raiment, lodging, and the comfortable societies of his own kind, what can a man desire more in these days of his travel ? Indeed, covetous, proud, and beastly minded men desire more, either to lay by them to look upon, or else to waste and spoil it by their lusts, while other Bretheren live in straits for the want of the use thereof. But the Laws and Faithful Officers of a Free Commonwealth do regulate the irrational conduct of such men.[6]

There were to be two kinds of storehouses. One was to contain raw materials and from it the workers were to draw the goods required for their several trades. The other was for finished products, which were to be issued to consumers as needed. No money would pass in either case :

[6] Quoted by L. H. Berens, in *The Digger Movement in the Days of the Commonwealth,* p. 218.

If any man or family want corn or other provisions, they may go to the Storehouses and fetch without money. If they want a horse to ride, go into the fields in Summer, or to the Common Stables in Winter, and receive one from the Keepers, and when your journey is performed, bring him where you had him, without money. If any want food or victuals, they may either go to the butchers' shops and receive what they want without money, or else go to the flocks of sheep or herds of cattle, and take and kill what meat is needful for their families, without buying and selling.[7]

Two difficulties in connection with such a scheme will occur to one habituated to capitalistic society: (1) how are demands or wants to be kept in check, and (2) will production be sufficient? Under the first heading, Winstanley appears to have relied upon "the Laws and Faithful Officers" of the commonwealth to regulate unreasonable actions of individual men, so that it appears that the greedy were to be disciplined in some manner. On the other hand, a good deal of reliance was placed upon education.

With respect to production, also, education was Winstanley's answer:

the Law of a Commonwealth doth require that not only a Father, but that all Overseers and Officers should make it their work to educate children in good manners, and to see them brought up in some trade or other, and to suffer no children in any Parish to live in idleness and youthful pleasures all their days, as many have been; but that they may be brought up like men and not like beasts. That so the Commonwealth may be planted with laborious and wise experienced men, and not with idle fools.[8]

And as boys are trained up in learning and in trades, so all maids shall be trained up in reading, sewing, kniting, spinning of linnen and woollen, music, and all other easy neat works, either for to furnish Storehouses with linnen and wooll cloth, or for the ornament of particular houses with needlework. If this course were taken, there would be no idle person or beggar in the Land, and much work would be done by that now lazy generation for the enlarging of the Common Treasury.[9]

Incidentally, no one was allowed to be trained wholly in book-learning, as were the scholars who lived in monarchial society, in case "through idleness they spend their time to find out policies to advance themselves to be Lords and Masters over their laboring brethren, which occasions all the trouble in the world."[10] Inventions were to be encouraged, by conferring honor on those who were responsible for them. Undoubtedly, Winstanley—like More before him—looked to the upbuilding of new standards of social approval and disapproval to a large extent to ensure the smooth working of his communistic scheme. Men might be trained to be industrious and not greedy, Winstanley thought, and any who happened to have longings in other directions could be kept in line by their fellows. But this was implied, rather than stated in a formal manner

[7] *Ibid.*, p. 217. [8] *Ibid.*, p. 214. [9] *Ibid.*, p. 215 [10] *Ibid.*

in his writings. Short of actual trial, it is doubtful whether settlement of the problem could have been carried much farther.

The project of the English Quaker, John Bellers (c. 1654–1725), may be linked with the ideas of the Diggers half a century before it appeared. Bellers's scheme was in the form of an appeal for subscriptions to establish what he called "A Colledge of Industry." The title of his book, like many others of its time, was long: *Proposals for Raising a Colledge of Industry of all useful Trades and Husbandry, with Profit for the Rich, A Plentiful Living for the Poor, and A Good Education for Youth. Which will be Advantage to the Government, by the Increase of the People, and their Riches* (London 1696). Bellers's plan was to establish a self-sufficing community of about three hundred persons, the capital being provided and the government undertaken by subscribers or stockholders. The production system was to be partly communistic. Based to some extent on individual abilities, promotion to a life of ease was held out as an inducement for good work. Distribution within the community was to be according to needs but the stockholders were to receive a return. The project, which in itself came to nothing, appears to have been the source of inspiration of the communistic proposals of Robert Owen, referred to below, and was so acknowledged by the latter writer.

Modern Proposals for Social Reform

Such writings as those described above had a certain contemporary influence, but the socialist movement of modern times dates from the close of the eighteenth century. Social conditions in the period of the industrial revolution provoked criticism and discontent. The prevailing political theories in England and France gave an equalitarian slant to the criticism. Locke and Rousseau had emphasized the liberty and equality of men, yet in practice it was obvious that the freedom of most men was limited by the necessity to sell their labor in order to obtain the means of subsistence. Gross inequality, rather than its opposite, characterized the distribution of wealth. In other words, of the three natural rights that had been recognized by Locke—liberty, equality, and property—one, namely property, appeared to be subverting the other two. As a result, the mass of mankind seemed to be doomed to continual labor. This argument led inevitably to the socialists' attack upon property rights and has been traced in Chapter IV. In the closing years of the eighteenth century, the French revolutionaries adopted the natural-rights slogan of "liberty, equality, and fraternity"; but the propertied middle classes dominated the Revolutionary governments and Locke's other natural right—that of property—received support throughout. Babeuf's protest and his fate have been referred to in Chapter IV. The confiscation of the lands of the Church and of emigrant nobles is to be regarded as a measure of political punishment rather than as an attack upon property as such, so that it was left to later socialist writers to assail property *per se*. In the course of their criticism of inequality, necessarily the socialists had to endeavor to elucidate what was meant by equality. What did equal distribution of wealth mean? Obviously, it could not mean an equal amount *per head,* since small children did not need so much as grown men. Still less could it refer to an equal portion *per worker,* or Brown, with a wife and twelve children, would have to support these from the same income as was received by his friend Smith, who was unmarried and had no dependents. Two general principles have been followed by socialists: (1) distribution on the basis of *desert* or *productive labor* has been suggested, as has (2) division on the basis of *consumptive needs.* These raise the questions of the *right of man to labor,* the *right to the produce of labor,* and the *right to subsistence.* The socialists have persistently declared that the existing individualist system is *unfair,* which calls forth the question *what is fair?* On examination, it is usually found that the distributional side of the answer is made to rest upon such contentions as the existence of the right to work, the right to enjoy the produce of one's work, and the right to means of support. This subject has received attention in Chapter IV.

It cannot be said that there has been agreement among the socialists as to the nature of the society which was to supplant the existing one. In general terms, it was accepted that private property over important fields should be abolished, but there has been disagreement as to exactly how far the abolition should go. Should all producers' and consumers' goods be socially owned, not merely land and factories, but dwelling houses, furniture, food, and suits of clothes? Or should property rights be permitted in consumption goods? If the latter, should this apply to all such goods, even houses, or only to less important items, like food and clothes? Should ownership be vested in the State, or in producers' groups? Are people to be given money wages and permitted to spend these as they choose, or is remuneration to be in kind, *i.e.,* in goods and services? What is to be the title of individuals to the receipt of their shares in distribution, the work they do, or the mere fact of the existence of their consumptive needs? Should production be organized by the State, by smaller groups recognized or set up for the purpose, like gilds or modern co-operatives, or left to individuals? Should groups or individuals be self-sufficing, or should there be specialization and therefore exchange? How is the new society to be established, by constitutional methods or by revolt? If the latter, should the procedure be by armed insurrection or by the weapon of the general strike? Is it necessary that the State set up the new commonwealth, or could this be relied upon to establish itself in the absence of State action? Is it to be maintained afterwards by State authority, or is the State to disappear once socialism has become established? All these possibilities have received some support.

The Anarchism of William Godwin

Foremost among anarchists and communists was William Godwin, who wrote when the French Revolution was disturbing men's minds. Godwin believed that the environment explained why man fell short of perfection. He thought that such vices as robbery and fraud originated in poverty and in the ostentation and tyranny of the rich. They are rendered permanent by legal penalties that made it impossible for the fallen people to raise themselves and by the continuance of that inequality of wealth which had caused the defects in the first instance. Government was responsible for these conditions, Godwin said. This thesis was developed in the famous *Enquiry Concerning Political Justice*:

> My propensities are the fruit of the impressions that have been made upon me, the good always preponderating, because the inherent nature of things is more powerful than any human institutions. The original sin of the worst men, is in the perverseness of these institutions, the opposition they produce between public and private good, the monopoly they create of advantages which reason directs to be left in common. What then can be more shameless than for society to make an example of those whom she has goaded to the breach of order, instead of amending her own institutions, which, by straining order into tyranny, produced the mischief? Who can tell how rapid would be our progress towards the total annihilation of civil delinquency, if we entered upon the business of reform in the right manner? [11]

With men in their existing state, Godwin affirmed, "a self-love of the narrowest kind is so deeply rooted in many of them" [12] that an entirely voluntary system was not immediately practicable. But he believed that institutions should be designed to assist in human improvement. Coercion — that is, government regulation or restraint — should be minimized and people encouraged to govern themselves:

> It is earnestly to be desired, that each man should be wise enough to govern himself without the intervention of any compulsory restraint; and, since government even in its best state is an evil, the object principally to be aimed at is, that we should have as little of it as the general peace of human society will permit.[13]

A prominent place in institutional reform was allotted to equalizing the distribution of wealth, Godwin's opinion on this subject having been given attention in Chapter IV. Briefly, he argued in favor of distribution according to consumptive needs and believed that the removal of inequality in distribution would effect enormous improvement in the

[11] 2nd ed., vol. 2, p. 251.
[12] 1st ed., London 1793. vol. 1, p. 137.
[13] 2nd ed., vol. 1, p. 201.

nature of mankind, so that coercion would no longer be necessary. In a chapter entitled, "Benefits Attendant on a System of Equality,"[14] Godwin declared,

> In a state of society where men lived in the midst of plenty, and where all shared alike the bounties of nature, these sentiments [*i.e.*, the spirit of oppression, envy, etc.] would inevitably expire. The narrow principle of selfishness would vanish. No man being obliged to guard his little store, or provide with anxiety and pain for his restless wants, each would lose his individual existence in the thought of the general good.[15]

Godwin's postulate — that men lived in the midst of plenty — is important. It is the point brought out in connection with the *Utopia* of Sir Thomas More. Godwin seemed to have in mind, like More, the achievement of plenty by *simplifying wants,* not merely by *increasing output.* In so far as a reduction in wants was contemplated, the resulting benefit in leisure and contentment cannot be regarded as directly due to equality. Granted that equality might reduce desires by making emulation less important, the benefit in the way of promoting human leisure — if it is to be regarded as a benefit — flows from the *reduction of wants,* not from *equality* as such.

To bring about a state of equality, Godwin considered that no action was necessary. The "inevitable progress of improvement" insensibly led toward equality,[16] he said. As men became better educated, they would lose their selfishness. This was not to say, however, that conscious action could not facilitate the change. The goal should be borne clearly in mind, in order that the progress toward it might be accelerated — for example, by the modification of the system of legal punishments.

The essential features of Godwin's doctrine — anarchism and communism — were neither of them new. In ancient Greece Aristippus and especially Zeno, in their teachings, had defended individual freedom against the power of the State, the latter strongly criticizing Plato's *Republic* in this connection. The same anarchistic ingredient was present in the Stoic-Roman-medieval concept of natural law. Godwin, however, is to be regarded as being at once the father of modern anarchism and of modern communism and his writings have exercised great influence in various directions — for example, they stimulated Malthus to write his well-known *Essay on the Principle of Population.*

The Industrial System of Saint-Simon

Entirely different were the theories of Saint-Simon. His thought was a reaction against the politics of the Revolution and the military system of Napoleon. In the Bourbon Restoration which followed the fall of the Empire, there seemed to be some danger that the return of the emigrant

[14] *Ibid.*, Book 8, Chap. 3. [15] *Ibid.*, vol. 2, p. 338. [16] *Ibid.*, vol. 2, p. 400.

nobles would injure the industry that had developed during the war period. Saint-Simon espoused the cause of industry. To his mind, it was not kings and royal officials who were important but industrialists and professional men. A parable in *L'Organisateur* (Paris 1819), which has not been translated, summarized his viewpoint. Here he asked his readers to consider which the country would feel more, (1) the loss of a number of the leading doctors, the best chemists, the most distinguished physiologists and bankers, the most prominent agriculturists, and so forth, or (2) a corresponding number of members of the Royal family and the nobility, ministers of State, and government officials. France, he declared, would no doubt be grieved over the latter loss but would be crippled by the former. So the conclusion was drawn that it was the professional and industrial classes, not statesmen or politicians, who were important. Saint-Simon advocated that chambers of professional men, industrialists, and scientists be entrusted with the government of society, with the object of increasing its productive efficiency. This he referred to as the *Industrial System* and he declared it to be the final system — the one for which all others were merely preparatory. He said that the distribution of incomes should be on the basis of the contributions made to production by the person concerned. For the formula, *to each according to his needs,* which Godwin had favored, there was substituted another, *to each according to his works*. Saint-Simon's view of the importance of industry to society, and the view that those should run it who are — technically — most competent to do so has been widely held at different times. It was the essential feature of the so-called *Technocracy,* which aroused interest a few years ago. Such an attitude is fundamentally different from that of Godwin. Godwin looked upon production as merely incidental to human character and human liberty. Saint-Simon put it in the front place.

The Self-Contained Communities of Owen and Fourier

While the Saint-Simonians were writing, Robert Owen (1771–1858), in Britain, and Charles Fourier (1772–1837), in France, advanced schemes of still different nature. Owen was a self-made factory-owner, who had become deeply concerned over the conditions under which the workers had to live in the rising industrial centers of his time, especially the position of child labor. As a result, he experimented with a system of education for the young people employed in his own factory at New Lanark, Scotland, and gave active support to the movement for factory legislation that found expression in the measure passed by the British parliament in 1819. Interesting himself in the distress of unemployed workers during the severe depression that followed the end of the Napoleonic Wars, he was led to recommend to his own county of Lanark and for general adoption the establishment of self-supporting villages, on the lines of those proposed by Bellers a century before. Each was to include 1200 persons, who would require 600 to 1800 acres of land for their support, the area varying according to the quality of the soil and the type of industry to be carried on. Buildings were to be erected in a parallelogram, containing school, kitchen, dining, sleeping, and sitting rooms, storehouses, and so forth. Wearing simple dress and eating plain food, the members of each community would produce according to their several abilities and partake of the produce according to their needs, that is, the system of production and distribution was to be communistic. Under these conditions, Owen argued, human selfishness would disappear :

> These new associations can scarcely be formed before it will be discovered that by the most simple and easy regulations all the natural wants of human nature may be abundantly supplied; and the principle of selfishness . . . will cease to exist for want of an adequate motive to produce it. It will be quite evident to all, that wealth of that kind which will alone be held in any estimation amongst them may be so easily created to exceed all their wants, that every desire for individual accumulation will be extinguished. To them individual accumulation of wealth will appear as irrational as to bottle up or store water in situations where there is more of this invaluable fluid than all can consume.[17]

Owen hoped that government authorities would be induced to establish such communities and was greatly disappointed when they failed to do so, especially since he had friends who were influential in official circles. As a result of this failure to obtain outside support, he himself established communities, at New Harmony in Indiana (where he purchased one ready-made, from the Rappites, a religious group), and at Queenwood, in Hampshire, England. Both these ventures resulted in financial loss, however, and ultimately closed down.

In the meantime, Fourier was conducting propaganda in favor of similar projects in France. Fourier came from a middle-class family, whose property had been lost in the Revolutionary period. Compelled to earn his own living, he wrote in his spare time. He was a dreamer, rather than a practical man like Owen, and he wrote as though he believed himself gifted with divine knowledge of the possibilities of future human evolution.

Fourier's objective was the harmonious development of human nature, free from the restrictions imposed by law and convention in existing society, such as marriage and private property. In other words, full play was to be given to human feelings or passions. To attain this, he projected communities, similar to those of Owen, terming them *phalansteries*. Large buildings were to be erected, giving accommodation to

[17] *Report to Lanark,* reprinted in *A New View of Society and Other Writings,* Everyman's Library, London 1927, pp. 288-289. Quoted by permission of J. M. Dent & Sons, Ltd., and E. P. Dutton & Co., Inc.

numerous persons and surrounded by sufficient land for maintenance. Fourier mentioned various numbers — 810, 1000, and 1620 — but his object was clear. He wanted to ensure that the group was large enough so that that all human talents would be represented:

among every 810 persons Nature distributes all the talents necessary for excelling in the different branches of human activity. Hence an Association of 1,000 persons would necessarily have in its ranks eminent performers of all kinds; that is, if the capacities of each were cultivated and developed from infancy, as would be the case in the Combined Order.[18]

The communities were not to be entirely independent. Fourier visualized their members co-operating to form industrial armies, for the purpose of carrying through large undertakings (he even referred to the reclamation of the Sahara desert!). Concert parties also were to travel between the various communities. His system of distribution, unlike that of Owen, rejected communism. Labor was to get five twelfths of the product, capital four twelfths, and management three twelfths. Even inheritance was not ruled out.

This social program was set forth first in the *Théorie des quatre mouvements* (2 vols., Lyons 1808) and expanded in later works. Considerable opposition was roused by these writings, due in no small degree to the support they gave to loose sex relationships, based upon passion and untrammeled by social ties. Fourier secured some followers, however, and, although he himself was too poor to finance the establishment of communities, certain of his supporters did so. As a result a number of these were set up, of which Brook Farm, organized in Massachusetts in 1841, is the best known J. B. A. Godin, a French manufacturer who had come under Fourier's influence, gave financial assistance and operated his own enterprise on Fourierist principles (ultimately it became a cooperative concern). Unless this enterprise is counted, all the Fourierist experiments failed, exactly as did those of Owen.

A member of the Oneida community, an American religious association, gave an interesting reason for the failure, referring especially to Owen's New Harmony scheme:

There are only two ways of governing such an institution as a Community; it must be done either by law or by grace. Owen got a company together and abolished law, but did not establish grace; and so, necessarily failed.[19]

What was meant here was that religious communities, such as the Oneida and Rappite villages, were run by "grace" or religious enthusiasm. In the absence of "grace," authority might suffice. According to this critic, Owen furnished neither. The membership of New Harmony included

[18] *Théorie des quatre mouvements,* translated by H. Clapp, Jr., as *The Social Destiny of Man, or Theory of the Four Movements,* N. Y. 1857, p. 140.

[19] J. H. Noyes, *History of American Socialisms,* Phila. 1870, p. 54.

a number of able people but they were individualistic and did not pull together, so constant bickerings led to the dissolution of the community. But the associations advocated by Owen and Fourier had another defect. They were intended to be self-sufficing or largely so, yet they were too small to admit of any considerable specialization of labor. Mass production was impossible. If the residents came together, knowing this and prepared to live simply for the attainment of their ideals, well and good. But Fourier claimed that the productive efficiency was one of the advantages of his associations :

> An Association, supposing it to number a thousand persons, offers such enormous advantages to industry, that the indifference which prevails on the subject is almost inexplicable. . . they [*i.e.,* economists] have perceived . . . that three hundred families associated together would have one granary kept in good order, instead of three hundred granaries kept in bad order; one dairy carefully attended to instead of three hundred dairies managed generally with extreme ignorance; that instead of sending a hundred milkmen to market, they would send but one; that in various cases, especially in Summer, they would have three or four large fires instead of three hundred small ones, etc., etc. These are some of the economies which have been recognized by different observers, who have not, however, indicated a twentieth part of the advantages which would result from Agricultural Association.[20]

It was, indeed, economic benefit which Fourier relied upon to a large extent to harmonize the interests of the many individuals gathered in each phalanstery :

> "How, in a word, absorb the jealousies of individuals in a plan of general and combined operations?" To this I reply — by the allurements of wealth and of pleasure. The strongest passion of the great majority of men, in the country as well as the city, is love of gain; and when they see an associated township, the chances being equal, yield three, five, seven times as much as a township of isolated families, and at the same time secure to all the associates the most varied enjoyments, they will forget all their rivalries and hasten to organize Association, which will extend itself at once, and without the least intervention of law, throughout all regions. . .[21]

Had Fourier's expectations of economic advantage proved correct, it is possible that his prophecy of rapid expansion of the association movement would have been realized. Both he and Owen wished to establish a few communities and fully expected that more would follow, until ultimately society was transformed. Instead, the examples disappeared and society remained unchanged.

The Co-operative Workshops of Louis Blanc

Associations of a different type were advocated by Louis Blanc (1811–1882). Blanc was the son of a French official in Spanish employment

[20] *The Social Destiny of Man,* p. 8. [21] *Ibid.,* p. 9.

during the period of Napoleonic domination. Later he became a journalist and in 1839 published in Paris a study entitled *Organisation du travail.*[22] In his literary work Blanc had taken the radical side during the struggles that preceded the revolution of 1848 and, on the outbreak of the latter, he became a socialist member of the provisional government and president of the so-called Luxembourg labor commission. In his *Organisation du travail,* Blanc had asserted the right of every man to subsistence and favored a society in which production was according to abilities and consumption on the basis of needs—a formula that appears to be as old as the Stoics and has been adopted as their own by modern communists.

For the realization of this aim, Blanc made certain proposals, including one to the effect that undertakings such as mines and railroads should be nationalized. State credits should be advanced to associations of workmen, he said, to enable them to purchase raw materials and tools and thus to engage in production without having to hire themselves to capitalists for the purpose. These associations were to be entirely different from those of Owen and Fourier. Where the earlier writers had advocated self-contained communities, Blanc favored co-operative associations of specialized producers. Their products were to be intended largely for the market, and the income resulting from their sale was to be used for the support of the members. As a practical measure, interest was to be paid on the capital used to establish the undertakings, but after this had been repaid the revenue was to be employed (1) as wages, (2) to maintain the infirm and contribute to other industries, and (3) to provide funds for extension, by supplying tools to new members. Thus Blanc hoped that the associations would expand over the entire field of industry.

The revolutionary government recognized the laborers' right to work, and for the attainment of this objective ordered the establishment of national workshops under the direction of an engineer, Émile Thomas (1822–1880). Thomas appears to have controlled them in accordance with the wishes of the antagonistic majority of the provisional government, so that, while seeming to fall in with Blanc's program, they discredited it. The guarantee of the right to work led the government into offering employment to all comers. Useless earthworks were constructed. The workshops of the groups of laborers on relief work became centers of political agitation. The government called some of the disaffected workers into the army. A revolt ensued, but it was speedily crushed and a period of reaction followed. The difficulties with which an official recognition of the right of all to work is associated have not been solved even today, as is shown by the complex problem presented by the continuance of large-scale public relief in western countries. With respect

[22] Translated by M. P. Dickoré as *Organization of Work,* Cincinnati 1911.

to co-operative workshops, aided by government credit, such as Blanc proposed, these face the problems of co-operation generally, on which subject something is said in a later section.

Christian Socialism[23]

Brief mention must be made of the Christian Socialist movement, which appeared in England after the failure of the Chartist agitation of the 1830's and 1840's. With a view to placing the working class in political control and so making possible far-reaching social reforms, a *People's Charter* had been prepared. Parliament was petitioned to enact the Charter but—though subsequently most of its points became law—it refused. The unrest continued and at times assumed revolutionary proportions. But the agitators met with a number of defeats and the movement collapsed. Yet there were those in the upper social strata who felt that something should be done to ameliorate the condition of the laboring class, and among them were the men who gave themselves the name of *Christian Socialists.* Thomas Hughes (1822–1896), who, though trained in the law and for a time a member of Parliament, is probably best known as the author of *Tom Brown's School Days,* joined the group. Two clergymen and college professors, J. F. D. Maurice (1805–1872), and Charles Kingsley (1819–1875), the latter a novelist of repute, also took part in the movement, as did E. Vansittart Neale (1810–1892), who later was active in British consumers' co-operative organizations.

Notwithstanding their choice of name, it is difficult to describe these men as out-and-out socialists. Kingsley, indeed, especially as he became older, advanced views that were in some respects ultra-conservative, looking upon the lords and bishops as the natural leaders of the people. But the Christian Socialists sought reform. How evil they regarded the existing society in one of its aspects is brought out in Kingsley's pamphlet on sweatshop tailoring, *Cheap Clothes and Nasty* (London 1850), and in his novel, *Alton Locke* (London 1850). Members of the group supported ameliorating laws—thus, they assisted in the enactment of the Industrial and Provident Societies Act of 1852, under which consumers' co-operatives developed, and sponsored the cause of the labor unions during the controversy of the 1860's and 1870's, referred to in Chapter XII. Though never more than a small body, therefore, the Christian Socialists were not without influence in the development of the modern movement for social reform, helping to prepare the ground for later developments.

[23] The English Christian Socialist movement, which is here dealt with, must be distinguished from that bearing the same name on the continent of Europe. The so-called Christian Socialist organizations of some Continental countries developed in opposition to socialist labor unions and political parties, one of the main factors behind their appearance being the opposition of religious bodies to the socialist program.

The Co-operative Movement

At this stage it seems well to refer to the rise of the co-operatives. In some respects, co-operation is a business movement, but it has its ideological side and it owes its inception to the same social protest as has given strength to the modern socialist movement.

Perhaps the most outstanding success among co-operative ventures has been the British consumers' co-operative store system. From a small beginning in the retail store of the *Rochdale Society of Equitable Pioneers,* established in 1844, an immense organization has arisen, conducting a very large percentage of the total trade in many industrial areas. Wholesale co-operatives exist in England and Scotland, to serve the needs of the local retail societies. Factories and land are owned, in Britain and abroad, to supply some of the goods sold in the stores. Banking, insurance, and building-loan enterprises are operated.

The Rochdale Pioneers grew out of unrest among a group of textile workers in Rochdale, Lancashire. A strike was mooted, as also was some form of political action. Finally co-operation carried the day. In connection with the Owenite agitation of some years previously, there had been considerable discussion among members of the working class respecting the establishment of co-operative villages, and certain enthusiasts in Rochdale revived this idea. It was decided to start a fund by small weekly subscriptions, the money to be used for trading purposes. The list of objectives of the association thus launched on its career makes interesting reading:

The establishment of a store for the sale of provisions, clothing, &c.

The building, purchasing or erecting a number of houses in which those members desiring to assist each other in improving their domestic and social conditions may reside.

To commence the manufacture of such articles as the Society may determine upon, for the employment of such members as may be without employment, or who may be suffering in consequence of repeated reductions in their wages.

As a further benefit and security to the members of the Society, the Society shall purchase or rent an estate or estates of land which shall be cultivated by the members who may be out of employment, or whose labour may be badly remunerated.

That for the promotion of sobriety, a Temperance Hotel be opened in one of the Society's houses as soon as convenient.

That as soon as practicable the Society shall proceed to arrange the powers of production, distribution, education and government; or, in other words to establish a self-supporting home-colony of united interests, or to assist other Societies in establishing such Colonies.[24]

[24] Quoted from F. Podmore, *Robert Owen,* 2 vols., London 1906, reprinted in 1 vol., London 1923, p. 584 of the reprint. By permission of George Allen & Unwin Ltd.

The scheme outlined in these sentences was obviously socialistic. Ultimately, the workers were to be self-employed, without the intervention of the capitalist. In the meantime, progress was to be made by providing work for those who had no employment or who were badly paid, and a retail store was to be established. As events turned out, this last objective came to the fore. Success in retail trading was spectacular and the more fundamental plan of reforming society was allowed to sink into the background. It is probably true that in the areas where consumers' co-operation is most important — that is, in the industrial north of England — there are many centers of population where more than half the inhabitants spend more than half of their incomes through the channel of the co-operative stores. Yet, for the most part, the individuals concerned remain wage-laborers employed in private capitalistic enterprises, exactly as were their forebears nearly a century ago, when the Rochdale Pioneers' society was established.

Much of the success of the retail co-operatives has rested upon practical points, such as the reservation of a portion of the profits for distribution to members in an annual dividend on purchases made by them. This dividend has become an institution among the working classes, being used for holiday savings, the purchase of the larger items of household equipment, and similar matters. Members are astonishingly loyal to the co-operatives and the steady and predictable nature of their business has given the stores some advantage. Again, it must be remembered that they grew up in England before the appearance of the modern chain store system, so were favored by the economies of mass selling that have enabled the chains to oust their small competitors in this country.

In addition to the retail stores, co-operation has been active over a wide field. The Danish societies for the purchase of farm requisites and the marketing of agricultural produce, the Raiffeisen land banks in Germany, and the British societies for financing home ownership, are examples that have achieved success. On the other hand, it must be recognized that the English-speaking countries and to some extent the continent of Europe are filled with the débris of failed schemes of co-operation and with co-operative organizations whose success has been no more than mediocre. The producers' co-operatives that were established in France in the middle of the last century, the farming projects set up by the British government in connection with the land settlements of the 1914–1918 war period, and the milk pool that dominated the southwestern Scotland dairy area in the late 1920's, as well as innumerable smaller ventures in the field of agricultural co-operation, instance co-operative enterprises that have proved unsuccessful.

For these failures various reasons can be assigned. Working men and small farmers do not always realize the necessity for efficient business management. Neither have they at all times appreciated the cost of the services necessary for handling produce. In consequence, they have compared, say, the dollar that a basket of fruit brings in the retail market with the thirty or forty cents received by the farmer, and, concluding that only co-operation is required to transfer most of the difference into the pockets of the producer, have hastened to set up a co-operative organization. Inexperienced management, coupled with the antagonism of other traders, has resulted in the failure of the new association to pay over to the farmers — in the long run — even the thirty or forty cents that they got from private traders, so the project has collapsed. Closer attention to the business side might have avoided the whole trouble. In agricultural marketing, especially, a large sum of public money has been expended in open or veiled subsidies of co-operative ventures. Educational institutions, for instance, have given them a good deal of free publicity and technical advice. In the absence of help of this kind, failures might have been even more common. Some of the most significant co-operative marketing projects of recent years have emphasized the control of production and of price at least as much as the economies and social benefits that attend mere working together. Organizations of this kind can be classed, quite properly, with producers' cartels or trusts. Here is discovered again one of the most common troubles of economics — the use of a single word, like co-operation, to cover a number of different things. A large organization whose principal purpose is to enable a group of producers to dominate a particular market, such as the Glasgow milk pool, appears to have as much affinity to the industrial trust or monopoly as to the socialist visions of Owen and Blanc.

Anarchists after Godwin

Possessed of a certain similarity to the co-operative movement are the doctrines of the anarchists, exemplified in the writings of William Godwin, to which reference has been made. The essential feature of anarchism, as distinct from other plans for social reform, is that it dispenses with government as this is ordinarily understood. According to the anarchists, men do not need authoritative coercion to ensure their proper behavior in society: they are capable of running society without government. The advocates of co-operation did something to indicate how this might be possible. Individuals would seek their mutual advantage by combining into voluntary associations, for productive and other purposes, reducing the function of government to the prevention of wrong-doing. Blanc's co-operation, however, was a State affair, since he relied upon State action to set up his producers' co-operatives. This is true, also, of Proudhon, who is classified commonly as an anarchist and whose ideas are referred to again below.

Godwin gave the State only a temporary and disappearing function. Its coercion of individuals was definitely harmful, he thought, perpetuating the evils against which it was directed. But it could not be swept away, in existing circumstances. Godwin believed that men's characters would have to be changed by the institution of equality and by the gradual lessening of coercion before government could be abolished altogether. Proudhon, who inherited the mantle of Godwin as leader of anarchistic thought, was a genuine proletarian, the son of a French artisan and educated by scholarships. His vigorous criticism of private property, mentioned in Chapter IV, identified him with the socialists. The revolution of 1848 brought him to the front. He became a member of the Assembly and later suffered imprisonment for his views. Like Blanc, he proposed to use the State to establish a new society. The method he favored was the provision of free credit for productive purposes, in the form of bank notes, repayable on the sale of the produce for which they were issued, but not bearing interest. The principle behind Proudhon's plan was that in existing society the worker had no capital and therefore was compelled to sell his labor to an employer. If credit were made available to him, this would become unnecessary. The capitalist system would then disappear, Proudhon thought, and in its stead there would arise one in which production continued without the intervention of the capitalist and which did not contain the class distinctions familiar in existing society. The same basic idea was responsible for the co-operative labor exchanges, advocated by Owen and others and described in Chapter IX. The true aim and purpose of government, in Proudhon's opinion, was to prevent the oppression of one class by another. In the new society, this oppression would be possible no longer, so that government would become redundant. Industry would run itself without government authority, Proudhon believed — an idea that shows traces of Saint-Simonian influence.[25]

"Max Stirner" (J. K. Schmidt), a German who made his living by teaching and translating, deserves mention here for his extreme anarchistic position. Freedom, according to Stirner, was power to do as one wanted, untrammeled by government control. He desired the attainment of this freedom, involving, of course, the abolition of government:

> The State always has the sole purpose to limit, tame, subordinate, the individual — to make him subject to some *generality* or other. . . Never does a State aim to bring in the free activity of individuals, but always that which is bound to the *purpose of the State*.[26]

But, in opposition to the State, I feel more and more clearly that there is still

[25] Proudhon advanced his doctrines in a number of books. Probably the *Idée générale de la révolution au XIX siècle* gives the best account. The works that have been translated (*Qu'est-ce que la propriété* and the first part of the *Système des contradictions économiques ou philosophie de la misère,* both translated by B. J. Tucker) give their author's criticism of existing society but not much information on his proposals concerning the new one.

[26] *The Ego and His Own,* p. 237.

left me a great might, the might over myself, *i.e.* over everything that pertains only to me and that *exists* only in being my own.[27]

Stirner said that the communists attacked the system that made the individual dependent upon other individuals, that is, on the capitalists. But communism would make him dependent on the social group, or community. Even more than Proudhon, Stirner proposed to make the individual independent of both capitalist and community—self-reliant and dependent only upon himself.

After Proudhon's death, Mikhail Bakunin (1814–1876) became recognized as the leader of European anarchism. Bakunin came of a Russian landowning family but—as he had resigned from the army and left Russia in protest against government methods—his estates were confiscated. He took part in the Dresden revolt of 1849 and was deported to Russia, where he spent some time as a prisoner in Siberia. He escaped, however, and for the remainder of his life engaged in agitation in western Europe, where his disagreement with Marx caused a split in the first socialist international organization.

Bakunin's general thesis was that the State was to be regarded as an instrument for the oppression of the working classes. It should be destroyed, therefore, he argued, when a system of anarchistic communism would appear in its place. Bakunin wished to dispense with the State because it was inherently objectionable. Government was not merely a denial of freedom to the governed, he declared: it even corrupted the governors themselves. Becoming privileged persons, though they gained "in politeness, in utilitarian and practical wisdom," they lost in spontaneity, and became sluggish:

It is the characteristic of privilege and of every privileged position to kill the mind and heart of men. The privileged man, whether politically or economically, is a man depraved in mind and heart. That is a social law which admits of no exception, and is as applicable to entire nations as to classes, corporations, and individuals. It is the law of equality, the supreme condition of liberty and humanity.[28]

The writings of Bakunin were fragmentary, the slim work on *God and the State,* which was first published in 1882 and has been quoted above, being the most significant. But he was an active servant in the cause of social revolution. Only force, he believed, could destroy the machinery of the State, and his program included the subversion of order by every possible means. *Nihilism* was the result. Open insurrection was fostered, as well as such acts as assassinations of government functionaries and bombings of buildings.

The history and thought of Prince P. A. Kropotkin (1842–1921) were similar in many respects. Possessed of an early acquaintance with the

[27] *Ibid.*, p. 268.

[28] *God and the State,* N. Y. n.d., p. 31.

Russian court, Kropotkin developed radical views during his student days but entered government service, principally engaging in scientific activity. After being imprisoned for conducting revolutionary agitation, he resided in western Europe and much of his writing was done there. Like Bakunin, Kropotkin looked to revolution to destroy the State, which he regarded as an instrument of oppression, but he said more than Bakunin had done on the nature of the society that was to succeed the present one.

Voluntary co-operation, or mutual aid, was Kropotkin's solution. This he said, had characterized men's lives from very early times and, in the absence of repression by the State, would form the basis of the future society. As stated in *Mutual Aid, a Factor of Evolution* (London 1902), Kropotkin's argument was as follows:

> neither the crushing powers of the centralized State nor the teachings of mutual hatred and pitiless struggle which came, adorned with the attributes of science, from obliging philosophers and sociologists, could weed out the feeling of human solidarity, deeply lodged in men's understanding and heart, because it has been nurtured by all our preceding evolution. What was the outcome of evolution since its earliest stages cannot be overpowered by one of the aspects of that same evolution. And the need of mutual aid and support which had lately taken refuge in the narrow circle of the family, or the slum neighbours, in the village, or the secret union of workers, re-asserts itself again, even in our modern society, and claims its rights to be, as it always has been, the chief leader towards future progress.[29]

A third member of the famous trio of Russian anarchists, Count Leo Tolstoy (1828–1910), opposed force in every form, including revolutionary activity. Instead, like Godwin, he appealed to reason to bring about the change. Basing his thesis on Christianity, Tolstoy argued that the pursuit of gain and the exercise of force were in contradiction to the Christian spirit. But some improvement was taking place, he believed. Already men were beginning to feel that it was immoral to be rich and, in consequence, they bequeathed their estates to charities. In the course of time, the Christian spirit would triumph, and oppression and force would disappear from the earth. Government, which was an instrument of violence, would cease to exist.

This general philosophy is expressed more completely in *The Kingdom of God Is Within You* (1893) than elsewhere in Tolstoy's writings but it permeates them all. Two passages from this work will serve to exemplify it:

> 'Very likely the State was needed and is still needed for all those purposes which you attribute to it,' says a man who has made the Christian understanding of life his own. 'But I know that on the one hand I no longer need

[29] 2nd ed. 1904, reprinted, London 1908, p. 292. Quoted by permission of William Heinemann, Ltd.

the State, and on the other I can no longer perform the actions that are necessary for its existence. Arrange what you need for your own lives. I cannot prove either the need or the harmfulness of government in general. I only know what I myself need and do not need, what I can do and what I cannot. I know for my own part that I do not need to divide myself from other nations, and so I cannot acknowledge my exclusive adherence to any nation or State nor subjection to any government. I know in my own case that I do not need all these governmental institutions that are produced by violence and arranged within the State, and I cannot deprive others who need my labour, in order to give it in the form of taxes to institutions I do not need and which as far as I know are harmful. I know that I need neither the government nor tribunals founded on violence, and therefore I cannot take part in either the one or the other. I know that I do not want either to attack other nations and slaughter them or to defend myself from them with arms, and so I cannot take part in wars or preparations for war. Very likely there are people who cannot help considering all this to be necessary and indispensable. I cannot dispute with them. All I know, know indubitably, is that as far as I am concerned I cannot do these things. And I cannot do them, not because such is my own personal will, but because such is the will of Him who sent me into life, and gave me an indubitable law for my guidance.[30]

And what do we want armies for, with their generals, and bands, and cavalry, and drums? What are they wanted for when there is no war and no one wants to conquer anybody? And even if there were a war, other nations would not let us profit by it, and the army will not fire on its own people.

And what are the judges and lawyers for, who in civil cases decide nothing according to justice, and in criminal affairs themselves recognize the uselessness of punishments?

And what are the tax-gatherers for, who exact the taxes reluctantly while what is really needed is easily collected without them?

And what is the use of the clergy, who have long since ceased to believe in what they have to preach?

And what is the use of capital in private hands, if it can be useful only after becoming public property?

And once they ask themselves these questions, men cannot fail to conclude that they ought not to support all these institutions which have become useless.[31]

Tolstoy's work as a whole needs no description. Its literary power has made it among the most influential of social protests. Its author was one of many Russians who applied themselves to remedying the evils of the society in which they grew up. Bakunin and Kropotkin were two others. The result was seen in the Revolution of 1917; but few would claim that the Soviet system which was then set up has as yet developed

[30] *The Works of Leo Tolstoy*, Centenary Edition, vol. 20, Oxford 1935, pp. 284-285. Quoted by permission of the Oxford University Press.

[31] *Ibid.*, pp. 327-328.

much conformity with the anarchistic society that was visualized by the Russians whose work has been examined in the present section. Whatever the Russian State has done, certainly it has not disappeared. Rather does the Hegelian idea of State-over-all appear to represent the position that has been reached.

The question of practicability arises, with respect to all anarchistic schemes. Is a society without government or coercion a workable thing? Granting the Godwin-Tolstoy assumptions of men's inherent equality and perfectibility, no doubt it is. But can these be granted? It must be remembered that man is an animal that has evolved through countless centuries of struggle, so can be expected to possess a certain inborn propensity to strive. The leadership idea of Renan, Nietzsche, Mosca, and Pareto—from which, indeed, Stirner was not altogether free—accords with this situation. On the other hand, it has to be admitted that men have lived for a very long time in society and that a measure of self-restraint has become second nature. But Godwin's point was that men will not need to be restrained from anti-social actions. Their own desires will lead them to help their fellows, not injure them. This point has been discussed in Chapter I, in connection with the Hegelian theory of a common will. Short of trial, perhaps little more can be done to give an answer. Yet it must be borne in mind that there has been some trial. Britain and the United States of America have been at peace for over a century, although their interests have conflicted in many ways. In some rural communities and small towns, where inequality of wealth is not great, order is kept without much difficulty. In the most vital social unit, the family, love rather than coercion is the ruling force. But, in the light of the social theories of Nietzsche and Pareto, can it not be concluded that some strong-armed individual or social group will arise and seize power in an anarchistic society? Tolstoy attempted to deal with this possibility, in a way, in *The Story of Ivan the Fool* (1885). Ivan was one of three brothers, all rulers. One was strong in arms, another was wealthy, but Ivan was neither. All saw their kingdoms invaded. The strong and the rich kingdoms fell, but Ivan's people received their conquerors without opposition and taught them better ways of living. Is this possible in practical life? Given suitable education and continuance of political authority during the learning period, some men think that it is. Only time and experimentation can tell. For nearly two thousand years (longer, if Stoicism is taken into account) men have attempted to set up a Kingdom of God upon earth and there are some who have not yet lost hope of its success.

Rodbertus

In classifying schemes of social reform, there is often set against the *Associative Socialism* of Owen and Fourier, and the anarchism of such men as Godwin and Bakunin, the *State Socialism* of the Germans, Rodbertus and Marx. This must now receive consideration.

Rodbertus was a man of some wealth, who, after a period of study and travel, settled on an estate in Pomerania, to manage this and take part in political affairs. Disagreeing with the government of which he had become a member, he retired to his estate and applied himself to social studies.

Rodbertus possessed a knowledge of Classical economics and appears to have been influenced by the doctrines of Saint-Simon and Sismondi. His main concern was with the distribution of wealth. He thought that the propertied classes — the landowners and capitalists — exploited the workers by possessing themselves of a portion of the produce of the labor of the latter group. Rodbertus did not believe, with Bastiat, that the capitalist's share would decline and that of the laborer increase. Instead, he thought that the contrary would be the case. This "law of the diminishing wage share" was what explained the recurrence of business crises,[32] according to Rodbertus.

But he believed that evolution would right things in due course. In the earliest stage of human history labor had been owned by the privileged classes, slavery being the rule. In the second period, namely that in which Rodbertus himself lived, land and capital were owned, but not labor. The laborers, however, were exploited. In the third stage, which lay in the future, Rodbertus said that production would be organized by the State and private property would be abolished, except for the property right of the worker in his own labor. Exploitation, therefore, would cease. Violent revolution was not needed to bring about the change, but Rodbertus advocated government action to mitigate existing evils and to help to reach the better state that was ahead.

To this end a scheme was put forward for an exchange system, based on labor.[33] The formula of Saint-Simon — to each according to his works, that is, to the worker the produce of his labor — was to be the principle governing wages. As long as private property was recognized, landowners and capitalists were to be allotted their share of the social income, but the benefits of progress were to go to the workers. The central position, both in the period of transition to socialism as well as in the socialist society which represented the final stage of economic evolution, was to be occupied by the State. In this emphasis on the State, Rodbertus, like his countrymen Marx and Lassalle, showed the effect of his German philosophical background.

Marx

Best known and most influential of nineteenth century socialists was the exiled German, Karl Marx. Some of the essential features of his

[32] See Chapter XV.

[33] This is described in Chapter IX.

doctrines were anticipated by others, as is shown in the chapters on Property, Valuation, and Business Prosperity and Depression. But Marx synthesized what came to him from his predecessors into a comprehensive body of ideas that has been of enormous significance in subsequent thought, providing arguments for socialist agitators in many countries, including the Russian Bolsheviks.

Marx offered not merely a vigorous criticism of existing society but a theory of change, leading to another society that, in his view at least, would be a better one. To the nature of the new system when fully established, however, he gave comparatively little attention.

Something was said in Chapter I respecting the Marxian theory of social development. It is now necessary to examine it in greater detail. The *Communist Manifesto,* of Marx and Engels, set forth the doctrine of class struggle in the following words:

> The history of all hitherto existing society is the history of class struggles. Freeman and slave, patrician and plebian, lord and serf, guild-master and journeyman, in a word, oppressor and oppressed, stood in constant opposition to one another, carried on an uninterrupted, now hidden, now open fight, a fight that each time ended, either in a revolutionary reconstitution of society at large, or in the common ruin of the contending classes.[34]

From the medieval serfs, ran the *Manifesto,* sprang the craftsmen of the early towns of Europe. With the expansion of markets due to geographical discoveries, however, the craft system became inadequate and factory production took its place, being developed by the bourgeois class. Under the new system a vast productive capacity had been created and new markets had to be found in other parts of the world:

> The need of a constantly expanding market for its products chases the bourgeoisie over the whole surface of the globe.[35]

The result was that the entire world was being brought into the focus of industrial civilization:

> The bourgeoisie, by the rapid development of all instruments of production, by the immensely facilitated means of communication, draws all, even the most barbarian, nations into civilization. The cheap prices of its commodities are the heavy artillery with which it batters down all Chinese walls, with which it forces the barbarians' intensely obstinate hatred of foreigners to capitulate. It compels all nations, on pain of extinction, to adopt the bourgeois mode of production; it compels them to introduce what it calls civilization into their midst, i.e., to become bourgeois themselves. In a word, it creates a world after its own image.[36]

Yet the immense powers of industrial production which had been developed under the system could not be kept under control. Commercial crises (*i.e.,* cyclical depressions in business) were the result:

[34] *Op. cit.,* p. 12. [35] *Ibid.,* p. 17. [36] *Ibid.,* pp. 17-18.

Modern bourgeois society . . . is like the sorcerer, who is no longer able to control the powers of the nether world whom he has called up by his spells. For many a decade past the history of industry and commerce is but the history of the revolt of modern productive forces against modern conditions of production, against the property relations that are the conditions for the existence of the bourgeoisie and of its rule. It is enough to mention the commercial crises that by their periodical return put on its trial, each time more threateningly, the existence of the entire bourgeois society. In these crises a great part not only of the existing products, but also of the previously created productive forces, are periodically destroyed.[37]

The Marxian theory of crises was not new with Marx. As is shown in Chapter XV, it had been elaborated early in the nineteenth century, and Rodbertus, among the socialists, was very prominently associated with it. But Marx made it an integral part of his theory of economic development. He said that the capitalist system was causing its own destruction. Depressions were not the only source of trouble. According to Marx, the position of the workers was deteriorating. Capital was becoming more and more concentrated in ownership. "One capitalist always kills many,"[38] while the propertyless working class, or proletariat, was increasing in size. As Marx said, in his chief work, *Capital*:

Along with the constantly diminishing number of the magnates of capital, who usurp and monopolise all advantages of this process of transformation [*i.e.*, manufacture], grows the mass of misery, oppression, slavery, degradation, exploitation; but with this too grows the revolt of the working-class, a class always increasing in numbers, and disciplined, united, organised by the very mechanism of the process of capitalist production itself. The monopoly of capital becomes a fetter upon the mode of production. . . Centralisation of the means of production and socialisation of labour at last reach a point when they become incompatible with their capitalist integument.[39]

Then the end would come:

The knell of capitalist private property sounds. The expropriators are expropriated.[40]

The workers would become so numerous, Marx declared, and the capitalists so few, that it would be a comparatively simple matter for the former to seize the reins of political power, thus raising the proletariat into the position of ruling class. This position they would use to possess themselves of economic power:

The proletariat will use its political supremacy, to wrest, by degrees, all capital from the bourgeoisie, to centralize all instruments of production in the hands of the state, i.e., of the proletariat organized as the ruling class. . .[41]

[37] *Ibid.*, pp. 19-20.
[38] *Capital*, vol. 1, Pt. 8, Chap. 32.
[39] *Ibid.*
[40] *Ibid.*
[41] *Communist Manifesto*, pp. 40-41.

Recognizing that the program might have to be varied in different countries, Marx and Engels submitted in the *Manifesto* a list of immediate proletarian objectives. These were as follows:

1. Abolition of property in land and application of land rent to public purposes.
2. A heavy progressive income tax.
3. Abolition of all rights of inheritance.
4. Confiscation of the property of emigrants and rebels.
5. Nationalization of banking.
6. Nationalization of transport undertakings.
7. Extension of nationally-owned manufactories, cultivation of waste land, and soil improvement generally, in accordance with a State plan.
8. Equal obligation of all to work, with the establishment of industrial armies, especially for agriculture.
9. Gradual elimination of the boundary marks between agriculture and industry, and town and country, with a more equable spreading of population over the land area.
10. Free education for all children. Abolition of child labor as then existing. Integration of education with industrial production.

After the program had been carried through to completion, the State, as it was known, would disappear. Class distinctions having gone, the class struggle would come to an end:

> When, in the course of development, class distinctions have disappeared, and all production has been concentrated in the hands of a vast association of the whole nation, the public power will lose its political character. Political power, properly so called, is merely the organized power of one class for oppressing another. If the proletariat during its contest with the bourgeoisie is compelled, by the force of circumstances, to organize itself as a class, if, by means of a revolution, it makes itself the ruling class, and, as such sweeps away by force the old conditions of production, then it will, along with these conditions, have swept away the conditions for the existence of class antagonisms, and of classes generally, and will thereby have abolished its own supremacy as a class. In place of the old bourgeois society, with its classes and class antagonisms, we shall have an association, in which the free development of each is the condition for the free development of all.[42]

The *Manifesto* ended with what was at once a threat and an appeal — a threat to the capitalists and a call to the workers to rise up and destroy their oppressors:

> The Communists disdain to conceal their views and aims. They openly declare that their ends can be attained only by the forcible overthrow of all existing social conditions. Let the ruling classes tremble at a Communist revolution. The proletarians have nothing to lose but their chains. They have a world to win. Working men of all countries, unite![43]

[42] *Ibid.*, p. 42.

[43] *Ibid.*, p. 58.

There appears to be some inconsistency between the ideas of Marx on revolution and his theory of social development, as outlined in Chapter I. If the Marxian theory of historical determination were correct (that is, if it were true that the course of history was governed by material factors), how could it be supposed that the thoughts of men could change it, whether these thoughts were expressed in agitation, revolution, or otherwise? Presumably, what his appeal was intended to do was to hasten the overturn which Marx believed economic circumstances had rendered inevitable.

The abolition of government was entirely consistent with the views of Marx respecting the nature of this institution. Historically, he thought, the State had been the political machine of the ruling class, the instrument whereby other groups had been dominated. Yet it may well be asked, how could society be expected to run itself without any government organization? Marx was greatly influenced by Hegel and there is little doubt that something in the nature of the "common will" of the Hegelians, discussed in Chapter I, was the basis of the socialist leader's expectation that society would be capable of operating without government. Thomas Hobbes, it will be remembered, made the assertion that in the absence of government there would be chaos, because of the conflict of individual interests. The followers of Hegel (of whom Marx was one) looked to a common will—that recognized a general interest—to avoid this difficulty. But, as has been indicated, Marx said very little concerning the nature of the society which he thought would succeed the existing one.

The closing words of the *Communist Manifesto,* quoted above, bring out one of the leading characteristics of Marxism. It was international. Where Rodbertus had thought in terms of the nation, Marx cut across international boundaries and appealed to the working classes of the whole world to combine for the purpose of ending their domination by the capitalists.

The *Manifesto* was written during 1847–1848, when Europe seethed with revolution. But the uprisings were suppressed and Europe continued much as before. Engels, editing the English translation of the first volume of *Das Kapital* in 1886, prophesied again:

> The decennial cycle of stagnation, prosperity, over-production and crisis, ever recurrent from 1825 to 1867, seems indeed to have run its course; but only to land us in the slough of despond of a permanent and chronic depression. The sighed-for period of prosperity will not come; as often as we seem to perceive its heralding symptoms, so often do they again vanish into air. Meanwhile, each succeeding winter brings up afresh the great question, "what to do with the unemployed;" but while the number of the unemployed keeps swelling from year to year, there is nobody to answer the question; and we

can almost calculate the moment when the unemployed, losing patience, will take their own fate into their own hands.[44]

In view of what has happened since 1848, it is clear that the Marxian prophecy has not proved correct. True, followers of Marx inspired and carried through the Bolshevik Revolution in Russia in 1917, but it was a breakdown caused by war, not capitalism, that gave them their chance. In its early stages, with the liquidation of non-proletarian classes, the Russian Revolution followed a Marxian course, but critics say that what has emerged is an authoritarian State on the Hegelian plan. The present rulers of Russia assert that, in so far as this condition exists, it is merely temporary. History alone can answer this claim.

On the other hand, in Germany, where it appeared to many that Marxism had its greatest opportunity of success, developments have gone otherwise. An authoritarian State has liquidated the Marxists, at least for the time being. The same is true of Italy. Undoubtedly the situation referred to by Bernstein and discussed below, namely the fact that capital did not become so concentrated as Marx expected, assisted in defeating the Marxian forecast. But, after all, history has not yet come to an end, and the Marxists, like other prophets who are disappointed in the present, may find consolation in the future.

Syndicalism

In France and Spain, towards the end of the nineteenth century, socialist theory tended to assume the form of syndicalism, named from the *syndicats* or labor unions of France. Unlike Blanc and Marx, who gave the political organization of the State a place in establishing the new order, the syndicalists expected the labor unions to overthrow the existing society and to perform important functions in operating its successor.

The social system contemplated by the syndicalists took the form of an industrial order, somewhat on the lines suggested by Saint-Simon. Industries would be operated by associations of workers, the nuclei being in existence already in the form of labor unions. These associations would own the means of production and their products would be exchanged through *Bourses du travail,* or labor exchanges. The new society was to be established by the use of labor's weapon of the strike. All unions were to strike at once and the general strike would overturn the existing system.

What is superficially the same idea, shorn of the revolutionary aspect, runs through the writings of the English *Gild Socialists,* of whom R. H. Tawney (1880–   ) and G. D. H. Cole (1889–   ) may be mentioned. The Gild Socialists, however, appear to visualize a central authority, the State, as being supreme, with the separate productive associations

[44] *Capital,* vol. 1, editor's preface.

existing only as creatures of the State. The social system contemplated by the German philosopher, J. G. Fichte, at an earlier date, had certain affinities with this plan. But where Fichte contemplated a common will and an authoritarian State, men like Tawney have incorporated democratic ideas.

The development of syndicalist thought in France accompanied the appearance of a decided division in the socialist ranks. On the one hand were the labor unions, whose objects were concerned with matters like wages and working conditions, and whose method was the strike. On the opposite side stood socialists whose aims were political and who used the ballot box and the legislature as their means of approach. The same division has existed in Britain in a certain degree, though the British labor unions have not followed their French counterparts in the direction of making syndicalist organization and the general strike the accepted program. None the less, the absorption of some British labor union leaders in parliamentary affairs has led to dissatisfaction among the rank and file of union members. *Direct action*—which in practice meant either sympathetic strikes or the general strike of the French syndicalists, according to circumstances—gained adherents. This was manifested in the *triple alliance* of miners, railwaymen, and road transport workers in the post-war period, and came to a head in the general strike of 1926.

The latter revealed the general strike weapon to be less effective than its supporters had expected. Undoubtedly cities might suffer great inconvenience from such a strike but experience demonstrated that the means of distributing essential commodities could be improvised. Also it was shown that a general strike might raise antagonism to the workers' cause from members of the outside public. What no doubt appears to some observers a more significant failure was in the German Nazi triumph of 1933. Though action by the labor unions was suggested, nothing was done and the unions permitted themselves to be dissolved without any real struggle. With respect to France, it must be remembered that that country is divided rather sharply politically. The strength of the socialist movement has been in the cities, especially Paris. The rural districts have been predominantly conservative. History has proved that it was relatively easy to make a revolution in Paris, but—unless 1789 is counted as an exception—so far, on every occasion when this has occurred, the conservative reaction, drawing its strength from the country districts, in the long run has prevailed. It is difficult to perceive that the general strike is especially suitable to such a situation.

Socialism by Evolution

As opposed to the *revolutionary socialism* of Marx and the syndicalists, must be set the ideas in the direction of *socialism by evolution,* or gradual change, which have found favor in a number of countries.

In Germany, Ferdinand Lassalle (1825–1864) supported a policy of gradualism. Lassalle, like Marx, was greatly influenced by Hegelian thought. He led a colorful career, being imprisoned in connection with the revolution of 1848. During a dispute between Bismarck and the Prussian liberals in 1862, Lassalle came forward with a proposal that the laboring class should enter politics on its own account. His general policy was laid down in the famous *Open Letter to the National Labor Association of Germany*.[45] In 1862 a working men's convention was held at Nuremberg and was adjourned with the intention of meeting a year later at Leipzig. In the meantime, Lassalle was invited to draw up a platform. The *Open Letter* was the result. The essential feature of Lassalle's program was the abolition of the wage system by the establishment of producers' co-operative associations :

The working class must become itself a monster employer : the whole a series of gigantic enterprises. By this means and by this alone, can amelioration come, and the iron and cruel law governing wages be abolished. The wages class, once become its own employer, the division between wages and profits of enterprise at once is removed : the wage disappears, and in its stead comes the certain and satisfying reward of labor honestly performed. The whole production of labor becomes the claim of the worker, unaffected by any employer. This method of the abolition of the profits of enterprise is peaceful, legal, and, withal, simple. Through free associations, the working classes organize themselves as their own employers, and, by the simple act, emancipate themselves from the system which gave the working class wages, at all times but a small part of the entire product : not more than is barely sufficient to support life, while the surplus falls to the share of the employing class, making them rich. Be assured that this is the only true method of release for the working class, all others being specious and illusory.[46]

Lassalle recognized that many industries were organized on a large scale (for instance, railroads and textile factories) and required a capital too large for the workers to provide out of their own resources. True to the Hegelian ideology, he called upon the State to render assistance :

For this very reason, it is the duty and becomes the business of the State to come to your rescue, to enable you to expedite and give form and vitality to the scheme so promising of betterment to the working class of the nation. The State ought to regard it as its holiest duty to assist in making certain the possibility of your self-organization and association ; for in your elevation lies the secret of the grandeur and completeness of the State.[47]

State credit to working men's associations was what Lassalle had in mind. Thus socialism would be given a beginning and from this he expected that it would spread through the entire field of industry.

[45] Translated by J. Ehmann and F. Bader, Cincinnati, n.d.

[46] *Ibid.*, pp. 19-20.

[47] *Ibid.*, p. 20.

How was the State to be moved to act in this manner? Lassalle found the answer in universal and direct suffrage, which would enable the workers to elect a sufficient number of representatives to the legislature to give them political influence.

Lassalle's life was cut short in a duel connected with an affair of the heart, but he helped to establish the organization that grew into the German Social Democratic Party. In due course this came to wield considerable influence upon official policy, though perhaps not so much as Lassalle had forecast.

No less significant were the *Socialists of the Chair* (*i.e.,* professorial chair), a body of German university teachers. At a congress held at Eisenach in 1872 there was established the *Verein für Sozialpolitik,* or Social Policy Union, to which adhered a number of academic supporters of social reform, of whom Gustav von Schmoller was probably the best known to English readers. Like Lassalle, members of the Union assigned to the State the task of reforming society. Change by legislation was their program. In the next generation, through the social insurance legislation of Bismarck—designed in part to circumvent the socialists—Germany advanced a considerable way along this path. Other countries have followed suit.

Toward the turn of the century the standard of gradualism was raised within the camp of organized German socialism by Eduard Bernstein (1850–1932). Bernstein called for a revision of the aims of the socialist movement on the ground that the theories of Marx, which hitherto had been accepted by the socialists, had been proved incorrect. Marx had argued that the capitalist system would destroy itself but Bernstein pointed out that this had not happened. Where Marx had forecast that wealth would become aggregated into the hands of a small section of the people, the intermediate class of small-propertied persons failed to disappear. Indeed, it was growing in importance. Not merely were there some important industries, of which agriculture was the chief, that were unaffected by the trend towards large-scale organization, but the rise of the joint stock company, or corporation, made possible a wide dispersion of ownership in the case of great concerns. Even supposing that a successful revolution transferred power to the socialists, Bernstein said that the problem to be faced by the State in taking over and operating industry would be immense. Further, it was wrong to regard the workers as a single class, with a united interest. They were divided into many groups, possessing divergent interests. The industrial workers, whom Marx had regarded as the working class *par excellence,* was everywhere a minority of the total population. Bernstein concluded that the Marxian revolution was impracticable and that the attainment of socialism must be a gradual process. Continual pressure by the labor unions as well as political action were necessary, Bernstein said, not preparation for insurrection. Bernstein's views — which obtained the name *Revisionism* — were set forth in a number of writings[48] but the influence of Marxism in German official socialist circles was too great for them to be adopted as the official policy. However, a Revisionist minority remained active; and even the majority group, though formally Marxist, was lukewarm towards the idea of social revolution.

In other countries the evolutionary attitude was adopted widely. In France Marxian doctrines had never predominated, and French socialist politicians did not hesitate to ally themselves with liberals outside the socialist party. The same was true of Britain. The Fabian Society, named from a Roman general famous for his gradualist strategy, was established in 1883–1884 and maintained an evolutionary position. Among its members have been such influential socialists as the dramatist, George Bernard Shaw (1856–), and the social workers, Sidney (1859–1947)[49] and Beatrice (1858–1943) Webb. The Parliamentary Labour Party for a long time worked in alliance with the non-socialist Liberal Party. But, in recent years, criticism of such collaboration has increased and official policy now opposes formal links with non-socialist parties, though some working together takes place and there is no sanction of revolutionary objectives. The differences between the various countries are largely in emphasis, however, because in all of them — even in the United States of America — both revolutionary and gradualist wings of the socialist movement have been represented.

The measures favored by the evolutionaries — such as increasing government control of business, gradual expansion of national and municipal ownership of productive enterprises, and reduction of inequality by taxation and the extension of free social services — have made great headway. As yet there is no sign of the trend ceasing. Without doubt in many countries the granting of the franchise to the working class has been influential in this development. But recently democratic institutions have not appeared to possess the vigor they promised in former years, and it is *etatism,* or authoritarianism of the Hegelian type, rather than socialism, that has been responsible for some of the more spectacular changes.

Fascism and National Socialism

This development—expressed as it was in Italian Fascism and the National Socialism of Germany, as well as in corresponding tendencies in other countries — has both similarities to, and differences from, the socialist schemes that have been described. Theoretically and practically, there is some ground for regarding it as the child of an alliance between socialism and Romantic nationalism.

[48] *Die Voraussetzungen des Sozialismus und die Aufgaben der Sozialdemokratie,* 1899, translated by E. C. Harvey as *Evolutionary Socialism,* N. Y. 1911, may be consulted.

[49] Later Lord Passfield.

Its political basis was that of the Hegelian State, with its general will and inherent inequality; to which was added, quite logically, the social leadership conception of Renan, Mosca, and Pareto, referred to in Chapter I. Centralization was emphasized and there was a ruling class, recruited from various social groups within the State. Private property was permitted but subjected to the condition that it must be used in accordance with the common purpose—a situation that is in full accord with the Romantic theories discussed in Chapter IV. The principle of industrial self-regulation, which has come down from the gilds of medieval times and was given prominence in the writings of Fichte and the syndicalists, was incorporated to some extent. Nationalism was enthroned. The group whose will was to be served was that united by ties of blood and language, so that Jews were pushed out of Germany while Germans were brought back from abroad.

There was little here that was really new. The plan of Plato's *Republic*—particularly its hierarchy of classes and its control over men's minds—may be considered in the minds of some to justify the claim that its author was one of the first Fascists or Nazis. Mussolini's supporters admitted that they had received inspiration from Renan and Pareto, as well as from the syndicalists. German National Socialism had roots in the philosophy of Fichte and Hegel.

Perhaps the developments in Europe during the past few years are too close at hand to be placed in proper perspective but already one conclusion seems to have emerged. It was not merely a matter of Germany and Italy going in one direction and the rest of the western world choosing a different path. In many respects Soviet Russia—professedly based on Marxism—appears singularly like the authoritarian States of Central Europe. Even countries that are still called democratic contain authoritarian elements. Thus, a British legal dignitary[50] felt it necessary to attack the growth of the power of bureaucracy in his own country; while critics of the National Industrial Recovery Act, and of the New Deal generally, have drawn parallels between tendencies that have disclosed themselves in the United States and those so marked in contemporary Europe. But it rests with historians who can look back from the vantage point of the future to give an adequate account of all this.

Summary of Chapter

Social protest is an ancient phenomenon. In the fourth century B.C., when Greece was becoming more individualistic, Plato advocated a return to a system incorporating a higher degree of socialism. Early Christian teachers gave a certain amount of support to communism. The *Utopia* of Sir Thomas More depicted a communist society in the sixteenth cen-

[50] Lord Hewart (1870–1943), Lord Chief Justice, 1922–1940.

tury. A hundred years later the Diggers attempted to establish one in England.

But the modern movement for social reform can be dated from the industrial revolution. Alike only in offering a vigorous criticism of existing social arrangements, reformers have put forward all manner of schemes. Absence of government on the one hand and government domination on the other, small self-contained communities and nationally owned and organized large-scale industries, have been suggested. Distribution of income according to work done and on the basis of consumptive needs have received support. Some reformers have favored revolutionary methods: others have believed in the possibility of evolutionary change. One of the most remarkable of social experiments—Soviet Russia in our own day—was professedly modelled on the ideas of Karl Marx, the outstanding socialist of the nineteenth century. Yet it shows resemblance to Italian Fascism and German National Socialism, partly, no doubt, because of a common ancestry in Hegelian theory.

CHAPTER VI

ECONOMIC NATIONALISM

The term *economic nationalism* must be distinguished from another that is used in this book, namely *national economics*. The latter refers to the conception of economics as *State policy*. The idea behind it is that national resources and objectives can be co-ordinated, just as in individual economics the individual considers the balancing of his personal wants and the means of satisfying them. Entirely different from this is the idea of *economic nationalism,* or self-sufficiency. Granted that there is to be a national economic policy, it does not necessarily follow that this will be directed towards self-sufficiency. The nation's policy, indeed, may be the opposite one of promoting free exchange with other countries. It has often happened that advocates of national economic policies have also supported economic self-sufficiency but the difference between the two concepts must be borne in mind. In the main, in this volume, formal treatment of national economics is relegated to the concluding chapter, which deals with the scope and method of economics, while economic self-sufficiency forms the topic of the present chapter. Anything like complete division between the two, however, is impossible of achievement.

Economic nationalism can be described as a special case of sentiment in favor of group or area self-reliance—the idea that a social group or a district under a particular government shall be independent of other groups or areas. Economic self-reliance, in this broad sense, antedates the modern State and goes back to very early times. It is also found in areas that are much smaller than the State, as when it is argued that purchases should be made from local tradesmen or jobs given to home-town residents in preference to outsiders. On a national basis, at different times in human history it has been so important as to feature prominently in economic discussion, as during the mercantile period and again in our own time.

Self-Sufficiency in Early Times

In general, it may be said that self-reliance is characteristic of primitive society, but there are important exceptions to this rule. Coast-dwelling, fishing communities are met with, regularly handing over portions of their catches to inland agricultural tribes, in return for some of the produce of the latter. Villages are composed of potters, who barter the utensils they make for fruits collected by their neighbors. Trading groups range over a wide area, living on the profits resulting from their transactions. Such conditions may not be the most primitive imaginable but they are found among peoples who pass as savages at the present time. No doubt among these uncivilized tribes there are men, who, remembering the wars of yester-year, point out the risks attending this specialization. If so, these commentators are entirely comparable with some twentieth century economic nationalists. Unfortunately, no evidence is available on the subject.

It is clear that Homeric Greece was in a large degree self-sufficing and that there came to be more dependence on external commerce as time passed by and specialization developed. The remarks of the classical philosophers on the subject of self-sufficiency suggest little sympathy with the growth of specialization. Aristotle, indeed, went so far as to assert that there was general agreement on the merit of self-reliance:

every one would agree in praising the territory which is most entirely self-sufficing; and that must be the territory which is all-producing, for to have all things and to want nothing is sufficiency.[1]

But, long before Aristotle taught, under Solon manufactures were encouraged. Athens outgrew her resources in the way of food and pursued a policy of importing grain (for whose production Greece was not well suited) and fish from the Black Sea area, paying for these commodities by exporting wine and fine goods, such as pottery and jewelry.

Rome went through the same evolution. Whereas the Latin communities were self-sufficing in early times, later there was extensive area-specialization. An outstanding example was seen in the heavy shipments of grain from the African provinces and other portions of the outer Empire to the Imperial city. Taken as a whole, however, the Empire was largely self-supporting. An interesting sidelight on the Christian position during the later Imperial period was referred to in Chapter II. Tertullian exhorted believers to be content with what was produced locally, instead of demanding imported luxuries, but as simplicity rather than self-sufficiency appears to have been the teacher's objective, the subject is more appropriately treated under the heading of wealth.

The middle ages were characterized by a high degree of economic localism. This was true especially of the towns. Gild and municipal authorities did their best to foster the interests of local traders and manufacturers. Outside merchants were forbidden to deal directly with the local consumers, while privileges were purchased from the king and inter-municipal agreements entered into for the purpose of assisting home traders who fared abroad.

Mercantilism

With the rise of the modern State, centralized regulation succeeded the local control of medieval times and policies of economic self-sufficiency were everywhere put into force.

[1] *The Works of Aristotle*, vol. 10, *Politica*, 1326b.

Mercantilist Objectives

The German economist, Gustav von Schmoller (1838–1917), has seen the explanation of this development in the desire of the governments of the new States to weld these into unities, destroying the old particularism within their areas and making themselves strong against their enemies outside. Passages from Schmoller's essay on *The Mercantile System* show this point of view:

The seventeenth century had just managed to fight its way up from local sentiment to national sentiment; international law as yet scarcely existed. The old bonds which had held together Catholic states had been broken; all the intellectual movement of the time centred in the new national life; and the stronger and sounder beat the pulse of that life, the more it felt its individuality, the more inevitable was it that it should bar itself against the world outside with a harsh egoism. Each new political community that forms itself must be carried along by a strong and exclusive feeling of community; these are the roots of its strength. The struggle for self-sufficiency and independence is as natural to it as the spirit of violent rivalry which hesitates at nothing in order to come up with, to surpass, and to crush the rivals in whom it always sees enemies. It was the law of autarchy by which the commercial policy of those times was exclusively guided. The endeavour after autarchy naturally shews itself in an especially violent and one-sided form in the youth of nations.[2]

In proportion as the economic interests of whole states, after much agitation of public opinion, found a rallying-point in certain generally accepted postulates, there could not fail to arise the thought of a national policy, of protection by the state against the outside world, and of the support by the state of great national interests in their struggle with foreign countries. The conception of a national agriculture, of a national industry, of national shipping and fisheries, of national currency and banking systems, of a national division of labour, and of a national trade must have arisen before the need was felt of transforming old municipal and territorial institutions into national and state ones. But, as soon as that had taken place, it must have seemed a matter of course that the whole power of the state, in relation to other countries as well as at home, should be placed at the service of these collective interests; just as the political power of the towns and territories had served their municipal and district interests.[3]

Francis Bacon, an English statesman who lived during the mercantile period, and William Cunningham, an economic historian of more modern times, put the matter somewhat differently. Not the *unity* of the State (that is, the idea of the State as a coherent entity) but its *power*

[2] *The Mercantile System and its Historical Significance* (translated from a chapter of *Studien über die wirthschaftliche Politik Friedrichs des Grossen* 1884), N. Y. 1895, reprinted 1931, p. 62. Quoted by permission of The Macmillan Company. The word *autarchy*, meaning self-sufficiency, was suggested by a passage in the writings of Aristotle.

[3] *Ibid.*, p. 59.

(the strength and influence exercised by that entity) was what was aimed at, according to these writers. Thus, Bacon declared of King Henry VII, who ruled England from 1485 to 1509, that

The king also, having care to make his realm potent, as well by sea as by land, for the better maintenance of the navy, ordained, "That wines and woads from the parts of Gascoign and Languedoc should not be brought but in English bottoms;" bowing the ancient policy of this estate, from consideration of plenty to consideration of power. For that almost all the ancient statutes incite by all means merchant-strangers to bring in all sorts of commodities; having for end cheapness, and not looking to the point of state concerning the naval power.[4]

Cunningham's account was as follows:

While the structure of society was being recast, and the recognised principles of economic morality were only derided, there seemed to be complete moral chaos; but there was one factor which was strong enough to reduce the anarchy to order again; men were forced in their dealings to have a due regard to the *power of the state*; this is the central idea in the commercial systems of the Reformation and post-Reformation periods.

Hitherto we have seen it come into play as limiting and restricting particular changes which seemed to be fraught with danger. The power of the nation was affected by the use of foreign shipping, and therefore native vessels were to be preferred; so too, the export of bullion was prohibited as it led to the impoverishment of the realm. Any importation which interfered with the employment of the people, the woolgrowing and clothmaking, which threatened the food supply, and the unthrifty games, which interfered with their military training, were all authoritatively checked; but as time passed on, the desire of advancing the national power came to be much more powerful; it was the ruling ambition, and the whole commercial and agricultural system was formed on this basis. As it came gradually into clear consciousness it became, not a restrictive and limiting, but a formative force, and under its guidance commercial enterprise and industrial skill were stimulated, while they were combined into a great national economic system. . .

When this aim was consciously and persistently pursued as the main end of mercantile regulations there was an entire reversal of the principles which had actuated such a ruler as Edward III. [King 1327–1377]; the first signs of tentative efforts in the new direction may be found in the complaints of the Good Parliament and the Statutes of Richard II. [King 1377–1400]. Edward had legislated in the interests of the consumers and with the view of providing *plenty*; the parliaments of Richard II. took another turn, and insisted on introducing conditions which eventually, as they were worked out in subsequent centuries, favoured the growth of English *power*. It is only when we cast our eyes forward that we see the full importance of the

[4] *The History of the Reign of King Henry the Seventh* (London 1622), reprinted in *The Moral and Historical Works of Lord Bacon* (Bohn's Library), London 1862, p. 361.

changes . . . and that they really laid the foundations of the famous mercantile system.[5]

Bacon and Cunningham wrote in England, where the central government was strong and unity was not a very significant problem after the end of the fifteenth century. Schmoller had in mind conditions in Germany—and especially Prussia—during the transition from medievalism to the modern State. No doubt this explains the difference in viewpoints.

Although good enough for ordinary purposes, strictly speaking, it is incorrect to refer to the new policy as nationalistic. Broadly, it can be said that the tendency was for the political units, or States, to be identical with the groups of people tied together by blood, religion, language, and customs, that are called nations. But the identification was not complete. Even Elizabeth's "England" included the distinct nation of Wales, while the State called Austria embraced a heterogeneous collection of peoples. Until the nineteenth century, the Italian nation was broken up into a number of separate States. The same was true of Germany even more recently. Mercantilist policy was State policy, therefore, not national policy, though on the political side a ruling motive was the desire of governments to make the State and the nation identical. By restricting contacts with the outside, while destroying separatism or localism within the State, something could be done in this direction.

In Chapter II there was some discussion of the theory put forward by Heckscher recently, to the effect that Mercantilism represented a change in the attitude of men to goods. Whereas, as Bacon and Cunningham said, the regulations of earlier times aimed at plenty of goods (or *provision* in Heckscher's terminology), the newer policy showed a distrust of goods, which was displayed in a long series of measures designed to protect the country against imports and to foster the exportation of home-produced commodities.

Another view of Mercantilist ideology, now fairly generally abandoned, is that it was grounded on an identification of money and wealth, which led the various governments to endeavor to maintain a favorable balance of trade for the purpose of accumulating the precious metals. This interpretation, to which some reference has been made in Chapter II, receives further attention in Chapter XIV.

Commentators on Mercantilist literature, including Adam Smith, have pointed out that some of the leading writers responsible for it had a pecuniary interest in the policies that they advocated. They were connected with foreign trade and were open to the suspicion of having ulterior motives in commercial policy. Thus, Thomas Mun was a director of the

[5] W. Cunningham, *The Growth of English Industry and Commerce*, vol. 1, 4th ed., 1905, pp. 467-470.

East India Company, whose principal business was the importation of Asiatic luxuries into Britain; Sir Josiah Child (1630–1699) was governor of the same company; while Edward Misselden was a member of the Merchant Adventurers Company, which exported English cloth to northern Europe. It happened that the early 1620's witnessed a serious depression in English industry and that both the East India and Merchant Adventurers companies were subjected to criticism. Mun's *Discourse of Trade* and Misselden's works on *Free Trade* and *The Circle of Commerce,* discussed elsewhere, can be interpreted as defenses against this attack. But, if the real objectives of men like Mun and Misselden were to further their own private interests, at least the argument of the general or State interest was used to hide them. Misselden's statement on the subject is worth quoting:

It is true, I am a brother, though unworthy of that worthie *Society* [*i.e.,* the Merchant Adventurers Company] : and so I am of other Companies also : and so also I am a member, though one of the least, of that great Commonwealth of this Kingdom : wherein I have learnt to preferre, that publique, to all these particular obligations.[6]

One wonders how far Misselden's contemporaries were convinced!

Whatever be the motive behind them, Mercantilist arguments appear to have carried conviction to the minds of contemporary statesmen. Far-reaching plans of industrial and commercial development, through tariff protection and other means, were put under way in the various countries of western Europe during the sixteenth, seventeenth, and early eighteenth centuries. Mercantilist statesmen did not try to make their States entirely independent of others in the economic sphere. Not an absence of trade with other countries but a favorable balance, that is to say, an excess of exports (other than specie), was what they desired. It now becomes necessary to examine Mercantilist policy.

Mercantilist General Policy

As an early example of Mercantilist argument, *A Discourse of the Common Weal of this Realm of England* may be quoted again. One of the characters appearing in the *Discourse,* the Doctor, discussing the case of an English paper-maker, who had been driven out of business because he could not manufacture his commodity "as good cheap as that came from beyonde the seaze" (*i.e.,* imported from overseas), declared,

but I would have ether the paper staied from cumminge in, or els so burdined with custome that, by that time it came hether, oure men might afforde theire paper better cheape than straungers might doe theires, the custome considered.[7]

[6] *The Circle of Commerce,* p. 65.

[7] *Op. cit.,* p. 66.

That is to say, the Doctor favored the imposition of a customs duty that would enable the home manufacturers to sell as cheaply as the foreigners, allowing for the duty.

Barthélémy de Laffemas (1545–1612) and Antoine de Montchrétien or Montchrestien (c. 1576–1621) in France, Thomas Mun (1571–1641) in England, and Philipp Wilhelm von Hornigk (also spelled Horneck, Hornick, and Hoerningk (1638–1713) in Austria, set out schemes for the guidance of their respective States. Laffemas was at first tailor to King Henry IV of France and later Controller-General of Commerce. He wrote on the advantages that would accrue to his country from the development of industries, giving especial attention to the question of raw material for silk-manufacture. Montchrétien was a manufacturer of hardware and perhaps of particular interest in the history of economic thought by reason of the fact that he published the first book to contain the name *political economy* in its title, the *Traicté de l'économie politique* (Rouen 1615). Thomas Mun is of more importance to English-speaking students. As has been mentioned, Mun was connected with the (English) East India Company, which imported luxury goods in exchange for silver sent to the East. There is little doubt that one of his reasons for writing on the subject of trade—perhaps, indeed, his only reason—was to justify the operations of his company. If there were one activity that was as bad as importing luxuries, in the minds of the men of that time, it was exporting silver. Luxurious consumption was objectionable alike to God and to the State, while the exportation of specie had been legislated against for centuries. Mun's purpose was to show how both of these actions—offensive as they might appear at first sight—were in the long run for the good of the State. It was not opposed to State policy to send out silver, he argued, if in due course more silver came back in return. Nor was the importation of luxuries really harmful, for they could be sold to the residents of other European countries at a profit. In any event, Mun declared that Britishers would insist on having Eastern commodities, and, if British merchants refused to supply the demand, foreigners would do so at a greater cost. Also, there were incidental advantages accruing from the company's traffic, such as the maintenance of shipping that would be useful in the event of war.

Mun put forward a comprehensive plan, directed towards increasing the "wealth and treasure" of the nation, at least according to his claim. Against such a short-sighted policy as would put a ban on the operations of his company because they appeared to conflict with the immediate interest of the nation, Mun advocated the longer view. In his *England's Treasure by Forraign Trade. or, The Balance of our Forraign Trade is The Rule of our Treasure* (published posthumously, London 1664), the merit of this was illustrated by a parable :

For if we only behold the actions of the husbandman in the seed-time when he casteth away much good corn into the ground, we will rather accompt him a mad man than a husbandman : but when we consider his labours in the harvest which is the end of his endeavours, we find the worth and plentiful encrease of his actions.[8]

In this work Mun made a number of suggestions respecting State economic policy. Waste land should be cultivated, he thought. Importation would be lessened "if we would soberly refrain from excessive consumption of forraign wares in our diet and rayment." In exportation, regard should be had not merely to the home country's superfluities but to its neighbors' wants. Goods should be exported in the country's own ships in preference to those of foreigners, in order to secure the income from transport charges for the national benefit. "The frugal expending likewise of our own natural wealth might advance much yearly to be exported unto strangers." Britain should fish her own seas and not leave them to the Dutch. She might make profits by acting as a distributive depot, importing Asiatic spices, silks, and indigo (presumably through the agency of the East India Company), for the purpose of re-selling to continental buyers at a profit. Trade to distant countries should be fostered, because its profits were greater than in the case of nearby trade. Even money should be exported if the ultimate result were the accumulation of an increased quantity in return. "It were policie and profit for the State to suffer manufactures made of forraign Materials to be exported custome-free" but native wares should not be taxed too heavily or their export sales would be injured. In general, according to Mun, it was good for Englishmen to work hard and consume little, selling their surplus to foreigners and, incidentally, having a tender regard for the kind of traffic in which the East India Company was engaged. Truly, this was a dreary outlook for those who were not—like Mun—stockholders in that company.

Hornigk possessed an entirely different background from that of Mun. Born in Mainz, Germany, he moved to Vienna with his father and later entered the service of a South German prince. His best known work, *Oesterreich über alles, wann es nur will* (1684),[9] belongs to the Viennese period. Austria's fortunes were then in eclipse and Hornigk made a number of proposals with the object of restoring them. His thesis was that, if the greatness of a country consisted of its surplus of specie and other goods necessary or useful for its subsistence, without dependence on other countries, it followed that the national economy should be arranged on self-sufficing lines. If this were not entirely feasible, then there should be as little dependence as possible on other nations.

[8] p. 50.

[9] Selections from this work have been translated by A. E. Monroe in *Early Economic Thought*, pp. 221-243.

Hornigk formulated nine rules designed to achieve this objective : (1) The country's natural resources should be fully explored. (2) Raw materials should be elaborated at home, to avoid payment to foreigners for manufacturing, which was costly. (3) The Austrian people should be trained to engage in useful activities, instructors being brought from abroad if necessary. (4) The precious metals should not be exported or hoarded but always kept in circulation. (5) The Austrians should abstain from consuming foreign goods as far as possible, especially luxuries. (6) When imports were necessary, they should be purchased directly from those who had produced them and should be paid for, not in specie, but in goods produced in Austria. (7) Further, necessary imports should be brought in as raw materials and elaborated at home. (8) Foreign markets should be sought for the surplus products of the country. (9) Where the home supply of a commodity was adequate, imports should be forbidden, notwithstanding considerations of friendship or political alliances. Even when the home-produced article was inferior to that made abroad, the former should be preferred. Given the observation of these maxims, Hornigk believed that Austria, which, when he wrote, was undeveloped industrially, would surpass other nations in wealth. Hence the title of the book, which means *Austria over all, if only she will.*

The idea that protection of a nation's industries from foreign competition affords employment to its people, or at least prevents unemployment, appeared from time to time in Mercantilist thought. It found expression in England, as early as the fifteenth century, Acts of Parliament being passed in 1455 and 1463, laying unemployment in the home textile industry at the door of foreign competition and enacting protective measures. A century later, the Doctor in *A Discourse of the Common Weal of this Realm of England,* arguing in favor of a bonus or reward to those who introduced a new industry, took up this position :

In venis [*i.e.,* Venice] as I heard, and in many other places beyonde the sea, they weare rewarded and cherished, everie man that bringes in anie new arte or mistorie [mistery = craft] whearby the people might be set aworke. . .[10]

A hundred years afterwards, Petty discussed the subject :

Suppose the Hollander outdo us by more art, were it not better to draw over a number of their choice Workmen, or send our more ingenious men thither to learn. . . Nevertheless, if the Hollanders advantages in making Cloth be but small and few in comparison of ours, that is, if they have but a little the better of us, then I conceive that Prohibitions to export Wool may sufficiently turn the scales. . . As for prohibition of Importations, I say that it needs not be, until they much exceed our Exportations. For if we should think it hard to give good necessary Cloth for debauching Wines, yet if we cannot dispose of our Cloth to others, 'twere better to give it for

[10] *Op. cit.,* p. 89.

Wine or worse, then to cease making it; nay, better to burn a thousand mens labours for a time, then to let those thousand men by non-employment lose their faculty of labouring.[11]

Petty appears to have had in mind the unemployment that appeared from time to time in the English clothing industry, referred to in Chapter XV. Labor was visualized as an overhead cost. In Petty's opinion, it was better to make some use of the efforts of specialized cloth-makers than see them wasted altogether. Indeed, having regard to the loss of skill that resulted from unemployment, he thought it preferable to permit the cloth to be manufactured and destroyed rather than to allow the workers to remain unoccupied. Many modern students of unemployment will sympathize with this point of view. But, unlike that of some later writers, Petty's employment argument was directed against protection (on the ground that it would diminish exports), instead of being in its favor.

Another idea formulated by some Mercantilist writers was that of assisting infant industries. A suggestion of this appeared in the passage from the *Discourse of the Common Weal,* quoted above. Andrew Yarranton (c. 1616–1685), an Englishman who seems to have been, at different times, soldier, engineer, and agricultural investigator, made certain proposals of this nature in his *England's Improvement by Sea and Land* (London 1677). Among a number of suggestions advanced for the furtherance of English industry, Yarranton mentioned a seven-year import duty on Swedish, Flemish, and Spanish iron, and on Dutch and German linen, for the purpose of establishing these industries on a commercial scale in England. The plan of Daniel Defoe (c. 1660–1731) for the encouragement of English manufactures of such type as would not prejudice the important woolen industry, set forth in *An Humble Proposal to the People of England for the Encrease of their Trade and Encouragement of their Manufactures* (London 1729), fell into this class.

The monetary schemes that formed an important aspect of Mercantilist thought, are dealt with in Chapters XIV and XV.

All in all, one may conclude that the public good that was aimed at by the Mercantilists was a prosperous and contented State, independent of others for the means of its existence.

Mercantilist Legislation

In the various countries of western Europe a body of regulations came into existence on lines in keeping with the writings mentioned in the last section. Thus, in Britain, there were measures restricting the importation of manufactured goods that competed with home products. The immigration of Continental artisans was encouraged at various times.

[11] *The Economic Writings of Sir William Petty,* vol. 1, *A Treatise of Taxes & Contributions* (first published London 1662), pp. 59-60.

Emigration of skilled British workmen and exportation of machinery were forbidden. Attempts were made to ensure that the colonies would develop along lines that made them useful to the home country, by acting as sources of supply for raw materials and markets for finished products. The growth of colonial enterprises that competed with those of the mother country was discouraged. To assist the British mercantile marine — a source of profit in peace and a recruiting ground for the navy in time of war — the navigation acts required colonial goods to be carried in British or colonial ships. They had to be transported to Britain in the first instance, so that she should gain from the entrepôt trade. Wages and hours of labor were regulated, poor laws passed, enclosures of arable land forbidden — a numerous and contented people, industriously working in the service of the State, being the objective. Some features of this policy are discussed below.

The patents of monopoly. Especially interesting were the licenses or patents of monopoly, that were granted in England during the Elizabethan and Stuart reigns. To promote new industries or naturalize in England activities that had grown up abroad, exclusive manufacturing rights, somewhat like modern patents, were conferred upon individuals or groups. An example was the glass industry. Medieval Englishmen were content with open spaces for windows, or used horn substitutes, but by the sixteenth century a number of glass-makers were at work, many of them immigrants. The quality of the English product was inferior to that of the Continental manufacturers, however, and in 1567 a patent was granted to two Flanders glass-makers for the introduction of the Lorraine method of manufacture. Though this did not prove very successful, the industry expanded, especially as further immigrations took place. In 1574 a patent for drinking glasses was granted to an Italian, despite opposition from British manufacturers. On expiry, its reversion was conferred upon one Sir Jerome Bowes, for no greater reasons than personal services to the Crown and payment of an annual rental. This incident brings out one of the defects of the patent system. Some of the grants were honest attempts to reward inventors or those who introduced foreign processes, but others were nothing more than subsidies to individuals, who happened to be in personal or political favor, and were entirely devoid of economic justification. As a result, there was considerable public opposition to the patents. Even where the grant was in the nature of a reward for useful service in innovation, it excluded others from employing the protected process. An agitation grew up, one of whose results was the Statute of Monopolies, passed in 1624. This law condemned patents of monopoly, with certain exceptions (including new inventions, which were to be protected for fourteen years). Abuses were not ended, however, because it remained possible to justify a patent whose real reason was elsewhere (*e.g.*, personal favor) by the assertion that an improvement in manufacturing processes was to be effected. None the less, the patents were important in economic history, representing the beginnings of modern patent legislation as well as a forecast of later schemes for the development of infant industries.

Protection from foreign imports. The efficacy of import duties and prohibitions as a means of developing home industries was realized quite early. In England in 1258 the Oxford Parliament endeavored to help the clothing industry by enjoining that wool was not to be exported nor cloth imported. The reign of Edward III in the next century saw further assistance to the same industry, by a number of import prohibitions as well as by the encouragement of immigrant weavers. After a period of free trade, Edward IV (King 1461–1483) returned to a protectionist policy, which his Tudor successors continued. On the continent of Europe similar programs were followed, for example, the city of Hamburg prohibited the importation of beer from the surrounding area, and its neighbor, Lübeck, that of harness. Such regulations became a characteristic feature of Mercantilism. Thus, in 1563, the English government forbade the importation of a long list of commodities "being ready wrought" (*i.e.*, manufactured), including girdles, knives, and gloves, and the number of prohibited articles was increased later. The government of James I (King 1603–1625) imposed duties—prohibitory in the case of cloth—on imported articles, it being declared that

> If it be agreeable to the rule of nature to prefer our own people before strangers, then is it much more reasonable that the manufactures of other nations should be charged with impositions than that the people of our own kingdom should not be set on work.[12]

Dowell, the historian of English taxation, commented upon the situation which existed a century later (in 1713–1714), in the following terms:

> The popular feeling on the subject [of import duties] had calmed down, the principles of the protective system were in the ascendant, and the manufacturers of the articles proposed for taxation submitted, with pleasure, to taxes which fell eventually upon the consumers of the articles taxed, and were accompanied with duties on foreign articles of the same description at rates which, practically prohibitory, secured to them a monopoly in the home market. Candles, and leather, and paper, and paper-hangings, and pasteboard, and printed, painted, or stained silks, linens and calicoes, and soap, and starch, and gilt and silver wire all ranged as contributories to the revenue in our fiscal list, which now included most of the principal manufactures in existence in England. . .[13]

[12] *The Rates of Marchandizes as they are set downe in the Booke of Rates* (James I), quoted by E. Lipson, in *The Economic History of England*, vol. 3, p. 15.

[13] S. Dowell, *A History of Taxation and Taxes in England from the Earliest Times to the Year 1885*, 4 vols., 2nd ed., London 1888, vol. 4, pp. 282-283. Longmans.

One of the most remarkable cases of infant industry protection was largely accidental. A contest between English woolen manufacturers and the East India Company had ended in a victory for the former, the government prohibiting the use of Asiatic silk goods and calicoes (cottons), which had been imported by the company to the detriment of the English woolen industry. As the prohibition was somewhat ineffective, it was reinforced by a further act in 1721, which forbade the use of calicoes altogether, whatever their source. For a time there existed a doubt as to whether fustian goods (*i.e.*, those made of a mixture of cotton and linen) were included in the ban, but this was set at rest by a law passed in 1736. Fustians were permitted and the Lancashire fustian manufacture grew apace. As technique improved, the Lancashire producers became able to turn out pure cotton cloth. Had the prohibition of this been continued, it would have prevented the rise of this English industry. Instead, it was removed. It is a strange historical paradox that English cotton manufacture, which later was to be identified so closely with the agitation for free trade, owed in no small degree its own establishment to a protective measure.

The Limitations of Mercantilist Trade Policy

Not all the Mercantilists were satisfied that their policy of aiming at an export surplus could be pursued indefinitely. Even Mun admitted that the accumulation of specie would raise prices. He suggested a policy of lending:

> lest when wee have gained some store of mony by trade, wee lose it again by not trading with our mony.[14]

Mun mentioned the example of an Italian duke who endeavored to "enlarge his trade by issuing out to his Merchants great sums of money for very small profit." He was prepared, also, in the last resort, to mitigate his rule against luxurious consumption:

> Lastly, all kind of Bounty and Pomp is not to be avoided, for if we should become so frugal, that we would use few or no Forraign wares, how shall we then vent [*i.e.*, sell] our own commodities? what will become of our Ships, Mariners, Munitions, our poor Artificers, and many others? doe we hope that other Countreys will afford us money for All our wares, without buying or bartering for Some of theirs? this would prove a vain expectation; it is more safe and sure to run a middle course by spending moderately, which will purchase treasure plentifully.[15]

Sir James Steuart (later Denham, 1712–1780) said much the same thing. Steuart was an economic writer of the period immediately before the appearance of the *Wealth of Nations* and gave general support to

[14] *England's Treasure by Forraign Trade*, p. 44.

[15] *Ibid.*, pp. 148-149.

Mercantilist doctrines. His book, *An Inquiry into the Principles of Political Œconomy: Being an Essay on the Science of Domestic Policy in Free Nations* (2 vols., London 1767), was the first in English to incorporate the term *political economy* in its title. In this work, Steuart remarked:

We must encourage œconomy, frugality, and a simplicity of manners, discourage the consumption of every thing that can be exported, and excite a taste for superfluity in neighbouring nations. When such a system can no more be supported to its full extent, by the scale of foreign demand becoming positively lighter; then in order to set the balance even again, without taking any thing out of the heavy scale, and to preserve and give bread to those who have enriched the state; an additional home consumption, proportioned to the deficiency of foreign demand, must be encouraged. For were the same simplicity of manners still kept up, the infallible consequence would be a forced restitution of the balance, by the distress, misery, and at last extinction of the supernumerary workmen.[16]

Though couched in language that is explained by Steuart's theory of economic equilibrium, it is evident that the author visualized some such situation as had been referred to by Mun.

Theorists of Free Trade

Early Critics of Mercantilism

Toward the end of the seventeenth century in England, critics of Mercantilism began to appear. Roger Coke, who lived during the latter half of the century and was a grandson of the famous judge, Sir Edward Coke, was one of the earliest of these. In *A Treatise (Wherein is demonstrated that the Church and State of England are in Equal Danger with the Trade of it)* (4 parts, London 1671–1675), Coke attacked the policy of government interference with imports. It was likely to provoke retaliation on the part of foreigners, he argued, and this would result in a diminution of English exports. By removing the stimulus of foreign competition, it reduced the efficiency of home manufactures and led to monopoly, with its accompaniment of inferior quality and dearness of the product. These arguments appeared many times in later writings.

Nicholas Barbon, in *A Discourse of Trade,* referred to earlier in this volume, repudiated the Mercantilist belief that the importation of foreign goods hindered the sale of English articles. Englishmen purchased imported commodities for the sake of variety, Barbon said, while foreigners did the same with English products. As a result, more goods were sold than would be the case if no trade existed—an ingenious argument, containing, possibly, a certain element of truth. Charles Davenant's views have been mentioned in Chapter III. Though tinged with the

[16] *The Works, Political, Metaphisical, and Chronological, of the Late Sir James Steuart of Coltness, Bart.,* 6 vols., London 1805, vol. 1, pp. 348-349.

prevailing opinion that the government should supervise trade, Davenant granted the assumption that commerce was capable of regulating itself and drew a general conclusion which was in favor of freedom from control.

David Hume

It is probably true that in Britain David Hume delivered the first effective onslaught upon Mercantilist trade policy. Hume demonstrated, lucidly and convincingly, that it was not merely *unnecessary* to promote the accumulation of specie by means of a favorable balance of trade. Such a plan was *self-defeating*, he declared. In the absence of government action, if money were scarce in Britain, commodity prices would fall. This would encourage exports, cause the balance of trade to become favorable, and so bring in specie from abroad. Conversely, if money were plentiful—that is, if the objective of the Mercantilists were attained—commodity prices would rise. British goods would be dear to foreigners and their sales would fall off, resulting in an unfavorable trade balance which would carry off some of the specie to other countries. Hume's examination of the relationship between money, prices, and the trade balance is studied in greater detail in Chapter XIV.

Like Mun before him and Steuart afterwards, Hume contemplated a future in which foreigners would be unwilling to buy British goods, at least on the scale to which his own generation was accustomed. Nations passed through a course of evolution in regard to trade, he said. In the early stage, while their own industries were undeveloped, they had much to gain by buying from foreigners. Men were taught new wants and were stimulated to satisfy them by their industry. When they had learned their lesson, a loss of foreign trade would not inconvenience them. Unable to sell goods for export, they could turn their activities to the home market. Thus :

> If we consult history, we shall find, that, in most nations, foreign trade has preceded any refinement in home manufactures, and given birth to domestic luxury. The temptation is stronger to make use of foreign commodities, which are ready for use, and which are entirely new to us, than to make improvements on any domestic commodity, which always advance by slow degrees, and never affect us by their novelty. The profit is also very great, in exporting what is superfluous at home, and what bears no price, to foreign nations, whose soil or climate is not favourable to that commodity. Thus men become acquainted with the *pleasures* of luxury and the *profits* of commerce ; and their *delicacy* and *industry*, being once awakened, carry them on to further improvements, in every branch of domestic as well as foreign trade. And this perhaps is the chief advantage which arises from a commerce with strangers. It rouses men from their indolence ; and presenting the gayer and more opulent part of the nation with objects of luxury, which they never before dreamed of, raises in them a desire of a more splen-

did way of life than what their ancestors enjoyed. And at the same time, the few merchants, who possess the secret of this importation and exportation, make great profits; and becoming rivals in wealth to the ancient nobility, tempt other adventurers to become their rivals in commerce. Imitation soon diffuses all those arts; while domestic manufacturers emulate the foreign in their improvements, and work up every home commodity to the utmost perfection of which it is susceptible. Their own steel and iron, in such laborious hands, become equal to the gold and rubies of the INDIES.

When the affairs of the society are once brought to this situation, a nation may lose most of its foreign trade, and yet continue a great and powerful people. If strangers will not take any particular commodity of ours, we must cease to labour in it. The same hands will turn themselves towards some refinement in other commodities, which may be wanted at home.[17]

Here Hume forecast something in the nature of the situation that appears to have arisen in Britain in recent years.

The Physiocrats

The French Physiocrats took up a position antagonistic to Mercantilist regulation. Though it was inherently unproductive, trade (whether local or international) was necessary, they thought, because people had to get from others the things that they did not themselves produce. Later economists argued that men exchanged things they had in such plenty that the marginal utility was low, for other goods possessed in so small a quantity that the marginal utility was high, and therefore gained by the exchange. But, with the possible exception of Turgot, the Physiocrats had no ideas of this kind. However, they saw the fallacious nature of the arguments used by some of the Mercantilists. For example, they appreciated that the result of a favorable balance of trade would be to raise prices, and that the foreign seller of a commodity did not necessarily pay the duty levied on its importation. After Turgot's accession to high financial office in the government service in 1774, one of his acts was to issue an edict virtually freeing imports and exports. The new policy had its purpose stated as follows:

to animate and extend the cultivation of the land, whose produce is the most real and certain wealth of a state; to maintain abundance by granaries and the entry of foreign corn; to prevent corn from falling to a price which would discourage the producer; to remove monopoly by shutting out private licence in favour of free and full competition; and by maintaining among different countries that communication of exchange of superfluities for necessities which is so conformable to the order established by Divine Providence.[18]

[17] *Essays and Treatises on Several Subjects,* vol. 1, *Of Commerce,* pp. 274-275.
[18] H. Higgs, *The Physiocrats.,* London 1897, p. 62. Quoted by permission of Macmillan & Co.; Ltd., and The Macmillan Company.

But, as was mentioned in Chapter III, the new order in France did not last long, failing to survive Turgot's fall from office in 1776.

Harris and Smith

In the meantime, in England, a more effective and lasting criticism came from the pen of Adam Smith. Joseph Harris (1702–1764), an official of the Mint, published a book entitled: *An Essay Upon Money and Coins* (London, Part 1, 1757, Part 2, 1758)[19] in which there was set forth a theory of international trade:

By the wise appointment of divine Providence, a mutual intercourse and commerce amongst men, is both conducive and necessary to their well being. Every man stands in need of the aid of others; and every country may reap advantages, by exchanging some of its superfluous products, natural or artificial, for those which it wants of foreign growth. . . Men are endued with various talents and propensities, which naturally dispose and fit them for different occupations; and are . . . under a necessity of betaking themselves to particular arts and employments. . . In like manner, as all countries differ more or less, either in the kinds or goodness of their products, natural or artificial; particular men find their advantages, which extend to communities in general, by trading with the remotest nations.[20]

Here was laid down the principle that Smith was to develop so successfully, the language and arguments being so like those of Smith that there is little doubt that Harris was the source of some, at least, of Smith's inspiration. However, Harris was not entirely free from Mercantilist ideas, because he declared:

Every nation should have a watchful eye over its foreign commerce; for it might so happen, that a trade which enriches the merchant, might impoverish the public.[21]

He said, also:

that trade is best, which tends most to promote industry at home, by finding employment for most hands; and which furnishes the nation with such foreign commodities, as are either useful and necessary for our defence, or more comfortable subsistence. And that trade is the worst, that exports the least of the product of labour; that furnishes materials for manufactures in other countries, which afterwards might interfere with some of its own; and which brings home unnecessary commodities, either soon perishable, or of a precarious value.[22]

Like Harris, Smith led up from the benefits of division of labor to those of international exchange:

[19] Reprinted in *A Select Collection of Scarce and Valuable Tracts on Money*, ed. J. R. McCulloch, London 1856, re-issued London 1933.

[20] *Ibid.*, issue of 1933, pp. 355-356. Quoted by permission of P. S. King & Son Ltd.

[21] *Ibid.*, p. 362.

[22] *Ibid.*

It is the maxim of every prudent master of a family, never to attempt to make at home what it will cost him more to make than to buy. The tailor does not attempt to make his own shoes, but buys them of the shoemaker. The shoemaker does not attempt to make his own clothes, but employs a tailor. The farmer attempts to make neither the one nor the other, but employs those different artificers. All of them find it for their interest to employ their whole industry in a way in which they have some advantage over their neighbours, and to purchase with a part of its produce, or what is the same thing, with the price of a part of it, whatever else they have occasion for.

What is prudence in the conduct of every private family, can scarce be folly in that of a great kingdom. If a foreign country can supply us with a commodity cheaper than we ourselves can make it, better buy it of them with some part of the produce of our own industry, employed in a way in which we have some advantage. . .

The natural advantages which one country has over another in producing particular commodities are sometimes so great, that it is acknowledged by all the world to be in vain to struggle with them. By means of glasses, hot-beds, and hot-walls, very good grapes can be raised in Scotland, and very good wine too can be made of them at about thirty times the expense for which at least equally good can be brought from foreign countries. Would it be a reasonable law to prohibit the importation of all foreign wines, merely to encourage the making of claret and burgundy in Scotland? But if there would be a manifest absurdity in turning towards any employment, thirty times more of the capital and industry of the country, than would be necessary to purchase from foreign countries an equal quantity of the commodities wanted, there must be an absurdity, though not altogether so glaring, yet exactly of the same kind, in turning towards any such employment a thirtieth, or even a three hundredth part more of either. Whether the advantages which one country has over another, be natural or acquired, is in this respect of no consequence. As long as the one country has those advantages and the other wants them, it will always be more advantageous for the latter, rather to buy of the former, than to make.[23]

But, according to Smith, in practice men had disregarded the economic advantages of free exchange. Certain types of foreign trade had been fostered artificially, and capital and labor had been attracted into them from the other employments to which, in the absence of interference, they would have flowed. The British Empire had been organized on Mercantilist principles:

A great empire has been established for the sole purpose of raising up a nation of customers who should be obliged to buy from the shops of our different producers, all the goods with which these could supply them. For the sake of that little enhancement of price which this monopoly might afford our producers, the home-consumers have been burdened with the whole expense of maintaining and defending that empire. . . It cannot be very difficult to determine who have been the contrivers of this whole mercantile

[23] *Wealth of Nations,* Bk. 4, Chap. 2.

system; not the consumers, we may believe, whose interest has been entirely neglected; but the producers, whose interest has been so carefully attended to; and among this latter class our merchants and manufacturers have been by far the principal architects.[24]

Smith was prepared to grant that an industry necessary for defense should be protected. Also he thought that when a tax was imposed on home production, a corresponding import duty should be levied on competing goods from abroad. Retaliatory duties were a matter for careful consideration, he said. The same was true of the removal of customs levies on articles that had been protected for a time. As for these last, Smith considered the employment problem, which has been mentioned in connection with the writings of Sir William Petty. Where the industry concerned employed a large number of workmen,

Humanity may in this case require that the freedom of trade should be restored only by slow gradations, and with a good deal of reserve and circumspection. Were those high duties and prohibitions taken away all at once, cheaper foreign goods of the same kind might be poured so fast into the home market, as to deprive all at once many thousands of our people of their ordinary employment and means of subsistence. The disorder which this would occasion might no doubt be very considerable.[25]

But, commented Smith, the importance of this factor "would, in all probability . . . be much less than is commonly imagined." Foreign competition might not destroy the home industry, he said, and even if it did so, it by no means followed that those who were thrown out of work would fail to secure other employment.

Smith, however, did not believe that free trade would come to pass:

To expect, indeed, that the freedom of trade should ever be entirely restored in Great Britain, is as absurd as to expect that an Oceana or Utopia should ever be established in it. Not only the prejudices of the public, but what is much more unconquerable, the private interests of many individuals, irresistibly oppose it.[26]

The "monopoly," which had been erected by the protectionist legislation of the past, Smith said, had become so powerful as to be able to intimidate the government:

This monopoly has so much increased the number of some particular tribes of them [*i.e.*, manufacturers], that, like an overgrown standing army, they have become formidable to the government, and upon many occasions intimidate the legislature. The member of parliament who supports every proposal for strengthening this monopoly, is sure to acquire not only the reputation of understanding trade, but great popularity and influence with an order of men whose numbers and wealth render them of great importance. If he opposes them, on the contrary, and still more if he has authority enough to

[24] *Ibid.*, Bk. 4, Chap. 8. [25] *Ibid.*, Bk. 4, Chap. 2. [26] *Ibid.*

be able to thwart them, neither the most acknowledged probity, nor the highest rank, nor the greatest public services, can protect him from the most infamous abuse and detraction, from personal insults, nor sometimes from real danger, arising from the insolent outrage of furious and disappointed monopolists.[27]

Smith assailed Mun's contention that trade to distant countries was more advantageous than nearby commerce, declaring that, on the contrary, near and especially home trade was the more economical. Here the author of the *Wealth of Nations* appears to have had in mind two points: (1) that some of the capital employed in distant trade gave employment to foreigners and (2) that distant trade consumed more time. Possibly what he was driving at under the last heading was some conception of diminishing returns on capital—that if capital were scarce it had better be employed at home—but his whole argument here was very confused.

Notwithstanding his own prophecy to the contrary, Smith's polemic in favor of free trade was successful. Its effects were not seen immediately, because for a large part of the succeeding forty years England was engaged in a life-and-death struggle with France and was more concerned with victory than with economic gain. France, during this period, built up through the *Continental System* a degree of self-sufficiency, embracing her own territory and that of her allies as well as of conquered countries. This had a motive opposite to that which drove the Central Powers in the European war of 1914–1918 into economic isolation. France and the French allies in the Napoleonic Wars, in effect, blockaded themselves by refusing ingress to British goods for the purpose of ruining England's commercial prosperity. At the same time, French industries received encouragement, the sugar beet industry providing a notable example.

The Success of the Free Trade Arguments

The conclusion of the war began a period of controversy respecting British commercial policy, during the course of which, not merely trade itself, but the subjects of population and diminishing returns received attention. The free traders held that Britain would be wealthier if she were to concentrate on manufacturing, where her advantage was apparent, using manufactured products to purchase the necessary food and raw materials, than would be the case if she produced the latter commodities herself. The arguments of the economists were closely connected with their theories of production costs—the laws of increasing and diminishing returns. It was thought that manufactures were subject to decreasing costs as their output expanded, while the production of raw materials showed the opposite tendency. The subject is discussed in

[27] *Ibid.*

Chapter VIII. Probably the practical success of the free trade argument was due less to the merits of the arguments by which it was supported than to the favorable environment in which they were formulated. For various reasons, the industrial revolution of the latter half of the eighteenth century had been mainly a British phenomenon. Britain faced the Atlantic Ocean, which had become the world's chief artery of commerce. She was defended from invasion by the narrow seas. She possessed an abundant supply of coal and, in Lancashire, a climate that was very favorable to cotton spinning. In England there appeared the series of inventions that was to revolutionize the iron and textile industries. Britain was victorious in the Napoleonic Wars and her shipping dominated the trade lanes of the world. Her colonies spread over the habitable globe. On the other hand, the territories of her competitors had been devastated by years of warfare. So it came about that British manufacturers led the world and that free trade meant freedom for British merchants to conquer the markets of the earth. The Reform Act of 1832 increased the political power of the manufacturers and traders, who found it in their interest that Britain should follow the advice of the economists by removing barriers to international trade.

The result was seen in the measures that removed Mercantilist legislation from the Statute Book. Under the leadership of Richard Cobden (1804–1865) and John Bright (1811–1889), the latter a prominent cotton manufacturer, the Anti-Corn Law League was organized at Manchester in 1838–1839. The League conducted a vigorous agitation not merely against the corn laws but in favor of free trade generally. A serious famine due to the failure of the Irish potato crop induced the Prime Minister, Sir Robert Peel (1788–1850), to side with the free trade group and a repealing law was passed in 1846, the duties themselves disappearing in 1849. The navigation acts were abrogated in the latter year, while the tariff revisions undertaken by W. E. Gladstone (1809–1898) in 1853 and 1860 virtually removed protection from the British fiscal system.

For a time it seemed possible that other European countries would follow suit. In France Bastiat pamphleteered in favor of free trade in an engaging series of papers of which the *Petition of the Manufacturers of Candles, Wax-lights, Lamps, Candlesticks, Street Lamps, Snuffers, Extinguishers, and of the Producers of Oil, Tallow, Resin, Alcohol, and, Generally, of Everything Connected with Lighting,* for protection against the competition of sunlight,[28] is best worth quoting:

[28] Printed in *Sophismes économiques* (Paris 1846), translated by P. J. Stirling as *Economic Sophisms.* Reprinted London and N. Y. 1909 and 1921. It is of interest that the London issue of 1909 (under the title of *Fallacies of Protection*) was used as campaign material in the political struggle then proceeding in England on the subject of tariffs. It had a foreword by H. H. Asquith (later Earl of Oxford and Asquith), British Prime Minister.

To Messieurs the Members of the Chamber of Deputies.

GENTLEMEN—You are on the right road. You reject abstract theories, and have little consideration for cheapness and plenty. Your chief care is the interest of the producer. You desire to protect him from foreign competition, and reserve the *national market* for *national industry*.

We are about to offer you an admirable opportunity of applying your—what shall we call it?—your theory? No; nothing is more deceptive than theory—your doctrine? your system? your principle? But you dislike doctrines, you abhor systems, and as for principles you deny that there are any in social economy. We shall say, then, your practice—your practice without theory and without principle.

We are suffering from the intolerable competition of a foreign rival, placed, it would seem, in a condition so far superior to ours for the production of light that he absolutely *inundates* our *national market* with it at a price fabulously reduced. The moment he shows himself our trade leaves us—all consumers apply to him; and a branch of native industry, having countless ramifications, is all at once rendered completely stagnant. This rival, who is no other than the sun, wages war to the knife against us, and we suspect that he has been raised up by *perfidious Albion* (good policy as times go); inasmuch as he displays towards that haughty island a circumspection with which he dispenses in our case.

What we pray for is, that it may please you to pass a law ordering the shutting up of all windows, skylights, dormer-windows, outside and inside shutters, curtains, blinds, bull's-eyes; in a word, of all openings, holes, chinks, clefts, and fissures, by or through which the light of the sun has been in use to enter houses, to the prejudice of the meritorious manufactures with which we flatter ourselves we have accommodated our country—a country which, in gratitude, ought not to abandon us now to a strife so unequal.[29]

This seems to be an expansion of *The Humble Petition of the Colliers, Cooks, . . .* attributed to John Arbuthnot, but by some to Swift, which depicted the ruin that would be caused by the use of focused sunshine instead of fires, and moonbeams instead of tallow candles.

Following a visit to England, Bastiat founded the *Association pour la liberté des échanges* at Bordeaux in 1846, to conduct propaganda on the lines of that of the English Anti-Corn Law League. But the free traders were weaker in France than across the Channel. The revolution of 1848 supervened; but the establishment of the Second Empire resulted, after 1852, in a lowering of tariffs. In 1860, by the Cobden-Chevalier treaty, the French government entered into an agreement with Britain for reciprocal reductions in import duties. A protectionist revival soon set in, however, becoming pronounced after 1875, and France turned her back on the free trade policy. A similar change in sentiment was seen in Germany. From 1850 the Prussian government moved in the directions of free trade, negotiating with France in 1862 a treaty similar

[29] pp. 60-61 of the re-issue of 1921. Quoted by permission of Ernest Benn Ltd. and G. P. Putnam's Sons.

to the Franco-British pact of 1860. Agreements on the same lines were reached with other German States and with Austria but, from 1879, the trend was again towards protection, the fact that tariffs received the support of the Prussian statesman, Bismarck, being a notable influence.

Modern Protectionist Theories

Infant Industry Protection

It is very evident that few other countries were in England's position in relation to free trade. It was all very well for British economists to argue that, in existing circumstances, foreigners could gain by buying the goods that were cheaply produced in Britain, paying for them by their own raw materials. But undeveloped nations looked forward to achieving in some degree the position already attained by Britain and were not satisfied to continue indefinitely on the existing basis. The newly-created United States of America was in some respects the most suitable of the younger nations for industrial development, so it was perhaps natural that in this country there should arise a protest against the policy of *laissez faire* in international trade.

Hamilton's Report on Manufactures. In 1791 Alexander Hamilton (1757–1804) submitted to the American House of Representatives his famous *Report on Manufactures.* Hamilton commenced by asserting that the expediency of fostering manufacturing in America was generally admitted:

> The expediency of encouraging manufactures in the United States, which was not long since deemed very questionable, appears at this time to be pretty generally admitted. The embarrassments which have obstructed the progress of our external trade, have led to serious reflections on the necessity of enlarging the sphere of our domestic commerce. The restrictive regulations, which, in foreign markets, abridge the vent of the increasing surplus of our agricultural produce, serve to beget an earnest desire that a more extensive demand for that surplus may be created at home; and the complete success which has rewarded manufacturing enterprise in some valuable branches, conspiring with the promising symptoms which attend some less mature essays in others, justify a hope that the obstacles to the growth of this species of industry are less formidable than they were apprehended to be. . .[30]

Hamilton proceeded to attempt to convince any remaining objectors by examining Adam Smith's arguments in some detail and offering a refutation of them. Unlike Smith, he refused to concede that agriculture was more productive than manufacturing.[31] He enumerated a number

[30] *Report on Manufactures,* communicated to the House of Representatives, 1791, reprinted in *The Works of Alexander Hamilton,* ed. H. C. Lodge, 9 vols., N. Y. 1885, vol. 3, p. 294. Quoted by permission of G. P. Putnam's Sons.

[31] See Chapter VIII.

of benefits conferred by the development of manufactures. They gave considerable scope to the division of labor and, more than agriculture, to the employment of machinery; they offered work to classes of people who would be idle otherwise, such as those with physical disabilities, and women and children; they promoted immigration from foreign countries; they provided greater opportunity for the "diversity of talents and dispositions, which discriminate men from each other"; they offered a more varied field for enterprise; and they created a secure demand for the surplus produce of the soil. Hamilton pointed out that some of the industrial nations of Europe were dependent upon foreign sources of supply of raw materials more than would be the case with American manufacturers and that, though wages were higher in the United States, transport costs would be saved. Capital was scarce in the United States, and this was a usual argument against the development of manufactures, but Hamilton thought that foreign capital might be used. Instead of being looked upon as a rival, such capital should be regarded as "a most valuable auxiliary." The independence and security of a country demanded that it should possess within itself the essentials of national supply—that is, food, habitation, clothing, and defense—Hamilton said. To those people who referred to the conflict of interest between the industrial North and the agricultural South, he replied that mutual wants were one of the strongest links in political association. In the *Report* there was submitted a list of commodities whose production might be encouraged, bounties being favored for the purpose, because—among other reasons—they avoided "the inconvenience of a temporary augmentation of price." Hamilton remarked, very sensibly, that it would be a questionable policy to continue bounties on manufactures that had been long established, but "in new undertakings, they are as justifiable as they are oftentimes necessary."

To determine what industries should be assisted, five tests were laid down: (1) the extent to which America furnished the necessary raw materials, (2) the degree to which labor could be substituted by machinery (because labor was dear in America), (3) the ease with which the policy could be carried out in practice, (4) the extent of the uses to which the article could be applied, and (5) its value for purposes of defense. On the administrative side, a body of commissioners was to be set up, controlling a fund supported by protective duties and used for bounties and other methods of industrial encouragement. Such a fund, Hamilton thought, would be ample, because

> There is little room to hope, that the progress of manufactures will so equally keep pace with the progress of population, as to prevent even a gradual augmentation of the product of the duties on imported articles.[32]

[32] *Report on Manufactures,* p. 413.

As has been shown earlier in this chapter, arguments for the protection of infant industries were not new with Hamilton. In the sixteenth century they were advocated in *A Discourse of the Common Weal of this Realm of England,* the author stating that they existed already in Venice and elsewhere. Some of the English monopolies of a later date professed as their object the establishment in England of manufactures which had grown up abroad. But Hamilton's arguments were prominent in the American discussions during the early part of the nineteenth century, in which this country's system of industrial protection arose. Possibly the most significant factor in the appearance of this protection was the interference with commerce that was caused by the Revolutionary and Napoleonic Wars. In the Revolutionary period trade with England (which was then the main source of supply for manufactured articles) was impeded. This situation reappeared during the non-intercourse period (when commercial relations were suspended) and in the succeeding war of 1812–1815). Limitation of British competition provided an opportunity for numerous small manufacturers to establish themselves, particularly in the northeastern part of the country. Severe injury was done to some of these, when trade with Britain was resumed, and undoubtedly the unwillingness of the Americans to see this happen continually did much to explain the success of the protectionist arguments, especially after 1815.

German nationalist philosophy and Friedrich List. About the same time a strong development of nationalist sentiment was apparent in Germany. The country was divided politically and the States of the Rhineland were overrun by the armies of Napoleon. Prussia had challenged the French and suffered a heavy defeat, which resulted in a period of stocktaking and reform. From that time is to be dated the rise of modern Germany, for as the nineteenth century wore on it became increasingly clear that Prussia was bent on a policy of national unification that would bring the lesser German States under her leadership. The conditions that Schmoller had described in Prussia herself at an earlier date, and identified by him with Mercantilism, were spread widely over the German country in the nineteenth century. National unity became the aim, and tariff policy—through the Zollverein, or customs union—was one of the instruments by which Prussia furthered this objective.

A strong vein of nationalism was apparent in German philosophy. As early as 1800, before the debacle of Jena, when Napoleon overthrew the Prussians, the philosopher Fichte had developed the conception of a self-sufficing nation, in his *Der geschlossene Handelsstaat* (The Closed, or Exclusive, Commercial State). Hegel's emphasis on the political ends of the State rather than the "capricious" wants of individuals, and the historical and evolutionary outlook which he gave to German philosophy, had their logical result in the writings of List.

What mattered to Hegel and List were not the riches of individuals, which Adam Smith had declared to be wealth of nations, but the wider objectives of the nation—the *good of the State,* whatever this was. Thus, in *The National System of Political Economy,* List said:

> The system of the school [*i.e.,* the school of Adam Smith] suffers . . . from three main defects: firstly, from boundless *cosmopolitanism,* which neither recognizes the principle of nationality, nor takes into consideration the satisfaction of its interests; secondly, from a dead *materialism,* which everywhere regards chiefly the mere exchangeable value of things without taking into consideration the mental and political, the present and the future interests, and the productive powers of the nation; thirdly, from a *disorganising particularism* and *individualism,* which, ignoring the nature and character of social labour and the operation of the union of powers in their higher consequences, considers private industry only as it would develop itself under a state of free interchange with society (i.e. with the whole human race) were that race not divided into separate national societies.
>
> Between each individual and entire humanity, however, stands THE NATION, with its special language and literature, with its peculiar origin and history, with its special manners and customs, laws and institutions, with the claims of all these for existence, independence, perfection, and continuance for the future, and with its separate territory; a society which, united by a thousand ties of mind and of interests, combines itself into one independent whole, which recognises the law of right for and within itself, and in its united character is still opposed to other societies of a similar kind in their national liberty, and consequently can only under the existing conditions of the world maintain self-existence and independence by its own power and resources. As the individual chiefly obtains by means of the nation and in the nation mental culture, power of production, security, and prosperity, so is the civilisation of the human race only conceivable and possible by means of the civilisation and development of the individual nations.[33]

Further, List believed that society was an evolving thing. He thought that what was good for the nation at one time might be quite unsuitable at another. This was the essence of List's thesis against freedom of trade. When in the United States of America, he had seen the position of American manufactures and become familiar with the arguments that were being used to justify protection, including those of Hamilton. Returning to Germany, he applied the ideas he had gained from his American sojourn to the industrial problem of his mother country. In the *National System,* he asserted that there were several stages in the economic evolution of a nation, these having been listed in Chapter I of

[33] *Op. cit.,* p. 141.

this book. America and Germany, he argued, were in the fourth of these stages, namely, that of agriculture with a limited amount of manufactures catering for the home market. Britain, on the other hand, had reached the fifth and final stage, where her manufactures were full-grown and could maintain themselves in worldwide trade. From the viewpoint of Germany and America, it was not sufficient that those countries remain in their existing position, List considered. They should endeavor to attain that already occupied by Great Britain. At least, they should become self-sufficing.

The true political economy, with which Smith had not concerned himself, List said, was

> that policy which each separate nation had to obey to make progress in its economical conditions.[34]

If, as—according to List—Smith and his supporters assumed, there existed a universal union of nations and a guarantee of everlasting peace, the principle of international trade might be justified. But List asserted that in fact such a system was non-existent. The nations were divided. With the industrial predominance of Great Britain, free trade was extending the market for English goods over all countries and developing England as "one immense manufacturing city." Yet in List's view, it was not for the best good that such a degree of specialization should arise. Diversification of industry was advantageous:

> *the reciprocal exchange between manufacturing power and agricultural power is so much greater, the closer the agriculturist and manufacturer are placed to one another, and the less they are liable to be interrupted in the exchange of their various products by accidents of all kinds.*[35]

The United States had some experience of such accidents. But the benefit of home manufactures to an agricultural country was not confined to the avoidance of risk of trade interruption. In List's opinion, the nation could not be considered fully developed unless it had a variety of occupations:

> The whole social state of a nation will be chiefly *determined by the principle of the variety and division of occupations and the co-operation of its productive powers. . . The most important division of occupations, and the most important co-operation of productive powers in material production, is that of agriculture and manufacture.* Both depend mutually upon one another. . . *A nation which only carries on agriculture, is an individual who in his material production lacks one arm.*[36]

Admitting that all countries could not produce every commodity—(for instance, tea and cotton production required special climatic conditions), List argued that countries in the temperate zone were favored by

[34] *Ibid.*, p. 97. [35] *Ibid.*, p. 127. [36] *Ibid.*, pp. 129-130.

nature, and their inhabitants owed it to themselves and to the world, not merely to develop their own productive powers to the highest possible point, but to make the tropical lands tributary to them.

To foster manufactures in such a country as Germany, which had the possibility of developing them, a system of protection was recommended. Import duties were to be introduced gradually, in order that as little damage as possible might be done to vested interests. List considered the size of these duties and concluded :

It may in general be assumed that where any technical industry cannot be established by means of an original protection of forty to sixty per cent. and cannot continue to maintain itself under a continued protection of twenty to thirty per cent. the fundamental conditions of manufacturing power are lacking.[37]

Exactly why List chose these figures, and not others one half as large or twice as much, was not made clear.

Since the duties were intended to stimulate manufactures, in List's system tariffs on agricultural products were ruled out. Raw materials should be permitted to enter the country freely or subjected only to revenue duties, he believed The policy should be timed to go into operation when conditions were suitable for industrial development. The duties imposed under it should be regarded as a measure of industrial education, continued during the educational process and brought to an end when this was completed.

John Stuart Mill. The idea of infant industry protection was referred to by John Stuart Mill, who made it the basis of a famous exception to the general principle of free trade. List had written before Mill. Yet it was not the German but the less well-known Scottish-American, John Rae, whom Mill mentioned. Mill admitted that in one particular circumstance protection was justifiable :

The only case in which, on mere principles of political economy, protecting duties can be defensible, is when they are imposed temporarily (especially in a young and rising nation) in hopes of naturalizing a foreign industry, in itself perfectly suitable to the circumstances of the country. The superiority of one country over another in a branch of production, often arises only from having begun it sooner. There may be no inherent advantage on one part, or disadvantage on the other, but only a present superiority of acquired skill and experience. A country which has this skill and experience yet to acquire, may in other respects be better adapted to the production than those which were earlier in the field : and besides, it is a just remark of Mr. Rae, that nothing has a greater tendency to promote improvements in any branch of production, than its trial under a new set of conditions. But it cannot be expected that individuals should, at their own risk, or rather to their

[37] *Ibid.*, p. 251.

certain loss, introduce a new manufacture, and bear the burthen of carrying it on until the producers have been educated up to the level of those with whom the processes are traditional. A protecting duty, continued for a reasonable time, might sometimes be the least inconvenient mode in which a nation can tax itself for the support of such an experiment. But it is essential that the protection should be confined to cases in which there is good ground of assurance that the industry which it fosters will after a time be able to dispense with it; nor should the domestic producers ever be allowed to expect that it will be continued to them beyond the time necessary for a fair trial of what they are capable of accomplishing.[38]

Mill later withdrew his support, but many economists have accepted the theoretical validity of his argument. In mass-production industries (that is, those whose costs decline rapidly with expansion of output), it may well happen that the small factories of a country, where the industry is yet new and undeveloped, cannot compete in costs with the larger and more firmly established plants elsewhere. Yet, if and when the new factories reach a scale comparable to that of their older competitors, they may be able to undercut the latter in their local market, because of the costs of importation, not only maintaining themselves but recouping to the nation the costs of the early protection. This is Mill's case and it is possible that there have been numerous examples in the development of young countries, including the United States of America and the British self-governing dominions. To exemplify the kind of claim that is commonly made by those interested in an infant industry, for protection from foreign competition, an extract may be given from the *Report of the Customs Tariff Commission* (1934–1935), appointed to study the problem as it affected the Union of South Africa:

It was pointed out on behalf of African Explosives and Industries that superphosphates could be produced profitably if the turnover were on a sufficiently large scale. The company could point to the fact that in regard to explosives they had reached the stage when they could do without protection. They had every expectation of being able to reach the same position with superphosphates if given protection for a period of five years. Up to the present, their fertilizer plants had been run at a loss. Your Commission was strongly impressed with the probability that this industry, if given protection, would be able in a short time to achieve an independent economic basis, and therefore to shed that protection.[39]

The opposition to protection of this nature has been on practical grounds. Where there exists a possibility that protection might be granted, every fond parent of an infant industry becomes a claimant for public assistance. Moreover, as has been pointed out frequently with reference to the United States, the protected infants resolutely refuse to

[38] *Principles of Political Economy,* Bk. 5, Chap. 10, Sect. 1.

[39] *Report,* Pretoria 1936, p. 72.

grow up, or to admit that they have reached a sufficient state of maturity to justify the withdrawal of the protection. But, in spite of these difficulties, the young countries have chosen to follow the course advocated by Hamilton and List, by imposing protective tariffs on imports for the purpose of building up home manufactures. How far the latter would have come into existence without this assistance cannot be determined. Whatever be the explanation, manufacturing industries have arisen in the United States and in such British dominions as the Union of South Africa, while Britain's own factories suffer eclipse.

Carey and Patten

The State of Pennsylvania gave rise to the leading American school of protectionists. Henry C. Carey, whose father was a friend of List's during the stay of the German writer in this country, was the leader of this group. Carey went beyond the position of List and Mill, who justified protection merely as a temporary measure. He supported it *per se.*

First, Carey followed List in emphasizing the effect upon human development of a many-sided industry. Diversified activity "furnishes employment for every variety of human faculty," he said. On the other hand, area-specialization and international trade

> — forbidding this development — limits the range of employment, and compels whole populations to employ themselves in scratching the earth, in the carriage of merchandise, or in the work of exchange. . .[40]

Next, like Hamilton, Carey referred to the saving in the cost of carriage that would attend the development of manufactures in America. But this was not a valid argument, as John Stuart Mill pointed out, because the cost of carriage of imported goods was a form of protection to the home-produced commodity, and imports came in only if manufacturing costs were low enough, in the countries from which the goods were brought, to compensate for the cost of transport.

In addition, Carey argued that the export of agricultural commodities diminished the natural stock of fertilizing ingredients possessed by the country concerned. "The planter," he said, was "steadily giving more of his raw materials, and receiving less in exchange for them" and the result was "exhaustion of the soil, and weakness of the State."[41] Mill admitted that export of farm produce exhausted the soil but replied that, when it ceased to pay better to break up new land than to manure the old, America would either become an importer of fertilizer or, "without protecting duties, grow corn for herself only and, manufacturing for herself, will make her manure, as Mr. Carey desires, at home."[42]

[40] *Principles of Social Science,* 3 vols., Phila. 1858–1859, reprinted 1877, vol. 2, pp. 241-242.

[41] *Ibid.,* vol. 2, p. vii. [42] *Principles of Political Economy,* Bk. 5, Chap. 10, Sect. 1.

Mill's conclusion, therefore, was that Carey's economic arguments for protection (other than assistance to infant industries) were "totally invalid," but the English writer admitted that the American, like many other protectionists, rested the case for import duties partly on non-economic considerations.

S. N. Patten (1852–1922), who taught economics for many years in the University of Pennsylvania, used arguments for protection that were akin to those of Carey. Producers should be near together, Patten said:

> The policy of a government desiring to develop its land most fully must necessarily be one that will create in the vicinity of each class of lands a demand for all that group of products which is necessary for its best use.[43]

Patten also mentioned the factor of soil deterioration, resulting from specialization in such products as cotton, wheat, and tobacco. He added that systematic protection of goods that had been elaborated or manufactured had the effect of raising their prices relative to the products of natural monopolies:

> A systematic protection of all producers will have the effect of raising the value of all commodities produced by them and of lowering the value of the products of natural monopolies; while a policy of free-trade, if fully adopted by a country, will create a high value of the products of natural monopolies and, through the increased competition which results, a low value for other commodities. . . Thus foreign trade causes the wealth of the country to be distributed in a different way from what it would be if there were no foreign trade of this kind. The classes gaining from the growth of natural monopolies have a greater share out of the total production of the nation than they would have if the natural resources of the country were used for the production of those commodities consumed at home.[44]

Here Patten meant that there would be more sales of the monopolized products under free trade than under protection, because the latter policy would diminish exports as well as imports. But this would be true only if the increased industrial development that followed from the adoption of a protective policy were insufficient to compensate for the falling off of foreign sales. This, clearly, would depend on the nature of the product and on similar factors. For example, a "natural monopoly" that ministered to some industrial use might not be developed at all in the absence of local manufactures, if the transport cost of its product in raw form were high. Some other source, nearer to the foreign demand, might be utilized instead.

On the subject of infant industries, Patten pointed out, quite correctly, that these were not merely representative of an early stage in national development. They were "something that a nation will always have as

[43] *The Economic Basis of Protection,* Phila. 1890, p. 31. Quoted by permission of J. B. Lippincott Company.

[44] *Ibid.,* pp. 39-40.

long as it remains in a dynamic condition."[45] The naturalization — to use Mill's word — in England and America of the dye industry developed in Germany, and in England and Germany of the automobile industry first established in the United States, are twentieth century examples of this situation.

Fundamentally, it can be said that both Carey and Patten had ideas that possessed considerable similarity to those of List. The ideal of all three writers was a nation developed as an entity — many-sided and self-reliant — as opposed to one that functioned only as a specialized member of a world economy.

The Employment Argument Again

Outside the special case of infant industries, the rank and file of economists in the English-speaking countries have opposed protection with virtual unanimity, taking their stand on Adam Smith's argument that it is economical that areas should specialize in those forms of production for which they are most suited. Following Smith, they have conceded that special attention should be paid to industries needed for purposes of defense; but the needs and risks of war have been regarded as something that economists, as such, have no special competence to assess.

But some writers have recognized other exceptions to the general rule of free trade, besides that mentioned by Mill. Thus, Cournot supported the employment argument, ventilated by others in earlier times. According to Cournot, what is now called *friction* or *immobility* in the labor market might justify protection in certain circumstances. The French writer was considering a case discussed by J. B. Say, concerning the shipping industry. A Dutch shipowner was supposed to be able to carry hemp for the French government from Riga to Havre at an out-of-pocket cost of 35 francs a ton, and to offer to perform the work for 40 francs, leaving a profit of 5 francs for himself. French shipowners wanted 55 francs for the same service, which cost them 50 francs. Cournot raised the question of whether Adam Smith and his followers were right in concluding that such trade ought to be given to the Dutch. The conclusion was correct, Cournot argued, only if the assumption were made that the French workers who had been trained as sailors or shipbuilders, and the French owners of ships, could move their labor and capital elsewhere and obtain an equivalent return. But such a supposition was "gratuitous," said Cournot, and the inference was that in this case the home industry should be favored.[46]

The Classical assumption of inter-occupational mobility of labor and capital is a very real disability when it is sought to apply the theory of

[45] *Ibid.*, p. 97.

[46] See *Researches into the Mathematical Principles of the Theory of Wealth*, pp. 167-170.

international trade, advanced by the Classical economists, to a society that is characterized to a very large extent by immobilities. Undoubtedly, this fact is one reason why protectionist policies have received strong political support in recent years. But the point should not be over-emphasized. Immobility is not always or indeed often a permanent condition. Given sufficient time, existing workers die and are replaced by a new generation. Even mature men can be trained for other jobs. Capital equipment does not last forever. It follows that immobility is mainly an argument for short-term protection and then only for such forms of assistance as will promote adjustment, rather than merely continue a maladjusted situation.

Henry Sidgwick made a point of some significance in his book, *The Principles of Political Economy*. He said that the Classical advocates of free trade had as their objective the maximization of individual happiness, irrespective of nationality. From the standpoint of the nation — which, Sidgwick said, was that taken by governments — this was objectionable :

> It is often assumed, expressly or tacitly, that when a class in a given nation can obtain any kind of commodities cheaper through foreign trade, the nation as a whole must be benefited by their so obtaining it. What is overlooked is the possibility that the portion of the nation from which employment is withdrawn by the change cannot be employed *within their own country* without a loss of utility on the whole greater than the gain from the cheaper foreign supply of the commodities they were producing before the change. . . I think it must be admitted in any theoretical treatment of the subject that in order to realise the economic advantage obtainable by free trade between two countries, a displacement of labour and capital out of one of the countries may be necessary : so that the *aggregate* wealth of the persons living *in one of the countries* may be reduced by the change.[47]

Applying Sidgwick's statement to the example studied by Cournot, it can be said that, if *maximum individual happiness* be the criterion (irrespective of whether those who are happy are of French or Dutch nationality), then it is immaterial that employment is taken away from Frenchmen and given to the Dutch. The French, it is true, for a time may be left unemployed, but Dutchmen, who otherwise would be out of work, find jobs. Even if the assumption here made of the existence of reserves of unemployed laborers be removed, the maximum happiness principle still supports free trade if the unemployed French shipworkers can move to Holland and secure employment in their old trade in that country. But it must be remembered that the French government is not expected to give attention to the happiness of the residents of Holland. France alone is in its care. In this situation, undoubtedly it will prefer the happiness of its subjects over that of foreigners ; and, in all probability, it will not remain unmoved if a mass migration of Frenchmen to Holland occurs.

[47] *Op. cit.*, p. 495.

Why, then, did economists like Ricardo and J. S. Mill expect governments to take a different view? Partly, no doubt, because liberalism was in fashion in England in the first half of the nineteenth century and nationalism unpopular, but also possibly because of Britain's special position as a colonizing nation. Ricardo ruled out international mobility of the productive factors and certainly in his days the practical difficulties attending movement were great. But Mill discussed emigration at some length. When Ricardo and Mill wrote, British institutions were spread over a large proportion of the empty spaces of the world, so that the Britisher who went abroad was not required to forego his cultural heritage in quite the same manner as must the migrating Swede, German, and Italian. In the twentieth century barriers to movement in the form of government restrictions have made emigration very difficult, so that men who lose their positions because of shifts in demand to the products of some other country, until they can move into other occupations, remain as recipients of public relief in the land of their birth. This situation gives the employment argument for protective tariffs greater force than it would possess if mobility (including migration) were easier.

History shows many examples of protectionist policy carried through largely to defend established industries. Already it has been mentioned that one reason for the growth of the United States tariff in the early part of the nineteenth century was the possibility that local manufactures (which had grown up during the period of trade interruption connected with the Napoleonic Wars) would be destroyed by free commerce. The Union of South Africa furnished an almost complete parallel after the war of 1914–1918. The protection given to agricultural products by the German tariffs of 1885 and 1887 was partially explained by the severity of competition from the new countries overseas. Every newspaper reader is aware of the political influence of this argument at the present time, when protection is the order of the day.

The Conservation of Natural Resources

In reviewing the writings of Carey and Patten, earlier in this chapter, reference was made to the arguments of these economists in favor of limiting the development of industries that depleted the natural resources of the country. Free trade, Carey asserted, led some countries — including America in his own time — to specialize in agriculture, exhausting the soil.

The English economist, W. S. Jevons, in his book on *The Coal Question,* raised the same point with regard to the mineral resources of England. According to Jevons, unlimited free trade was leading to a rapid exhaustion of the coalfields. Once this situation was realized, he thought that two schools of thought would develop:

Some will wish to hold to our adopted principles, and leave commerce and the consumption of coal unchecked even to the last—while others, subordinating commerce to purposes of a higher nature, will tend to the prohibition of coal exports, the restriction of trade, and the adoption of every means of sparing the fuel which makes our welfare and supports our influence upon the nations of the world.[48]

Jevons's reference to such considerations as being "of a higher nature" recalls the hierarchy of motives suggested in his *The Theory of Political Economy,* discussed in Chapter II. Here Jevons was placing the interest of the nation, as Müller and List regarded it, above the immediate self-interests of individuals.

An outstanding case of protection for the purpose of conserving natural resources is to be found in the economic policy of the Union of South Africa. That country depends very largely on the gold mining industry. Confronted by the possibility—if not the likelihood—that unrestricted exploitation of the mines would lead to their early exhaustion, without any parallel rise of other industries to take the place of gold, the government has adopted a policy of industrial diversification. The expansion of mining is being checked, while encouragement is given to agriculture and manufactures. Thus the Union has become more self-sufficing than would have been the case under a free trade system and it is hoped that its prosperity will prove more lasting.[49] Here the issue is clearly drawn between the maximization of individual wealth and the continuing prosperity of a nation. There is no doubt whatever that individual wealth would be greater if investors and laborers were permitted unrestricted entry into gold mining, than when they are encouraged to enter agriculture and manufacture under South African conditions, providing that mobility of capital and labor is possible when the gold mines become exhausted. But this assumption cannot be granted, at least with respect to much of the labor employed in the mines. The fact that the European miners are themselves immigrants or have descended from immigrants does not mean that their own successors will be able or willing to migrate. The negroes who make up the great majority of mine employees are likely to experience greater difficulty in moving away. From the individual standpoint, therefore, if a long view be taken, there is much to be said for the government policy. Still more potent is the fact that the problem is not regarded as an individual one but a question for the nation. If gold mining disappears and nothing has been built up in its place, South Africa is likely to revert to the arid pastoral culture which existed within its borders before gold was discovered—a situation which South African statesmen do not appear to be prepared to contemplate.

[48] p. xviii.

[49] The policy is described in an article by the writer in the *American Economic Review,* Menasha 1938.

Pareto

An ingenious argument for protection has been furnished by the Italian economist and sociologist, Pareto.[50] Confronted by the situation that abstract economic theory (*i.e.*, the theory of the Classical and Neo-Classical schools, to which Pareto himself adhered) gave general support to free trade but that legislators preferred protection—without, apparently, any injurious results, Pareto sought an explanation.

He distinguished between (1) the direct economic effects of protection, (2) the indirect economic effects, and (3) the general social effects. The direct effects he admitted to be harmful to the production of wealth, as Adam Smith had said. But, on the other hand, Pareto thought that the indirect economic effects might be beneficial. He said that the existence of a system of protection permitted able men to rise to controlling positions in industry, with the result that production was increased. On this point, it should be said that many economists have assumed the opposite to be true, namely, that—in the absence of foreign competition to keep them on their mettle—industrial managers would become slack and inefficient. No statistics exist to prove either argument, so the two assertions can only be set against each other.

Pareto's position on protection was closely linked with his general social theory, which has been referred to in Chapter I. The social effect of protection, he thought, was that it assisted the circulation of the élite, or class of leaders, by allowing clever men to rise to power.

Whatever is concluded respecting such a theory, certainly it is true that wealth has increased in spite of the growth of protection in Europe and elsewhere in recent decades. However, this proves nothing. Protection might have fostered the growth of wealth, as Pareto argued, but it is equally possible that wealth might have advanced more rapidly had there been less protection.

The Modern Growth of Economic Nationalism

Whatever be the cause, protection and, indeed, economic nationalism generally have grown in strength in recent years. As was seen in the earlier chapters of this book, the basic philosophy of Locke and Smith was individualistic and had room for the nation only in so far as it served the purposes of the individual. But the Hegelians gave a more prominent place to the State and even the later English utilitarians recognized that the State organization might function over a wide field. With the passage of time, men's thoughts on economics have become less individualistic and more political or social. As has often been the case, the ideas of practical people seemed to move in advance of those of academicians, with the result that much of the economic literature in this field has been highly critical of the new tendency.

[50] *See The Mind and Society*, vol. 4, pp. 1544-1566.

The latter part of the nineteenth and the early years of the twentieth centuries witnessed a scramble among European nations for territory in the newly opened up continent of Africa, very like that which had taken place between Mercantilist powers for Asiatic and American possessions at an earlier date. The war of 1914–1918 did a great deal to exaggerate nationalistic feelings and, though there was much talk of internationalism in the immediate post-war period, the peace settlement laid the ground for further intensification of the spirit of nationalism. The powers that had come late in the struggle for colonies — Germany, Italy, and Japan — were opposed to those that had built up extensive empires in an earlier period, namely Britain and France.

Protection took on renewed significance. During the war, trade had been interrupted and driven into fresh channels. Industries had been developed that faced destruction in the event that commerce was made free again. This was as true of the manufacture in England of commodities that formerly had been imported from Germany as of industries established in the self-governing dominions to elaborate goods that previously had been bought from British makers. This was one factor that helped to wean England from her free trade allegiance as well as to encourage protectionist legislation in the newer countries overseas.

The onset of depression after 1929 gave considerable encouragement to economic nationalism. When there were thousands — or even millions — of workers unemployed in domestic industries, it seemed only sensible to many people that the influx of competitive goods of foreign manufacture should be prevented. Unbalanced exchanges and currency depreciation led nations to adopt the Mercantilist policy of encouraging exports and discouraging imports. The possibility of war caused statesmen to inaugurate programs of national self-sufficiency. The reduction of exports, due to protective policies elsewhere, had the same effect, because the lack of foreign exchange forced restriction of imports. Quota systems and barter agreements became the rule and foreign trade was canalized on lines often more influenced by political than by economic considerations.

On the economic side, the correlation of protectionist sentiments — and, indeed, of government economic activity as a whole — with industrial depression has been marked. It must be borne in mind that the most powerful support for *laissez faire* came from the commercial and industrial interests who were themselves its beneficiaries. The triumph of the anti-corn law agitation in Britain and the continued popular successes of the free trade Liberal Party rested in part on the fact that the industrialists were convinced that manufacturing costs would be brought and kept low by the admission of imports free of duty. To the working class, which, as time passed by, obtained more political power, cheap food had a wide appeal. Whatever the manufacturers thought about it, the subsistence theory of wages was not accepted by working men.[51] There grew up the conviction that free trade meant not merely cheap bread but the continued prosperity of British industry, with returns in dividends to stockholders and steady employment at good wages for the workers.

Even the countries on the continent of Europe moved in a free trade direction during the period of general industrial prosperity that accompanied rising price levels during the third quarter of the nineteenth century. They turned over to protection, and to government regulation generally, when manufacturing industry and agriculture became depressed in the declining price period that commenced about 1875. Protection was favored by the British statesman, Joseph Chamberlain, during the early years of the twentieth century, but in a period of business prosperity it fought a losing battle. The situation was otherwise in the depression that followed the 1920 boom, and especially after 1929. To reason from a simple correlation of two factors, in this case protectionist sentiment and industrial depression, however, is always fraught with danger as a logical procedure. The most that can be said of this particular example is that it might to taken as suggesting one of the factors that have been at work.

Predominantly, in recent discussions, the prosperity of man *as a producer,* rather than his interest *as a consumer,* has received attention, as appeared to be the case in the Mercantilist period. Yet these are notable examples of the opposite situation, as under the Labour government in Britain a few years ago, when the consumers' co-operatives formed an influential pressure group. For the most part it seems evident that men are better organized as producers than as consumers, so that the producer is powerful and articulate while the consumer's interest goes by default. According to Adam Smith, "Consumption is the sole end and purpose of all production; and the interest of the producer ought to be attended to, only so far as it may be necessary for promoting that of the consumer."[52] Perhaps some historian of the twentieth century will make comments about the men of the present day, comparable to those that were penned by Bacon, Cunningham, and Heckscher on their Mercantilist predecessors, that they have bent the aim of national policy from consideration of plenty towards something else. But it must be remembered that there are many individuals living today who do not associate plenty with free trade. They fear that with institutions as at present organized—monopolies, pressure groups, and legislatures only too anxious to interfere in commercial affairs—freedom of international trade may

[51] See Chapter XII for an account of this theory.

[52] *Wealth of Nations,* Bk. 4, Chap. 8.

mean severe fluctuations in the course of business. They prefer the income-stability and security that they think are offered by protection. Granting that, in a period long enough to give mobility to the productive factors, free trade may increase wealth, two problems confront the individual: (1) what share of the total wealth does he receive? and (2) what occurs when mobility is impossible? Until free traders are able to furnish convincing answers to these questions (which go back at least as far as the fifteenth century), they are unlikely to wean practical men from their protectionist affiliations.

But it must be recognized that economic arguments have been by no means alone in the field. Assistance to agriculture in Europe has been justified by the pleas that country people are physically fitter than townsmen and that a strong peasant class confers an element of political stability on its nation. Self-sufficiency in case of war or other interruption to world trade, national unity, and other factors, have been of great significance. It is idle to examine the recent growth of economic nationalism without recognizing that the position and functions of the State have been emphasized in other spheres in the same period. Economic nationalism is too intimately part of a wider collectivism to be entirely understandable in isolation.

Summary of Chapter

Arguments in favor of local self-sufficiency are found in early writings but after the end of the middle ages the subject assumed great importance. With the rise of the great States of western Europe, economic regulation — which previously had been largely localized or particularized — was placed on a national basis. Central governments actively pursued policies of economic independence for the purpose of giving unity and strength to their States. The body of Mercantilist literature is to be related to this period. Much of it dealt with foreign trade and some of the chief writings were penned by men with a personal interest in trading concerns.

As years passed by, the decline of royal absolutism and the growing tendency to emphasize individual ends caused trade regulation to recede into the background. Once the maximization of individual riches was accepted as a social objective, economic nationalism was open to serious objections. These were set forth in the works of Hume, Smith, and others. Yet protection was not without its defenders, even from the standpoint of individual riches. The infant industry argument, associated with the names of Hamilton, List, and Mill, has been of special significance, as have the views of those who have advocated the restriction of international trade to maintain home employment and to conserve natural resources. But even more than has been the case with many other subjects that economists have discussed, the economic aspect of the problem had been by no means decisive and practical policy has been developed more in face of the economists' opposition than with their approval. With the lapse of time and the growth of feeling that national or social aims should receive attention, *laissez faire* in international trade has suffered some eclipse.

CHAPTER VII

POPULATION

Early Thought and Practice

It is sometimes said that population has received attention only recently as an economic problem. The reason given is that, in the early stages of human development, natural resources were plentiful relative to the number of people dependent upon them for their subsistence. In these circumstances, an increase in numbers raised no difficulties. With the passage of time and continued growth of population, however, a scarcity of resources revealed itself, it is stated, so population began to arouse interest.

The Customs of Savages

This belief is ill-founded. Possessed of a limited knowledge of his environment and of very crude production techniques, primitive man appears to have had just as much trouble as his modern descendants in making ends meet. Accordingly, population has long been a problem to the savage, whether recognized or not. This has been made abundantly clear by A. M. Carr-Saunders (1886–), a leading British writer on the subject of population, in his book on *The Population Problem: A Study in Human Evolution* (Oxford 1922). In this work there was presented a large body of evidence, drawn from various sources, respecting the practices of primitive people. It was shown that regulation of population increase was and is quite customary in savage societies. Postponement of marriage, bans on cohabitation for an extended period following childbirth, the exposure of infants, and similar social customs, furnished effective barriers against any undue growth of population, along with such better-known phenomena as wars and famines. In other words, what were termed by Malthus the *preventive checks* to population growth, as well as the *positive checks,* were operative even in the earliest times. Birth control may be new enough, in its existing methods, but as a general principle it appears to have been familiar to man for a very long time. This fact must be borne in mind in relation to the background of any study of population theories.

The Classical World

As in other fields, the writers of early Greece were more concerned with the elaboration of rules and the formulation of policies than with scientific theorizing. Thus Plato, in his *Republic,* associated the defense of a State with the number of its inhabitants and insisted that there should be a sufficiently large number of people for the preservation of independence. In the planned States of the *Republic* and the *Laws,* as in some States of the present, people were included among the things which were to be planned. The State visualized in the *Laws* was to have 5040 families, and methods were indicated for the preservation of this number:

> they in whom generation is affluent may be made to refrain, and, on the other hand, special care may be taken to increase the number of births by rewards and stigmas, or we may meet the evil by the elder men giving advice and administering rebuke to the younger. . .[1]

If, notwithstanding this, there were too many births, "owing to the too great love of those who live together, and we are at our wits' end"—to use Plato's words—

> there is still the old device often mentioned by us of sending out a colony. . . If, on the other hand, there come a wave bearing a deluge of disease, or a plague of war, and the inhabitants become much fewer than the appointed number by reason of bereavement, we ought not to introduce citizens of spurious birth and education, if this can be avoided; but even God is said not to be able to fight against necessity.[2]

So, in the last resort, Plato was prepared to admit immigrants. His ideas on eugenics, or control of quality, were very thorough-going. In the society described in the *Republic,* not only were the best of each sex to be mated as often as possible and the inferior as seldom as possible—apparently by careful scrutinizing of the list of invitations to be issued in connection with official hymeneal festivals—but undesirable children were to be killed off and only those with praiseworthy characteristics raised to maturity. Plato recognized that the people might not approve of this sort of thing, so he observed:

> Now these goings on must be a secret which the rulers only know, or there will be a further danger of our herd, as the guardians may be termed, breaking out into rebellion.[3]

As for the children, this difficulty was to be met by removing all infants from the care of their parents, immediately after birth, so that the latter would never know of their destruction, if this should occur. Thus, numbers and quality of people were to be regulated. In view of the present situation (as regards both numbers and quality), there might be something to be said for modern governments giving their attention to Plato.

Even Aristotle, who rejected Plato's communistic ideas generally, was quite prepared to control marriage and birth rates. First, he considered

[1] *The Dialogues of Plato,* vol. 5, *Laws,* p. 123.
[2] *Ibid.*
[3] *Ibid.,* vol. 3, *Republic,* p. 153. It was the guardians or administrators who were to be cared for in this way.

the numbers necessary for a State, deciding the question largely on political grounds:

> A state, then, only begins to exist when it has attained a population sufficient for a good life in the political community: it may indeed, if it somewhat exceed this number, be a greater state. But, as I was saying, there must be a limit.[4]

This limit Aristotle found in the administrative difficulties attending a large political unit. For example, "in an over-populous state foreigners and metics will readily acquire the rights of citizens, for who will find them out?" This statement forecast one of the troubles of twentieth century America.

Having settled the matter of numbers in the State to his own satisfaction, Aristotle went on to consider how extensive its territory should be, that is, over what area these numbers should be scattered. This, he saw, was at least partly an economic matter:

> In size and extent it [*i.e.*, the State] should be such as may enable the inhabitants to live at once temperately and liberally in the enjoyment of leisure.[5]

Some may consider this statement to be anticipatory of the optimum theory of population, discussed later. Aristotle, however, as has been noticed elsewhere, attached only a limited importance to wealth, so it could not be expected that he would follow up the point. On the practical side, he was just as willing as Plato to control both numbers and quality of children.

Roman thought went little beyond the formulation of measures designed to stimulate population growth among citizens, whose declining birth rate caused concern—an early experience of a problem that has assumed significance in our own days. About the time of the birth of Christ, under the Emperor Augustus, penalties were imposed on men who were not married, and rewards given for marriage and the birth of offspring. For instance, Romans with three children were exempted from certain troublesome offices, and inheritance by unmarried or childless persons was restricted. The statement made by Augustus in defense of his laws is worth quotation:

> While sickness and war snatch away so many citizens, what must become of this state if marriages are no longer contracted? the city does not consist of houses, of porticos, of public places, but of inhabitants. You do not see men . . . starting out of the earth to take care of your affairs. . . My only view is the perpetuity of the republic.[6]

[4] *The Works of Aristotle*, vol. 9, *Politica*, 1326b. [5] *Ibid.*

[6] Contracted by Montesquieu, *The Spirit of Laws*, vol. 2, pp. 151-152.

The Middle Ages and Early Modern Times

Christianity, on its more ascetic side, contained the seeds of a serious population difficulty. Lusts of the flesh were frowned upon and some teachers went so far as to favor complete abstention from sexual intercourse, which would have brought population to the point of extinction at the end of a single generation. Fortunately for the future of the human race, this attitude received no wide support, at least outside the religious leaders or bodies themselves—for whom celibacy offered a prospect of undivided allegiance to spiritual well-doing. At first, the clergy were allowed to marry; and, though clerical marriages were generally stamped out during the middle ages, the rank and file of believers were always permitted to marry and have children. Thus, Aquinas, while declaring that virginity was preferable to marriage, on the question of "whether no venereal act can be without sin," stated,

> A sin, in human acts, is that which is against the order of reason. Now the order of reason consists in its ordering everything to its end in a fitting manner. Wherefore it is no sin if one, by the dictate of reason, makes use of certain things in a fitting manner and order for the end to which they are adapted, provided this end be something truly good. Now just as the preservation of the bodily nature of one individual is a true good, so, too, is the preservation of the nature of the human species a very great good. And just as the use of food is directed to the preservation of life in the individual, so is the use of venereal acts directed to the preservation of the whole human race. Hence Augustine says . . . *What food is to a man's well being, such is sexual intercourse to the welfare of the whole human race.* Wherefore just as the use of food can be without sin, if it be taken in due manner and order, as required for the welfare of the body, so also the use of venereal acts can be without sin, provided they be performed in due manner and order, in keeping with the end of human procreation.[7]

As in similar writings of Aquinas and others, what was at issue was not economics but Christian ethics, and, characteristically, the Church in general and Aquinas in particular offered a solution that could be followed practically by the world.

The economic aspect of population was not neglected altogether. Jordanes (sixth century), for example, a Goth and historian of his nation, referred to population pressure in his writings. As the middle ages gave place to modern times, Machiavelli's *Discorsi . . . sopra la prima deca di Tito Livio* (1521), recognized the operation of such checks as famine and disease. Later still, Bacon's *Of Vicissitude of Things* mentioned population growth as one of the reasons for war and suggested the possibility of people not marrying nor generating "except they know means to live":

[7] *Summa theologica,* Pt. 2, Second Pt., Q. 153, Art. 2.

The great accessions and unions of kingdoms do likewise stir up wars : for when a state grows to an over-power, it is like a great flood, that will be sure to overflow ; as it hath been seen in the states of Rome, Turkey, Spain, and others. Look when the world hath fewest barbarous people, but such as commonly will not marry, or generate, except they know means to live (as it is almost everywhere at this day, except Tartary), there is no danger of inundations of people ; but when there be great shoals of people, which go on to populate, without foreseeing means of life and sustentation, it is of necessity that once in an age or two they discharge a portion of their people upon other nations, which the ancient northern people were wont to do by lot ; casting lots what part should stay at home, and what should seek their fortunes.[8]

Bacon's phrase, "as it is almost everywhere at this day," is very significant. Apparently the English statesman had few fears of the nature of those entertained by Malthus two centuries afterwards.

Political Arithmetic

The study of population on a quantitative basis began with the writings on what is commonly called *Political Arithmetic* that appeared toward the end of the seventeenth century. The names of John Graunt (1620–1674), Sir William Petty, Gregory King (1648–1712), and Charles Davenant deserve mention.

Graunt was a London tradesman who made a hobby of what now would be called vital statistics. Petty displayed ingenuity as an inventor and taught anatomy at Oxford before going to Ireland to survey lands forfeited in the wars of the period. There he obtained an estate. In connection with his Irish survey he collected economic data and his writings abound in deductions made from this. King worked mainly on genealogy but was of a mathematical turn of mind and made estimates of the current population and production of England. Davenant had duties that gave him an interest in King's figures and he incorporated them in his own writings. These men had the common characteristic that their studies were on realistic lines, and population was a subject to which they devoted particular attention. Graunt's examination of the death returns (*bills of mortality*) of the city of London and adjoining areas is a landmark in the history of vital statistics, establishing such generalizations as that death rates tend to be higher in urban than in rural localities and greater during the early and late years of life than in the middle period. Such matters are outside the subject of this chapter but Graunt's comment on the relatively low rate of growth of city population is worth quoting:

When I consider, That in the Country seventy are Born for fifty eight Buried, and that before the year 1600 the like happened in *London*, I con-

[8] Reprinted in *The Moral and Historical Works of Lord Bacon,* p. 156.

sidered, whether a City, as it becomes more *populous,* doth not, for that very cause, become more *unhealthful*: and inclined to believe, that *London* now is more *unhealthful* than heretofore; partly for that it is more populous, but chiefly because I have heard, that sixty years ago few *Sea-Coals* [*i.e.*, coal brought by sea from the Newcastle area] were burnt in *London,* which are now universally used.[9]

Some of Petty's ideas are interesting, also. For example, in *A Treatise of Taxes & Contributions,* he said:

Fewness of people, is real poverty; and a Nation wherein are Eight Millions of people, are more than twice as rich as the same scope of Land wherein are but Four. . .[10]

Thus Petty took the opposite position from that assumed by Malthus, postulating increasing returns as population rose, instead of the diminishing-returns tendency which worried the latter author. Petty's reason for this is curious:

For the same Governours which are the great charge, may serve near as well, for the greater, as the lesser number.[11]

Perhaps a present-day American, contrasting the town-meeting governments of the early settlements with the elaborate and expensive administrations of the twentieth century, may draw a different conclusion. However, Petty added:

If the people be so few, as that they can live, *Ex sponte Creatis,* or with little labour, such as is Grazing, &c. they become wholly without Art.[12]

Here there was suggested an economic reason for increasing returns as population grew. In his *Political Arithmetick,* the same writer attributed the wealth of the Dutch, in part, to the fact that

Men may live near each other, for their mutual assistance in Trade.[13]

He listed several advantages attending population increase:

1. Suppose some great Fabrick were in Building by a Thousand Men, shall not much more time be spared if they lived all upon a Thousand Acres, then if they were forced to live upon ten times as large a Scope of Land.
2. The charge of the cure of their Souls, and the Ministry would be far greater in one case than in the other; as also of mutual defence in case of Invasion, and even of Thieves and Robbers: Moreover the charge

[9] *Natural and Political Observations mentioned in a Following Index, and made upon the Bills of Mortality,* London 1662, 5th ed., London 1676, reprinted in *The Economic Writings of Sir William Petty,* vol. 2, pp. 393-394. The authorship of the *Observations* has been disputed, some attributing the work to Petty. The evidence on the subject is reviewed on pp. xxxix-liv of the volume from which this passage is taken, where a conclusion in favor of Graunt is reached. Petty, however, certainly edited the 5th edition, reprinted in his *Economic Writings.*

[10] *Ibid.*, vol. 1, p. 34. [11] *Ibid.* [12] *Ibid.* [13] *Ibid.*, p. 255.

> of the administration of Justice would be much easier, where Witnesses and Parties may be easily summoned, Attendance less expensive, when Mens Actions would be better known, when wrongs and injuries could not be covered, as in thin peopled places they are.
>
> Lastly, those who live in solitary places, must be their own Soldiers, Divines, Physicians, and Lawyers; and must have their Houses stored with necessary Provisions (like a Ship going upon a long Voyage,) to the great wast, and needless expence of such Provisions.[14]

Petty, obviously, was not troubled about population increase, although, as will be noted in the chapter on Rent, he was not blind to the fact that a growth in numbers of people would have a tendency to raise the price of food. From the economic standpoint, it appears that England, in Petty's view, was under-populated and would gain by an increase in numbers. Perhaps, though, Petty was too anxious about the advancement of his plans concerning the disposal of Irish land and people for his comments to be entirely impartial on such matters.

The Malthusian Theory

With the industrial revolution, the population of England and Wales advanced by leaps and bounds. From about five and a half millions in 1700, it had risen to around six and a half by 1750, and to nine in 1800. By 1850, it stood at eighteen millions. It was not to be expected that such an increase would pass unnoticed by economic theorists. Moreover, along with the rise in population, there was at times considerable distress. Widespread rural enclosures, together with the continuance of an unsatisfactory poor law, meant severe poverty in some districts, resulting in burdens on the parishes for its alleviation. Business depressions made their appearance from time to time. This was particularly true in the lulls that occurred during the Napoleonic struggle and especially after peace was concluded. That the population theory commonly associated with the name of T. R. Malthus should arouse great interest in such a situation is understandable. Malthus offered no new theory but rather formulated with some precision and presented very forcefully an old idea, in circumstances where it seemed to assume tremendous practical significance.

The essentials of the theory can be stated briefly. Population tends to increase in a geometric proportion (*i.e.,* 2:4:8:16, etc.), being limited only by certain checks. These are (1) positive checks, that is, vice and misery arising from the pressure of population upon the means of subsistence, and (2) preventive checks, under which heading Malthus included moral restraint. The positive and preventive checks are mutually exclusive, since, to the extent that the latter are in force, the former are inoperative.

[14] *Ibid.,* pp. 255-256.

Forerunners of Malthus

Though commonly associated with the name of Malthus, the basic idea dates from long before his time. Mention has been made of some of the earlier suggestions of such a theory. In the sixteenth and seventeenth centuries a number of statements appeared, containing one or more ingredients of the Malthusian theory.

Mercantilists and Political Arithmeticians. Both Mun and Locke held beliefs on the subject of wages which rested on the postulate that population possessed an unlimited capacity to increase at a fixed subsistence minimum.[15]

Petty used the conception of a geometric rate of increase in *Another Essay in Political Arithmetick, Concerning the Growth of the City of London: With the Measures, Periods, Causes, and Consequences thereof* 1682 (London 1683):

> For supposing the eight *Persons* who came out of the *Ark, Increased* by a Progressive doubling in every 10 Years, might grow in the first 100 Years after the *Flood* from 8 to 8000, and that in 350 Years after the *Flood* (when abouts *Noah* dyed) to one Million, and by this time 1682, to 320 Millions (which by rational conjecture, are thought to be now in the World) it will not be hard to compute, how in the intermediate Years, the *Growths* may be made. . .[16]

Petty himself made such a computation, assuming that the doubling period was ten years at the beginning of the period which had elapsed between the time of Adam and Eve and his own day, and twelve hundred years at the end.

Johann Peter Süssmilch (1707 or 1708–1767), a Prussian army chaplain who was interested in demography, not only made use of the conception of a geometric rate of increase but gave startling data respecting the influence of epidemics in checking population growth. These, incidentally, were quoted later by Malthus in support of his own arguments.

Montesquieu, Cantillon, and Steuart. Montesquieu referred to the tendency of people to marry (and have children) whenever the means of subsistence permitted it:

> Wherever a place is found in which two persons can live commodiously, there they enter into marriage. Nature has a sufficient propensity to it, when unrestrained by the difficulty of subsistence.[17]

True to the evolutionary attitude displayed in all his writings, Montesquieu went on to declare that the rate of increase depended upon the stage of development reached by the society concerned:

15 See Chapter XII.

16 *The Economic Writings of Sir William Petty,* vol. 2, p. 465.

17 *The Spirit of Laws,* vol. 2, p. 139.

A rising people increase and multiply extremely. This is, because with them it would be a great inconvenience to live in celibacy; and none to have many children. The contrary of which is the case when a nation is formed.[18]

The explanation is not very lucid, though the second portion of it may have reference to the problem of subsistence. Montesquieu was emphatic in saying that births were not unchecked in practice :

The females of brutes have an almost constant fecundity. But in the human species, the manner of thinking, the character, the passions, the humour, the caprice, the idea of preserving beauty, the pain of child-bearing, and the fatigue of a too numerous family, obstruct propagation a thousand different ways.[19]

To this, even the most modern reader can only reply, "Very true!" Obviously, however, this last statement conflicts with that first quoted, unless the two refer—as well they might—to different social classes or stages in social evolution. Finally, Montesquieu gave an account of population changes in the past and of the measures whereby various rulers had endeavored to control the number of people, mentioning the laws of Augustus in Rome, those of Louis XIV in France not long before Montesquieu's own time, and others.

Cantillon's population theory is worth attention :

Experience shews that Trees, Plants and other Vegetables can be increased to any Quantity which the Extent of Ground laid out for them can support. The same Experience shews that all kinds of the Animal Creation are to be multiplied to any Quantity which the Land allotted to them can support. . . In a word, we can multiply all sorts of Animals in such numbers as we wish to maintain even to infinity if we could find lands to infinity to nourish them; and the multiplication of Animals has no other bounds than the greater or less means allotted for their subsistence. It is not to be doubted that if all Land were devoted to the simple sustenance of Man the race would increase up to the number that the Land would support in the manner to be explained.[20]

Cantillon compared the population situations in China and among the American Indians with that in Europe; that in various classes of Europeans in his time; and that at different times. In the course of his comparisons, he had occasion to point out that

a Man who lives on Bread, Garlic and Roots, wears only hempen garments, coarse Linen, Wooden Shoes, and drinks only water, like many Peasants in the South of France, can live on the produce of an Acre and a half of Land of medium goodness, yielding a sixfold harvest and resting once in

[18] *Ibid.*

[19] *Ibid.*, p. 132.

[20] *Essai sur la nature du commerce en général*, translated by H. Higgs, London 1931, pp. 65-67. Quoted by permission of Macmillan & Co., Ltd., and The Macmillan Company.

3 years. On the other hand a grown-up Man who wears leather Shoes, Stockings, Woollen Cloth, who lives in a House and has a change of Linen, a Bed, Chairs, Table, and other necessaries, drinks moderately of Beer or Wine, eats every day Meat, Butter, Cheese, Bread, Vegetables, etc. sufficiently and yet moderately needs for all that the produce of 4 to 5 acres of land of medium quality.[21]

He then generalized :

I assumed that most men desire nothing better than to marry if they are set in a position to keep their Families in the same style as they are content to live themselves. That is, if a Man is satisfied with the produce of an Acre and a half of Land he will marry if he is sure of having enough to keep his Family in the same way. But if he is only satisfied with the produce of 5 to 10 Acres he will be in no hurry to marry unless he thinks he can bring up his Family in the same manner.[22]

Thus Cantillon did not assert that population necessarily increased to the limits set by the bare minimum of subsistence. Men had *varying standards of living,* he thought, and these set bounds upon their willingness to multiply. In other words, the subsistence standard was not fixed, as far as multiplication was concerned, but was a matter of human decision.

Cantillon proceeded to use this conception in attacking calculations respecting rates of population increase, such as had been made by Gregory King in England :

If seventeen centuries ago there were 26 millions of people in Italy, now reduced to 6 millions at most, how can it be determined by the progressions of Mr. King that England which today contains 5 or 6 millions of Inhabitants will probably have 13 millions in a certain number of years? We see daily that Englishmen, in general, consume more of the produce of the Land than their Fathers did, and this is the real reason why there are fewer Inhabitants than in the past.[23]

Incidentally, Cantillon gave the example popularized by Malthus, namely the North American Colonies, to represent a situation in which there was no check upon population increase :

Men multiply like Mice in a barn if they have unlimited Means of Subsistence; and the English in the Colonies will become more numerous in proportion in three generations than they would be in thirty in England, because in the Colonies they find for cultivation new tracts of land from which they drive the Savages.[24]

[21] *Ibid.*, p. 71.

[22] *Ibid.*, p. 77. See Chapter XII for the similar views expressed by Ricardo and by Malthus in his *Political Economy*.

[23] *Ibid.*, p. 83. King's calculations were contained in *Natural and Political Observations and Conclusions upon the State and Condition of England, London* 1696, reprinted Baltimore 1936.

[24] *Ibid.*

As Cantillon stated it, with a subsistence standard that depended on the will of the people concerned, the population principle was less open to objection than was the case in the *Essay* of Malthus.

Sir James Steuart discussed the subject of population on Malthusian lines in his *Inquiry into the Principles of Political Œconomy*:

Thus the generative faculty resembles a spring loaded with a weight, which always exerts itself in proportion to the diminution of resistance : when food has remained some time without augmentation or diminution, generation will carry numbers as high as possible; if then food come to be diminished, the spring is overpowered; the force of it becomes less than nothing. Inhabitants will diminish, at least, in proportion to the overcharge. If, upon the other hand, food be increased, the spring which stood at o, will begin to exert itself in proportion as the resistance diminishes; people will begin to be better fed; they will multiply, and, in proportion as they increase in numbers, the food will become scarce again.[25]

The positive checks had their place :

That the generative faculty in man (which we have compared to a spring), and the care and love we have for our children, first prompt us to multiply, and then engage us to divide what we have with our little ones. Thus from dividing and subdividing it happens, that in every country where food is limited to a certain quantity, the inhabitants must be subsisted in a regular progression, descending down from plenty and ample subsistence, to the last periods of want, and even sometimes starving for hunger.

Although the examples of this last extremity are not common in some countries, yet I believe they are more so than is generally imagined; and the other stages of want are productive of many diseases, and of a decay which extinguishes the faculty of generation, or which weakens it, so as to produce children less vigorous and less healthy. I appeal to experience, if this reasoning be not just.[26]

Those born of parents whose subsistence is precarious, or which is proportioned only to their own physical necessary only, have a precarious existence, and will undoubtedly begin their life by being beggars. Many such will perish for want of food, but many more for want of ease; their mendicity will be accompanied with that of their parents, and the whole will go to ruin. . .[27]

Like the Mercantilist he was, Steuart hastened to call in the State to put things right :

as by far the greater part of inhabitants are in the lower classes, it becomes the duty of a statesman to provide against such evils, if he intends, usefully to increase the number of his people.[28]

I believe, it will be found, that a sufficient abundance of children are born already; and that we have neither occasion for concubinage, or polygamy,

[25] *The Works . . . of the Late Sir James Steuart* . . . vol. 1, pp. 25-26.
[26] *Ibid.*, p. 26. [27] *Ibid.*, p. 94. [28] *Ibid.*, p. 94.

to increase their numbers. But we want a right method of taking care of those we have, in order to produce a multiplication proportioned to the possibility of our providing nourishment and employment. I have therefore proposed, that a statesman, well informed of the situation of his people, the state of every class, the number of marriages found in each, should say, let a particular encouragement be given to so many marriages among the lower classes and let these be distributed in a certain proportion for every parish, city, borough, &c. in the country; let rules be laid down to direct a preference, in case of a competition, between different couples; and let the consequence of this approbation be, to relieve the parents of all children above what they can maintain, as has been said. I propose no new limitations upon marriage, because I am a friend to liberty, and because such limitations would shock the spirit of the times. I therefore would strongly recommend hospitals for foundlings over all the country; and still more strongly the frugal maintenance of children in such hospitals, and their being bred up early to fill and recruit the lowest classes of the people.[29]

Steuart seems to have been more concerned over a possible shortage of children than an excess.

The Physiocrats had the conception of population increasing up to the minimum of subsistence. P. S. Dupont de Nemours (1739–1817), one of the leading members of the school, indeed, gave the arithmetical example mentioned by Malthus later—the American colonies of England doubling their population every twenty-five years, owing to the plenitude of the means of subsistence available to their inhabitants.

Adam Smith. Smith used this illustration also, giving in outline the general Malthusian theory, but—and the limitation is important—he restricted it to the poorer classes:

Every species of animals naturally multiplies in proportion to the means of their subsistence, and no species can ever multiply beyond it. But in civilized society it is only among the inferior ranks of people that the scantiness of subsistence can set limits to the further multiplication of the human species; and it can do so in no other way than by destroying a great part of the children which their fruitful marriages produce.

The liberal reward of labour, by enabling them to provide better for their children, and consequently to bring up a greater number, naturally tends to widen and extend those limits. It deserves to be remarked too, that it necessarily does this as nearly as possible in the proportion which the demand for labour requires. If this demand is continually increasing, the reward of labour must necessarily encourage in such a manner the marriage and multiplication of labourers, as may enable them to supply that continually increasing demand by a continually increasing population. If the reward should at any time be less than what was requisite for this purpose, the deficiency of hands would soon raise it; and if it should at any time be more, their excessive multiplication would soon lower it to this necessary

[29] *Ibid.*, pp. 97-98.

rate. The market would be so much under-stocked with labour in the one case, and so much over-stocked in the other, as would soon force back its price to that proper rate which the circumstances of the society required. It is in this manner that the demand for men, like that for any other commodity, necessarily regulates the production of men; quickens it when it goes on too slowly, and stops it when it advances too fast. It is this demand which regulates and determines the state of propagation in all the different countries of the world, in North America, in Europe, and in China; which renders it rapidly progressive in the first, slow and gradual in the second, and altogether stationary in the last.[30]

On the subject of checks, Smith remarked:

Poverty, thought it no doubt discourages, does not always prevent marriage. It seems even to be favourable to generation. A half-starved Highland woman frequently bears more than twenty children, while a pampered fine lady is often incapable of bearing any, and is generally exhausted by two or three. Barrenness, so frequent among women of fashion, is very rare among those of inferior station. Luxury, in the fair sex, while it inflames perhaps the passion for enjoyment, seems always to weaken, and frequently to destroy altogether, the powers of generation.

But poverty, though it does not prevent the generation, is extremely unfavourable to the rearing of children. The tender plant is produced, but in so cold a soil, and so severe a climate, soon withers and dies. It is not uncommon, I have been frequently told, in the Highlands of Scotland, for a mother who has borne twenty children not to have two alive. . . This great mortality, however, will everywhere be found chiefly among the children of the common people, who cannot afford to tend them with the same care as those of better station. Though their marriages are generally more fruitful than those of people of fashion, a smaller proportion of their children arrive at maturity.[31]

Apparently, therefore, the man who has been called the father of political economy divided society into classes, so far as the rate of multiplication was concerned, forecasting the views of later writers on this subject.

Franklin and Price. Among pre-Malthusian writers on population, the American, Benjamin Franklin (1706–1790), deserves mention. In his *Observations Concerning the Increase of Mankind, Peopling of Countries, &c.* (Boston 1755),[32] Franklin remarked that births were regulated by the means of support. Subsistence acted as a check on population, through the operation of what Malthus was to call "moral restraint." If the means of subsistence were inadequate, Franklin said that marriage was deferred or abstained from altogether. This accounted for the low rate of increase in cities and old-settled countries, as compared with America:

[30] *The Wealth of Nations*, Bk. 1, Chap. 8. [31] *Ibid.*

[32] Reprinted as Extra Number 63 in the *Magazine of History with Notes and Queries*, vol. 16, N. Y. 1918.

For people increase in proportion to the number of marriages, and that is greater in proportion to the ease and convenience of supporting a family. When families can be easily supported, more persons marry, and earlier in life.

In cities, where all trades, occupations and offices are full, many delay marrying, till they can see how to bear the charges of a family; which charges are greater in cities, as Luxury is more common: many live single during life, and continue servants to families, journeymen to Trades, &c. hence cities do not by natural generation supply themselves with inhabitants; the deaths are more than the births.

In countries full settled, the case must be nearly the same; all Lands being occupied and improved to the heighth; those who cannot get land must labour for others that have it; when labourers are plenty their wages will be low; by low wages a family is supported with difficulty; this difficulty deters many from marriage, who therefore long continue servants and single. Only as Cities take supplies of people from the country, and thereby make a little more room in the country, Marriage is a little more incourag'd there, and the births exceed the deaths. . .

Land being thus plenty in *America,* and so cheap as that a labouring man that understands Husbandry, can in a short time save money enough to purchase a piece of new Land sufficient for a plantation, whereupon he may subsist a family; such are not afraid to marry; for if they even look enough forward to consider how their children when grown up are to be provided for, they see that more Land is to be had at rates equally easy, all circumstances considered.

Hence Marriages in *America* are more general, and more generally early, than in *Europe.* And if it is reckoned there, that there is but one marriage per annum among a hundred persons, perhaps we may here reckon two; and if in *Europe* they have but four Births to a marriage (many of their marriages being late) we may here reckon eight, of which if one half grow up, and our marriages are made, reckoning one with another at twenty years of age our people must at least be doubled every twenty years.[33]

Later in the work, however, presumably to allow a safe margin, doubling of population was supposed to take place every twenty-five years.

Then, Franklin developed the important point that neither emigration nor immigration affected the rate of population growth, providing that the quality of the migrants was the same as that of the home population. If people left the country, their places were soon filled by the newly-born. If they come in, they merely crowded out home-born babies:

The importation of foreigners into a country that has as many inhabitants as the present employments and provisions for subsistence will bear, will be in the end no increase of people; unless the new comers have more industry and frugality than the natives, and then they will provide more Subsistence, and increase in the country; but they will gradually eat the natives out. Nor is it necessary to bring in foreigners to fill up any occasional vacancy

[33] *Ibid.,* pp. 217-218.

in a country; for such vacancy . . . will soon be filled by natural generation. Who can now find the vacancy made in *Sweden, France* or other warlike nations, by the Plague of heroism forty Years ago; in *France* by the expulsion of the Protestants; in *England* by the settlement of her Colonies; or in *Guinea,* by one hundred years' exportation of slaves, that has blacken'd half *America?* The thinness of inhabitants in *Spain* is owing to national pride and idleness, and other causes, rather than to the expulsion of the *Moors,* or to the making of new settlements.[34]

So, with his mind on maintaining the predominantly British character of the American people, Franklin opposed the immigration of Germans into Pennsylvania,

who will shortly be so numerous as to Germanize us instead of our Anglifying them, and will never adopt our language or customs, any more than they can acquire our complexion.[35]

Had he followed to its logical conclusion his own argument respecting the effect of immigration on numbers, Franklin might have gone further and opposed all immigration whatever.

Shortly afterwards Richard Price (1723–1791), a British clergyman who was friendly with Franklin, similarly related migration to population. Where Franklin had before him the special condition of a new country, receiving immigrants, Price considered the case of an emigrating country, namely Great Britain. He wrote:

Unless the Kingdom is made a prison to its inhabitants, these migrations cannot be prevented, nor do I think they have any great tendency to produce depopulation. When a number of people quit a country there is more employment and greater plenty of the means of subsistence left for those who remain; and the vacancy is soon filled up.[36]

Granting the principle that population tends to increase rapidly within the confines set by subsistence, the Franklin-Price theory follows as a matter of course. It is the logical result of applying the Malthusian principle of population to the problem of migration. But certain qualifications are required. In the first place, other things being equal, it is clear that a population growth based on home-born babies may not coincide in point of time with one resulting from the immigration of adults. Second, experience has shown that migratory streams contain a large majority of males, which is likely to upset the numbers of births. Moreover, the situation developed later that Americans – especially city-dwellers – ceased to show their old fertility and southern and eastern European immigrants, among whom "restraint" was less effective, did most to fill American cradles. But the problem of declining birth rates must be left to a later section.

[34] *Ibid.*, pp. 222-223. [35] *Ibid.*, p. 224.

[36] Quoted by J. Bonar, in *Theories of Population from Raleigh to Arthur Young,* London 1931, pp. 204-205. Quoted by permission of George Allen & Unwin Ltd.

Malthus

Godwin's forecast. Malthus's famous book, *An Essay on the Principle of Population, as It Affects the Future Improvement of Society, with Remarks on the Speculations of Mr. Godwin, M. Condorcet, and Other Writers* (London 1798), was the result of a controversy of some interest in connection with the development of socialist thought. Robert Wallace (1697–1771), a Scottish minister of religion of some distinction, in a work entitled *Various Prospects of Mankind, Nature, and Providence* (London 1761), had considered the possibility of an ideal form of government based on social and economic equality, like the *Utopia* of Sir Thomas More. He concluded that the increase of population that could be expected to result from such a system rendered it impracticable. William Godwin, in his *Enquiry Concerning Political Justice* opposed this view, remarking that

> Three fourths of the habitable globe is now uncultivated. The parts already cultivated are capable of immeasurable improvement. Myriads of centuries of still increasing population may pass away, and the earth be still found sufficient for the subsistence of its inhabitants. . . It would be truly absurd to shrink from a scheme of essential benefit to mankind, lest they should be too happy, and by necessary consequence at some distant period too populous.[37]

Godwin himself looked on the distant future with no concern:

> One tendency of a cultivated and virtuous mind is to diminish our eagerness for the gratifications of sense. They please at present by their novelty, that is, because we know not how to eliminate them. They decay in the decline of life, indirectly because the system refuses them, but directly and principally because they no longer excite the ardour of the mind. The gratifications of sense please at present by their imposture. We soon learn to despise the mere animal function, which, apart from the delusions of intellect, would be nearly the same in all cases; and to value it only as it happens to be relieved by personal charms or mental excellence. We absurdly imagine that no better road can be found to the sympathy and intercourse of minds. But a slight attention might convince us that this is a false road full of danger and deception. Why should I esteem another, or by that other be esteemed? For this reason only, because esteem is due, and only so far as it is due.
>
> The men therefore whom we are supposing to exist, when the earth shall refuse itself to a more extended population, will probably cease to propagate. They will no longer have any motive, either of error or reason, to induce them. The whole will be a people of men, and not of children. Generation will not succeed generation, nor truth have in a certain degree to recommence her career at the end of every thirty years. There will be no war, no crimes, no administration of justice as it is called, and no gov-

[37] *An Enquiry Concerning Political Justice,* 2nd ed., vol. 2, p. 376.

ernment. Beside this, there will be no disease, no anguish, no melancholy and no resentment. Every man will seek with ineffable ardour the good of all.[38]

The reply of Malthus. This was the target against which Malthus directed his *Essay*. His thoughts appear to have been developed in discussions with his father on the subject. The first edition of the *Essay* was published anonymously and at once caused considerable discussion. A mere outline, it was followed by a second edition, carrying an amended title: *An Essay on the Principle of Population; or, A View of its Past and Present Effects on Human Happiness; with an Inquiry into Our Prospects Respecting the Future Removal or Mitigation of the Evils which It Occasions* (London 1803). Like the title, the work itself was expanded, containing a large volume of evidence supporting its conclusions and a lengthy explanation of various expedients bearing on the problem of population. In this work Malthus argued that population was not a problem that would arise myriads of centuries in the future, as Godwin had asserted. It was immediate:

Through the animal and vegetable kingdoms Nature has scattered the seeds of life abroad with the most profuse and liberal hand; but has been comparatively sparing in the room and the nourishment necessary to rear them. The germs of existence contained in this spot of earth, with ample food, and ample room to expand in, would fill millions of worlds in the course of a few thousand years. Necessity, that imperious all-pervading law of nature, restrains them within the prescribed bounds. The race of plants and the race of animals shrink under this great restrictive law; and the race of man cannot by any efforts of reason escape from it.

In plants and animals the view of the subject is simple. They are all impelled by a powerful instinct to the increase of their species; and this instinct is interrupted by no reasoning or doubts about providing for their offspring. Wherever, therefore, there is liberty, the power of increase is exerted; and the superabundant effects are repressed afterwards by want of room and nourishment, which is common to plants and animals; and among animals, by their becoming the prey of each other.

The effects of this check on man are more complicated. Impelled to the increase of his species by an equally powerful instinct, reason interrupts his career, and asks him whether he may not bring beings into the world, for whom he cannot provide the means of support. If he attend to this natural suggestion, the restriction too frequently produces vice. If he hear it not, the human race will be constantly endeavouring to increase beyond the means of subsistence. But as by that law of our nature which makes food necessary to the life of man, population can never actually increase beyond the lowest nourishment capable of supporting it; a strong check on population, from the difficulty of acquiring food, must be constantly in operation. This difficulty must fall somewhere; and must necessarily be severely felt in

[38] *Ibid.*, pp. 384-385.

some or other of the various forms of misery, or the fear of misery, by a large portion of mankind.[39]

Malthus then made a comparison between what would be the natural increase of population if "left to exert itself with perfect freedom," and "what might be expected to be the rate of increase in the productions of the earth, under the most favourable circumstances of human industry." Remarking that, with respect to the former of these, "in no state that we have known, has the power of population been left to exert itself with perfect freedom," he added,

In the northern states of America, where the means of subsistence have been more ample, the manners of the people more pure, and the checks to early marriages fewer, than in any of the modern states of Europe, the population was found to double itself for some successive periods every twenty-five years.[40]

Malthus said that in some circumstances the rate of increase was greater than this, so he considered that he was playing safe in taking twenty-five years as the doubling period:

It may safely be pronounced therefore, that population when unchecked goes on doubling itself every twenty-five years, or increases in a geometrical ratio.[41]

As for the food supply, difficulties loomed up:

The rate according to which the productions of the earth may be supposed to increase, it will not be so easy to determine. Of this, however, we may be perfectly certain, that the ratio of their increase must be totally of a different nature from the ratio of the increase of population. A thousand millions are just as easily doubled every twenty-five years by the power of population as a thousand. But the food to support the increase from the greater number will by no means be obtained with the same facility. Man is necessarily confined in room. When acre has been added to acre till all the fertile land is occupied, the yearly increase of food must depend upon the amelioration of the land already in possession. This is a stream, which, from the nature of all soils, instead of increasing, must be gradually diminishing.[42]

Again, to be safe,

Let us suppose that the yearly additions which might be made to the former average produce, instead of decreasing, which they certainly would do, were to remain the same; and that the produce of this island might be increased every twenty-five years, by a quantity equal to what it at present produces: the most enthusiastic speculator cannot suppose a greater increase than this. In a few centuries it would make every acre of land in the island like a garden.[43]

[39] 2nd ed., pp. 2-3. [40] *Ibid.*, p. 4. [41] *Ibid.*, p. 5. [42] *Ibid.* [43] *Ibid.*, p. 7.

they are acting directly contrary to the will of God, and bringing down upon themselves various diseases, which might all, or in a great part, have been avoided, if they had attended to the repeated admonitions which he gives, by the general laws of nature, to every being capable of reason.[49]

To improve the living conditions of the poor, Malthus said, it was not enough that the absolute quantity of subsistence should be raised. This would only encourage a further increase in population. It was population that required to be dealt with:

It [*i.e.*, to attempt to proportion food to population] would appear to be setting the tortoise to catch the hare. Finding, therefore, that, from the laws of nature, we could not proportion the food to the population, our next attempt should naturally be to proportion the population to the food. If we can persuade the hare to go to sleep, the tortoise may have some chance of overtaking her.[50]

"Nothing," declared Malthus, "would so effectively counteract the mischiefs occasioned by Mr. Paine's Rights of Man, as a general knowledge of the real rights of man." He went on,

What these rights are, it is not my business at present to explain; but there is one right, which man has generally been thought to possess, which I am confident he neither does, nor can, possess, a right to subsistence when his labour will not fairly purchase it. . . A man who is born into a world already possessed, if he cannot get subsistence from his parents on whom he has a just demand, and if the society do not want his labour, has no claim of *right* to the smallest portion of food, and, in fact, has no business to be where he is. At Nature's mighty feast there is no vacant cover for him. She tells him to be gone, and will quickly execute her own orders, if he do not work upon the compassion of some of her guests. If these guests get up and make room for him, other intruders immediately appear demanding the same favour. The report of a provision for all that come, fills the hall with numerous claimants. The order and harmony of the feast is disturbed, the plenty that before reigned is changed into scarcity; and the happiness of the guests is destroyed by the spectacle of misery and dependence in every part of the hall, and by the clamorous importunity of those, who are justly enraged at not finding the provision which they had been taught to expect. The guests learn too late their error, in counteracting those strict orders to all intruders, issued by the great mistress of the feast, who, wishing that all her guests should have plenty, and knowing that she could not provide for unlimited numbers, humanely refused to admit fresh comers when her table was already full.[51]

No wonder that Malthus was attacked by the humanitarians! His theory had obvious connections with the principle of diminishing returns. Had it been possible for the returns per unit of labor applied to remain stable, notwithstanding continued multiplication of the number

[49] *Ibid.*, pp. 507-508. [50] *Ibid.*, p. 509. [51] *Ibid.*, pp. 531-532.

of laborers, population could increase indefinitely without the appearance of the checks mentioned by Malthus. The theory, too, was the foundation of the long-run subsistence theory of wages, dealt with in Chapter XII. In the main, it can be said that its acceptance among the British Classical economists was complete. Senior, it is true, forecast some changes in ideas [52] but, as was typical of his writings, he did not develop his modifications sufficiently to make any very important impression on current opinion. John Stuart Mill, whose work dominated British economic thought during the third quarter of the nineteenth century, not only accepted Malthusianism but went even further than Malthus himself in bewailing the gloominess of the population outlook and in seeking means for its amelioration.

Post-Malthusian Theories

Godwin and Place

One of the first important attacks on Malthus came from William Godwin, whose writing had provoked the *Essay* in the first instance. In 1820, Godwin published a book entitled *Of Population. An Enquiry concerning the Power of Increase in the Numbers of Mankind, being an Answer to Mr. Malthus's Essay on that Subject* (London). Godwin's work was diffuse and had little effect on current thought but it contained some ideas of significance.

Godwin refused to admit that population behaved as Malthus asserted. He was particularly critical of the Malthusian theory of geometrical progression. In some cases he granted that there had been rapid multiplication but he said that in others growth had been slow or non-existent. He pointed out that the Swedish figures, which went back to the middle of the eighteenth century (before most countries began to gather statistics regularly), displayed comparatively little increase. Indeed, history revealed many examples of countries once populous that later lost considerable numbers of their people.

Further, Godwin argued that subsistence could be made to increase at a rate that would keep pace with population. He referred to the manner in which the famous agriculturist, Thomas Coke (1754–1842, Earl of Leicester of Holkham from 1837) had raised the productivity of his Norfolk estate. What Coke had been able to do, Godwin said, others could accomplish. The consciousness of this, he thought, should prevent "any sober man . . . from preaching up Mr. Malthus's doctrine of depopulation." [53] A scarcity of food that would limit population growth was declared to be so remote that it "might fairly be left to Providence." [54]

Evidently, much of what Godwin said was in opposition not so much

[52] The views of Senior are referred to in a later section.

[53] p. 494.

[54] *Ibid.*, p. 455.

to the principles of Malthus as to the conclusions that the Malthusians drew from these principles. The geometrical rate of increase applied only in the absence of checks, according to Malthus, so that Godwin's historical data merely demonstrated the efficacy of the checks. Yet, since he placed less emphasis on the propensity of population to increase, Godwin saw a smaller need for checks. As he said of Sweden,

in a country, not liable to the inroad of savage conquerors, nor to the perhaps still more destructive influences of a government framed for the misery of its subjects, absolute desolation is not to be expected.[55]

But Godwin's general conclusions were at complete variance with those of Malthus. Where the earlier writer had drawn a dark picture of the future, Godwin saw nothing to worry about. In the light of more than a century of experience since he wrote, it is possible to say that, to date, it is his estimate which has been borne out by events, rather than that of Malthus.

Yet Francis Place (1771–1854), in his *Illustrations and Proofs of the Principle of Population: including an Examination of the Proposed Remedies of Mr. Malthus, and a Reply to the Objections of Mr. Godwin and Others* (London 1822), described Godwin's book as "a plausible attempt" to refute Malthus and one "utterly destitute of proof."[56] The title of Place's work indicated its purpose and conclusion. Malthus's "principle" stood, Place believed, notwithstanding what Godwin had said against it. But incidentally Place developed in the book his own ideas respecting checks to population and especially those on the deliberate limitation of families, or birth control:

if without any thing which should have the appearance of immediate self-interest in the teacher, at the expence of the scholar; if without what to the people may appear like canting; if without airs of superiority and dictation; if without figure and metaphor, means were adopted to show them [*i.e.*, the working people] how the market came to be overstocked with labour; that this was the cause of the low rates of wages—that it was impossible for real wages to rise, so as to enable them to live in comfort while they continued to keep the supply above the demand;—if it were clearly shown to them, that inevitable poverty and misery would result from marrying and having a family while this state of things continued; if familiar instances were collected of the poverty and misery, the crime and disgrace, to which indiscreet marriages too frequently led; if it were shown, that overstocking the market, even in a small degree, with labour, inevitably deteriorated the condition of every working man;—if all this were clearly and familiarly shown, on the one side, and if, on the other, it was as clearly shown, that by abstaining from marriage for even a few years, the supply of labour might be brought rather under the demand; that, when so, its price, like that of bread, or meat, or potatoes, when scarce, would rise, and might, by their abstinence from marriage, be raised so high as to enable

[55] *Ibid.*, p. 351.

[56] p. ix.

them to maintain themselves respectably, and give many of them a fair chance of rising in the world; — if a hundredth, perhaps a thousandth part of the pains, were taken to teach these truths that are taken to teach dogmas, a great change for the better might, in no considerable space of time, be expected to take place in the appearance and the habits of the people. If above all, it were once clearly understood, that it was not disreputable for married persons to avail themselves of such precautionary means as would, without being injurious to health, or destructive of female delicacy, prevent conception, a sufficient check might at once be given to the increase of population beyond the means of subsistence; vice and misery, to a prodigious extent, might be removed from society, and the object of Mr. Malthus, Mr. Godwin, and of every philanthropic person, be promoted, by the increase of comfort, of intelligence, and of moral conduct, in the mass of the population.

The course recommended will, I am fully persuaded, at some period be pursued by the people, even if left to themselves. The intellectual progress they have for several years past been making, the desire for information of all kinds, which is abroad in the world, and particularly in this country, cannot fail to lead them to the discovery of the true causes of their poverty and degradation, not the least of which they will find to be in overstocking the market with labour, by too rapidly producing children, and for which they will not fail to find and to apply remedies.[57]

Something should be said of the life of Place, as this helps to explain his views. Born and reared in poor circumstances in London, he married at nineteen years of age and in twenty-six years had fifteen children, five of whom died in childhood. In his early life on the London streets, he had become acquainted with the temptations to which unmarried young men were subjected. His wife appears to have been a powerful influence for good in his life and, in the course of time, he became a prosperous tailor. He was interested in social problems and his home became a meeting place of London reformers. The book from which the quoted passage has been taken was his only one and the ideas it expressed were obviously based on his own experience. It offered an alternative to the moral restraint of which Malthus had spoken, which really meant postponement of marriage. As Place said of himself and three others — one of whom was the elder Mill and who among them were said to have had thirty-six children — "rare fellows we to teach moral restraint."[58]

It may be doubted whether the cause assigned by Place in the passage — desire to raise the wage rate by restricting the supply of labor — has been to any extent responsible for the growing popularity of birth control. Rather has the economic motive been that of increasing the standard of life by spreading the wage received among fewer persons, in a smaller family. But at all events, the second half of the nineteenth

[57] *Ibid.*, pp. 164-166.

[58] p. 10 of the editor's introduction to a reprint of Place's book, Boston 1930 (ed. N. E. Himes). Quoted by permission of Houghton Mifflin Company.

century witnessed a steady and continuous decline in the birth rate over a large part of the western world. To Place and Senior, the possibility of a falling birth rate was but a ray of hope among the gloomy forebodings of their time. By the fourth quarter of the century, however, a slackening of population growth, accompanying a rising standard of living on the part of the masses of the people, became sufficiently obvious to be looked upon as a matter for congratulation, removing the fears raised by the Malthusian writers.

Bastiat, Carey, and George

In the middle of the nineteenth century, the Malthusian theory was subjected to severe attack from outside England. Bastiat in France, and Carey in the United States of America, challenged the principle of diminishing returns on its dynamic side, upon which the population theory was based.[59]

Like Petty before him, Bastiat pointed out that some advantages attended a larger population, giving a new and more optimistic direction to population theory.

Adam Smith had fitted population into his general system of economic harmony. The demand for men necessarily regulated the production of men, Smith said, so that economic equilibrium was preserved. The writings of Malthus had disturbed this harmonious conception. According to Malthus, in view of the tendency for numbers to increase, economic equilibrium on the population side was maintained only at the expense of the misery involved in the positive checks, or, alternately, by moral restraint. Malthus, therefore, introduced an important source of discord into Smith's self-adjusting and harmonious system, and provided one of the features that was to qualify economics for the opprobrious title of "the dismal science." In accordance with his general outlook, Bastiat endeavored to restore harmony in the field of population theory. This he did, to his own satisfaction, by removing the need for the objectionable checks. Economic benefit followed from the growth of population, said Bastiat. A tendency towards increasing returns was substituted for that in the direction of diminishing returns, so the checks became unnecessary. The following passage from Bastiat's chief work, *Harmonies of Political Economy*, gives his point of view :

> Does not a street of equal length render more service in Paris than in a remote village? Is not a mile of railway of more use in the Department of the Seine than in the Department of the Landes? Is not a London merchant content with smaller profits on account of the greater amount of business which he transacts? In everything we shall discover two sets of exchange agencies at work, which although identical in kind, act very

[59] This subject is dealt with in the following chapter.

differently, according as they operate in a densely or a thinly peopled locality.

The density of population not only enables us to reap more advantage from the machinery of exchange, it permits us to improve that machinery, and increase its power. Where the population is condensed, these improvements are advantageous, because they save us more efforts than they exact; but where the population is scattered and thin-spread, they exact more efforts than they save.

On leaving the metropolis for a time, and going to reside in a small provincial town, one is astonished to find that in many instances the most ordinary *services* can only be obtained at great expense, and with time and difficulty.

It is not the material part of the commercial mechanism only which is turned to account and improved by the single circumstance of the density of population, but the moral part also. When men are massed together, they have more facility in dividing their employments, in uniting their powers, and in combining to found churches and schools, to provide for their common security, to establish banks and insurance companies, in a word, to procure themselves all the common enjoyments with a much smaller proportion of efforts.[60]

In America, Henry C. Carey took up a similar attitude. The procreative function, in common with all others, he said, had to be related to the circumstances in which it was exercised. The consolidation or enclosure of land in England had driven the laborers from the soil, while improvements in machinery rendered their labor redundant in the factories and "the poor were thus made poorer and weaker, as the rich grew richer and stronger."[61] The Irish policy of the British government had contributed to the distress by driving Irishmen to the sister island. The repeal of the corn laws made things worse. These facts concerned Britain, it is true, but, in Carey's opinion, the advocates of the Malthusian theory had mistaken the results of local factors for a general principle. In different circumstances, the so-called law of Malthus was inapplicable:

Pioneer life, where property and person are reasonably secure, is, as has been shown, favorable to increase of numbers – isolated men having little occasion for the exercise of any faculties but those by which the physical powers are stimulated, leaving the mental ones in a great degree undeveloped. Reasoning *à priori*, therefore, it is to the former provinces, and present States, of North America, we should look for the most rapid growth of numbers, and there it is we find it.[62]

The rapid growth of the North American population Carey viewed from the standpoint of Bastiat, rather than that of Malthus:

The whole [world] was given for man's use – to be by him subdued; and yet, how small is the portion he has, as yet, subjected to his use! Look

[60] *Harmonies of Political Economy*, pp. 113-114.
[61] *Principles of Social Science*, vol. 3, pp. 287-288.
[62] *Ibid.*, p. 293.

almost where we may, the richer soils remain unoccupied – Switzerland abounding in population, while the rich lands of the lower Danube are lying waste – men gathering together on the slopes of the Andes, while the rich soils of the Orinoco and the Amazon remain in a state of nature – France and Germany, Italy and Ireland, presenting, on a smaller scale, a state of things precisely similar. Seeing these facts, we are led, and that too necessarily, to the belief, that man has made but little progress in the execution of the divine command; and yet, turn in what direction we may, we are met by the assertion that all the poverty and wretchedness of mankind is due to the one great error in the divine laws, in virtue of which, population tends to increase more rapidly than the food and other raw materials required for the satisfaction of his wants, and the maintenance of his powers.[63]

That man may increase, there must be increase in the supply of food. That the latter may increase, mankind must grow in numbers – it being only by means of the growing power of association and combination, that man is enabled to control and direct the earth's forces, and to pass from the condition of nature's slave, to that of nature's master. Population makes the food come from the richer soils, with constant increase in the return to labor; whereas depopulation drives men back to the poorer ones, with constant decline in the ability to obtain the necessary supplies of food and clothing.[64]

The "wild man of the prairies," Carey said, found the supplies of buffaloes and prairie dogs declining from year to year but, as population expanded, vegetable food was substituted for that derived from animals and the mineral world was brought into co-operation. More people, indeed, were required to remedy the deficiency of carbonic acid thus arising, so that, for the dismal prophecies of Malthus there was substituted a conception of

simple and beautiful laws by the action of which the supply of food and other raw materials is adjusted to meet the wants, and gratify the tastes, of an increasing population. . .[65]

The outlook of Henry George was much the same:

We have, in modern times, seen many communities advance in population. Have they not at the same time advanced even more rapidly in wealth? We see many communities still increasing in population. Are they not also increasing their wealth still faster? . . . Where will you find wealth devoted with the most lavishness to non-productive use – costly buildings, fine furniture, luxurious equipages, statues, pictures, pleasure gardens and yachts? Is it not where population is densest, rather than where it is sparsest? Where will you find in largest proportion those whom the general production suffices to keep without productive labor on their part – men of income and of elegant leisure, thieves, policemen, menial servants, lawyers, men of letters, and the like? Is it not where population is dense rather than where it is sparse? Whence is it that capital overflows for remunerative invest-

[63] *Ibid.*, pp. 330-331. [64] *Ibid*, p. 313. [65] *Ibid.*, p. 325.

ment? Is it not from densely populated countries to sparsely populated countries? These things conclusively show that wealth is greatest where population is densest; that the production of wealth to a given amount of labor increases as population increases. These things are apparent wherever we turn our eyes. On the same level of civilization, the same stage of the productive arts, government, etc., the most populous countries are always the most wealthy.[66]

This conclusion is doubtful, to say the least, because other factors than mere density of population explain the growth in national wealth. But George did not allow his argument to rest upon such a generalization. He gave a reason, which was substantially that of Petty[67] and Bastiat. Aggregation of population increased productivity:

And the reason of this is obvious. For, even if the increase of population does reduce the power of the natural factor of wealth, by compelling a resort to poorer soils, etc., it yet so vastly increases the power of the human factor as to more than compensate. Twenty men working together will, where nature is niggardly, produce more than twenty times the wealth that one man can produce where nature is most bountiful. The denser the population the more minute becomes the subdivision of labor, the greater the economies of production and distribution, and, hence, the very reverse of the Malthusian doctrine is true; and, within the limits which we have any reason to suppose increase would still go on, in any given state of civilization a greater number of people can produce a larger proportionate amount of wealth, and more fully supply their wants, than can a smaller number.[68]

There can be little question that the opinions of Carey and George, like those of Malthus on the opposite side, were largely explained by environmental considerations. In the middle of the nineteenth century America was sparsely settled and possessed immense resources susceptible of fuller development. The time was remote when the United States would be as thickly peopled as was the England in which Malthus wrote. But it was one thing to say that population had not reached a point at which it pressed upon the means of subsistence and quite another to argue that there was a continuing tendency for output per head to increase as population advanced. The latter appeared to be the position of Bastiat and Carey.

The Optimum Theory of Population

On the basis of the writings discussed above, the optimum theory was formulated. According to this theory, there were two tendencies, not one, resulting from the growth of population. If people were very

[66] *Progress and Poverty*, pp. 127-128.
[67] See Chapter VIII, p. 386.
[68] *Progress and Poverty*, pp. 133-134.

thinly scattered, average productivity would rise when population grew. If population were unduly dense, productivity would fall with further growth in numbers of people. Between the two extremes lay a best or *optimum* point, at which production per head was at its maximum.

Henry Sidgwick laid the foundation of this idea in his *Principles of Political Economy*:

It is in examining the nature of the ultimate barrier to increase of population, affirmed in the second of the propositions above given,[69] that we come upon what has been called the Law of Diminishing Returns. Before discussing this, it should be observed that the greater rapidity in the increase of population which we have supposed would involve necessarily a smaller proportion of workers to non-workers. Assuming, however, that the arts of industry were sufficiently developed to enable this smaller proportion, duly aided by instruments, to provide adequate nourishment, clothing, &c., for the whole population, and that no greater proportion of the produce of labour took the form of luxuries; it is evident that if the productiveness of labour did not diminish, the increase of population might go on until it was checked by non-preventable diseases due to overcrowding. The "Law of Diminishing Returns," then, affirms that the productiveness of labour does tend to diminish, as the proportion of labourers to land increases, after a certain degree of density of population – much below what would be on other grounds insanitary – has been reached. *The degree of density, it should be observed, varies with the development of the industrial arts, and the accumulation of capital; and it tends to be continually advanced by the progress of invention,* provided that, through the accumulation of capital, the improvement of processes which invention renders possible is actually realised. The necessity – to which Carey drew attention – of thus limiting the scope of the law of diminishing returns to communities of a certain density is now generally recognised. In fact, in a thinly-peopled country we have to note a tendency to increasing returns; every additional labourer tends to make labour on the average more productive, since he enables the whole body of labourers to realise more fully the advantages of co-operation. And this tendency to increasing returns continues to operate, in all branches of industry except agriculture and mining, without any known limit from density of population, except such as arises from sanitary considerations. The closer human beings live to one another, the greater tends to be the quantum of utility derived from a given quantum of labour in conveyance and communication; the greater, therefore, tends to be the development of co-operation by exchange; and as the scale on which each particular branch of manufacture may be profitably organised becomes thus proportionally

[69] The second proposition read as follows:

> Secondly, it may be affirmed that if the process of doubling and re-doubling of the population were continued, upon any given portion of the earth's surface, the means of subsistence obtainable from the region in question would within a certain time become barely sufficient to support the population; so that the supposed increase could no longer continue, – the time at which this stoppage would be reached varying, of course, with the density of the population.

larger, the production itself tends correspondingly to become more economical. . .[70]

The statement made by Sir Edward West, in his *Essay on the Application of Capital to Land,* (London 1815), discussed in the following chapter, contained the essential ingredients of the optimum theory. West said that, as population grew, increased specialization tended to make labor more productive. But, on the other hand, the necessity to utilize poorer land tended to render it less productive. West considered that the latter tendency was the more significant, that is, he accepted the general Malthusian position. Sidgwick was more careful. He declared that the point at which diminishing returns commenced depended upon circumstances impossible to forecast with accuracy:

as other things do not remain the same, as on the contrary the improvement in the arts of industry – including improvement in the system of co-operation through exchange with less densely peopled countries – is continually going on, a tendency of growing population to decrease proportional produce in England is continually counteracted by the tendency of industrial progress to increase it; and our evidence does not enable us to lay down any concrete law, formulating the actual influence which the two forces combined may be expected to exercise in determining the average produce per head for a given density of population. If indeed we excluded Foreign Trade, we might confidently affirm that no degree of improvement in industry known to us by experience could counteract the effect in decreasing the average productiveness of labour which the actual rate of increase of population in England would cause; so that the decrease in average supply must soon check the rate of increase. But then this exclusion of Foreign Trade makes such an affirmation purely abstract and hypothetical. . . If the dream of Free-Traders were realised, if all the world were willing to allow free ingress to our manufactures, it seems to be quite possible that the whole of England might become almost as thickly populated as Middlesex, without any decrease in the average productiveness of her labour.[71]

Sidgwick did not use the term *optimum population,* nor, indeed, did he develop the conception of a *best point* with any precision – it was implied in his writings rather than brought out formally. But he made clear that there was a point of maximum returns (or produce) per head; and that its position depended on circumstances and was subject to change if these altered, especially that it moved upward with the progress of invention and improvement generally. Here, therefore, were all the essentials of the optimum theory of population, as developed by Cannan and Carr-Saunders later.

But Sidgwick, good utilitarian that he was, indicated a different possibility. He was interested in human happiness and he recognized that this offered two entirely different criteria. In addition to that of *greatest*

[70] *Op. cit.,* pp. 150-151, italics ours.

[71] *Ibid.,* pp. 154-155.

happiness per head, which was related to the greatest wealth or produce per head of the optimum theory, there was an alternative, *greatest total happiness*. Allowing for the happiness of those who were yet unborn, it was possible that total happiness might be increased by permitting population to advance beyond the point of maximum happiness per head. This is brought out by Sidgwick in his work on *The Methods of Ethics* (London 1874, 7th edition, London 1907):

Assuming, then, that the average happiness of human beings is a positive quantity, it seems clear that, supposing the average happiness enjoyed remains undiminished, Utilitarianism directs us to make the number enjoying it as great as possible. But if we foresee as possible that an increase in numbers will be accompanied by a decrease in average happiness or *vice versa*, a point arises which has not only never been formally noticed, but which seems to have been substantially overlooked by many Utilitarians. For if we take Utilitarianism to prescribe, as the ultimate end of action, happiness on the whole, and not any individual's happiness, unless considered as an element of the whole, it would follow that, if the additional population enjoy on the whole positive happiness, we ought to weigh the amount of happiness gained by the extra number against the amount lost by the remainder. So that, strictly conceived, the point up to which, on Utilitarian principles, population ought to be encouraged to increase, is not that at which average happiness is the greatest possible,—as appears to be often assumed by political economists of the school of Malthus—but that at which the product formed by multiplying the number of persons living into the amount of average happiness reaches its maximum.[72]

It is to be regretted that more attention has not been given to this idea by population writers.

The Theory That a Higher Standard of Life Diminishes the Number of Births

Another line of criticism of the Malthusian theory concerned the effect of a higher living standard on the rate of population increase. Adam Smith, as has been seen, believed that it was "only among the inferior ranks of people" that the scantiness of subsistence set limits to the multiplication of the human species. Further Smith commented on the difference in the rates of reproduction of rich and poor. By implication, this position was accepted by Malthus and his followers. It was the poor about whom they were concerned and it was to this class that their homilies were addressed. The Classical writers on population—more plentifully supplied with this world's goods—did not stop to ask what was the condition in their own class, or their conclusions might have been given less general applicability.

A noteworthy assault on this shortcoming came from Thomas Double-

[72] pp. 415-416. Quoted by permission of Macmillan & Co., Ltd., and The Macmillan Company.

day (1790–1870), an English radical reformer, in *The True Law of Population shewn to be connected with the Food of the People* (London 1841). On the basis of a diversity of data ranging from the burgesses of his own city of Newcastle-upon-Tyne, to the literature of early Greece, with comments upon the breeding of flower plants and the behavior of sheep by the way, Doubleday propounded the theory that

The GREAT GENERAL LAW then, which, as it seems, really regulates the increase or decrease both of vegetable and of animal life, is this, that whenever a *species* or *genus* is *endangered,* a corresponding effort is invariably made by nature for its preservation and continuance, by an increase of fecundity or fertility; and that this especially takes places whenever such danger arises from a diminution of proper nourishment or food, so that consequently the state of depletion, or the deplethoric state, is favourable to fertility; and that on the other hand, the plethoric state, or state of repletion, is unfavourable to fertility, in the ratio of the intensity of each state, and this probably throughout nature universally, in the vegetable as well as the animal world; further, that as applied to mankind this law produces the following consequences, and acts thus: —

There is in all societies a constant increase going on amongst that portion of it which is the worst supplied with food; in short, amongst the poorest. Amongst those in the state of affluence, and well supplied with food and luxuries, a constant decrease goes on. Amongst those who form the mean or medium between these two opposite states — that is to say, amongst those who are tolerably well supplied with good food, and not overworked, nor yet idle — population is stationary. Hence it follows that it is upon the *numerical proportion* which these three states bear to each other in any society that increase or decrease upon the whole depends.[73]

Now, of course, this "great general law" may be looked at askance, but it is a well-known fact that birth rates are high among the poor.

Even before Doubleday wrote, the socialist, William Thompson, gave the lie direct to Malthus in his book, *An Inquiry into the Principles of the Distribution of Wealth most conducive to Human Happiness*:

There is no disposition or physical interest amongst mankind, elevated but one step over the merest savage existence, if even in that state, to breed beyond their absolute comforts, whatever they may be: and as these comforts increase, accompanied as they are with an increase of knowledge, the tendency to improvident breeding, uniformly decreases with their increase. Not a single instance can be quoted from history, or from the conduct of any living community, of over-breeding taking place in consequence of increased comfort alone, where all expedients of insecurity had been removed.[74]

Thompson admitted that a rate of increase beyond the means of subsistence was physically possible but said that human prudence held it in check:

[73] 3rd ed., London 1853, pp. 5-6.

[74] *Op. cit.*, p. 426.

In the physical constitution of man, there is a possibility of increasing the numbers of his kind at a quicker rate than the quantity of food. There is also a physical possibility of increasing the number of sheep or of silk-worms beyond the quantity of food (grass, roots, or leaves) necessary for their support. But who ever inferred from thence that human prudence was not sufficient, by means of the most obvious calculation, to limit this possibility of increase of these useful animals, to the food to be afforded them, and the purposes to be derived to man from their existence? As this power of breeding in their own species, is fully as much under the controul of human beings, as the same power in any animals which they rear; why should not the same principles of prudence be used in regulating the increase of men, as in regulating the increase of sheep or silk-worms?[75]

Sir Archibald Alison (1792–1867), Scottish lawyer and historian, in a work entitled *The Principles of Population, and their connection with Human Happiness* (2 vols., Edinburgh and London 1840), developed the point more exhaustively and in relation to its historical background.

The preface to the book expressed Alison's point of view:

It is the aim of the author in the following pages to show, that the same Invisible Hand and Irresistible Agency directs and pervades the social destinies of the species . . . that there is no permanent or lasting cause of distress which presses on the human species in any changes of its progress. . .[76]

Alison believed that population did not inevitably press against the means of subsistence. Instead, as population expanded, factors came into play that restricted further growth. Several of these were mentioned. First came the development of human reason. Savages acted according to their instincts—hence, according to Alison, the population principle operated among them without restraint—but civilization brought habits of prudence. Even in advanced societies, Alison said, division of labor and the growth of cities degraded the laboring classes, so that in their actions they became comparable with savages, education being a possible remedy. A more important factor was the extension of what Alison called *artificial wants* among the people. Specialization of labor opened up the possibility of gratifying acquired wants. The acquisition of one comfort or means of gratification excited desires for others. No limits could be set to such wants, as the highest objects of luxury in one generation became the comforts of the next, and the absolute necessities of a few generations later. In this connection, Alison made the interesting comment that

There is no greater evil to the lower orders of a country than to have the wealth which is the fruit of their labour spent at a distance from themselves, because in that case they have no opportunity of acquiring either the habits of industry, or the ideas of comfort which are essential to their well-being,

[75] *Ibid.*, pp. 535-536.

[76] Vol. 1, pp. xiii-xiv.

and population is furnished with the means of increase, while no scope for the development of its limitations is afforded.[77]

The factor of acquired wants, Alison regarded as the most influential in controlling population:

This great and important change which ensues, in the progress of society, in the habits and desires of all its members, is the principal counterpoise which Nature has provided to the principle of population.[78]

Alison said that the savage—knowing nothing of luxuries—had no stimulus to limit population. But it was quite otherwise with civilized man, for the indulgence of his acquired wants was incompatible with a rapid increase of population. Early marriage and numerous children would make it impossible to satisfy these wants. Men's desire to preserve their positions in the social scale, to accumulate property, and to rise in rank, encouraged family limitation.

In civilized societies, only among the poor was population increase rapid, Alison remarked. The rich, and the "middling ranks of society," increased very slowly. What was needed in order to diminish the birth rate of the poorer class was to make artificial wants "descend so far as to influence the conduct of the majority of their members."[79] Alison was of the opinion that this already was the case with the English poor, though not with those of Ireland. Were it not for the influx of Irish immigrants, he said, "the condition of the people in all parts of the island [*i.e.*, Britain] would be comparatively comfortable."[80]

In America, somewhat earlier, John Rae had discussed the extent of saving among members of different social classes and expressed the view that the middle classes deferred marriage for the purpose of raising their families in the social scale, a practice that was not found among the laborers.[81]

The Englishman, Senior, like Alison and for much the same reason, looked upon the future of population with less concern than was shown by Malthus:

It appears, therefore, that habits of prudence in contracting marriage, and of considerable superfluous expenditure, afford the only permanent protection against a population pressing so closely on the means of subsistence as to be continually incurring the misery of the positive checks. And as the former habits exist only in a civilized, and the latter only in an opulent society, it appears equally clear that, as a nation advances in civilization and opulence, the positive checks are likely to be superseded by the preventive. If this be true, the evil of a redundant population, or, to speak more intelligibly, of a population too numerous to be adequately and regularly supplied with necessaries, is likely to diminish in the progress of improvement. As wealth increases, what were the luxuries of one generation become the decencies of

[77] *Ibid.*, p. 109.
[78] *Ibid.*
[79] *Ibid.*, p. 113.
[80] *Ibid.*, p. 114.
[81] See Chapter XI, p. 544.

their successors. Not only a taste for additional comfort and convenience, but a feeling of degradation in their absence, becomes more and more widely diffused. The increase in many respects of the productive powers of labour must enable increased comforts to be enjoyed by increased numbers; and as it is the more beneficial, so it appears to be the more natural course of events that increased comfort should not only accompany but rather precede increase of numbers.[82]

Senior, however, was not prepared to grant that the outlook was entirely satisfactory:

But although we believe that, as civilization advances, the pressure of population on subsistence is a decreasing evil, we are far from denying the prevalence of this pressure in all long settled-Countries; indeed in all Countries except those which are the seats of colonies applying the knowledge of the old Country to an unoccupied territory. We believe that there are few portions of Europe the inhabitants of which would not now be richer if their numbers were fewer, and would not be richer hereafter if they were now to retard the rate at which their population is increasing. No plan for social improvement can be complete unless it embrace the means both of increasing the production of wealth and of preventing population from making a proportionate advance.[83]

History has shown the groundlessness of the Malthusian fears and the general correctness of the beliefs of Alison and those who thought like him. Since they wrote, birth rates have diminished and wealth per head has increased substantially.

Pearl's Theory

Reference should be made to the theory respecting population growth, advanced recently by Raymond Pearl (1879–1940), an American biologist.[84] Pearl's argument was that population growth typically takes the form of a flattened and sloping S-shape curve, such as appears at the top of page 355.

He examined the rate of growth of both vegetable and animal populations as well as those exhibited by human societies. The body weight of a pumpkin (reflecting the number of cell units), the number of yeast cells in a population of that material, the rate of growth of a tadpole's tail, the number of fruit flies that appeared in a culture of banana jelly, and the population of such countries as France, Germany, and the United States of America, all fitted into his pattern, mathematical formulae being calculated to represent the exact form of the various growth curves. Though this has the form of a biological explanation, it has economic implications.

[82] *Political Economy*, p. 42. [83] *Ibid.*

[84] See *The Biology of Population Growth*, N. Y. 1925. The material in this section is reproduced by permission of Alfred A. Knopf, Inc.

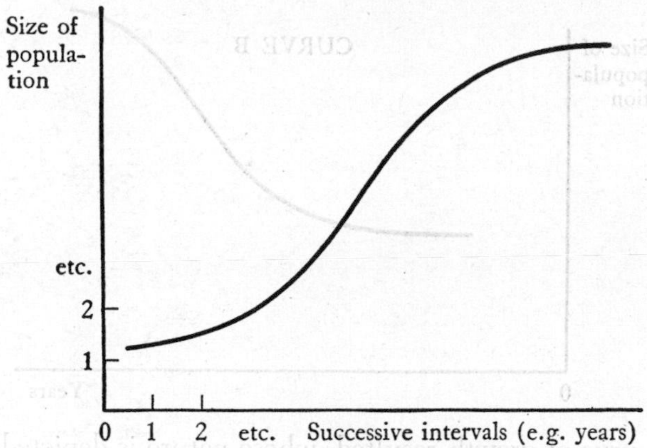

The lower portions of Pearl's curves correspond to the American colonies in the Malthusian example, where population was increasing in geometric progression and the checks had not yet put in an appearance. The upper parts can be interpreted in terms of the gradual emergence of some form of check. It is evident that there are many possible checks or limiting factors in the biological world — food, air, water, and the difficulties of transporting nutriment and waste products in a specialized economy of cells, such as exists in the case of the pumpkin or the tadpole's tail. Malthus, of course, fixed his mind on one of these limiting factors, that of the food supply, though — as events have suggested since he wrote — there are others, even in the case of human societies.

Pearl's graph of the population of Germany in the nineteenth century is especially interesting. This population started on a course of the type of Curve A below, with a relatively small maximum :

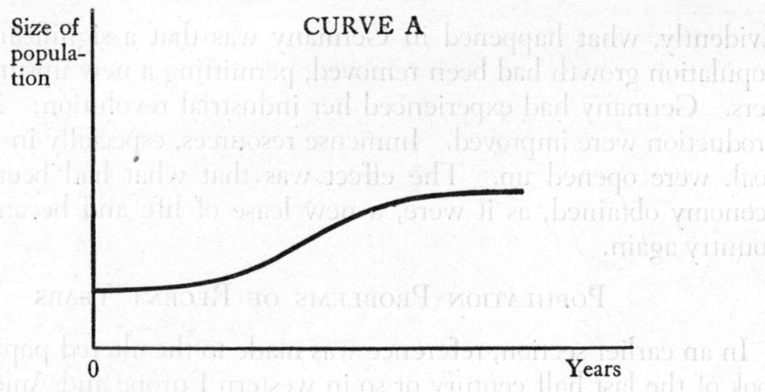

Then, it left this curve and embarked upon another of different form, with a higher maximum, shown as Curve B :

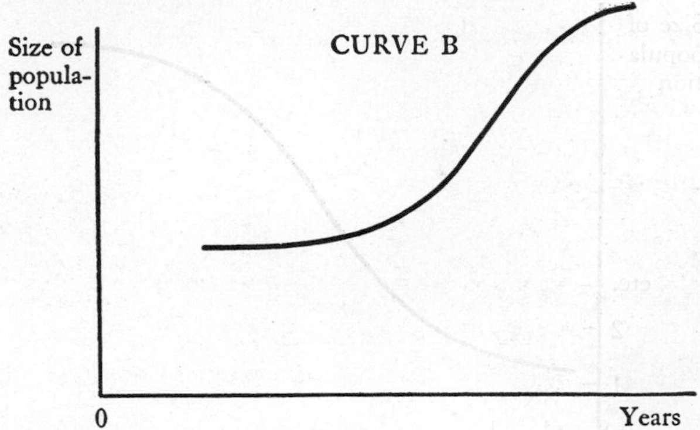

A complex curve of growth resulted, whose nature is depicted in the following figure:

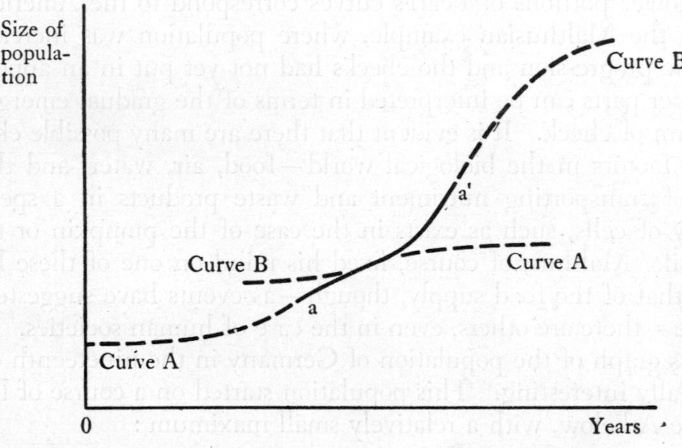

(Line a a' represents German population 1820-1910)

Evidently, what happened in Germany was that a significant check to population growth had been removed, permitting a new upsurge in numbers. Germany had experienced her industrial revolution. Methods of production were improved. Immense resources, especially in the form of coal, were opened up. The effect was that what had been a mature economy obtained, as it were, a new lease of life and became a young country again.

Population Problems of Recent Years

In an earlier section, reference was made to the altered population outlook of the last half century or so in western Europe and America. One result is that a new population problem, not of numbers, but of quality, has emerged. Not merely have birth rates fallen, they have declined most among the wealthier and better-educated classes of society, leaving recruitment to come from the poorer groups. People may be poor because they have been ill-treated or unfortunate, but too often they are in this position because they are inefficient and — at least according to some studies — of less than average intelligence. With an eye to the extent to which desirable traits are being passed on to the next generation, sociologists have become increasingly concerned about this problem.

But the very severity of the fall in birth rates is doing something to remove the fear respecting future population on grounds of quality, because the diminution in births is being carried into the poorer classes of society, through the spread of knowledge of birth control devices and other factors.

On the subject of numbers, however, a new fear is arising: concern is being expressed that there will be too few people rather than too many. With respect to England, for instance, alarming figures have been presented by Enid Charles (Mrs. Lancelot Hogben, 1894–), in a recent memorandum entitled *The Effect of Present Trends in Fertility and Mortality upon the Future Population of England and Wales and upon its Age Composition.*[85] One of the calculations whose results are given in this publication, on the assumption that birth and death rates continue to fall in accordance with recent experience, indicates that the population of England and Wales in 2035 A.D. will be less than five millions, that is, considerably smaller than the population of London at the present time. Other countries of northern and western Europe appear to be in a similar predicament, and the same is true of the United States. Perhaps a world that was not split into contending nations might look with equanimity upon a declining population, but not so that existing at the present time. Hence, in some countries, measures are being taken for the purpose of stimulating marriages and births. Thus family endowment[86] has found support in certain countries — notably France — in the hope that it might have a favorable effect on births. In this manner are the facts of the twentieth century answering the forebodings of the nineteenth. Yet it must be borne in mind that such forecasts as that to which reference has just been made rest merely upon the projection of present tendencies into the future. Factors that cannot now be discerned may upset them completely, just as those unforeseen by Malthus removed the fears aroused by the theory of that great writer on the subject of population.

Summary of Chapter

Numbers of people appear to have been a problem from the earliest times. Practices aiming at the control of population are widespread

[85] *Royal Economic Society Memorandum,* No. 55, London 1935.

[86] Family endowment is a scheme whereby the wage is made to depend on the family requirements of the worker concerned. Commonly a flat rate is paid per worker, plus additional allowances for children.

among savages and comments on numbers appear in the writings of the ancient philosophers. Imperial Rome took active measures to stimulate births in the citizen class. Occasional remarks on the subject of population are found in medieval literature, and the Political Arithmeticians of the late seventeenth and early eighteenth centuries gave it considerable attention.

Modern thought on population has centered round the celebrated "principle" of Malthus. Malthus argued that the human race had a tendency to multiply beyond the means of subsistence and that this was kept in check either by physical factors (such as shortage of food) or by moral restraint. In its essentials, this theory had been stated long before the time of the economist whose name it bears and it was the peculiar situation in England when he wrote which gave it special point.

The Malthusian principle was assailed by Bastiat, Carey, and others, and the optimum theory of later years may be looked upon as a synthesis of the ideas of Malthus and those of his opponents. Even in the early part of the century there were some writers who believed that the principle applied, if at all, only to the poorer classes of society. It was suggested that a rising standard of life might diminish births, rather than increase them as Malthus had asserted. As is well known, in the century or so that is covered by accurate statistics, living standards have risen greatly but births have declined.

The population problem has changed in its nature. Where Malthus argued that there was a danger of *too many* people, later writers (noting that the less successful social groups were breeding faster than the more successful) pointed to *quality* or type. Finally, quality has become a less serious problem, as the decline in births has affected the lower social strata. But, in view of divergencies in birth trends among different nations, in countries where births are falling most a new problem of numbers — that of *too few* — has made its appearance.

CHAPTER VIII

PRODUCTION

Economists commonly define *production* as the creation of goods and services that satisfy human wants. A minimum amount of these is necessary for life but, if all that men wanted were forthcoming without any special effort on their part, production need receive no attention. A tiny population residing in a region of great natural resources may do nothing beyond gathering whatever its members think is useful but it must be remembered that fruit does not fall into the mouth nor clothes shape themselves, even in such a delectable spot. A certain amount of bodily activity is beneficial in itself, however, and the Arcadia that has been mentioned may be so well endowed by nature that effort does not require to pass this point. This situation is not entirely imaginary, because some tropical and sub-tropical areas impress the visitor in this way.

A question is raised similar to that which has agitated economists with respect to wealth. Just as it has been asked whether *all useful things* should be designated wealth, or only those that happened to be *scarce relative to human wants,* so it can be inquired whether the creation of all things possessing utility is to be counted as production, or merely those that are scarce. The answer to the second question has been considered to follow from that returned to the first, and the theory of production has been shaped accordingly. But the matter can be carried farther. Is the use of the word *production* to be restricted to the result of efforts and sacrifices *not in themselves considered desirable* (*i.e.,* those undertaken *for the product*)? Or, are all efforts and sacrifices that bring forth a useful product to be looked upon as production, even though they are put forward *for their own sakes* rather than because a product results? That is, are fish caught for fun during vacation time to be counted on the same basis as those obtained by a person regularly employed in fishing and regarding his task as laborious? The fish caught for the sheer joy of fishing may not be distinguishable from those caught by a tired man in the rain, for no other reason than that he must eat. This situation is true of other occupations. Some of the work done by an enthusiastic doctor, teacher, or writer would be undertaken, no doubt, for mere love of these activities, but how much would be so performed is impossible to determine, even by the individuals concerned. The theory of production has not progressed far enough to differentiate between the produce of work done for other reasons and that of activity specially directed towards the securing of a product. As was seen in Chapter IV, the theory of distribution has advanced beyond this, because it has distinguished between *necessary payments* and *unnecessary payments,* or surpluses.

One solution of such difficulties as that brought to light by the fishing example is to include efforts and sacrifices, on the one hand, and product on the other, in a common denominator. Happiness and utility have been made to serve this purpose in Classical and Neo-Classical economics. The utility obtained by the vacationing angler from his activity is taken into account along with that yielded by the fish he catches. In the case of the professional fisherman, the corresponding calculation is represented by the utility of the fish caught, less the disutility involved in the work of fishing. Jevons produced a set of curves which recognized that even professional fishermen get some pleasure out of their tasks.[1] In general, however, the implications of this situation on production have been neglected. The amount of the product or the utility yielded by this, together with the toil and trouble of getting it, are what have been brought into production calculations.

Early Times

A great deal of what was said in the chapter on wealth is applicable to production, because it depends on what importance men attach to wealth whether they show more or less concern in producing it. The savage, whose desires are limited, for this reason sets bounds on his productive activity. If his bodily wants are easily satisfied, he spends most of his time on something else. He enjoys social contacts, music, dancing, singing, etc. He fights, sleeps, or merely lazes around. If the criterion of happiness or utility be applied, perhaps the savage "produces" as much as a twentieth century American. But usually it is not; so it is said that the level of production is low in primitive societies. Much nonsense is spoken on the subject of raising the standard of life of backward peoples because of an inadequate appreciation of this point.

It would be wrong to assume, however, that the savage works little because he deliberately chooses other ways of spending his time. As was emphasized at the beginning of the book, often he does not decide such things on any rational basis but adopts the standards and customs of his group. In primitive communities, therefore production is largely on a customary basis and change is slow. That change is not unknown, though, is made clear by such circumstances as the concentration on crop production to the exclusion of cattle, developed by those tribes of the cattle-loving Bantu people who have spread into the tsetse-fly regions of central Africa, where cattle cannot be kept successfully. Another example is the rapid alteration in native standards of production which is taking place at present in all parts of Africa that have come under the influence of the white man. This feature was discussed in Chapter II.

[1] See Chapter IX.

It has already been shown that the ancient Greek philosophers and their successors in Rome did not attach much importance to wealth or, therefore, to production. This was even more true of the teachers of the early Christian Church. Yet it has been noted that ample evidence is available to demonstrate that many of the common people of those times were of a different mind. The rise of the Greek cities and, still more, of the Roman Empire witnessed an economic development that was not paralleled again until the close of the middle ages. In Rome, especially, industry and commerce were given attention, not disfavored as was to a large extent the case during the succeeding medieval period.

Some of the modern ideas respecting production theory were not unknown even in the ancient world. The *Book of Genesis,* for example, contains a suggestion of the principle of diminishing returns:

> And Abram was very rich in cattle, in silver, and in gold. . . And Lot, also, which went with Abram, had flocks, and herds, and tents. And the land was not able to bear them, that they might dwell together: for their substance was great, so that they could not dwell together.[2]

The pseudo-Aristotelian *Œconomica* had something to say on the technique of good management:

> The sayings of the Persian and the Libyan may not come amiss; the former of whom, when asked what was the best thing to fatten a horse, replied, 'His master's eye', while the Libyan, when asked what was the best manure, answered, 'The landowner's foot-prints.'[3]

This work contained, also, a hint of the productive advantages of division of labor:

> He who intends to practice economy aright ought to be fully acquainted with the places in which his labour lies and to be naturally endowed with good parts. . .[4]

Even earlier, in his *Republic,* Plato had gone so far as to attribute the establishment of society to men's appreciation of the benefit of specialization in assisting production. In this connection, the following dialogue was recounted:

S. (*Socrates*): I am myself reminded that we are not all alike; there are diversities of natures among us which are adapted to different occupations.

A. (*Adeimantus*): Very true.

S.: And will you have a work better done when the workman has many occupations, or when he has only one?

A.: When he has only one.

S.: Further, there can be no doubt that a work is spoilt when not done at the right time?

[2] *Genesis,* 13, vs. 2-6.

[3] *The Works of Aristotle,* vol. 10, *Oeconomica,* 1345a.

[4] *Ibid.,* 1345b.

A. : No doubt.

S. : For business is not disposed to wait until the doer of the business is at leisure; but the doer must follow up what he is doing, and make the business his first object.

A. : He must.

S. : And if so, we must infer that all things are produced more plentifully and easily and of a better quality when one man does one thing which is natural to him and does it at the right time, and leaves other things.[5]

Varro (116–27 B.C.) is an example of a Roman writer who made comments on production. In his *Rerum rusticarum*,[6] he referred to the way in which market factors influenced the selection of the product:

Those estates which have a suitable market in the neighbourhood for the sale of their produce, and can thence obtain what is needed for the farm, are so far profitable. . . Thus close to a city it pays to cultivate gardens on a large scale, fields of violets and roses, for instance, and many other things which a city welcomes. . .[7]

In the same book reference was made to the usefulness of rewards in stimulating output:

You should quicken the interest of the overseers in their work by means of rewards. . .[8]

Other matters of like nature were discussed.

In the early Christian period considerable attention was given to the form of production. The question of what occupations should be engaged in (and therefore what commodities should be produced) was regarded as highly important. In production, as in everything else, the Christian man was to be a servant of God, occupying himself only in those activities that received the divine favor. But occasionally, especially as time went by, comments appeared on the efficiency of production. A notable example was *The Rules of Saint Robert*, written by Robert Grosseteste, Bishop of Lincoln, about 1240, to assist the widowed Countess of Lincoln in the management of her estate. The Bishop advised that the Countess

discreetly and gently ask if your people do well, and how your corn is growing, and how profitable your ploughs and stock are, and make these demands openly, and your knowledge shall be much respected.[9]

Other suggestions were made, such as forbidding dinners and suppers out of the manorial hall, "for from this arises waste, and no honour to the lord or lady." This sort of language might be acceptable enough, when

[5] *The Dialogues of Plato*, vol. 3, *Republic*, p. 50.

[6] Translated by L. Storr-Best as *Varro on Farming*, London 1912.

[7] p. 47 of the translation. Quoted by permission of G. Bell & Sons, Ltd.

[8] *Ibid.*, p. 51.

[9] Translated in E. Lamond's edition of *Walter of Henley's Husbandry*, p. 141.

coming from a taverner or a merchant, but it is hardly the kind of speech that one would have expected from a bishop! Walter of Henley, who seems to have been a lord's bailiff or manager, wrote about the same time on similar lines.

Modern Writers on the Nature of Production

As the middle ages gave place to modern times and thought developed along Mercantilist lines, the new ideas on wealth were reflected in the attitude taken with respect to production. Men were encouraged to make or import commodities conducing to the good of the State. Articles of obvious usefulness, like simple food and clothes, or those that could be sold abroad in exchange for gold and silver, were preferred over luxury goods.

Except for the water-diamond comparison, which appears to have been got from John Law and is mentioned in Chapter IX of this volume, the first book of Adam Smith's *Wealth of Nations* was relatively free from the ancient discrimination between desirable and undesirable, or useful and useless, activity. Professional men were not criticized as being unproductive but, instead, were regarded with some favor, their higher remuneration being explained by the training they required. But, in later portions of the work, Smith distinguished sharply between what he called *productive* and *unproductive* labor. The difference between the two turned upon whether the labor did or did not fix itself in a vendible commodity. To be counted as productive, according to Smith, labor had to (a) add to value and (b) be incorporated in a commodity:

There is one sort of labour which adds to the value of the subject upon which it is bestowed: there is another which has no such effect. The former, as it produces a value, may be called productive; the latter, unproductive labour. Thus the labour of a manufacturer adds, generally, to the value of the materials which he works upon, that of his own maintenance, and of his master's profit. The labour of a menial servant, on the contrary, adds to the value of nothing. . . A man grows rich by employing a multitude of manufacturers: he grows poor, by maintaining a multitude of menial servants. The labour of the latter, however, has its value, and deserves its reward as well as that of the former. But the labour of the manufacturer fixes and realises itself in some particular subject or vendible commodity, which lasts for some time at least after that labour is past. It is, as it were, a certain quantity of labour stocked and stored up to be employed, if necessary, upon some other occasion. That subject, or what is the same thing, the price of that subject, can afterward, if necessary, put into motion a quantity of labour equal to that which had originally produced it. The labour of the menial servant, on the contrary, does not fix or realise itself in any particular subject or vendible commodity. His services generally perish in the very instant of their performance, and seldom leave any trace of value behind them, for which an equal quantity of service could afterward be procured. The labour of some of the most respectable orders in the society is, like that of menial servants, unproductive of any value, and does not fix or realise itself in any permanent subject, or vendible commodity, which endures after that labour is past, and for which an equal quantity of labour could afterward be procured.[10]

In the class of unproductive laborers, Smith proceeded to include some of the "gravest and most important" as well as some of the "most frivolous" professions. Kings, churchmen, physicians, opera dancers, and buffoons were lumped together in this category. In writing of the subject, Smith referred to the views of the Physiocrats. As is shown later, this group of economists attached a different meaning to the word *productive*.

According to the test that Smith applied, the labor employed in making both wool and tennis balls would be classed as productive, but not, for instance, that of a medical man. To say that a physician who was engaged in saving life was less productive than a manufacturer of tennis balls would have seemed peculiar, no doubt, to the sixteenth century author of *A Discourse of the Common Weal of this Realm of England*.[11] But Smith was considering the accumulation of capital and it was perfectly proper for him to say that some types of labor—even that done on tennis balls—added to accumulated capital (consumers' capital, in this case), while others—including the services of physicians—did not. The removal of an inflamed appendix or the curing of a bad attack of influenza adds nothing to capital, as this is ordinarily calculated, however large may be the utility yielded to the patient concerned. Smith's thoughts, however, seem to have carried him beyond this point. His language suggests that he took the view, still common among prudent persons, that there was *more merit* in making something that lasted, than in producing an article that was ephemeral.

Lauderdale repudiated Smith's distinction between productive and unproductive labor:

If . . . wealth is regarded in its true light, as consisting of the abundance of the objects of men's desire, it is impossible to discern why that should not be considered as wealth which tends to the satisfaction of man's immediate desires [*e.g.*, the labor of menial servants], as well as that which is stocked and stored up for the satisfaction of his future desires [which Smith called productive]; and, in truth, there is no one who has criticised the distinction, which rests the value of commodities on their durability, with greater acrimony than the person who wishes to make the distinction betwixt productive and unproductive labour depend merely upon the duration of its produce [*i.e.*, Smith]. "We do not (says he) reckon that trade disadvantageous, which consists in the exchange of the hardware of England for the wines of France, and yet hardware is a very durable commodity, and was it not for this continual exportation, might, too, be accumulated for ages to-

[10] Bk. 2, Chap. 3.

[11] See Chapter II, p. 92.

gether, to the incredible augmentation of the pots and pans of the country." Again: It is a losing trade, it is said, "which a workman carries on with the ale-house; and the trade which a manufacturing nation would naturally carry on with a wine country, may be considered a trade of the same nature. I [*i.e.,* Smith] answer, That the trade with the ale-house is not necessarily a losing trade."

It appears, therefore, impossible to contend, that the labour of the manufacturer and artist, or even the labour of that class whose services perish at the moment, are not, as well as that of the husbandman, to be considered as productive of wealth.[12]

Thus, according to Lauderdale, any kind of activity that furthered the satisfaction of men's desires was to be regarded as productive, whether its produce was consumed at the moment of its appearance or some time in the future.

J. B. Say in France, and J. R. McCulloch (1789–1864) in England, abandoned Smith's position for that of Lauderdale. Discussing "immaterial products, or values consumed at the moment of production," in his *Traité d'économie politique,* the former of these writers remarked :

Smith will not allow the name of products to the results of these branches of industry [*i.e.,* the services rendered by the physician, musician, or actor, which Say called "immaterial products"]. Labour so bestowed he calls unproductive : an error he was led into by his definition of wealth, which he defines to consist of things bearing a value capable of being preserved, instead of extending the name to all things bearing exchangeable value : consequently, excluding products consumed as soon as created. The industry of the physician, however, as well as that of the public functionary, the advocate or the judge, which are all of them of the same class, satisfies wants of so essential a nature, that without those professions no society could exist. Are not, then, the fruits of their labour real? They are so far so, as to be purchased at the price of other and material products, which Smith allows to be wealth; and by the repetition of this kind of barter, the producers of immaterial products acquire fortunes.

To descend to items of pure amusement, it cannot be denied, that the representation of a good comedy gives as solid a pleasure as a box of comfits or a discharge of fireworks, which are products, even within Smith's definition. Nor can I discover any sound reason, why the talent of the painter should be deemed productive, and not the talent of the musician.[13]

McCulloch, a government official and member of the British Classical School in the period between Ricardo and J. S. Mill, discussed the same subject in *The Principles of Political Economy* (Edinburgh 1825, 4th edition, Edinburgh 1849) :

The manufacturer is not a producer of matter, but of utility only. And is it not obvious that the menial servant belongs to the same class, and is also a

[12] *An Inquiry into the Nature and Origin of Public Wealth,* pp. 152-153.

[13] *A Treatise on Political Economy,* p. 120.

producer of utility? It is universally allowed that the husbandman who raises corn, beef, and other articles of provision, is a productive labourer; but if so, why is the cook or menial servant who prepares and dresses these articles, and fits them for use, to be set down as unproductive? It is clear that there is no difference whatever in the nature of their services—that they are either both productive, or both unproductive.[14]

Senior took the same view. John Stuart Mill formally agreed with Smith but only in respect of terminology. Mill accepted Smith's definition of production, involving realization in a tangible commodity, but, having done so, he admitted the Lauderdale-Say-McCulloch argument that services not so realized might be valuable to mankind.

In general it can be said that the attitude of later economists of the Neo-Classical School has been that it is no business of the economist to say which commodities are useful and which are not, but for the consumer to decide what he wants and for the economist to leave any consideration of the merit of this decision to the moralist.[15] On the other hand, this view has been subjected to severe criticism from such writers as List, Ruskin, and Veblen—the Romanticists and the Institutionalists. First, it is asserted that the Classical and Neo-Classical definition of wealth and production is too narrow, excluding many things that are desirable from the standpoint of the group or the nation. Second, in another way it is claimed to be too wide, because it includes some commodities that are injurious. Ruskin's views on the subject are of interest, by reason of the fact that this writer confined the name *wealth* to goods and services of which he approved and coined another word, *illth*, for those that failed to secure his approbation. Labor that produced wealth as so defrned, that is, labor that brought into existence what Ruskin called "the means of life," was positive or productive, in his estimation, but that which destroyed or harmed life was negative or unproductive.

The Factors of Production

The Productivity of Land

Land and labor the sources of production. Seventeenth and early eighteenth century writers looked upon land and labor as the agents or factors responsible for production. The philosopher, Thomas Hobbes, set the fashion. Discussing the economic aspect of the Commonwealth, or State, in his *Leviathan,* he said,

As for the plenty of matter, it is a thing limited by nature, to those commodities, which from the two breasts of our common mother, land and sea, God usually either freely giveth, or for labour selleth to mankind.[16]

[14] 4th ed., p. 585.
[15] See, for example, the passage from *The Economics of Enterprise,* by H. J. Davenport, quoted in Chapter XVI, p. 723.
[16] *The English Works of Thomas Hobbes,* vol. 3, p. 232.

John Graunt's *Natural and Political Observations . . . upon the Bills of Mortality* contained a similar statement. Graunt was interested in vital statistics. In considering State policy with respect to marriage, he had occasion to comment :

Hands being the Father, as Lands are the Mother and Womb of Wealth.[17]

Sir William Petty, who also wrote on economic statistics and, indeed, has been credited with the last-named work, made much the same remark in his *Treatise of Taxes & Contributions:*

That Labour is the Father and active principle of Wealth, as Lands are the Mother.[18]

Cantillon began his *Essai sur la nature du commerce en général* with the following paragraph :

The Land is the Source or Matter from whence all Wealth is produced. The Labour of man is the Form which produces it : and Wealth in itself is nothing but the Maintenance, Conveniencies, and Superfluities of Life.[19]

In none of these passages was capital mentioned. Land and labor received full credit as being the sources of production.

The idea that only labor that is employed in cultivating land is productive. Next came a group of economic writers, the French Physiocrats, who refused the attribute of "productive" even to labor, at least unless it was applied to land. Land alone, they believed, was the source of production.

Cantillon pointed the way. Chapter 12 of his *Essai* had the title :

All Classes of Individuals in a State subsist or are enriched at the Expense of the Proprietors of Land.[20]

Developing this, the author said :

If the Prince and the Proprietors of Land close their Estates and will not suffer them to be cultivated it is clear that there would be neither Food nor Rayment for any of the Inhabitants; consequently all the Individuals are supported not only by the produce of the Land which is cultivated for the benefit of the Owners but also at the Expense of these same Owners from whose property they derive all that they have.[21]

This cannot be said to prove that only land is productive, because the argument can be turned round and used to justify a statement that labor alone is productive. Just as land was supposed by Cantillon to be withdrawn by its proprietors, so labor might be withheld. If no labor were employed on the land, then nothing would be produced. Cantillon, however, was satisfied with his demonstration and proceeded to say that

[17] Reprinted in *The Economic Writings of Sir William Petty,* vol. 2, p. 377.
[18] *Ibid.,* vol. 1, p. 68. [19] *Op. cit.,* p. 3. [20] *Ibid.,* p. 43. [21] *Ibid.*

the farmers generally received two thirds and the landowners one third of the produce. He referred, also, to the way in which other citizens were supported by the produce of land. Then he returned to his first point:

> But let this Matter be how it will, if we examine the Means by which an Inhabitant is supported it will always appear in returning back to the Fountain-Head, that these Means arise from the Land of the Proprietor either in the two thirds reserved by the Farmer, or the one third which remains to the Landlord.[22]

The Physiocrats made this an essential feature of their distribution theory. They said that only when labor was employed on land did it produce a surplus over what was required for its maintenance. Out of this surplus all other classes in the State were supported. Agriculture alone was productive, therefore: all other occupations were unproductive or stipendiary: Thus, Quesnay laid down the first maxim of government:

> Let the sovereign and the nation never forget that land is the only source of wealth and that it is agriculture which multiplies it.[23]

Turgot, in his *Réflexions sur la formation et la distribution des richesses*,[24] written in 1766 for the information of two young Chinese students, and published in 1769–1770, stated:

> *The Husbandman is the only person whose labour produces something over and above the wages of the labour. He is therefore the sole source of all wealth.*[25]

Under this heading, Turgot said:

> The land pays him directly the price of his labour, independently of any other man or any agreement. Nature does not bargain with him to oblige him to content himself with what is absolutely necessary. What she grants is proportioned neither to his wants, nor to a contractual valuation of the price of his days of labour. It is the physical result of the fertility of the soil, and of the wisdom, far more than of the laboriousness, of the means which he has employed to render it fertile. As soon as the labour of the Husbandman produces more than his wants, he can, with this superfluity that nature accords him as a pure gift, over and above the wages of his toil, buy the labour of the other members of the society. The latter, in selling to him, gain only their livelihood; but the Husbandman gathers, beyond his subsistence, a wealth which is independent and disposable, which he has bought and which he sells. He is, therefore, the sole source of the riches,

[22] *Ibid.*, p. 45.

[23] *Maximes générales du gouvernement économique d'un royaume agricole* (Versailles 1758), reprinted in *Œuvres économiques et philosophiques de F. Quesnay*, p. 331. Translated.

[24] Translated as *Reflections on the Formation and the Distribution of Riches*, London and N. Y. 1898. There is also an earlier translation, dated 1795.

[25] 1898 translation, p. 9. Quoted by permission of The Macmillan Company.

which, by their circulation, animate all the labours of the society; because he is the only one whose labour produces over and above the wages of the labour.[26]

In the section that followed, Turgot divided society into two classes on this basis, one *productive* (the cultivators of the soil) and the other *stipendiary, sterile,* or *unproductive* (the artisans). The comments made in other portions of the book and in the Physiocratic writings generally made it clear that the school regarded all labor that was not employed in the cultivation of land as unproductive. Turgot, indeed, in Section 18 of the *Réflexions,* made the following statement:

We can then distinguish the two non-disposable classes as the *productive class,* which is that of the Cultivators, and the *barren class,* which includes all the other stipendiary members of the Society.[27]

His *disposable class* was that of proprietors of land who, "not being bound by the need of subsistence to a particular labour, can be employed for the general needs of the Society, such as war and the administration of justice, either by a personal service, or by the payment of a part of their revenue with which the State or the Society may engage men to discharge these functions."[28]

Commerce was classified by the Physiocrats as unproductive, like industry, but it is not altogether clear what was the position of mining. It was similar to agriculture in that it utilized natural resources but Turgot refused to admit that it was productive. Land produced an annual fruit, he argued, whereas a mine was itself the garnered fruit.

In assessing the Physiocratic doctrine, it is necessary to inquire what such writers as Turgot meant by the word *productive.* If it were physical production, then in the state of knowledge of the physical sciences current in the middle of the eighteenth century, when the school flourished, it must have seemed reasonable enough to consider that only agriculture was productive. A farmer threw seed upon the surface of the soil and it was returned tenfold. Nothing like this appeared to result from the labor of artisans or officials. At the best, the latter only changed the form of the materials on which they were employed, making leather into shoes or yarn into cloth. Nowadays, it is well known that the farmer creates matter no more than the artisan, and that the materials from which the increment in the crop, as compared with the seed, are present beforehand in the soil, air, water, and fertilizer.

But it is evident that physical production was not what the Physiocrats had in mind when they asserted that only agriculture was productive. Their thoughts were on the *net product,* or surplus, which they supposed to result from agricultural operations. They believed that the artisan sold his output for a payment that was sufficient to cover (a) his produc-

[26] *Ibid.* [27] *Ibid.,* p. 17. [28] *Ibid.,* p. 15.

tion costs and (b) subsistence wages for himself. The cultivator, on the other hand, they thought, as the result of his labor, received more than this. He got (a) his production costs and (b) his subsistence wages, as before, but in addition he obtained (c) a surplus, which was paid to the landlord in the form of rent. In this sense, therefore, "productive" meant *productive of a surplus*. In other words, according to the Physiocrats, for some reason the produce of the soil exchanged for more than enough to cover the maintenance of the cultivators. This point receives attention in Chapter X.

The Physiocrats were not alone in attaching special importance to agriculture. In America Benjamin Franklin appears to have been influenced by Physiocratic ideas. Living in a country where farming was the chief industry and where such manufacture and trade as existed ministered primarily to the needs of the agriculturists, it was understandable that Franklin should agree with the Physiocrats on the importance of the agricultural industry. The passage given below brings out his position :

> there seem to be but three ways for a nation to acquire wealth. The first is by *war*, as the Romans did, in plundering their conquered neighbours. This is *robbery*. The second by *commerce*, which is generally *cheating*. The third by *agriculture*, the only *honest way*, wherein man receives a real increase of the seed thrown into the ground, in a kind of continued miracle, wrought by the hand of God in his favour, as a reward for his innocent life and his virtuous industry.[29]

The Scotsman, Sir James Steuart, discussing the multiplication of mankind in *An Inquiry into Principles of Political Œconomy*, stated,

> the most essential requisite for population, is that of agriculture, or the providing of subsistence. Upon this all the rest depends. .[30]

> A people, therefore, who have an industrious turn, will multiply in proportion to the superfluity produced by their farmers. . .[31]

This led to Steuart's theory of population, commented upon in Chapter VII. The solid truth behind Steuart's view on agriculture is the fact that subsistence is the most vital need of man. Other things can be had by a society only in as far as its productive power is in excess of that required to cover the elementary needs of subsistence. No doubt this gives a certain priority to agriculture in any economic hierarchy. It may be that the productive powers of some modern societies are so great that men now have to give little attention to the primary need of subsistence but, unquestionably, other communities in the past have stood closer to the sub-

[29] *The Writings of Benjamin Franklin*, ed. A. H. Smyth, 10 vols., N. Y. 1905-1907, vol. 1, pp. 148-149. Quoted by permission of The Macmillan Company.

[30] *The Works . . . of the late Sir James Steuart . . .* vol. 1, p. 32.

[31] *Ibid.*, pp. 35-36.

sistence minimum and, indeed, some do so at the present time. The primacy of subsistence is conceded by diminishing utility theorists, when they depict the first increments of income possessing a great utility. But this affords no justification for the Physiocratic theory, whatever may be conceded in respect of the more general statement of Steuart.

Agriculture more productive than other occupations. Adam Smith went halfway towards accepting the Physiocratic idea. Admitting the superiority of agriculture in production, he thought that *less productive,* not *unproductive,* was the designation to apply to industry and commerce.

Though Smith described the Physiocratic system as "perhaps, the nearest approximation to the truth that has yet been published upon the subject of political economy," he criticized it rather severely:

> The capital error of this system, however, seems to lie in its representing the class of artificers, manufacturers, and merchants, as altogether barren and unproductive.[32]

To demonstrate the truth of this statement, Smith pointed out that even the latter class "reproduces annually the value of its own annual consumption, and continues, at least, the existence of the stock or capital which maintains and employs it." He went on to a simile:

> But upon this account alone the denomination of barren and unproductive should seem to be very improperly applied to it. We should not call a marriage barren or unproductive, though it produced only a son and a daughter, to replace the father and mother, and though it did not increase the number of the human species, but only continued it as it was before. Farmers and country labourers, indeed, over and above the stock which maintains and employs them, reproduce annually a neat [*i.e.,* net] produce, a free rent to the landlord. As a marriage which affords three children is certainly more productive than one which affords only two; so the labour of farmers and country labourers is certainly more productive than that of merchants, artificers, and manufacturers. The superior produce of the one class, however, does not render the other barren or unproductive.[33]

Having compromised with the Physiocratic doctrine in this manner, Smith brought in his own criterion of productiveness. The labor of artificers was to be regarded as productive because it fixed or realized itself in a vendible commodity. In this connection it is of interest to note that the author of the *Wealth of Nations* appeared to deny his earlier claim that agriculture was more productive than other occupations, for he said that

> farmers and country labourers can no more augment, without parsimony, the real revenue, the annual produce of the land and labour of their society, than artificers, manufacturers, and merchants.[34]

[32] *Wealth of Nations,* Bk. 4, Chap. 9. [33] *Ibid.* [34] *Ibid.*

Finally, Smith expressed the opinion, mentioned later in this chapter, that manufactures were a more suitable field for division of labor than was agriculture — which might have led him to the conclusion that labor employed in the former field was more productive than that engaged in the latter. Instead of reaching this judgment, however, he was content to call quits :

In this respect, therefore, the class of cultivators can have no sort of advantage over that of artificers and manufacturers.[35]

This cannot be said to square with the lesson drawn from his two- and three-child family comparison.

Agriculture on a par with other occupations. The American statesman Alexander Hamilton took issue with Smith on this subject. Making the case for protection of infant industries in the United States of America which has been discussed in Chapter VI, Hamilton considered the claim that labor spent in manufactures was unproductive as compared with that employed in agriculture. He admitted the importance of agriculture as such :

It ought readily to be conceded that the cultivation of the earth, as the primary and most certain source of national supply, as the immediate and chief source of subsistence to man, as the principal source of those materials which constitute the nutriment of other kinds of labor, as including a state most favorable to the freedom and independence of the human mind — one, perhaps, most conducive to the multiplication of the human species, has intrinsically a strong claim to pre-eminence over every other kind of industry.[36]

He proceeded, however :

But, that it has a title to any thing like an exclusive predilection, in any country, ought to be admitted with great caution ; that it is even more productive than every other branch of industry, requires more evidence than has yet been given in support of the position.[37]

Hamilton then considered the views of the Physiocrats and of Adam Smith, quoting extensively from the *Wealth of Nations.* Smith, he conceded, had denied the exclusive productiveness of agriculture but, on the other hand, had asserted its superiority. The argument which appeared in the *Wealth of Nations,* to the effect that, in agriculture "nature co-operates with man," Hamilton described as "quaint and superficial." Next, an attack was made upon Smith's assertion that the existence of rent demonstrated the superior productivity of cultivation. The difference was verbal rather than one of substance, Hamilton said :

[35] *Ibid.*
[36] *Report on Manufactures,* in *The Works of Alexander Hamilton,* vol. 3, p. 297.
[37] *Ibid.,* pp. 297-298.

It is easily discernible, that what, in the first instance, is divided into two parts, under the denomination of the ordinary profit of the stock of the farmer and rent to the landlord, is, in the second instance, united under the general appellation of the ordinary profit on the stock of the undertaker; and that this formal or verbal distribution constitutes the whole difference in the two cases. It seems to have been overlooked, that the land is itself a stock or capital, advanced or lent by its owner to the occupier or tenant, and that the rent he receives is only the ordinary profit of a certain stock in land, not managed by the proprietor himself, but by another, to whom he lends or lets it, and who, on his part, advances a second capital, to stock and improve the land, upon which he also receives the usual profit. . .

The rent, therefore, accruing to the proprietor of the land, far from being a criterion of exclusive productiveness, as has been argued, is no criterion even of superior productiveness. The question must still be, whether the surplus, after defraying expenses, of a given capital, employed in the purchase and improvement of a piece of land, is greater or less than that of a like capital, employed in the prosecution of a manufactory; or whether the whole value produced from a given capital and a given quantity of labor, employed in one way, be greater or less than the whole value produced from an equal capital and an equal quantity of labor, employed in the other way; or rather, perhaps, whether the business of agriculture, or that of manufactures, will yield the greater product, according to a compound ratio of the quantity of the capital and the quantity of labor which are employed in the one or in the other.[38]

Hamilton's questions were not well put. Once the land was capitalized, presumably on the basis of its earning power or rental, it became a truism to say that this earning power was no more than represented the profit or interest on the capital involved. But at all events he saw through the Physiocratic assertion of the unique productivity of agriculture.

Ricardo, in his theory of rent, changed altogether the ground of debate. Instead of asking, *Is land productive?* Ricardo inquired, *Why is rent paid?* In seeking an answer, he found—contrary to what the Physiocrats appeared to assume—that rent was not paid for land as such. Some land, namely that on the margin of cultivation, yielded no rent. Only superior soils or situations brought a rent to those who owned the land concerned. If being *productive* meant *surplus-producing,* as it had done to the Physiocrats, Ricardo said that not all land possessed this quality but only some of it. Furthermore, a long series of writers after Ricardo showed that the capacity to yield a surplus was not peculiar to land. Labor and capital, in appropriate circumstances, produced surpluses comparable to that returned by land. Fuller treatment of this subject must be reserved to later chapters.

[38] *Ibid.*, pp. 303-304.

The Productivity of Labor

Earlier in this chapter it was seen that Sir William Petty and his contemporaries placed labor on an equal footing with land as a factor of production. Reference to the treatment of rent, later in this book, however, will reveal that Petty had some comprehension of the Ricardian theory, whose implications respecting the productivity of labor are examined below.

The Physiocrats thought that labor produced enough to maintain itself and nothing more, at least except when employed in cultivating land. That labor was unproductive followed from the Physiocratic definition of productiveness. Production, to the Physiocrats, meant calling into existence a surplus above maintenance. Maintenance itself was excluded.

According to Adam Smith, some labor was productive and some was not, the test being whether the labor fixed or realized itself in a vendible commodity, that is whether or not it was incorporated in producers' or consumers' capital goods.

In the meantime, John Locke — who was interested, not in production, but in appropriation — had offered the basis of a labor theory. In his view, labor put the greatest part of the value into every commodity; from which it followed that labor was mainly responsible for production. Adam Smith moved away from this position. Though it had been true in the past, Smith said, it was so no longer, and value was now largely explained by the scarcity of land and capital, as well as by labor. Ricardo, coming next in line, refused to accept Smith's abandonment of Locke's idea. Ricardo did not study production as such, but a production theory was implied in his general doctrine. At the margin of cultivation, according to the Ricardian theory, land produced nothing. Here the product was explained entirely by capital and labor. Superior land produced the additional product, which was to be credited to superiority. But capital was merely labor which had been expended in the past on the construction of equipment and, therefore, could be assimilated to labor generally. At the margin of cultivation, labor accounted for the entire product. In other words, in Ricardo's view, labor was not merely productive: it was the only factor that possessed this quality, excluding the additional product created by the generosity of Providence in furnishing superior land. Karl Marx, and the socialists generally, gave a ready acceptance to this theory. It is examined in some detail in Chapter IX.

As was shown in Chapter IV, the socialists asserted the laborer's right to the whole of the produce. It was postulated that the worker had produced the article and, from this assumption, it was reasoned that he had a right to its enjoyment. It did not worry the socialists to be informed that, unaided by land or capital, the laborer could not produce so much as he could when he enjoyed the assistance of these other agents.

Capital was eliminated on the ground that—except in so far as it represented merely past labor, to be remunerated on a labor basis—it was merely the result of exploitative power. Land was a gift of God, intended for the free use of mankind, not something to be monopolized by whoever happened to secure possession of it. What the socialists thought, therefore, was not that labor alone produced everything but that labor, aided by the free gifts of God, did so.

The Productivity of Capital

Capital as the maintenance of laborers. From very early times writers on economic matters have accepted that land and labor made some sort of contributions to production. On the other hand, many teachers have gone out of their way to deny that capital was productive. Aristotle informed his students that money was barren, and this viewpoint was prominent in the ideas of the medieval Canonists. Even at the end of the seventeenth century men like Petty and Cantillon were speaking of land and labor as the factors of production. Yet Cantillon brought capital into his system as a productive factor:

> The Land naturally produces, aided by human Labour, 4, 10, 20, 50, 100, 150 times the amount of corn sown upon it, according to the fertility of the soil and the industry of the inhabitants. It multiplies Fruits and Cattle. The Farmer who conducts the working of it has generally two thirds of the produce, one third pays his expenses and upkeep, the other remains for the profit of his enterprise. If the Farmer have enough capital to carry on his enterprise, if he have the needful tools and instruments, horses for ploughing, cattle to make the Land pay, etc. he will take for himself after paying all expenses a third of the produce of his Farm. But if a competent Labourer who lives from day to day on his wages and has no capital, can find some one willing to lend him land or money to buy some, he will be able to give the Lender all the third rent, or third part of the produce of a Farm of which he will become the Farmer or Undertaker.[39]

There is nothing here to show *how* capital is productive. Land + labor + capital was said to produce three rents, of which the laborer who possessed no capital must be content with one, whereas the farmer, who had capital, was able to secure two. The productivity of capital evidently explained the second, but how the process operated Cantillon neglected to say.

Of the Physiocrats, Turgot devoted considerable attention to capital, which he called *circulating wealth*. This existed in the form of cattle even prior to the appearance of agriculture. Capital was accumulated out of the annual produce and was necessary for the employment of labor, being advanced by the capitalist to the laborer (to cover the maintenance of the latter during the productive process) and recouped

[39] *Essai sur la nature du commerce en général*, p. 201.

out of the resulting produce. Capital was necessary, also, for the purpose of equipment. It was an essential part of what later came to be called the roundabout method of production:

All the various kinds of labours, whether in the cultivation of the land, in industry, or in Commerce, require advances. Even if one should till the land with one's hands, it would be necessary to sow before reaping: it would be necessary to live until after the harvest. The more perfect and energetic the cultivation of the land becomes, the more considerable are these advances. There is need of cattle, of implements of husbandry, of buildings to hold the cattle and store the produce; it is necessary to pay a number of persons proportioned to the extent of the undertaking, and to enable them to subsist until the harvest. It is only by means of considerable advances that we obtain a large return, and that the lands produce a good deal of revenue. In every craft, whatever it may be, it is necessary that the Workman should have tools in advance, that he should have a sufficient quantity of the materials upon which he has to labour; it is necessary that he should subsist while waiting for the sale of his finished goods.[40]

Adam Smith's position was much the same. He said that laborers who owned no stock or capital had to obtain tools and subsistence from capitalists, or they could not produce. But neither Turgot nor Smith demonstrated in what manner capital was productive, that is, how it happened that the worker who possessed tools could produce more than he who had none. Perhaps they thought that this was self-evident.

Capital as a substitute for labor. Lauderdale offered an explanation. Equipment was productive, he said, because it *saved or economized labor.* A product obtained by combining with land a small quantity of labor together with some capital was just like a similar one incorporating the same quantity of land and no capital but more labor. It followed that the capital so used must be regarded as being as productive as the labor it replaced.

Petty had forecast this idea in *The Political Anatomy of Ireland* (London 1691, probably written in 1672). Petty applied it, however, not so much to material capital goods as to knowledge (in other words, to the *spiritual capital* of Müller and List, dealt with later):

if by such Simple Labour I could dig and prepare for Seed a hundred Acres in a thousand days; suppose then, I spend a hundred days in studying a more compendious way, and in contriving Tools for the same purpose; but in all that hundred days dig nothing, but in the remaining nine hundred days I dig two hundred Acres of Ground; then I say, that the said Art which cost but one hundred days Invention is worth one Mans labour for ever; because the new Art, and one Man, perform'd as much as two Men could have done without it.[41]

[40] *Reflections on the Formation and the Distribution of Riches*, p. 45.
[41] *The Economic Writings of Sir William Petty*, vol. 1, p. 182.

Lauderdale enumerated several ways in which capital might be employed: (1) building and obtaining machinery, (2) procuring the raw materials necessary for manufacture, and transporting them, as well as the finished products, to their destination, (3) foreign trade, (4) agriculture, and (5) monetary circulation. In all these cases, Lauderdale said, the capital produces a profit

either—*from its supplanting a portion of labour, which would otherwise be performed by the hand of man*; or—*from its performing a portion of labour, which is beyond the reach of the personal exertion of man to accomplish.*[42]

This statement was supported as follows:

That we may perceive how the profit of capital thus employed arises from supplanting labour, let us consider the effect of a capital vested in machinery, in that first employment of man, the cultivation of the ground. The moment he places a portion of capital in the acquisition of a spade, one man must obviously, in the course of a day, be able, with his spade, to prepare as much land for receiving seed, as fifty could, by the use of their nails. Thus, this portion of capital supplants the necessity of the labour of forty-nine men.[43]

Unlike Böhm-Bawerk and others who wrote on the subject later, Lauderdale did not look at capital as necessarily productive. He mentioned the possibility that a stocking loom might not add to the number of stockings turned out by its operator. In such an event, he said that the machine,

though it executed the stockings in the greatest perfection, would be set aside as useless, merely because incapable of supplanting any portion of labour.[44]

If accumulation took place in excess, Lauderdale said, the public must suffer. Not only would consumption be discouraged but more capital would be created than was necessary:

By the creation of a quantity of capital more than is requisite for the moment, a thing, however much esteemed, is produced in such a quantity, that the whole cannot be employed,—a part ceases to be an object of desire; and as things, when no longer scarce, can form no part of individual riches, so, when no longer objects of desire, they form neither a portion of individual riches nor of wealth.—The finest palaces in the world stand empty at Delhi, unoccupied and undesired; and the spacious warehouses at Antwerp, serve only as monuments of her departed commerce.[45]

Modern writers would say that, failing errors in forecasting (such as took place at Antwerp), this could only happen if there were such a large supply of capital that its marginal productivity declined to zero. Though

[42] *An Inquiry into the Nature and Origin of Public Wealth,* p. 161.
[43] *Ibid.*, pp. 162-163. [44] *Ibid.*, p. 166. [45] *Ibid.*, pp. 220-221.

(Innsbruck 1889)[53], contained the author's positive or constructive contribution.

Expounding his own theory in the later volume, Böhm-Bawerk commenced by asserting that

Present goods are, as a rule, worth more than future goods of like kind and number.[54]

This proposition, he said, was "the kernal and centre" of the interest theory presented in the book. Böhm-Bawerk advanced three reasons for thinking that present goods were worth more than future goods: (1) present wants were apt to be more intense or greater than future wants; (2) people underestimated the needs of the future, so (mistakenly) thought that present wants were greater than those of the future; (3) present goods had a "technical superiority" over future goods, in that they could be used to produce other goods, so that a certain quantity of present goods was equivalent to a greater quantity of goods in the future (by reason of the increment of product). On the last, Böhm-Bawerk wrote:

It is an elementary fact of experience that methods of production which take time are more productive. That is to say, given the same quantity of productive instruments, the lengthier the productive method employed the greater the quantity of products that can be obtained.[55]

in this third cause, we have a quite universally valid reason for present goods having a greater value than future.[56]

To illustrate this by an example as simple as it is well worn. Imagine, with Roscher, a tribe of fisher-folk without capital, subsisting on fish left in pools on the shore by the ebb-tide and caught with the bare hand. Here a labourer may catch and eat three fish a day. If he had a boat and net he could catch thirty fish a day, instead of three. But he cannot have these tools, for their making would cost him a month's time and labour, and, in the meantime, he would have nothing to live upon. To save himself from starvation he must continue his wretched and costly fishing by hand. But now someone cleverer than the rest borrows ninety fish, promising, against the loan, to give back a hundred and eighty fish after one month. With the borrowed fish he supports himself during a month, makes a boat and net, and, during the next month, catches nine hundred fish instead of ninety. From this take, not only can he make the stipulated payment of a hundred and eighty fish, but he retains a considerable net gain to himself. . .[57]

This, of course, is the well-known principle of the productivity of capital. Böhm-Bawerk—unlike Lauderdale and the English economist, J. M.

[53] Translated, also by W. Smart, as *The Positive Theory of Capital*, London 1891. Additions to this work have been translated by W. A. Scott and S. Feilbogen as *Recent Literature on Interest (1884–1899)*, N. Y. 1903.

[54] *The Positive Theory of Capital*, p. 237. Quoted by permission of G. E. Stechert & Co.

[55] *Ibid.*, p. 260.

[56] *Ibid.*, p. 271.

[57] *Ibid.*

Keynes, in his recent writings — seemed unable to visualize a situation in which no additional opportunities existed for the profitable use of capital, so he said that his principle was universally valid. This point receives attention in Chapter XI.

As was the case with Senior, Böhm-Bawerk recognized that capital was not an independent factor of production, distinct from land and labor. It was an amalgamation or synthesis of these two factors, the willingness of the possessor to wait for the product being a necessary condition for capital to come into existence. Böhm-Bawerk examined in some detail the nature of capital. Most of it was composed of intermediate goods — those standing between raw materials on which no labor had been expended and finished goods ready for consumption. Production by the aid of capital was said to be *indirect* or *roundabout,* in that consumers' goods were not produced by direct application of labor to natural materials but only at the end of an indirect or roundabout process. The addition of more capital to the productive process lengthened it or made it more roundabout. To understand such a term as "lengthening the process of production," it must be borne in mind that what was involved was not *time* as a simple factor but time multiplied by *amount of capital goods concerned,* so that the process could be said to be longer or more roundabout even though it occupied no more time, if more capital were used for the same time.

Böhm-Bawerk's explanation of capital is a familiar part of modern economic theory. It covers what is now often called *producers' capital* as distinct from what is known as *consumers' capital,* that is, finished goods ready for consumption. But Senior's name, *abstinence,* which referred to an important ingredient of capital as Böhm-Bawerk visualized it, has gone out of fashion. As the German socialist Lassalle pointed out, it appeared somewhat ridiculous to speak of a wealthy capitalist, surfeited with consumption goods, as "abstaining" when he saved income that it did not occur to him to spend. Realizing that some of the capital supply — perhaps a good deal of it — comes from such sources, economists have tended to choose names less open to criticism, such as *waiting,* favored by Alfred Marshall, and the *capital disposal* of Cassel.

Digression on capital as capitalized earning-power. A number of modern writers have emphasized the value aspect of capital and looked upon it as capitalized earning-power. Instead of regarding capital as something material — the tangible equipment which assists in the roundabout method of production — they have regarded it as a value. What does a man speak of as his capital? The property he possesses that has a value on the market, namely such things as his house and furniture, his stocks and bonds, his deposits at the bank. These things are valuable, not because they are tangible or even because they represent tangible things, but because they have earning-power. The market capitalizes the income that is expected to accrue from their utilization—income received directly in satisfactions or in the form of money. Moreover, the market capitalizes intangible things that possess earning-power, such as a franchise or the goodwill attached to a trading business, just as much as it capitalizes tangibles like factory buildings and machinery. Further, the market accords no value (other than what they are worth when broken up for different uses) to tangibles that have lost their earning-power—an obsolete building or machine, for example.

The views of H. D. MacLeod on the subject of wealth, mentioned in Chapter II, forecast this attitude respecting the nature of capital. It has been developed especially by Thorstein Veblen, in his book on *The Theory of Business Enterprise* (New York 1904). The American economist Irving Fisher (1867–1947) has used the idea, in *The Nature of Capital and Income* (New York 1906) and later writings,[58] to explain *capital values,* as distinct from capital goods (on which his position is essentially that of Böhm-Bawerk).

Obviously, to speak of capital in MacLeod's sense as being productive is illogical. The fact that an income accrues is what explains the existence of the capital—the latter being merely a present value attached to expected future increments of the former. This point has been of some significance in connection with government regulation of the rates charged by railroads and public utilities generally. Some individuals have claimed that the rates should be fixed so as to allow a fair return on the market capitalization. Since the market merely capitalizes expected earnings (which depend on rates), clearly such a claim is nonsensical.

The immaterial or spiritual capital of the Romanticists. In Chapter II some mention was made of the conception of wealth held by Adam Müller and Friedrich List. To these men wealth was not merely tangible goods and services of obvious personal usefulness. It embraced the entire culture of a social group, of a nation.

A correlative of this idea of wealth was one of immaterial or spiritual capital, in the shape of the cultural heritage built up by a people and passed from one generation to another. As ideas and institutions that had come over from the past, and were incorporated in "immaterial capital," obviously helped to build up the culture of the present (that is, they contributed to the wealth of the nation, as Müller and List defined it), it followed that immaterial capital was productive. But this immaterial or spiritual capital was not merely productive of immaterial wealth: it assisted in the production of tangible goods and services. Knowledge, security, the habit of co-operation, and similar factors, made it possible for men to produce more material wealth than they could have done in

[58] See Chapter XI, p. 547.

the absence of these assistants. The passage from the writings of Petty, quoted earlier in this chapter,[59] will serve to demonstrate the truth of this contention.

It is evident that the Romanticists have made a good point here. But it is by no means clear that it has been neglected entirely by the Classical and Neo-Classical economists. Bentham, whose writings exercised great influence on these economists, had given considerable attention to the importance of security (from the aggression of others, from arbitrary dispossession by the government, etc.) as a factor influencing the volume of production. Sidgwick, and other economists of his period, incorporated this argument in their teachings. The difference between the Germans and the English writers on this subject, such as Sidgwick, was that the latter defined capital so as to exclude security and other institutional factors, and therefore found it necessary to refer to the latter as extraneous influences which, though important in relation to production, were non-economic; whereas Müller and List gave capital a more comprehensive definition. In other words, the difference turned on divergent views on terminology and the delimitation of the social sciences.

Organization As a Factor of Production

The last fifty years have witnessed an attempt—notably on the part of Alfred Marshall—to set up a fourth agent or factor of production, namely *business organization* or *enterprise*. Though the conception of organization as a productive element has been of service in connection with exposition and inquiry, as a factor of production it can be considered to represent merely a special kind of labor, that of initiation, direction, and supervision. The matter cannot be dismissed with this statement but, since it is intimately connected with some of the problems discussed under the heading of profits, it is convenient to reserve treatment of it to the chapter on that subject.

The Laws of Returns

An ever-present problem in the world has been that of the relationship between input and output, between the quantities of the factors of production used in productive operations and the amount of the resulting produce. Quite early there was evidence that men noticed that difficulty was experienced in expanding output on the basis of a fixed supply of one of the productive agents, land in particular. A passage from the *Book of Genesis*, quoted at the beginning of this chapter, attributed the parting of Abram and Lot to this circumstance. The flocks possessed by the two men could not be fed on a limited pasturage so well as on a larger area, so they agreed to part.

[59] See p. 376.

The Principle of Diminishing Returns

From time to time, in subsequent years, writers referred to the effect of population growth in terms that implied an underlying knowledge of the same principle of diminishing returns, some of these being mentioned in Chapter VII. But a comprehensive and lucid formulation of the principle awaited the work of the Physiocrat, Turgot. In his *Observations sur la mémoire de M. de Saint-Peravy,* written about 1768, Turgot stated,

Granting to the author of this essay that, in a state of ordinary good cultivation, the annual advances return two hundred and fifty to the hundred, it is more than probable that if the advances were increased by degrees up to the point at which they return nothing, each increment would be less and less productive. . . If, instead of the advances being increased by equal increments beyond the point where they return the most, on the contrary they are diminished, the same change in the proportion will be found. It is not only conceivable but it is certain that very small advances will give a profit much less than very large advances, and that in a proportion much less than that of the advances. If *two thousand livres* return *five thousand, one thousand* will perhaps not return *fifteen hundred,* and *five hundred* not return *six hundred.* Seed sown on soil naturally fertile, but without any preparation, would be an advance almost entirely lost. If it were once cultivated, the produce would be greater, cultivating a second, a third time, might not simply double and triple, but quadruple or decuple the produce, which thus will increase in a greater proportion than the advances increase, and that up to a certain point, at which the produce will be as great as possible, in comparison with the advances. Beyond this point, if the advances are increased further, the produce will increase also, but less, and always less and less until, the fecundity of the earth being exhausted, and art unable to add anything, additional advances will add nothing to the produce.

I observe that it would be an error to imagine that the point where the advances return the most which is possible, is the most advantageous which the cultivation can attain, because, although the new advances do not return quite as much as did the preceding advances, if they return enough to augment the net product of the soil, it is advantageous to apply them. . .[60]

Thus Turgot appreciated that there was a point of greatest returns (per unit of capital applied), when capital was applied to an area of land. On either side of this point — that is, when less or more capital was used — the returns per unit of capital declined. But, further, when the costs of the capital were taken into account, he argued that the cultivator need not stop his applications at the point of maximum returns. It would pay him to continue beyond this, adding capital as long as the extra returns which were secured were more than enough to counterbalance

[60] Reprinted in *Œuvres de M. Turgot,* 9 vols., Paris 1808, vol. 4, pp. 316-318. Translated.

the cost of the capital applied. The theory can be represented in graphical form, though Turgot himself did not use this type of exposition, thus:

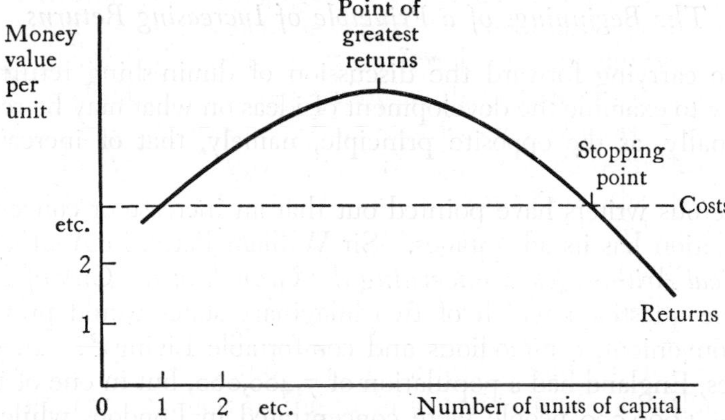

Few writers have offered a statement of the principle of varying returns clearer and more concise than that of Turgot.

In Scotland, shortly afterwards, the writings of James Anderson (1739–1808), bore on the problem. In the corn law controversy, which arose in Britain at the conclusion of the Napoleonic Wars, a number of the disputants dealt with it. Bounties on the exportation of grain and duties on importation, which had been brought over from an earlier period, became a matter of discussion after 1750. Readers of the *Wealth of Nations* will remember the antagonism displayed by Smith to these laws. During the war years prices were at levels that were very satisfactory to the farmers; but, as the Napoleonic conflict neared its close, an agitation sprang up from the landed interest in favor of re-establishing the corn law system on a basis that would offer protection to British farmers in the post-war period. Not only politicians but leading economists took sides. Malthus pamphleteered in favor of protection and Ricardo wrote on the opposite side. The result was seen in the protective measure of 1815 and its modifications, which, a quarter of a century afterwards, became the target of free trade opposition.

During this period Britain was passing through her industrial revolution and the population was expanding rapidly. Whereas in former times grain was exported in good years and imported in seasons of dearth, importation now took place more commonly and in larger quantities. The country was to a large extent self-sufficing in regard to grain, however, even after the end of the Napoleonic Wars, so that, when plentiful harvests coincided with the post-war price slump, the protective corn law was inadequate to preserve the prosperity of British farming. But those who looked ahead had no difficulty in prophesying that the population would soon pass beyond the capacity of the home country's fields to feed

very difficult to get even implements for his husbandry, without the aid of the smith and the carpenter; and they again, find it their interest to truck with him for what they want, instead of tilling the ground themselves. In building and furnishing a house, the business becomes still more complex; and more variety of arts are necessary. And should any one undertake to provide a coat only, by going himself through the various operations of shearing the wool, carding, spinning, weaving, tucking, &c. half the labour and toil in his own particular profession, would not only have equipped him with a better garment, but also procured him other necessaries.[63]

The enthusiasm displayed by Adam Smith on the subject is well known. Chapter 1 of the first book of the *Wealth of Nations* dealt with it and began:

The greatest improvement in the productive powers of labour, and the greater part of the skill, dexterity, and judgment with which it is any where directed, or applied, seem to have been the effects of the division of labour.

Smith proceeded to illustrate, giving pin-making as an example of a business conducted on mass-production lines:

One man draws the wire, another straights it, a third cuts it, a fourth points it, a fifth grinds it at the top for receiving the head; to make the head requires two or three distinct operations; to put it on is a peculiar business, to whiten the pins is another; it is even a trade by itself to put them into the paper; and the important business of making a pin is, in this manner, divided into about eighteen distinct operations, which, in some manufactories, are all performed by distinct hands, though in others the same man will perform two or three of them. I have seen a small manufactory of this kind where ten men only were employed, and where some of them consequently performed two or three distinct operations. But though they were very poor, and therefore but indifferently accommodated with the necessary machinery, they could, when they exerted themselves, make among them about twelve pounds of pins in a day. There are in a pound upwards of four thousand pins of a middling size. Those ten persons, therefore, could make among them upwards of forty-eight thousand pins in a day. Each person, therefore, making a tenth part of forty-eight thousand pins, might be considered as making four thousand eight hundred pins in a day. But if they had all wrought separately and independently, and without any of them having been educated to this peculiar business, they certainly could not each of them have made twenty, perhaps not one pin in a day; that is, certainly, not the two hundred and fortieth, perhaps not the four thousand eight hundredth part of what they are at present capable of performing, in consequence of a proper division and combination of their different operations.[64]

Smith next made the case a general one:

In every other art and manufacture, the effects of the division of labour are

[63] *A Select Collection of Scarce and Valuable Tracts on Money*, pp. 357-358.
[64] Book 1, Chap. 1.

similar to what they are in this very trifling one : though in many of them, the labour can neither be so much subdivided, nor reduced to so great a simplicity of operation. The division of labour, however, so far as it can be introduced, occasions, in every art, a proportionable increase of the productive powers of labour.[65]

The advantages of specialization were listed by Smith. It improved the dexterity of the workman, saved time in passing between different tasks, and led to the invention of machinery.

Much later in his book Smith argued that division of labor was more likely to take place in manufactures than in agriculture :

the labour of artificers and manufacturers, as it is capable of being more subdivided, and the labour of each workman reduced to a greater simplicity of operation, than is that of farmers and country labourers, so it is likewise capable of both these sorts of improvement [*i.e.*, in machinery and in the worker's skill] in a much higher degree.[66]

None of these statements contains anything on the side of increasing returns that is comparable to Turgot's enunciation of the principle of diminishing returns. Petty suggested a principle of increasing returns. Where Turgot had said that, if excessive increments of capital were expended on a constant quantity of land, beyond a certain point the returns would fall off, Petty argued that if increments of population were added to a unit area of land the returns would increase. The English writer visualized no early stage at which returns would behave in the opposite fashion, while Turgot accepted that returns would increase up to a maximum and only fall off thereafter. Had Petty used a graph—which, of course, he did not—his representation would have been as follows :

With the necessary alterations in units, Quesnay's formulation was very similar. Harris reasoned that an increased aggregation of people (his small- and large-society comparison) meant more division of labor, which

[65] *Ibid.* [66] *Ibid.*, Bk. 4, Chap. 9.

in turn was accompanied by higher production per head. What Smith said, on the other hand, was that division of labor was applicable more to manufacturing industry than to agriculture. A number of later writers followed Smith in this comparison.

The Relationship Between the Two Principles

It is now possible to return to the subject of diminishing returns. As has been noticed, Turgot developed what today is sometimes called the law of proportionality. If one factor of production remains in fixed supply—as was the case with land in Turgot's example—and a variable factor is added, increment by increment, a point of greatest returns is discernible. On either side of this optimum point returns decline.

The problem which confronted English writers about 1815 was also one of proportionality. But it was on a grander scale. In their problem the fixed area of land was Great Britain, and what was being added, unit by unit, was the population of that island. So economists like Ricardo theorized as to how returns would behave as the population expanded.

West, Malthus, and Ricardo. One of the most interesting contributions was that of Sir Edward West (1783–1828), a lawyer who later distinguished himself in India. He appears to have had an interest in economics and joined in the corn law controversy. The title of his pamphlet, *An Essay on the Application of Capital to Land, with Observations shewing the Impolicy of any great Restriction of the Importation of Corn, and that the bounty of 1688 did not lower the price of it* (London 1815), brings out the political purpose of the study.

West set out to demonstrate the truth of the principle of diminishing returns, which he said had occurred to him some years before. He stated it in a dynamic form:

> in the progress of the improvement of cultivation the raising of rude produce becomes progressively more expensive, or, in other words, the ratio of the net produce of land to its gross produce is continually diminishing.[67]

The "progress of the improvement of cultivation," it should be explained, really meant, not what the words imply, but the changes that took place as population increased. But, although his principle was dynamic, West's demonstration of its truth was static. If, *at a time,* recourse were had to poorer soils, or the rich soils were cultivated more intensively, he said that the returns per unit of capital and labor applied to land would fall off. This, he assumed, was what would happen when population increased:

> As each cultivator is driven into a narrower compass by the pressure of population, he is obliged to till soils which are comparatively ungrateful and

[67] *An Essay on the Application of Capital to Land,* reprinted Baltimore 1903, p. 9. Quoted by permission of The Johns Hopkins Press.

exhausted : the cattle are fed on artificial grasses ; and expensive manures are brought from a distance to enable the land to yield successive crops, instead of being left, when exhausted, as in the earlier stages of improvement, to renovate itself.[68]

West made it quite clear that there were two possibilities. Poorer land could be brought under cultivation, or land already farmed could be tilled more intensively :

The additional work bestowed upon land must be expended either in bringing fresh land into cultivation, or in cultivating more highly that already in tillage.[69]

The latter, of course, was what Turgot had studied. The former, as is indicated in Chapter X, had been dealt with by Anderson. So far, therefore, West had said nothing new. But he now remembered Adam Smith's remarks about the influence of division of labor in the direction of increasing returns, which Smith had said was applicable more to manufactures than to agriculture, and made his complete statement as follows :

It appears, therefore, that in the progress of improvement an equal quantity of work extracts from the soil a gradually diminishing return ; and that, therefore, the whole quantity of work bestowed on land in the progress of improvement, extracts from the soil a gradually diminishing proportionate return. But the quantity of work which can be done by a given number of hands is increased in the progress of improvement, by means of the subdivision of labour and machinery even in agriculture. Such increase then of the quantity of work which can be performed by the same number of hands in agriculture, may either more than compensate, or just compensate, or fall short of compensating the diminution of the return of the same quantity of work. In the first of which cases labour in agriculture would become absolutely more productive ; in the second would remain always equally productive ; in the last would become absolutely less productive.[70]

West thus considered that agriculture was subject to two tendencies : (1) one towards diminishing returns, owing to the increased cost of securing food from poorer soil and of working better land more intensively, and (2) one in the direction of increasing returns, due to division of labor. The question arose, which of the two was the more influential in agriculture ? West came to the conclusion that the first was the more important. Further, balancing agriculture's tendency to diminishing returns with that of manufacture in the other direction, he judged that the former would predominate, so that the returns to labor *as a whole* would fall off :

It follows therefore that labour cannot be always equally productive in agriculture in the progress of improvement ; and, a fortiori, that the produc-

[68] *Ibid.*, p. 13. [69] *Ibid.*, p. 14. [70] *Ibid.*, pp. 15-16.

tive powers of labour cannot increase, but that they must become gradually less productive in the progress of improvement. And not only less productive, but so much less productive that the continual increase of the effective powers of labour in manufactures does not compensate for their continued diminution in agriculture.[71]

T. R. Malthus considered the same problem in a pamphlet entitled *An Inquiry into the Nature and Progress of Rent, and the Principles by which it is Regulated* (London 1815). Like West, Malthus endeavored to assess the relative significances of the tendencies towards diminishing and increasing returns. The former rested on the need for recourse to poorer soils as population expanded, as West had said. But the statement made by Malthus on increasing returns was somewhat different. Where West had spoken of the gains from specialization of labor, Malthus referred broadly to improvements in agriculture, which included not merely the advantages of large-scale production, but any benefits resulting from new inventions and scientific discoveries. The conclusion, respecting agriculture and manufacturing, was the same as had been reached by West. Diminishing returns (or increasing costs) obtained for agriculture, whereas the opposite was true of manufactures :

With regard to improvements in agriculture, which in similar soils is the great cause which retards the advance of price [*i.e.*, of the price or cost of the produce] compared with the advance [in the quantity] of produce; although they are sometimes very powerful, they are rarely found sufficient to balance the necessity of applying to poorer land, or inferior machines. In this respect, raw produce is essentially different from manufactures. The real price of manufactures, the quantity of labour and capital necessary to produce a given quantity of them, is almost constantly diminishing; while the quantity of labour and capital, necessary to procure the last addition that has been made to the raw produce of a rich and advancing country, is almost constantly increasing.[72]

Ricardo's views were much the same. As population expanded, he said, poorer land would be brought under cultivation and the good soil farmed more intensively, so that the returns per unit of capital and labor applied to the land would fall off. Ricardo believed that improvements were of little avail to check the process. They counteracted the tendency towards diminishing returns, if their immediate effect only were considered, but in the long run they stimulated the growth of population so were of no benefit.

Senior. Nassau Senior continued the distinction between agriculture and manufactures that had been made by Smith and West. His "Fourth Elementary Proposition" ran :

[71] *Ibid.*, p. 19.

[72] Reprint, Baltimore 1903, p. 38. Quoted by permission of The Johns Hopkins Press.

That, agricultural skill remaining the same, additional Labour employed on the land within a given district produces in general a less proportionate return, or, in other words, that though, with every increase of the labour bestowed, the aggregate return is increased, the increase of the return is not in proportion to the increase of the Labour.[73]

Developing this proposition, he stated, in heavy type, that

Additional Labour when employed in Manufactures is MORE, when employed in Agriculture is LESS, efficient in proportion.[74]

The difference between the two, Senior argued, was due to the circumstance that the volume of production was elastic in agriculture but not in manufactures:

No additional labour or machinery can work up a pound of raw cotton into more than a pound of manufactured cotton; but the same bushel of seed-corn, and the same rood of land, according to the labour and skill with which they are treated, may produce four bushels, or eight bushels, or sixteen.[75]

Senior's argument here was fallacious. He forgot to ask, as he should have done, what would happen to the cost of growing cotton if the output that was required expanded considerably, by reason of an increase in the scale of textile operations. Had he done so, he would have discovered that pounds of manufactured cotton were in the same situation as bushels of grain. More intensive production from existing cotton lands, or resort to poorer soil, would increase the cost of producing cotton just as was the case with grain.

Senior inquired into the problem that had agitated West, Malthus, and Ricardo. What would be the effect on returns of an increase of population? He stated the general rule that the return to labor expended in agriculture tended to decline as the amount of such labor increased. But he qualified this by referring to the existence of a countervailing tendency for labor to become more skilful. In the century which preceded the time Senior wrote, indeed, he thought that the latter had been more important than the former, so that—on balance—returns in agriculture had risen:

More efficient implements, a better rotation of crops, a greater division of labour, in short, improvements in the art of agriculture, generally accompany the increase of agricultural labour. They always accompany that increase when it is accompanied by an increase of the capital as well as of the population of a Country; and they always counteract, and often outweigh, the inferiority or diminished proportional powers of the soil to which they are applied. The total amount of the annual agricultural produce of Great Britain has much more than doubled during the last hundred years; but

[73] *Political Economy*, p. 26. [74] *Ibid.*, p. 81. [75] *Ibid.*, p. 83.

it is highly improbable that the amount of labour annually employed in agriculture has also doubled.[76]

It was possible, Senior thought, though "certainly not probable," that an equal rate of progress might be maintained in the next hundred years. But he believed that this could not go on indefinitely.

In the case of manufactures, on the other hand,

every increase in the number of manufacturing labourers is accompanied not merely by a corresponding, but by an increased productive power.[77]

The only check that need be feared, he said, was the increased difficulty of importing raw materials and food. Senior's views here bear the imprint of their environment. When he wrote, British industry was expanding by leaps and bounds. Year by year, factories were producing more goods and producing them more cheaply, and there seemed no limit to the process of industrial expansion, other than that which Senior visualized.

J. S. Mill. About the same time as Senior was writing in England, the French mathematician Cournot, in his *Recherches sur les principes mathématiques de la théorie des richesses,* offered an algebraic formulation of the laws of increasing and diminishing returns. Just before, Samuel Bailey (1791–1870), an Englishman of inherited means who devoted himself to writing and public work, had attacked the Ricardian theory of value in *A Critical Dissertation on the Nature, Measure, and Causes of Value: Chiefly in Reference to the Writings of Mr. Ricardo and His Followers* (London 1825). This book gave a threefold classification of commodities.

First came products that were monopolized; then those "in the production of which some persons possess greater facilities than the rest of the community, and which therefore the competition of the latter cannot increase, except at a greater cost." Lastly, there were goods "in the production of which competition operates without restraint." The second case was that of diminishing returns, or increasing costs. Production had "no assignable boundary" and was "limited by the watchful competition, which is ever ready to act upon it the moment it [*i.e.,* value] has exceeded a particular point." Grain, raw produce in general, and minerals were grouped by Bailey in this category. The third class covered what is now called constant and increasing returns, or constant and diminishing costs.[78]

John Stuart Mill, in his *Principles of Political Economy,* gave a classification on the same lines as that of Bailey. In considering the subject of value, Mill said that two factors were required to confer value upon a

[76] *Ibid.,* p. 86. [77] *Ibid.*

[78] Reprint, London 1931, pp. 185-198. Quoted by permission of the London School of Economics and Political Science.

commodity: (1) utility and (2) difficulty of attainment. There were, he commented, three kinds of difficulty of attainment. First, the case of absolute limitation of supply, as with rare books and pictures. Second was the situation in which commodities were reproducible without limit, for all practicable purposes, and, as would appear from Mill's language, without increase in cost. This embraced the cases of constant and increasing returns and, according to Mill, it included "the majority of all things that are bought and sold." It was, of course, Bailey's third category. Finally came the case, "intermediate between the two preceding," where multiplication of product was possible to an unlimited extent, subject to the condition that

> Only a limited quantity can be produced at a given cost: if more is wanted, it must be produced at a greater cost.[79]

This was Bailey's second class, that of diminishing returns, and to it, in Mill's opinion, there belonged agricultural produce and "generally all the rude produce of the earth."

Evidently the writings of Bailey and Mill represented a change from the position that had been taken by West. But this cannot be regarded as an improvement. West looked upon diminishing and increasing returns as two *states* or *conditions of production,* through which any commodity might pass but with the probability that agricultural products were in the former and manufactures in the latter situation. On the other hand, with Bailey and Mill, diminishing and increasing returns referred to *two sets of commodities,* with the implication that the same product could not pass from one to the other.

Carey and Bastiat. In the meantime, H. C. Carey had delivered a frontal attack on the theory of diminishing returns in its dynamic aspect. In *The Past, the Present, and the Future* (Philadelphia 1848) and other writings, Carey asserted that there was no tendency for the returns to labor to decline as population increased. Instead, he declared that the opposite was the case. Men settled first, he said, not on rich land, as Ricardo had stated, but on poor soil. The earliest settlements were made on treeless uplands, for example, and only at a later stage did farmers bring under cultivation the inherently more fertile bottom land which required preparatory treatment in the way of clearing or drainage. According to Carey, therefore, the progress of cultivation was not from more to less fertile soil but in the opposite direction, with the result that the returns to labor *increased,* instead of diminishing. Carey gave numerous historical illustrations, drawn from America and elsewhere, in support of this thesis, and concluded:

> How far all this is true, we must leave to the reader to judge. All others

[79] Bk. 3, Chap. 2, Sect. 2.

of the laws of nature are broad and universally true, and we are disposed to hope that he may now agree with us in believing that there is one law, and one alone, for food, light, air, clothing, and fuel : and that man, in all and every case, commences with the worst machinery and proceeds onward to the best; thus enabled, with the growth of wealth, population, and the habit of union, to obtain with constantly diminishing labour an increased supply of all the necessaries, conveniences, comforts, and luxuries of life.[80]

The Frenchman Bastiat also denied the practical applicability of the principle of diminishing returns. In effect, he gave Petty's argument that the aggregation of population led to economies in production. On this basis, he controverted the Malthusian belief that a growth in population was accompanied by a decline in the productivity of labor.

The arguments of Carey and Bastiat have been examined in Chapter VII and need not be repeated here. It is in place, however, to refer to John Stuart Mill's reply. The Englishman conceded to Carey the possibility that the statements of the latter, concerning the historical progress of land settlement, were correct. But Mill refused to grant that this upset his own theory :

As far as words go, Mr. Carey has a good case against several of the highest authorities in political economy, who certainly did enunciate in too universal a manner the law which they laid down, not remarking that it is not true of the first cultivation in a newly settled country. Where population is thin and capital scanty, land which requires a large outlay to render it fit for tillage must remain untilled; though such lands, when their time has come, often yield a greater produce than those earlier cultivated, not only absolutely, but proportionally to the labour employed, even if we include that which has been expended in originally fitting them for cultivation. But it is not pretended that the law of diminishing return was operative from the very beginning of society : and though some political economists may have believed it to come into operation earlier than it does, it begins quite early enough to support the conclusions they founded on it. Mr. Carey will hardly assert that in any old country — in England or France, for example — the lands left waste are, or have for centuries been, more naturally fertile than those under tillage. Judging even by his own imperfect test, that of local situation — how imperfect I need not stop to point out — is it true that in England or France at the present day the uncultivated part of the soil consists of the plains and valleys, and the cultivated, of the hills? Every one knows, on the contrary, that it is the high lands and thin soils which are left to nature, and when the progress of population demands an increase of cultivation, the extension is from the plains to the hills. Once in a century, perhaps, a Bedford Level may be drained, or a Lake of Harlem pumped out : but these are slight and transient exceptions to the normal progress of things; and in old countries which are at all advanced in civilization, little of this sort remains to be done.[81]

[80] *The Past, the Present, and the Future,* p. 50.

[81] *Ibid.,* Bk. 1, Chap. 12, Sect. 3.

Thus, as an answer to an argument based on the course of early settlement, Mill referred Carey to what was happening in nineteenth century Europe. But Mill gave no recognition to the circumstance upon which Senior had commented, namely, that even in eighteenth and nineteenth century Britain the returns to labor had increased, not diminished.

In fact, of course, Malthus, Ricardo, West, and Mill had noticed the existence of two antagonistic tendencies. As population increased, other things being equal, men had resort to poorer land and also cultivated the better land more intensively, so that production costs tended to rise. On the other hand, as population became more concentrated, again other things remaining the same, certain economies arose — savings in transportation and communication, for instance. Furthermore, as the population multiplied, the other things ceased to remain the same, because improvements of various kinds were introduced, lowering the costs of production. Looking into the future, Mill — like Ricardo and West before him — prophesied that the tendency towards diminishing returns would prevail. The present generation, glancing backwards over the period that has passed by since West and Mill ventured their prophecy, must admit that the forecast has proved incorrect, so far at all events. What Senior said about the century before he wrote has proved to be equally applicable to that which followed his time.

Sidgwick. In Chapter VII it was shown how Sidgwick tied together the diminishing and increasing returns principles with respect to population growth. The static aspect, he accepted as proved :

> That the application of labour in agriculture is subject, in a certain sense, to the condition of Diminishing Returns may be considered to be an established doctrine : that is to say, it is universally admitted by competent persons that, in a country in which population has reached a certain point of density, the agricultural produce needed is obtained partly by processes more costly than would be required if the total amount needed were less.[82]

On the dynamic side, however, Sidgwick left behind the earlier writers by declaring that the evidence available did not justify a definite conclusion as to the relative magnitudes of the two conflicting tendencies.

The Neo-Classical School. As has been seen, through a large part of the nineteenth century, economists discussed the laws of returns with special reference to population changes. That is, they discussed the man-land ratio in its dynamic aspect. They also tended to make a commodity or industrial classification. Diminishing returns applied to agriculture, they thought, increasing returns to manufactures.

Marshall wrote when England was more highly industrialized. Large plants had arisen in many industries and the economies of mass produc-

[82] *The Principles of Political Economy*, pp. 151-152.

tion were increasingly evident. Yet, like his predecessors, Marshall did not question that these economies had a special applicability to manufactures, as distinct from agriculture :

we say broadly that while the part which nature plays in production shows a tendency to diminishing return, the part which man plays shows a tendency to increasing return.[83]

Marshall continued the West-Ricardo-Senior-Mill tradition in defining the principle of diminishing returns so as to refer only to the application of other factors to land :

The law of or *statement of tendency to Diminishing Return* may be provisionally worded thus : An increase in the capital and labour applied in the cultivation of land causes *in general* a less than proportionate increase in the amount of produce raised, unless it happens to coincide with an improvement in the arts of agriculture.[84]

The law or principle of increasing returns, Marshall stated thus :

An increase of labour and capital leads generally to improved organization, which increases the efficiency of the work of labour and capital.[85]

He proceeded :

in those industries which are not engaged in raising raw produce an increase of labour and capital generally gives a return increased more than in proportion ; and further this improved organization tends to diminish or even override any increased resistance which nature may offer to raising increased amounts of raw produce.[86]

A *law of constant return* operated, Marshall said, when the two tendencies balanced each other.

In the statement of the principle of diminishing return, here quoted, Marshall was dealing with the proportionality of the productive factors. More capital and labor applied to the same quantity of land, other things being equal, meant that returns, per unit of capital and labor, would decline. Marshall might have asked — as did his English contemporary, P. H. Wicksteed, and the American J. B. Clark — what would happen if some other factor were kept in fixed supply, and land were varied ? In his book on *The Distribution of Wealth* (New York 1899), J. B. Clark (1847–1938), who taught economics at Columbia University for many years and may be regarded as the leader of the Neo-Classical School of economists in the United States, gave an interesting series of diagrams on this subject. Labeled and somewhat simplified, these were as follows : [87]

[83] *Principles of Economics*, p. 318.
[84] *Ibid.*, p. 150. [85] *Ibid.*, p. 318. [86] *Ibid.*
[87] See *The Distribution of Wealth*, Chap. 13. Reproduced by permission of The Macmillan Company.

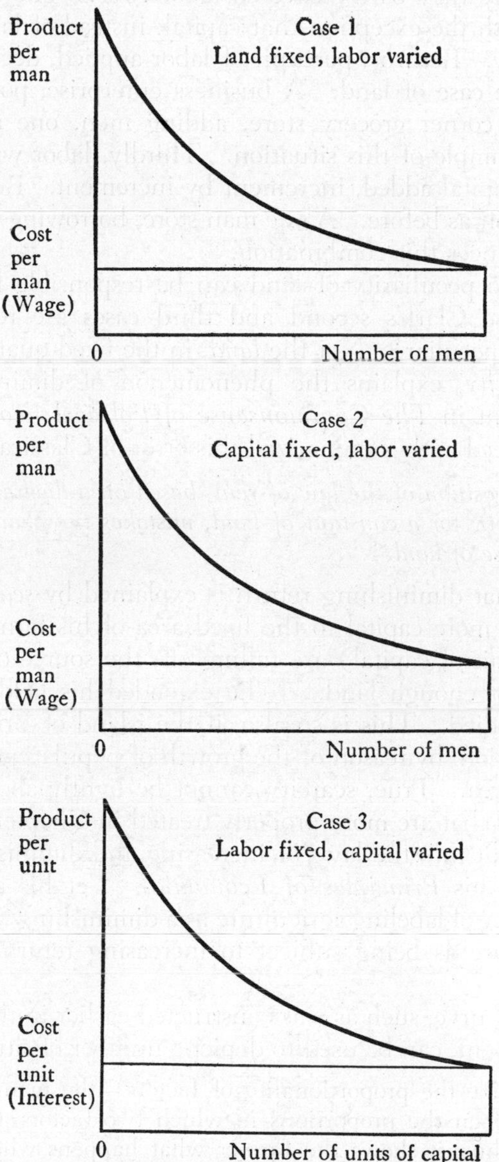

Except that Clark's figure included no early stage of increasing returns, the first graph is almost identical with that constructed from Turgot's statement and depicted in a previous section of this chapter. To a fixed quantity of land, labor was added, unit by unit, and the return (per unit of labor) declined as the quantity of labor was increased. Application ceased, at least under economic management, when returns had fallen to a point where they barely covered labor costs. The second diagram was similar, with the exception that capital, instead of land, was kept at a fixed quantity. Returns, per unit of labor applied, declined exactly as they did in the case of land. A business enterprise, possessing a fixed capital — say a corner grocery store, adding men, one after another — serves as an example of this situation. Thirdly, labor was kept fixed in quantity and capital added, increment by increment. Returns, per unit of capital, fell off as before. A one-man store, borrowing successive units of capital, instances this combination.

Evidently, no peculiarity of land can be responsible for diminishing returns, because Clark's second and third cases are realistic enough. What, then, is peculiar? Not the *land*, in the fixed quantity of this factor, but its *fixity*, explains the phenomenon of diminishing returns. Speaking of rent in *The Commonsense of Political Economy* (London 1910), Wicksteed aptly summarized this error of Classical economics:

The current exposition of the law of rent, based on a diagram of "decreasing returns" to labour, for a constant of land, mistakes the characteristics of the constant for those of land.[88]

The truth is that diminishing return is explained by *scarcity*. When a farmer, adding more capital to the fixed area of his farm, finds that his returns (per unit of capital) are falling off, the source of the trouble is that he has not enough land. If he extended his fields, the situation would be remedied. This is so also, if the island of Britain should get into a like position, by reason of the growth of population (and therefore labor) on its area. True, scarcity cannot be lightly abolished, but this raises questions that are more properly treated in Chapter IX.

Marshall went into the laws of increasing and diminishing returns in some detail in his *Principles of Economics*. Yet his adhesion to the Classical practice of labeling agriculture as a diminishing returns industry, and manufacture as being subject to increasing returns, led him into difficulties.

The returns curve, such as was constructed earlier in this chapter from Turgot's statement, can be used to depict a number of situations:

1. It may describe the proportionality of factors — the manner in which returns vary when the proportions in which two factors are combined are changed. Thus, it shows the farmer what happens when he uses more land and less labor in producing his crop.
2. It may refer to population: that is, it may indicate what happens to returns when the number of people on the fixed area of England increases. This, of course, is merely proportionality upon a larger scale.
3. It may be applicable to plant size. For example, it may show what is the effect upon returns of increasing the size of a farm or steel plant.

[88] Reprinted in 2 vols., London 1933, vol. 2, p. 550. Quoted by permission of George Routledge & Sons Ltd.

4. The third case can be extended, to cover size of firm, or to put the problem differently, how many plants per firm, that is, what is the best scale of financial or entrepreneural unit, as distinct from the technical unit called a plant? It must be remembered that some firms, especially large corporations, own numerous plants.

At times, Marshall appeared to confuse these various problems. In his contrast of agriculture with manufacture he was comparing two things entirely different. He believed that agriculture operated under conditions of diminishing returns because there his question was the first or the second of those listed above — quite commonly the second. Returns fell off, because, to obtain more produce, either inferior land had to be brought under cultivation, or land already farmed must receive more intensive tillage. But with manufacture, what often seemed to be in his mind was the third case. The economies of mass production came into play as the size of plant increased, lowering production costs. Against the Classical question of how returns from the land varied when population increased, and the agricultural industry was required to expand its operations, Marshall should have asked how the costs of manufactured cotton fared when the *cotton manufacturing industry* increased in scale. Instead, he seemed to inquire what resulted when *cotton factories* increased in size. Had he compared the two industries, he would have noticed that an expansion of cotton manufacture implied taking land from other uses, attracting labor from elsewhere, and taxing the capital supply to a greater extent, exactly as was the case with wheat. Wicksteed's comment on the matter is worth quotation:

In books on Political Economy our attention is called to the following facts. If successive doses or increments of labour (or labour and capital) are applied to a piece of land, we find that, at any rate after a certain point, doubling the amount of labour does not double the product. As we increase the amount of labour, therefore, each successive increment secures a smaller return in the shape of product. This is called the "law of diminishing returns," and is said to apply generally to agricultural and extractive industries. On the other hand, if an industry such as that of the cotton or iron trade so increases that, say, twice as much labour (or labour and capital) is employed on it as before, it will generally be found that the result is more than a doubled product. This is said to illustrate the "law of increasing returns," and to apply generally to manufactures.

When the statements are made thus baldly the reader can hardly fail to see that the two "laws" are in no sense co-ordinate, and cannot be regarded as standing side by side. . . The cases are not parallel. In stating the law of diminishing returns, it is assumed that the factor of land is constant, and if, when a number of factors co-operate to produce a result, you double some of them without doubling others, of course you cannot expect to double the result. If you double the pastry without doubling the apples, you do not double the pie. If you double the diners without doubling the dinner, or double the dinner without doubling the diners, you do not double the dining experience. In like manner if you double the land without doubling the operations on it, or double the operations without doubling the land, you cannot expect to double the crop. This principle would apply to manufactures just as much as to agriculture. If, for example, you had doubled the number of hands, retaining the same machinery and buildings, or if you had doubled the raw material without doubling the labour bestowed upon elaborating it, or if you had doubled the labour bestowed on the same raw material, you could in no case expect the exact doubling (or other proportionate increase) of the product. . . There are circumstances under which any of these operations might more than double the total result. If a business were desperately under-staffed or under-stocked, for instance, doubling the defective factor might more than double the effect of the whole; but if doubling any one of these factors without doubling the others exactly doubled the efficiency of the concern, it would only be a coincidence; and "after a certain point" it would certainly less than double it. The "law of diminishing returns," then, is really no more than an axiomatic statement of a universal principle that applies equally to all forms of industry, and to a great range of non-industrial experiences as well.[89]

This point was elaborated by other writers, contemporary with Wicksteed, notably H. J. Davenport and T. N. Carver in the United States of America.

Thus, after a century of service as a principle of population, the law of diminishing returns reappears where Turgot had placed it, as a question of proportionality of productive factors. Indeed, some economists, such as Davenport, have given it this name. But Turgot dealt only with the capital-land ratio. Modern economists deal, not merely with the proportions of capital, labor, and land that are combined together in the productive process, but with other questions such as size of plant and scale of firm.

Summary of Chapter

At all times men have asked questions concerning the relative merits of different forms of activity: how did this or that occupation accord with the ultimate end of human endeavor? The ancient philosophers, the teachers of the early Church, and the Mercantilists answered such inquires in their several ways.

With the emergence of modern economics in the eighteenth and early nineteenth centuries, however, a controversy developed whose connection with ethical judgments was less evident. The study of wealth led to that of the production of wealth and so economists asked what employments could be classed as productive. The French Physiocrats believed that the word "productive" should be reserved for occupations which brought forth a *surplus above maintenance*, and they thought that the

[89] *Ibid.*, pp. 527-529.

cultivation of land alone was in this position. While offering a compromise, Adam Smith set up a different test. Only where the product possessed *lasting power* should labor be called productive, he argued. But his successors insisted that all activities that satisfied human wants should be designated as productive and – though not without opposition from some Romantic writers – this view has been accepted widely since.

Closely connected with the last problem has been the question of what factors are responsible for production. Land and labor were in that position, according to Petty. Land alone should receive credit, the Physiocrats believed, while a long series of writers – many of them socialists – have asserted that only labor was productive. Several explanations have been offered for the inclusion of capital. Certain economists, notably Alfred Marshall, have made a case for a fourth factor, namely "organization" or "enterprise."

Perhaps the most absorbing topic studied under the heading of production has been that of laws of returns. Suggested as early as the *Book of Genesis* and of special interest to writers on population at different times, the so-called law of diminishing returns has played an important part in the history of economic ideas. Against it, Petty and others put forward a law or tendency to increasing returns. In recent years there has been considerable clarification of thought in this field. The static and dynamic aspects of the laws have been distinguished and it has been made clear that they are not merely applicable to the ratio of labor or capital to land, but to such other problems as the size of the industrial plant and the scale of the business enterprise.

CHAPTER IX

VALUE

It is a commonplace of economics that exchange is necessary only in so far as production has passed beyond the self-sufficing basis and has become specialized. Accordingly, since the trend has been in the direction of increased specialization and interdependence, it can be said that exchange has become progressively more significant. This statement needs some qualification, however, because development has not been uniformly in one direction. Moreover, even in the twentieth century, there are immense gaps in the exchange system. One of the principal social units of the present time — the family — operates almost entirely on communistic principles. Each member contributes according to his or her capacity and the produce is shared according to needs. In the usual case, the father works outside the home, while the mother performs the duties associated with the household, and the children are reared at the expense of the parents until they are able to fend for themselves. In turn, perhaps, the parents are taken care of in old age by their children.

But, outside the family, many transfers take place on a gift and return-gift basis. Notwithstanding that the larders of the two families are equally well stocked, the Smiths accept an invitation to dinner with the Browns and invite the latter to their own home in due course. Numerous people spend considerable time before Christmas selecting presents for friends who could do as well — if not better — for themselves, realizing that the latter are engaged in similar activity. Formally, the gifts are made without any relation to return, yet nothing is more familiar than the annual revision of gift lists for the purpose of deleting the names of those who neglected to remember the donor the year before.

The fact of exchange raises the problem of valuation. On what basis are commodities to be exchanged for each other? A specialist manufacturer of arrow-heads or shoes exchanges his product for the catch of a fisherman. The rate of exchange of arrow-heads against fishes settles how many hours the maker of the former must spend in chipping stones in order that he may eat his fill.

As was seen in Chapter IV, from early times means have existed through which the division of incomes based upon rates of exchange (like the arrow-head : fish transaction just mentioned) has been altered or supplemented in some way or other, by taxation, public relief, charity, etc. But exchange has furnished the primary method of distributing incomes for large groups of the population, especially in recent times. Valuation is fundamental to much of what appears in the chapters dealing with distribution. The price of land in terms of other things (that is, its *value*) represents the income of the landowner in modern society; the price of capital, that of the capitalist; the price of labor, the income of the working man; and only in the light of ideas on price or value can distribution theories be understood.

Exchange and Valuation in Primitive Communities

From time to time statements are met to the effect that barter is the standard form of primitive exchange, but this is very far from being the case. Malinowski lists no fewer than seven ways of transferring goods and services among the Melanesian Islanders, where his studies were conducted: (1) pure gifts, made without hope of reward, such as the presents of a father to his children; (2) customary transferences, repaid irregularly and without strict equivalence, exemplified by the food that custom decrees should be given after harvest by the cultivator to his wife's brothers; (3) recompense for services rendered, for example, those of a magician; (4) gifts that are returned in an economically equivalent form, though the equivalence may not be exact—the gift and return-gift arrangement mentioned above; (5) exchange of goods against privileges, titles, and non-material possessions, like the right to execute a particular dance; (6) ceremonial barter, with deferred payment—a peculiar social custom of the Melanesian Islanders; (7) ordinary trade on a barter basis, such as takes place between the inhabitants of agricultural or fishing villages and the makers of ornaments—the latter group being regarded, incidentally, with great disdain by the former.[1] While other investigators, in different localities, could prepare classifications showing considerable variation from that of Malinowski, the list serves to illustrate the complexity of primitive exchange. Sometimes it is found that transactions are unheard of in primitive communities, in respect of things that are quite commonly bought and sold in advanced societies. Thus there was no thought of trade in land among the South African Bantu before white settlement. On the other hand, primitive people are found buying and selling under circumstances where commercial exchange is not customary in civilized society, like the instance mentioned in Chapter IV of a young American Indian purchasing from his mother the right to use a ceremonial paint. In some of the types of exchange mentioned, there is an obvious necessity for some system of valuation. In others, all idea of valuation of the commodity exchanged is ruled out. What appears on the surface to be barter on commercial lines in fact may be quite different. Thus, Firth, writing on the customs of the New Zealand Maori, declared in connection with exchange among these people that the use of the word *barter* is misleading:

[1] Malinowski, B., *Argonauts of the Western Pacific*, Chap. 6.

Barter essentially implies some agreement as to the rates of exchange, a practice quite foreign to the Maori mode of conducting matters. No stipulation was made by the donor as to the amount of the commodity which must be given in exchange, and no bargaining or haggling of any kind took place. Such would not be *tika* ("correct"), to all appearances the affair was one of gift for gift.[2]

Firth explained that the usual plan in this form of exchange was to make a present and convey, by some means or other, a hint of what was desired in return. No equivalence was laid down and to expect this was not in accordance with Maori ideas of what was right and proper. Return gifts, indeed, were often more lavish than those which had preceded them, so that the giver should appear to have more than fulfilled his obligation. It would be wrong, however, to conclude from this that the savage has no idea of valuation. He has his standards for things that are familiar to him. Gifts are often keenly appraised by their recipients, even though custom demands that they shall appear to be ignored when they are made. Open-handed generosity is not pushed too far. Firth recounts a story of a Maori who used to frequent a path along which neighboring fishermen returned home with their catches. He hailed the passers-by with the declaration, "I am very fond of that food," when, in accordance with local custom, it was handed to him. The frequency of such incidents aroused resentment among the villagers, who raised a war party and slew him. Apparently Maori etiquette preferred this violent method of ending his importunities to refusing him food, which shows the strength of a social custom of generosity. To give unwillingly or to refuse to give at all was looked upon as disreputable. Yet there must be some form of reciprocity, or at least no unreasonable frequency in the occasions which called for gifts, or trouble ensued. African travelers have many times recounted how gifts made in accordance with custom on the occasion of a visit, while seemingly neglected by the recipient at the time, were in fact shrewdly estimated. Observers who are acquainted with primitive people tell stories of the almost unlimited patience displayed by a colored bargainer and of his willingness to walk several miles for the purpose of securing an article at a lower rate. This, at least, is the case in southern Africa. So here, as well as elsewhere, there is found to be considerable difficulty in fitting primitive people into a simple pattern.

The Ancient World

In Chapter I it was noticed how, from the self-sufficing primitive social units of an earlier time, specialized industry and commerce emerged in the Mediterranean countries. The Phœnicians were notable traders and

[2] Firth, R., *Primitive Economics of the New Zealand Maori,* p. 403.

in some instances trafficked very far afield. Not only did they, like the Greeks, settle at various points on the shores of the Mediterranean Sea, but they even reached Britain on their voyages. The eastern Mediterranean, especially, became an important trading area, the products of one portion being exchanged for those of another. In addition to this inter-area trade, there was considerable local exchange. City-dwellers had to buy their food from outside, and one specialized craftsman or professional worker exchanged his product for that of another.

The unfavorable comments made by Plato and Aristotle on the subject of trade have been noticed. But the fact of its existence had to be recognized and the Greek philosophers showed the same ethical approach to the problem of valuation as was displayed in other portions of their economic and political writings. Plato—who seemed to regard value as something inherent in a commodity—taught that the profits of retail trade should be regulated. This function he assigned to the guardians or administrators of his State:

> the guardians of the law should meet and take counsel with those who have experience of the several kinds of retail trade, as we before commanded concerning adulteration (which is a matter akin to this), and when they meet they shall consider what amount of receipts, after deducting expenses, will produce a moderate gain to the retail trades, and they shall fix in writing and strictly maintain what they find to be the right percentage of profit. . . And so retail trade will benefit every one, and do the least possible injury to those in the state who practise it.[3]

Aristotle distinguished between use and exchange, between use value and exchange value, and spoke of exchange as arising naturally:

> For example, a shoe is used for wear, and is used for exchange; both are uses of the shoe. . . The same may be said of all possessions, for the art of exchange extends to all of them, and it arises at first from what is natural, from the circumstance that some have too little, others too much.[4]

Exchange should be *fair* or *just*, Aristotle said. Of what was just, he appeared to offer two criteria. First, there was a suggestion that the utilities of the commodities to the buyers and sellers respectively should be taken into account: "the just is intermediate between a sort of gain and a sort of loss . . . it consists in having an equal amount before and after the transaction."[5] Second, the labor-time involved in production was brought in, allowing for the difference in social status of the producers, for the problem of distributive justice was "to divide the distributable honour or reward into parts which are to one another as are the merits of

[3] *The Dialogues of Plato*, vol. 5, *Laws*, p. 307.
[4] *The Works of Aristotle*, vol. 10, *Politica*, 1257a.
[5] *Ibid.*, vol. 9, *Ethica Nicomachea*, 1132b.

the persons who are to participate."[6] Aristotle's statement on the subject was as follows:

Now proportionate return is secured by cross-conjunction. . . The builder, then, must get from the shoemaker the latter's work, and must himself give him in return his own. If, then, first there is proportionate equality of goods, and then reciprocal action takes place, the result we mention will be effected. If not, the bargain is not equal, and does not hold; for there is nothing to prevent the work of the one being better than that of the other; they must therefore be equated. (And this is true of the other arts also. . .) For it is not two doctors that associate for exchange, but a doctor and a farmer, or in general people who are different and unequal; but these must be equated. . . There will, then, be reciprocity when the terms have been equated so that as farmer is to shoemaker, the amount of the shoemaker's work is to that of the farmer's work for which it exchanges.[7]

As this passage is far from lucid, the explanation furnished by W. D. Ross, Aristotle's translator, may be examined:

The working of 'proportionate reciprocity' is not very clearly described by Aristotle, but seems to be as follows. A and B are workers in different trades, and will normally be of different degrees of 'worth'. Their products, therefore, will also have unequal worth, i.e. (though Aristotle does not expressly reduce the question to one of time) if $A = nB$, C (what A makes, say, in an hour) will be worth n times as much as D (what B makes in an hour). A fair exchange will then take place if A gets nD and B gets 1C; i.e. if A gives what it takes him an hour to make, in exchange for what it takes B n hours to make.[8]

This was the basis of Aquinas's teachings on *just price,* at a later date.

Both Plato and Aristotle were considering what *should be,* not *what was,* and their doctrines have been hailed by some as forerunners of the "just price" theory of the middle ages.

Roman law appears to have made prices a matter of free bargaining, for the most part, though the rescript of Diocletian about the year 300 is sometimes mentioned as evidence to the contrary. However, it is now fairly clear that Diocletian's action was neither new nor of the significance that some historians have implied. Under both Domitian (Emperor 81–96) and Marcus Aurelius (Emperor 161–180), certain prices were regulated in time of scarcity, and the example appears to have been followed from time to time in later reigns. Except perhaps temporarily, the control measures do not seem to have been very effective.[9]

[6] *Ibid.,* 1131b, Editor's footnote.

[7] *Ibid.,* vol. 9, *Ethica Nicomachea,* p. 1133a.

[8] *Ibid.*

[9] See M. Rostovtzeff, *The Social and Economic History of the Roman Empire,* Oxford 1926, p. 463.

Christian Ideas to the Reformation

The Early Christian Teachings

Characteristic of the medieval Christian attitude on value was the conception of a "just price," which should be fair to both parties in the transaction. St. Paul had exhorted:

Furthermore then we beseech you, brethren, and exhort you by the Lord Jesus. . . That no man go beyond and defraud his brother in any matter: because that the Lord is the avenger of all such, as we also have forewarned you and testified.[10]

Lactantius taught that the buyer should inform the seller of any good qualities possessed by the articles offered him, that were unknown to the seller, while the latter should reveal defects in the commodities that he offered for sale:

by these things it appears that he is the wisest man who prefers to perish rather than to commit an injury, that he may preserve that sense of duty by which he is distinguished from the dumb creation. For he who does not point out the error of one who is offering the gold for sale, in order that he may buy it for a small sum, or he who does not avow that he is offering for sale a runaway slave or an infected house, having an eye to his own gain or advantage, is not a wise man . . . but crafty and cunning. Now craftiness and cunning exist in the dumb animals also: either when they lie in wait for others . . . or when they avoid the snares of others in various ways. But wisdom falls to man alone. For wisdom is understanding either with the purpose of doing that which is good and right, or for the abstaining from improper words and deeds. Now a wise man never gives himself to the pursuit of gain, because he despises these earthly advantages: nor does he allow any one to be deceived, because it is the duty of a good man to correct the errors of men. . .[11]

It is commonly said that the early Fathers did not try to discover any theoretical basis for valuation. This is not altogether correct. Tertullian, notably, did so. Discussing female dress, this teacher said that things were valued or prized for their scarcity:

It is only from their rarity and outlandishness that all these things possess their grace; in short, within their own native limits they are not held of so high worth. Abundance is always contumelious toward itself. There are some barbarians with whom, because gold is indigenous and plentiful, it is customary to keep (the criminals) in their convict establishments chained with gold, and to lade the wicked with riches — the more guilty, the more wealthy.[12]

[10] *Thessalonians* I, 4, vv. 1-6.
[11] *Ante-Nicene Christian Library,* vol. 21, *The Divine Institutes,* p. 334.
[12] *Ibid.,* vol. 11, *On Female Dress,* p. 311.

Religious Thought at the Close of the Medieval Period

But it was left to Albertus and Aquinas to consider the subject more fully. Following Aristotle, they adopted the concept of labor-cost. Though Aquinas did not define cost in any precise manner, he made it clear that the parties to an exchange should be remunerated in accordance with their position in society. In other words, *custom* and *status* were taken as the standard of justice. Here, also, Aquinas appeared to be following Aristotle; but his ideas were in full accord with medieval sentiment, which regarded justice in terms of the hierarchy of classes that was characteristic of the then-existing social system.

Considering the question of whether the same principle of justice should apply in both distribution and exchange—*i.e.*, whether *fair* or *just wages* should be governed by the same rules as regulated *just prices* —Aquinas laid it down that

> in distributive justice a person receives all the more of the common goods, according as he holds a more prominent position in the community. This prominence in an aristocratic community is gauged according to virtue, in an oligarchy according to wealth, in a democracy according to liberty, and in various ways according to various forms of community. Hence in distributive justice the mean is observed, not according to equality between thing and thing, but according to proportion between things and persons: in such a way that even as one person surpasses another, so that which is given to one person surpasses that which is allotted to another. . . On the other hand in commutations [*i.e.*, exchanges] something is delivered to an individual on account of something of his that has been received, as may be seen chiefly in selling and buying. . . Hence it is necessary to equalize thing with thing, so that the one person should pay back to the other just so much as he has become richer out of that which belonged to the other.[13]

Aquinas may have had in mind some conception of the varying utility of a commodity to different individuals—a point mentioned later—when he wrote the second of these passages. If so, he qualified it immediately by another reference to the social station of the exchangers:

> In actions and passions a person's station affects the quantity of a thing: for it is a greater injury to strike a prince than a private person. Hence in distributive justice a person's station is considered in itself, whereas in commutative justice it is considered in so far as it causes a diversity of things.[14]

Exactly what Aquinas meant by this statement is not clear but at least the station of the exchangers was mentioned, even in respect of "commutative justice," which referred to sale prices. Brief reflection is enough to show that in an exchange economy the two forms of justice are closely associated, because incomes (distributive justice) are determined by the

[13] *Summa theologica*, Pt. 2, Second Pt., Q. 61, Art. 2. [14] *Ibid.*

prices received from the sale of the commodities produced (commutative justice) and medieval practice gave full recognition to this. The "just price" of Aquinas and his contemporaries was the price that was adequate, but no more than adequate, to cover costs of production as based on the accustomed standards of living of the producers concerned.

Elsewhere Aquinas elaborated his ideas on lines not greatly different from those of Lactantius. Sellers should reveal any defects that had come to their knowledge in the commodities sold and, even where they were ignorant of the existence of defects, they were none the less to make restitution if these came to light afterwards. In determining the "just price" — and this represents an advance on the earlier teacher — both the loss suffered by the seller from parting with the commodity and the gain the buyer derived from its acquisition were to be taken into account :

we may speak of buying and selling, considered as accidentally tending to the advantage of one party, and to the disadvantage of the other : for instance, when a man has great need of a certain thing, while another man will suffer if he be without it. In such a case the just price will depend not only on the thing sold, but on the loss which the sale brings on the seller. And thus it will be lawful to sell a thing for more than it is worth in itself [whatever this means — probably its production cost on the basis already indicated] though the price paid be not more than it is worth to the owner. Yet if the one man derive a great advantage by becoming possessed of the other man's property, and the seller be not at a loss through being without that thing, the latter ought not to raise the price, because the advantage accruing to the buyer, is not due to the seller, but to a circumstance affecting the buyer. Now no man should sell what is not his, though he may charge for the loss he suffers. On the other hand if a man find that he derives great advantage from something he has bought, he may, of his own accord, pay the seller something over and above : and this pertains to his honesty.[15]

Here Aquinas clearly recognized that the usefulness of the article exchanged might be greater to one of the parties than to the other and thought that justice would be done by some kind of compromise. Evidently, what were at stake were the producer's and consumer's surpluses of modern economic terminology. Further, he admitted that the "just price" could not be determined with any great precision :

the just price of things is not fixed with mathematical precision, but depends on a kind of estimate, so that a slight addition or subtraction would not seem to destroy the equality of justice.[16]

In conclusion, Aquinas gave an opinion on the legitimacy of windfall capital profits arising with the passage of time, and of gains due to exchange transactions :

[15] *Ibid.*, Q. 77, Art. 1.

[16] *Ibid.*

if he sells at a higher price something that has changed for the better, he would seem to receive the reward of his labour. . . If . . . he buys not for sale but for possession, and afterwards, for some reason wishes to sell, it is not a trade transaction even if he sell at a profit. For he may lawfully do this, either because he has bettered the thing, or because the value of the thing has changed with the change of place or time, or on account of the danger he incurs in transferring the thing from one place to another, or again in having it carried by another.[17]

As the middle ages gave place to modern times, Church teachers did much to reconcile the doctrine of "just price" with the needs of an expanding commerce. Long before, Chrysostom had justified profit from trading in cases where the commodity was transformed. Alexander of Hales, in the thirteenth century, did the same in respect of goods that were transported. By this time, also, risk had become generally accepted as a title to mercantile gain. The Englishman, Richard of Middleton, said that goods were appreciated more where they were scarce than where they were plentiful (a modern writer would argue that they possess a greater marginal utility where they are scarce). The merchant, who bought at the local price that was looked upon as "just" in an area of plenty, and sold at the "just price" in a deficit area, made a profit on the transaction, it is true. But Richard believed that this merchant was performing a useful service and that his gain could not be regarded as a sinful one.[18] Duns Scotus took much the same view. As long as profits were in keeping with the merchant's station in life and there was no fraud, remuneration was legitimate, he believed. In Italy Bernardin of Siena (1380–1444) and Antoninus, Archbishop of Florence (1389–1459), justified prices that allowed for risks and the utilities of time and place. As a result, the old idea of a "just price" as something inherent in the commodity passed away and, in its stead, appeared a value that was more flexible and more in accordance with modern thought. Antoninus, indeed, recognized different levels of "just price," of which the higher might be charged in respect of credit sales. As a juristic conception, however, the ethical price was fighting a losing battle. Medieval regulation gave place to Mercantilism and this, in turn, to individualistic competition.

Medieval Price Data

An examination of historical records is enlightening. A large number of transactions in the middle ages consisted of those in which the producer dealt directly with the consumer. Agriculturists carried surplus produce to market for sale to townsmen. Craftsmen prepared articles to

[17] *Ibid.*, Q. 77, Art. 4.

[18] For an account of the views of Richard on trade and price, see M. Beer, *Early British Economics from the XIIIth to the middle of the XVIIIth century*, London 1938, pp. 40-43.

order or carried only a small stock of goods of their own making, which they sold to customers as these came along. What was at issue in such cases was whether either party should be permitted to enrich himself at the other's expense. Aquinas argued, in effect, that price should not be determined by the accidents of immediate need on either side but that it should satisfy the accepted canons of justice. A man in his bargains should follow the Christian way of life and should not endeavor to profit by another's misfortunes. Justice was done, Aquinas thought, if prices were such that the parties concerned could maintain their accustomed standards of life. The only form of government regulation that Aquinas himself appears to have recommended was that of weights and measures, but the inevitable result of the general acceptance of the Christian position on "just price," in a world where human frailty led to frequent departures from it in practice, was that municipalities, gilds, and even central governments interfered in the market in various ways. In England, where at that time the national government was more important than in some other countries, the great staples of life — bread and ale — were given attention by this authority. Assizes or courts, supported by royal authority from 1202, laid down the price of the loaf on a sliding scale governed by variations in the price of grain. But, even in England, much of the regulation was local. Craft gilds prescribed standards of quality and schedules of prices, often subject to municipal approval, employing officials or searchers to see that these were observed. Yet trade in many articles could not be controlled in this way. It was an underlying assumption of the common law[19] that the free workings of competition would result in a measure of fairness to the parties concerned. Actions in restraint of trade, including engrossing (which would be called "cornering" today), forestalling (*i.e.*, buying up commodities on their way to market), and regrating (purchase for resale in the same market)[20] were forbidden.

In fact, notwithstanding the general opinion that medieval prices were governed by custom and regulation, market conditions had much to do with determining prices. Reference to the tables published by the English economic historian, J. E. Thorold Rogers, in his *History of Agriculture and Prices in England* (1259–1793) (7 vols., Oxford 1866–1902), will demonstrate this. There were periods of relative scarcity and plenty in the middle ages, just as in modern times. Indeed, because of difficulties of transport, unusually favorable or unfavorable weather conditions seem to have had a greater effect than at present in the areas affected by

[19] *i.e.*, law that has grown up by usage, as distinct from statute law, based on formal acts of the governing body.

[20] But see W. G. Ashley, *An Introduction to English Economic History and Theory*, 2 vols., London 1888–1893, vol. 1, p. 182, for earlier usage of these words.

them. The result was seen at times in very wide price variations, of which the following is an example :[21]

Average Prices of Grain per Quarter in 1287 and 1290*						
	Wheat	*Barley*	*Oats*	*Beans*	*Peas*	*Rye*
English currency — shillings and pence						
1287 1290	2*s*. 10*d*. 6*s*. 5*d*.	2*s*. 6*d*. 4*s*. 6*d*.	1*s*. 6*d*. 2*s*. 7*d*.	1*s*. 10*d*. 4*s*. 4*d*.	2*s*. 0*d*. 4*s*. 0*d*.	2*s*. 3*d*. 5*s*. 7*d*.
Equivalent in present-day U. S. currency at par — dollars						
1287 1290	.68 1.54	.60 1.08	.36 .62	.44 1.04	.48 .96	.54 1.34
* Years of plenty and of dearth respectively.						

Even with respect to wages, considerable fluctuations were not unknown. Rogers declared that

> The immediate effect of the Plague [*i.e.*, the Black Death in the middle of the fourteenth century] was to double the wages of labour ; in some districts, to raise the rate even beyond this.[22]

The year-to-year piece rates shown by Rogers sometimes displayed marked variation. For instance, $2\frac{1}{2}$*d*. was paid in the east of England for threshing a quarter of wheat in 1298 and 4d. in 1299, though mostly the changes were less than this. It is worth mentioning, however, that at the time of the Black Death the government took measures to deal with the situation, ordering laborers to serve out the terms of their contracts at the old figure. Ultimately, however, wages appear to have risen by about 50 per cent, the regulatory measures proving ineffective in view of the scarcity of labor.

In the light of these data, it appears that in practice the factors of custom and "just price" may have been less significant in valuation at the close of the middle ages than has been commonly believed, and that such exhortations as those of Aquinas were aimed not only at regulatory authorities but at private people in their dealings, with a view to bringing them nearer to the Christian standard than they might have been otherwise.

[21] *A History of Agriculture and Prices in England*, vol. 1, pp. 228-229. Quoted by permission of the Oxford University Press.

[22] *Ibid.*, p. 265.

Competitive Pricing in the Modern World

The decline of scholastic authority, the escape of industry and trade from gild and Mercantilist regulation, and the accompanying rise of competition, had their logical result on value theory in the attempts made by various economic writers to construct a theory of competitive valuation.

Early Theories

Mention should be made first of Nicholas Barbon. Treating "Of the Value and Price of Wares" in *A Discourse of Trade,* published in 1690, this writer advanced what was in the main a utility theory:

> The Value of all Wares arise from their Use; Things of no Use, have no Value, as the *English* Phrase is, *They are good for nothing.*
>
> The Use of Things, are to supply the Wants and Necessities of Man: There are Two General Wants that Mankind is born with; the Wants of the Body, and the Wants of the Mind; To supply these two Necessities, all things under the Sun become useful, and therefore have a Value.[23]

Price was a matter of supply and demand according to Barbon; demand itself being determined by utility:

> The Price of Wares is the present Value; And ariseth by Computing the occasions or use for them, with the Quantity to serve that Occasion; for the Value of things depending on the use of them, the *Over-pluss* of Those Wares, which are more than can be used, become worth nothing; So that Plenty, in respect of the occasion, makes things cheap; and Scarcity, dear.[24]

Locke wrote on similar lines in *Some Considerations of the Lowering of Interest and Raising the Value of Money* (London 1691):

> The vent [*i.e.,* sale] of any thing depends upon its necessity or usefulness; as convenience or opinion, guided by fancy, or fashion, shall determine. The vent of any commodity comes to be increased, or decreased, as a greater part of the running cash of the nation is designed to be laid out, by several people at the same time, rather in that, than another; as we see in the change of fashions.[25]

After a statement of the quantity theory of money, which is given attention in Chapter XIV of this book, Locke passed on to distinguish between goods absolutely necessary to life and those which were less necessary. It is possible that he had it in mind that the demand for the former was inelastic and for the latter more or less elastic, but his words do not make this altogether clear:

> There is nothing more confirmed, by daily experience, than that men give any portion of money for whatsoever is absolutely necessary, rather than go

[23] *Op. cit.,* pp. 13-14. [24] *Ibid.,* p. 15.

[25] *The Works of John Locke,* vol. 5, pp. 30-31.

without it. And in such things, the scarcity of them alone makes their prices. As for example : let us suppose half an ounce of silver, or half a crown now in England, is worth a bushel of wheat : but should there be next year a great scarcity of wheat in England, and a proportionable want of all other food, five ounces of silver would, perhaps, in exchange purchase but one bushel of wheat : so that money would be then nine-tenths less worth in respect of food, though at the same value it was before, in respect of other things, that kept their former proportion, in their quantity and consumption. By the like proportions, of increase and decrease, does the value of things, more or less convenient, rise and fall, in respect of money; only with this difference, that things absolutely necessary for life must be had at any rate; but things convenient will be had only as they stand in preference with other conveniences. . .[26]

John Law's explanation is of some interest, if only for his use of the water-diamond comparison made famous subsequently by Adam Smith. Treating of "How goods are valued," in Chapter 1 of his *Money and Trade Consider'd; with a Proposal for Supplying the Nation with Money* (Glasgow 1705, 2nd ed., London 1720), Law said :

Goods have a Value from the Uses they are apply'd to; and their Value is Greater or Lesser, not so much from their more or less valuable, or necessary Uses : as from the greater or lesser Quantity of them in proportion to the Demand for them. *Example.* Water is of great use, yet of little Value; because the Quantity of Water is much greater than the Demand for it. Diamonds are of little use, yet of great Value, because the Demand for Diamonds is much greater, than the Quantity of them. Goods of the same kind differ in Value, from any difference in their Quality. . . Goods change their Value, from any Change in their Quantity, or in the Demand for them. *(Ex.)* If Oats be in greater Quantity than last year, and the Demand the same, or lesser, Oats will be less valuable.[27]

Crude and short as were the ideas of Barbon, Locke, and Law, they contained the germs of later theory.

Another theory of some interest for the manner in which it foreshadowed later ideas was that of the Physiocrat, Turgot. Turgot said that if a man could choose between objects appropriate to his use, he would prefer one to another and allow in his mind for the difference in their values. Values (by which Turgot meant utilities) were not fixed but changed from one moment to another, according to variation in need. Turgot illustrated this by saying that when a savage was hungry, he would think more of a morsel of game than of many bears' skins, but when his hunger was satisfied and he became cold, the skins would seem to him to be more precious. Secondly, Turgot remarked, not merely present needs but those of the future were taken into account. Thirdly, came difficulty of attainment. As between two things of equal utility,

[26] *Ibid.*, p. 31.

[27] 2nd ed., p. 4.

the higher value would be attributed to that which was more difficult to procure. This, Turgot commented, was the reason why water, notwithstanding its usefulness, was not regarded as valuable in well-watered countries, though in deserts it had an infinite value. Turgot proceeded to say that exchange resulted from the different positions of men in relation to commodities. Savages, with more fish than they could eat, exchanged with others who had skins in plenty but nothing to eat, to the mutual satisfaction of the exchangers. The seller of fish gained utility, because his surplus and hitherto useless fish procured him the skins he needed to keep his warm, while the seller of skins was in the opposite position.

In this discussion Turgot came close to the theory advanced by Walras and Jevons afterwards but, as he did not bring in the principle of diminishing utility, he failed to give his theory the precision of that of later writers.

The Cost of Production Theory of Cantillon and Smith

In the theories that have been mentioned above, an endeavor was made to explain value in terms of market factors, but inquiring minds soon began to probe behind temporary market circumstances in an attempt to explain value. Quite early, cost of production was suggested as the reason behind price differences. Cantillon adopted this explanation. He said that market prices were in the first instance determined by the supply and demand immediately forthcoming :

> Suppose the Butchers on one side and the Buyers on the other. The price of Meat will be settled after some altercations, and a pound of Beef will be in value to a piece of silver pretty nearly as the whole Beef offered for sale in the Market is to all the silver brought there to buy Beef. This proportion is come at by bargaining. The Butcher keeps up his Price according to the number of Buyers he sees; the Buyers, on their side, offer less according as they think the Butcher will have less sale : the Price set by some is usually followed by others. Some are more clever in puffing up their wares, other in running them down. Though this method of fixing Market prices has no exact or geometrical foundation, since it often depends upon the eagerness or easy temperament of a few Buyers or Sellers, it does not seem that it could be done in any more convenient way. It is clear that the quantity of Produce or of Merchandise offered for sale, in proportion to the demand or number of Buyers, is the basis on which is fixed or always supposed to be fixed the actual Market Prices; and that in general these prices do not vary much from the intrinsic value.[28]

Cantillon spoke of commodities having an "intrinsic value." Defining what he called the "Price or intrinsic value" of a thing as "the measure of the quantity of Land and of Labour entering into its production, hav-

[28] *Essai sur la nature du commerce en générale,* pp. 117-119.

with these more useful commodities : for whatever bread is worth more than acorns, wine than water, and cloth or silk, than leaves, skins, or moss, that is wholly owing to labour and industry : the one of these being the food and raiment which unassisted nature furnishes us with : the other, provisions which our industry and pains prepare for us; which how much they exceed the other in value, when any one hath computed, he will then see how much labour makes the far greatest part of the value of things we enjoy in this world : and the ground which produces the materials, is scarce to be reckoned in, as any, or, at most, but a very small part of it : so little, that even amongst us, land that is left wholly to nature, that hath no improvement of pasturage, tillage, or planting, is called, as indeed it is, waste; and we shall find the benefit of it amount to little more than nothing. . .

It is labour then which puts the greatest part of the value upon land, without which it would scarcely be worth any thing : it is to that we owe the greatest part of all its useful products; for all that the straw, bran, bread, of that acre of wheat, is worth more than the product of an acre of as good land, which lies waste, is all the effect of labour. . .[34]

Thus land in its natural state, according to Locke, was worth practically nothing. He came to this conclusion, apparently, from examining the "waste," or common land, which still existed in large tracts in Britain when he wrote. He ignored completely the aspect which later was to interest Ricardo, namely that land lay waste because it was infertile or unfavorably located, and that part of the product of cultivated soil was the result of the superior quality or situation of the latter.

Capital Locke dealt with by explaining that it was *past labor,* that is, labor that had been incorporated in the past in instruments or other equipment :

it is not barely the ploughman's pains, the reaper's and thresher's toil, and the baker's sweat, is to be counted into the bread we eat; the labour of those who broke the oxen, who digged and wrought the iron and stones, who felled and framed the timber employed about the plough, mill, oven, or any other utensils, which are a vast number, requisite to this corn, from its being seed to be sown, to its being made bread, must all be charged on the account of labour, and received as an effect of that. . . It would be a strange "catalogue of things, that industry provided and made use of, about every loaf of bread," before it came to our use, if we could trace them; iron, wood, leather, bark, timber, stone, bricks, coals, lime, cloth, dyeing, drugs, pitch, tar, masts, ropes, and all the materials made use of in the ship, that brought any of the commodities used by any of the workmen, to any part of the work : all which it would be almost impossible, at least too long, to reckon up.[35]

Locke's labor theory of value as presented in his *Two Treatises,* quoted above, may seem at first sight inconsistent with his supply and demand theory of price, set out in *Some Considerations of the Lowering*

[34] *The Works of John Locke,* vol. 5, pp. 362-363.
[35] *Ibid.,* p. 363.

of Interest and Raising the Value of Money, mentioned earlier in this chapter. But the difference is more apparent than real, because in the pamphlet on interest Locke was obviously considering market value, whereas in the *Two Treatises* he was reaching towards something more fundamental. Probably it can be said that his position was similar to that of Cantillon and even Marshall : over short periods he thought that market demand and supply were the significant factors in determining price, but, over longer periods, cost of production (which with Locke was mainly labor) was the important influence.

Adam Smith. Smith said that labor was the ultimate standard of value :

Every man is rich or poor according to the degree in which he can afford to enjoy the necessaries, conveniencies, and amusements of human life. But after the division of labour has once thoroughly taken place, it is but a very small part of these with which a man's own labour can supply him. The far greater part of them he must derive from the labour of other people, and he must be rich or poor according to the quantity of that labour which he can command, or which he can afford to purchase. The value of any commodity, therefore, to the person who possesses it, and who means not to use or consume it himself, but to exchange it for other commodities, is equal to the quantity of labour which it enables him to purchase or command. Labour, therefore, is the real measure of the exchangeable value of all commodities. The real price of every thing, what every thing really costs to the man who wants to acquire it, is the toil and trouble of acquiring it. What every thing is really worth to the man who has acquired it, and who wants to dispose of it or exchange it for something else, is the toil and trouble which it can save to himself, and which it can impose upon other people. What is bought with money or with goods is purchased by labour, as much as what we acquire by the toil of our own body.[36]

While the general drift of Smith's argument is clear, analysis shows some confusion. The writer once heard of a doctor who, owed ten dollars for a minor operation performed on an impecunious carpenter, accepted payment in the form of repairs to his home. The operation, as described by the carpenter, took twenty minutes of the doctor's time : the repairs occupied two days of that of the carpenter. The two were exchanged voluntarily and at standard rates, so presumably they were of equal value. What was this value in terms of labor, twenty minutes or two days ? Or should the criterion be the lengths of time that would have been taken by the respective parties to do their own jobs ? The doctor guessed that he might have repaired his house in a couple of weeks but agreed that, at best, he would have performed the task in an inferior manner. The carpenter, on the other hand, admitted that he could not have operated on himself at all. Here there are four possibil-

[36] *Wealth of Nations,* Bk. 1., Chap. 5.

ities of labor value — twenty minutes, two days, a couple of weeks, and something which is entirely unreal and incalculable. Smith made no choice between them, though he appears to have been cognizant of the difficulty. It was unnecessary for him to go further into the subject, because, in his opinion, labor no longer served as a measure of value in any practical way. It was the "real measure" of the exchangeable value of all commodities but "not that by which their value is commonly estimated."[37]

As was said in Chapter IV, Smith believed that only in the earliest stages of society did commodities exchange on the basis of the labor they had cost to produce. After capital had been accumulated and land had become scarce and privately owned, the owners of these factors were able to obtain payment for their use, so that cost ceased to be represented by labor only and came to include profit and rent, at least, according to Smith. Thus he was led to the cost of production theory of value that has received attention in an earlier section.

Incidentally, Smith indicated one of the practical difficulties of basing value on labor. Labor was of varying quality:

> It is often difficult to ascertain the proportion between two different quantities of labour. The time spent in two different sorts of work will not always alone determine this proportion. The different degrees of hardship endured, and of ingenuity exercised, must likewise be taken into account. There may be more labour in an hour's hard work, than in two hours' easy business; or an hour's application to a trade which it cost ten years' labour to learn, than in a month's industry, at an ordinary and obvious employment. But it is not easy to find any accurate measure either of hardship or ingenuity. In exchanging indeed the different productions of different sorts of labour for one another, some allowance is commonly made for both. It is adjusted, however, not by any accurate measure, but by the higgling and bargaining of the market, according to that sort of rough equality which, though not exact, is sufficient for carrying on the business of common life.[38]

This point was of little significance to Smith, who regarded the labor explanation of value as inapplicable to contemporary society, but it was to cause trouble to Ricardo and Marx, whose views were different.

David Ricardo. Ricardo made the theory a cardinal feature of his system of economics. His career is interesting. The son of a successful Jewish stockbroker of London, Ricardo was severed from his family by adoption of the Christian faith on his marriage. Thrown on his own resources, he accumulated sufficient capital on the stock exchange to retire from business at an early age, devoting himself to parliamentary duties and economic study. Possessed of a keen analytical mind, he showed a propensity to reduce everything to simple principles, commonly, his critics

[37] *Ibid.* [38] *Ibid.*

said, drawn from the commercial background of the city of London, with which he was familiar.

Studying value in his *Principles of Political Economy and Taxation* (London 1817), unlike Cantillon and Smith, Ricardo confined himself to competitive conditions. Where Cantillon and Smith had distinguished between short-term market values and long-term or normal values based on production costs, Ricardo ignored the former with virtual completeness. He recognized that not all commodities were produced under competitive conditions but ruled out those which were not so produced, considering them exceptional :

> Possessing utility, commodities derive their exchangeable value from two sources : from their scarcity, and from the quantity of labour required to obtain them. There are some commodities, the value of which is determined by their scarcity alone. No labour can increase the quantity of such goods, and therefore their value cannot be lowered by an increased supply. Some rare statues and pictures, scarce books and coins, wines of a peculiar quality, which can be made only from grapes grown on a particular soil, of which there is a very limited quantity, are all of this description. Their value is wholly independent of the quantity of labour originally necessary to produce them, and varies with the varying wealth and inclinations of those who are desirous to possess them. These commodities, however, form a very small part of the mass of commodities daily exchanged in the market. By far the greatest part of those goods which are the objects of desire, are procured by labour ; and they may be multiplied, not in one country alone, but in many, almost without any assignable limit, if we are disposed to bestow the labour necessary to obtain them. In speaking, then, of commodities, of their exchangeable value, and of the laws which regulate their relative prices, we mean always such commodities only as can be increased in quantity by the exertion of human industry, and on the production of which competition operates without restraint.[39]

In Ricardo's time, enterprises were smaller than is common today and it is probable that the assumption of free competition had more reality than would be the case in the twentieth century. But even when Ricardo wrote, as Cantillon and Smith had pointed out, forms of production were such that the prices determined by competition were not fully applicable to the short period. It is too much to claim that Ricardo had no appreciation of this : he stated it clearly when discussing wages, for example.[40] But it is difficult to understand why Ricardo—whose writings on money displayed his interest in economic dynamics—neglected this aspect almost entirely in his work on principles. After all, the factories and ships of 1817 took many years to wear out and specialized workers had to face losses if their skill became obsolete. The

[39] *Principles of Political Economy and Taxation*, in *The Works of David Ricardo*, ed. by J. R. McCulloch, pp. 9-10.

[40] See the passage quoted in Chapter XII, p. 574, and footnote to that passage.

plight of the English hand-loom weavers in the early part of the nineteenth century was a demonstration of this fact. Probably the explanation of Ricardo's position was that he thought, like Senior later,[41] that political economy should deal with general tendencies, rather than with the particular circumstances of the moment.

In respect of commodities produced under competitive conditions, to which his book on *Principles of Political Economy and Taxation* was devoted, Ricardo rejected Smith's opinion that the labor basis of valuation had ceased to be applicable. Even in the contemporary world the value of commodities depended on labor, he said:

> The value of a commodity, or the quantity of any other commodity for which it will exchange, depends on the relative quantity of labour which is necessary for its production. . .[42]

The cost of land was immaterial, in Ricardo's view, not because land as such produced little, as Locke had argued, but because only the superior qualities of land produced anything. The price of grain was governed by its production cost on the poorest land that was under cultivation, where no rent had to be paid. Grain produced on better land had to meet a rent equivalent only to the superior advantages of the soil on which it was grown. Rent, therefore, was not a part of cost. Capital Ricardo dealt with on the lines followed by Locke. It was past labor incorporated in equipment:

> Not only the labour applied immediately to commodities affect their value, but the labour also which is bestowed on the implements, tools, and buildings, with which such labour is assisted.[43]

Ricardo pointed out that, even in the early stages of society, where Smith admitted that the labor basis of valuation was operative, some tools were necessary. He went on,

> If we look to a state of society in which greater improvements have been made, and in which arts and commerce flourish, we shall still find that commodities vary in value comformably with this principle: in estimating the exchangeable value of stockings, for example, we shall find that their value, comparatively with other things, depends on the total quantity of labour necessary to manufacture them, and bring them to market. First, there is the labour necessary to cultivate the land on which the raw cotton is grown; secondly, the labour of conveying the cotton to the country where the stockings are to be manufactured, which includes a portion of the labour bestowed in building the ship in which it is conveyed, and which is charged in the freight of the goods; thirdly, the labour of the spinner and weaver; fourthly, a portion of the labour of the engineer, smith, and carpenter, who erected the buildings and machinery, by the help of which they are made;

[41] See p. 435.

[42] *Ibid.*, p. 9, section heading.

[43] *Ibid.*, p. 16, section heading.

fifthly, the labour of the retail dealer, and of many others, whom it is unnecessary further to particularize. The aggregate sum of these various kinds of labour, determines the quantity of other things for which these stockings will exchange, while the same consideration of the various quantities of labour which have been bestowed on those other things, will equally govern the portion of them which will be given for the stockings.[44]

This is almost identical with Locke's statement on the same subject.

Obviously, labor varied in quality, as Adam Smith had remarked. Notwithstanding the greater importance of the point to his theory, Ricardo went no farther than Smith in dealing with it, except to assert that the allowances made for quality differences had become a matter of custom:

In speaking, however, of labour, as being the foundation of all value, and the relative quantity of labour as almost exclusively determining the relative value of commodities, I must not be supposed to be inattentive to the different qualities of labour, and the difficulty of comparing an hour's or a day's labour, in one employment, with the same duration of labour in another. The estimation in which different qualities of labour are held, comes soon to be adjusted in the market with sufficient precision for all practical purposes, and depends much on the comparative skill of the labourer, and intensity of the labour performed. The scale, when once formed, is liable to little variation. If a day's labour of a working jeweller be more valuable than a day's labour of a common labourer, it has long ago been adjusted, and placed in its proper position in the scale of value.[45]

This burked the issue, rather than offered a reasonable explanation.

The socialist theory of surplus value. Such a theory was a veritable godsend to the socialists. They believed that in some way the workers were exploited by the capitalists and the Ricardian theory of value appeared to furnish a scientific basis for this belief. Following Rousseau, the socialists Thompson, Gray, and Bray developed the theory of capitalistic exploitation which was described in Chapter IV. Rodbertus and Marx made it a prominent feature of their work.

Thompson's opinions on value were set forth in his *Inquiry into the Principles of the Distribution of Wealth Most Conducive to Human Happiness.* They will be made clear by the following passage from that work. Thompson was considering the just remuneration of capital and said:

The labourer pays five pounds a year for a house. The house costs fifty pounds, and is calculated to last fifty or one hundred years. By the labourer's measure of the use of this article of capital, he should pay one pound or ten shillings a year rent for the yearly loss in value, according to the time the house would be in consuming [*i.e.,* for depreciation], with a trifling surplus to repay the trouble of the owner — say five shillings a year out of each

[44] *Ibid.,* p. 17. [45] *Ibid.,* pp. 14-15.

of a hundred houses, or as many as it would employ one man to superintend, amounting to twenty-five pounds a year — to enable him to enjoy as much as any of the operative labourers. Fifteen to twenty-five shillings a year rent, instead of one hundred shillings, would be for this item the charge on the labourer. For the use of the capital of his employer, it would be in about the same proportion, or something more in consequence of the more perishable nature of the capital employed; that part which consists in machinery not being liable to last as long as the house.[46]

Thompson was stating two sides of the case, those of the employer and the laborer respectively. The passage gave the view of the latter and Thompson made it evident that he supported it. When the worker paid a hundred shillings for house rent, he was defrauded of from seventy-five to eighty-five shillings, according to whether the house was estimated to last fifty or a hundred years. This seventy-five or eighty-five shillings was the "surplus value" of Karl Marx.

Bray set forth the same general idea, in his *Labour's Wrongs and Labour's Remedy*:

If a just system of exchange were acted upon, the value of all articles would be determined by the entire cost of production; *and equal values should always exchange for equal values.* If, for instance, it take a hatter one day to make a hat, and a shoemaker the same time to make a pair of shoes — supposing the material used by each to be of the same value — and they exchange these articles with each other, they are not only mutually but equally benefited: the advantage derived by either party cannot be a disadvantage to the other, as each has given the same amount of labour, and the materials made use of by each were of equal value.[47]

But Bray said that, if under the same conditions the hatter were to obtain two pairs of shoes in exchange for a hat, the exchange would be unjust. The hatter would secure the equivalent of two days' labor of the shoemaker for only one day of his own. This was what happened when the worker sold his labor to the capitalist, Bray believed, and it was the gain received from this unjust exchange that enabled the capitalist to "live in luxury and idleness," while the laborer was doomed to "incessant toil." According to Bray,

The whole transaction, therefore, plainly shews that the capitalists and proprietors do no more than give the working man, for his labour of one week, a part of the wealth which they obtained from him the week before. . . The wealth which the capitalist appears to give in exchange for the workman's labour was generated neither by the labour nor the riches of the capitalist, but it was originally obtained by the labour of the workman; and it is still daily taken from him, by a fraudulent system of unequal exchanges. The whole transaction, therefore, between the producer and the capitalist, is a palpable deception, a mere farce: it is, in fact, in thousands of instances,

[46] *Op. cit.*, pp. 167-168. [47] *Op. cit.*, p. 48.

no other than a barefaced though legalised robbery, by means of which the capitalists and proprietors contrive to fasten themselves upon the productive class, and suck from them their whole substance.[48]

As Marx referred to Bray's writings in a book which preceded *Capital,* there seems little doubt that the American-English socialist was one of the sources of his inspiration.

The views of Marx on the subject of value were given in *Capital.* This voluminous treatise was an attack upon the capitalist system. Among other things, it described, along lines suggested in the books of Thompson and Bray, the process whereby the capitalists exploited the workers. As was the case with Thompson and Bray, to Marx value had a certain ethical meaning. He spoke of it as though it were an inherent quality or worth, rather than a ratio reached by the higgling of the market. Yet, also, he seemed to think that it was market value.

To Marx, value was crystallized human labor. In his words, the value of any commodity was the "labour-time socially necessary" for its production. This, in turn, was defined as the labor-time "required to produce an article under the normal conditions of production, and with the average degree of skill and intensity prevalent at the time."[49] Marx had no conception of marginal cost, speaking of "average" skill and intensity of labor, though his term "socially necessary" precluded waste:

Though the capitalist have a hobby, and use a gold instead of a steel spindle, yet the only labour that counts for anything in the value of the yarn is that which would be required to produce a steel spindle, because no more is necessary under the given social conditions.[50]

The Locke-Ricardo explanation of capital, reducing this factor to past labor incorporated in instruments, was adopted by Marx, but he improved considerably on Ricardo in his treatment of different qualities of labor. He started similarly to the English writer:

Skilled labour counts only as simple labour intensified, or rather, as multiplied simple labour, a given quantity of skilled being considered equal to a greater quantity of simple labour. Experience shows that this reduction is constantly being made. A commodity may be the product of the most skilled labour, but its value, by equating it to the product of simple unskilled labour, represents a definite quantity of the latter labour alone. The different proportions in which the different sorts of labour are reduced to unskilled labour as their standard, are established by a social process that goes on behind the backs of the producers, and, consequently, appear to be fixed by custom.[51]

But, unlike Ricardo, Marx endeavored to elucidate the process by which the values of the different classes of labor were determined:

[48] *Ibid.,* pp. 49-50.
[49] *Capital,* vol. 1, Pt. 1, Chap. 1, Sect. 1.
[50] *Ibid.,* Pt. 3, Chap. 7, Sect. 2.
[51] *Ibid.,* Pt. 1, Chap. 1, Sect. 2.

All labour of a higher or more complicated character than average labour is expenditure of labour-power of a more costly kind, labour-power whose production has cost more time and labour, and which therefore has a higher value, than unskilled or simple labour-power.[52]

Reference to the passage dealing with this subject, quoted earlier in the chapter from Smith's *Wealth of Nations,* will show that Smith had the same idea. An hour's application in a trade that had taken ten years to learn was compared, by that writer, to a month's labor at an "ordinary and obvious employment."

On the basis of the labor theory of value as thus set forth, Marx elaborated his celebrated theory of surplus value. According to Marx, value of labor was the labor-cost of its maintenance and reproduction. As the productive process went on, this value (including the value of past labor incorporated in raw materials and equipment) was transferred to the commodity produced:

While the labourer is at work, his labour constantly undergoes a transformation: from being motion, it becomes an object without motion, from being the labourer working it becomes the thing produced. At the end of one hour's spinning, that act is represented by a definite quantity of yarn; in other words, a definite quantity of labor, namely that of one hour, has become embodied in the cotton.[53]

For the worker to produce, instruments and maintenance were necessary, Marx said. Since the laborer himself did not possess these, he had to sell his labor to the capitalist. It was not necessary, however, for the latter to pay to the worker the full value of his product. Here, Marx brought in another of the Classical theories, the subsistence theory of wages. He believed that the capitalist remunerated his labor on a cost basis. He paid enough to cover the labor-costs of maintenance and reproduction but no more. In other words, the capitalist paid for labor at its value as defined above. But he (the capitalist) did not permit the laborer to cease productive operations immediately sufficient value had been transferred to the product to cover its labor-cost. The worker was required to continue for a longer time and so produce a surplus value for the benefit of the capitalist:

the labour-process may continue beyond the time necessary to reproduce and incorporate in the product a mere equivalent for the value of the labour-power. Instead of the six hours that are sufficient for the latter purpose, the process may continue for twelve hours. The action of labour-power, therefore, not only reproduces its own value, but produces value over and above it. This surplus value is the difference between the value of the product and the value of the elements consumed in the formation of that product, in other words, of the means of production and the labour-power.[54]

[52] *Ibid.,* Pt. 3, Chap. 7, Sect. 2. [53] *Ibid.* [54] *Ibid.,* Pt. 3, Chap. 8.

The result was impressive:

By turning his money into commodities that serve as the material elements of a new product, and as factors in the labour-process, by incorporating living labour in their dead substance, the capitalist at the same time converts value, *i.e.*, past, materialised, and dead labour into capital, into value big with value, a live monster that is fruitful and multiplies.[55]

That is to say, to take the figures quoted in the previous passage, having obtained a surplus value equivalent to six hours' labor, the capitalist uses this to purchase more labor and so to procure for himself a still greater quantity of surplus value. This, indeed, according to Marx, was how capitalists became rich.

As stated, the labor theory of value is open to certain objections. Marx himself appreciated that market values might change after labor has been incorporated in the commodities concerned. What happened to value in such a case? Marx answered as follows:

The value of a commodity, it is true, is determined by the quantity of labour contained in it, but this quantity is itself limited by social conditions. If the time socially necessary for the production of any commodity alters—and a given quantity of cotton represents, after a bad harvest, more labour than after a good one—*all previously existing commodities of the same class are affected,* because they are, as it were, only individuals of the species, and their value at any given time is measured by the labour socially necessary, *i.e.*, by the labour necessary for their production under the then existing social conditions.[56]

Thus Marx seems to have contemplated a reproduction-cost interpretation of his "labour-time socially necessary" definition of value.

Marx neglected those commodities that possessed value but for whose production no labor was required and also those that were valued disproportionately to the labor incorporated in them (the "rare statues and pictures," etc., of Ricardo. Further, except that he referred to a tendency toward monopoly, he gave no convincing explanation of why it did not happen that competition caused the surplus value to disappear. Under conditions where the output of a single firm is small in relation to the total production of the industry (as was probably the case at the middle of the nineteenth century in the English textile industry, from which Marx drew many of his examples), any expansion in the output of one firm could have little effect on the market price of the commodity produced. The surplus value, per unit of output, therefore, would remain virtually unchanged. More units being produced, it follows that the total surplus value received by the firm would be increased. Obviously,

[55] *Ibid.*, Pt. 3, Chap. 7, Sect. 2.
[56] *Ibid.*, Pt: 3, Chap. 8. Italics ours.

the firm would be under an inducement to expand its output. Not merely one but all firms in the industry would be in this position. Yet, if all expand, the market price of the product would decline, causing the surplus value to diminish and ultimately to disappear. Such is the criticism which can be levied against the Marxian theory of surplus value in the light of modern ideas on competitive equilibrium.

But it is not apparent that the theory of Marx is open to some of the objections that have been advanced against it by subsequent writers. Thus, it has been asked why—if labor alone had a capacity to produce surplus value—the employer did not use as much labor and as little capital as possible. On this point, it must be remembered that to Marx capital was merely stored-up labor, presumably with the same capacity to produce surplus value as was possessed by other labor. Moreover, that Marx was not unfamiliar with the "laws of returns" or "principle of proportionality" is shown by the following passage, taken from the concluding volume of *Capital*, published by Engels after the death of its author:

> If five laborers produce ten times as many commodities as formerly, this does not increase the outlay for fixed capital tenfold; although the value of this part of the constant capital [*i.e.*, the capital invested in equipment] increases with the development of the productive process, it does not increase by any means in the same proportion with them.[57]

This states the principle of increasing returns on capital as production expands.

Proposals for reform. The labor theory of value led to some remarkable results in the way of suggestions for social reform. If, as Locke, Smith, and Marx seemed to make clear, the explanation of why the laborer did not receive the full value of his product was that those who owned the soil and the stock of capital goods used this ownership to exploit the working man, why not abolish property altogether? This subject has been discussed in Chapter IV. Alternatively, why not enable the worker to escape from his position of servitude by making available to him a supply of capital through the government? This, in effect, was the proposal of Proudhon and, in a sense, of Lassalle. Lastly, might it not be possible to establish some equitable system of exchange, that valued commodities on a labor basis and made it unnecessary for the workers to depend upon the capitalists? This suggestion received a trial.

Robert Owen, in his *Report to the County of Lanark* in 1817, declared that

> The genuine principle of barter was, to exchange the supposed prime cost of, or value of labour in, one article, against the prime cost of, or amount of

[57] *Ibid.*, vol. 3, p. 305. Quoted by permission of Charles H. Kerr & Company.

labour contained in any other article. This is the only equitable principle of exchange. . .[58]

Owen, like Smith, said that this system obtained in early times but had since been given up. He looked forward to its re-introduction and considered that

substantial improvement in the progress of society may be easily effected by exchanging all articles with each other at their prime cost, or with reference to the amount of labour in each, which can be equitably ascertained, and by permitting the exchange to be made through a convenient medium to represent this value, and which will thus represent a real and unchanging value, and be issued only as substantial wealth increases.[59]

Extended consideration of social arrangements would be necessary before it could be said how much of the necessities and comforts of life a day's labor would yield to the worker on this equitable basis, Owen said, but he hazarded the guess that it would amount to not less than what at the time could be purchased for five shillings ($1.25).

From time to time in the years following—years of labor ferment as they were—Owen and his followers advocated action on the lines thus laid down. It appears that one Josiah Warren, who had taken part in Owen's communistic experiment at New Harmony, Indiana, put such a plan into action at Cincinnati in 1827 and certainly he fathered a scheme of the kind at New Harmony itself in 1842. Between these dates, however, another Owenite, Dr. King, proposed labor exchanges in London and Brighton, England, and in 1832 one was opened in London, a branch being established in Birmingham the following year.

The principle upon which this scheme was based was that producers should sell their produce to the exchange in return for labor notes (a form of paper currency), entitling them to receive so many units of other men's labor. These notes were to be spent in purchasing commodities from the exchange. The system speedily collapsed. The basic difficulty appears to have been that of valuation. If the exchange authorities accepted the producer's word for how long it had taken him to produce his commodity, they might be cheated. Even if the figure given were cor-

[58] *A New View of Society and Other Writings*, p. 262. The source of inspiration here was probably Bellers's *Proposals for Raising a Colledge of Industry* to which Owen gave some credit for his village community idea. Bellers said, on pp. 11-12 of this work,

This colledge-fellowship will make labour, and not money, the standard to value all necessaries by. . . And when people have their whole dependence of trading by money, if that fails, or is corrupted, they are next door to ruine; and the poor stand still, because the rich have no money to employ them, tho' they have the same land and hands to provide victuals and cloaths, as ever they had. . .

This passage is of interest, also, because it hints at the views of Owen and others on the cause of business depressions. See Chapter XVI.

[59] *Ibid.*, p. 263.

rect, the worker might have taken an unduly long time on his task. He might be what is sometimes called nowadays a sub-marginal worker, unable to produce efficiently. The exchange officials were left with the alternative of making their own valuation of commodities offered for sale. This had its own difficulties, because what individual could be expected to value all products with exactness? Had the exchange followed the course of securing expert valuations, the scheme might have been workable, but it would have involved the abandonment of the labor basis of valuation. Faced with the competition of the exchange, tradesmen accepted labor notes in their stores. Like the workers who had received them in exchange for commodities, they expended the notes in the purchase of such goods from the exchange stock as seemed to be priced cheaply. Articles priced dearly were left on the exchange shelves, and the result was seen in a depreciation in the value of the notes, coincident with that of the commodities that they represented.

Other writers, notably the socialists, Bray and Gray, advanced exchange projects of similar nature, and, in Germany, Rodbertus formulated a scheme possessing a certain relationship to that of Owen. Rodbertus was aiming, not at introducing a new system in an experimental manner into existing society, but at a more comprehensive social reform. In his plan the State was to regulate wages and commodity prices on a basis that would ensure rewards proportional to normal labor-cost. Allowance was to be made for the conditions of labor in different industries and for variations in the quality of individual labor. Thus, a normal ten-hour day in industry as a whole might be represented by a six-hour day in mining, while an inferior worker would not get the full wage for his day's work. Wages were to be paid, not in money of the ordinary kind, but in notes entitling the recipients to goods whose production had required an equivalent labor-time. As long as capital and land remained private property, it would be necessary for the State to decide what proportions of the product should go to these factors, the remainder being distributed among the working class. Adjustments would be needed from time to time, Rodbertus said, as the productivity of industry changed, with the object of permitting the wage-earner to share in the benefits of economic progress.

Notwithstanding the theoretical objections and practical difficulties attending valuation on a labor basis, such as were experienced in the operation of Owen's labor exchanges, the labor theory of value has exercised tremendous influence on men's minds. If it is interpreted to mean that market prices are governed in actuality by labor-cost, obviously it is incorrect. At best, it can be no more than a tendency. The difference between a fact and a tendency is sometimes very great. Thus it may be true that, given a sufficiently long period, profits tend to equality, yet a chewing gum company may average for years over thirty per cent profit on its capital while a steel manufacturing enterprise or railroad operates at a loss. Even as a statement of tendency, the labor theory of value cannot be substantiated, as long as natural materials and capital are scarce in relation to the demands for them, and have to be paid for. Its appeal, however, lies not in any claim it possesses to be a statement of fact. Many people believe that merit is to be measured in a rough and ready way by labor, and that the difference they perceive between market values and labor-costs represents undeserved surpluses which go to capitalists and landowners. To individuals who take this view valuation on a labor basis is not so much *factual* as *ethical*—not a matter of *what is* but of *what should be.* They feel that there is a social offense in a condition in which, to use the words of John Stuart Mill, the produce of labor is "apportioned as we now see it, almost in an inverse ratio to the labour."[60] Though Mill's statement is nearly a century old, it remains in the minds of many men a true description of the distribution of work and rewards in industrial society. The labor theory of value, no doubt, had its seeds in certain ideas of the British Classical School of economists, but its soil has been the social inequality that exists in the modern world and its cultivators those who have felt dissatisfied. It has been the belief of many social critics that distribution based on the labor principle would be more just than the system that has ruled in practice. In this has lain the real strength of the labor theory of value.

The Cost of Production Theories of Senior and Mill

Like Marx, Senior built on the work of Smith and Ricardo, but, unlike Marx, he abandoned Ricardo's past-labor explanation of capital and developed instead the other alternative which Ricardo had suggested—the concept of interest as payment for waiting or abstinence. According to Senior, capital was not merely past labor, incorporated in materials and instruments. It was labor and natural materials, together with a third factor, namely abstinence. Senior pointed out that the expenditure of labor upon a commodity was not always necessary to confer value:

> Mr. Malthus, Colonel Torrens, and the other Economists who consider labour, using that word in its popular sense, as a necessary constituent of wealth, appear to have been led to that opinion by observing, first, that some quality besides mere utility is necessary to value; secondly, that all those things which are useful, and are acquired by labour, are valuable; and thirdly, that almost everything which is valuable *has* required some labour for its acquisition. But the fact that that circumstance is not essential to value will be demonstrated if we can suppose a case in which value could exist without it. If, while carelessly lounging along the sea-shore, I were to pick up a pearl, would it have no value? Mr. M'Culloch would answer, that the value of the pearl was the result of my appropriative industry in

[60] *Principles of Political Economy,* Bk. 2, Chap. 1, Sect. 3.

stooping to pick it up. Suppose then that I met with it while eating an oyster? Supposing that aerolites consisted of gold, would they have no value? Or, suppose that meteoric iron were the only form in which that metal were produced, would not the iron supplied from heaven be far more valuable than any existing metal? It is true that, wherever there is utility, the addition of labour as necessary to production constitutes value, because, the supply of labour being limited, it follows that the object, to the supply of which it is necessary, is by that very necessity limited in supply. But any other cause limiting supply is just as efficient a cause of value in an article as the necessity of labour to its production. And, in fact, if all the commodities used by man were supplied by nature without any intervention whatever of human labour, but were supplied in precisely the same quantities as they now are, there is no reason to suppose either that they would cease to be valuable, or would exchange in any other than the present proportions.[61]

Ricardo had admitted that in exceptional cases (which he said could be neglected) value was not related to labor. But Senior looked upon the point as more fundamental. According to Senior, it was not labor but scarcity (which may—or may not—be explained by labour) which conferred value.

Senior proceeded to say that abstinence, as well as labor, was necessary for production. What Senior meant by this has been explained in Chapter VII. Abstinence, like labor, he declared, was a sacrifice, so that the real cost of production, which determined price, became not merely labor only but labor and abstinence:

The obstacle to the supply of those commodities which are produced by labour and abstinence, with that assistance only from nature which every one can command, consists solely in the difficulty of finding persons ready to submit to the labour and abstinence necessary to their production. In other words, their supply is limited by the cost of their production.[62]

With respect to those commodities, or, to speak more accurately, with respect to the value of those parts or attributes of commodities, which are the subjects of equal competition, which may be produced by all persons with equal advantages, the cost of production to the producer and the cost of production to the consumer are the same. Their price, therefore, represents the aggregate amount of the labour and abstinence necessary to continue their production. If their price should fall lower, the wages or the profits of those employed in their production must fall below the average remuneration of the labour and abstinence that must be undergone if their production is to be continued. In time, therefore, it is discontinued or diminished, until the value of the product has been raised by the diminution of the supply. If the price should rise beyond the cost of their production, the producers must receive more than an average remuneration for their sacrifices. As soon as this has been discovered, capital and industry flow towards the employment

[61] *Political Economy*, pp. 23-24. [62] *Ibid.*, p. 97.

which, by this supposition, offers extraordinary advantages. Those who formerly were purchasers, or persons on their behalf, turn producers themselves, until the increased supply has equalized the price with the cost of production.[63]

Except that the rent of land was excluded by Senior, this economist offered a theory very similar to that of Smith. He said that the values of commodities must cover the necessary remuneration of the productive factors. But Senior recognized that competition was not free in the *short run*. Prices could rise or fall before adjustment took place, he said:

But though, under free competition, cost of production is the regulator of price, its influence is subject to much occasional interruption. Its operation can be supposed to be perfect only if we suppose that there are no disturbing causes, that capital and labour can be at once transferred, and without loss, from one employment to another, and that every producer has full information of the profit to be derived from every mode of production. But it is obvious that these suppositions have no resemblance to the truth. A large portion of the capital essential to production consists of buildings, machinery, and other implements, the results of much time and labour, and of little service for any except their existing purposes. A still larger portion consists of knowledge and of intellectual and bodily dexterity, applicable only to the processes in which those qualities were originally acquired. Again, the advantage derived from any given business depends so much upon the dexterity and the judgment with which it is managed, that few capitalists can estimate, except upon an average of some years, the amount of their own profits, and still fewer can estimate those of their neighbours. Established businesses, therefore, may survive the causes in which they originated, and become gradually extinguished as their comparative unprofitableness is discovered, and the labourers and capital engaged in them wear away without being replaced; and, on the other hand, other employments are inadequately supplied with the capital and industry which they could profitably absorb.[64]

This obviously raised the whole problem of rigidities in production, on which so much work has been done by Marshall and others in recent years. Senior thus admitted that his principles of competition represented only a long-term tendency, but consoled himself with the belief that

Political economy does not deal with particular facts, but with general tendencies, and when we assign to cost of production the power of regulating price in cases of equal competition, we mean to describe it not as a point to which price is attached, but as a centre of oscillation which it is always endeavouring to approach.[65]

Some of Senior's other references to non-competitive conditions receive attention elsewhere.

[63] *Ibid.*, p. 101. [64] *Ibid.*, p. 102. [65] *Ibid.*

John Stuart Mill accepted Senior's addition of abstinence to cost of production and made one or two alterations of his own. As was noticed in Chapter VII, Mill recognized that cost conditions may vary, bringing in what are commonly called the "laws of returns." Like Senior, he thought that the statement that value must be adequate to cover cost of production represented only a long-run tendency:

Persons whose capital is already embarked, and cannot be easily extricated, will persevere for a considerable time without profit, and have been known to persevere even at a loss, in hope of better times. But they will not do so indefinitely, or when there is nothing to indicate that times are likely to improve. No new capital will be invested in an employment, unless there be an expectation not only of some profit, but of a profit as great (regard being had to the degree of eligibility of the employment in other respects) as can be hoped for in any other occupation at that time and place. When such profit is evidently not to be had, if people do not actually withdraw their capital, they at least abstain from replacing it when consumed. The cost of production, together with the ordinary profit, may therefore be called the *necessary* price, or value, of all things made by labour and capital. Nobody willingly produces in the prospect of loss. Whoever does so, does it under a miscalculation, which he corrects as fast as he is able. . . As a general rule, then, things tend to exchange for one another at such values as will enable each producer to be repaid the cost of production with the ordinary profit; in other words, such as will give to all producers the same rate of profit on their outlay.[66]

But Mill changed the basis of cost discussion from *real costs* (in the form of labor and abstinence, to which Ricardo and Senior had referred) to *money costs*, that is, wages and profit:

It will have been observed that Ricardo expresses himself as if the *quantity* of labour which it costs to produce a commodity and bring it to market, were the only thing on which its value depended. But since the cost of production to the capitalist is not labour but wages, and since wages may be either greater or less, the quantity of labour being the same; it would seem that the value of the product cannot be determined solely by the quantity of labour, but by the quantity together with the remuneration; and that values must partly depend on wages.[67]

Mill said that "the maxim laid down by some of the best political economists," that wages did not govern value, was applicable only to *general wages*. If all wages rose or fell equally, he said, relative values would be unaffected.[68] He argued, however, that this was certainly not true of *relative wages*. If wages in a particular employment rose more than elsewhere, relative values would reflect the change. The same

[66] *Principles of Political Economy,* Bk. 3, Chap. 3, Sect. 1.
[67] *Ibid.,* Bk. 3, Chap. 4, Sect. 2.
[68] Obviously, this was only true if the same proportion of labor were used in the various occupations, or if other costs moved similarly to wages.

applied to the rate of profit, that is, the price of capital. This aspect of Mill's theory roused the ire of one who regarded himself in general as a disciple of Mill, namely, J. E. Cairnes:

> Of all ideas within the range of economic speculation, the two most profoundly opposed to each other are cost and the reward of cost – the sacrifice incurred by man in productive industry, and the return made by nature to man upon that sacrifice. All industrial progress consists in altering the proportion between these two things; in increasing the remuneration in relation to the cost, or in diminishing the cost in relation to the remuneration. Cost and remuneration are thus economic antitheses of each other; so completely so, that a small cost and a large remuneration are exactly equivalent expressions. Now, in the analysis of cost of production which I have quoted [*i.e.*, that of Mill], these two opposites are identified; and cost, which is sacrifice, cost, which is what man pays to nature for her industrial rewards, is said to consist of wages and profits, that is to say, of what nature yields to man in return for his industrial sacrifices.[69]

The source of conflict between Cairnes and Mill was that the single word *cost* was being used to cover entirely different things. Mill was looking at production from the standpoint of the *enterpriser*, to whom the cost of labor was certainly the wage paid. Cairnes's viewpoint was equally correct with respect to the *laborer* and to *society*. The laborer's cost was toil and trouble and, presumably, he would be willing to work only if this cost were covered, and perhaps more than covered, by the wage he received. The same was true from the wider angle of society. Total real cost in terms of efforts and sacrifices was one thing, total income was another; and economic progress consisted, as Cairnes pointed out, in widening the margin between the two. If, without affecting production, the wage were raised, could it be said that labor-cost had risen? From Mill's standpoint of the enterpriser this was what happened, with the result that, if the price of the product remained unchanged, the enterpriser's profit was lessened. But the toil and trouble of laboring had not gone up because of the fact that the laborer's share of the product had increased.

On the cost side of value theory, Marshall took over from Mill at this point.

The Classical Theory of International Values

Before leaving the subject of Classical value theory, something should be said about the ideas of Ricardo and his successors on international exchange, that is, on the principles of value operative in foreign trade.

Ricardo specifically excepted international trade from his general rule that commodities exchanged at ratios which represented their relative

[69] *Some Leading Principles of Political Economy, Newly Expounded*, p. 45.

costs in terms of labor. In the chapter of his *Principles of Political Economy and Taxation* that was devoted to foreign trade, he declared:

In one and the same country, profits are, generally speaking, always on the same level; or differ only as the employment of capital may be more or less secure and agreeable. It is not so between different countries. If the profits of capital employed in Yorkshire, should exceed those of capital employed in London, capital would speedily move from London to Yorkshire, and an equality of profits would be effected; but if in consequence of the diminished rate of production in the lands of England, from the increase of capital and population, wages should rise, and profits fall, it would not follow that capital and population would necessarily move from England to Holland, or Spain, or Russia, where profits might be higher.[70]

In other words, according to Ricardo, there was mobility of capital and labor *within a country* (the Yorkshire-London case) but not *between countries.*

What, then, determined international values? Ricardo gave an arithmetical example. He supposed England to be so circumstanced that a certain quantity of cloth required the labor of 100 men for a year to make it, and that the amount of wine for which it exchanged on the market absorbed the labor of 120 men over the same period. In Portugal, on the other hand, only 80 men were required to produce the wine and only 90 needed for the cloth. Undoubtedly, it would be advantageous that both wine and cloth should be produced in Portugal, but immobility of the productive factors prevented this, Ricardo said. Capital and labor could not move from England to Portugal. Portugal, therefore, would concentrate on wine, where her productive advantage was greater, while England would produce cloth, in whose manufacture her disadvantage was less. The price of cloth in terms of wine could not rise beyond the point at which it would pay the Portuguese to produce cloth, nor fall below the level at which England would produce wine. Ricardo thus recognized that relative or *comparative* costs set limits on the rates of exchange in international trade but gave no explanation as to where, between these limits, exchange would in fact take place.

John Stuart Mill carried the matter further in the first of his *Essays on Some Unsettled Questions of Political Economy* (London 1844). Mill dealt with a point that had interested an earlier writer, Robert Torrens (1780–1864), a retired army colonel who served in parliament and was interested in economic questions. In *The Economists Refuted* (London 1808), published before Ricardo's work on international values appeared, Torrens argued that the gain from international exchange was divided in variable proportions between the parties concerned. Mill carried the matter farther. He made it clear that Ricardo's principle of comparative

[70] *The Works of David Ricardo,* p. 76.

costs merely indicated a zone or range within which trade might take place with advantage to both parties. Between the limits set by comparative costs, the value at which commodities exchanged was determined by the relative strengths of the demand by each country for the product of the other, subject to the condition that in equilibrium imports just paid for exports:

It may be considered, therefore, as established, that when two countries trade together in two commodities, the exchange value of these commodities relatively to each other will adjust itself to the inclinations and circumstances of the consumers on both sides, in such manner that the quantities required by each country, of the articles which it imports from its neighbours, shall be exactly sufficient to pay for one another. As the inclinations and circumstances of consumers cannot be reduced to any rule, so neither can the proportions in which the two commodities will be interchanged. We know that the limits within which the variation is confined, are the ratio between their costs of production in the one country, and the ratio between their costs of production in the other.[71]

What ensured that exports and imports would balance in the long run, of course, was the manner in which any lack of balance would affect specie movements, a subject that is discussed in Chapter XIV. Mill did not seem to perceive that the condition that exports and imports should balance could be satisfied by more than one rate of exchange between the commodities but his reference to the factor of relative intensities of demand made this point of little significance.

J. E. Cairnes made an important contribution to the theory of international values. Cairnes challenged Ricardo's assumptions of intranational mobility of the productive factors and international immobility:

The assumption commonly made in treatises of Political Economy is that, as between occupations and localities within the same country, the freedom of movement for capital and labor is perfect, while, as between nations, capital and labor move with difficulty or not at all. In strictness neither member of this assumption can be maintained.[72]

Cairnes pointed out that, while capital moved easily within a country, this was not altogether true of labor. He said, too, that international migration of capital and labor took place on a large scale. However, he concluded that in general within a country there was sufficient mobility for profits to gravitate to the same level and that, in spite of international migration, this was not the case between countries:

It thus appears, alike with regard to labor and capital, that notwithstanding a certain amount of international mobility in these instruments of production, the impediments to their transference from country to country are yet

[71] Quoted in *Principles of Political Economy,* Bk. 3, Chap. 18, Sect. 2.
[72] *Some Leading Principles of Political Economy, Newly Expounded,* p. 302.

sufficiently great to prevent effective competition from taking place between the industries of different countries, such as is really operative in each separate country over a very large proportion of its domestic industry.[73]

But in his treatment of wages, Cairnes paid special attention to the phenomenon of non-competing groups of trades.[74] Within such a group, he said, mobility of labor was possible, but between groups it could not take place. Equality of wages could not be reached between the groups, at least through the operation of an equalizing flow from high-wage to low-wage occupations. That is to say, the position as between the non-competing groups was exactly what Ricardo and Mill had supposed to be applicable to international trade. Within the groups exchanges tended to take place on a basis that equated the costs of production of the commodities exchanged, but between the groups the basis was reciprocal demand (which Mill had applied to international trade). Because of this, Cairnes commented that, strictly speaking, it was incorrect to speak of domestic trade as taking place on the basis of cost of production and international exchange on that of reciprocal demand :

It is thus clear that no hard and fast line can be drawn between domestic and international trade founded on the character of the obstacles presented to the movements of labor and capital; and it must, therefore, be owned that the terms "international" and "domestic" do not accurately express the distinction which it is designed to make. What we want is a term which would cover all that portion of the trade of mankind carried on between localities sufficiently separated from each other, whether by moral or physical obstacles, to prevent the action, as between producers in the trading localities, of effective industrial competition, and which would exclude the trade carried on under those more favorable conditions where industrial competition is effective. So far as I know, there is no one word that accurately meets this requirement. "International" is that which perhaps comes most nearly to what we want.[75]

Thus, with Cairnes, value theory was formally established on the foundation of *cost of production* where exchanges took place under conditions where mobility of the factors of production was possible, and *reciprocal demand* where mobility did not obtain. Cairnes's position was that the latter situation had special applicability to the field of international trade but that it was not confined to this field. Many subsequent writers on the theory of foreign trade have followed this precedent.

The Marginal Theory

Early writers. To understand later developments, it is necessary to go back to an earlier period. Some examination has been given to the work

[73] *Ibid.*, p. 305.

[74] See Chapter XII.

[75] *Some Leading Principles of Political Economy, Newly Expounded*, p. 306.

of Barbon, Law, and Turgot, who based value on utility. One of the most remarkable early writers on value was Lauderdale, who argued that both utility and scarcity were essential to value. He indicated the causes of variations in value, as follows:

> The value of every commodity, it has been observed, may be altered:
> 1. By a diminution in its quantity;
> 2. By an increase in its quantity;
> 3. By an increase of demand;
> 4. By a diminution of demand.[76]

Earlier in his book Lauderdale had given eight causes of variation in value, the four here mentioned, and "the same four circumstances, in relation to the commodity we have adopted as a measure of value" (*i.e.*, money). Obviously, he was speaking of price, in modern terminology, not value.

Lauderdale then proceeded to discuss the relation between the intensity of men's desires for a commodity and its value. Giving sugar as an example, he said:

> It is obvious, that the desire of mankind to continue their usual enjoyments, must, with certainty, raise the price of every commodity of which the quantity is diminished: this rise of value must undoubtedly, in some instances, check the demand for it; and that again tends to counteract the effects the diminution of the quantity of the commodity would otherwise have in raising its value. The rise of value, therefore, of any one commodity, in consequence of the diminution of its quantity, must be regulated by the perseverance of the consumers in their desire to enjoy the same quantity; which must universally depend on the nature of the commodity in which the scarcity exists; as the obstinacy in attempting to acquire the same quantity of it, must be proportioned to the degree of inclination which either necessity, habit, or taste, has created for it. Thus, though we have known grain, meat, and other articles of first necessity, in certain situations, and under certain circumstances, rise in value from one to fifty, articles of taste or luxury have hardly, in any instance, ever been found to rise to double or triple their usual value. The diminution of quantity, therefore, must raise the price of different commodities in different degrees, having always a more powerful effect in proportion to the degree in which the commodity itself appears necessary.[77]

Here was not merely a statement that demand was elastic but one that included the view that elasticity depended on the nature of the commodity: the demand for necessities displayed little elasticity, Lauderdale said, that for luxuries a great deal.

Elsewhere, Lauderdale mentioned, as had Cantillon and Smith, that when relative values changed, production was altered to suit:

[76] *An Inquiry into the Nature and Origin of Public Wealth*, p. 58.
[77] *Ibid.*, pp. 65-66.

when variations in value are created by an increase of demand for any commodity, the industry of the community is not alone directed to increase the production of that article, by the extraordinary encouragement derived from its augmented value; for a part of the industry is at the same time called off from the formation and production of other articles, by the discouragement which a diminution in their value creates; as was exemplified in the effects of an increased demand for sugar in raising the price of that article, and in depressing the value of wine, butchers-meat and mustard, and consequently that of various other articles.

In like manner, when variation in value is occasioned by a diminution of demand, it discourages the production of the commodity for which the demand is diminished, not alone by the great reduction of its value; for, at the same time, new and highly advantageous channels of industry are pointed out for those who were employed in producing it, by the extension of demand for, and consequent rise in, the value of other commodities, which it has been made apparent must take place.[78]

Thus in summary form were presented the essential features of the modern concept of economic equilibrium. On the production side, Lauderdale followed the lines laid down by Locke, Cantillon, and Smith; but on the side of demand he incorporated something of the utility theory, which later was to characterize the Marginal School.

More lucid and complete with respect to the relationship between utility and value was *A Lecture on the Notion of Value,*[79] by W. F. Lloyd (1794–1853), who taught economics at Oxford in the 1830's. After pointing out that the elementary wants of primitive people were soon satiated and that it was only the infinite variety of the wants of members of civilized societies which made the passion for wealth insatiable, Lloyd passed on to examine what happened to utility and value as satiation was approached:

We have come to the conclusion, that an increase of quantity will at length exhaust, or satisfy to the utmost, the demand for any specific object of desire. Having reached this point, let us now inquire, what happens, with respect to value, at the time when the demand or want is thus fully satisfied? It will be found that, in the case of every commodity, its value vanishes at the very instant of satisfaction.[80]

Water was given as an example.

To illustrate what is now called the principle of diminishing utility, Lloyd gave a hypothetical case of the type familiar to readers of modern textbooks:

Let us suppose the case of an hungry man having one ounce, and only one ounce of food at his command. To him, this ounce is obviously of very

[78] *Ibid.*, pp. 108-109.

[79] Delivered at Oxford in 1833 and published in 1837. Reprinted in *Economic History,* London 1927.

[80] *Economic History,* vol. 1, pp. 171-172.

great importance. Suppose him now to have two ounces. These are still of great importance; but the importance of the second is not equal to that of the single ounce. In other words, he would not suffer so much from parting with one of his two ounces, retaining one for himself, as he would suffer, when he had only one ounce, by parting with that one, and so retaining none. The importance of a third ounce is still less than that of the second; so likewise of a fourth, until at length, in the continual increase of the number of ounces, we come to a point, when, "through that infallible specific, eating," the appetite is entirely or nearly lost, and when, with respect to a single ounce, it is a matter of indifference whether it is parted with or retained. Thus while he is scantily supplied with food, he holds a given portion of it in great esteem—in other words, he sets a great value on it; when his supply is increased, his esteem for a given quantity is lessened, or, in other words, he sets a less value on it.[81]

Like Lauderdale, Lloyd appreciated that commodities had different elasticities of demand, and, moreover, he drew a distinction between the *extent* (or amount) of demand and its *elasticity* (or response to price changes). Likening demands to springs, Lloyd said that they may be compared absolutely or relatively. The utility of grain after an abundant harvest was comparable with a weak spring; that of grain in times of scarcity with a strong one. Here Lloyd had in mind what is now called the *extent* of demand. But, he said, utilities possessed another quality found in springs: they had different degrees of responsiveness or sensitivity. *Elasticity* was what Lloyd meant by this. *Total utility* was likewise distinguished from *marginal utility* and value identified not merely with the latter but also with cost of production, whichever might be the lesser:

To obtain the idea of the utility of an object, imagine what would happen, what inconvenience would arise, from the loss, not of that object alone, but of the whole species to which that object belongs [*i.e.*, total utility]. Thus, to obtain the idea of the utility of water, imagine the predicament we should be in, were we deprived, not of a pailful which may chance to be before our eyes, and may stand destined to some particular use, but of the whole element of water. But value . . . attaches to an object in possession, which, consequently, cannot be unlimited in quantity. To obtain, therefore, the idea of value, imagine yourselves deprived, not, as before, of the whole of the species, but only of the possession of a certain definite quantity. Take again, for example, the instance of the pail of water, and suppose it to be overturned. Its value would then be estimable, either by the inconvenience which would be felt, supposing the particular want which it was intended to supply to remain unsatisfied [*i.e.*, marginal utility], or by the trouble of going to the well again, whichever might be least [*i.e.*, cost of production].[82]

Senior, also, recognized the principle of diminishing utility. After remarking that "the mere necessities of life are few and simple," he went

[81] *Ibid.*, p. 172.

[82] *Ibid.*, pp. 175-176.

on to say that "no man is satisfied with so limited a range of enjoyment," but demands variety and even luxury:

It is obvious, however, that our desires do not aim so much at quantity as at diversity. Not only are there limits to the pleasure which commodities of any given class can afford, but the pleasure diminishes in a rapidly increasing ratio long before those limits are reached. Two articles of the same kind will seldom afford twice the pleasure of one, and still less will ten give five times the pleasure of two. In proportion, therefore, as any article is abundant, the number of those who are provided with it, and do not wish, or wish but little, to increase their provision, is likely to be great; and, so far as they are concerned, the additional supply loses all, or nearly all, its utility. And in proportion to its scarcity the number of those who are in want of it, and the degree in which they want it, are likely to be increased; and its utility, or, in other words, the pleasure which the possession of a given quantity of it will afford, increases proportionally.[83]

On the supply side, as has been mentioned earlier in this chapter, Senior saw that the supply of a commodity was conditioned by the difficulty of increasing it, that is, by the cost of producing an additional quantity. Thus Senior, like Lauderdale, had at hand the essential ingredients of Marshall's two-sided theory of value. He failed to synthesize them, however, and, notwithstanding his appreciation of the facts of demand, gave his formal support to the cost of production theory of value.

The Irish economist and judge, Mountiford Longfield (1802–1884) and the German landowner, J. H. von Thünen (1783–1850), about the same time as Senior was writing in England, both anticipated in a remarkable way the marginal theory of value which came to the front in later years. But the work of these men was concerned primarily with distribution, rather than with value theory proper, and so is left for consideration to later chapters. It should be mentioned, however, that a French engineer, A. J. É. J. Dupuit (1804–1866), gave a detailed presentation of the principle of diminishing utility, illustrated by graphs and worked out in some of its implications. Dupuit was interested in public transport and water supply, and studied the benefits furnished by undertakings in these fields. He described diminishing utility in terms similar to those used in Lloyd's lecture and published a graph which brought out the conception of consumers' surplus, subsequently popularized by Marshall. Dupuit's curve was constructed by representing the utility derived by the consumer, from each increment of the commodity purchased, by the sum of money he was just willing to pay for it. From this, Dupuit reached the conclusion drawn by Marshall later, namely that the consumer would pay for every unit that price which the last-

[83] *Political Economy*, pp. 11-12.

consumed or marginal increment was worth to him. Since the other units consumed had a higher utility than had this last one, it followed that the consumer received a surplus of utility (which Dupuit called *relative utility* and Marshall named *consumers' surplus*) on the portions consumed earlier.[84]

Another Continental writer, whose work anticipated that of the Marginal School of 1870 and afterwards, was the German Hermann Heinrich Gossen (1810–1858). In a book entitled *Entwickelung der Gesetze des menschlichen Verkehrs und der daraus-fliessenden Regeln für menschliches Handeln* (Brunswick 1854), Gossen put forward doctrines which were in some respects almost identical with those published by the Englishman, W. S. Jevons, in *The Theory of Political Economy* (1871). So similar, indeed, were the views of the two writers that in the second edition of his own book, issued in 1879, Jevons thought it necessary to disclaim any knowledge of Gossen's work when his first edition had appeared.[85] Gossen's work was published in Germany when the Historical School was dominant in that country and, although he himself had high expectations of its results, it was received with such little favor that its author ordered the destruction of the remainder of the edition a short time before his death. Because they were more influential and also because they are available in English, Jevons's writings are preferred here to exemplify marginal theory.

W. S. Jevons and his contemporaries. Soon events took a new turn. Around 1870 there arose in three different countries of Europe a new school of economists. Carl Menger (1840–1921) in Austria, M. E. L. Walras (1834–1910) in Switzerland, and W. S. Jevons in England, writing more or less simultaneously, put forward a system of economic principles based on utility. As has been shown in this chapter and elsewhere, some of the essential ideas of the group were by no means new. But in economics they had been regarded as unorthodox and, to a large extent, had been neglected. After 1870, however, they rapidly assumed a dominant position in western Europe, at least outside Germany, where the Historical School retained its powerful position.

In Chapter II it was indicated that Jevons went back to Bentham for his leading theory and treated economics as a "Calculus of Pleasure and Pain." Economics, he said,

> must be founded upon a full and accurate investigation of the conditions of utility; and, to understand this element, we must necessarily examine the

[84] Dupuit's chief papers on economic subjects have been reprinted in the original French under the title of *De l'utilité et de sa mesure,* Turin 1933. A good account of his work appears in Palgrave's *Dictionary of Political Economy*, vol. 1.

[85] Gossen's theories are described in Palgrave's *Dictionary of Political Economy,* vol. 2.

wants and desires of man. We, first of all, need a theory of the consumption of wealth.[86]

Using language similar to that of Lloyd, he gave a figure [87] to illustrate the utility derived by an individual consuming ten successive units of food in twenty-four hours :

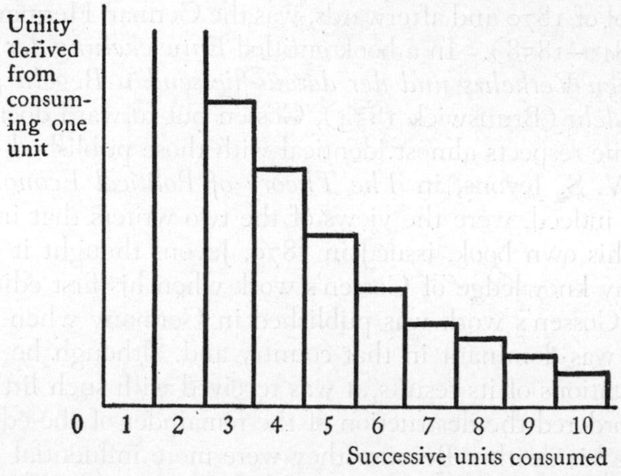

Jevons appreciated that the step-like nature of his diagram was due to the large size of the successive increments of food, in relation to the whole. The smaller the increments, the more nearly the graph which portrayed diminishing utility would be to the form of a continuous curve. For single individuals, it was absurd to speak of infinitely small quantities of food relative to the whole, but for an entire nation this was not unreasonable, Jevons said. Accordingly he proceeded to represent diminishing utility by a curve, as Dupuit had done before him : [88]

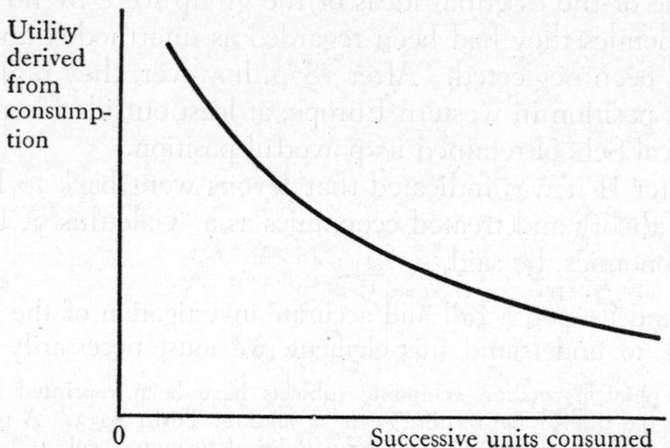

[86] *The Theory of Political Economy*, p. 39.
[87] *Ibid.*, p. 46.
[88] *Ibid.*, p. 49, simplified.

The utility obtained from the last or marginal increment consumed Jevons called the *final degree of utility*, but later it came to bear the name *marginal utility*.

On this basis, Jevons elaborated his theory of exchange. A person possessing a large quantity of commodity *A*, finds that the utility of the last increment to him is small. If he has none of commodity *B*, the utility of an increment of it to him is large. He gains, therefore, by exchanging a unit of *A* for one of *B*. Likewise he experiences a gain, though one of less extent, by exchanging a second unit of *A* for another increment of *B*, and so on. As he parts with units of commodity *A*, the utility to him of the marginal unit rises. As he receives *B*, the utility yielded by the last increment of this commodity falls. He ceases to exchange when he experiences no further gain by handing over *A* in exchange for *B*. Indeed, if he proceeded beyond the point at which it is immaterial to him whether he has a unit of *A* or of *B* he would lose. Jevons declared therefore that

The ratio of exchange of any two commodities will be the reciprocal of the ratio of the final degrees of utility of the quantities of commodity available for consumption after the exchange is completed.[89]

That is to say, in modern terminology, values conform with marginal utilities.

This theory Jevons illustrated by the following diagram:[90]

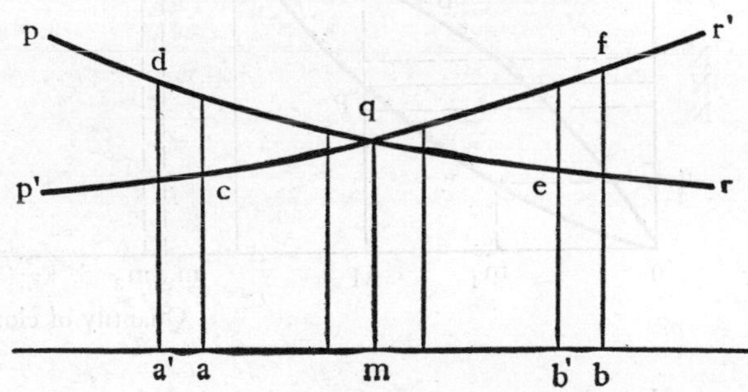

p q r is the utility curve of one of the commodities, say *A*, measured from *p*; *p' q r'* is that of the other, say *B*, measured from *r'*. An exchange of a quantity of *A* equal to *b' b*, causes the person who possessed it to lose utility equal to *b' b e*. But the quantity *b' b* which he gets of commodity *B* in exchange, returns to him a utility of *b' b f*, which is greater. It follows that his gain from exchange is equal to *b' b* multiplied by *e f*. The other party to the exchange, when he gives away his quantity *a' a*

[89] *Ibid.*, p. 95.

[90] *Ibid.*, p. 97.

(which is equal to $b' b$) of commodity B, loses utility of $a' a c$, but obtains in return a quantity of A which has a utility to him of $a' a d$. He gains, therefore, the utility represented by $a' a$ multiplied by $c d$. If exchanges were carried beyond the point m, the exchangers would lose. The possessor of A will be willing to exchange some of his stock for B as long as this point is not passed and the same is true of the individual who owns B. The ratio of exchange that is finally reached is such that the last unit of A that is exchanged, as well as that of B received in return, possesses a utility equivalent to $m q$. In other words, commodities exchange at ratios such that their marginal utilities are equal.

In *The Pure Theory of Foreign Trade,* circulated privately in 1879,[91] Marshall gave an interesting construction to represent the gains resulting from exchange. He illustrated England's demand for German linen, and Germany's demand for English cloth, by a pair of curves, $O E$ and $O G$ in the diagram that appears below: [92]

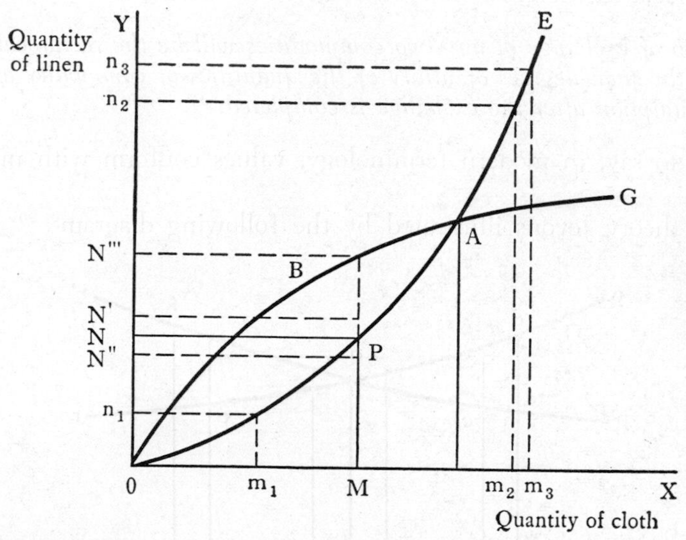

$O E$ is so drawn that from any point, say P, a horizontal line drawn to $O Y$ gives the amount of cloth that England is willing to exchange for the quantity of German linen represented by the corresponding vertical line drawn to $O X$. Thus, England is willing to give $P N$ of cloth in return for $P M$ of German linen.

[91] Reprinted in *The Pure Theory of Foreign Trade and The Pure Theory of Domestic Values,* London 1930.

[92] *Ibid.,* fig. 1, opposite p. 28. Modified for purposes of exposition. Reproduced by permission of the London School of Economics and Political Science.

of Economics, mentioned him only in a footnote. It was left to Marshall to synthesize for general use the ideas of Jevons and others, respecting demand, with those of Ricardo and John Stuart Mill, on cost of production and supply, giving to the English-speaking world a broader foundation for value theory than had been furnished by either of the antecedent schools.

Marshall. Probably it is true that the bulk of the economic writings which have appeared in English since 1890, in their treatment of the problem of value, have been based on the ideas of J. B. Clark and Alfred Marshall, especially the latter. American students, to a large extent, obtained their ideas on the marginal theory of value directly or indirectly from Clark, but that economist's main work was on distribution and is appropriately treated in Chapters XII and XIII, as well as in Chapter VIII. Even in the United States Marshall's writings had great influence, and in Britain his theories were supreme. Marshall taught at Cambridge for a large part of his life and fathered the group of Neo-Classical economists that is commonly referred to as the Cambridge School.

Notwithstanding the great influence of Marshall's work, it contained little that was altogether new. There was a shifting of emphasis, a reduction in the importance attached to this aspect, an elaboration in the direction of that, with the several parts knit together into a coherent and convincing whole. Marshall's training and outlook harked back to J. S. Mill and at first he resisted the influence of W. S. Jevons. Even later, he never admitted such conceptions as pleasure and pain into the prominent position in economic thought assigned to them by Jevons. Not *pleasures* as psychological reactions but factual *demands* were what mattered to Marshall. Therefore, while he took over the apparatus and main conclusions of the Jevonsian system, he discarded as something which was outside economics the psychological ideas which lay behind them.

But just as he drew on the ideas of Jevons, so Marshall incorporated in his theories the doctrines of Mill on the side of production. Not utility alone, nor cost of production alone, but both of these factors, according to Marshall, were necessary to explain value. They interacted with each other:

> We might as reasonably dispute whether it is the upper or the under blade of a pair of scissors that cuts a piece of paper, as whether value is governed by utility [as Jevons said] or cost of production [as Mill had maintained]. It is true that when one blade is held still, and the cutting is effected by moving the other, we may say with careless brevity that the cutting is done by the second; but the statement is not strictly accurate, and is to be excused only so long as it claims to be merely a popular and not a strictly scientific account of what happens.[108]

[108] *Principles of Economics,* p. 348.

This is essentially nothing more than was represented by Jenkin's figures and by the graph that Jevons had offered in connection with his theory of labor. Jevons's curve depicting the pleasure and pain of labor was the equivalent of a cost curve, for the pains of the labor undergone were the subjective costs of production.

Of Marshall's treatment of demand little needs to be added to what has been said already. His incorporation of the conception of consumers' surplus into a measure of social good was important, but it has received attention elsewhere.[109] It was in production that Marshall's contribution to economic theory was most important. As was mentioned in Chapter VIII, following up a distinction that had been made by Mill and his predecessors of the Classical School, Marshall identified three cases, according to whether an expansion of output was accompanied by rising unit costs (diminishing returns), by constant unit costs (constant returns), or by falling unit costs (increasing returns), the second being a condition in which tendencies in the first and last directions counterbalanced each other. In addition, he devoted special attention to the influence of time on value. Again he recognized three conditions: (1) a period too short for any production to take place, (2) one where supply could be increased with the aid of existing factors of production but where there was insufficient time for the quantities of the factors themselves to be adjusted, and (3) a period long enough for adjustments in the supplies of the factors of production to be made. In the shortest period, except for such influences as storage and sellers' fears of "spoiling the market" by sales at unusually low prices, production costs were of little significance. Supply was fixed and the strength of the demand was what governed prices. In this situation, incomes arising from the sale of the product were in the nature of rents, not being needed to stimulate the supply. In the intermediate time period, some expenses (called prime, special, or variable costs) had to be met for production to continue, except when producers were prepared to undergo losses to keep their customers and staffs together during temporary slumps in business. But other items of expenditure (fixed, overhead, or supplementary costs) were independent of output, as was the case with those representing machinery or buildings, and any returns on their account were rents. Lastly, in the long run, or normal period, excluding payments for land or other permanent advantages, all expenses became variable, because all productive factors were withdrawable. Thus,

> we may conclude that, *as a general rule,* the shorter the period which we are considering, the greater must be the share of our attention which is given to the influence of demand on value; and the longer the period, the more important will be the influence of cost of production on value.[110]

[109] See Chapter III, pp. 165-166.

[110] *Ibid.*, p. 349.

To sum up then as regards short periods. The supply of specialized skill and ability, of suitable machinery and other material capital, and of the appropriate industrial organization has not time to be fully adapted to demand; but the producers have to adjust their supply to the demand as best they can with the appliances already at their disposal. On the one hand there is not time materially to increase those appliances if the supply of them is deficient; and on the other, if the supply is excessive, some of them must remain imperfectly employed, since there is not time for the supply to be much reduced by gradual decay, and by conversion into other uses. Variations in the particular income derived from them do not *for the time* affect perceptibly the supply; and do not directly affect the price of the commodities produced by them. The income is a surplus of net receipts over prime cost; (that is, it has something of the nature of a rent. . .). But unless it is sufficient to cover in the long run a fair share of the general costs of the business, production will gradually fall off. In this way a controlling influence over the relatively quick movements of supply price during short periods is exercised by causes in the background which range over a long period. . .[111]

Both Cantillon and Smith had said something about short-term divergencies in market prices from the long-term norm set by production costs. The same is true of Senior and John Stuart Mill. What Marshall did was to develop this feature of value theory. Marshall lived in an age of capitalistic production. A large percentage of the expenditure incurred for productive purposes, in many industries, was for long-lasting and specialized equipment. Once capital had been embarked in the construction of such equipment, it could not be freed or mobilized for other uses, so its owners had to be content with whatever remuneration they could obtain from its employment. On the other hand, profitable businesses were protected, in some measure, by the large expense and long time necessary for competitors to enter their field, and therefore might manage to sell their products above cost for substantial periods. According to Marshall, the cost to which price tended to correspond in the long run was the *marginal cost,* that is, the cost of the most expensive increment of the product obtained by utilizing inefficient factors of production or by working others intensively and at great expense. Whenever price was in excess of marginal costs, expansion of output was encouraged. New firms were attracted to the industry and existing businesses stimulated to produce a greater quantity. Conversely, when price fell below marginal costs, there was an inducement to contract output. Inefficient firms or plants might shut down and others operate on a reduced scale.

Böhm-Bawerk and Wieser. Harking back to Jevons's contemporary, Menger, and following a different path from that chosen by Marshall, a group of Austrian economists—of whom, along with Menger himself,

[111] *Ibid.*, pp. 376-377.

the most notable figures were Böhm-Bawerk and Wieser—built up another variety of the marginal theory of value.

As opposed to Marshall's *cost of production* (that is, cost required to induce the productive use of the factors responsible for production), Wieser developed a conception of *alternative, opportunity,* or *transfer* costs. According to Wieser, costs were not prices necessary to call forth supplies of the factors of production (that is, to induce these factors to produce at all); they were the payments that were needed to attract the productive factors from the other uses open to them. The cost of an agent of production, therefore, was the price required to exclude the next highest bid for its services. Wieser's statements on this subject may be quoted:

Productive elements which admit of only one kind of employment, do not share the multiplicity of conditions necessary for the emergence of what we recognise as costs. A mineral spring, which can be used only by drawing off its contents and putting them into bottles, must, obviously, stand in a quite different relation to the value of the product from the unskilled labour which fills the bottles, but is capable of a hundred other uses besides.[112]

Whenever the business man speaks of incurring costs, he has in mind the quantity of productive means required to achieve a certain end; but the associated idea of a sacrifice which his efforts demand is also aroused. In what does this sacrifice consist? What, for example, is the cost to the producer of devoting certain quantities of iron from his supply to the manufacture of some specific product? The sacrifice consists in the exclusion or limitation of possibilities by which other products might have been turned out, had the material not been devoted to one particular product. Our definition in an earlier connection made clear that cost-productive-means are productive agents which are widely scattered and have manifold uses. As such they promise a profitable yield in many directions. But the realization of one of these necessarily involves a loss of all the others. It is this sacrifice that is predicated in the concept of costs. . .[113]

This view of costs was popularized in America by H. J. Davenport. It was described in that writer's book on *The Economics of Enterprise*, as follows:

We are in substance seeking a formula for human choices in the field of production. Here choice follows the psychological law valid for all human activity: *men follow the line of least sacrifice*. . . Only where, between two lines of agreeable work, one chooses that line which in process and product affords the larger satisfaction of wants is the formula of *the maximizing of pleasure* adequate. But the formula of *the minimizing of sacrifice* is everywhere sufficiently inclusive. For the man who works because he finds work pleasant, it would be a sacrifice to refrain from work; he chooses that line

[112] *Natural Value*, p. 175.

[113] *Theorie der gesellschaftlichen Wirtschaft* (Tubingen 1914), translated by A. F. Hinrichs as *Social Economics*, N. Y. 1927; pp. 99-100 of the translation. Quoted by permission of the Adelphi Company.

of work which he prefers, in view both of the pleasures of the activity and of the accompanying compensations in productiveness. He ceases to work at the point where continuance would be the greater sacrifice. The man to whom all effort is irksome chooses that line of activity which, in view both of the quality of the work and of its compensation, involves the smallest sacrifice. For him who prefers idleness to activity, activity would mean the larger sacrifice. This principle of minimizing sacrifice is, then, the generalization for which we are seeking. . .

So far then as he planned his work rationally, Crusoe was continually turning his efforts to that undone thing, the doing of which had come to be of leading importance — subject all the while, of course, to the condition that it was worth the labor penalties involved. At a certain point fishing was abandoned for game : More fish were refused in the interest of more game. The game cost fish, or the fish cost game ; since the work which would produce either fish or game was applied to game and withdrawn from fish. The limit upon production, the cost barrier, was reached at the first one of two margins, — the margin of effort and of displaced recreation, or the margin of displaced alternative product. These displacements of possible products, these foregoings of alternative openings, these sacrifices of some second thing in the process of getting some particular thing, are perhaps best indicated under the term *opportunity costs*. To go without fish to get game or to raise wheat upon terms of foregoing the raising of corn may be taken as illustrative of one of the simplest aspects of this doctrine of opportunity cost. . .

Suppose, for example, that a child has been given both a pear and a peach ; that some predatory boy tries to seize them ; and that the only method of saving either is to drop one, say the pear, in the wayside weeds, and to run for shelter with the peach while the aggressor is picking up the pear : What has the peach cost ? True the peach was a gift. In a certain sense, therefore, it cost nothing. Nevertheless it is retained only on terms of foregoing the pear. The term *cost* seems not quite satisfactory to cover the case. Perhaps *displacement* or *foregoing* would be preferable. Or, if one offers you your choice between a ride and an evening at the theater, it is awkward to say that the acceptance of the one is at the cost of the other. Yet the resistance to the taking of the one is the letting go of the other. . . Or, if with a dollar which you have earned you are at choice between buying a book or a pocket knife, and finally buy the book, the resistance overcome is best expressed, not by the labor devoted to the earning of the dollar, and not by the dollar itself, but by the alternative application of the dollar. . . The highest cost of the book, the best test or measure of its worth to you, was in the significance of its strongest competitor, the knife.[114]

It is evident that costs, on the definition of Wieser and Davenport, are not merely disutilities or pains suffered by reason of the labor and abstinence involved in production. They include utilities or pleasures sacrificed. The cost of a wooden plow to a savage, for instance, is not merely the toil and trouble of making it but the most desirable thing that has

[114] *Op. cit.*, pp. 59-61.

to be foregone in order that the plow may be procured—which may be the fish that would have been caught had the savage chosen to spend his time fishing instead of constructing the plow (*i.e.*, the most attractive "alternative"). The pains or disutilities of labor are only effective costs if the savage's "next preference" is idleness.

The usefulness of such a concept in understanding the disposal of economic resources will be appreciated. In so far as men guide their conduct by enlightened self-interest, they direct resources into the channels that appear to be most attractive, selecting those that are able to outbid the rest. This principle has been familiar in economic literature from the time of Cantillon and Smith : what was new with Wieser and Davenport was its special application to the problem of cost. Acceptance of the doctrine that costs are displaced opportunities was to some extent a logical consequence of the emphasis placed by Wieser upon the short period. But the principle had the effect that the Austrian group of economists, of which Wieser was a member, got away from Marshall's two-sided theory of value, with cost of production on the one hand and demand or utility on the other. Since costs represented alternative utilities, both supply and demand came to depend on utility.

Another idea developed by the Austrians was what is sometimes called "the reversibility of the supply curve." Wicksteed, especially, the leading English follower of the Austrian group, was associated with this principle. So was Böhm-Bawerk. It was admitted that trade did not always take place between one set of people who were suppliers and another who were demanders, but that persons who were suppliers at high prices might enter the market and buy when prices fell to lower levels. Even under short-run conditions, when production could not take place, supply was not definite but depended on price, since this had to be high enough to exclude the bids of the present possessors, some of whom would retain their ownership if the price were sufficiently low. Böhm-Bawerk's famous example of a horse market illustrated this. Ten prospective buyers and eight sellers were assumed to be confronting one another in the market, with schedules as follows : [115]

Buyers		*Sellers*	
A_1 values a horse at (and will buy at any price under this amount) . . .	£30	B_1 values a horse at (and will sell at any price above this amount)	£10
A_2 " " " " "	£28	B_2 " " " " " "	£11
A_3 " " " " "	£26	B_3 " " " " " "	£15
A_4 " " " " "	£24	B_4 " " " " " "	£17
A_5 " " " " "	£22	B_5 " " " " " "	£20
A_6 " " " " "	£21	B_6 " " " " " "	£21.10s.
A_7 " " " " "	£20	B_7 " " " " " "	£25
A_8 " " " " "	£18	B_8 " " " " " "	£26
A_9 " " " " "	£17		
A_{10} " " " " "	£15		

115 *The Positive Theory of Capital*, p. 203.

It must be admitted, however, that while this situation may be true enough of a horse market, in which the suppliers are farmers who themselves have use for horses or at least possess grassland upon which they can graze, it is quite inapplicable to the ordinary run of modern specialized markets. Automobile manufacturers cannot use more than a very small percentage of the cars which their factories produce. Dentists, for physical reasons, cannot ordinarily serve themselves. On the other hand, where dealers have access to storage facilities, the reversibility of the supply curve is not only real but of everyday occurrence, as traders add to their stocks by making purchases when prices decline to low levels and reduce these stocks by sales when prices rise. Thus it is seen that the Austrian economists provided a different basis for the supply curve or schedule from that adopted by Marshall. Supply was conditioned, not by the cost of *calling into existence* a commodity or its factors of production, but by the price necessary to *exclude other uses, including that of the supplier himself*. Obviously, this conception is more pertinent in the short run than that of Marshall, who, indeed, went some way toward admitting it in respect to his "temporary equilibrium" in the short period during which production was impossible. Marshall's cost of production concept was more applicable to the longer periods which were his chief concern.

Another significant feature of the Austrian theory was Böhm-Bawerk's "law of the marginal pairs." Instead of continuous curves, crossing at the point of equilibrium, such as those of Jevons, Jenkin, and Marshall, Böhm-Bawerk took account of the fact that often demand and supply were not divisible into small fractions (so as to give continuous curves) but altered by relatively large increments, leading to discontinuities. This was true of the horse market. A person could not buy or sell a fraction of a horse but only an entire animal. So it happened that, in the case of the horse market example given above, demand and supply overlapped by as much as 10s. (*i.e.*, ten shillings or two and a half dollars), leaving this range as a field for bargaining. Between £21 and £21. 10s. in the illustration, there were five buyers and five sellers in the market. With small markets and large units of commodity—the market for houses or farms in a particular locality, for instance—overlaps of large dimensions are quite common. Thus the writer remembers being told by a real estate dealer of a case where only one buyer appeared when a certain house was offered for sale. The deal was consummated and afterwards, in conversation, it was learned that the buyer would have been prepared to go nearly $2000 above the bottom price at which the seller was willing to sell.

The mathematical equilibrium theorists. A further variant of the marginal theory goes back to M. E. L. Walras. Instead of balancing curves of schedules that represented the demand and supply of a single commodity (in the manner favored by Jevons, Marshall, and the Austrians), Walras aimed at presenting a statement of economic equilibrium that comprehended all commodities and all productive factors.

Clearly, the demand for an article is influenced not only by its price but by the prices of other goods. For instance, the demand for coffee is not only governed by the price of coffee, diminishing if this rises and increasing when it falls. If complementary goods, like milk, sugar, or cups, rise in price, a cup of coffee as ordinarily consumed will cost more, so that the demand for coffee will fall just as certainly as if coffee itself had increased in price. The demand for these articles is evidently a joint one and the situation was recognized as such and dealt with by Marshall. But other and, in some cases, more remote influences are at work. If competing goods, such as beer or tea, become cheaper, while coffee remains at its old price, to some extent the consumer shifts his demand for drinks to beer and tea, diminishing the demand for coffee and causing the price of this commodity to become lower. If radio sets or automobiles get dearer, the consumer, in order to continue to afford these items, may stint to some extent his consumption of coffee. Further, if it happens that a staple commodity such as bread falls in price, the consumer may choose to devote an increased proportion of his income to the purchase of more elaborate foods, with the surprising result that the demand for the article that has got cheaper (*i.e.*, bread) *diminishes*. Thus, not merely one price and one commodity, but all prices and all commodities, possess significance in determining demand. In other words, to take the case of coffee, the equation of demand is not $D = {}^{f}\,{}^{p}$ coffee, where $D =$ the demand for coffee, ^{p} coffee $=$ the price of this commodity, and ${}^{f} =$ a definite mathematical function, but $D = {}^{f}$ (^{p} coffee, ^{p} milk, ^{p} sugar, ^{p} cups, ^{p} tea, ^{p} beer, ^{p} radios, ^{p} automobiles . . . ${}^{p}n$), where ^{p} coffee, ^{p} milk, etc., are the prices of these articles, and n is the total number of commodities. The same is true of supply. If rubber becomes dearer, land, labor, and capital may be attracted from coffee to rubber growing and the supply of the former commodity may be diminished, causing its price to increase. Factors of production that are mobile between different uses, are apportioned, not merely according to the demand for their services in one of these, but with reference to the demands of all. If one factor of production becomes cheaper, relative to another, the cheaper factor tends to be substituted for the dearer in productive operations. If, say, because of an increased propensity of people to save, the supply of new capital increases without a corresponding increase in the supply of labor, capital becomes relatively cheaper and supplants in some uses the dearer labor, Marshall's *principle of substitution* referred to this situation. With Marshall, however, the principle of substitution was, as it were, off the main track of theoretical presentation. The neatly balancing and readily understandable curves of supply and demand, expressed by the equations $S = fp$ and $D = fp$ (where S = supply, D = demand, f = a definite function, and p = price), occupied the center. Walras's formulae for economic equilibrium were too complicated to admit of any complete graphical representation. Two dimensions can be depicted on a plane surface, three in a solid, but Walras's equations had innumerable dimensions and geometric representation was impossible. Resort was had, therefore, to simultaneous equations for resolution, and, at the price of this complexity, there was presented a comprehensive picture of economic equilibrium. Marshall's curves were of an *other things being equal* nature. They showed how the demand for coffee, and the supply, would vary if the price of this commodity changed, on the assumption that all other prices remained unaltered. The formulae of Walras brought in the other prices. A notable group of economists have followed suit, including Wicksell and Cassel in Sweden, and Pareto at Lausanne.[116]

The use of marginal cost and marginal revenue curves. In the last few years, there has come into use a form of graphical representation that, for some purposes, is a decided improvement on the curves used by Jevons and Marshall. The curves used by these older writers depicted totals and averages. At a price of, say, 25 cents, a hundred articles would be produced. At 50 cents, three hundred, and so on until at $2.50 production rises to five thousand. Quantity and cost *per unit* (that is to say, *average costs*) are what are given here. Income from sales may be represented in the same fashion. At a price of 25 cents, twenty thousand articles would be sold. At $2.50, sales would amount, say, to only five hundred. Here, again, are quantity and *revenue per article,* or *average revenue.* The new technique has added the concepts of *marginal cost* and *marginal revenue.* The advance has been developed in a number of writings, of which *Notes on Supply* (*Economic Journal* 1930) and *The Economics of Imperfect Competition* (London 1933), by the Cambridge economists R. F. Harrod (1900–   ) and Joan Robinson (1903–   ), respectively, and *The Theory of Monopolistic Competition* (Cambridge, Mass. 1933), by the Harvard teacher E. H. Chamberlin (1899–   ), are deserving of special mention.

The marginal cost is, of course, the cost of adding an extra unit of output. If this cost is below the average, the effect of adding another unit (at lower cost) is to *bring down* the average. If, on the other hand,

[116] English presentations of the ideas of this group of economists are available in K. Wicksell's *Lectures on Political Economy* (translated by G. Classen, 2 vols.), vol. 1, London 1934, G. Cassel's *Theory of Social Economy,* and the recent study by J. R. Hicks on *Value and Capital.*

the cost of an additional unit is more than the average, producing it will *raise* the average. It follows, therefore, that the curves, when constructed, have forms such as the following:

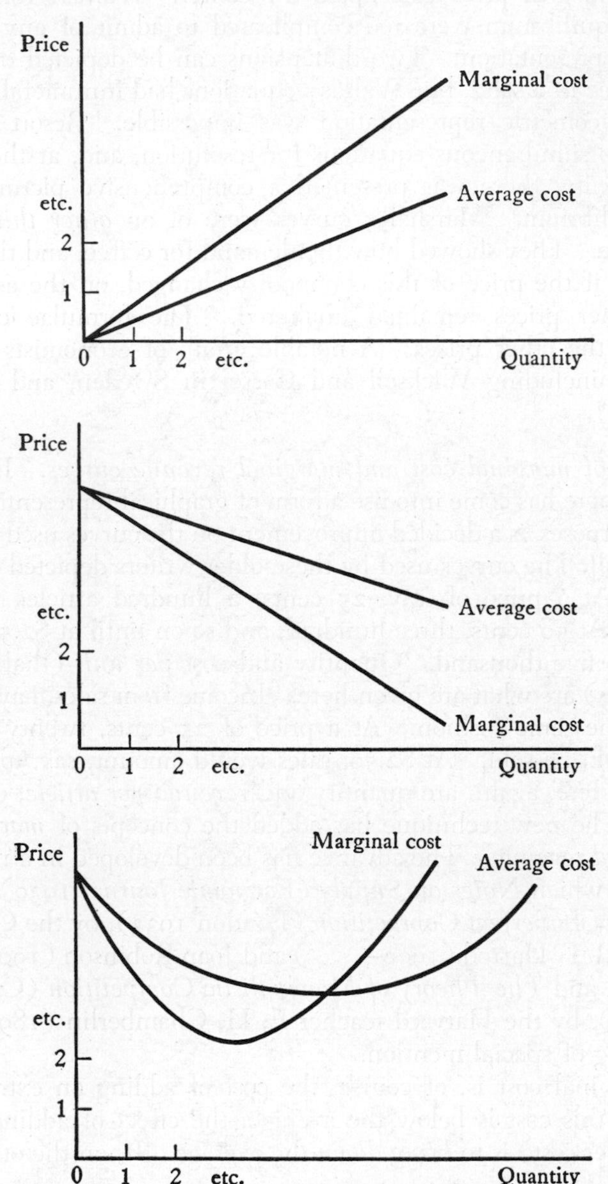

Under competitive conditions, it is argued that a producer will bring forth an output of such size that (1) marginal revenue equals marginal cost and (2) average revenue equals average cost, giving a construction[117] of the following nature:

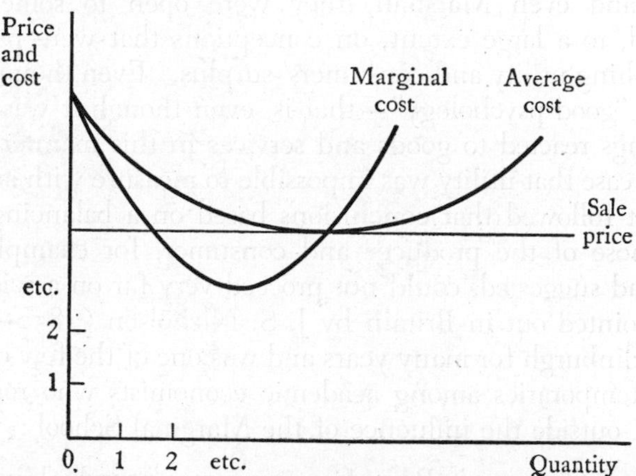

It can be seen readily why this is the case. That producers will carry their production as far as the point where the revenue from the marginal increment of output just covers the cost of this increment is a commonplace of marginal theory. Marginal revenue therefore approximately equals marginal cost. But if, in the case of the least efficient firm in the industry, average revenue is less than average cost, then the firm concerned is losing money and must ultimately go out of business, causing the supply of the commodity in the market to fall off. The price therefore rises, increasing the average revenue of the remaining firms. On the other hand, if average revenue for the marginal or least efficient firm in the industry is greater than average cost, new firms will come in, lowering prices and therefore bringing down average revenues. But what of the firms that are more advantageously situated? Clearly, they owe their advantage to some non-competitive situation, such as a more favorable location, better business management, etc. The extra returns which result from these superiorities are surpluses or rents, so that it can be said that, if rents are included in cost, then all firms are in the position of the least efficient firm with respect to the balancing of average revenue and average costs. And, *under the influence of competition* these non-competitive advantages tend to disappear. So that it can be said that *in a condition of perfect competition such advantages are non-existent,* and that marginal revenue equals marginal cost and average revenue equals average cost.

[117] Under competitive conditions, it is assumed that the output of a single firm is very small relative to the whole market, so that it can be increased without affecting materially the sale price of the product. To the individual firm, therefore, demand is virtually completely elastic, and the sale price line represents both average and marginal revenues. See the discussion of Cournot's work, appearing on pp. 470-471.

Criticism. In one form or other, the marginal theories have been dominant in the last half-century. As expressed by W. S. Jevons, the Austrians, and even Marshall, they were open to some objections. They rested, to a large extent, on conceptions that were psychological, like diminishing utility and consumers' surplus. Even though they were accepted as "good psychology" — that is, even though it was agreed that men's feelings reacted to goods and services in this manner — it still remained the case that utility was impossible to measure with any accuracy. From this it followed that conclusions based on a balancing of relative utilities (those of the producer and consumer, for example), such as Marshall had suggested, could not proceed very far on a scientific basis. This was pointed out in Britain by J. S. Nicholson (1850–1927), who taught at Edinburgh for many years and was one of the few of Marshall's British contemporaries among academic economists who remained to a large extent outside the influence of the Marginal School:

> If the idea of Consumer's Rent [*i.e.*, consumers' surplus] were intended simply to explain the varying degrees of satisfaction derived from spending money in various ways — in other words, if it were intended simply for the explication of certain conceptions — the hypothetical character of the measurements assumed might be passed over. But Professor Marshall definitely states that 'the exact measurement of the Consumer's Rent in a market has already a great theoretical interest, and may become of high practical importance.' He applies the notion also to such definite concrete problems as the imposition of taxes and the bestowal of bounties. . . Stripped of its technical phraseology, this amounts to saying that a government, with advantage to the *community*, might tax bread and coals to give a bounty on calico and matches. . . A paradox of this kind is only presentable when arrayed in hypotheses. . .[118]

Nicholson proceeded to examine the hypotheses, and reached the conclusion that

> No expansion of the formula, 'the more we have the less we want,' can be a sufficient substitute for the enumeration of the many and various actual conditions which govern the consumption of wealth, and the prices of commodities and services.[119]

Nicholson was only one of a number of objectors among economists to the psychological assumptions that lay behind some of the marginal theories. As was noticed in Chapter II, the result was seen in an attempt to formulate the marginal theory of value in a manner that avoided the need for assumptions of this nature. The idea of balancing the pleasure of consumption against the pain of production was left behind, and, in

[118] *Principles of Political Economy,* 3 vols., London 1893-1901, vol. 1, 1893, p. 63. Quoted by permission of A. & C. Black Ltd., and The Macmillan Company.

[119] *Ibid.,* p. 65. This passage was deleted in the second edition (1902) but Nicholson's general position remained unchanged.

its place, was put an equilibrium of demand and supply as evidenced in the market. On this basis, Cassel and others were able to give allegiance to marginal principles while offering a vigorous criticism of the psychology of Jevons and his group. Yet there were economists, including Nicholson, who declined to accept this solution. Demand, they said, was complex. Conscious choice between alternatives—a fundamental principle of the marginal system—was one factor, they agreed. But there were others, such as custom. People bought some things because they were so accustomed, without giving the subject a moment's thought. A certain price, like that of the morning newspaper or a doctor's fee, became likewise a matter of custom, and both demand and supply adjusted themselves to the customary price. Customs changed as time went on: for instance, the heavy gold chains and ostrich-plumed hats which delighted members of an earlier generation, ceased to be wanted and produced. Economists who emphasized such factors had little patience with the nicely-balanced curves and intricate mathematical equations that attracted their Neo-Classical contemporaries, based as these were on assumptions concerning the background. They had more interest in studying the background itself. Hence, the antagonistic attitude of such men as Schmoller and Veblen towards the marginal theory of value.

After all, it is evident that equations of the form of $D = fp$, which represent demand as a function of price, are applicable only in so far as demand is actually governed by price. Every non-price influence on demand has the effect of reducing the correlation between demand and price; and if the volume of such influences is sufficiently large it becomes pointless to make use of the equation at all.

Pareto's reply to such critics of mathematical economics was pungent. "Alas, good soul," he said to the objector, "mathematical economics helps, at least, to a rough understanding of the effects of the interdependence of economic phenomena, while your gabble shows absolutely nothing!" [120] Obviously this was an over-statement, because institutional studies have brought to light a great deal. On the other hand, probably the rank and file of present-day economists will agree that there is enough connection between demand and price to serve as the basis of a generalization of the "other things being equal" type. Criticism can always be parried by a reference to the type of "other things" that must be considered, together with a refusal to estimate their relative significance in particular situations. For it is evident that conditions change a good deal. Custom may be significant over long periods, as when a house lease is renewed from year to year without much attention to market conditions. But when its influence is broken—for example, when the tenant moves to a new district—bargains may become highly competitive.

[120] *The Mind and Society*, vol. 1, p. 20.

Monopoly

Early Monopolistic Situations

An examination of historical records shows that monopoly was an ancient phenomenon. A Roman trader might possess a supply of corn in time of scarcity and, in the absence of some form of public control, charge a high price to his customers. A medieval merchant might "engross" the available stock of a certain commodity. A craft gild might have on its membership roll all the local producers of the article in which it is interested. An association of overseas traders might hold the sole right to engage in a particular form of traffic. There is evidence to the effect that such situations were often abused. For example, the British company of Merchant Adventurers (originally a group of trading gilds but later a chartered company, chiefly employed in the export of cloth) was attacked at various times for the manner in which it excluded prospective traders from the field. This policy was avowed by the company and justified by the plea that "Our trade is too narrow for our traders" (*i.e.*, the trade was overcrowded).[121] The charter of the British East India Company, granted in 1600, conferred upon the company "the whole, entire and only trade" to and from the East Indies, and this company in its turn became subject to opposition on the ground of its monopolistic power.

The Classical Economists

It is sometimes said that the British Classical economists built up a system of economics based on competition and neglected monopoly. This is incorrect. Not only did some of them recognize the limitations of competition in the short run but they admitted the existence of monopolistic situations of more lasting nature. This was particularly true of Adam Smith.

It was an essential part of Smith's equilibrium theory, like that of Cantillon, that market prices could rise above or fall below production cost in the short run. This brought the possibility of temporary profits or losses, which disappeared in the long run, when prices tended to correspond to the costs of production. Smith's reference to the price of black cloth during a public mourning is classic :

> Such fluctuations affect both the value and the rate either of wages or of profit, according as the market happens to be either over-stocked or under-stocked with commodities or with labour; with work done, or with work to be done. A public mourning raises the price of black cloth (with which the market is almost always under-stocked upon such occasions), and augments the profits of the merchants who possess any considerable quantity of it. It

[121] E. Lipson, *The Economic History of England*, vol. 2, London 1931, p. 216. Quoted by permission of A. & C. Black Ltd., and The Macmillan Company.

has no effect upon the wages of the weavers. The market is under-stocked with commodities, not with labour; with work done, not with work to be done. It raises the wages of journeymen tailors. The market is here under-stocked with labour. There is an effectual demand for more labour, for more work to be done than can be had. It sinks the price of coloured silks and cloths, and thereby reduces the profits of the merchants who have any considerable quantity of them upon hand. It sinks too the wages of the workmen employed in preparing such commodities, for which all demand is stopped for six months, perhaps for a twelvemonth. The market is here over-stocked both with commodities and with labour.[122]

The general reasoning here is clear. A temporary shortage of black clothes raised the price of the tailors who could make them and also of the cloth that went into their manufacture. But the demand for weavers was unaffected, either because the scarcity was too temporary in its nature to justify making more cloth or because weavers could make this type of material instead of that which might have been used otherwise. Both cases were possible and it is not evident which of them Smith had in mind. Colored silks and cloths were in the opposite situation.

Smith remarked that, notwithstanding the existence of fluctuations of this kind, market price was "continually gravitating" towards the cost of production. Those who made exceptional profits were careful to conceal them, to prevent an influx of rivals, and sometimes they were successful for a time:

If the market is at a great distance from the residence of those who supply it, they may sometimes be able to keep the secret for several years together, and may so long enjoy their extraordinary profits without any new rivals.[123]

A dyer who has found the means of producing a particular colour with materials which cost only half the price of those commonly made use of, may, with good management, enjoy the advantage of his discovery as long as he lives, and even leave it as a legacy to his posterity.[124]

In the case of some "singular and esteemed productions" of land, like wines from some of the vineyards of France, the commodities may "continue for whole centuries" to be sold at a price in excess of the cost of production, this fact being reflected in high land values. Such monopolies, Smith thought, may even be permanent:

Such enhancements of the market price are evidently the effect of natural causes which may hinder the effectual demand from ever being fully supplied, and which may continue, therefore, to operate for ever.[125]

Trading franchises did not escape his attention, as is shown in a later passage.[126]

[122] *Wealth of Nations,* Bk. 1, Chap. 7. [123] *Ibid.* [124] *Ibid.* [125] *Ibid.*

[126] See the extract referred to in Footnote 130.

Smith gave examples of other monopolistic situations :

People of the same trade seldom meet together, even for merriment and diversion, but the conversation ends in a conspiracy against the public; or in some contrivance to raise prices.[127]

We rarely hear, it has been said, of the combinations of masters, though frequently of those of workmen. But whoever imagines, upon this account, that masters rarely combine, is as ignorant of the world as of the subject. Masters are always and everywhere in a sort of tacit, but constant and uniform, combination, not to raise the wages of labour above their actual rate. To violate this combination is everywhere a most unpopular action, and a sort of reproach to a master among his neighbours and equals. We seldom, indeed, hear of this combination, because it is the usual, and one may say, the natural state of things which nobody ever hears of. Masters too sometimes enter into particular combinations to sink the wages of labour even below this rate. These are always conducted with the utmost silence and secrecy, till the moment of execution, and when the workmen yield, as they sometimes do, without resistance, though severely felt by them, they are never heard of by other people. Such combinations, however, are frequently resisted by a contrary defensive combination of the workmen; who sometimes too, without any provocation of this kind, combine of their own accord to raise the price of their labour. Their usual pretences are, sometimes the high price of provisions; sometimes the great profit which their masters make by their work. But whether their combinations be offensive or defensive, they are always abundantly heard of.[128]

Smith spoke of land as a monopoly and took occasion to remark that its price was determined on monopoly principles :

The rent of land . . . is naturally a monopoly price. It is not at all proportioned to what the landlord may have laid out upon the improvement of the land, or to what he can afford to take; but to what the farmer can afford to give.[129]

This brings out Smith's theory of monopoly price, which had been stated earlier in his book :

A monopoly granted either to an individual or to a trading company has the same effect as a secret in trade or manufactures. The monopolists, by keeping the market constantly under-stocked, by never fully supplying the effectual demand, sell their commodities much above their natural price, and raise their emoluments, whether they consist in wages or profit, greatly above their natural rate. The price of a monopoly is upon every occasion the highest which can be got. The natural price, or the price of free competition, on the contrary, is the lowest which can be taken, not upon every occasion indeed, but for any considerable time together. The one is upon every occasion the highest which can be squeezed out of the buyers, or

[127] *Ibid.*, Bk. 1, Chap. 10, Pt. 2.
[128] *Ibid.*, Bk. 1, Chap. 8.
[129] *Ibid.*, Bk. 1, Chap. 11.

which, it is supposed, they will consent to give : the other is the lowest which the sellers can commonly afford to take, and at the same time continue their business.[130]

It is plain that Smith had only part of the truth here, unless, indeed, the monopolists were short-sighted. Seeking to maximize their profits (an assumption which Smith seems to have made, like many later writers on monopoly), the monopolists restricted the supply of their commodity which went on to the market. Thereby, they secured a higher price than could have been obtained had they produced all that could be sold at a price sufficient to cover production costs. But this did not mean that it would pay them to obtain the highest possible price. Profit is a function of two dimensions : (1) excess of price over cost, and (2) number of articles sold. It is easy to demonstrate that the highest price "which can be got" would, where the demand is at all elastic, cut down sales to such an extent as to lower the monopolist's profit. Smith, who paid no attention to elasticity of demand, failed to perceive this point.

Ricardo's theory of value was limited to conditions of competitive production, as was mentioned earlier in this chapter, but it will be remembered that he admitted certain exceptions—the "rare statues and pictures," etc., whose value was independent of the quantity of labor required to produce them. These were in fixed supply and their value depended on "the varying wealth and inclinations of those who are desirous to possess them." Such cases were exceptional, however, in Ricardo's opinion, and could be neglected. But this was not the case with land. Ricardo assumed that land, as such, was plentiful but that the better soils were scarce, with the result that the owners of the more fertile tracts could exact from their users a price that had no relation to any labor that might be involved in settling the land and rendering it suitable for cultivation. Rent, therefore, according to Ricardo, was a monopoly price, as Smith had said, though Ricardo himself did not make this altogether clear.

An early critic of Ricardian doctrines, Samuel Bailey, took Ricardo to task for the emphasis he had placed on competitive production and the manner in which he had neglected monopoly. Having stated a number of objections to Ricardo's value theory in his book, *A Critical Dissertation on the Nature, Measures, and Causes of Value,* Bailey commented :

Mr. Ricardo did not, evidently, allow sufficient importance to that source of value which he calls scarcity; nor did he consistently bear in mind, that it was the very same principle which enabled the owner of land, or of mines, of more than common fertility, to raise the value of their articles beyond what would afford the customary profit. Instead of scarcity, or, in other words, monopoly, or protection from competition, being an unimportant source of value, and the commodities which owe their value to it forming a

[130] *Ibid.,* Bk. 1, Chap. 7.

Marshall

Marshall wrote along lines that represented a logical advance from the position of J. S. Mill. He realized that, in the long run or normal period, the possibility of adjusting the supplies of the productive factors and transferring them between different uses made for competitive pricing. But he saw also that, in shorter periods, such adjustments and transfers could be, at best, only incomplete. Reference has been made already to this aspect of Marshall's work.

In addition, he furnished a lucid and comprehensive treatment of monopoly pricing, using curves to show how the monopolist, pursuing his greatest advantage, would determine the supply or price of the commodity produced. But Marshall was not content to limit his study to this case. He considered another, in which the monopolist regarded consumers' surplus as equally desirable with monopoly profit. Admitting that monopolists who regarded benefit to others as equally important to that received by themselves might be uncommon, Marshall introduced a compromise arrangement in which the monopolist producer counted two units of consumers' surplus as being on the same plane of attractiveness as one unit of profit to himself. Graphs were supplied, to elucidate the actions of these kindly-disposed monopolists.

Here, evidently, Marshall was attempting to be realistic. He recognized that even monopolists were not necessarily so selfish that they considered only their own interests. In any event, Marshall argued, there were instances where it paid the monopolists to sell at lower prices than would maximize immediate profits. A railroad, for example, may sacrifice present gain to develop in its area a thriving community, productive of future business and profits. With respect to publicly-owned monopolies, of which there were many, he commented,

when a municipality undertakes the supply of gas or water, or facilities for transport by improved roads, by new bridges, or by tramways, the question always arises whether the scale of charges should be high, so as to afford a good net revenue and relieve the pressure on the rates [*i.e.*, local taxes]; or should be low, so as to increase consumers' surplus.[135]

Economists and politicians have been accustomed to revile the monopolist and, undoubtedly, experience has afforded considerable justification for this attitude. Yet, probably benevolence is no more unusual as a motive within the breast of monopolists than elsewhere among mankind. The writer remembers being in the home of a certain poor family when the local doctor (a monopolist) called to visit a sick member. Having performed his medical duties, the doctor left on the table, not an account for services rendered, calculated on the basis that would maximize his own income, but a gift of £1 ($5.00). Obviously, if such practices were

[135] *Principles of Economics*, p. 487.

characteristic of monopolists, monopoly would be less important as a practical problem than it is. Even if benevolence be regarded as non-existent, or ruled out, it is evident that monopolists have to take a long view. Policies that would maximize profits immediately may arouse a public clamor, which might be reflected in adverse legislation or in a falling off of demand for the commodity produced. Further, as Marshall pointed out, a large number of monopolies are owned by central and local government bodies, especially in the field of public utilities. Here, it is reasonable to expect that the operating authorities have considerable regard to the interests of consumers, who are often broadly identical with the owning groups.

Imperfect Competition After Cournot

It is difficult to imagine a market situation in which there is no fear of competition. If there be excluded such competition as that existing between a monopolized product and the other articles that compete with it for inclusion in the consumer's purchase list, it is obvious that many cases of monopoly rest on institutional factors. This is true of so-called "natural monopolies." Thus, supposing that all the diamonds of the world came from a single mine, owned by a monopolistic corporation, what would confer the monopoly power would not be *nature* but the *property right* that barred out other diggers, exactly as with the franchise of a public utility concern or the patent of an industrial enterprise. This fact restricts the exercise of monopoly power. What laws have given, they can take away, so that a monopolist who passes beyond the limits of social approval does so at his own risk. A utility undertaking developed on the basis of a franchise, therefore, may find itself facing the risk of destruction or competition, and this limits its control of prices. Further, the authority that establishes the monopoly power may condition it in some way. In Britain, for instance, a patentee is not permitted to follow the dog-in-the-manger policy of refusing to manufacture something for which he possesses exclusive rights. If he refuses to produce the patented article, his rights lapse. Again, franchises have often been granted for utility undertakings, subject to provisions for rate regulation.

The line of demarcation between commodities (including services) is not hard and fast. Mr. Brown may have a perfect monopoly of "Brown's Centerville Bread" and some consumers may be greatly attached to this product, but with respect to his sales to other buyers he may be in active competition with numerous manufacturers of brands that satisfy the same need on the part of the consumer. Bread, itself, must compete with other foods in some degree. This situation was allowed for, no doubt, in the demand curves that Marshall used in his monopoly graphs, but it must be admitted that it goes a long way towards breaking down the separation of value into two compartments—competi-

Specialist Literature

Reference may be made to the literature that has appeared in applied economics, as distinct from pure theory. Economists concerned with some of the practical aspects of business have had to face theoretical problems involved in their specialities. The work that has been done on the subject of railway rates will serve as an example.

Railroad service has been highly monopolistic, at certain times and places, and in other instances subject to severe competition. Its provision requires expensive equipment of a specialized and long-lasting nature. Its product—transportation—is itself semi-specialized, in that one form of traffic requires equipment which is to some extent different from that needed for another. Freight cars are different from the corresponding passenger rolling stock, refrigerator cars for fruit traffic from cars intended to carry coal. As between the various types of transport, costs cannot be divided with any completeness, because specialization is only partial and many costs are incurred for more than one class of traffic. Because of this, it has been argued, notably by the American, F. W. Taussig,[138] that railway rates are a special case of *joint costs,* a subject to which Marshall and others had given attention. Opponents of this view, such as the English economists, W. M. Ackworth, R. Y. Edgeworth, and A. C. Pigou,[139] have emphasized the extent to which cost adjustments can be made as between different types of traffic, so that the product—transportation—is made to appear more homogeneous. From this angle, variations in the charges made for this homogeneous service seem to rest, not upon differences in cost, but on those in the value of the services rendered. The railroads thus become classified as discriminating monopolies, whose selling prices (*i.e.*, rates) are determined by what the traffic will bear.

Much ground is common to the disputants. It is evident that the *special* or *prime* costs of carrying particular parcels of traffic must be met in the short run, and that in the long run *all costs* must be covered if the railway undertakings are to continue. It is clear, too, that costs that can be allocated specifically between different classes of traffic must be met from the receipts of these branches and that there must be sufficient surplus over such costs to meet those expenses that are joint and cannot be divided. All this is familiar to readers of Marshall. What is at issue, therefore, is the emphasis to be given to the various aspects. To what extent can there be said to be competition and how far monopoly? How completely can costs be divided? What time period is in mind? Is the

[138] See Taussig, *A Contribution to the Theory of Railway Rates, Quarterly Journal of Economics* 1891.

[139] See R. Y. Edgeworth, *Contributions to the Theory of Railway Rates, Economic Journal,* 1911–1912, reprinted in *Papers Relating to Political Economy,* vol. 1, and A. C. Pigou, *Wealth and Welfare,* London 1912, and *The Economics of Welfare.*

problem one of how railroad managers *do* in fact arrange their rate schedules, or how, having in mind the public interest, they *should* fix rates? Or is it a question of the principles which should underlie the decisions of regulatory bodies when dealing with corporations which presumably are able to take care of their own interests? Evidently, this leads to the subject of price regulation in general.

Regulated Values Again

Government Measures to Control Monopoly

The criticism to which some of the early trading companies were subjected, on the grounds of their monopolistic practices, has been mentioned. In the latter part of the eighteenth century, the East India Company was controlled by the British government in various ways. Not merely was it taxed, but a maximum rate of dividend was prescribed by law, and parliament even interfered with the price of its tea. This obviously anticipated the modern policy regarding public utilities.

Undoubtedly the most important development of recent years, in the field of practical valuation, has been this tendency towards authoritative price determination. The rise of monopolies or partial monopolies has led to a serious problem of social control. It has been feared—not without justice in some instances—that monopolistic institutions might exploit consumers and sellers of the factors of production, especially the laboring class.

One line of approach has been the prohibition or destruction of monopolies, that is, the enforcement of competition. Thus, the Sherman Act of 1890, in America, enabled the government in the early years of the present century to prosecute a number of trusts and, in some instances, to break them up, an example being the dissolution of the old American Tobacco Company. The ban on railway amalgamations in Britain, following the report of the Cardwell Committee in 1853, was of similar nature. Another case was the agreement between the British banks and the Treasury, sequential to the proceedings of the Committee on Amalgamations of 1918, to the effect that no further bank mergers would take place without Treasury consent. With the passage of time, however, sentiment has changed and there is no longer the same emphasis on preserving competition for the purpose of protecting the consumer, though feeling in favor of this kind of action has not altogether disappeared.

Instead, the tendency is for monopolies to be permitted to exist but to be subjected to some form of control. The British railways were regulated to some extent from their infancy and systematic rate control came in 1888–1893. In America the Granger laws of the 1870's established the principle of State regulation of railroad rates, and control by the State public service commissions of the rates charged by other utility under-

been fought out in legislative assemblies and law courts. Some of the leading decisions in this country have been the effect of the protection afforded by the Federal Constitution to property rights. In the *Smyth vs. Ames* case of 1897, a ruling of the regulatory body of the State of Nebraska was contested on the ground that railroad rates established by it were unduly low. The Supreme Court found that, as a matter of fact, the rates were confiscatory and, therefore, illegal. The judges went on to indicate some of the factors that should be taken into account in rate determination:

> the basis of all calculations as to the reasonableness of rates to be charged by a corporation maintaining a highway under legislative sanction must be the fair value of the property being used by it for the convenience of the public. And in order to ascertain that value, the original cost of construction, the amount expended in permanent improvements, the amount and market value of its bonds and stock, the present as compared with the original cost of construction, the probable earning capacity of the property under particular rates prescribed by statute, and the sum required to meet operating expenses, are all matters for consideration, and are to be given such weight as may be just and right in each case. We do not say that there may not be other matters to be regarded in estimating the value of the property. What the company is entitled to ask is a fair return upon the value of that which is employed for the public convenience. On the other hand, what the public is entitled to demand is that no more be exacted from it for the use of a public highway than the services rendered by it are reasonably worth.[140]

Here were set up two different criteria; (1) fair return on fair value of the property, and (2) value of the services rendered. Serious problems were raised. What percentage return was to be considered as fair? How was the capital value to be calculated? Several factors were mentioned as being significant in arriving at capital value but how was it to be determined what weight was "just and right" with respect to each of them?

The Transportation Act of 1920 laid it down that the regulatory commissioners should adjust rates so that the carriers as a whole, or in groups, should earn a fair return on their capital—5½ per cent being indicated. With respect to the first two years of the Act's operation, it was provided that an additional amount of ½ per cent might be allowed for improvements and betterments, and this was in fact granted in 1920. In 1922, however, the permissible rate was lowered to 5¾ per cent, at which level it remained until the law was changed in 1933. It was declared that this provision for a percentage return was not a guarantee to the railroads and subsequent events demonstrated their incapacity to earn the

[140] 169 U. S., pp. 546–547.

establishment of widely varying percentage returns, each case being considered on its merits. The Bluefield decision of 1923 resulted in the interesting formula that a utility was entitled to earn a return equal to that made currently in the same part of the country on other businesses involving corresponding risks and uncertainties, but uncertainties are too difficult to assess for such a ruling to be meaningful.

One of the most outstanding controversies has been that relating to the basis of valuation of assets. What weight, if any, should be given to the costs of reproduction? Though suggested in earlier cases, the problem did not become very important until after the war of 1914–1918, when inflation had raised construction costs substantially. In the Southwestern Bell Telephone case of 1923, the court ruled that a public service commission order which made no allowance for increased construction costs was unconstitutional. In the Hope Natural Gas case of 1944, however, the court accepted the original cost basis. Original investment, prudently made, now receives wide support as a basis for rate-making.

The Economic Factors

The whole subject has been one of hot debate. Fairness is not an economic conception, yet economic factors are at work. If rates are fixed so low that capital is not reinvested in the regulated industry and new funds are not forthcoming, then people's wants will go unsatisfied, at least so far as private enterprise is concerned. In the case of some of the disputants, it seems possible that this result is intended—public ownership being the goal. But it is evident that public ownership will not remove the necessity for the supply price of capital to be met and low rates may be illusory if they are only maintained because the general public underwrites the risks involved.

The Transportation Act of 1933, modifying the law of 1920, already referred to, laid down the principle that railroad rates were to be determined with due regard to their effect on the movement of traffic and the maintenance of an adequate and efficient transportation service. But even this economic criterion was attended by difficulties. For instance, just how much regard should there be for the effect of rate reductions in stimulating the movement of traffic? How long could rates be forced, consistent with the furnishing of railway service? In view of the high percentage of total costs represented by relatively long-lasting equipment, it is clear that, without causing the railroads to suspend operation, rates could be reduced, over short periods, considerably below what would ensure the maintenance of railway service in the long run. Short-term costs would be covered and traffic would continue to be carried by the existing equipment, yet there would be no motive for the replacement of the latter.

This brings out a major point in the controversy. People seem to feel

society, and thus cover the whole of production. The prices of the factors of production, too, are thus determined through the principle of scarcity. The demand of consumers is indirectly a demand for factors of production, which demand can be adequately restricted only by placing suitable prices on the factors of production. The principle of scarcity thus has exactly the same application to the socialist economy as to the present economic system, except that in a socialist society subject to a single rational control it would, in fact, have to be maintained much more completely than is possible under the present system.[142]

But this idea has been contested, notably by the Austrian economist, Ludwig von Mises. Mises has argued that competition is necessary for the scientific distribution of productive resources. Competition between consumers governs the prices of goods and services ready for consumption. The entrepreneur guides the factors of production into the appropriate channels. Thus are the wants of consumers brought into adjustment with the supplies of scarce means to meet these wants, so as to maximize satisfaction and minimize production costs. Under socialism, or any form of centralized planning, such adjustment on any scientific basis would be impossible, Mises contended, because there would be no private ownership of the factors of production and therefore no real competitive market for their services. Without such a market, the calculations whereby wants and scarce means are brought into relationship with each other in the individualistic economy would be impracticable. As costs cannot be calculated, there would be no method of knowing which is the more economic of alternative means to achieve the same end. In the absence of these calculations, decisions must be made on the basis of vague valuations. This thesis was set forth by Mises in his book on *Socialism*. The passage given below will serve to exemplify the argument :

Suppose, for instance, that the socialist commonwealth was contemplating a new railway line. Would a new railway line be a good thing? If so, which of many possible routes should it cover? Under a system of private ownership we could use money calculations to decide such questions. The new line would cheapen the transportation of certain articles, and, on this basis, we could estimate whether the reduction in transport charges would be great enough to counterweigh the expenditure which the building and running of the line would involve. Such a calculation could be made only in money. We could not do it by comparing various classes of expenditure and savings in kind. If it is out of the question to reduce to a common unit the quantities of various kinds of skilled and unskilled labour, iron, coal, building materials of different kinds, machinery and the other things which the building and upkeep of railways necessitate, then it is impossible to make them the subject of economic calculation. We can make systematic economic plans only when all the commodities which we have to take into account can be assimilated to money. True, money calculations are in-

[142] *The Theory of Social Economy*, pp. 134-135.

complete. True, they have profound deficiencies. But we have nothing better to put in their place. And under sound monetary conditions they suffice for practical purposes. If we abandon them, economic calculation becomes absolutely impossible. This is not to say that the socialist community would be entirely at a loss. It would decide for or against the proposed undertaking and issue an edict. But, at best, such a decision would be based on vague valuations. It could not be based on exact calculations of value.[143]

Lionel Robbins and F. A. von Hayek, also have argued that a calculated price equilibrium (without any real market) is impracticable. Various writers have controverted this, endeavoring to develop systems of valuation that are suitable to a collectivist economy and proving the practicability of such systems to their own satisfaction, if not to that of others.

Obviously, the possibility of solution turns on whether or not it is possible to devise a system of factor prices that will reflect the relative scarcities of the factors of production, in the absence of private enterprise and private ownership. But it must be recognized that many socialists—bearing in mind the extent of monopoly and the manner in which consumer choices are influenced by advertising in our present society—doubt whether authoritarian direction is likely to be less rational. The practicability of such direction is not in question. There is no doubt whatever that the government of a collectivist State could decide how the factors of production are to be disposed of and what commodities are to be produced. What Mises questioned is whether, in the absence of a free market that reflects the relative scarcities of the productive factors and the intensities of demands for the various products, economic considerations can receive proper attention. Further, it has been asked whether a socialist system can be devised that will permit individual freedom of choice with regard to consumers' goods, going beyond a mere nominal selection of articles that the planning authority has decided to make available. Obviously this problem is associated with the other and in neither case is experience in authoritarian societies of much value in reaching a solution. In reviewing the literature that has come into existence in recent years on the subject, it seems impossible to resist the conclusion that the line of division between the two sides turns on the broader political and philosophical views of the contestants. Those who have given their allegiance to socialism or authoritarianism on other grounds do not appear to be perturbed by the thesis of Mises that, under collectivism, probably productive resources would be used wastefully. On the other hand, convinced opponents of collectivist philosophies seem unlikely to be converted to them by any demonstration of the practicability of socialist pricing.

[143] *Op. cit.*, pp. 121-122. Quoted by permission of Jonathan Cape Ltd., and The Macmillan Company.

something akin to the modern rent in the sense of representing the commercial value of the property concerned.[1]

Chapter IV should be referred to in connection with the emergence of property rights in the ancient world. Individual ownership and use seem to have evolved out of some sort of social use and control, but it is clear that, by the time of Roman dominance, there was something approaching free trade in land, at least in certain areas. In due course, however, individual ownership and competitive bargaining respecting land, such as they were, declined with the rise of the feudal system.

The Evolution of the Land System from Feudal Times

Landholding was an integral part of feudal organization. There was a two-way system of rights and duties. Land was held. Payments were made by the holder to him from whom he held it. But the payments were not for the land as such, in the manner familiar in tenancy bargains of the twentieth century. Often the man who made them was himself unfree and paid dues *as a person* rather than *as a holder of land.* But even in the middle ages there were some freemen who were in a position to drive bargains, concerning land and services, that partook more of the nature of the modern contract.

This class of freemen grew in numbers with the passage of time, and the same appears to have been true of what may be called free land, that is, land that was outside the two-way ties of the medieval system. In England, after the Black Death of the fourteenth century, large numbers of serfs fled from their manors to become freemen elsewhere. The enclosure movement in the sixteenth century had the effect of conferring freedom on many more. A considerable number of these men became tenants of the modern type, holding land by virtue of payments that they contracted to make in return.

The means by which medieval landholding was transformed into modern property ownership have been described in Chapter IV. The feudal estates either (1) were broken into small peasant proprietorships by the abolition or commutation of the cultivators' dues, or (2) became the personal property of the lords by the destruction of the connection of the serfs with the soil. In England, most of the land was rented out to tenant farmers, but on the Continent extensive areas were farmed by noblemen and, in France especially, considerable sales to townsmen and others took place.

When what is now the United States of America and the British self-governing dominions were opened up, much of the land passed into the possession of cultivators at an early stage. But even these coun-

[1] See *Primitive Economics of the New Zealand Maori,* pp. 285-286. Firth mentions that it is not the *payment* but the *offer of payment* which implies a recognition of ownership. Often it is refused, because to accept it might be regarded as an admission of a right of continuing occupancy.

which they could be commuted, were worth over 2 shillings (48 cents) per acre. At their market value, the customary payments were calculated to amount to about 3 shillings and 9 pence (90 cents) per acre. Obviously, on the basis of these figures, it would pay a serf to leave the manor and become a tenant elsewhere. He would give up land for which he paid labor services worth in the market as much as 90 cents, and which required 48 cents to commute them, for land just as good but costing only 21½ cents. It is no matter for surprise, therefore, to learn from economic historians that many serfs abandoned their manors and went to other lords as tenants. True, their former masters had a legal right to reclaim the runaways, but tracing them must have been a difficult, if not impossible, task.

Great stability existed in the payments made for land in the subsequent period. According to the author quoted above, nearly all the Forncett land that had formerly been subject to labor services had been converted into leaseholds with money rents by 1406. The figures make clear that these money rentals failed completely to reflect the inflation of prices (and presumably of farming profits) that took place in the latter half of the sixteenth century. Indeed, rents declined in face of rising commodity prices. In 1527–1528, the total rent roll of the manor was £55 (say $275), whereas it had fallen to £47 ($235) by 1604–1605. Rogers's *History of Agriculture and Prices in England* gives decennial average prices for wheat as follows: 1521–1530 7 shillings and 6 pence ($1.80) per quarter, 1603–1612 35 shillings and 3½ pence ($8.57) per quarter — a rise of between three and four hundred per cent. Other commodity prices shared this increase. Moreover, the diminution in money rental does not fully reflect the fall that took place in the cultivators' payments. The extinction of serfdom as a legal condition, which in Forncett was completed in 1575, meant the disappearance of other dues for which the peasant was liable, such as the fines payable on inheritance.

Rents in the Seventeenth and Eighteenth Centuries

Both custom and competition appear to have been important in seventeenth century England. The eminent Nonconformist preacher, Richard Baxter, in his *Christian Directory*, gave some attention to the problem of land rent, as well he might in offering a set of rules for the guidance of practical men in a country which was predominantly agricultural. Baxter asked:

> *Is it lawful for a mean* [*i.e.*, poor] *man, who must needs make the best of it, to purchase tenanted Land of a liberal Landlord, who setteth his Tenants a much better pennyworth* [*i.e.*, gives them a better bargain] *that the buyer can afford?* [4]

[4] *A Christian Directory*, Pt. 4, p. 140.

tries have not been free from the problem of large proprietorships. Quebec, in the early days of French settlement, had a feudal system modeled on that of the mother country. In Australia and New Zealand considerable areas of land — some of which later proved suitable for closer settlement — were granted to graziers and land companies. In the United States a few large properties are still to be found, notably the Scully estates in the Middle West. The South has its own problem of large plantations, now often cultivated in small tracts by share-croppers. In the richer agricultural areas of America, much of the land originally granted in homestead lots is rented to tenants. Practically all the empty agricultural areas of the world, that have come into the possession of English-speaking settlers, were opened up after private property and free renting had become established in Europe. It was only to be expected, therefore, that modern European — and particularly British — ideas on land bargaining would be reflected in the land policies of these newer countries. But in spite of this, the bulk of the land was not sold or rented indiscriminately by the several governments. It was handed to settlers, subject to obligations like residence and cultivation. Those responsible for public policy in the new countries were able to perceive that the development of the empty lands would be influenced by the manner in which individuals were permitted to acquire title to the soil. In consequence, free trade in land played a small part in the growth of these young countries. There are exceptions, but in general it can be said that unrestricted bargaining in land appeared in the newer parts of the English-speaking world only after the obligations of the early settlers had been fulfilled.

The Beginnings of Commercial Renting

It is evident that something in the nature of a free market in land arose in England when free tenants began to rent land in the fourteenth, fifteenth, and sixteenth centuries, and it has been common to date the beginning of commercial renting from this period. It was believed that the enclosure movement, associated with the prosperity of sheep farming in the sixteenth century, had a widespread influence in this connection. Before then, the argument ran, payments in connection with the occupancy of land were on a customary basis. Afterwards, the principle formulated by Ricardo started to operate. Farmers competed with each other for the possession of land. Their profits had to cover (1) subsistence wages and (2) the ordinary return on capital. Anything remaining from the product went in rent to the landowner.

Recent research has shown that the significance of the early enclosures has been exaggerated, the area affected by them being much smaller than was thought formerly. The question arises, what view is to be taken respecting the emergence of competitive renting?

In the first place, it appears possible that something allied to the Ricardian principle operated even before the appearance of commercial tenancy. The serfs of the middle ages were, in the eyes of the law, the property of their lords and could be "tallaged" or taxed at the will of the latter. In these circumstances, evidently the lords could tallage their serfs to such an extent as to leave them merely with a minimum for subsistence, taking the whole surplus produce into their own possession. That such a situation was not unknown is suggested by a statement in *Fleta*,[2] a treatise on English common law dated about 1290 and apparently written for the guidance of landlords and their officials. The author, whose identity is uncertain, recommended that inquiry should be made, with respect to the serfs,

of each what they are worth for tallage, without committing waste or impoverishment, and how much their works [*i.e.*, labor services] and dues are worth and how much is given in rent each year. . .[3]

The tallage was an additional levy, imposed by the lord at will. What the writer of this passage appears to have had in mind, therefore, was that all other payments made by the peasants should be taken into account in order to discover whether, in view of their subsistence needs, they could be tallaged farther. Here was no customary rent or fixed payment but a situation in which any surplus that existed above the subsistence minimum might find its way, through the tallage, into the landlord's pockets.

Yet it must be recognized that custom was very influential in governing the dues paid by the peasants to their lords. It is unlikely that the lords' officials kept close checks upon what the serfs could pay, adjusting tallages to suit, as *Fleta* advised. Probably, only in the event of something unusual arising, such as a peasant becoming obviously well off, or an alteration in economic conditions that affected the whole system of ordered relationships, was much done in the way of adjustment of dues. The Black Death of 1348–1349 was an instance of this kind. Many peasant holdings lost their occupants by death. Labor services fell off. Landlords could not handle the land on their own account because of the scarcity of labor. The result was that it became possible for the surviving peasants to rent vacant land at rates far lower than was represented by the dues on their customary land. A writer on English economic history, F. G. Davenport, in *The Economic Development of a Norfolk Manor 1086–1565* (Cambridge 1906), gave the information that money rents on the manor of Forncett, Norfolk, in 1376–1378 (after the Black Death), averaged 10¾ pence (21½ cents) per acre. The customary services due from such land, estimated at the low rate for

[2] The work was said to have been written in the Fleet Prison, London. This explains the title. Extracts are translated in *The Manor Farm*, by F. H. Cripps-Day, London 1931.
[3] *Ibid.*, p. 46. Quoted by permission of the author and B. Quaritch, Ltd.

The answer, Baxter said, depended on whether a tenant "hath by custome a half-title to his easier Rent" and whether the alternative was an even more oppressive purchaser.

A similar answer was given to the question of whether a landlord might raise rentals. A rise to the full value of the land was unjust, Baxter remarked, where a tenant had been accustomed to a lower rent. Further,

The common case in *England* is, that the Landlords are of the Nobility or Gentry, and the Tenants are poor men, who have nothing but what they get by their hard labour out of the Land which they hold : And in this case some abatement of the full worth is but such a necessary Mercy, as may be called Justice.[5]

ordinarily the common sort of Tenants in England should have so much abated of the fullest worth, that they may comfortably live on it, and follow their labours with cheerfulness of mind, and liberty to serve God in their families, and to mind the matters of their salvation, and not to be necessitated to such toil, and care, and pinching want, as shall make them liker Slaves than Freemen, and make their lives uncomfortable to them, and make them unfit to serve God in their families, and seasonably mind eternal things.[6]

This is probably what Thomas Aquinas would have said, had he asked the same question four centuries earlier. Baxter's argument was ethical but he had been a clergyman in a country town for much of his life and probably knew a good deal about farm rents. He spoke as if it were quite common for rents to be "easier" than the full worth of the land justified, but also as though the opposite case existed, namely that of rack-renting. Frequently, he referred to the influence of custom. The reference made, in the first of the passages quoted above from the *Christian Directory*, to the position of the "mean man" as compared with that of the "liberal landlord" seems broadly representative of a situation existing in England for many years. Large landowners have not always been meticulous in exacting the full competitive value of land from their tenants, whereas small owners who have purchased farms as investments and expected them to furnish an adequate income have often given greater attention to this point.

Rogers quoted an English agricultural work published some time before Baxter wrote, Norden's *The Surveyor's Dialogue* (1607), as evidence of the existence of competitive renting. Norden was concerned in defending the surveyors and land agents against the charge that they incited landlords to raise rents. Tenants were their own enemies in this respect, he said, by bidding against each other for farms :

And, should any that is in authority in this case (who in duty is not to hinder the lord) or the lord himself inhibit such hot spirits to climb as

[5] *Ibid.*, p. 141. [6] *Ibid.*

sowing, picking of choice seed instead of taking it promiscuously, steeping it instead of using it wholly unprepared, and manuring the ground with salt instead of rotten straw, &c) then will the Rent be as much more advanced, as the excess of encrease exceeds that of the labour [*i.e.*, Ricardo's *intensive* margin].[13]

In other words, if the counties near London could not produce all the produce necessary, it must be grown in those farther afield and its price must rise to cover the additional transport cost. But at the same time the land near at hand would be farmed more intensively. In either case, rent would represent the difference between the cost of production and the returns from the sale of the produce.

Finally in a letter to a correspondent, Petty wrote that as people multiplied rents rose proportionally:

I conclude, that as People double faster now then they did in former Ages, so ye Rents of Lands must also rise proportionably, and ye number of years Purchase also. . . .[14]

And, in *A Treatise of Ireland* (1687), he commented:

If the Rents of the Lands of England and Wales be 11 Millions, when the People are but 7 Millions, then the Addition of another Million will make the Rents $\frac{1}{7}$ Part more than now, and the Number of Year's Purchase will be $\frac{1}{7}$ more also. . . .[15]

If these statements are compared with the theory set forth by Ricardo more than a century afterwards, it will be found that Petty anticipated some of the main ideas of the later economist.

Turgot. Cantillon and the Physiocrats appear to have regarded the rent of land as in some way the gift of God to the landowners. They thought that Providence had so arranged matters that labor employed on land gave rise to a product greater than that which could be obtained by utilizing the labor in any other employment. The additional amount went as rent to the owners of the land.

When land was cultivated, there was applied (1) labor and (2) capital in the form of tools and workers' maintenance. According to the Physiocrats, the labor must be remunerated sufficiently to cover the cost of its subsistence. The capital had to be restored. What was left of the produce after these two payments were met constituted rent. It was a unique surplus arising in the economic system. This aspect of the Physiocratic theory has been discussed in Chapter VIII and requires no attention here.

[13] *Ibid.*, p. 52.

[14] *Ibid.*, p. 467 (footnote). The reference to an increase in number of years' purchase refers to a fall in the rate of interest at which the rent was capitalized. It was customary to speak of land as worth so many years' purchase (*i.e.*, so many annual rents).

[15] *Ibid.*, p. 564.

high for the lord's advantage as the ladder of their own will, or supposed ability, will reach? I should think it a greater madness for a lord wilfully to refuse what is so voluntarily offered, and so willingly given.[7]

On the other hand, Rogers himself repeatedly mentioned the great stability of land rents.[8] It seems likely that both custom and competition were operative, therefore, even at an early date. Below, it will be argued that this was true later.

About the time of Baxter, Gregory King, in giving figures of British incomes, estimated the rent of land at about one third of the total produce. Davenant modified King's data somewhat, and put rent at about one quarter of the produce of corn land. Petty gave rent as one fourth of total income. Cantillon said that it amounted to one third of the produce of land, but he was speaking of France, where conditions differed from those in England. Feudal dues, which in England had disappeared long before, persisted in many parts of France in the eighteenth century. Moreover, in France rents commonly took the form of a share of the produce (as in present-day America), instead of the cash rents which were usual in Britain. According to Arthur Young, the English agricultural writer who described rural conditions in France in 1787–1789 (about fifty years after Cantillon wrote), tenancies of the English type—where cultivators rented for cash direct from the landowner—were not unknown. But a large percentage of the land was in *metayage*, or share tenancy, much of it being leased from its owners by middlemen for cash and sub-let by the latter to small farmers on a share basis. The proportion of the produce paid by the cultivators as rent, and the amount of capital that they furnished, varied to some extent, as they do in modern America. Young, incidentally, was severely critical of the French system of tenancy. From his comments, it appears evident that custom exercised a good deal of influence in determining the rentals to be paid, and that the system was such that the benefits of improvements went largely to the landlords. As a result, enterprise was deterred. Had competition been operative, and especially had long leases been granted, the farmer might have been able to retain a sufficient proportion of the extra product for which his labors were responsible, to stimulate him to efficiency. This, at least, was the argument of the English writer.

Modern Theories of Rent

The Emergence of the Ricardian Theory

Petty. As may be expected, mindful of the importance of agriculture and of land rent in national income, seventeenth and eighteenth century writers on economics gave some attention to the theoretical explanation of rent.

[7] *A History of Agriculture and Prices in England,* vol. 5, p. 42.

[8] See *Ibid., vol.* 4, pp. 725, 739; vol. 5, pp. 801-802.

In *A Treatise of Taxes & Contributions,* Petty asserted that rent represented a surplus, the balance of the produce of land after the costs of cultivation had been met:

Suppose a man could with his own hands plant a certain scope of Land with Corn, that is, could Digg, or Plough, Harrow, Weed, Reap, Carry home, Thresh, and Winnow so much as the Husbandry of this Land requires; and had withal Seed wherewith to sowe the same. I say, that when this man hath subducted his seed out of the proceed of his Harvest, and also, what himself hath both eaten and given to others in exchange for Clothes, and other Natural necessaries; that the remainder of Corn is the natural and true Rent of the Land for that year; and the *medium* of seven years, or rather of so many years as makes up the Cycle, within which Dearths and Plenties make their revolution, doth give the ordinary Rent of the Land in Corn.[9]

Petty said that the corn would exchange for the amount of silver that could be produced in the same time by a man who went to a country where this metal was available, refined it and transported it to the corn grower.[10]

If corn were dear, rents were higher proportionately:

for as great need of money heightens Exchange, so doth great need of Corn raise the price of that likewise, and consequently of the Rent of the Land that bears Corn, and lastly of the Land it self. . .[11]

Petty perceived clearly the effect of location and transport costs on rent. He gave examples of corn growing forty miles from London and only one mile away, saying that at the latter place the price of corn would be higher by the cost of transport for the additional thirty-nine miles. With perishable commodities, the "hazard of corrupting" had to be added also.

Hence it comes to pass, that Lands intrinsically alike near populous places . . . will not onely yield more Rent for these Reasons, but also more years purchase then in remote places, by reason of the pleasure and honour extraordinary of having Lands there. . .[12]

He showed an understanding of the two ways by which produce could be increased—the "extensive" and "intensive" methods made familiar by Ricardo later:

For if the said five Shires [*i.e.,* near to London] did already produce as much Commodity, as by all endeavour was possible; then what is wanting must be brought from a far, and that which is near, advanced in price accordingly [*i.e.,* Ricardo's *extensive* margin]; or if by the said Shires by greater labour then now is used, (as by digging instead of Ploughing, setting instead of

[9] *The Economic Writings of Sir William Petty,* vol. 1, p. 43.
[10] Compare with Senior's theory of the value of money. See Chapter XIV.
[11] *The Economic Writings of Sir William Petty,* vol. 1, p. 48. [12] *Ibid.,* p. 49.

But Turgot offered an explanation of rent which suggested that of Ricardo. As has been indicated earlier in this chapter, the French system of land tenure in the eighteenth century was somewhat complex. Many of the feudal lords did not lease their land directly to cultivators but rented it in large parcels to enterprisers, who, in turn, leased it in small plots to peasants on a share-rent basis. Discussing the rent paid by the enterprisers (or undertakers), Turgot argued,

The competition of rich Undertakers in agriculture fixes the current price of leases in proportion to the fertility of the land and the price at which its products are sold, always according to the calculations the Farmers make, both of their expenses and of the profits they ought to draw from their advances: they cannot give the Proprietor more than the surplus. But, when the competition among them is very keen, they give him all this surplus, the Proprietor only letting his land to him who offers the highest rent.[16]

That is to say, the enterprisers (undertakers or farmers) expected to get a return on their capital that—according to Turgot's views on profits—was comparable with the income obtainable from other investments of capital. Any product above what was required to give this profit might be paid in rent to the landlords. How much was so paid depended on the intensity of the competition for leases but in no case could the enterprisers afford to pay to the owners more than the entire surplus. The cultivators, who rented from the enterprisers, received profits that were, in effect, subsistence wages. If the enterprisers discussed by Turgot be regarded as the equivalent of the farmers of Ricardo's England, and the French cultivators as comparable with English farm laborers, then Turgot's explanation of the situation becomes similar to that of Ricardo. The main difference seems to be that, where Turgot spoke as if the enterprisers might pay to the landlords *anything up to the entire surplus produce,* Ricardo asserted that competition would force them to pay this amount.

Adam Smith. Smith discussed rent, but did so without presenting an unequivocal theory. At one point in the *Wealth of Nations,* he seemed to support the Physiocratic belief that rent was an attribute of land as such:

But land, in almost any situation, produces a greater quantity of food than what is sufficient to maintain all the labour necessary for bringing it to market in the most liberal way in which that labour is ever maintained. The surplus too is always more than sufficient to replace the stock which employed that labour, together with its profits. Something, therefore, always remains for a rent to the landlord.[17]

[16] *Reflections on the Formation and the Distribution of Riches,* p. 56.
[17] Bk. 1, Chap. 11, Part 1.

Obviously, "always" and "in almost any situation" are not consistent with each other. "Always" represented the Physiocratic position, but "in almost any situation" suggested that Smith had doubts.

Earlier in the same chapter, however, Smith had spoken of rent as being governed by the principle now coupled with the name of Ricardo :

Rent, considered as the price paid for the use of land, is naturally the highest which the tenant can afford to pay in the actual circumstances of the land. In adjusting the terms of the lease, the landlord endeavours to leave him [*i.e.*, the tenant] no greater share of the produce than what is sufficient to keep up the stock from which he furnishes the seed, pays the labour, and purchases and maintains the cattle, and other instruments of husbandry, together with the ordinary profits of farming stock in the neighbourhood. This is evidently the smallest share with which the tenant can content himself, without being a loser, and the landlord seldom means to leave him any more. Whatever part of the produce, or, what is the same thing, whatever part of its price, is over and above this share, he naturally endeavours to reserve to himself as the rent of his land, which is evidently the highest the tenant can afford to pay in the actual circumstances of the land.[18]

Smith remarked that the rent of land varied with fertility and situation, land that was more fertile or nearer to market commanding a higher rent. But he neglected to say whether or not there were some "actual circumstances" of land that were so disadvantageous that the cultivator could afford to pay no rent whatever for its use. Indeed, he seemed almost to align himself definitely with the Physiocrats on this point, when he commented,

The rent of land, it may be thought, is frequently no more than a reasonable profit or interest for the stock laid out by the landlord upon its improvement. This, no doubt, may be partly the case on some occasions; for it can scarce ever be more than partly the case. The landlord demands a rent even for unimproved land, and the supposed interest or profit upon the expense of improvement is generally an addition to this original rent.[19]

But, again, "scarce ever" left a loophole.

The question of whether rent was coincident with surplus produce (surplus in the sense of being in excess of that required to cover the ordinary remuneration of capital and labor) was ventilated :

Sometimes, indeed, the liberality, more frequently the ignorance, of the landlord, makes him accept of somewhat less than this portion; and sometimes too, though more rarely, the ignorance of the tenant makes him undertake to pay somewhat more, or to content himself with somewhat less, than the ordinary profits of farming stock in the neighbourhood.[20]

Here, Smith evidently agreed with Turgot that rent and surplus were not necessarily identical, yet, a page or so afterwards, he declared that the rent of land was "a monopoly price." He proceeded :

[18] Bk. I, Chap. II. [19] *Ibid.* [20] *Ibid.*

depend on the difference in the quality of these two portions of land."[25] If population be augmented further, land of still poorer quality must be taken into cultivation, when "rent immediately commences on the second, and it is regulated as before" by the difference in the productive capacities of the land. Ricardo went on to make a general statement:

Thus suppose land—No. 1, 2, 3,—to yield, with an equal employment of capital and labour, a net produce of 100, 90, and 80 quarters of corn. In a new country, where there is an abundance of fertile land compared with the population, and where therefore it is only necessary to cultivate No. 1, the whole net produce will belong to the cultivator, and will be the profits of the stock which he advances. As soon as population had so far increased as to make it necessary to cultivate No. 2, from which ninety quarters only can be obtained after supporting the labourers, rent would commence on No. 1; for either there must be two rates of profit on agricultural capital, or ten quarters, or the value of ten quarters must be withdrawn from the produce of No. 1, for some other purpose. Whether the proprietor of the land, or any other person, cultivated No. 1, these ten quarters would equally constitute rent; for the cultivator of No. 2 would get the same result with his capital, whether he cultivated No. 1, paying ten quarters for rent, or continued to cultivate No. 2, paying no rent. In the same manner it might be shown that when No. 3 is brought into cultivation, the rent of No. 2 must be ten quarters, or the value of ten quarters, whilst the rent of No. 1 would rise to twenty quarters; for the cultivator of No. 3 would have the same profits whether he paid twenty quarters for the rent of No. 1, ten quarters for the rent of No. 2, or cultivated No. 3 free of all rent.[26]

Clearly, this is Anderson's reason for rent—the fact that the lands which are cultivated vary in fertility.

But Ricardo proceeded to consider the possibility that better soils might be cultivated more intensively, as an alternative to extending cultivation to poorer land:

It often, and, indeed, commonly happens, that before No. 2, 3, 4, or 5, or the inferior lands are cultivated, capital can be employed more productively on those lands which are already in cultivation. It may perhaps be found, that by doubling the original capital employed on No. 1, though the produce will not be doubled, will not be increased by 100 quarters, it may be increased by eighty-five quarters, and that this quantity exceeds what could be obtained by employing the same capital on land No. 3. In such a case, capital will be preferably employed on the old land, and will equally create a rent; for rent is always the difference between the produce obtained by the employment of two equal quantities of capital and labour.[27]

This, of course, is a corollary of the principle of diminishing returns, which was discussed in Chapter VIII.

[25] *The Works of David Ricardo, Principles of Political Economy and Taxation,* p. 36.
[26] *Ibid.,* p. 36. [27] *Ibid.,* pp. 36-37.

Evidently Ricardo believed that the price of grain was determined by the cost of that portion of the supply that was most expensive to obtain. The most costly grain was (1) that produced on the *extensive margin* of cultivation, that is, on the poorest land which paid to cultivate, and (2) that obtained on the *intensive margin,* that is, the last and most expensive increment of the product secured by intensive cultivation of the good land. The difference between price, as so determined, and cost, in any particular circumstances, was rent, according to Ricardo. Rent arose, therefore, (1) on land which was better than the poorest in cultivation and (2) in the case of the earlier and less expensive increments of expenditure on good soil. Thus, Ricardo was able to say:

The reason, then, why raw produce rises in comparative value [as population increases], is because more labour is employed in the production of the last portion obtained, and not because a rent is paid to the landlord. The value of corn is regulated by the quantity of labour bestowed on its production on that quality of land, or with that portion of capital, which pays no rent. Corn is not high because a rent is paid, but a rent is paid because corn is high; and it has been justly observed, that no reduction would take place in the price of corn, although landlords should forego the whole of their rent. Such a measure would only enable some farmers to live like gentlemen, but would not diminish the quantity of labour necessary to raise raw produce on the least productive land in cultivation.[28]

Applying this theory to the Britain in which he lived, Ricardo drew the conclusion that, other things remaining the same, grain prices and land rents would rise as population increased, though improvements in agriculture would operate in the reverse direction:

The rise of rent is always the effect of the increasing wealth of the country, and of the difficulty of providing food for its augmented population.[29]

The exchangeable value of all commodities rises as the difficulties of their production increase. If, then, new difficulties occur in the production of corn, from more labour being necessary, whilst no more labour is required to produce gold, silver, cloth, linen, &c., the exchangeable value of corn will necessarily rise, as compared with those things. On the contrary, facilities in the production of corn, or of any other commodity of whatever kind, which shall afford the same produce for less labour, will lower its exchangeable value. Thus we see that improvements in agriculture, or in the implements of husbandry, lower the exchangeable value of corn; improvements in the machinery connected with the manufacture of cotton, lower the exchangeable value of cotton goods. . .[30]

According to the wage theory which Ricardo accepted, wages stood at

[28] *Ibid.,* pp. 38-39. [29] *Ibid.,* p. 40.

[30] *An Essay on the Influence of a Low Price of Corn on the Profits of Stock, Shewing the Inexpediency of Restrictions on Importation,* London 1815, *ibid.,* p. 377.

In Chapter IX the possibility was suggested that Ricardo, who, after all, was a man of considerable practical knowledge in commercial affairs, did not look upon his theory as anything more than an underlying tendency. But, if this were the case, he failed to state it definitely, and so left himself open to attack. Practical conditions, in the minds of some critics, did not accord with the Ricardian abstraction.

In the field of rent theory, the principal opponent was Richard Jones (1790–1855), who succeeded Malthus as professor of political economy in the East India Company's college at Haileybury. In 1831 Jones published in London the first (and only) part of *An Essay on the Distribution of Wealth and on the Sources of Taxation.* This dealt entirely with rent. In it Jones presented a mass of evidence dealing with land tenure in various countries. The *labor* or *serf rents* which had been carried over in some parts of Europe from the middle ages were dealt with. Next came the *metayer* or *share rents* of France and Italy, then the *ryot rents* of India and other Eastern countries, and the *cotter* (or cottier) *rents* of Ireland. Not until the last of seven chapters was reached did *farmers' rents,* of which Ricardo had treated, receive attention. Even under this last heading, Jones's conclusions were not in complete accordance with those of Ricardo. But the chief feature of the *Essay* was not there. It lay in the list of rents which existed in practice but to which the Ricardian principle was inapplicable:

The existence of rents upon the metayer system, is in no degree dependent upon the existence of different qualities of soil or of different returns to the stock and labor employed. The landlords of any country who, with small quantities of stock, have quantities of land, sufficient to enable a body of peasant laborers to maintain themselves, would continue to derive a revenue as landowners from sharing in the produce of the industry of those laborers, though all the lands in the country were perfectly equal in quality. . .[36]

The existence and progress of rents under the ryot system is in no degree dependent upon the existence of different qualities of soil, or different returns to the stock and labor employed on each. The sovereign proprietor has the means of enabling a body of laborers to maintain themselves, who without the machinery of the earth with which he supplies them, must starve. This would secure him a share in the produce of their labor, though all the lands were perfectly equal in quality. Ryot rents may increase from two causes, from an increase of the whole produce, effected by the greater skill, industry, and efficiency of the tenant: or from an increase of the sovereign's proportion of the produce; the produce itself remaining the same, and the tenant's share becoming less. . .[37]

The existence of rent, under a system of cottier tenants, is in no degree dependent upon the existence of different qualities of soil, or of different returns to the stock and labor employed. Where, as has been repeatedly

[36] *Essay*, p. 105.

[37] *Ibid.*, p. 140.

observed, no funds sufficient to support the body of laborers, are in existence, they must raise food themselves from the earth, or starve; and this circumstance would make them tributory to the landlords, and give rise to rents, and, as their number increased, to very high rents, though all the lands were perfectly equal in quality. Cottier rents, like other peasant rents, may increase from two causes; first, from an increase of the whole produce, of which increase the landlord takes the whole or a part. Or, the produce remaining stationary, they may increase from an augmentation of the landlord's share, that of the tenant being diminished to the exact amount of the additional rent.[38]

What Jones had in mind here was, not merely the existence of what have since been called *scarcity rents* (as distinct from the *differential rents* of Ricardo, but also the significance of what now would be referred to as institutional factors in governing rents of the nature he discussed. Thus, under the metayage system, custom might decree that one half of the produce should be paid as rent to the landowner, or the ruler's sovereignty might confer upon him the right to receive a certain rent from the ryot or peasant, these rents being to a large extent apart from the influence of competition. Granting the assumptions on which the Ricardian theory was based, this theory might be quite correct. What Jones asserted was the irrelevance of these assumptions to the conditions he described.

J. E. Thorold Rogers (1823–1890), in his *History of Agriculture and Prices in England,* went so far as to question the applicability of the Ricardian assumptions even to nineteenth century England:

Rent may be of two kinds: — An economic rent, strictly so defined, in which the tenant-farmer, having theoretically entire discretion in adopting and continuing his calling, and absolute facility for transferring his tenure from one holding to another without appreciable loss, procures the mean rate of profit which other industrial avocations are reputed to have, in the following of which capital and skill are fluid and mobile, and can therefore be employed with no more risk in one direction than another. This is the theory of profit held by economists of the speculative school, who having derived their illustrations mainly from the modern money market, have written about agricultural and manufacturing capital as though it could be manipulated with almost as much ease as a balance at a banker's or an investment in consols can be. But it is almost superfluous to say that such an economic rent has never been in existence. It is true that the freedom of a tenant in the first occupancy of agricultural land is apparently perfect. I say apparently, for there may and generally does exist an urgent demand for the material on which to exercise capital and skill, especially if the industry be the only one possible, and therefore the discretion in making a contract for occupancy is or has been generally curtailed. But immediately on the tenant entering into possession his freedom is at an end. He can-

[38] *Ibid.*, pp. 153-154.

but to mean *economic surplus*. A payment is said to be in the category of a surplus when it is unnecessary from the standpoint of production, that is, when production continues unchanged in its absence.

Ricardo looked upon land rent in this light. But this did not apply to the whole of what was called by this name in popular terminology. In the lay mind, rent was then, as it still is, the entire payment that falls to be made for the use of land or buildings. Ricardo defined rent to include only part of this payment:

> Rent is that portion of the produce of the earth which is paid to the landlord for the use of the original and indestructible powers of the soil.[41]

Natural advantages, like position, were included among the "original and indestructible" powers for which rent was paid, but not improvements. These latter were capital, according to Ricardo, and were remunerated as such.

In this manner a number of more recent writers have regarded rent, and the term *economic rent* has been coined to distinguish the Ricardian meaning from the popular one. By definition, economic rent is a surplus. Something that is "original and indestructible" was not produced in the expectation of receiving a price for its use, nor will it be withdrawn if such a price be not paid. An original and indestructible agent of production goes on producing, therefore, regardless of whether or not it is remunerated. Obviously, granting Ricardo's assumptions of originality and indestructibility, it is incontestable that rent is a surplus.

But can they be granted? Senior pointed out that not all the attributes of land, possessing permanent value, were original. Some had been put there by man:

> When an estate has been for some time leased to a careful tenant, it generally receives permanent ameliorations, which enable the owner, at the expiration of the lease, to obtain a higher rent. A bog worth 2s. [say 50 cents] annually an acre, may be converted into arable or pasture worth annually £2 [say $10]. Is the increase of revenue rent or profit? It arises from an additional fertility, now inseparably attached to the land. It is received by the owner without sacrifice on his part. It is, in fact, undistinguishable from the previous rent. On the other hand, its existence is owing to the abstinence of the farmer, who devoted to a distant object, the amelioration of the land, labour which he might have employed in producing immediate enjoyment for himself. If the owner of the estate had farmed it himself, and had directed labour to be employed on its permanent improvement, the additional produce occasioned by those improvements would clearly have been termed profit. It appears, therefore, most convenient to term it profit when occasioned by the improvements made by a tenant. In fact, these improvements are as consistently to be termed capital as a dock or a cotton mill. . .

[41] *The Works of David Ricardo, Principles of Political Economy and Taxation*, p. 34.

> We may be asked, then, whether the improvements which form the greater part of the value of the soil of every well-cultivated district are all, and for ever, to be termed capital? Whether the payments received from his tenants by the present owner of a Lincolnshire estate, reclaimed by the Romans from the sea, are to be termed, not rent but profit on the capital which was expended fifteen centuries ago?[42]

Senior's own answer to the question thus formulated was that the distinction of profit from rent, and therefore of capital from land, ceased "as soon as the capital . . . has become . . . the property of a person to whose abstinence and exertions it did not owe its creation."[43]

Whatever may be thought of this reply, it is evident that Senior had placed his finger upon an important point. Once a permanent improvement had been undertaken, it was in the same position as an original power of the soil. It was immobile and, therefore, its remuneration was unnecessary from the standpoint of production. In other words, any income to which it gave rise was just as much a surplus as was the rent of land. The position is that what passes for land in the different portions of the globe is not land as the Creator left it but land plus the changes which man has made to it, in the form of clearing, drainage, irrigation, etc. In the ordinary case, it has become quite impossible to ascertain how much of the productive value of the land is due to the original powers and how much to the improvements which have been made by man.

The American economist, F. A. Walker, considered this subject in his *Political Economy*. Walker said,

> the consideration of greatest importance in computing the cost of "producing" farms, is that, in general, agricultural improvements are compensated, and are expected to be compensated, upon the principle of those annuities in which a certain number of annual payments both yield due interest on the purchase money and extinguish the capital itself, as when a man for $1,000 (on which the normal interest would be $50 or $60) purchases the right to receive $120 a year for a certain term, with no claim on the principal thereafter.
>
> Now, is this so, or is it not? Let us satisfy our minds on this point; for if the proposition just now stated is correct, it disposes effectually of the argument against the economic doctrine of rent derived from the fact of expenditures in "producing" farms.
>
> That this proposition is correct, is, I think, proved conclusively by the fact, abundantly established by English experience, that *there are few classes of improvements known to agriculture which a tenant for 33 years will not make at his own expense,* notwithstanding the certainty that he will cease to enjoy the benefit of them at the expiry of his lease.[44]

[42] *Political Economy*, pp. 128-129. [43] *Ibid.*, p. 129.
[44] pp. 398-399. Quoted by permission of Henry Holt and Company, Inc.

those in the improvements) to others. The annual rental payable was determined by outside valuation.

In southern Ireland, however, this practice was not followed, and the result was chaos. An intense land hunger prevailed which led prospective farmers to offer rents that were far beyond their capacity to pay. Eviction from the land was held above their heads, when the rents fell into arrears, and in many instances tenants lost their holdings. Unable to get what they considered to be their rights by legal procedure, they resorted to illegal methods. If a new tenant bought the rights of an outgoer from the latter, he was allowed to take possession undisturbed. But a man who merely rented a farm from which his predecessor had been evicted and who paid nothing to the outgoing tenant, was liable to be boycotted, forcibly dispossessed, or even murdered. The land war was rendered all the more bitter by reason of the fact that political and religious issues were at stake.

In an attempt to settle the problem the British government, under the leadership of W. E. Gladstone, passed laws in 1870 and 1881, which, in effect, extended the Ulster Custom to all Ireland. What had gained the name of the *three F's* in the agitation responsible for the Acts were conceded, namely "fair rents," "fixity of tenure," and "freedom of sale." Rents were to be adjudicated. Tenants were not to be dispossessed arbitrarily from their holdings. If they wished to leave, they were to be free to sell their interests, the purchasers being granted the right of entry in their stead.

In 1886 the system that had been established in Ireland earlier was, in some measure, applied to the Scottish Highlands, where a problem somewhat similar to that of Ireland existed. Rent regulation and security of tenure, but not complete freedom of sale, were granted to the Scottish peasants. The law of 1886 paved the way for more comprehensive legislation in 1911. As in Ireland, the government was given powers to take over large estates, subject to the payment of compensation, and break them into smaller plots. Tenant ownership of improvements was continued. The farmers might assign their holdings to relatives but might not dispose of them to others. In the absence of relatives, the public authority entrusted with administering the scheme sought a new tenant, who was required to compensate the outgoer for his improvements. A land court determined rents and other matters arising out of the plan.

In the areas of larger farms and commercial agriculture, in Great Britain outside the Highland area of Scotland, a different plan has been followed. There the landowners, not the cultivators, own the permanent improvements, so that the problem has been less serious. But in order that improvements by the tenant shall not be discouraged, provision has been made for compensation for improvements made by him during his tenancy. Nominally the landowner, but in fact the incoming tenant, takes over the improvements at a valuation. A series of Agricultural Holdings Acts, of which those passed in 1883 and 1923 were the most important, govern the procedure.

But the Agricultural Holdings Acts have done more than this. They have conferred upon British tenants a certain amount of security of tenure. Providing the tenants are not remiss in ways laid down in the laws, they cannot be removed from their holdings without being compensated for "disturbance." In cases of dispute rents are determined by arbitration. As the disturbance compensation is ordinarily not less than one nor more than two years' rental of the farm concerned, it is fairly effective in conferring security of occupancy.

The result of the whole series of British laws has been to divide ownership. Though the English legislation has not especially laid this down, it is clear that such is its effect. This was still more true in Ireland. The tenants were granted certain rights of continuance of their tenancies. In Ireland these rights were saleable and brought in considerable sums to outgoing tenants, for the payments made by new tenants at entry were usually substantially more than was represented by the tangible improvements owned by former occupants of the farms. Even in England, though such sales are not recognized by law, they sometimes occur.

Obviously, a mere right of occupancy is valuable only if the rental payable for the farm is less than represents its full worth to the tenant. In Ireland this was certainly the case. The demand for farms was very intense and their number was limited, so that competitive rents would have been very high. The effect of the system set up in Ireland was to prevent the entire amount of this competitive rental from going to the landlord, who, incidentally, was often an absentee residing in England. The land commissioners appointed under the Irish laws lowered rents considerably, not merely during the depression that continued until the 1890's, but even after commodity prices and agricultural prosperity took an upward trend in 1896. The commissioners obviously adopted a standard of "fair rents" that was remote from any competitive valuation. They recognized that the Irish farmers were very poor. Working in Ireland and especially in the rural areas of that country, where public opinion was strongly in favor of the tenants, perhaps it was to be expected that the commissioners would act as they did. At all events, they raised the standard of life of the Irish peasants by lowering rents.

But the land problem of Ireland was not solved. The Irish wanted to own their own farms. The landlords, feeling that their interests had been neglected, were willing to sell the land. The result was seen in the land purchase law of 1903, under which most of the farm land of Ireland was transferred to the cultivators.

In Great Britain the plan has been less definite in its results. Rent

CHAPTER XI

INTEREST

Interest is income accruing in respect of the use of capital and, as such, has been a subject of controversy from very early times. Men have asked if the payment of interest could be supported on ethical grounds, and, if so, upon what basis it ought to be calculated. Aside from this moral aspect, there has been theorizing on the problems of why interest is paid, what determines its rate, and what would be the result if a different rate were fixed by law or if interest were made illegal altogether. This chapter traces the manner in which such questions have been asked and answered at different times in human history.

Interest in Early Times

Savage Societies

It is commonly believed that interest is unknown in savage communities. The historian Tacitus (c. 55–120) commented to this effect with respect to the German tribes in the Roman period. Recent researches have demonstrated the existence in some primitive communities of a form of exchange that possesses a *prima facie* resemblance to lending at interest, namely, that of the *gift and return gift.* An article is presented by one individual to another, with the understanding that the recipient is obligated to make some form of return in due course. The return gift is ordinarily more lavish than was its predecessor and, at first sight, it appears that the additional amount is interest. But careful investigators have concluded that there is no parallel between the two. Custom prescribes that the generosity displayed in the original gift shall be repaid by still greater generosity. What is observed is a social standard of generous conduct, therefore, rather than anything in the nature of interest on loans. The practice is worth bearing in mind, however, as representing a possible origin of interest.

The Ancient World

Records show that interest was common in the early societies of the Eastern Mediterranean-Persian Gulf area, namely Babylon, Egypt, and Greece. Rates were high, being of the order of 12 to 20 per cent per year. Debtors who were unable to meet their engagements were often enslaved. The reforms of Solon, to which reference has been made elsewhere, were partly aimed at this situation.

Plato forbade loans at interest, saying, in the *Laws,* "no one shall . . .

lend money upon interest."[1] But as he added immediately afterwards, "and the borrower should be under no obligation to repay either capital or interest," it is not clear that he was opposing interest as such. Later in the same work, the philosopher explicitly permitted interest as a penalty for delay in making contractual payments:

And let him who, having already received the work in exchange, does not pay the price in the time agreed, pay double the price; and if a year has elapsed, although interest is not to be taken on loans, yet for every drachma which he owes to the contractor let him pay a monthly interest of an obol.[2]

An obol was one sixth of a drachma, so that this was equivalent to an interest rate of 200 per cent yearly. However, evidently this was a penalty for non-fulfillment of an obligation and the inclusion of the words "although interest is not to be taken on loans" may be considered evidence that Plato was opposed to interest in the ordinary way.

Aristotle's condemnation of interest is well-known:

The most hated sort [of wealth-getting], and with the greatest reason, is usury, which makes a gain out of money itself, and not from the natural object of it. For money was intended to be used in exchange, but not to increase at interest. And this term interest, which means the birth of money from money, is applied to the breeding of money because the offspring resembles the parent. Wherefore of all modes of getting wealth this is the most unnatural.[3]

Aristotle's argument seems to have been directed against the charging of interest on loans made for unproductive purposes. Undoubtedly many of the borrowers of ancient Greece, like those of the present day, wanted the money to finance consumption. In these circumstances, it was not unreasonable for Aristotle to oppose interest. Money did not "breed," when it was used unproductively, so it was true to say in this case that interest was "unnatural." It was claiming an offspring from something whose nature was such that it produced no offspring. But it would have been difficult to defeat, on these grounds, a claim to interest on loans that were used productively. If a man took money that had been lent to him and invested it in livestock, which bred and multiplied, it was difficult to argue that money was unproductive.

Aristotle's attitude on usury is to be associated with his antagonism to commercialism generally and to the disfavor he showed towards occupations that he thought were unmanly or lacking in dignity. Often the usurer himself was not only an inferior citizen but he ruined those who should have been upholders of the State. Yet to the Greek philosopher the merchant was only a little less culpable than the usurer.

The position in Rome was not greatly different from that in Greece.

[1] *The Dialogues of Plato*, vol. 5, p. 124.

[2] *Ibid.*, pp. 308-309.

[3] *The Works of Aristotle*. vol. 9, *Politica*, 1258b.

ages so that, as late as the thirteenth century, Thomas Aquinas was able to say,

To take usury for money lent is unjust in itself, because this is to sell what does not exist. . .[8]

Here Aquinas was using Aristotle's argument, to the effect that money was barren. It was not denied that capital, properly used, yielded a profit; but the profit was credited to labor, not to the capital with which that labor was assisted. The position was stated by Antoninus thus:

Money is not profitable of itself alone, nor can it multiply itself, but it may become profitable through its employment by merchants. . .[9]

This is the question that has interested the socialists. A product results from the co-operation of capital, labor, and natural materials. Which of these factors is to be given the credit for producing it? In its different aspects, the problem has been discussed in Chapters IV and VIII and needs no further attention at this juncture.

Exceptions to the prohibition. But, by this time, the ban on usury had ceased to be complete. Aquinas admitted certain exceptions to the general prohibition. He refused to sanction interest in respect of loans of goods that were destroyed in use, such as food:

if a man wanted to sell wine separately from the use of the wine, he would be selling the same thing twice, or he would be selling what does not exist, wherefore he would evidently commit a sin of injustice. In like manner he commits an injustice who lends wine or wheat, and asks for double payment, viz. one, the return of the thing in equal measure, the other, the price of the use, which is called usury.[10]

It was otherwise, Aquinas thought, with things that were not so destroyed. In their case, it was possible to sell the use as well as sell the articles themselves. A man might hand over to another the ownership of a house, while retaining for himself the right to use it for a time, or he might grant the right of use, while keeping the ownership himself. Rent therefore might be charged for the use of a house, and possession demanded at the conclusion of the renting period.

Obviously, this argument could be used to justify receiving income, not only from houses but from land and, indeed, from any form of productive property. Moreover, notwithstanding his prohibition of *taking* or demanding interest, Aquinas tolerated its being *given.* It was unjust for the lender to require interest to be paid but a borrower need have no scruples in paying it:

[8] *Summa theologica,* Pt. 2, Second Pt., Q. 78, Art. 1.

[9] G. O'Brien, *An Essay on Medieval Economic Teaching,* London 1920, p. 181. Longmans.

[10] *Summa theologica,* Pt. 2, Second Pt., Q. 78, Art. 1.

It is by no means lawful to induce a man to sin, yet it is lawful to make use of another's sin for a good end, since even God uses all sin for some good. . . . Accordingly . . . it is by no means lawful to induce a man to lend under a condition of usury : yet it is lawful to borrow for usury from a man who is ready to do so and is a usurer by profession ; provided the borrower have a good end in view, such as the relief of his own or another's need.[11]

In view of the situation of his time, when the principal lenders included the Jews, who were not subjected to the Christian prohibition of usury, the exception was significant.

Aquinas dealt with interest in connection with the problem of restitution. If one man deprived another of something that he might have enjoyed, it was just that the former should make restitution. Two cases were distinguishable. Being deprived of his goods for a time, the owner might realize a loss : for instance, he might have to replace them at a heavy cost. On the other hand, he might merely lose his chance of profiting from the use of the goods. Aquinas thought that the former was a just title to compensation but that the latter was not. These were the cases of *damnum emergens* and *lucrum cessans*, respectively, and the distinction between them is at least as old as the teachings of Accursius (1182–1260), at Bologna.

Aquinas was not making an innovation in accepting realized loss as a title to interest payment ; Alexander of Hales had done so before him. Further, some of the contemporaries of Aquinas even justified interest in the alternative instance, that of loss of profit, and this position became more general during the fourteenth and fifteenth centuries.

Broadly, it can be said that an increasing list of exceptions to the ban on usury was permitted, in addition to those discussed already. Contracts of bottomry, representing a combination of loan and insurance on a ship and cargo, made their appearance in Italy as early as the beginning of the thirteenth century. Penalties for non-payment of advances at their due dates were allowed to be incorporated in loan contracts, as long as there was some period of free lending, however short this might be. Such penalties, in practice, often merely represented interest. The *triple contract* was an ingenious method of evading the prohibition of usury. Partnership agreements had always been lawful. A contract of assurance was unobjectionable. So it followed that *A* could contract a partnership with *B*, and insure with *C* against loss of capital, as well as with *D* against fluctuations in the profits of the partnership. Why, therefore, should all these contracts not be legal when made between *A* and *B*? In this case, however, the net result was a loan at interest, because *A* was furnishing *B* with capital at what amounted to a fixed rate of interest. Some theologians[12] argued that the triple contract was

[11] *Ibid.*, Art. 4. [12] Notably Johann Eck (1486–1543), Luther's great opponent.

for prudence in this respect. Beyond question, the general currency given to his approval of usury was justified neither by the form of Calvin's statement nor by his avowed intentions, but probably this applies to many other declarations that have proved of historic significance.

Regulation of Interest After the Middle Ages

Interest Control in Retreat

In practice, even in these countries that embraced the Reformation, the secular legislation that had grown up during the middle ages, prohibiting or regulating interest, did not disappear at once. In England the prohibition was repealed in 1545, a maximum rate of 10 per cent being substituted. This was reduced in 1624 to 8 per cent and later in the same century a further reduction took place to 6 per cent. In 1713 the maximum was lowered again to 5 per cent. This percentage stood (with exceptions applicable only to the Bank of England and the short-term money market) until 1854, when the practice of regulating interest was abandoned. It was natural, therefore, that economic writers should discuss the subject of interest control.

The Views of the Theorists

The closing years of the seventeenth century witnessed a controversy on this subject in England. Some Mercantilists, notably Sir Josiah Child, advocated a reduction in the legal maximum, but this was opposed by other authorities, including North. The arguments used receive some attention later in this chapter, as well as in Chapter XV, but it is of interest to note here that Petty, Locke, and North asserted that it was pointless to attempt to regulate the interest rate. This, they said, was determined by supply and demand, and found its own level, regardless of laws on the matter.

Half a century later the French Physiocrats devoted some attention to the problem. Except for Turgot, whose ideas are considered elsewhere, they appear to have reached a logical conclusion from their own theory of production, namely, that interest was indefensible in the case of loans made to commerce and manufactures, but justifiable when credit was extended for agricultural purposes. According to the Physiocrats, commercial and industrial occupations were unproductive, because they gave rise to no surplus. From this it followed that if people engaged in them had to meet interest payments they could only pass them on to others, or suffer themselves. Agriculture, on the other hand, was a productive employment, and individuals who raised loans to engage in it could meet the interest obligations out of the resulting product.

Adam Smith opposed legal prohibitions of interest, such as had been common in former times, remarking that

This regulation, instead of preventing, has been found from experience to increase the evil of usury; the debtor being obliged to pay not only for the use of the money, but for the risk which his creditor runs by accepting a compensation for that use. He is obliged, if one may say so, to insure his creditor from the penalties of usury.[15]

However, in spite of the general support which he gave to *laissez faire,* Smith was prepared to support the existing law that fixed a maximum rate of interest, considering that the then legal maximum of 5 per cent was, "perhaps, as proper as any."[16] If the legal rate were higher, he said, "the greater part of the money which was to be lent" would go to "prodigals and projectors," instead of to "sober people" who were unable or unwilling to pay high rates.

Jeremy Bentham took Smith to task for this attitude, in his *Defence of Usury* (written in 1787 but not printed until 1816). Bentham's subtitle indicates the nature of his conclusions: "Showing the Impolicy of the present Legal Restraints on the terms of Pecuniary Bargains." There was appended a special letter to Adam Smith, "on the Discouragements opposed by the above Restraints to the Progress of Inventive Industry."

The *Defence* took the form of a series of "Letters to a Friend," and in the introductory one of these its author stated his general position on the subject of usury:

the proposition I have been accustomed to lay down to myself on this subject is the following one, viz. that *no man of ripe years and of sound mind, acting freely, and with his eyes open, ought to be hindered, with a view to his advantage, from making such bargain, in the way of obtaining money, as he thinks fit: nor* (what is a necessary consequence) *anybody hindered from supplying him, upon any terms he thinks proper to accede to.*[17]

In the succeeding letters Bentham listed the borrowing classes who were supposed to be benefited by the law against usury—the prodigals, the indigent, the "rashly enterprising" and the "simple"—and proved to his own satisfaction that the regulation did more harm than good. He argued that, in so far as these classes were able to borrow at the low legal rate, they were encouraged unduly, while the operation of the measure often made it impossible for them to borrow at all. In the appended letter to Smith, Bentham quoted the latter's arguments against the great economist himself:

"To give the monopoly of the home market to the produce of domestic industry in any particular art or manufacture, is in some measure to direct private people in what manner they ought to employ their capitals, and must in almost all cases be either a useless or a hurtful regulation."—Thus far

[15] *Wealth of Nations,* Bk. 2, Chap. 4.
[16] *Ibid.*
[17] *The Works of Jeremy Bentham,* vol. 3, p. 3.

Interest in Modern Economic Theory

During the middle ages there was little attempt to explain the fact of interest. That it existed was well recognized: otherwise there would have been no occasion for religious teachers to devote as much attention as they did to the subject. If medieval writers had been as greatly concerned with economics as with ethics, they might have asked why borrowers were willing to pay interest and lenders able to demand it. Then they might have perceived that the prohibition which they supported had the effect of driving the business of lending into subterranean channels and so causing interest to be higher than would have obtained in its absence. But this aspect was neglected.

This has not been the case with more modern writers. Many of them have delimited their field of study so as to exclude moral considerations and have approached the problem of interest from the standpoint of economics. *What is, and why it is,* has been asked, not *what should be.* Yet there have been important exceptions, notably among the socialists. It is necessary to examine these modern theories.

The Exploitation Theory

The kernel of the medieval prohibition of usury was the belief that interest was unjust and represented exploitation of the borrower. Shorn of its religious aspect, this idea was continued in modern times by a series of writers, beginning with Locke and running through Smith and Sismondi to the socialists.

Locke and Smith. As was shown in Chapter IV, both John Locke and Adam Smith suggested what amounted to an exploitation theory of interest. In the early stages of society, before land and capital had become private property, they thought that the laborer received the entire produce of his work. This was no longer true in modern life, Smith explained, and his choice of language seemed to imply that the situation was brought about by the grasping natures of capitalists and landowners.

Sismondi. Basing his arguments on Smith's work, Sismondi developed this idea further, along lines made familiar in Chapter IV. He said that labor was the source of wealth but, in modern society, because of the private ownership of land and capital, the worker had no command over these aids to production. He had to sell his labor, therefore, to the proprietors of the other factors. Since the laborer's need for subsistence was more intense that his employer's requirement for labor, the wage bargain was unfavorable to the worker, who received merely enough to subsist upon. It might have been expected that Sismondi would pass from a statement of this theory to a condemnation of interest, but he did the opposite. He justified it. Just as the landlord earned his rent by the labor he expended in settling the land, as Locke had argued, so, Sismondi said, the capitalist rested his claim on the labor of accumulation. The only difference between the three justifications, which all rested on labor, was in point of time. The laborer's right to income was dependent upon his present industry: those of the landlord and the capitalist were based on the labor of the past. Sismondi, therefore, beginning with the idea of exploitation, arrived at a labor explanation of interest.

A little thought will serve the show that this argument is invalid as a theory of interest. Even if Sismondi's thesis be accepted, all that is justified is the replacement or amortization of capital on the basis of its labor cost of production: the labor incorporated in capital goods should be recompensed with an equal quantity of labor. There is nothing in Sismondi's argument to demonstrate why the remuneration should include an additional amount in respect of interest.

Ricardo, Rodbertus, and Marx. Ricardo's labor theory of value, described in Chapter IX, had as a corollary an exploitation theory of interest, as Marx perceived. Ricardo argued that incomes other than rent were determined by the productivity of capital and labor on the worst land in cultivation, the benefit of the superiority of better land going in rent to its owners. Labor was paid on a subsistence basis. Capital was merely past labor stored up in instruments and, as such, was entitled to a reward. This, as was indicated when the writings of Sismondi on this subject were discussed, covered amortization of capital but not interest in addition. If interest arose, presumably it was devoid of any labor justification. Ricardo's alternative suggestion, namely, that interest in some way represented payment for *time,* has received attention in Chapter VIII.

It was left to the socialist writers to bring out the implications of the Ricardian labor theory, but their contributions were treated in Chapters IV and IX and require no further description here. Suffice it to say that they reverted to the medieval attitude of denying any right to interest on capital. They admitted that the labor incorporated in capital goods was productive, but this was *as labor,* they said, not *as capital* or *time.* Time, as such, according to the socialists, required no remuneration, and it was only the position of economic power occupied by the propertied classes which enabled them to demand one. Obviously, the soundness of this argument turned upon the necessity or otherwise of payment for the use of capital. The statement of Böhm-Bawerk on this subject, in his *Capital and Interest,* is worth quoting:

> The perfectly just proposition that the labourer should receive the entire value of his product may be understood to mean, either that the labourer should *now* receive the entire *present* value of his product, or should receive the entire *future* value of his product *in the future.* But Rodbertus and

His answer was:

The same as limiting the Exportation of Money; and there may be as well Laws for limiting Exchange also: For Interest always carrieth with it an Ensurance *praemium,* which is very casual, besides that of Forbearance: For Instance, in *Ireland* there was a time when Land (the highest Security) was sold for 2 years Purchase: It was then naturally just to take 20, 30, or 40 *per Cent.* Interest; whereas there the Law allows but 10. And since that time, Land being risen to 12 Years purchase, responsible Men will not give above 8. And insolent [insolvent?] men will offer *Cent. per Cent.* notwithstanding the Law.[31]

North's view was the same. Interest was not a matter for State control, he believed. It was governed by supply and demand. If Holland had low interest (as Child and his supporters pointed out), this was not because of the existence of laws to this effect but because of a plenitude of lenders in relation to borrowers:

These things consider'd, it will be found, that as plenty makes cheapness in other things, as Corn, Wool, &c. when they come to Market in greater Quantities than there are buyers to deal for, the Price will fall; so if there be more Lenders than Borrowers, Interest will also fall; wherefore it is not low Interest makes Trade, but Trade increasing, the Stock of the Nation makes Interest low. It is said, that in *Holland* Interest is lower than in *England.* I answer, It is; because their Stock is greater than ours. I cannot hear that they ever made a Law to restrain Interest, but am certainly Informed, that at this day, the Currant Interest between Merchant and Merchant, when they disburse Money for each others Account, is 6 *per Cent* and the Law justifies it.[32]

It is not altogether clear what North had in mind here. Were the Dutch able to borrow at low interest because they were industrious and frugal, and so saved a great deal? Or was the explanation that Holland had plenty of money? North mentioned the Bank of Amsterdam, but in connection with public finance rather than with the creation of currency—though, of course, money was involved.[33] He spoke of "lenders," not savers, but he also referred to "stock" or capital. On the whole, perhaps it can be concluded that he thought of interest as being governed by the supply of capital, through savings, instead of by the supply of money as such.

The Capital or Waiting Theory

What has been for almost a century the dominant explanation of interest has turned, not upon money, but upon the use or command over capital.

The production of both producers' and consumers' goods takes time.

[31] *The Economic Writings of Sir William Petty,* vol. 2, pp. 447-448.

[32] *Discourses upon Trade,* p. 18.

[33] See Chapter XIV, p. 649.

Even after the goods reach their final form, time elapses before they are entirely used up. From the first preparation of soil for the wheat crop, to the eating of the bread which results, may be eighteen months or so in the ordinary way. Further, by taking into account the time required to construct the equipment employed in growing and processing the wheat, the length of time involved can be increased almost indefinitely. One might consider the case of the coal, that was used to smelt the iron, from which the foundry machines were made, that manufactured the implements utilized in cultivation – reaching back in a house-that-Jack-built fashion in a process that appears to have no definite starting point. The consumption of final goods may be a very long process. Bread is eaten a day or two after it leaves the baker's oven but an automobile gives service for several years, while a house lasts fifty or a hundred years.

Production costs have to be met from day to day over the production period. The income from the product, to gain which these costs were incurred, accrues afterwards. In the case of a house, it comes in as a stream of satisfactions over the half-century or more that the house is occupied. To obtain these satisfactions, there must be contributed (a) the natural materials needed, (b) labor, and (c) waiting. It may be that society is so situated that any one of these three factors is so plentiful that it can be had for nothing, so that no price need be paid on its account and no other means of rationing it pursued. This is the case, no doubt, with the mud and reeds of the African negro's hut or the logs from which the cabin of the Canadian backwoodsman is constructed. If such a situation were to arise with respect to waiting, interest would be non-existent. So many men would be willing to make interest-free loans, that no one who wanted credit need go without it.

This has not been the case in modern society. The demand for loans and their supply have been such that interest has emerged. Demanders have bid against each other for the scarce supply of capital, causing a price to be determined in the market. But other situations can be imagined. For example, loyal acceptance of a religious prohibition of interest may have the effect that favoritism settles the distribution of loans. This favoritism may itself be socially determined, as when religious tenets support loans to the poor as opposed to those intended to finance trading enterprises. In so far as the medieval ban on usury was effective, this, broadly, can be said to have been its result. Another environment that can be visualized is when an authoritative State refuses to permit competitive bidding for the use of capital and itself undertakes the apportionment of loans between the various possible uses, by some form of rationing. This practice has obtained to an important extent in Soviet Russia, with respect to the supply of capital to public enterprises.

But, in western Europe, from the decline of religious and temporal

This, of course, is an extension of the proverb "the devil finds work for idle hands to do."

With this idea in his mind, Hume attacked the problem of the relationship between money and the rate of interest. He offered two solutions, one of them applicable to Spain and the other to England and France.

In the case of Spain in the sixteenth and seventeenth centuries, when specie was received from the American mines, Hume said that the first effect was to increase lending and lower the interest rate:

> In the conquering country [*i.e.*, Spain], it is natural to imagine, that this new acquisition of money will fall into a few hands, and be gathered into large sums, which seek a secure revenue, either by the purchase of land or by interest; and consequently the same effect follows, for a little time, as if there had been a great accession of industry and commerce. The encrease of lenders above the borrowers sinks the interest; and so much the faster, if those, who have acquired those large sums, find no industry or commerce in the state, and no method of employing their money but by lending it at interest.[40]

But this circumstance was only temporary:

> after this new mass of gold and silver has been digested, and has circulated through the whole state, affairs will soon return to their former situation; while the landlords and the new money-holders, living idly, squander above their income; and the former daily contract debt, and the latter encroach on their stock till its final extinction. The whole money may still be in the state, and make itself felt by an encrease of prices: But not being now collected into any large masses or stocks, the disproportion between the borrowers and lenders is the same as formerly, and consequently the high interest returns.[41]

Thus, in Hume's opinion, there was no lasting effect upon interest, apparently because the Spanish people failed to develop habits of industry and frugality.

It was quite otherwise, he thought, in such countries as England and France, which had no mines. Through trade with other countries, like Spain, which possessed mines, an influx of specie had the effect of raising commodity prices. During the rise, profits were stimulated and commerce and industry expanded, Hume's explanation of this process being given in Chapter XV. This growth of commerce increased frugality. The supply of capital was augmented and the rate of interest was diminished:

> when commerce has become extensive, and employs large stocks, there must arise rivalships among the merchants, which diminish the profits of trade, at the same time that they encrease the trade itself. The low profits of merchandize induce the merchan's to accept more willingly of a low interest,

[40] *Ibid.*, p. 318.

[41] *Ibid.*, p. 319.

when they leave off business, and begin to indulge themselves in ease and indolence. It is needless, therefore, to enquire which of these circumstances, to wit, *low interest or low profits*, is the cause, and which the effect? They both arise from an extensive commerce, and mutually forward each other. No man will accept of low profits, where he can have high interest; and no man will accept of low interest, where he can have high profits. An extensive commerce, by producing large stocks, diminishes both interest and profits; and is always assisted, in its diminution of the one, by the proportional sinking of the other.[42]

As to the reduction of interest, which has followed in ENGLAND, FRANCE, and other kingdoms of EUROPE, that have no mines, it has been gradual; and has not proceeded from the encrease of money, considered merely in itself, but from that of industry, which is the natural effect of the former encrease, in that interval, before it raises the price of labour and provisions.[43]

That the stimulus imparted to industry by rising prices could have such effects upon the structure of industry and men's frames of mind was explained by the long-drawn-out nature of the process, lasting, as it did, in the case that Hume discussed, for a century and a half or more.

Hume, therefore, presented two theories. According to the first—which he applied to Spain—the supply of money, acting through the loan market, governed interest rates. In respect of the earliest stage, Hume was in agreement with such writers as Petty, but he went beyond his predecessors in arguing that the effect would be temporary. It would disappear, apparently (though Hume did not say this specifically), when price levels had become adjusted to the altered volume of money. The other theory—worked out in the England-France example—was that, in the period of price adjustment, men's habits would be changed, resulting in permanent effects upon the interest rate. His particular case was one of rising prices, expanding industry, increased savings, and a lowered interest rate; but the argument he used would have been equally applicable the opposite way round. Presumably falling prices would discourage industry, diminish savings, and raise interest.

There were two evident shortcomings in Hume's statement. Why did he not, in the England-France instance, bring in the initial stage of lowered interest caused by an influx of new money into the loan market? Presumably, the explanation lay in his assumption that the Englishmen and Frenchmen who received the additional money did so in small sums and used it in trade. Still, having regard to what Hume had to say on the correlation of profits and interest, this might have been expected to produce at least a temporary fall in interest rates. Perhaps he felt that to admit this would have been playing into the hands of those whose interest theories he was criticizing. Secondly, why did Hume deny to Spain the assumption that he made with respect to England and France, that rising

[42] *Ibid.*, pp. 315-316.

[43] *Ibid.*, pp. 319-320.

prices would expand industry and so increase men's propensity to save? As far as can be judged, the distinction was made because Hume did not believe that the Spanish people had the necessary inherent capacity for commercial undertakings, or their habits were too fixed for any such change to be made.

In spite of these shortcomings, however, Hume's interest theory was highly suggestive. It anticipated the work of such economists as Turgot, Senior, and Böhm-Bawerk, who developed interest theories based on saving or forbearance. In its emphasis on habit and national character, it gave a foretaste of the ideas of the German Historical School and the American Institutionalists. Still more, as will be seen later, it contained some of the essential ingredients of the theory recently propounded by the English economist, J. M. Keynes.

Turgot. Like Hume, Turgot controverted the theory that interest was merely a matter of the quantity of money. "Money has two different valuations in commerce,"[44] he said. One concerned its purchasing power over commodities: the other had reference to the interest rate. The two were independent:

These two valuations are independent of each other, & are governed by quite different principles.[45]

Amplifying this statement, Turgot proceeded:

Money may be very common in ordinary commerce, may there have very little value, may answer to a very small quantity of commodities, and the interest of money may at the same time be very high.

Suppose that when there are *a million ounces of silver* circulating in commerce, *an ounce of silver* is given in the market for a measure of corn. Suppose there comes into the State, it matters not how, *a second million* ounces of silver, and that this increase is distributed to every purse in the same proportion as the first million, so that the man who before had two ounces of silver now has four. The silver considered as a mass of metal will certainly diminish in price, or, what is the same thing, commodities will be paid for more dearly; and, to get the measure of corn which we got before with an ounce of silver, it will be necessary to give a good deal more silver, and perhaps *two ounces* instead of *one.* But it by no means will follow from thence that the interest of money falls, if all this money is carried to market and employed in the current expenditure of those who possess it, as by supposition the first million ounces were; for the interest of money falls only when there is more money to lend, in proportion to the wants of borrowers, than there was before. But the money which is carried to market is not to lend; it is the money which is placed in reserve, the accumulated capitals, that are lent; and so far from the increase of money in the market, or the diminution of its price in relation to com-

[44] *Reflections on the Formation and the Distribution of Riches*, p. 74.
[45] *Ibid.*, p. 75.

modities in ordinary trade, infallibly and by immediate sequence bringing about a decrease of the interest of money, it may on the contrary happen that the very cause which increases the money in the market, and which increases the prices of other commodities by lowering the price of money, is precisely that which increases the hire of money or the rate of interest.[46]

It was not the quantity of money as such, therefore, in Turgot's opinion, but that of capital, which influenced the interest rate. By capital was meant either commodities that were not required for the immediate subsistence of their owner, or money that could be employed to purchase such commodities. The supply that affected interest was not money from the mines but savings, that is, the excess of production over consumption. This, in relation to the demand, governed the rate of interest:

The price of interest depends immediately upon the relation between the demand of the borrowers and the offer of the lenders; & this relation depends chiefly on the quantity of moveable riches accumulated, by the saving of revenues & of annual products, to form capitals withal, whether these capitals exist in money or in any other kind of effects having a value in commerce.[47]

As Hume had said, the supply of savings and the demand for capital depended largely on men's propensities to save and to spend:

The spirit of economy in a nation tends to augment incessantly the sum of its capitals, to increase the number of lenders, to diminish that of borrowers. The habit of luxury has precisely the contrary effect. . .[48]

The historical lowering of interest rates, which Petty, Hume, and others had sought to explain, Turgot regarded as a proof that in Europe, in general, economy had prevailed over luxury. Unlike Hume, the French writer made no attempt to connect the fall in interest with the increase that had taken place in the quantity of money. From all appearances, if he thought of the matter at all, he regarded the fact that the two changes took place together as a mere coincidence.

The Physiocrat, however, dealt with a problem to which Hume had given no attention, that of why interest was paid at all. Like other members of the French school, Turgot believed that the rent of land was a surplus and that the State could tax it without injuring production. Asking if this were true also of interest on capital, he gave the answer that it was not:

If this return [*i.e.*, interest] is diminished, the capitalist will withdraw his money, and the undertaking will come to an end. This return ought, then, to be inviolable, and enjoy an entire immunity, because it is the price of an advance, made to an undertaking, without which the undertaking could not go on. To touch it, would be to augment the price of advances in all

[46] *Ibid.*, pp. 75-76. [47] *Ibid.*, p. 78. [48] *Ibid.*, p. 80.

undertakings, and consequently to lessen the undertakings themselves, that is to say, agriculture, industry and commerce.[49]

In other words, in Turgot's opinion, interest was like wages in that it contained no surplus.

The Classical economists. Adam Smith made no addition to the waiting theory and, indeed, his treatment of the subject of interest was decidedly inferior to that of Hume. Ricardo's solitary hint that capital goods might require a remuneration in excess of that corresponding to the labor incorporated in them, to compensate for the waiting undergone, was mentioned in Chapter VIII.

On the other hand, J. B. Say, who admitted he owed much to Hume, formally made interest a matter of the supply of and demand for what he called disposable or loanable capital:

the more abundant is the disposable capital, in proportion to the multiplicity of its employments, the lower will the interest of borrowed capital fall.[50]

What he meant by disposable capital was made clear by the following passage:

it is essential to pay strict attention to the meaning of the term, *supply of disposable capital*; for this alone can have any influence upon the rate of interest; it is only so much capital, as the owners have both the power and the will to dispose of, that can be said to be in circulation. A capital already vested and engaged in production or otherwise, is no longer on the market, and therefore no longer forms a part of the total circulating capital; its owner is no longer a competitor of other owners in the business of lending, unless the employment be one, from which capital may be easily disengaged and transferred to other objects. Thus, capital lent to a trader, and liable to be withdrawn from his hands at short notice, and *a fortiori,* capital employed in the discount of bills of exchange, which is one way of lending among commercial men, is capital readily disposable and transferable to any other channel of employment, which the owner may judge convenient. . .

But capital embarked in the construction of a mill, or other fabric, or even in a moveable of small dimensions, is fixed capital, which being no longer available for any other purpose, is withdrawn from the mass of circulating capital, and can no longer yield any other benefit than that of the product wherein it has been vested. Nor should it be lost sight of, that even though the mill or other fabric be sold, its value, as capital, is not by that means restored to circulation; it has merely passed from one proprietor to another. On the other hand, the disposable value, wherewith the buyer has made the purchase, is not thrown out of circulation, having merely passed from his into the seller's hands. The sale neither increases nor diminishes the mass of floating capital in the market.[51]

[49] *Ibid.,* p. 93.

[50] *A Treatise on Political Economy,* p. 349.

[51] *Ibid.,* p. 350.

Thus, like Marshall later, Say recognized that the interest obtainable on loans was quite different from the returns yielded from old investments of capital. He saw that the profit that was expected to accrue from capital investment was an important factor in explaining the demand for loans, but he kept the two distinct.

With respect to loans, Say said that risk was significant:

the ratio of the premium of insurance, which frequently forms the greater portion of what is called interest, depends on the degree of security presented to the lender; which security consists in three circumstances: – 1. The safety of the mode of employment; 2. The personal ability and character of the borrower; 3. The good government of the country he happens to reside in.[52]

Fluidity was a consideration, also:

Among the circumstances incident to the nature of the employment, which influence the rate of interest, the duration of the loan must not be forgotten; *ceteris paribus,* interest is lower when the lender can withdraw his funds at pleasure, or at least in a very short period; and that both on account of the positive advantage of having capital readily at command, and because there is less dread of a risk, which may probably be avoided by timely retreat.[53]

Senior's contribution was his elucidation of the nature of capital, mentioned in Chapter VIII. According to Senior, capital was composed of three elements, (1) natural materials, (2) labor, and (3) abstinence. The last was just as necessary as the other two. It was defined as follows:

the conduct of a person who either abstains from the unproductive use of what he can command, or designedly prefers the production of remote to that of immediate results.[54]

Like labor, abstinence was disagreeable, so it

must therefore be called into exertion by the prospect of its specific remuneration . . . by the hope of profit. . .[55]

That is to say, what Senior called profit, but what in this chapter is being treated as interest, was necessary in order that saving might be stimulated. John Stuart Mill took the same line.

Time preference in consumption before Böhm-Bawerk. The opinion that men tend to undervalue present pleasures as compared with those arising in the future is as old as Aristotle. The exception made on this ground by John Locke, to the general rule that men know best what is for their good, will be remembered.[56] Samuel Bailey, attacking the

[52] *Ibid.*, p. 346.
[53] *Ibid.*, pp. 346-347.
[54] *Political Economy*, p. 58.
[55] *Ibid.*, p. 185.
[56] See Chapter II, p. 99.

seem to be the desire of personal, and family aggrandizement, and a wish, conjoined with the pursuit of both, to rank high in the estimation of the world. The acquisition of fortune, is a road open to the ambition of all men, and, in the present days, is the only road open to that of most men. The mere desire to rise in the world, and envy of the superiority of other men, may excite many to enter on this path, and preserve them steadily in it.[63]

This, of course, accords with Rae's comments on men's attitude toward wealth, referred to in Chapter II. Rae did not approve altogether of such actions and remarked that they must be "kept in strict check," or "disorders" would break out.

Rae recognized that the strength of the desire to accumulate wealth varied in different societies. Living, as he did, in the early period of American settlement, it was natural for him to say something about conditions among the Indians. The life of a hunter, Rae opined, was unfavorable to accumulation. On the other hand, a pastoral civilization "implies a considerable degree of care and foresight."[64] Even within the same social framework, differences existed between individuals. Like Hume, Rae thought that owners of landed estates were apt to be prodigal. Discussing marriage, he commented that "men of even moderate fortune" commonly defer this step "until they have a prospect of raising their families above their own rank." The laboring classes, on the other side, thought only of "immediate sensual gratifications."[65]

John Stuart Mill drew on Rae's work. Discussing the minimum rate of profit and the relationship between the interest rate and the volume of savings, Mill said that the desire to accumulate wealth depended on

the comparative estimate made by the people of that place and era, of future interests when weighed against present.[66]

On the other hand, the "disposition to employ capital productively" was influenced by the degree of security that existed, which led to the subject of risk. But, like his predecessors in the British Classical School, Mill failed to distinguish between interest and profits, so was prevented from developing any adequate theory of interest.

Böhm-Bawerk and his predecessors in marginal productivity theory. The Austrian economist, Eugen von Böhm-Bawerk, developed the time-preference idea of capital supply, in his *The Positive Theory of Capital.* Böhm-Bawerk made the same statement as Rae, to the effect that men prefer present to future satisfactions:

Present goods are, as a rule, worth more than future goods of like kind and number.[67]

[63] *Ibid.*, pp. 59-60.
[64] *Ibid.*, p. 79.
[65] *Ibid.*, pp. 230-231.
[66] *Principles of Political Economy*, Bk. 4, Chap. 4, Sect. 3.
[67] *Op. cit.*, p. 237.

Like Rae, Böhm-Bawerk admitted that people varied in their emphasis on the present as compared with the future. A peasant who had reaped a poor harvest, a laborer who was starving, and beginners who were impoverished but expected to be better off later in life (such as young artists and budding doctors), were only too ready to promise, in return for a loan, a considerably higher repayment in the future. The contrary also occurred. A fifty year old clerk who possessed a good present income but faced the probability of being poor when his earning power ceased, was an example. Böhm-Bawerk said that, in some cases, an emphasis on present goods was justified, because present needs were greater than those likely to arise in the future. In general, however, he believed that men underestimated the intensity of their future needs. For this there were three reasons: (1) want of imagination, which prevented them from picturing the intensity of their future desires, (2) weakness of character, which made them unable to resist their present cravings, and (3) the uncertainty of human life.

But, in addition, present goods possessed an *economic superiority* over future goods, Böhm-Bawerk argued, because they made it possible for more goods to exist in the future. Labor, when assisted by tools, could produce more than labor not so aided. It followed that the capital that was represented by tools had a present value greater than the same amount of capital in the future, say next year. A certain amount of capital this year was equivalent, not to the same amount a year hence, but to this, plus something extra in the shape of the product to which it could rise in the meantime. In other words, present goods were worth more than future goods because capital was productive.

As a result of these factors, Böhm-Bawerk said, people were prepared to pay a premium or *agio* for present goods. That is to say, they were willing to pay interest. What determined the rate of this interest? It was here that Böhm-Bawerk made a notable advance over Senior and Rae. He brought in the conception of diminishing productivity. Successive units of capital would add less and less to the product, when used to assist labor in the productive process. The rate of interest must be such that it did not exceed the product of the last increment of capital employed in production:

> The rate [of interest] is determined by the productiveness of the last economic extension of process, in such a way that the amount of capital making the extension possible must bear a less interest than the surplus return obtained by means of it. . .[68]

By "extension of process," Böhm-Bawerk meant making production more roundabout, that is, using more capital. Excluding complications from discontinuities caused by the fact that capital increments are of finite

[68] *Ibid.*, p. xxxix.

thinking that his income will rise after graduation. An aging man realizes that shortly his earning-power will decline.

Were it not for such factors, it might be concluded that people would have to be compensated to induce them to save. A man with a steady income of $2500 a year, for example, saves $500 in one year to spend in a later one. In the year of the saving, his income falls to $2000. When the savings are spent, it rises to $3000. Assuming that his wants are the same in the two periods, the income from $2000 to $2500 has greater utility than that between $2500 and $3000. From this it follows that a loss of utility arises from the saving process. The same would be true of borrowing in anticipation of future income.

According to Landry and Fisher, the rate of interest is that which equates lending and borrowing as so explained. As thus stated, there appears little reference to the productivity of capital. But this is only apparent, because productivity affects the relationship between the present and future utilities which are being compared. Fisher recognized this fact when, on the title page of *The Theory of Interest,* he mentioned two factors, (1) impatience to spend and (2) opportunity to invest. Thus it becomes clear that the Landry-Fisher theory is really an amplification of that of Böhm-Bawerk.

The theory of Böhm-Bawerk, Landry, and Fisher has had considerable popularity in recent years but it is open to certain objections. In the first place, it is not necessarily—perhaps not even largely—true that an individual foregoes present satisfactions in order that he may consume more (*i.e.*, capital plus interest) in the future. Often he saves in order to receive an investment income in the future, without any intention of consuming the accumulated capital itself.[70] On the psychological side, can it be assumed that the man who spends only $2000 out of a regular income of $2500, to invest the difference, really loses in immediate satisfactions? Security is a factor. Earning-power may come to an end through illness or unemployment, and investments are a form of insurance against this contingency. When the satisfaction got from security is added to that obtained from consumable goods, the total may be as great as would be yielded by spending the entire income on consumables. An individual whose desire for security is great does not necessarily lose, therefore, even though he receives no interest whatever. Böhm-Bawerk's assumption of a time preference in favor of the present falls to the ground in this situation. Lastly, the Böhm-Bawerk—Fisher theory assumes rational choice. Men are supposed to set against each other the utilities promised by alternative courses of action and select the one that maximizes utility. Yet from the time of Aristotle it has been recognized that

[70] On this subject, the two articles by F. H. Knight on *The Quantity of Capital and the Rate of Interest* (*The Journal of Political Economy,* Chicago 1936) may be consulted.

rational choice is only one factor in a complex human make-up. Undoubtedly, much saving is habitual or the result of business customs and standards, such as those that measure commercial prudence and success by reserve fund allocations and business extension.

Non-psychological explanations. Because of difficulties such as have been indicated above, some economists of the Marginal School have endeavored to avoid psychological explanations of why people lend and borrow. Instead, they have concentrated on the facts of lending and borrowing. Put in an extreme form, so as to contrast with the theory of Landry and Fisher, the reasoning is as follows: People lend and borrow. Capital can be used productively. The rate of interest is determined by the supply and demand in the market. No doubt psychological factors of some kind stand behind the actions of lenders and borrowers, but this is a matter for psychologists to go into (if they care to do so), not something lying within the province of an economist who possesses no special knowledge of psychology. Davenport and Cassel are associated with this general position, but even the work of these writers is not free from psychological implications. Davenport, for example, said in *The Economics of Enterprise*:

> For each individual, consumption (spending) stops and saving (investment) begins . . . where the advantages from saving, whatever these advantages may be, make an appeal strong enough to displace present consumption.[71]

This assumes that men make a rational choice between alternatives, when, in fact, other motives, such as custom, may be at work. Cassel, as is shown in a later section of this chapter, built up a theory concerning the supply of capital, that turned upon men's decisions to consume some of their capital as interest falls. This theory was supported, not, as might have been expected, by statistics showing that such was in fact the case, but by figures to demonstrate that there was an inducement for individuals to behave in this fashion.

The Form of the Supply Curve of Capital

Higher interest encourages saving. It now becomes necessary to give some attention to the nature of the reaction of savings to the interest rate.

Senior spoke as though abstinence, like labor, increased in supply in response to higher remuneration:

> as the rate of wages depends in a great measure on the number of labourers, and the rate of profit on the amount of capital, both high wages and high profits have a tendency to produce their own diminution. High wages, by stimulating an increase of population, and therefore an increase of the number of labourers, and high profits, by occasioning an increase of capital.[72]

[71] *Op. cit.*, p. 363.

[72] *Political Economy*, p. 140.

the funds destined for the maintenance of productive labour receive no augmentation from the revenue of those who ought naturally to augment them the most. The capital of the country instead of increasing gradually dwindles away. . .[78]

W. L. Sargant (1809–1889), a Birmingham manufacturer who was interested in economics, in his *Recent Political Economy* (London 1867), offered an arithmetical illustration of the manner in which higher interest might be expected to diminish savings:

A clerk calculates that when his family have married away from his house, he shall be able to live on £80 a year. If interest were as low as in Holland formerly [2 per cent], it would require £4000 to supply this moderate income: at 5 per cent., £1600 would suffice: at 10 per cent., £800. As interest rises the necessary savings diminish.[79]

Fleeming Jenkin made the same point, in his article on *Trade Unions: How Far Legitimate* (*North British Review*, 1868):

No manufacturer has come before the Commission [*i.e.*, the Trade Union Commission of 1867–1869] to say, 'I have always, or generally, diminished my business whenever I have had to give increased wages;' and yet, whenever a man does continue his business at the original rate of production, with increased wages and constant, or nearly constant, receipts, he is increasing the wages fund or his circulating capital in the face of a diminished profit. . .

The greatest portion of the circulating capital of a country constituting its wages fund is of this nature. Year by year the savings of other classes add to this fund, but it is mainly composed of the price received by the manufacturer for his produce, a portion of which he habitually re-invests in the payment of labour without any conscious effort to save. We now assert that the proportion which he does so re-invest is not necessarily smaller because wages are larger or profits smaller. A manufacturer will generally work his mill or factory to the utmost so long as he does obtain a profit; he does not voluntarily set aside a certain sum for wages, diminishing and increasing that sum according to profits, but he employs as many men as he can, and pays them what he must. How this 'must' is determined, shall be considered further on. Obviously there is a limit to action of this sort. Any conscious savings he will generally invest in other undertakings, and if his profits fall below a certain point, he will endeavour in all ways to divert the use of his fixed capital to other objects. He may be unable to control his personal expenditure; and so, if wages rise and profits fall beyond a certain point, his contribution to the wages fund will diminish, and possibly disappear, owing to his ruin. But how is this certain point to be determined? Are all manufacturers habitually carrying on their business at such profits, that should these diminish they will diminish their annual payments in wages? We think not, and if not, the wages fund may increase in the face of diminished profits.

[78] Bk. 4, Chap. 7, Part 3.
[79] p. 76. Quoted by permission of Williams & Norgate Ltd.

Let us turn to the second class of capitalists, men who, not being manufacturers, save to invest money, with the object of obtaining an assured income as the reward of their saving. . . Will these savings be increased or diminished as the rate of interest is high or low? On the other hand, a high rate of interest is a greater temptation to investment than a low one; but then with a low rate of interest, a much larger given sum must be invested to return a given income, and a given ideal income, of say 1,000 £. per annum, is generally the object of investors of this class. Is it clear that the saving for investment in countries with a high average rate of interest is greater in proportion to the incomes than in countries where a low rate of interest obtains? We doubt it extremely; indeed, we entirely disbelieve that saving increases in proportion to the rate of interest to be obtained. We do not believe that men determine if they can get 10 per cent. that they will invest 1,000 £., but that if they can only get 5 per cent. they will spend it. The contrary proposition is more nearly true: if men can get 10 per cent. for their money they will consider they have made a sufficient provision for their family by investing 10,000 £.; if they can only get 5 per cent. they feel compelled to invest 20,000 £. before retiring from business. In fine, both with the manufacturer re-investing old savings in his own business, and the professional man investing new savings, diminished profits on capital lead to diminished expenditure, and not always or generally to diminished saving.[80]

In the first portion of this passage, Jenkin was at least as much concerned with demolishing the wage fund theory as dealing with the relationship between profits and savings. His idea seems to have been that profits contained, in most cases, an element of surplus which could be taken away without affecting the business man's willingness to re-invest his earnings. In the second portion, Jenkin's argument was identical with that of Sargant.

Sidney and Beatrice Webb, English socialists who have collaborated in many works on labor and social problems, in their *Industrial Democracy* (2 vols., London 1897), dealt with the same problem as Jenkin, that is, the effect on savings of wage increases. Their conclusion was that people at different income levels would react in various ways to a change in the rate of interest:

The strongest motives for saving—the desire to provide for sickness and old age, or for the future maintenance of children—go on, as the hoards of the French peasantry show, whether profit or interest is reaped or not. . . At the other end of the social scale, though possibly for a different reason, accumulation appears to proceed with equal indifference to the rate of profit. The annual savings of the Astors and Vanderbilts, the periodic re-investment of income by the Cavendishes and Grosvenors, the automatic accumulation of the Rothschilds, do not, as a matter of fact, depend on how much per cent these millionaires expect to get for their new capital, but on the amount of sheer surplus over and above their current habits of expenditure. It is,

[80] F. Jenkin, *The Graphic Representation of the Laws of Supply and Demand, and other Essays on Political Economy*, pp. 10-11.

lation of wealth. For though with man's growing command over the resources of nature, he may continue to save much even with a low rate of interest; yet while human nature remains as it is every fall in that rate is likely to cause many more people to save less than to save more than they would otherwise have done.[88]

No factual evidence was submitted, so the conclusion represented nothing more than Marshall's opinion.

J. S. Nicholson held a different view. In his *Principles of Political Economy,* Nicholson listed a number of factors. Some operated to increase saving when interest rose and others worked in the reverse direction. A third group, like security, had no connection with the interest rate. The net effect, he thought, was indeterminate:

The truth is . . . the growth of material capital depends upon a number of variables, of which the rate of interest is only one, and is, furthermore, indeterminate in its effect.[89]

Nicholson's list of variables is itself of some interest. Not merely the division of the stream of production between present and future satisfactions, but the size of the stream itself and the manner in which income was distributed between the various sections of the population, were taken into account. Protection by and against the government (here Nicholson followed Mill), as well as the existence of facilities for investment, had their place. Indeed, it can be said that this writer went a long way in offering what may be called a historical or institutional interpretation of interest and capital accumulation.

Schmoller, in his *Grundriss der allgemeinen Volkswirtschaftlehre* Leipzig 1900–1904), gave figures, showing a historic tendency for interest to fall.[90] During the period from 1820 to 1845, in western Europe, interest declined from 5 to 3½ per cent. By the sixties, it had risen to 5—7 per cent again, but after 1873 it receded to 2½—3 per cent. Schmoller considered that it was not unlikely that the rate might decline to 2 or even to 1½ per cent in the twentieth century. On the basis of these data, it appears that the assumption that a decline in the interest rate lowers the supply of capital cannot be supported. The lessening rate of interest over the period Schmoller studied was accompanied, not by a diminution in the capital supply but by a great increase. Moreover, in those countries where interest declined most, the greatest amount of capital was accumulated.

Yet it must be appreciated that simple correlations, such as that drawn here, have limited usefulness. It is true that the rate of interest has shown a declining tendency. It is also true that savings have grown.

[88] *Ibid.,* p. 235. [89] *Op. cit.,* vol. 1, p. 394.

[90] Schmoller's figures appear in an extract from his work, reprinted in *Selected Readings in Economics,* by C. J. Bullock, Boston 1907, pp. 563-568.

But it is two centuries since North commented upon the association between low interest and the riches of Holland, and pointed out that the former might be explained by the latter.

It is interesting to note that Friedrich von Wieser and other economists of the Marginal School have given attention to the phenomenon of declining interest rates. Their explanation has followed that of North. According to Wieser, interest has fallen because the supply of capital has increased relative to the demand. Thus,

> During the entire course of economic development the trend of the rate of productive interest is downward. Despite all technical progress, *the increase of capital reduces its marginal yield.*[91]

It was the opinion of Ricardo and J. S. Mill that the tendency would be for interest to fall; but their forecast was based on a particular view concerning the future of population. On marginal principles, all that was required for interest to decline was that capital should become more plentiful in comparison with the other factors of production. This is what Wieser said had happened "During the entire course of economic development." It will be remembered that both Hume and Turgot explained the reduction in interest, that they observed in earlier years, by a relative increase in the capital supply.

But historical evidence cannot be regarded as conclusive on how the interest rate and the supply of capital are related *at a time*. Over a long period economic conditions change. Innumerable writers have commented that part of the apparent fall in interest may be due to lessened risks attending investment. The possibility that a higher level of real income (and therefore a greater capacity to save) may be accompanied by increased saving should be borne in mind. The history of interest rates, like many other historical phenomena, appears too complex to be explicable in terms of a single factor.

Interest, Capital-Ownership, and the Length of Human Life

A novel idea in interest theory has been put forward in this century by Gustav Cassel, in *The Nature and Necessity of Interest* (London 1903) and *The Theory of Social Economy*.

Cassel, in effect, offered a capital supply curve of peculiar shape. Above an interest rate of about $2\frac{1}{2}$ per cent, he was prepared to admit that the effect of the rate of interest upon the supply of capital was not marked. For such reasons as were indicated by earlier writers, he thought that opposing tendencies were at work, and that these might be considered to balance each other.

But below this level, according to Cassel, the situation was altogether different. Society being constituted as it was, most of the capital was in

[91] *Social Economics*, p. 348. Italics ours.

used to define the short-term money-market rate on loans—and the *rate of interest* proper (*i.e.*, the long-term rate of interest on capital). The rate of discount, Nicholson said, depended on the demand and supply of loanable money: the rate of interest was governed by the demand and supply on loanable capital. Credit concerned one, savings the other.[97] The Dutch economist, N. G. Pierson, some of whose monetary theories are discussed in Chapter XIV, followed a similar line in his *Leerboek der staathuishoudkunde* (2 vols., Haarlem 1884–1890).[98] Pierson, however, argued that there was not merely a one-way connection between the supply of money and the short-term interest rate: the link was two-sided. An increase in the quantity of money or credit might be alternately a cause and a result of a reduction in the interest rate.[99] In America H. J. Davenport, in *The Economics of Enterprise,* studied the relationship between the short-term market rate of interest and the long-term rate, on lines suggesting the work of Wicksell in Sweden, discussed in Chapter XV.[100] But the whole matter was clearly tied up with price movements and with changes in the volume of business activity. It is therefore appropriate that fuller consideration of the leading theories in this field should be reserved to Chapter XV. At all events, the ground was laid for some of the more recent theories of interest, notably that of Keynes, studied in the next section.

Schumpeter and Keynes

Can interest be made to disappear? Probably it is true that, until recently, most economists believed that a negative answer was beyond all question, at least so long as society retained anything like its present form.

Joseph A. Schumpeter (1883–), now teaching at Harvard University, has argued in his *Theorie der wirtschaftlichen Entwicklung* (2nd edition Munich 1926)[101] that the existence of interest is largely a phenomenon of economic dynamics. Producers introduce innovations that return an excess above their cost, so that an income accrues out of which interest can be met. The demand for capital caused by the existence of opportunities for profitable investment explains why existing rates of interest have to be paid. In an economy where inventions and new processes were unknown, only consumption loans could explain interest and the rate would be insignificant. Interest, therefore, in Schumpeter's opinion, is mainly the result of economic progress.

In Chapter XIII it will be shown that J. B. Clark and Alfred Marshall

[97] *Op. cit.*, vol. 2, London and N. Y. 1897; see pp. 215-229.

[98] Translated by A. A. Wotzel as *Principles of Economics,* 2 vols., London 1902–1912.

[99] See vol. 1 of the translation, pp. 225-232.

[100] See especially Chap. 18 of *The Economics of Enterprise.*

[101] Translated by R. Opie as *The Theory of Economic Development,* Cambridge, Mass. 1934.

offered an explanation of profits very similar to this, but these economists assumed that a positive rate of interest was needed to call forth a supply of capital adequate to meet the requirements of society. Schumpeter asserts that this would be much less true — if it were true at all — in a static economy. In the middle of the nineteenth century, as is mentioned in Chapter XIII also, John Stuart Mill admitted that inventions had the effect of maintaining the rate of interest — Mill spoke of profits — above its possible minimum. Schumpeter's theory, in effect, is that this minimum is close to zero.

Even more spectacular is the theory of the Cambridge economist, J. M. Keynes, as set forth in *The General Theory of Employment Interest and Money*. People invest, said Keynes, not for income in the way of interest, but for speculative gains or capital appreciation. In a changing economy they make forecasts that they hope will turn out better than those of others. In the light of what they think is their far-sightedness or luck, they out-bid others for investments or factors of production, expecting to profit when events move in their favor. The gains that can be made in this manner far outweigh (or individuals think they outweigh) the modest returns associated with what are considered to be safe investments, Keynes argued. Speculation would continue on this basis, he believed, regardless of the interest rate and even though interest were non-existent. In these circumstances, according to Keynes, the rate of interest is purely conventional and, given suitable methods, could be lowered indefinitely:

> *Any* level of interest which is accepted with sufficient conviction as *likely* to be durable *will* be durable; subject, of course, in a changing society to fluctuations for all kinds of reasons round the expected normal.[102]

A high interest rate, indeed, discourages savings, Keynes thought, because of its depressing effect on industrial activity and therefore on the incomes out of which savings are made.

In his view, what determines the rate of interest is *liquidity preference,* that is, men's preference between holding funds in liquid form (as cash and bank balances) and owning investments. If individuals try to convert investments into liquid funds, by selling them in a market in which cash is scarce, investments fall in value, of course (which is the same as saying that interest rises). On the other hand, if liquid funds be made plentiful, interest can be lessened. In other words, an easy credit policy or one of liberal government expenditure lowers interest rates. This is part of the recognized theory of money and banking and is referred to in Chapter XIV.

But, Keynes argued, such policies stimulate industrial activity.[103] In

[102] *The General Theory of Employment Interest and Money,* p. 203. Quoted by permission of Macmillan & Co., Ltd. and Harcourt, Brace and Company, Inc.

[103] See Chapter XV.

power were used for the manufacture of very durable equipment, they would have to be drawn, to a very large extent, from the satisfaction of current needs, and society would be reduced to a condition in which men, with tremendous efforts, and while suffering the greatest privation, would build Egyptian pyramids for the edification of future ages.[106]

Keynes made no real attempt to deal with such arguments. He emphasized the other side, the productive capacity of society under conditions of full employment of the factors of production. In the year Keynes's book appeared, 1936, Sir William Beveridge analyzed the data on British unemployment and reached the conclusion that, although its volume was large, most of it was to be attributed to non-cyclical factors.[107] This suggested that the prospects of increasing industrial output by abolishing cyclical unemployment were less bright than Keynes believed. On the other hand, the high levels to which production was pushed during the war years since that time have given added hope to Keynes's followers.

The war has been fought without the high interest rates that have accompanied many previous wars and this again gives support to the Keynesian theory. It may be unnecessary to postulate continuance of conditions which have explained the height of interest rates in the past. The economic development of past centuries has been characterized by enormous growth in (1) population and (2) production and consumption per head. Demands for capital, therefore, have been greater than would be the case in a stabler economy. Aside from wartime developments which may prove temporary, population growth has slackened and signs exist that the future movement may be downwards. Architects of ideal societies, like Sir Thomas More, visualized communities in which wants were simpler and leisure greater than has been the case in the practical world. A good deal of high-pressure salesmanship seems to be necessary to keep consumption in its present trend. May it not happen that the people of the future will prefer more leisure to further spectacular advances in output? Inventions will continue, presumably, and it must be remembered that many of these economize the use of capital. In this situation, the demands for capital may grow less intense, unless, indeed, men insist on having a destructive war every few years. What about the supply of capital? Since the savings of individuals come largely from the rich, with greater equality of wealth they may be expected to lessen. On the other hand, public savings are becoming more important. But there is much here that is quite imponderable. Thus, contemporary forecasts regarding population may prove entirely inaccurate. Evidently, estimating the future is a task even more complex than understanding the past.

[106] *The Theory of Social Economy*, p. 225.

[107] In a paper read before the British Association for the Advancement of Science.

Summary of Chapter

A strong feeling against interest on loans was evident in the ancient world and the middle ages. Commonly maximum rates were fixed by law, and for a considerable period in the middle ages interest was prohibited altogether. But a growing list of exceptions to the ban were admitted, allowing trade to develop with the aid of borrowed capital. The reformer Calvin recognized interest to be justified, though with qualifications. In countries that remained Catholic the old prohibition faded into the background. It is noteworthy, however, that the practice of fixing maximum rates of interest has persisted and even grown in recent years.

Writers on economic subjects in modern times have formulated a number of interest theories. To the socialists, interest on capital has represented exploitation of the workers and has been explained by the possession of property rights by the capitalists. The belief that interest was governed by the supply of and demand for money was prevalent among Mercantilist writers. The supply of capital or "waiting," in relation to the demand for this factor, has been the explanation most widely adopted by teachers of economics in recent years. It has been generally accepted that the demand for capital is largely determined by the rate of interest but there has been a diversity of opinion on the relationship of the supply (a matter of the rate of saving and of using up capital) to the interest rate.

With respect to the short run, economists have long recognized that interest is governed by money-market conditions. Recently the money-market aspect has been incorporated in general theory by J. M. Keynes, who has stated a somewhat revolutionary interest theory.

CHAPTER XII

WAGES

The Evolution of the Labor Market

In earlier chapters it has been shown that a labor market, in the sense of free laborers offering their services in return for wages, was by no means the general situation in the past.

Slavery and Serfdom

Slavery and serfdom, or bondage, made their appearance quite early in human history. Prisoners of war and wrong-doers were often enslaved or thrown into bondage. Debt seems to have been another means whereby men got into this position. In the ancient world a large part of the manual labor was performed by bondmen or slaves, and this was true even of skilled tasks and supervisory duties. During the middle ages slavery became less important but bondage was widespread and, indeed, lasted in central and eastern Europe until recent times. Slavery persisted on a considerable scale in Africa and Asia, and when Europeans opened up settlements overseas slavery appeared in some of them. South Africa and the United States of America provide examples.

Slave labor. An owner of slaves often regarded them merely as a source of income, through the produce of their labor. But slaves had to be supported in some manner and it must have happened sometimes in early societies, as it did in modern times, that slavery proved an expensive source of labor. The English economist, J. E. Cairnes, in his book on *The Slave Power* (London 1862), written in connection with slavery in the States of the Confederacy, emphasized this point, as did the American, F. A. Walker. The statement in Walker's book on *The Wages Question* (New York 1876) may be quoted to illustrate the argument used in this connection :

> The inferiority of the labor of the slave to that of the freeman, even of the lowest industrial grade, is proverbial. Slave labor is always and everywhere ineffective and wasteful because it has not its reward. No matter how complete the authority of the master over the person and the life, he cannot command all the faculties of his slave. The slave may be made to work, but he can not be made to think ; he may be made to work, but he can not be kept from waste ; to work indeed, but not with energy. Energy is not to be commanded, it must be called forth by hope, ambition, and aspiration. The whip only stimulates the flesh on which it is laid. It does not reach the parts of man where lie the springs of action. No brutality of rule can evoke even the

whole physical power of a human being. The man himself, even if he would, can not render his own best service unless some passion of the higher nature, love, gratitude, or hope, be awakened.[1]

Yet it must be remembered that such penalties as the whip were not the only inducements to activity under a slave system. Rewards, in the shape of promotion to supervisory positions and privileges of various kinds, were not unknown. The remarks of the early Roman writer, Varro, on the subject of slaves are of some interest. With an eye on replacement costs, Varro commented that it paid better in an unhealthy district to use hired laborers than slaves. In a healthy locality (in view of the inefficiency of slave labor) hired workers were better for the more important tasks. Then he went on to consider incentive, saying:

The goodwill of the overseers you should win by an occasional mark of esteem, and you ought to discuss, too, with the best of the labourers, the farm-work that is to be done, for where this is the case their sense of inferiority is lessened, and they feel that they are held in some account by their master. Their enthusiasm for work is increased by treatment more generous than usual, by better food and clothing, by occasional exemption from work, or the permission to graze a beast of their own on the farm, and by other privileges of the same kind – so that any who are given too hard a task, or too severe a punishment, may thus be consoled, and their goodwill and kindly feeling towards the master be restored.[2]

Probably many modern industrial psychologists would agree with Varro. Further, the attention being given to the problem of incentive at present shows that it has not disappeared even with the abolition of slavery, though no doubt it has become less serious. Lastly, it is evident that the factors that brought slavery to an end were not merely economic. The slave-owners of the Confederate States, who bore the impact of the economic loss that resulted from the productive inefficiency of slavery, fought for its maintenance. Even though some compensation was paid, the slaveholders of the Cape of Good Hope were highly incensed when the British government freed the slaves in that country. To a large extent it was the growth of moral antagonism to slavery in the northern part of the United States, and in Great Britain, respectively, which brought about these abolitions.

Bondage. Bondage or serfdom is a state intermediate between slavery (where the servant is owned by the master, like a chattel) and free labor (where temporary contracts are entered into voluntarily between servant and master). The serfs of former times were not at liberty to go where they pleased but were tied to the soil, that is, to the estates of their lords. Yet they had more personal and economic freedom than had the slaves.

[1] pp. 73-74.

[2] *Varro on Farming*, p. 52.

Serfdom was widespread in western Europe in the middle ages and existed in the east of that continent until recent times, the serfs on Russian estates being emancipated only in 1861.

Records are available that show how the medieval system of serfdom operated. An example is the anonymous *Seneschaucie,* attributed to the reign of the English king Edward I in the late thirteenth and early fourteenth centuries. This document states the duties of the various officials of the manor, or village community. The seneschal, or chief agent of the lord, had general oversight over the estate. Among other duties, he had to supervise the bailiffs of the various manors. The bailiff had to see that the lower officials performed their work properly and that the peasants worked in the lord's fields in accordance with their several duties. A provost or reeve was elected by the villagers on each manor, to regulate the agricultural practices in consultation with the bailiff. The hayward superintended the grassland. The cowherd had charge of the cattle, the shepherd of the sheep, etc. The ruling principle was obvious. The lord was supreme but he governed through a hierarchy of officials. The villagers—serfs and freemen—possessed limited rights of self-government or at least of consultation. The lord's officers were expected to preserve order in the community and, acting in their master's interests, to endeavor to exact from the manor as much produce as possible for the lord's use.

What provided the incentive in such a system? Legally, as has been shown elsewhere, the servile cultivators could be tallaged or taxed of all their produce. In practice, however, their dues (in labor, produce, or money) became in a large measure fixed by custom, so that they could accumulate possessions from what remained to them after these dues were paid. But if they became noticeably rich, a tallage was likely to descend upon them; and, in any event, the entire village was a productive unit and its common rules prevented the more enterprising men from forging ahead. Probably the subsistence principle of wages, accepted by the British Classical economists in later times, represented the nearest approach in modern economic ideas to an explanation of the manner in which the servile labor of the middle ages was remunerated.

But, in a sense, this appears to have had a somewhat general application in medieval times, to free labor as well as to that of serfs. The principle of a "just price" for commodities and services, discussed in Chapter IX, meant that the producers of all goods should be remunerated on a basis that provided them with an income adequate to maintain their accustomed station in life. In other words, every producer was to receive a subsistence wage, but the level of subsistence that determined the amount of this wage was a variable quantity, being high or low according to the social station of the individual concerned.

The Growth of Wage Labor

Something with a certain resemblance to wage labor has been found even in savage societies. Specialized craftsmen have existed, subsisting on the returns received from their work. Large-scale tasks, such as hut-building, have employed numerous workers, called together for the purpose. Firth speaks of the manner in which this labor was remunerated among the New Zealand Maori. In the case of unskilled labor, like dragging heavy timbers from the forest, "the daily provisioning and the concluding feast were sufficient reward" but more valuable gifts were given in return for work of a skilled nature. However,

> There was no exact standard, nor anything resembling a definite price for such work. A rough scale of values was in operation, and according to the length of time taken, the acknowledged skill of the expert, and the social importance of the work, the gifts made in return would tend to vary.[3]

This labor was part of a complex social organization and the rewards given for it were intended to demonstrate the generosity of those who gave them as well as to satisfy the workers who had contributed to the performance of the task. They were not something merely individual and contractual, as the modern wage is likely to appear.

Free wage labor, paid on a contractual or customary basis, evidently existed in the ancient world and, to some extent at least, throughout the middle ages. But with the passage of time more and more of the serfs became free. The younger sons of peasant cultivators, to whom the lord could grant no land, no doubt hired themselves as laborers, especially in the towns. Runaway serfs were another source of supply. The rise in wages that occurred after the Black Death appears to have been responsible for an extensive breaking-away of serfs from their manorial allegiance. The enclosure of the open fields of the villages for sheep farming in England during the sixteenth century threw a considerable number of laborers on the market. The situation in the rising towns was particularly interesting. Some of the cities had a practice whereby residence within the walls for a year and a day conferred freedom on those who had escaped from obligations elsewhere. From time to time, manorial lords endeavored to assert their rights over city burgesses on the ground that they were runaway serfs. But with the decline of labor services such actions were commonly designed to levy tallages on those who had become wealthy, rather than to enforce the ancient rights to labor service. Sometimes individual lords freed their serfs, as a death-bed act or otherwise, while in certain countries there were large scale emancipations, notably that which took place in Russia in 1861. Lastly, there is no

[3] *Primitive Economics of the New Zealand Maori*, p. 294.

Mun, Locke, and Davenant all discussed taxes in a manner that involved acceptance of the subsistence theory of wages. Thus:

Neither are these heavy Contributions [*i.e.,* taxes] so hurtful to the happinesse of the people, as they are commonly esteemed: for as the food and rayment of the poor is made dear by Excise, so doth the price of their labour rise in proportion; whereby the burden (if any be) is still upon the rich, who are either idle, or at least work not in this kind, yet have they the use and are the great consumers of the poors labour. . .[6]

supposing no more charges in raising it [*i.e.,* government revenue], than of a land-tax, and that there are only three millions to be paid, it is evident that, to do this, out of commodities, they must, to the consumer, be raised a quarter in their price. . . Let us see now who, at long-run, must pay this quarter, and where it will light. It is plain, the merchant and broker neither will, nor can; for, if he pays a quarter more for commodities than he did, he will sell them at a price proportionably raised. The poor labourer and handicraftsman cannot: for he just lives from hand to mouth already, and all his food, clothing and utensils, costing a quarter more than they did before, either his wages must rise with the price of things, to make him live; or else, not being able to maintain himself and family by his labour, he comes to the parish [*i.e.,* becomes a recipient of public relief]. . .[7]

The Dutch, whose labour and manufactures are dear by reason of home excises, can notwithstanding sell cheap abroad, because this disadvantage they labour under is balanced by the parsimonious temper of their people: But in England, where this frugality is hardly to be introduced, if the duties upon our home consumption are so large as to raise considerably the price of labour and manufacture, all our commodities for exportation must by degrees so advance in the prime value, that they cannot be sold at a rate which will give them vent in foreign markets. . .[8]

In the last of these passages, Davenant's reference to the effect of the duties in raising the price of labor and manufactures illustrates the subsistence theory.

Something in the nature of a subsistence theory of wages was also an important feature of Physiocratic doctrine. What ensured that the surplus produce resulting from the labor of cultivators found its way into the pockets of landowners was the circumstance that the former received for their labor only sufficient for their maintenance. Turgot stated the subsistence theory in a formal manner:

The mere Workman, who has only his arms and his industry, has nothing except in so far as he succeeds in selling his toil to others. He sells it more

[6] Mun, *England's Treasure by Forraign Trade,* p. 154.

[7] *Some Considerations of the Lowering of Interest and Raising the Value of Money,* in *The Works of John Locke,* vol. 5, p. 57.

[8] *An Essay upon the Probable Methods of making a People Gainers in the Balance of Trade* (London 1699), reprinted in *The Political and Commercial Works of . . . Charles D'Avenant,* vol. 2, pp. 199-200.

or less dear; but this price, more or less high as it may be, does not depend upon himself alone: it results from the agreement which he makes with him who pays his labour. The latter pays him as little as he can; as he has the choice among a great number of Workmen, he prefers the one who works cheapest. The Workmen are therefore obliged to lower the price, in competition with one another. In every kind of work it cannot fail to happen . . . that the wages of the workman are limited to what is necessary to procure him his subsistence.[9]

Adam Smith accepted the subsistence theory only with important modifications. In Chapter VII it was shown that Smith believed that the principle that population multiplied up to the limits set by subsistence had a certain validity, but he confined its operation to the poorer classes. Even then, he considered that it was not always applicable. Subsistence, Smith thought, put a *bottom limit* on wages:

A man must always live by his work, and his wages must at least be sufficient to maintain him. They must even upon most occasions be somewhat more; otherwise it would be impossible for him to bring up a family, and the race of such workmen could not last beyond the first generation.[10]

But the demand for labor might raise wages above this lower limit and, in Great Britain in his time, Smith thought that wages were "evidently more than what is precisely necessary to enable the labourer to bring up a family." Three reasons were given by Smith for this opinion. (1) There was a distinction between the amounts of the summer and winter wages. If the latter, which were lower, were adequate to cover subsistence, it followed that the former were more than was sufficient for this purpose. (2) The money wage was more stable than the price of provisions. If it were enough to cover the latter when this was high, it was more than enough when it was low. This was true both of seasonal and longer-term movements. (3) Changes in the prices of food and of labor—which, according to the subsistence theory, should coincide—were frequently in the opposite direction. Obviously, here Smith was attempting to controvert a long-term principle by arguments based on the short term. Even in the poorest families some necessary expenditure can be adjusted to a certain extent in point of time and, in any event, many short-term ups and downs of births are averaged out in the number of people of working age.

In connection with his discussion, however, Smith presented an interesting possibility. He was considering the difference in wages between England and Scotland. In Scotland, where the workers' food was "in general much inferior to that of their neighbours of the same rank in England," wages were lower. Smith said that this difference in feeding standards was an effect, not a cause:

[9] *Reflections on the Formation and the Distribution of Riches*, p. 8.
[10] *Wealth of Nations*, Bk. 1, Chap. 8.

those means of subsistence; in other words, the value of labour-power is the value of the means of subsistence necessary for the maintenance of the labourer.[17]

As to the nature of the subsistence standard, Marx followed Ricardo and Malthus in saying that it was not fixed, but he incorporated in it his own concept of historical evolution :

His [*i.e.,* the worker's] means of subsistence must therefore be sufficient to maintain him in his normal state as a labouring individual. His natural wants, such as food, clothing, fuel, and housing, vary according to the climatic and other physical conditions of his country. On the other hand, the number and extent of his so-called necessary wants, as also the modes of satisfying them, are themselves the product of historical development, and depend therefore to a great extent on the degree of civilisation of a country, more particularly on the conditions under which, and consequently on the habits and degree of comfort in which, the class of free labourers has been formed.[18]

Marx made a great point of his belief that the workers' standards of subsistence were being forced down under the system of capitalism :

The modern laborer . . . instead of rising with the progress of industry, sinks deeper and deeper below the conditions of existence of his own class. He becomes a pauper, and pauperism develops more rapidly than population and wealth. And here it becomes evident, that the bourgeoisie is unfit any longer to be the ruling class in society. . . It is unfit to rule because it is incompetent to assure an existence to its slave within his slavery, because it cannot help letting him sink into such a state that it has to feed him, instead of being fed by him.[19]

Rodbertus accepted the subsistence theory of wages and argued that its operation in face of a rising standard of industrial output had the effect of lowering the share of the product that was received by the workers. This is the celebrated *law of the diminishing wage share* and Rodbertus used it to explain the existence of business depressions :

According to this theory, pauperism and commerical crises spring from *one and the same* cause. . . This circumstance is *that when the distribution of the national product is left to itself, certain circumstances connected with the development of society produce this effect*: THAT WITH INCREASING PRODUCTIVENESS OF THE LABOUR OF SOCIETY, THE WAGES OF THE LABOURING CLASSES BECOME AN EVER SMALLER PORTION OF THE NATIONAL PRODUCT.[20]

The socialist, Lassalle, gave the subsistence theory considerable notoriety under the name of the *iron, or brazen, law of wages*. This Lassalle stated as follows :

[17] *Capital,* Pt. 2, Chap. 6. [18] *Ibid.* [19] *Communist Manifesto,* p. 29.

[20] *Overproduction and Crises,* translated by J. Franklin, London 1898, reprinted 1908, pp. 70-71. Quoted by permission of George Allen & Unwin Ltd. Rodbertus's theory of crises receives attention in Chapter XV.

There is no gain saying the assurance that the wages of a people are regulated by their ordinary habits of living, those habits conforming to the limits of existence and propagation. This is the cruel, rigorous law that governs wages under the present system.[21]

Here the theory was back in its early starkness. Lassalle asserted that the standard of subsistence was the minimum required for the maintenance and propagation of the working class, and that this determined the wage rate.

More recently, some economists have made a certain amount of use of the conception of subsistence wages as one factor that is supposed to lie behind the long-run supply of labor. Marshall, for example, said:

There is a constant tendency towards a position of normal equilibrium, in which the supply of each of these agents [the agents of production, "human as well as material"] shall stand in such a relation to the demand for its services, as to give to those who have provided the supply a sufficient reward for their efforts and sacrifices. If the economic conditions of the country remained stationary sufficiently long . . . both machines and human beings would earn generally an amount that corresponded fairly with their cost of rearing and training, conventional necessaries as well as those things which are strictly necessary being reckoned for. But conventional necessaries may change under the influence of non-economic causes, even while economic conditions themselves are stationary: and this change would affect the supply of labor. . .[22]

In Marshall's opinion, though considerable time was needed to bring about adjustments in the labor supply, on the whole the wage corresponded "in the long run fairly well to the *real* cost of producing" the labor concerned.[23] To this extent — though, as will be shown below, not without argument — the subsistence theory has received a degree of acceptance in recent years.

The theory that higher wages diminish the supply. But a different view, diametrically opposed to that last discussed, has made its appearance. Observing that birth rates are lowest among the social groups whose living standards are highest, writers have suggested that high wages, by raising the standard of life, reduce the birth rate and therefore diminish the labor supply.

The development of this idea, as a population theory, has been traced in some detail in Chapter VII. Here it must suffice to say that it is true that (1) living standards and real wages have risen over a period of time, (2) birth rates have declined during the same interval, and (3) even at the same time those social groups that receive high incomes and real wages tend to have small families. But the mere correlation of higher

[21] *Open Letter to the National Labor Association of Germany*, p. 14.

[22] *Principles of Economics*, p. 577.

[23] *Ibid.*, p. 661.

posed taxes for the purpose of compelling the negroes to work for wages and, finding that they left their employments when sufficient money had been accumulated to pay the taxes, proposed additional levies for the purpose of stimulating further labor. The less the sum per day that the natives received for working, the more days it was necessary for them to work. It was quite possible that the poor of Britain in the seventeenth and eighteenth centuries, when men like Petty and Young were writing, behaved similarly.

Obviously, what is essential to the operation of such a principle is the existence of a fixed need or standard of subsistence. Income is earned to cover this need but nothing is desired beyond it. Anything in the nature of an elastic scale of wants would render the principle ineffective and, since elasticity of wants is a correlative of what is termed civilization, this particular type of wage reaction is to be expected among relatively uncivilized people. But, given the assumption of inelasticity of wants, there is no reason why it should be confined to backward societies or classes within a society. Standards of living and of wants tend to be rather rigid among all social groups, so that even among relatively advanced people the quantity of work done may decline if wages are raised considerably. This phenomenon was observed among British munition workers in some instances during the war of 1914–1918, for example.

Subsistence and the Efficiency of Labor

It is evident that the number of people, is only one factor affecting the labor supply. Quantity of work done per person is equally important. The short-run theory described above bore on this subject, but only in so far as the standard of subsistence was fixed. Adam Smith offered another idea. He said that a higher rate of wages, by increasing the productive efficiency of the working man, might, to some extent at least, pay for itself:

The liberal reward of labour, as it encourages the propagation, so it increases the industry of the common people. The wages of labour are the encouragement of industry, which, like every other human quality, improves in proportion to the encouragement it receives. A plentiful subsistence increases the bodily strength of the labourer, and the comfortable hope of bettering his condition, and of ending his days perhaps in ease of plenty, animates him to exert that strength to the utmost. Where wages are high, accordingly, we shall always find the workmen more active, diligent, and expeditious, than where they are low; in England, for example, than in Scotland; in the neighbourhood of great towns, than in remote country places. Some workmen indeed, when they can earn in four days what will maintain them through the week, will be idle the other three. This, however, is by no means the greater part.[28]

[28] *Wealth of Nations*, Bk. 1, Chap. 8.

Thus, while Smith agreed that in some cases the workers might perform less work when wages were high (the theory last considered), in Britain in his day he thought that the majority behaved otherwise. Obviously this opinion conflicted with that of Arthur Young respecting the same date and country, but Young was speaking of rural laborers especially and it is not unreasonable to expect that the wants of such workers would be less elastic than those of townsmen. Smith, indeed, said that the propensity of workmen to become more industrious, if they were offered a higher wage as an inducement to do so, was so marked that it might go to extremes and injure the laborers themselves :

> Workmen . . . when they are liberally paid by the piece, are very apt to overwork themselves, and to ruin their health and constitution in a few years.[29]

If this were the case, a high wage — however effective as a short-run stimulant to labor — would defeat itself in the long run. But Smith held out the possibility that, if care were exercised and such extremes avoided, what has since been called *the economy of high wages principle* would operate. Productive efficiency would rise to compensate for the higher wages.

Though to a large extent neglected by the later Classical economists, this point has been emphasized in more recent literature, notably by the German economist, Lujo Brentano (1844–1931). It has been used to support public expenditure on education and on social services generally and has been advocated by some industrial leaders, of whom the automobile manufacturer, Henry Ford, is an outstanding example.

Few people now doubt that there is an element of truth in it. As was shown earlier in the chapter, even in the ancient world and the middle ages suggestions were not wanting that higher "wages" might be profitable to the "employer" in certain circumstances, for instance, the "better food and clothing" and "occasional exemption from work" which Varro proposed for slave laborers. Varro, and many later writers who have dealt with the slave system, have mentioned the advantages of permitting the slaves to marry and raise families, not merely to keep up the labor supply but to make the slaves more contented and to increase their efficiency. In those areas of the African continent where, not long ago, it was thought necessary to raise native taxes to bring forth a greater supply of labor, wants now are showing elasticity, and some observers are arguing that an increase in the rate of wages may pay for itself by augmenting the production of the native workers.

The Wages Fund Theory

Through the first half of the nineteenth century, along with the subsistence explanation described on pages 571 to 577 above, went the *wages*

[29] *Ibid.*

hire; nor fall, except either by a diminution of the funds devoted to paying labour, or by an increase in the number of the labourers to be paid.[37]

As W. S. Jevons pointed out later, Mill's statement went far towards reducing the wages fund doctrine to a tautology. The capital that was incorporated in the fund was no longer regarded as identical with the whole capital of the community but only with that portion of this which was devoted to the payment of laborers and presumably was a matter for decision. Next, the fund included more than capital. Any income employed to hire labor was part of the fund and the amount of this, likewise, appeared to rest on decisions. Lastly, the capital-plus-income fund was divided, not among the entire population, but only among that section that worked for wages. Once these qualifications were introduced, the wages fund idea meant very little.

As to the disposition of the fund, Mill recognized that this was not simply a question of competition. Custom was of some significance and, in fact, in England, there were few kinds of labor in which the remuneration would not be lower than it was, "if the employer took full advantage of competition."

The wages fund theory led to an important practical conclusion. At intervals labor agitation was in the public eye. If it were the fact, as advocates of the theory believed, that wages were determined by an arithmetical process, in which the fund was the dividend and the number of its sharers the divisor, then it followed, as James Mill had said, that the only possible means of raising wages was either to increase the size of the fund by savings or to diminish the number of people among whom it was divided. All that labor unions could hope to do in such a situation was to increase the share of one class of workers at the expense of others. Thus, John Stuart Mill commented:

> Those combinations [*i.e.*, labor unions] always fail to uphold wages at an artificial rate, unless they also limit the number of competitors. . . these partial combinations, in so far as they do succeed in keeping up the wages of any trade by limiting its numbers, might be looked upon as simply intrenching around a particular spot against the inroads of over-population, and making the wages of the class depend upon their own rate of increase, instead of depending on that of a more reckless and improvident class than themselves.[38]

So that Mill, though denying that labor unions could assist the working class as a whole, cannot be described as being altogether unfavorable to their activities. It was in connection with the labor union aspect that the wages fund theory was to meet its defeat.

[37] *Principles of Political Economy*, Bk. 2, Chap. 11, Sect. 1.
[38] *Ibid.*, Bk. 2, Chap. 14, Sect. 6.

The attack on the wages fund theory. In Germany the wage fund theory met effective opposition. A productivity theory had been suggested in Thünen's *Der isolierte Staat.* F. B. W. von Hermann (1795–1868) argued that the real demander for labor was not the employer, as the English economists appeared to assume, but the consumer of the product. It followed that in the last resort the wage depended on what the consumer was willing to pay for this product. Brentano developed the same idea, criticizing especially the idea of a fixed wage fund. The amount expended on wages, Brentano said, was not predetermined but depended on employers' decisions. An increased demand for goods by the consumer, for example, would encourage capitalists to devote more money to the employment of labor.[39]

In England, Senior, though formally supporting the wage fund theory, put his finger on a weak point when he admitted that the size of the fund was not independent of the productivity of labor.[40] But not until the latter part of the 1860's was the theory seriously questioned. At that time labor unionism became a matter of heated controversy. Numerous unions had been formed but their existence and policies were subjected to severe criticism. Acts of violence had taken place, culminating in an explosion at Sheffield. A court decision had been given that denied protection to union funds on the ground that the unions were not legal associations. The government appointed a commission of inquiry and certain legislation resulted, whose effect was to recognize the unions. In these circumstances, it was only to be expected that the wage fund doctrine would receive attention. As Fleeming Jenkin pointed out, in reviewing the report of the government commission, according to the theory,

> wages depend simply on the ratio between the capital employed as wages and the number of persons to be paid; and unless by augmenting the capital or by diminishing the number, in other words, by augmenting the demand or diminishing the supply, no permanent alteration in wages can be effected. The question for those who wish to raise the wages of labour is, not how to divide the existing wages fund in a manner more favourable to the working man, but how to increase competition for his labour among employers; in other words, how to increase the wages fund. Trade-unions, far from even aiming at this end, drive capital away from trade by harrassing employers, diminishing profits, and increasing risks. Therefore, in the long run they tend to diminish wages, and though for a little while they may obtain an increase from an employer working, for instance, under a penalty, the increase is only temporary, and is little, if at all, short of a theft from that employer. But while they fail to increase wages, they do increase the cost of produc-

[39] See J. W. Crook, *German Wage Theories,* N. Y. 1898.

[40] *Political Economy,* p. 173 ff.

ance of a *magnum opus* on labor affairs: "Its wrongful claims and rightful dues, its actual present and possible future" was the sub-title.

On the subject of the wages fund, Thornton did not deny that wages were paid out of capital. In fact, he stated explicitly that they were paid out of capital in the hands of employers. His argument was that the amount of the employers' resources devoted to the payment of wages was a matter of decision:

If there really were a national fund the whole of which must necessarily be applied to the payment of wages, that fund could be no other than an aggregate of smaller similar funds possessed by the several individuals who composed the employing part of the nation. Does, then, any individual employer possess any such fund? Is there any specific portion of any individual's capital which the owner must necessarily expend upon labour? . . . is there any law fixing the amount of his domestic expenditure, and thereby fixing likewise the balance available for his industrial operations? May he not spend more or less on his family and himself according to his fancy – in the one case having more, in the other less, left for the conduct of his business? . . . And be it observed, fixity or definiteness is the very essence of the supposed wages fund. No one denies that some amount or other must within any given period be disbursed in the form of wages. The only question is, whether that amount be determinate or indeterminate. If indeterminate, it cannot of course be divided, and might as well not exist for any power it possesses of performing the sole function of a wages fund, that, viz., of yielding a quotient that would indicate the average rate of wages.[45]

Finally, in *The Wages Question,* Walker asserted that "The wages of the laborer are paid out of the product of his industry"[46]:

. . . the employer purchases labor with a view to the product of the labor; and the kind and amount of that product determine what wages he can afford to pay. He must, in the long run, pay less than that product, less by a sum which is to constitute his own profits. If that product is to be greater, he can afford to pay more; if it is to be smaller, he must, for his own interest, pay less. It is, then, for the sake of future production that the laborers are employed, not at all because the employer has possession of a fund which he must disburse; and it is the value of the product, such as it is likely to prove, which determines the amount of the wages that can be paid, not at all the amount of wealth which the employer has in possession or can command. Thus it is production, not capital, which furnishes the motive for employment and the measure of wages.[47]

Obviously, these writings contained not merely a negative criticism of the wages fund theory but also a positive contribution. Wages were *not* paid out of a fund of predetermined size, it was said: they *were* paid from the produce resulting from the employment of labor.

[45] 2nd ed., London 1870, pp. 84-85.

[46] *Op. cit.*, heading of Chapter 8.

[47] *Ibid.*, pp. 129-130.

Writing on Thornton's book in the *Fortnightly Review* in 1869, John Stuart Mill admitted the force of that critic's arguments. Mill considered that the results of the discussion were "not yet ripe for incorporation in a general treatise on Political Economy,"[48] however, so was content to re-issue his *Principles of Political Economy* with the statements of the wages fund doctrine which have been quoted above and with only a footnote to put curious readers on the track of Thornton's work.

Later supporters. Notwithstanding Mill's retraction, J. E. Cairnes attempted to restore the wages fund doctrine in his *Some Leading Principles of Political Economy Newly Expounded.* Even later, the American, F. W. Taussig (1859–1940), in his book on *Wages and Capital* (New York 1896), supported the theory in a different form. The position taken by Taussig was that *real wages* (that is, the goods and services that the worker gets when he spends his money wages) are at any time definite in their amount. They are represented by the consumers' goods available for purchasing at the time the wages are spent. It follows from this that a rise in money wages would be reflected only in a higher price level for the articles purchased by the wage-earners and not by any increase in the real wage rate. Conversely, a decline in money wages lowers the prices of the goods and services bought by the laborers, so that real wages remain stable.

Given the assumptions (1) that a definite quantity of commodities and services are available to the workers for their consumption, and (2) that the entire wage, or a fixed percentage of it, is spent on purchasing these articles, there is an element of truth in Taussig's theory. But can these postulates be admitted? Suppose that money wages are increased, diminishing the money incomes of the employers or capitalists, the real wage rate can rise if either (1) the workers save a greater percentage of their incomes than formerly—that is, accept part of their real wage in investment goods, or (2) the persons other than wage-earners purchase fewer consumers' goods, leaving more of these latter for the workers. If the long view be taken, the theory clearly falls to the ground. Few people believe that a substantial shift-over of money incomes from employers or capitalists to wage-earners (although perhaps immediately resulting in higher prices for a relatively inelastic supply of consumers' goods) would not stimulate the output of the commodities and services upon which wages are spent, thereby raising real wages.

The Residual Theory

Another wage theory that has exercised a certain amount of influence is the idea that wages are a residue, being what remains of the product after the other shares (rent, interest, and perhaps profits) have been deducted.

[48] *Op. cit.*, preface to 7th ed.

to have perceived that the quantity of labor available was one of the factors that influenced the demand for capital, so that his "independent" determination of interest was fallacious. Jevons's theory of interest, likewise — though its author did not seem to realize this fact — left the capitalist disputing with the laborer for the residual product of industry, rent alone being independently determined. It was left to men like J. B. Clark and Marshall, in their marginal theory of value and distribution, to explain these points.

Something in the nature of a residual wage theory has been offered, however, in recent years. Keynes, in *The General Theory of Employment Interest and Money,* has offered a theory that goes a long way toward being an independent explanation of the mechanism of interest determination. Reference was made to this theory in the previous chapter. If it be accepted, labor appears to be enthroned as the residuary legatee and the beneficiary of future progress in productivity.

The Marginal Productivity Theory

Walker wrote at a time when, in the various countries, the work of Jevons, Walras, and Menger was being seriously considered. Jevons, as a member of the Marginal School of economists, might have been expected to present a wage theory in accordance with marginal principles.[52] As was seen in the preceding section, however, he failed to do so.

As early as the seventeenth century, in *The Political Anatomy of Ireland,* Sir William Petty had advanced a theory that identified wages with the produce of the labor concerned :

> suppose two Acres of Pasture-land inclosed, and put thereinto a wean'd Calf, which I suppose in twelve Months will become 1 C. heavier in eatable Flesh ; then 1 C. weight of such Flesh, which I suppose fifty days Food, and the Interest of the Value of the Calf, is the value or years Rent of the Land. But if a mans labour — — for a year can make the said Land to yield more than sixty days Food of the same, or of any other kind, then that overplus of days food is the Wages of the Man. . .[53]

Even before Jevons wrote, Thünen in Germany and Longfield in Britain had laid some of the foundations of a theory of distribution based, not merely on produce, but on the produce of the marginal or least effective increment of the factor of production concerned, that is to say, on marginal productivity. But the distributional theories of Thünen and Longfield were somewhat fragmentary and failed to receive any wide attention, and it was not until the close of the nineteenth century that Wicksteed and J. B. Clark produced a well-rounded marginal productivity theory of distribution.

[52] See Chapter II.
[53] *The Economic Writings of Sir William Petty,* vol. 1, p. 181.

This theory explained wages, interest, and rent on marginal principles. Just as the values of commodities represented the rates at which these exchanged on the margins where buyers and sellers were indifferent, so with the values of the factors of production. Wages conformed to the rate at which labor exchanged for commodities, on the margin where the entrepreneur was indifferent whether he employed the labor or not. Land and capital being kept constant in amounts, as successive laborers were hired the addition made to the produce by each succeeding man declined (this is the operation of the principle of diminishing returns). The employer continued to hire these men as long as they added more to the product than he had to pay them in wages. In due course, however, a point was reached at which the addition to the produce was just balanced by the cost of making it, that is, by the wage. Here, the business manager was indifferent. Beyond this point, the employment of additional laborers would be unprofitable, because the increments of product resulting from their work would fall short of the wages they had to be paid. The same argument applied to capital and land.

The general principle that the factors of production — including labor — were remunerated according to their marginal productivity was stated by Wicksteed in *An Essay on the Co-ordination of the Laws of Distribution* (London 1894), as follows:

> The general law of distribution, then . . . amounts simply to this: — That the share in the product which falls to any factor, no matter what be the character of that factor or of the service which it renders, is determined by the amount per unit which the concern, as a whole, would find it pay to allow to that factor sooner than have a portion of it withdrawn from co-operation. So stated the theorem may seem self-evident. And so indeed it is. Everyone knows that if a man "is not worth his salt" he is discharged, that if an employer cannot profitably keep all his hands at work he dismisses some of them (unless actuated by motives other than those usually described as "economic"), that if a machine is expected to "eat its head off" it is not bought, that unless I expect a piece of land to pay its own rent I do not take it for industrial purposes, and so on.[54]

Clark's formulation of the principle, with respect to labor, is of interest. In the use of both land and capital there existed an extensive and intensive margin, the extensive margin representing the poorest land or machines utilized, and the intensive margin the last and least productive employment of superior land or machines. The amount added to the product by the employment of labor on either of these margins (which, under the influence of competition tended to be the same) was called, by Clark, the *specific product of labor*. This, through competitive bargaining, he said, went to the laborer as wages:

[54] Reprinted London 1932, pp. 10-11 of the reprint. Quoted by permission of the London School of Economics and Political Science.

was not unopposed. For example, Marshall criticized it in the following language:

This doctrine [*i.e.*, marginal productivity] has sometimes been put forward as a theory of wages. But there is no valid ground for any such pretension. The doctrine that the earnings of a worker tend to be equal to the net product of his work, has by itself no real meaning; since in order to estimate net product, we have to take for granted all the expenses of production of the commodity on which he works, other than his own wages. But though this objection is valid against the claim that it contains a theory of wages; it is not valid against a claim that the doctrine throws into clear light the action of one of the causes that govern wages.[58]

At first sight, this appears to be a serious criticism of Clark. But actually all that Marshall meant was that, not labor alone, but capital and land also, had to be taken into account on the side of supply or production, as well as consumers' wants on the side of demand, in determining wages. In other words, according to Marshall, marginal theory did not offer an independent theory of wages but a comprehensive explanation of value and distribution, all the parts of which were inter-dependent. Probably no one realized this better than Clark and, indeed, it was the thesis of his *Distribution of Wealth*.

The theory received wide acceptance and forms the basis of much teaching on economics at present. Yet numberless teachers and students have been worried by its obvious inapplicability to many of the conditions of practical life. As Clark submitted it, it professed to be no more than a statement of *tendencies*. It depended on conditions like knowledge, rational choice, and the possibility of switching the factors of production between the various employments open to them, in other words on all that is implied by the word competition. The practical situation may be that the owners of the only steel plant in a locality are bargaining with a labor union representative of the workers and sufficiently powerful to enforce a shut-down if need be. The owners can withdraw the entire plant, by closing its doors in a lock-out. The workers can withdraw the whole labor force, in a strike. In either event, the product disappears altogether. What is the productivity of labor and of capital in such circumstances? The withdrawal of either destroys the whole product. Even though profits fall much below the level that would encourage capitalists to renew the buildings and machinery, it may pay the owners to continue operation while the plant remains in working order. Similarly with the workers. Although wages reach a level at which an insufficient number of new entrants to the working force come forward, yet many of those already employed may consider it worth their while to stay in their jobs. Because of the inability of capital, labor, and land, to be moved easily between different employments, it follows that in the

[58] *Principles of Economics*, p. 518.

short run the *total product* is likely to be the prize in a free-for-all fight between the owners of the factors of production. Indeed, mindful of the aspect of taxation, the government also may be considered to join in. Only where additions or withdrawals can take place, does the principle apply that marginal increments of product govern the remuneration of the productive factors. On the other hand, it must be conceded that the assumption of competition has more validity in the long than in the short run, so that as a statement of *tendencies* the marginal productivity theory is not without some application. Even here, however, its applicability is not complete, if only for the reasons that men's actions are not entirely rational and that self-interest is not the only human motive.

Theories of Differential Wages

The theories that have been described were primarily concerned with what is commonly called the *general rate of wages*. But writers at various times have studied wage disparities between different occupations. The comments of Aristotle and Thomas Aquinas on this subject will be borne in mind. To both of these philosophers, a man's worth was something which depended on the standard of life that social custom sanctioned for his class.

Cantillon, Harris, and Smith

Cantillon was one of the earliest of modern writers to consider in any detail the problem of wage discrepancies. His explanation was based largely on the assumption that workers could move between different occupations, and would be attracted to or repelled from the several employments according to their various amenities :

The Crafts which require most Time in training or most Ingenuity and Industry must necessarily be the best paid. . .

The Arts and Crafts which are accompanied by risks and dangers like those of Founders, Mariners, Silver miners, etc. ought to be paid in proportion to the risks.

When over and above the dangers skill is needed they ought to be paid still more, e.g. Pilots, Divers, Engineers, etc.[59]

But, somewhat surprisingly, Cantillon added,

When Capacity and trustworthiness are needed the labour is paid still more highly, as in the case of Jewellers, Bookkeepers, Cashiers and others.[60]

This last is of entirely different character from the others. The first three referred to features which made the various occupations more or less attractive *to the workers concerned,* that is, to the prospective entrants. Not so the last. It is largely immaterial to the worker whether the em-

[59] *Essai sur la nature du commerce en général,* p. 21. [60] *Ibid.*

ployer has to trust him or not, but the question of whether he is trustworthy might be highly important *to the employer* in the case of certain positions.

Cantillon's theory of population contained an interesting implication respecting wage differences. Some men were prepared to reproduce their kind on a very low subsistence level, he said, but others demanded a higher standard before they were willing to marry. If these differences in standards were related to employments, as no doubt they were in practice, the result would be that workers who were accustomed to a high standard of life maintained this by keeping their rate of reproduction low. Those who customarily had a low standard, were kept in poverty by their rapid multiplication. Cantillon himself did not draw this conclusion respecting wage rates, but it followed from his population theory.

Joseph Harris, who appears to have made considerable use of Cantillon's *Essai,* mentioned the same factors, in his *Essay upon Money and Coins,* in explaining why "Mechanics earn more than labourers, &c.":

To bring up a child to a trade, there is not only an expence in fitting him out, and during his apprenticeship, but also a risque [risk] of his dying before he is out of his time; from which considerations a mechanic is entitled to better wages than a common labourer: And as any given trade is attended with greater risques of any sort, requires more skill, more trust, more expence in setting up, &c. the artificer will be entitled to still better wages. In like manner those professions that require genius, great confidence, a liberal education, &c. have a right to be rewarded proportionably.[61]

Adam Smith followed Cantillon's list rather closely and there seems little doubt that it represented his source of inspiration on this subject, either directly or through Harris:

First, the wages of labour vary with the ease or hardship, the cleanliness or dirtiness, the honourableness or dishonourableness of the employment. Thus in most cases, take the year round, a journeyman tailor earns less than a journeyman weaver. His work is much easier. A journeyman weaver earns less than a journeyman smith. His work is not always easier, but it is much cleanlier. A journeyman blacksmith, though an artificer, seldom earns so much in twelve hours, as a collier [*i.e.,* coal miner], who is only a labourer, does in eight. His work is not quite so dirty, is less dangerous, and is carried on in day-light, and above ground. Honour makes a great part of the reward of all honourable professions. In point of pecuniary gain, all things considered, they are generally under-recompensed. . . Disgrace has the contrary effect. The trade of a butcher is a brutal and odious business; but it is in most places more profitable than the greater part of common trades. The most detestable of all employments, that of public executioner, is, in proportion to the quantity of work done, better paid than any common trade whatever. . .

61 *A Select Collection of Scarce and Valuable Tracts on Money,* p. 355.

Secondly, the wages of labour vary with the easiness and cheapness, or the difficulty and expense of learning the business. . . The difference between the wages of skilled labour and those of common labour is founded upon this principle. . . Education in the ingenious arts and in the liberal professions is still more tedious and expensive. The pecuniary recompense, therefore, of painters and sculptors, of lawyers and physicians, ought to be much more liberal : and it is so accordingly. . .
Thirdly, the wages of labour in different occupations vary with the constancy or inconstancy of employment. Employment is much more constant in some trades than in others. In the greater part of manufactures, a journeyman may be pretty sure of employment almost every day in the year that he is able to work. A mason or bricklayer, on the contrary, can work neither in hard frost nor in foul weather, and his employment at all other times depends upon the occasional calls of his customers. He is liable, in consequence, to be frequently without any. What he earns, therefore, while he is employed, must not only maintain him while he is idle, but make him some compensation for those anxious and desponding moments which the thought of so precarious a situation must sometimes occasion. . .
Fourthly, the wages of labour vary according to the small or great trust which must be reposed in the workmen. The wages of goldsmiths and jewellers are everywhere superior to those of many other workmen, not only of equal, but of much superior ingenuity; on account of the precious materials with which they are intrusted. We trust our health to the physician; our fortune, and sometimes our life and reputation, to the lawyer and attorney. Such confidence could not safely be reposed in people of a very mean or low condition. Their reward must be such, therefore, as may give them that rank in the society which so important a trust requires. . .
Fifthly, the wages of labour in different employments vary according to the probability or improbability of success in them. . . In the greater part of mechanic trades, success is almost certain; but very uncertain in the liberal professions.[62]

In connection with the last factor, Smith commented that the "overweening conceit which the greater part of men have of their own abilities" led them to overestimate their chance of success, with the result that wages in uncertain occupations were not, on the average, sufficiently high to compensate for the risk of failure involved in entering them.

Except for the fourth of these reasons for wage differences, the assumption was that men could exercise a choice between the several employments and that they were able and willing to move one way or another according to the relative attractiveness of the different occupations. In this situation, the wage rate acted so as to equalize the various attractions. But Cantillon's exceptional factor, that of *trust,* continued to occupy a place in the list.

[62] *Wealth of Nations,* Bk. 1, Chap. 10, Pt. 1.

Ricardo and Marx

Ricardo went off on a different track. As was pointed out in Chapter IX, he might have been expected to conclude from his general theory of value that wage differences were explained by variations in the costs of producing the several classes of labor. Labor that required long training, for example, cost more in terms of subsistence than did labor of a simpler kind. But Ricardo failed to develop this idea and it was his successor in value theory, Karl Marx, who put forward this explanation. What Ricardo himself said on the subject has been referred to in Chapter IX.[63]

Senior and Mill

Senior reproduced the Cantillon-Harris-Smith list of reasons for wage differences. Giving Smith as his authority, Senior mentioned (1) agreeableness of the occupation, (2) facility of learning it, (3) constancy of employment, (4) trustworthiness, and (5) probability of success. But he made two important additions: (6) "Variations occasioned by the difficulty of Transferring Labour and Capital from one employment to another" and (7) similar variations explained by the difficulty of movement "from one country to another." The reference to capital was explained, it should be said, by the fact that both Smith and Senior dealt with wages and profits together in this connection. With reference to the added factors, Senior said,

> great inequalities are found which cannot be accounted for by any circumstances leading men to prefer one employment to another, and which therefore continue only in consequence of the difficulties experienced by the labourers and the capitalists in changing their employments.[64]

This difficulty of movement, he continued, was "the principal evil of a high state of civilisation" and it existed "in proportion to the division of labour."[65] The obstacles to movement that existed within a locality were even greater when different localities were considered, because then not only the occupation but the place of abode had to be changed.

John Stuart Mill placed even more emphasis on the difficulties of movement. After considering cases in which inter-occupational mobility existed, he remarked that there were instances where wage variations were explained by a different principle. The goldsmiths and jewelers, who had served to exemplify the Cantillon-Smith case of "great trust" were in this position. Trustworthy people were scarce, Mill said, with the result that

> The superiority of reward is not here the consequence of competition, but of its absence: not a compensation for disadvantages inherent in the employ-

[63] See p. 425. [64] *Political Economy*, p. 217. [65] *Ibid.*

ment, but an extra advantage; a kind of monopoly price, the effect not of a legal, but of what has been termed a natural monopoly. If all labourers were trustworthy, it would not be necessary to give extra pay to working goldsmiths on account of the trust. The degree of integrity required being supposed to be uncommon, those who can make it appear that they possess it are able to take advantage of the peculiarity, and obtain higher pay in proportion to its rarity. This opens a class of considerations which Adam Smith, and most other political economists, have taken into far too little account. . .[66]

Mill was quite prepared to grant that skilled employments had to yield a sufficient additional remuneration, as compared with those in which skill was not required, to cover the extra costs incurred in training. But he said that in addition to this factor there was another, namely monopoly. Smith had referred to the influence of the apprenticeship laws in this connection, but Mill commented that, "independently of these or any other artificial monopolies":

there is a natural monopoly in favour of skilled labourers against the unskilled, which makes the difference of reward exceed, sometimes in a manifold proportion, what is sufficient merely to equalize their advantages. If unskilled labourers had it in their power to compete with skilled, by merely taking the trouble of learning the trade, the difference of wages might not exceed what would compensate them for that trouble, at the ordinary rate at which labour is remunerated. But the fact that a course of instruction is required, of even a low degree of costliness, or that the labourer must be maintained for a considerable time from other sources, suffices everywhere to exclude the great body of the labouring people from the possibility of any such competition.[67]

Thus, against the Cantillon-Smith list of competitive factors (neglecting the non-competitive one of "trust") was set the opposite situation of monopoly. The argument of Senior and Mill was obviously correct, as was that of Cantillon and Smith, granting in each case the necessary assumptions. Where Cantillon postulated freedom of choice, Mill assumed the absence of this freedom. The question arose, accordingly, how far was it true that competition existed? This was the problem to which Cairnes applied himself.

Longfield and Cairnes

In his *Lectures on Political Economy,* Longfield had attempted to rationalize the theory of occupational mobility. After admitting that mobility was impossible between employments that were widely separated in the social scale, such as lawyers and bricklayers, he declared that competition operated through a chain of intermediate professions, within which movement was possible:

[66] *Principles of Political Economy,* Bk. 2, Chap. 14, Sect. 2. [67] *Ibid.*

Increased profits of bricklayers, or the diminished gains of barristers, will not induce any person to become a bricklayer who would otherwise become a barrister. Neither will the diminished profits of bricklayers, or the increased gains of barristers, enable a man who would otherwise become a bricklayer, to pursue the profession of the bar, and by his competition reduce the gains of the profession to their proper level. This may be the case, and yet the due proportion between the gains of those two professions, so remote from each other, may be preserved by means of the intermediate professions. These act as media of communication. The effects of competition will reduce or raise the advantages of the trade of the bricklayer to the level of other employments which are filled by the same class of persons. It will moreover exert an immediate influence over the trades of a rank one degree higher, that is, in those trades which require a somewhat more tedious or expensive education, and therefore on an average receive higher emoluments, and are filled by a wealthier class of persons. For there are always some who would be influenced in the choice of trades approaching each other in expenses and emoluments, by slight additional circumstances of relative advantages or disadvantages in either. Thus trades one degree higher are brought to their level of advantages; and mounting step by step, even the most distant professions will preserve the natural proportion between their emoluments, as the emoluments of each profession will preserve their fair proportion to those of the profession of equal rank, and to those of all professions of a rank one degree immediately above or below it, and thus a series of communication is established between the lowest and the highest.[68]

It was on such a foundation that J. E. Cairnes built up his conception of *non-competing groups* in the labor market. The aim of this writer's *Some Leading Principles of Political Economy Newly Expounded* was to recast certain of the Classical economic doctrines in the light of the criticisms to which they had been subjected or to which they appeared to be open. In the section on value, mention was made of differential wages. Cairnes grouped occupations on the basis that movement was possible within each particular class but difficult or impossible between the several categories. He mentioned four groups: (1) Unskilled labor, or trades where little skill was needed. (2) Artisans, such as carpenters or masons. (3) Producers and dealers "of a higher order," whose activities demanded qualifications which could be obtained only by "persons of substantial means and fair educational opportunities," like civil engineers, chemists, and "the superior class of retail tradesman" (*i.e.*, storekeeper). (4) Persons "still more favourably circumstanced, whose ampler means would give them a still wider choice," including members of the learned professions and business executives.

Cairnes regarded this grouping only as a general one, but none the less he thought it was of some importance:

[68] *Op. cit.*, pp. 84-85.

No doubt the various ranks and classes fade into each other by imperceptible gradations, and individuals from all classes are constantly passing up or dropping down; but while this is so, it is nevertheless true that the average workman, from whatever rank he be taken, finds his power of competition limited for practical purposes to a certain range of occupations, so that, however high the rates of remuneration in those which lie beyond may rise, he is excluded from sharing them. We are thus compelled to recognise the existence of non-competing industrial groups as a feature of our social economy. . .[69]

Cairnes made this conception a basic feature of his comparison between domestic and international values, as has been noticed in Chapter IX.

Assessment

The theories that have been outlined contained two opposite principles in sharp juxtaposition. (1) Where labor can and does move readily in response to wage differences, it is supposed that relative wages will reflect only the varying attractiveness of the several occupations. (2) On the other hand, where mobility does not exist, the products of labor will exchange on the basis of relative intensities of demand and supply, and this will be reflected in wage rates. Competition is the ruling force in the first case, immobility or monopoly in the second. Either case may represent the truth in a particular instance. To take an example, if doctors' earnings are high relative to those received by plumbers, there are two possibilities: (1) Plumbers, or their sons, may be able to train as doctors, causing the supply of medical men to increase and that of plumbers to decline, lowering the wage differential to a point where it does no more than compensate the additional cost of becoming a doctor, the bother of being called out of bed at nights, etc. (2) Alternatively, plumbers or their sons may not be able to enter the medical profession, in which case the demand of medical practitioners for the services of plumbers, on the one hand, and the need of plumbers for medical assistance, on the other, will settle the matter (neglecting complications caused by the existence of other employments).

Cairnes grouped employments on this basis. In the example just given, case (1) refers to employments within a single non-competing group, case (2) to those in different groups. But this classification is unreal. It is apparent that there may be immobility over short periods in cases in which movement can take place over a period of time. Take the doctor-plumber example. It may be quite true to say that a practicing plumber has no hope of becoming a medical man, however attractive the remuneration of the latter appears to him compared with his plumber's wage. Yet his son may move across the gap between the two employments. Prob-

[69] *Op. cit.*, pp. 67-68.

ably the generalization can be made that mobility is to a large extent a function of time. The wages of a coal miner may be very low for many years without causing him to leave mining and enter another industry. Coal mining communities may be so isolated and self-contained that it is difficult even for the sons of present-day miners to find entry into other occupations. But given sufficient time, the possibility of movement becomes brighter. That is to say, the lines of demarcation between non-competing groups tend to fade away with the passage of time.

It is highly significant that the earlier writers should emphasize mobility and the later ones point to the difficulties of movement. Probably it is true that movement has tended to become more difficult as industrial occupations have become more specialized. On the other hand, the widespread nature of mechanization has increased the number of opportunities for what may be called horizontal mobility. A machine minder may move without difficulty between one industry and another, and the same is true of an office worker. Yet movement between machine and office desk within a single firm or industry may be virtually impossible.

The growth of specialization has broken up the labor market. In the short run, at all events, mobility is often so difficult that it seems artificial to speak of *the labor market,* or *the general rate of wages.* The truth seems to be that in the short period there are an enormous number of separate labor markets, each with its individual wage rate. Demands for an undifferentiated factor—labor—seem to be almost non-existent. He whose digestive system is out of order needs the services of a doctor. His neighbor, whose domestic drains are giving trouble, calls for a plumber. Both of them, perhaps, could give employment to someone active enough to mow lawns satisfactorily. None of these, not even the last (which comes closest), is really a demand for labor in general. The same applies to supply. An excellent doctor may be able to sell insurance at a pinch but could be expected to prove completely unsuccessful in manufacturing automobiles. Yet, as has been said, some of these limitations tend to dissolve away in the course of time.

In this situation it is natural that such writers as Cassel,[70] whose emphasis is on short-term equilibrium, tend to reject the conception of a single labor market, while economists whose concern has been with the longer view have continued to speak of such a market and to think in terms of a general wage rate.

Customary and Authoritarian Wages in Modern Times

The influence of custom on wage determination in modern times has been stressed by Sidney and Beatrice Webb, in their book on *Industrial Democracy.* This was a realistic study of the British labor market and some of its terminology is significant. "The right to a trade," "Progression

[70] See *The Theory of Social Economy,* Bk. 2, Chap. 8.

within the trade," "The device of restriction of numbers," "The device of the common rule"—these are among its section headings, and they characterize ideas that have more in common with medieval society than with individualistic competition. The Webbs used these terms to define some of the practices whereby the labor unionist of the late nineteenth century sought to protect his economic position. Men who had been trained legitimately in a particular employment (*i.e.*, who had passed through apprenticeship) claimed an exclusive right to practice it, shutting out other workers who had not entered in the regular manner. The unions restricted entry into the trades they covered and controlled promotion or progression from one level to another, in the interests of those who had already passed through the barriers. By the enforcement of common rules or standards respecting wages and hours of labor, one worker was prevented from undercutting others and thereby advancing himself at the expense of his fellows.

All this appears monopolistic and, indeed, the practices that have been mentioned represented a deliberate attempt on the part of organized workers to raise wages by restricting the supply of labor. The craft or skilled trade unions, with which the Webbs' study largely dealt and which dominated British labor unionism for some decades after 1850, were in a peculiarly favorable situation in this respect. In the skilled trades in which they operated, as Mill had pointed out, the time and expense required for training gave a measure of monopoly power to those who had passed through it. This power was exercised, not merely at the expense of the employer of labor, but against the consumer, as well as in opposition to the interests of other groups of workers.

Notwithstanding this monopolistic position, it seems evident that custom has been an influential factor behind the standards that the various labor regulations have sought to enforce. The different groups of workers had been accustomed to occupying their several positions in the industrial hierarchy. A skilled engineer, carpenter, or spinner, was among the élite of the labor world and had a higher standard than, say, a coal miner. But the miner in his turn was better off than a common laborer. Each had his own particular level, with its attendant advantages and disadvantages. He had come to take it as a matter of course and to regard it as a right, for which, in the last resort, he was prepared to struggle bitterly. It was a world in which, to a large extent, custom was right and what was right had might, as Malinowski said of the savage society in the Trobriand Islands. It was the outlook of medieval Europe, which had led Thomas Aquinas to conclude that distributive justice was done if men were remunerated sufficiently to meet their accustomed standards of living. It has not disappeared altogether in labor affairs, even today.

But as time has passed by, the position of the skilled workers has deteriorated, because the increased use of machinery in industry has made skilled craftsmanship less important and so has undermined the foundation on which many of the union restrictions rested. The result has been to place labor unionism on an industrial basis more than before, with mass bargaining — often involving strike threats or even actual withdrawals of labor — replacing the less spectacular methods that were relied upon by the skilled craft groups.

Along with this development has gone another in the direction of authoritative regulation of the labor market. For more than a century in England working conditions in the factories have been controlled. Starting in the State of Victoria in Australia in 1896 and spreading to England in the Trade Boards Act of 1909, government bodies have been set up to deal with wages and working conditions in the poorly-paid and unorganized trades, where labor unionism has been ineffective. Such devices as public inquiry and delay, and even compulsory arbitration of labor disputes, have been given force of law in different countries, while numerous governments have established conciliation services. In part, the motive behind such legislation has been that of public convenience. Strikes in important industries are responsible for considerable annoyance and even injury to members of the general public. But partly the purpose has been adjudication between the parties concerned. As has been pointed out in other chapters of this book, the paternal outlook that characterized government in the medieval and mercantile periods seems to have returned, and labor regulation is by no means an insignificant feature of this development.

The thought that is behind this movement may be exemplified by the famous Harvester judgment, promulgated in 1907 by Mr. Justice Higgins, President of the Australian Commonwealth Arbitration Court. Higgins took as his wage standard "the normal needs of the average employee regarded as a human being living in a civilised community" but did not define this in specific living requirements. However, he laid it down that 42 shillings (about 10 dollars) weekly were needed to maintain a family of five on this standard. This ruling served as the basis of Australian wage determination for many years, the money amount being adjusted by reference to a price index.[71] The acceptance of a standard of living criterion of wage rates has been widespread in public wage fixation. It was laid down in the English act of 1563, mentioned earlier in this chapter, and has been basic to many recent wage decisions. It has had important repercussions on the labor market. Thus, some South African wage determinations have used the "European" (*i.e.*, white) standard of living in determining the wage rate, with the intention that the "Non-European" (*i.e.*, colored) worker — whose productivity falls below that which would justify the wage so fixed — shall be driven out of the

[71] See F. C. Benham, *The Prosperity of Australia* London 1928, 2nd ed. 1930, pp. 190-192.

industry concerned. In other instances, "sweated" establishments have been legislated out of existence, by fixing a wage that was beyond their capacity to pay.

Summary of Chapter

What was said in Chapter X, respecting the integration of payments associated with land and the social system as a whole in early times, has equal applicability to labor. Though there are evidences of the existence of a competitive labor market to some extent much earlier, not until the break-up of medieval social organization did a free labor market become characteristic of industry.

Some of the Mercantilists, as well as the Physiocrats and the British Classical writers, accepted a long-run theory of wages that tied the latter to the subsistence needs of the worker. Men like Petty and Child believed that in the short run the rigidity of the worker's living standard would cause him to withdraw some of his labor if the wage were increased, and compel him to work more if the wage were reduced. Some economists, of whom Adam Smith was one of the most outstanding, argued that higher wages would promote efficiency and therefore increase the volume of work done. The wages fund theory furnished an account of the mechanism of the labor-demand: it was said that capital was set aside and utilized for the employment of labor. But this theory was abandoned when it came to be realized that there was no such thing as a fixed allocation of funds for the remuneration of workers, and that wages did not depend upon capital saved in the past but on produce called into existence in the present.

A residual explanation of wages had brief influence, it being argued that the other shares of income (rent, interest, and profits) were determined first, and that the worker received the balance of the product. This was soon superseded by the marginal theory, which visualized that the payments received by the owners of each of the factors of production were related to their several productive contributions on the margin where small additions or withdrawals could be made.

As distinct from the general rate of wages, which was the topic of these earlier theories, wage differences have received attention. Adam Smith based his explanation on the mobility of labor between the various employments. Later writings revealed a growing feeling that immobilities were important.

What may be called an institutional theory of wages appeared in *Industrial Democracy,* by Sidney and Beatrice Webb, who emphasized the connection between the wage and the accustomed standard of life of the worker, as well as his labor union practices.

Lately, authoritarian regulation has affected the labor market, as is the case in other fields.

CHAPTER XIII

PROFITS

The word *profits* has two meanings. First, there is the definition of the man-in-the-street, who ordinarily means the *entire return received by the business man* as the result of his operations. What is contributed to get this return is immaterial. Here may be a street pedlar, who, with a tiny investment in stock-on-hand, receives a reward that is mostly wages for his labor. There may be a wealthy and semi-retired partner in a financial firm, whose business income is mainly interest on capital. Yet both are looked upon as receiving profits. But in economics a different meaning of the word is often applied. Whatever *surplus* remains after there has been deducted, from the total income covered by profits as defined above, the portions that are properly wages, interest, and rent, is called *pure profit,* or simply *profit.* In this meaning, it is evidently possible for profit to be either positive or negative. If the business man makes an income that is in excess of wages for his labor, interest on his capital, and rent for any land he owns and uses for business purposes, then he has a positive pure profit. If his returns fall short of what are needed to cover wages, interest, and rent, his pure profit is negative.

The evolution of the theory of profits in economic literature, therefore, displays two aspects : (1) the differentiation or segregation of the various elements of business income and the clarification of the conception of surplus or pure profit and (2) the explanation of the manner in which pure profit is determined. These will be traced in turn.

The Differentiation of Business Income Into Its Component Parts

Early Ideas

Though formal analysis of business income has been a comparatively modern development, it would be wrong to assume that early writers had no understanding of the nature of profits. Aristotle and Aquinas, when they discussed the problem of what constituted a fair return to the producer or seller of an article, appreciated that this return was, in part at least, in the nature of wages for labor performed. The church teachers who discussed "just price" at the close of the middle ages realized that the merchant's return might contain elements of compensation for labor done on the product and for risks undergone, as well as interest on capital. They were specially concerned, indeed, with distinguishing the remuneration for labor and risk from that applicable to the use of capital, because they thought that the first two of these elements were justifiable, while the third was not.[1]

The Views of the Economists

Adam Smith and his predecessors. The Mercantilists commonly spoke as though business profits were largely returns on capital invested in trade, as was to be expected in view of the economic conditions of their time and the manner in which the Mercantilist writers emphasized foreign commerce. But it is evident that merchants traded to some extent on borrowed capital. Thus, Mun told of having received a loan of forty thousand crowns from the Duke of Tuscany, and Child declared that "most of our Trade" was "carried on by young Men that take up Money at Interest."[2] Obviously, in such cases, profits were not identical with interest, but rather were a residue after interest had been deducted.

Turgot wrote that merchants "All have this in common, that they purchase to sell again" and

their business depends upon advances which need to return with profit in order to be once more put into the undertaking.[3]

The Physiocrat writer said much the same thing about the business of those who cultivated the soil. Here, of course, no distinction was made between interest and profit.

Adam Smith took up this position more formally, for he headed his chapter on profits:[4] "Of the Profits of Stocks," "Stock" meaning capital. Speaking "Of the component Parts of the Price of Commodities,"[5] Smith expressed himself as follows:

The profits of stock, it may perhaps be thought, are only a different name for the wages of a particular sort of labour, the labour of inspection and direction. They are, however, altogether different, are regulated by quite different principles, and bear no proportion to the quantity, the hardship, or the ingenuity of this supposed labour of inspection and direction. They are regulated altogether by the value of the stock employed, and are greater or smaller in proportion to the extent of this stock.[6]

Smith said that there were three component parts of the price of commodities, namely, the rent of land, the wages of labor, and the profits of stock. He remarked:

When those three different sorts of revenue belong to different persons, they are readily distinguished; but when they belong to the same they are sometimes confounded with one another, at least in common language. A gentleman who farms a part of his own estate, after paying the expense of

[1] See Chapter IX, p. 412.
[2] *A New Discourse of Trade*, p. 19.
[3] *Reflections on the Formation and the Distribution of Riches*, p. 60.
[4] *Wealth of Nations*, Bk. 1, Chap. 9.
[5] *Ibid.*, Bk. 1. Chap. 6.
[6] *Ibid.*

cultivation, should gain both the rent of the landlord and the profit of the farmer. He is apt to denominate, however, his whole gain profit, and thus confounds rent with profit, at least in common language. . . Common farmers seldom employ any overseer to direct the general operations of the farm. They generally too work a good deal with their own hands, as ploughmen, harrowers, &c. What remains of the crop, after paying the rent, therefore, should not only replace to them their stock employed in cultivation, together with its ordinary profits, but pay them their wages which are due to them, both as labourers and overseers. Whatever remains, however, after paying the rent, and keeping up the stock, is called profit. But wages evidently make up a part of it. The farmer, by saving these wages, must necessarily gain them. Wages, therefore, are in this case confounded with profit. . . A gardener, who cultivates his own garden with his own hands, unites in his own person the three different characters of landlord, farmer, and labourer. His produce, therefore, should pay him the rent of the first, the profit of the second, and the wages of the third. The whole, however, is commonly considered as the earnings of his labour. Both rent and profit are, in this case, confounded with wages.[7]

Later in the book, Smith returned to the same topic :

Apothecaries' profit is become a by-word, denoting something uncommonly extravagant. This great apparent profit, however, is frequently no more than the reasonable wages of labour.[8]

What were merely reasonable wages for the apothecaries' labor, having regard to the skill and responsibility involved, Smith said, represented a high percentage return on the small capital employed in such a business.

It is clear, therefore, that Smith perceived the dangers that arose from the common use of the word profit. Yet he continually spoke as though profit were largely or entirely interest, or, at least, interest together with a payment for the risk to which the employment of capital was subjected. Time after time he referred to the "profits of stock" and even went on to make such statements as that which follows :

The profits of stock seem to be very little affected by the easiness or difficulty of learning the trade in which it is employed. All the different ways in which stock is commonly employed in great towns seem, in reality, to be almost equally easy and equally difficult to learn. One branch either of foreign or domestic trade cannot well be a much more intricate business than another.[9]

In view of the fact that, only a few pages afterwards, the discussion on apothecaries' profits appeared, the opinion quoted seems surprising.

Smith did not neglect risk, however :

The lowest ordinary rate of profit must always be something more than what is sufficient to compensate the occasional losses to which every em-

[7] *Ibid.* [8] *Ibid.*, Bk. 1, Chap. 10, Pt. 1. [9] *Ibid.*

ployment of stock is exposed. It is this surplus only which is neat [*i.e.,* net] or clear profit.[10]

Smith thought that, ordinarily, in such countries as Britain, one half of the so-called profit on stock could be regarded as interest on capital, and one half as payment for superintendence and risk; but he said that the proportions varied from one country to another:

> The proportion which the usual market rate of interest ought to bear to the ordinary rate of clear profit, necessarily varies as profit rises or falls. Double interest is in Great Britain reckoned, what the merchants call, a good, moderate, reasonable profit; terms which I apprehend mean no more than a common and usual profit. In a country where the ordinary rate of clear profit is eight or ten per cent. it may be reasonable that one half of it should go to interest, wherever business is carried on with borrowed money. The stock is at the risk of the borrower, who, as it were, insures it to the lender; and four or five per cent. may, in the greater part of trades, be both a sufficient profit upon the risk of this insurance, and a sufficient recompense for the trouble of employing the stock. But the proportion between interest and clear profit might not be the same in countries where the ordinary rate of profit was either a good deal lower, or a good deal higher. If it were a good deal lower, one half of it perhaps could not be afforded for interest; and more might be afforded if it were a good deal higher.[11]

Evidently Smith thought that interest varied more than did the remuneration of superintendence and risk.

David Ricardo. Ricardo followed Smith in speaking of profits as the "profits of stock," these words beginning his chapter on the topic.[12] But, except for this identification of profits with interest, his treatment of the subject was very different from that of Smith. The later writer was concerned with discovering laws or principles of distribution and his theory of profits was an integral part of his distribution theory. Smith had pointed out that there were three shares in distribution, wages, rent, and profits. Ricardo agreed. Wages stood at the subsistence level, he said. Rent was a differential payment. On the margin there was no rent, but better land commanded a rent in keeping with its superior quality. When stating his value theory, Ricardo appeared to assume that wages and rent were the only shares, wages including not merely payment for present labor but also for that done in the past in constructing capital equipment. In his chapter on profits, however, Ricardo seemed to abandon the idea of capital being rewarded on the basis of past labor. He spoke as if the return accruing to "stock" or capital were a residue of the product, after wages and rent had been deducted:

[10] *Ibid.,* Bk. 1, Chap. 9.

[11] *Ibid.*

[12] *Principles of Political Economy and Taxation,* Chap. 6.

We have seen that the price of corn is regulated by the quantity of labour necessary to produce it, with that portion of capital which pays no rent. We have seen, too, that all manufactured commodities rise and fall in price, in proportion as more or less labour becomes necessary for their production. Neither the farmer who cultivates that quantity of land, which regulates price [*i.e.*, that on the margin of cultivation], nor the manufacturer, who manufactures goods, sacrifice any portion of the produce for rent. The whole value of their commodities is divided into two portions only : one constitutes the profits of stock, the other the wages of labour. Supposing corn and manufactured goods always to sell at the same price, profits would be high or low in proportion as wages were low or high. But suppose corn to rise in price because more labour is necessary to produce it ; that cause will not raise the price of manufactured goods in the production of which no additional quantity of labour is required. If, then, wages continued the same, the profits of manufacturers would remain the same ; but if, as is absolutely certain, wages should rise with the rise of corn, then their profits would necessarily fall.[13]

Ricardo then proceeded to discuss what he called the "progress of society," that is, the changes that could be expected to take place as time passed and especially as population increased. This, it will be recalled, was a topic in which economists of Ricardo's period were intensely interested. The growth of population, Ricardo thought, would cause poorer land to be brought into cultivation and the better soil to be farmed more intensively. Rents would rise, therefore. Wages, being governed by the costs of subsistence, would rise in money amount with the increased price of corn, while real wages remained stable. But the produce of labor would decline, because of the operation of the principle of diminishing returns. Profits — being the residue — would fall off. This would happen, Ricardo argued, if other things remained the same. But, in fact, technical improvements would counteract the tendency towards diminishing returns and thus check the decline in the rate of profit :

The natural tendency of profits then is to fall ; for, in the progress of society and wealth, the additional quantity of food required is obtained by the sacrifice of more and more labour. This tendency, this gravitation as it were of profits, is happily checked at repeated intervals by the improvements in machinery connected with the production of necessaries, as well as by discoveries in the science of agriculture, which enable us to relinquish a portion of labour before required, and therefore to lower the price of the prime necessary of the labourer.[14]

Ricardo considered, however, that a decline in profits could not go on indefinitely. He believed that such a decline would check the accumulation of capital — which formed the wages fund — and therefore set a limit on the number of laborers that could be supported. Population growth, therefore, would cease :

[13] *The Works of David Ricardo,* p. 60.

[14] *Ibid.*, pp. 66-67.

The rise in the price of necessaries and in the wages of labour is, however, limited; for as soon as wages should be equal . . . to . . . the whole receipts of the farmer, there must be an end to accumulation; for no capital can then yield any profit whatever, and no additional labour can be demanded, and consequently population will have reached its highest point. Long, indeed, before this period, the very low rate of profits will have arrested all accumulation, and almost the whole produce of the country, after paying the labourers, will be the property of the owners of land and the receivers of tithes and taxes.[15]

Here is revealed the inconsistency of Ricardo's ideas respecting the remuneration received by owners of capital. If, as was said in the Ricardian theory of value, capital was past labor and was paid for as such, then, obviously, over a period long enough for Ricardo's assumption of competition to be applicable, capital also would receive subsistence wages, neither more nor less. Until the decline in profit impinged upon the subsistence wage of capital (*i.e.*, the subsistence of the laborer who produced for future use), there was no reason why savings should fall off at all. Beyond this point they would decline so heavily as effectively to prevent any further fall in the rate of profit. But why should it be presumed that profits were above subsistence wages in the first place? A past-labor theory of capital, such as Ricardo held, together with a subsistence theory of wages, involved the acceptance of a subsistence theory of profits.

John Stuart Mill. Mill held much the same opinion as Ricardo. As was mentioned in Chapter XI, he endeavored to answer the question, how low could the rate of profits (in the Ricardian sense, that is, return on capital) fall with the "progress of society." Having replied to this as well as he could, he expressed the view that, in countries that did not possess a large reserve of unused land,

the rate of profit is habitually within, as it were, a hand's breadth of the minimum, and the country therefore on the very verge of the stationary state.[16]

Mill hastened to add that he did not mean, by this statement, that the stationary state would soon be reached in the great countries of Europe, but rather that this would be the case if capital accumulation were to continue at its existing rate and "no circumstances having a tendency to raise the rate of profit occurred in the meantime."[17] Mill looked to such things as inventions to permit further growth in population. But innovations were not the only factors tending to maintain the rate of profit, in Mill's opinion. A great quantity of capital was wasted "in periods of over-trading and rash speculation, and in the commercial revulsions by

[15] *Ibid.*, p. 67.

[16] *Principles of Political Economy*, Bk. 4, Chap. 4, Sect. 4.

[17] *Ibid.*

which such times are always followed" (that is, in business depressions).[18] Further, there occurred a "perpetual outflow of capital into colonies or foreign countries, to seek higher profits than can be obtained at home."[19] This Mill regarded as one of the chief influences that kept up the rate of profit in England.

Clearly, behind all this was a substantial identification of profits with interest on capital. Yet, treating formally of profits in his book on distribution, Mill did something to split up business gains into their component elements. Of the profits or gains "which the possession of a capital enables a person to make," Mill said, "a part only is properly an equivalent for the use of the capital itself,"[20] that is, equivalent to *interest*. In addition, there was an element of *payment for risk*. Also, there was *remuneration for the labor employed* in operating the business:

> The rate of profit greatly exceeds the rate of interest. The surplus is partly compensation for risk. By lending his capital, on unexceptionable security, he [*i.e.*, the capitalist] runs little or no risk. But if he embarks in business on his own account, he always exposes his capital to some, and in many cases to very great, danger of partial or total loss. For this danger he must be compensated, otherwise he will not incur it. He must likewise be remunerated for the devotion of his time and labour. The control of the operations of industry usually belongs to the person who supplies the whole or the greatest part of the funds by which they are carried on, and who, according to the ordinary arrangement, is either alone interested, or is the person most interested (at least directly), in the result. To exercise this control with efficiency, if the concern is large and complicated, requires great assiduity, and often, no ordinary skill. This assiduity and skill must be remunerated.[21]

Mill recognized a diversity of cases. A business man might guarantee a fixed interest on borrowed capital, while he himself assumed both risk and exertion. A sleeping partner might furnish capital at his own risk to a business organizer whose own contribution was confined to labor. Again, a single individual might provide all the factors of production. Whatever the circumstances, the abstinence involved in supplying capital, the risks undergone, and the labor put forth, must all receive compensation. The "lowest rate of profit" that could "permanently exist," therefore, was

> that which is barely adequate, at the given place and time, to afford an equivalent for the abstinence, risk, and exertion implied in the employment of capital.[22]

[18] *Ibid.*, Sect. 5.

[19] *Ibid.*, Sect. 8.

[20] *Ibid.*, Bk. 2, Chap. 15, Sect. 1. Incidentally, Mill calculated this on the *alternative* or *opportunity cost* basis, "namely, as much as a solvent person would be willing to pay for the loan of it."

[21] *Ibid.*

[22] *Ibid.*, Sect. 2.

This, of course, was in accordance with Mill's theory of costs and factor prices generally.

Mill referred to the tendency of profits to be equalized under the influence of competition but he recognized that, where an element of monopoly was present, a relatively high rate of profit might persist for a considerable time. In the case of a business that could be carried on advantageously only on a large scale, for example, entry was restricted, he said, and profit might remain above the general level. The same was true of an industry based on a successful patent or other exclusive privilege. Such "Cases of extra profit analogous to rent," he commented in discussing the relation of rent to value, "are more frequent in the transactions of industry than is sometimes supposed."

J. B. Say. In the meantime, in France, Say had developed the theory of profits somewhat differently.

Say made a distinction between what were designated as the *profits of industry* and the *profits of capital,* instead of that between wages and profits which was usual in England. He said that the "profits of industry" included the wages of common labor and the remuneration received by those who followed scientific pursuits, as well as "the profits of the master-agent, or adventurer, in industry." [23] By the last-named type of income, Say meant the reward of the business organizer for whatever labor (including that of supervision or direction) he put into his enterprise. Commonly, Say admitted, the industrial organizer possessed capital of his own, which was used in the business, but this was not always the case. If the business organizer owned capital, then,

> he must be ranked *pro tanto* in the class of capitalists, and the benefits thence derived be set down as part of the profits of the capital so embarked.[24]

Because the two elements of remuneration for labor and that for capital were often combined (as Smith had said) in the recompense received by the enterpriser, people were likely to be confused on the subject of profits. This, according to Say, was what had occurred in English economic literature:

> Smith, and most of the English writers on this science, have omitted to notice this distinction; they comprise under the general head of the profit of capital, or stock, as they term it, many items, which evidently belong to the head of the profit of industry.[25]

Say proceeded to deal with the "profits of industry" and the "profits of capital" separately. In order to be in a position to earn "profits of industry," a man must have access to capital:

[23] *A Treatise on Political Economy,* Bk. 2, Chap. 7, heading of Sect. 3.

[24] *Ibid.,* p. 329.

[25] *Ibid.,* p. 354.

It is commonly requisite for the adventurer himself to provide the necessary funds. Not that he must be already rich; for he may work upon borrowed capital; but he must at least be solvent, and have the reputation of intelligence, prudence, probity, and regularity; and must be able, by the nature of his connections, to procure the loan of capital he may happen himself not to possess.[26]

These requisites, Say admitted, "shut out a great many competitors,"[27] the implication being that the semi-monopolistic position thus conferred helped to explain the difference between the remuneration of industry or enterprise and that of ordinary labor. But access to capital was not the only condition of entry into business enterprise. Certain personal qualities were required for successful management:

this kind of labour requires a combination of moral qualities, that are not often found together. Judgment, perseverence, and a knowledge of the world, as well as of business. He [*i.e.*, the enterpriser] is called upon to estimate, with tolerable accuracy, the importance of the specific product, the probable amount of the demand, and the means of its production: at one time, he must employ a great number of hands; at another, buy or order the raw material, collect labourers, find consumers, and give at all times a rigid attention to order and economy; in a word, he must possess the art of superintendence and administration. He must have a ready knack of calculation, to compare the charges of production with the probable value of the product when completed and brought to market. In the course of such complex operations, there are abundance of obstacles to be surmounted, of anxieties to be repressed, of misfortunes to be repaired, and of expedients to be devised.[28]

Those who were not possessed of these qualities were unsuccessful in their undertakings and their enterprises soon came to grief, Say said, leaving only the businesses that were more skillfully directed. Thus it happened that "the requisite capacity and talent limits the number of competitors for the business of adventurers."[29]

All types of business, Say agreed, did not necessitate the same degree of capacity and knowledge. A farmer, for instance, did not need so much as an enterpriser who traded to distant countries. It was the skilful adventurer "who directs the business of production, and is the centre of many bearings and relations," who "profits by the knowledge and by the ignorance of other people, and by every accidental advantage of production," who achieved the greatest success.[30]

Evidently, Say regarded business enterprise as being on a footing with other types of labor, but receiving a reward peculiar to its nature. This reward was partly *monopolistic,* since not all men could obtain entry into the profession of entrepreneur, because some did not possess the necessary

[26] *Ibid.*, p. 330.
[27] *Ibid.*, p. 330.
[28] *Ibid.*, pp. 330-331.
[29] *Ibid.*, p. 331.
[30] *Ibid.*, p. 332.

personal qualities and command of capital. But it was also *residual,* since the enterpriser guaranteed fixed payments to others while he himself undertook the risks attending production and trade.

The position that Say took with respect to the "profits of capital" has received some attention in Chapter XI. These profits were largely interest but also included an element of risk:

> Theory, therefore, leads to the presumption, which is confirmed by the test of experience, that the profit of capital is high, in proportion to the hazard of the adventure, and to the length of its duration.[31]

The inclusion of risk under both headings — the "profits of industry" and the "profits of capital" — is understood readily when it is remembered that, when capital is lent by one individual to another for business purposes, a certain amount of risk is undertaken by each of the parties. The borrower may lose his profits or wages of industry, because he has to meet the fixed interest payments and principal repayments. The lender runs the risk that the borrower's resources will prove inadequate.

Say's explanation of the process that regulated the profits of capital is of some interest:

> When a particular employment of capital, the trade with China, for instance, does not afford a profit proportionate, not only to the time of the detention, but likewise to the danger of loss, and the inconvenience of a long, perhaps a two years' duration of one single operation before the returns come to hand, a proportion of the capital is gradually withdrawn from that channel; the competition slackens, and the profits advance, until they rise high enough to attract fresh capital. This will serve also to explain, why the profits, derivable from a new mode of employment, are larger than those of common and ordinary employments, where the production and consumption have been well understood for years. In the former case, competition is deterred by the uncertainty of success; in the latter, allured by the security of the employment. In short, in this matter, as in all others, where the interests of mankind clash one with another, the ratio is determined by the relative demand and supply for each mode of employment of capital respectively.[32]

Here, evidently, is a statement to the effect that returns from various employments tend to be equalized in the long run, having regard to the risks attending them, but that substantial disparities may appear in the short run. As was noticed in Chapter IX, Senior and J. S. Mill said much the same thing in England later.

German writers in the early nineteenth century. In view of their relationship to the opinions of Say in France and to those of the later Classical economists in England, something should be said of the ideas of a group of German writers. F. B. W. von Hermann deserves men-

[31] *Ibid.,* p. 355.

[32] *Ibid.,* pp. 355-356.

tion. But even before Hermann produced his major economic work in 1832, Gottleib Hufeland (1761–1817), and K. H. Rau (1792–1870), had divided business profits into payment for risk and the remuneration of management. Hermann developed this point. The business man, he said, performed several functions. He combined the factors of production, directed and supervised the enterprise, and insured others against risk by guaranteeing them a fixed return while he himself assumed the risks of fluctuations in results. All these services were rewarded in the business profit. H. K. von Mangoldt (1824–1868) argued on similar lines.

The thought of Say and Hermann showed the effect of its Continental environment. French and German industries were organized on a smaller scale than was the case in England. That being so, the typical Continental business man used relatively less capital and more of his own labor than did his British counterpart, so that it was less reasonable to regard his gains as return on capital than was the case in Britain.

Marshall. Marshall's writings on profits followed that of Mill. What Marshall called the "Profits of capital and business power"[33] were resolvable into wages of management, interest on capital, and a premium for risk. As to the amount of the latter, like Adam Smith, Marshall thought that men were so constituted that they were apt to make insufficient allowance for failure when considering the attractiveness of risky employments. Those who succeeded in business were but a small proportion of the numbers who entered the field, so that

> to find the average profits of a trade we must not divide the aggregate profits made in it by the number of those who are reaping them, nor even by that number added to the number who have failed: but from the aggregate profits of the successful we must subtract the aggregate losses of those who have failed, and perhaps disappeared from the trade; and we must then divide the remainder by the sum of the numbers of those who have succeeded and those who have failed.[34]

It was probable, Marshall thought, that the true excess of "profits" over interest was not more than one half, on the average, and in some risky trades not more than one tenth, of what it was considered to be by those who had formed their opinion only by observing the returns of businesses that had proved successful. Undoubtedly, this statement is equally true today.

Marshall listed a factor that he called *organization*, along with land, labor, and capital as agents of production. This was the productive factor to which the "profits of capital and business power" were to be attributed. Behind this factor stood, not something obvious, like land or abstinence, but the institutional arrangements of modern business. When Adam

[33] *Principles of Economics*, Bk. 6, heading of Chap. 7.

[34] *Ibid.*, p. 621.

Smith wrote, the typical British enterpriser supervised the employment of his own capital, so it appeared reasonable enough to use the word profit for something that appeared broadly coincident with interest in many cases, though including a good deal of labor in others. By Marshall's time, however, the situation had changed over important fields of industry. Immense concerns had been built up but, because of the growth of the joint stock company or corporation, the ownership of capital was widespread. Management was in the hands of officials, some being large stockholders in the companies they controlled but others primarily salaried employees. Management and ownership of capital, which in Smith's day had commonly been in the hands of the same individuals, were now separated in many cases. Who is the entrepreneur and what is his remuneration in such circumstances? An individual may build up a thriving business and, in due course, sell it to the investing public for a price that capitalizes expectations of future gains. A company may fail to pay a dividend, yet the controlling group may do very well from directors' fees and profits gained from speculating on fluctuations in the price of the stock, which they, as insiders, have an excellent opportunity of forecasting. In either of these cases, the capital "put in" by the nominal owners may fail to receive its "normal remuneration." Are there then no "surpluses"? Again, the nominal controllers of a corporation—the common stockholders—may exercise no real control over the undertaking that they own. The Classical theory of enterprise and profits has an air of unreality under such conditions.

Marshall accepted that the remuneration of the business man was determined by the same principles as that of other classes of labor. It had to be adequate to maintain the supply of the services concerned. Individuals with special abilities received additional rewards—surplus incomes which partook of the nature of rents. Thus far, there was nothing peculiar to Marshall's theory of profit as distinct from his wage theory. But, in addition, he visualized what can be called *combination* (or *conjuncture*) *earnings,* resulting from the fact that, when properly combined in a going enterprise, the agents of production were more productive than when used separately:

> The earnings of a successful business, looked at from the point of view of the business man himself, are the aggregate of the earnings, firstly, of his own ability, secondly, of his plant and other material capital, and thirdly, of his good-will, or business organization and connection. But really it is more than the sum of these: for his efficiency depends partly on his being in that particular business; and if he were to sell it at a fair price, and then engage himself in another business, his income would probably be much diminished. The whole value of his business connection to him when working it is a notable instance of Conjuncture or Opportunity *value.*[35]

[35] *Ibid.,* p. 625.

But, in settling the disposal of the conjuncture earnings, the employees of the firm had to be taken into account:

> in some cases and for some purposes, nearly the whole income of a business may be regarded as a quasi-rent, that is an income determined for the time by the state of the market for its wares, with but little reference to the cost of preparing for their work the various things and persons engaged in it. In other words it is a *composite quasi-rent* divisible among the different persons in the business by bargaining, supplemented by custom and by notions of fairness. . . Thus the head clerk in a business has an acquaintance with men and things, the use of which he could in some cases sell at a high price to rival firms. But in other cases it is of a kind to be of no value save to the business in which he already is; and then his departure would perhaps injure it by several times the value of his salary, while probably he could not get half that salary elsewhere.[36]

This conjuncture value, however, when analyzed, appears to resolve itself into temporary gains resulting from the imperfections of competition. If anything sells for long at a higher price than the combined prices of its components, there is an inducement to enterprising men to bring the components into association and get the advantage of the augmented value, that is, to start new firms. The conjuncture gains resolve themselves, as Marshall himself perceived, into a special type of quasi-rent, which subject is discussed below.

It appears, then, that Marshall's case for a fourth factor falls to the ground theoretically, for the reason that what is embraced in it is resolvable into the other three factors—land, labor, and capital. A specialized class of laborers, often able, active, and willing to take great risks, but sometimes unscrupulous and risking only the funds of others, is what many economists identify with the "organization" or "enterprise" which makes up Marshall's fourth factor of production.

Economic Surpluses

The Classical Economists

As was shown in Chapter IX, Adam Smith recognized the existence of surpluses in prices, above production costs. Some of them were of a very temporary nature, such as the additional profits secured by merchants who happened to have a stock of black cloth on hand when a public mourning was declared. Trade secrets or grants of monopoly conferred a more lasting advantage on those who were fortunate enough to possess them, Smith said. Peculiar qualities of soil or situation were even more permanent, giving rise to rents.

J. B. Say, in his treatment of the "profits of capital," discussed earlier in this chapter and in Chapter XI, referred to the difference in the return obtained from old capital investments and that from new loans. The

[36] *Ibid.*, p. 626.

former was explained by the fortune that attended the chosen investment, Say considered.[37] John Stuart Mill's comment on the "Cases of extra profit analogous to rent" has been noticed. All three of these writers obviously anticipated Marshall's theory of *quasi-rent*. The German Hermann went so far as to refuse to differentiate between land and capital in regard to the nature of their remuneration. In each case, he said, the returns from the factor represented the differences between receipts and costs : in other words, they were rents ; and the factors from whose services they accrued were valued in the market by the process of capitalizing the rents.

Walker

F. A. Walker gave special attention to another point to which Say had referred, namely the question of the personal qualities required for success as an enterpriser. The American writer advanced a theory of profits that visualized a margin of no-profit enterprisers, with individuals possessed of superior abilities receiving profit as a sort of rent :

> we find, in the lower stratum of the industrial order . . . a "no-profits" class of employers. Notwithstanding all the magnificent premiums of business success, the men of real business power are not so many but that no small part of the posts of industry and trade are filled by men inadequately qualified, and who, consequently, have a very checkered career and realize for themselves, taking their whole lives together, a meager compensation, so meager that, for purposes of scientific reasoning, we may treat it as constituting no profits at all. Live they do, partly by legitimate toll upon the business that passes through their hands, partly at the cost of their creditors, with whom they make frequent compositions, partly at the expense of friends, or by the sacrifice of inherited means. This bare subsistence, obtained through so much of hard work, of anxiety, and often of humiliation, we regard as that minimum which, in economics, we can treat as *nil*. From this low point upwards, we measure profits.[38]

Here there was some ambiguity, because in so far as the enterprises concerned were able to levy "toll upon the business that passes through their hands," there existed some profit even on Walker's margin. But this does not alter his main thesis, that is, that profit represented a differential element.

Already, as was indicated in Chapter XII, Senior and John Stuart Mill had admitted that ordinary wages contained a differential element of this nature. Wages were often high because of the special ability possessed by the individuals who received them. To some extent, Walker's theory can be regarded as an extension of this idea to the "wages" of business enterprise. But there was a difference between Walker's position and that taken up by Senior and Mill. The English writers had assumed

[37] See the passage quoted in Chapter XI, p. 540. [38] *Political Economy*, p. 239.

(in the case of labor) or abstinence (with capital), together with payment for risk (in either instance). They seemed unconcerned about the fact that wages covered both toil and risk, yet some of them devoted much attention to the point that profit included remuneration for abstinence and risk. A reason that may appear plausible at first sight is that the risks of labor can be regarded as uninsurable in most cases, while capital can often be insured. But some risks of labor can be insured (accidents, for instance) and important risks attending the employment of capital (such as changes in future demand) are uninsurable.

The French economist, J. G. Courcelle-Seneuil (1813–1892), followed Say's segregation of interest from profits with the suggestion that profit should be regarded as payment for risk bearing. If capital could be borrowed in return for interest, and workers (including officials) were hired for wages and salaries, then profits remained as the remuneration of those who undertook business risks. F. B. Hawley (1843–1929), an American merchant who was interested in economics, took a similar view. His statement appears below:

> This theory asserts that the profit of an undertaking, or the residue of the product after the claims of land, capital, and labour (furnished by others or by the undertaker himself) are satisfied, is not the reward of management or co-ordination, but of the risks and responsibilities that the undertaker (usually spoken of as the Entrepreneur, but whom I prefer to designate as the Enterpriser) subjects himself to. And as no one, as a matter of business, subjects himself to risk for what he believes the actuarial value of the risk amounts to — in the calculation of which he is on the average correct — a net income accrues to Enterprise, as a whole, equal to the difference between the gains derived from undertakings, and the actual losses incurred in them. This net income, being manifestly an unpredetermined residue, must be a profit, and as there cannot be two unpredetermined residues in the same undertaking, profit is identified with the reward for the assumption of responsibility, especially, though not exclusively, that involved in ownership.[40]

Hawley's assertion that no one assumes risks unless he is paid to do so contains certain elements of weakness, even outside its postulate of rationality. Some men speculate on the racecourse and elsewhere, in spite of their knowledge that on the average a loss results. In other words, far from requiring payment for the assumption of risk, they appear willing to pay for the privilege. Further, risk-taking is not a matter of choice. He who abstains from committing himself in one direction, because of the risks involved, is apt to find that he has run into different dangers in another. Thus, today, men buy common stocks to avoid the dangers of inflation, as well as hold money to escape the risks attending common stock investment.

[40] *Enterprise and the Productive Process,* N. Y. 1907, pp. 106-107. Quoted by permission of G. P. Putnam's Sons.

Another difficulty is that risk-taking is not an independent factor. A penniless man cannot guarantee others against loss. The entrepreneur assumes risk in an ordinary business, because he engages his capital in it and enters into agreements with others (bondholders, wage-earners, etc.) to remunerate them at a fixed rate while he himself takes what is left, great or small as the case may be. In some instances the individual who contributes labor may be in a position to guarantee risks to some extent, as, for instance, when a doctor with a considerable reputation but little capital borrows money to finance the building of a clinic. Even there, however, the assets furnish a certain amount of security. The wage lien — given, say, in respect of a purchase of tools, by a worker with no capital but with regular employment — is perhaps the nearest approach to the assumption of risk by the factor, labor. But it is clear that whoever gives a guarantee against risk must have something with which to back the guarantee — commonly, of course, his capital.

More recently, F. H. Knight (1885–) of the University of Chicago, has done something to clarify the risk theory. In his *Risk, Uncertainty and Profit* (Boston 1921), Knight distinguished between *uncertainties*, which cannot be averaged out or insured against, and *risks*, which are calculable and insurable. According to Knight, profits are due to uncertainties, not to risks or to economic changes as such. Risks can be reduced to costs, by insurance. Provision can be made for those changes that are foreseen. Thus — to exemplify — it is simple for education authorities to adjust their provision for school buildings to changes in the birth rate, providing that these do not occur very rapidly. But uncertainty remains. Paper containers may attract demand from glass bottles and cans: armament programs may bring unexpected prosperity to airplane manufacturers. In Knight's view, it is the emergence of such situations which gives rise to profits and losses.

Yet it is in place to note that insurance is constantly reaching into new fields. Further, there are many ways other than that which is ordinarily called insurance whereby business uncertainties can be reduced. Common stocks are bought as a hedge against currency inflation. Forward dealings eliminate the risk of foreign exchange fluctuations. A can company undertakes the manufacture of paper containers: a glass concern invades the can field. A chemical firm invests large sums in corporations operating outside the chemical industry. Finally, the investment trust carries an extensive portfolio of diversified nature with a view to averaging out the uncertainties that attend the operation of specialized businesses.

Public Regulation and Business Profits

In Chapter IX something was said on the subject of public control of prices. But under the heading of profits it is necessary to supplement

CHAPTER XIV

MONEY

Since money is a medium of exchange, its historical significance has been closely related to that of exchange itself. In early times, and again during the middle ages, when production was largely on a subsistence basis, money was relatively unimportant. During the later Greek period and the age of Roman greatness, commerce was more highly developed and money played a part more comparable with that which it has assumed in the modern world.

An important feature of monetary history has been the extent to which the making of money has been monopolized by political authorities. If the money-material, whether this be shells or precious metal, can be procured by anyone and used as money without further ado, then the value of money is likely to be determined in the same way as that of other commodities. On the other hand, if money is made by a government authority or requires some form of public stamp before it becomes acceptable as currency, then there is a possibility that the manufacturing or stamping authority can control its value. An understanding of this is essential for the comprehension of monetary experience.

Money and Banking in the Ancient World

The Beginnings of Coinage

There is no difficulty in appreciating that a commodity whose value is comparatively stable, that can be recognized readily, is easy to transport, and has other convenient qualities, can gradually acquire the position of money. This seems to have been the manner in which the first metal moneys came into existence. There was an obvious advantage in having the money-material made up in suitable units, certified as to amount and quality, and coining started quite early. The kings of Lydia are said to have coined money as early as the seventh century before Christ and the practice spread to the Greek cities.

The coinage system was very convenient to the authorities, since they were able to profit by mixing alloy with the pure metal. Such adulteration of money appears to have occurred even in Lydia, so that currency debasement seems virtually as old as currency itself. According to the pseudo-Aristotelian *Œconomica,* the ancients played some quite modern tricks with their currencies. For example, Dionysius of Syracuse (c. 432–367 B.C.) is said to have halved the value of the drachma, just as the American government of 1934 reduced the value of the dollar by 41 per cent. Dionysius called in the coins, stamped every drachma as being of two drachmae in value, paid one of them for the coin brought in and used the other to pay off the public debt. Had the profit on America's revaluation of gold in 1934 been utilized to redeem government bonds, the parallel would have been almost complete.

The classical philosophers made certain comments on money. Aristotle gave what purported to be an account of its introduction :

When the inhabitants of one country became more dependent on those of another, and they imported what they needed, and exported what they had too much of, money necessarily came into use. For the various necessities of life are not easily carried about, and hence men agreed to employ in their dealings with each other something which was intrinsically useful and easily applicable to the purposes of life, for example, iron, silver, and the like. Of this the value was at first measured simply by size and weight, but in process of time they put a stamp upon it, to save the trouble of weighing and to mark the value.[1]

Here Aristotle evidently regarded the appearance of money as the product of economic necessity. In addition to serving as a means of exchange, it acted as a measure of value :

Money, then, acting as a measure, makes goods commensurate and equates them. . .[2]

As to the value of money, Aristotle spoke of this as being determined in the same way as was the value of other commodities, though money tended to have a more stable value :

Now the same thing happens to money itself as to goods – it is not always worth the same; yet it tends to be steadier.[3]

Yet, just before, the philosopher had offered an entirely different explanation of the value of money. He said that it was a matter of government decree :

money has become by convention a sort of representative of demand; and this is why it has the name 'money' (νόμισμα) – because it exists not by nature but by law (νόμος) and it is in our power to change it and make it useless.[4]

It will be seen later that these two theories of the value of money have continued to be important down to modern times.

Early Banking

Records are available which prove that what is now known as banking existed in various forms in the ancient world. The small size of the Greek and early Italian States made money-changing important after

[1] *The Works of Aristotle,* vol. 10, *Politica,* 1257a.
[2] *Ibid.,* vol. 9, *Ethica Nichomachea,* 1133b.
[3] *Ibid.*
[4] *Ibid.,* 1133a.

wool being the principal export at that time. Attempts were made to restrict the consumption of foreign luxuries by Englishmen, persons whose incomes were below a specified amount being forbidden from wearing certain articles specified by law. These measures did not prove very efficacious in increasing the flow of money for coining, and an official inquiry was held in 1382. The following questions were formulated:

1. Why did specie fail to come into England while that which was already there was carried out?
2. What remedy should be applied for the clipped and depreciated condition of the currency?
3. What should be done to make up the deficiency of coins of small value?
4. How should the relative values of gold and silver be regulated?
5. How could the importation of bad money be prevented?

The answer given by one witness, Richard of Aylesbury, who was either a merchant or a treasury official, to the first of these questions has seemed to some to forecast Mercantilist policy:

As to this, that no gold or silver comes into England, but that which is in England is carried beyond the sea, we maintain that if the merchandise which goes out of England be well and rightly governed, the money that is in England will remain and great plenty of money will come from beyond the sea, that is to say, let not more strange merchandise come within the realm than to the value of the denizen merchandise which passes out of the realm.[7]

But, unlike the Mercantilists, who thought a policy of this nature was sufficient, Aylesbury and his fellow witnesses favored supplementing it with such measures as prohibiting the exportation of coins, insisting that English contributions to the papal exchequer should be paid in goods instead of money, and forbidding the importation of coins (which were often light and bad) from other countries, especially from Scotland. The last of these recommendations brings out the difference between the ideas and problems of the fourteenth century and those that agitated Mercantilist statesmen at a later date.[8]

Monetary topics continued to arouse interest, not only in England but throughout western Europe, for, though there were differences in detail, the general evolution was similar. Reductions were made in the amount of metal contained in English standard money in 1411 and 1464. The result of these changes was that an ounce of sterling silver, which had been coined into 20 pennies in Saxon times and was equivalent to 21.6 pennies in 1290, in 1464 was coined into 40 pennies. Much the same

[7] A. E. Bland, P. A. Brown, and R. H. Tawney, *English Economic History: Select Documents*, p. 222.

[8] M. Beer, *Early British Economics*, pp. 76-80, may be consulted on this point.

situation applied to gold coins, which had come into use in England in the thirteenth century.

The Course of Prices

It is not clear that prices reflected fully this debasement of the currency. They rose after the Black Death, it is true, and some suspicion appears to have prevailed that this was connected with the reduction in the value of the currency made by Edward III. On the other hand, it must be appreciated that the production of commodities suffered severely, both during the epidemic and afterwards, because of the large number of deaths. The same money had less work to do and it could be expected that prices would rise. After this, however, throughout the remainder of the fourteenth and the entire fifteenth centuries, the tendency of prices was steady or even downwards. What seems to have happened is that the growth in the use of money absorbed the increased quantity of it that was made available from the mines as well as by currency debasement.

The Appearance of the Quantity Theory

The sixteenth century witnessed two important changes in English currency: (1) the debasements of Henry VIII and Edward VI, and (2) the influx of specie from the mines of Spanish America. By 1546 the debasements had carried the number of pennies equivalent to an ounce of silver to 133 and in 1551 it was as high as 266, though Elizabeth's recoinage of 1560 reduced it to 60. In France and elsewhere on the continent of Europe there were similar experiences. Exact indices of prices are not available but the data given in Rogers's *History of Agriculture and Prices in England* suggest that the general run of English prices more than doubled between 1500 and 1582 and doubled again during the period ending in 1702.

It was only to be expected that such a rise in prices—which occurred throughout western Europe—should arouse great interest. The author of *A Discourse of the Common Weal of this Realm of England* attributed the rise to currency debasement:

> even with the alteration of the coyne beganne this dearthe; and as the coine appered, so rose the price of thinges with all. . . I think this alteration of the coyne to be the first originall cause that straungers first selles theire wares dearer to us; and that makes all fermors and tennauntes, that rerethe any commoditie, agayne to sell the same dearer. . .[9]

Another manuscript, which incorporated the same material, mentioned the increased quantity of metal as an explanation of the higher prices. Discussing why "the aforesayd dearth of things . . . remayneth yet among us," the writer offered two reasons, of which the second was stated thus:

[9] *Op. cit.*, p. 104.

raign wares for our use and Consumptions, to the value of twenty hundred thousand pounds; By this order duly kept in our trading, we may rest assured that the Kingdom shall be enriched two hundred thousand pounds, which must be brought to us in so much Treasure; because that part of our stock which is not returned to us in wares must necessarily be brought home in treasure.[14]

It is the most generally received Opinion, and that not ill grounded, that this Ballance is to be taken by a strict Scrutiny of what Proportion the value of the Commodities exported out of this *Kingdom* bear to those Imported; *and if the Exports exceed the Imports,* it is concluded the *Nation* gets by the general course of its Trade, it being supposed that the over plus is Imported in *Bullion,* and so adds to the Treasure of the *Kingdom; Gold and Silver being taken for the measure and standard of Riches.*[15]

If it were really the case, as these passages seem to imply, that the Mercantilists identified wealth with the precious metals, obviously they were wrong. No doubt some writers made such a mistake. But, in Chapter II of this book reasons were given for rejecting the view that it was characteristic of the Mercantilists generally. Some of the most influential members of the group recognized that wealth was linked with useful goods and services, not merely with a store of money. True, they wished specie to be accumulated but this was not because they thought that it was wealth in itself. To the question of why the Mercantilists argued in favor of the accumulation of specie, a number of answers can be given.

In the first place, as is shown in Chapter XV, money was regarded as being in some way necessary for trade to be conducted and wealth to be produced. If there were not sufficient currency it was thought that industry and commerce would suffer.

Secondly, money was regarded as a store of value, useful because its possessor was able to command goods and services. Thus, Locke remarked, in *Some Consequences of the Lowering of Interest and Raising the Value of Money*:

Gold and silver, though they serve for few, yet they command all the conveniences of life, and therefore in a plenty of them consist riches.[16]

The vicissitudes of harvests and the needs of warfare made it appear desirable for the nation to have on hand some sort of reserve that could be drawn upon in case of need. The author of *A Discourse of the Common Weal of this Realm of England* stated this point:

For it is not enoughe for a prince or a realme to have sufficient [coin] for one yeare, and so to live as they saie from hand to mouthe, as we doe nowe,

[14] Mun, *England's Treasure by Forraign Trade,* pp. 11-12.
[15] Child, *A New Discourse of Trade,* p. 153.
[16] *The Works of John Locke,* vol. 5, p. 12.

but to have some store for sodeyne eventes, ether of warres or of dearthe. For yf we should have warres or dearthe, as we have had, and should nede ether artilerie, (municions,) or other aide of straungers, it is not the coine we have nowe could provide us that. And so likewise, yf we should have greate scarcitie of corne with in the realme, for the which we should be driven to fetche it from outewarde partes, it is not oure money would purchase it. . . Then, yf bothe warre and dearthe should come together, as it hathe ere this, howe should we doe? Surely we should be in a verie harde case, and muche in daunger of straungers. On the other side, yf theare weare some store of treasures with in the Realme, thoughe theare should happen bothe warres and dearthe, yet we should be able to abyde them for a yeare, or ii, or iii [*i.e.*, two or three years]. . . And money is, as it weare, a storehouse of anie commoditie ye would have . . . which may longest be kept withoute corruption, and easalest be carried two and fro for all exchange, (and) is most universally curraunte yf it be gold or silver.[17]

Mun went into this aspect with some care. A sovereign should endeavor to build up a reserve from annual contributions in peace time, which,

being well managed to advantage, it will become a great summe of money, able to make a long defence, which may end or divert the war.[18]

But not only a hoard of treasure should be thought of, money raised in peace should be expended to build up the national strength:

Neither are all the advances of Princes strictly tied to be massed up in treasure, for they have other no less necessary and profitable wayes to make them rich and powerfull, by issuing out continually a great part of the mony of their yearly Incomes to their subjects from whom it was first taken; as namely, by employing them to make Ships of War, with all the provisions thereunto belonging, to build and repair Forts, to buy and store up Corn in the Granaries of each Province for a years use (at least) aforehand, to serve in occasion of Dearth, which cannot be neglected by a State but with great danger, to erect Banks with their money for the encrease of their subjects trade, to maintain in their pay, Collonels, Captains, Souldiers, Commanders, Mariners, and others, both by Sea and Land, with good discipline, to fill their Store-houses (in sundry strong places) and to abound in Gunpowder, Brimstone, Saltpeter, Shot, Ordnance, Musquets, Swords, Pikes, Armours, Horses, and in many other such like Provisions fitting War; all which will make them to be feared abroad, and loved at home, especially if care be taken that all (as neer as possible) be made out of the Matter and Manufacture of their own subjects. . .[19]

Daniel Defoe was cynical enough to point out that one of the benefits of money was that it enabled people who had no taste for war themselves to hire mercenaries:

[17] *Op. cit.*, pp. 113-114.
[18] *England's Treasure by Forraign Trade*, p. 171.
[19] *Ibid.*, pp. 171-172.

North implied—the entire story. Experience has revealed that there may be extensive changes in commodity prices without the occurrence of sufficient movements of specie into or out of private stocks to counteract them. This circumstance does not appear to have been realized by North.

About the same time as North was writing, Locke formulated the quantity theory:

The change of this marketable value of any commodity, in respect of another commodity, or in respect of a standing, common measure, is not the altering of any intrinsic value, or quality, in the commodity . . . but the alteration of some proportion, which that commodity bears to something else. This proportion in all commodities, whereof money is one, is the proportion of their quantity to the vent [*i.e.*, demand].[25]

Money, whilst the same quantity of it is passing up and down the kingdom in trade, is really a standing measure of the falling and rising value of other things, in reference to one another: and the alteration of price is truly in them only. But if you increase, or lessen, the quantity of money, current in traffic, in any place, then the alteration of value is in the money: and, if at the same time wheat keep its proportion of vent to quantity, money, to speak truly, alters its worth, and wheat does not, though it sell for a greater, or less price, than it did before. For money, being looked upon as the standing measure of other commodities, men consider and speak of it still, as if it were a standing measure, though when it has varied its quantity, it is plain it is not. But the value or price of all commodities, amongst which money passing in trade is truly one, consisting in proportion, you alter this, as you do all other proportions, whether you increase one, or lessen the other.[26]

Locke showed that he had an appreciation of the importance of velocity of circulation. Considering how much money was required in proportion to trade, he remarked:

what proportion that is, is hard to determine; because it depends not barely on the quantity of money, but on the quickness of its circulation. The very same shilling may, at one time, pay twenty men in twenty days: at another, rest in the same hands one hundred days together.[27]

The volume of trade to be carried on by means of the money was also taken into account:

Supposing then, that we had now in England but half as much money as we had seven years ago, and yet had still as much yearly product of commodities, as many hands to work them, and as many brokers to disperse them, as before; and that the rest of the world we trade with had as much money as they had before, (for it is likely they should have more by our

[25] *Some Considerations of the Lowering of Interest and Raising the Value of Money*, in *The Works of John Locke*, vol. 5, p. 43.

[26] *Ibid.*, pp. 44-45. [27] *Ibid.*, p. 23.

moiety shared amongst them) it is certain that either half our rents should not be paid, half our commodities not vented, and half our labourers not employed, and so half the trade be clearly lost; or else, that every one of these must receive but half the money for their commodities and labour they did before, and but half so much as our neighbours do receive, for the same labour, and the same natural product at the same time.[28]

That is to say, half as much money would either (1) preserve the same price level for half the quantity of goods and services, or (2) maintain prices half as high for the entire quantity of goods and services.

Thus it seems clear that in Locke's opinion the price level of commodities varied *directly* with (a) the quantity of money and (b) its velocity, as well as *inversely* with (c) the volume of trade. The English philosopher's statements were crude and at times not very plain, but they contained the essentials of the quantity theory as commonly propounded two centuries and more afterwards.

A little later, Montesquieu, in *The Spirit of Laws,* stated the quantity theory in terms of arithmetic:

If since the discovery of the Indies, gold and silver have increased in Europe in the proportion of 1 to 20, the price of provisions and merchandizes must have been inhanced in proportion of 1 to 20. But if, on the other hand, the number of merchandizes has increased as 1 to 2, it necessarily follows, that the price of these merchandizes and provisions, having been raised in proportion of 1 to 20, and fallen in proportion of 1 to 2, it necessarily follows, I say, that the proportion is only as 1 to 10.[29]

Here Montesquieu offered what amounted to an equation of the following form:

$$\text{Price level of goods} = \frac{\text{Quantity of money}}{\text{Quantity of goods.}}$$

Nothing, however, was said here about velocity.

Cantillon. The French banker, Cantillon, worked out a theory of money in some detail, in his *Essai sur la nature du commerce en général.* The value of money was determined exactly as was the value of other commodities, he said:

As Gold, Silver, and Copper have an intrinsic value proportionable to the Land and Labour which enter into their production at the Mines added to the cost of their importation or introduction into States which have no Mines, the quantity of money, as of all other commodities, determines its value in the bargaining of the Market against other things.[30]

This passage stated two principles: (1) that the "intrinsic value" of the precious metals was determined by cost of production, and (2) that the quantity or supply available in the market governed their market value.

[28] *Ibid.*, p. 49. [29] *Op. cit.*, vol. 2, p. 97. [30] *Op. cit.*, p. 175.

productions on the part of Landlords and mine workers, the money produced by the Mines will necessarily go abroad to pay for the imports : this will gradually impoverish the State and render it in some sort dependent on the Foreigner to whom it is obliged to send money every year as it is drawn from the Mines.[34]

Cantillon said nothing about the manufacturers, who suffered in this fashion, changing their occupations to engage in mining, as might be expected to happen in circumstances such as he described. But he explored to some extent the manner in which the gains and injuries resulting from a price inflation were distributed between the various classes. He pointed out that the landlords, whose land was rented on leases, and the wage-earners, whose remuneration was relatively fixed, suffered harm by the rise in prices.

Cantillon recognized that the price rise need not be proportionate to the increase that took place in the quantity of money. Not only quantity, but velocity, he said, influenced the level of prices :

an acceleration or greater rapidity in circulation of money in exchange, is equivalent to an increase of actual money up to a point.[35]

The same was true of credit. Indeed, Cantillon remarked that one effect of an increase in the amount of currency available was that money tended to be used in some transactions where credit had sufficed previously :

this new quantity of money will spread itself in such a way that many who lived without handling money will now have some. Many purchases which used to be made on credit will now be made for cash, and there will therefore be greater rapidity in the circulation of money in England than there was before. From all this I conclude that by doubling the quantity of money in a State the prices of products and merchandise are not always doubled. A River which runs and winds about in its bed will not flow with double the speed when the amount of its water is doubled. The proportion of the dearness which the increased quantity of money brings about in the State will depend on the turn which this money will impart to consumption and circulation.[36]

The river simile was not well chosen, because if the velocity of the flow were doubled when the quantity was increased, the energy possessed by the moving water would be augmented in a greater proportion. None the less, the point Cantillon wished to make is quite clear. An increase in the quantity of money had other effects than that of increasing prices and the extent of the price rise which resulted was conditioned by the nature of these other effects.

[34] *Essai sur la nature du commerce en général,* pp. 163-167.

[35] *Ibid.,* p. 161.

[36] *Ibid.,* pp. 177-179.

Vanderlint and Hume. About the same time as Cantillon wrote, but before his *Essai* was published, there appeared in London a book entitled *Money answers all Things: or, An Essay to make Money Sufficiently plentiful Amongst all Ranks of People, and Increase our Foreign and Domestick Trade. . .* (London 1734), by a London merchant, Jacob Vanderlint (d. 1740). Among other matters, Vanderlint treated of the supply of money in a country such as England, which possessed no mines of gold or silver. This, asserted the author of the work, would regulate itself:

> no Inconvenience can arise by an unrestrained Trade, but very great Advantage; since if the Cash of the Nation be decreased by it . . . those Nations that get the Cash will certainly find every thing advance in Price, as the Cash increases amongst them. And if we, who part with the Money, make our Plenty great enough to make Labour sufficiently cheap, which is always constituted of the Price of Victuals and Drink, our Manufactures, and every thing else, will soon become so moderate as to turn the Balance of Trade in our Favor, and thereby fetch the Money back again.[37]

In other words, if one country experienced a rise in prices because of an addition to its stock of money, the relatively low price level of the country that had parted with the money would give a favorable balance of trade to the latter and cause specie to be brought back from the former country.

David Hume studied this problem and others connected with money. Unlike Cantillon and Vanderlint, who had practical concern with commercial affairs, Hume was interested only incidentally. But, in an essay with the title *Of the Balance of Trade,* he took occasion to assail the contemporary Mercantilist view that it was desirable for a country to have a favorable balance of trade. The fear that, if this were not attended to, gold and silver would flow abroad, Hume regarded as "almost in every case, a groundless apprehension":

> I should as soon dread, that all our springs and rivers should be exhausted, as that money should abandon a kingdom where there are people and industry.[38]

Though, according to Hume, fear of a wrong balance of trade "discovers itself, whenever one is out of humour with the ministry, or is in low spirits," in fact—beyond a temporary condition—it was an impossibility, he said. The explanation of this Hume found in the manner in which the quantity of money influenced commodity prices and international trade. A statement of the quantity theory was given in his essay *Of Money:*

> It seems a maxim almost self-evident, that the prices of every thing depend on the proportion between commodities and money, and that any consid-

[37] pp. 43-44. [38] *Essays and Treatises on Several Subjects,* vol. 1, p. 322.

For so much money and goods as lie dormant, or are out of currency and traffic, fall not within the present consideration.[44]

Having ruled out the influence of hoards in this manner, he was able to give a very precise formulation of the quantity theory:

the value of a given sum of money will be always, pretty exactly, in a reciprocal proportion to the sum total, or the whole quantity in circulation. . .[45]

One of the most interesting sections of the book is that which treats of changes in the value of money. Like Aristotle long before him, Harris said that money altered in value as did other commodities but that it was more stable in its value. Yet, nevertheless,

an increase or decrease of money will operate as surely, though by slower and more insensible degrees, as an increase or decrease of any commodity.[46]

He then proceeded to inquire why the price of goods had not risen in the same proportion as money had increased since the discovery of the "Indies." His answer was that the supply of commodities had been expanded:

the improvement of arts, lessen the values or prices of particular commodities; and the improvements of husbandry, in particular, lessen the prices of corn and cattle; and thence again, the price of labour will be lessened. From all these considerations, it is natural to suppose that the quantities of goods in *Europe,* have increased, since the discovery of the *Indies,* far beyond the people; and therefore, the value of any given commodity hath lessened, in proportion as the sum total or whole stock of commodities has been increased.[47]

Such, then, was the position that this aspect of monetary theory had reached before the inflation of the Napoleonic Wars period, for Adam Smith added nothing of significance to the expositions of Cantillon, Hume, and Harris. The volume of money, the extent of hoarding, the rapidity of circulation, and the output of goods and services to be exchanged, had all received recognition as factors influencing the price level.

Early Credit Inflations

It will have been noted that the early discussions on money were, for the most part, conducted in terms of hard money or metal. Yet, paper money received a certain amount of attention. Thus, as a remedy for scarcity of currency, in his *Quantulumcunque Concerning Money* Petty advocated, not measures aimed at the importation of specie, but the establishment of a bank:

[44] *Ibid.*, p. 391. [45] *Ibid.* [46] *Ibid.*, p. 396. [47] *Ibid.*, pp. 397-398.

Qu. 26. *What remedy is there if we have too little Money?*
Answ. We must erect a Bank, which well computed, doth almost double the Effect of our coined Money: And we have in *England* Materials for a Bank which shall furnish Stock enough to drive the Trade of the Whole Commercial World.[48]

At the time, it may be said, banks were operating successfully in some cities on the Continent, notably Amsterdam. Britishers were beginning to suspect that there might be a connection between the existence of such a bank and the commercial prosperity of Holland, though—as yet at all events—the Amsterdam institution merely accepted and transferred deposits and did not create credit.

North, also, thought that there was something to be said for a bank, at least to finance the government:

It might not be amiss in this place, to say somewhat of the Publick Banks that are in Forreign Parts, as *Amsterdam, Venice,* &c., but that is a Subject I have not time to dilate upon: I shall only say, that it is a cunning way of supplying the Government once with a great Sum; and as long as the Government stands, it is no loss to them that have the Credit, nor no great Inconveniency. . .[49]

North wrote this, it may be said, three years before the British government took the step of chartering the Bank of England.

John Law, first in his own country and later in France, advocated the establishment of a bank to issue paper currency. Law was the son of an Edinburgh goldsmith and, having got into trouble over a duel, fled to Holland. There he appears to have studied the operations of the Bank of Amsterdam. In 1705 he submitted a scheme for the establishment of a Scottish national bank. The cautious Scots, however, rejected Law's project, whereupon its author advanced similar proposals to various European governments, finally succeeding in obtaining powers to open a bank in France. The inglorious career of this institution is described below. In *Money and Trade Consider'd; with a Proposal for Supplying the Nation with Money,* Law wrote,

To supply the Nation with Money it is humbly propos'd, That 40 Commissioners be appointed by Parliament. . . That the Commissioners have power to coin Notes: Which Notes to be received in Payments where offer'd.[50]

Obviously, if such a scheme were workable, printing notes or otherwise issuing paper credit would be a much cheaper way of getting money than the onerous measures favored by some of the earlier Mercantilists. The question was its practicability.

[48] *The Economic Writings of Sir William Petty,* vol. 2, p. 446.
[49] *Discourses upon Trade,* p. 18.
[50] *Op. cit.,* p. 69.

change value of English money rose. Commodity prices fell, as did those of the precious metals. Security prices collapsed. A one fourth writing-up of the value of money (which is what the change amounted to, in view of the extent of the previous depreciation) might have been expected to have very serious consequences along this line. But the position seems to have been that internal prices had not fully reflected the fall in the exchange rate, so that there was a certain amount of "slack" to be taken in. This circumstance represented a degree of economic foundation for Locke's solution. Further, as is shown in Chapter XV, Locke did not believe that an increased volume of money stimulated business, so he did not foresee that a diminution in the volume of currency would lead to distress.

The experience of a few years later was even more alarming. In both England and France a wave of speculation developed, culminating in the collapse of the English "South Sea Bubble" of 1720 and that of Law's French bank in the same year. Law had set up the *Banque générale* in 1716, this later being converted into the *Banque royale* under government ownership. The *Compagnie de la Louisiana ou d'Occident* was established in 1717, for the purpose of developing the French colony of Louisiana, Law being a director. This company absorbed similar undertakings, founded to colonize other French dominions, and took the name of the *Compagnie des Indes.* It was granted important financial concessions in France, notably control of the mint, management of the national debt, and a farm of the tax revenues. In the meantime, the bank had received wide rights of note issue. Finally, the two institutions were amalgamated.

During the years 1716–1720, when these changes were going on in France, speculation rose rapidly and the currency became inflated. But in 1720, the year of the British "South Sea Bubble" crash, a crisis developed and the bank was forced to suspend payments. Panic followed, and the result in both England and France was to give a set-back to banking and company finance. Where Law had erred was that, while he expected a note issue to encourage trade,[53] he failed to allow for such a rise in prices and extension of speculation as actually took place. Instead of proceeding cautiously in the enlargement of banking operations, emboldened by an apparent success in the beginning years, he expanded rapidly and therefore added to, rather than checked, the speculative mania. History has shown that there are two ways of securing a cautious policy—placing cautious men in charge of operations and establishing a mechanism that itself forces a conservative policy. Human nature being as it is, probably the second offers more hope of success. It was not sufficient that Law's bank notes were backed by assets, even land. It was necessary that they be supported by *readily realizable* property and that

[53] See Chapter XV.

the reserve provisions should so operate as to check an over-issue of notes. This was the point on which turned the English bullionist discussion in the early years of the nineteenth century.

The English Controversy of the Restriction Period

The financial problems associated with the Napoleonic Wars gave a strong impetus to the study of monetary matters. Heavy war expenditures were accompanied by increased issues of bank notes. Commodity prices rose, as did those of the precious metals. There was "restriction" of specie payments, the Bank of England being ordered to suspend the convertibility of its notes into gold on demand. The foreign exchanges were upset, because similar conditions existed in the various countries. All this required explanation, which could not be given in terms of existing monetary theory. Hence arose what has become known as the bullionist controversy, in which—among other things—Ricardo made his reputation as an economist.

The participants in the discussion were ranged in two well-defined groups. On the one hand were those who criticized the monetary policies of the government and the Bank of England, Ricardo being a member of this group. Opposite stood those who defended official actions. Space does not permit a full examination of the controversy. Briefly, it can be said that the former group laid the blame for the depreciation of the currency upon the over-issue of Bank of England notes, while their opponents argued that the real cause of the depreciation must be sought elsewhere. A government committee of investigation was appointed (the so-called *Bullion Committee*), Ricardo having a large part in molding its report. This document accepted the arguments of the critics of the government and the bank, and advocated a return of bank notes to convertibility into specie at the pre-war standard. Such a measure would have been severely deflationary and might have caused a serious crisis, had it been adopted when it was proposed, that is, during the war. In fact, however, the report was rejected by parliament and not until some time after the peace was convertibility restored.

The Relation between the Private Banks and the Bank of England

One of the chief contributions made to monetary theory during the controversy resulted from the examination it involved into the relationship between the Bank of England note issues and the issues of the country banks. At that time banking organization in England was somewhat like that in the United States of America at the present day, in that a number of small banks existed all over the country. These local banks possessed the right to issue notes and the problem arose: what was the connection between their issues and the depreciation of the currency?

David Hume had already argued that currency was proportioned be-the debt in Britain contracted by his purchase. It will thus obviate the dearness of our articles : it will serve as a compensation to the foreigner for the loss which he would otherwise sustain by buying in our market. The fall of our exchange will, therefore, promote exportation and encourage importation [Thornton said "encourage" importation, although it is evident that in fact there would be discouragement, at least if importation into Britain was what he had in mind]. It will, in a great degree, prevent the high price of goods in Great Britain from producing that unfavourable balance of trade, which, for the sake of illustrating the subject, was supposed to exist.[55]

John Wheatley (flourished 1803–1822), another commentator on the monetary policy pursued in Great Britain during the wars, took the matter further. Thornton had dealt with a condition of unilateral inflation. He asked what would happen to the rate of exchange, supposing the currency of one country (England, in his case) were inflated. Wheatley considered a situation in which there might be inflation on both sides. He inquired what determined the exchange rate between two countries that had both depreciated their currencies. His answer was that the rate would be indicative of the relative degrees of inflation :

the course of exchange is the exclusive criterion of how far the currency of one country is augmented above the currency of another. . .[56]

Obviously, this suggests the *purchasing power parity theory* of the exchanges, which was developed by Cassel under similar conditions over a century later and described in a later section.

Monetary Theories Since 1821

The Cost of Production Theory of the Value of Money

Throughout the controversy just described, the underlying thought was that paper money should preserve its *specie value,* rather than that it should retain its *commodity value*. In other words, the ideal was that notes should be convertible into, or exchangeable for, a fixed quantity of specie, instead of a stable amount of consumable goods.

The value of specie had already been explained by Petty and Cantillon. According to these writers, the precious metals exchanged for other commodities in the ratio of their relative costs of production. Ricardo followed the same line in his *Principles of Political Economy and Taxation,* applying his general theory of value to the value of specie money :

Gold and silver, like all other commodities, are valuable only in proportion to the quantity of labour necessary to produce them and bring them

[55] *Ibid.*, pp. 200-201.
[56] *Remarks on Currency and Commerce,* London 1803, p. 207.

to market. Gold is about fifteen times dearer than silver, not because there is a greater demand for it, nor because the supply of silver is fifteen times greater than that of gold, but solely because fifteen times the quantity of labour is necessary to procure a given quantity of it.[57]

Senior developed this theory in some detail in his *Three Lectures on the cost of obtaining Money, and on some effects of Private and Government Paper Money,* delivered at Oxford in 1829 and printed the following year in London. In these lectures Senior applied himself to the question of wage differences between the various countries, explaining them in terms of the labor-cost of specie. Senior pointed out that in countries with no gold or silver mines these metals had to be procured by exporting other commodities. The greater the efficiency with which the latter were produced, he said, the higher wages would be in relation to the specie imported in exchange. In mining countries, on the other hand, the direct cost of producing the precious metals determined the wage scale. The foundation of this theory, of course, was the idea that all commodities (including the precious metals) exchanged at values determined by their relative costs of production.

A cost of production theory of the value of specie money is not incompatible with a quantity theory, since—given that coinage and melting down are unhampered—cost of production governs the quantity of money in circulation. If the value of circulating money is greater than its cost of production, then mining expands and more metal is presented for coinage. If, on the other hand, the value of money is less than its cost, mining contracts or ceases and money is melted down when required for non-monetary uses. John Stuart Mill made clear this connection between the cost of production and quantity theories of money in his *Principles of Political Economy*:

Since, however, the value of money really conforms, like that of other things, though more slowly, to its cost of production, some political economists have objected altogether to the statement that the value of money depends on its quantity combined with the rapidity of circulation; which, they think, is assuming a law for money that does not exist for any other commodity, when the truth is that it is governed by the very same laws. To this we may answer . . . that the statement in question assumes no peculiar law. It is simply the law of demand and supply, which is acknowledged to be applicable to all commodities, and which, in the case of money as of most other things, is controlled, but not set aside, by the law of cost of production, since cost of production would have no effect on value if it could have none on supply.[58]

Mill went on to say that the connection between the value of money and its quantity was really closer than was the case with other commodities,

[57] *The Works of David Ricardo,* p. 213.

[58] *Op. cit.,* Bk. 3, Chap. 9, Sect. 3.

law, trusting to ordinary banking principles—and especially to the necessity for bankers to ensure that they could meet their obligations in specie if need be—to prevent over-issue and consequent inflation of credit.

The currency school proved victorious and the Bank Charter Act of 1844 gave effect to the opinions of this group. A limit was set to the value of notes that the bank could issue without gold backing, notes beyond this amount being covered 100 per cent by gold. A proposal was made that additional issues should be permitted without gold cover, in times of crisis, but this failed to receive approval and from 1844 to 1928 the bank operated under conditions in which elasticity in the note issue was possible only by suspension of the charter act.

The underlying idea was that the monetary system was to be automatic in its operation. A rise in British prices, relative to those in other countries, would stimulate imports into Britain and discourage the country's exports. The exchanges would become unfavorable and gold would flow out. This would come either from the gold in circulation or from the reserve of the Bank of England but, in either event, the currency would be contracted by an amount equal to the gold that had been lost. Prices, therefore, would fall. Conversely, if British prices were low, a favorable balance of trade would cause gold to be imported, expanding the currency by the same amount and raising prices.

In practice both gold and Bank of England notes were held largely by the commercial banks as reserves against their customers' deposits. As long as the percentage of such backing held against deposits was kept constant, the system remained an automatic one. Whenever gold came into the country, deposits expanded by a multiple of the amount imported, this multiple corresponding to the reserve percentage (*e.g.*, if a 10 per cent reserve were kept, deposits expanded by ten times the amount of gold brought in; if the reserve were 5 per cent, deposits expanded twenty times). When gold was exported, deposits were forced to contract by the same multiple. But in practice the reserve percentage did not remain constant. When bank officials were optimistic, they allowed it to decline, so that deposits and notes expanded more than in proportion to the gold backing. On the other hand, when the outlook was dark, bankers permitted the reserve to expand, relative to deposits and note issues. No longer did the system operate automatically, therefore, strictly speaking. It was to some extent managed by decisions of bank directors to expand or contract credit. This subject is discussed further in Chapter XV.

The modus operandi. In the light of the changed banking situation, it was necessary to amend the current exposition of the connection between specie and prices. The link was no longer direct: it was indirect or roundabout. Specie affected bank reserves, which in their turn influenced bank credit and, through credit, commodity prices. Sir Robert Giffen (1837–1910), financial journalist and later government official and eminent statistician, as well as Henry Sidgwick, gave attention to this point. Their explanation was substantially the same. When gold came into the country, they said, it was deposited in the banks, increasing the reserve ratios of these institutions. Interest rates were lowered and lending encouraged. Traders borrowed from banks for the purpose of spending additional funds and it was this spending which raised commodity prices. The opposite chain of causes and effects came into operation when gold was exported. Bank reserves were depleted. Interest rates on advances were raised. This contracted loans and brought down commodity prices. Sidgwick's description of the process is worth quoting:

An increased supply of gold, not accompanied by a corresponding increase in the work that coin has to do (or a rise in the demand for gold otherwise caused), tends ultimately to lower the purchasing power of money relative to commodities generally; but, in the first stage of the process that leads to this result, the increment of coin—or in England of notes representing the new gold in the Issue Department of the Bank [*i.e.*, the Bank of England]—must pass through the hands of bankers, and so increase the amount of the medium of exchange that they have to lend. Hence the price paid for the use of money will tend to fall, and this fall will tend to cause increased borrowing, and consequent extended use of the medium of exchange; and then through the resulting rise in prices generally, the greater part of the new coin or bank-notes will gradually pass into ordinary circulation. Thus the fall in the purchasing power of money, consequent on an influx of gold, will normally establish itself through an antecedent and connected fall in the value of the use of money [*i.e.*, in interest].

In the same way, when gold has to leave a country, where the banking system is fully developed, in payment of commercial and other debts to foreigners, it will generally be taken chiefly from the reserves of banks; and the need of filling up the gap thus created will make it expedient for bankers to restrict their loans, and so tend to raise the rate of discount. The effect will generally be greater, the smaller the reserve of metal kept by the aggregate of banks, compared with the amount of the medium of exchange that they supply: hence it will be especially marked in such a banking system as our own, in which nearly the whole reserve of gold is kept by the Bank of England.[61]

The relation between gold and prices. Once the elasticity of bank reserves in such a situation was recognized, the theory of an arithmetical relationship between specie and prices became untenable. The amount of spending, and therefore the price of commodities, depended upon

[61] *The Principles of Political Economy*, p. 255. Here Sidgwick appears to argue that the rate of interest is governed by the supply of money, *i.e.*, loans. But this was only the short-term position, in his view. In the long term the influential factor was the volume of capital, depending on savings. The American, H. J. Davenport, and others made the same distinction, to which reference has been made in Chapter XI.

statement would be correct only if the reserve percentage maintained by the banks were infinitely elastic. Ordinarily, it has been argued that this is not possible because of the need for gold to meet foreign payments and for the internal circulation. As prices rise within a country, relative to those elsewhere, both of these factors cause a drain on the gold reserves. Even if prices rise uniformly in all countries, higher prices still necessitate more currency for internal use. An indefinite reduction in the reserve percentage is only possible, therefore, if (1) other countries keep "in step" and (2) if the standard metal be not employed for currency purposes. Whatever could be said with respect to (1), the condition mentioned under (2) was inapplicable in Laughlin's days. The second criticism is that Laughlin himself admitted that means of payment were not being created so fast as the production of some important goods expanded. This is what his reference to the causes of lower commodity prices meant. His argument appears to have turned on the assumption that the prices of these staple commodities should be allowed to fall with a decline in their production costs, so that the difference between Laughlin and such writers as Giffen can be considered to rest on an issue that has become more prominent in recent monetary discussion : should *prices* or *costs* be kept stable?

After 1896 events seemed to favor the arguments of the quantity theorists. The technical advances in production, which Laughlin had stressed in explaining the price decline of 1873–1896, continued unabated, yet prices began to rise. Laughlin was able to point to such factors as the advance in wage rates and the rise of taxation but, to the supporters of the quantity theory, it was the unparalleled expansion of gold production due to the opening up of the Witwatersrand which explained the change. Laughlin's factors were real enough but, with respect to them, 1896 did not stand out as a watershed in the manner that it did in relation to gold output.

The quantity equation of Irving Fisher. The quantity theory of the twentieth century owes more to Irving Fisher, perhaps, than to any other writer. Possessed of a mathematical turn of mind, Fisher offered a formula incorporating the main factors that earlier economists had recognized to be involved in the relationship between money and prices. The quantity of money, its velocity of turnover, and the volume of goods and services that were to be exchanged, all had their part in the Fisher equation. This, in its simple form, was expressed as follows :

$$P = \frac{M\ V}{T}$$

where $P =$ the general level of prices, $M =$ the quantity of money, $V =$ the velocity of money, and $T =$ the volume of trade, that is, the amount of goods and services to be exchanged. Expanded, the equation was:

$$P = \frac{MV + M'V'}{T}$$

where $P =$ the general level of prices, as before, $M =$ the quantity of cash, $V =$ the velocity of turnover of this cash, $M' =$ the volume of "deposit currency" or bank deposits, and V' the velocity of turnover of the deposits, and T the amount of goods and services requiring to be exchanged.

Fisher was not the first to attempt a mathematical formulation of the quantity theory. As early as 1840, Sir J. W. Lubbock (1803–1865), an English banker who was interested in astronomy and mathematics, gave a formula somewhat like that used by Fisher. But, like his fellow-countryman E. W. Kemmerer (1875–1945) shortly before, Fisher attempted a statistical verification of the quantity theory. Supported in his book on *The Purchasing Power of Money* (New York 1911) by a large volume of data, Fisher's presentation has had great influence.

In the Fisher equation, the purely quantity theory has disappeared, giving place to a *quantity-velocity-volume of trade* interpretation of the price level. Yet what does this mean? It is evident that, in practice, the several terms of the Fisher formula are not independent variables. They are inter-connected. If the volume of currency is being expanded rapidly, so that people fear a price inflation, there is a rush to spend money and velocity rises, exaggerating the effect of the increased volume of money. Again, as has been pointed out by many writers,[70] a rising price level is stimulating to business, so that the T of the Fisher equation is increased, thereby counteracting, to some extent, the tendency of prices to rise. It is, in fact, very surprising, in view of the attention which has been given in economic theory to the quantity of money, to notice what small alterations in the quantity of money (including bank credit) accompany great changes in general prices. Thus the price collapses of 1920–1921 and 1929–1931 were accompanied by only minor reductions in the volume of British bank deposits. On the other hand, the decline in velocity was considerable. But velocity represents merely the rapidity with which those who possess money spend it and, for this part of the formula to become meaningful, it is necessary to look behind the mathematical expression of velocity to men's decisions as to what to do with their money. Obviously, even if the formal correctness of the Fisher equation be granted, it has an altogether different meaning from that which was in the minds of the early quantity theorists. As an elucidation of the mechanics involved in the price level, it is admirable, but as an explanation of causation it has serious shortcomings.

[70] See Chapter XV.

develop an unfavorable trade balance with Britain and the dollar value of the British currency unit would rise. Conversely, if the British pound stood above $5, British exports would be discouraged and those of America stimulated. The British trade balance would become unfavorable and the value of the pound would fall.

Though the theory achieved considerable popularity, it was soon assailed. J. M. Keynes argued that, if the price levels that were taken into account were those of *commodities entering into international trade,* then the theory was "little more than a truism." Allowing for transport costs, foreign trade took place only if exchange rates compensated differences in purchasing power. But if, as Cassel seemed to intend, the *general price levels* were compared, Keynes said that, though some relationship between price level ratios and exchange rates was to be expected, this was not necessarily a precise or immediate one.[75] The force of this criticism must be granted.

The Cassel theory has been attacked from another direction. J. H. Williams (1887–), in America, Bertrand Nogaro (1880–) in France,[76] and Karl Helfferich (1872–1924) in Germany, have pointed to cases where the internal price levels and the volumes of currency issued have been *determined by* the exchange rate. In other words, these writers have shown that the chain of cause and effect can be the opposite from what is implied by the purchasing power parity theory. Helfferich's description of the situation in Germany during the post-war inflation brings this out:

> First came the depreciation of the German currency by the overburdening of Germany with international liabilities and by the French policy of violence. Thence followed a rise in the prices of all imported commodities. This led to a general rise in prices and wages, which in turn led to a greater demand for currency by the public and by the financial authorities of the Reich; and finally, the greater calls upon the Reichsbank from the public and the financial administration of the Reich led to an increase in the note issue. In contrast therefore, to the widely held view, it is not "inflation" but the depreciation of the currency which is the first link in this chain of cause and effect.[77]

Helfferich was not only a leading writer on money in Germany, but served as finance minister during the war of 1914–1918, later occupying other important official positions. As a patriotic German, he was

[75] See *Monetary Reform,* London and N. Y. 1924, and *A Treatise on Money,* London and N. Y. 1930, especially vol. 1, pp. 72-74 of the latter work.

[76] See J. H. Williams, *German Foreign Trade and the Reparation Payments, Quarterly Journal of Economics* 1922, and B. Nogaro, *Modern Monetary Systems,* London 1927 (translation of *La monnaie,* Paris 1924).

[77] K. Helfferich, *Money* (translation of *Das Geld,* 6th ed. 1923), 2 vols., London 1927, vol. 2, p. 601. Quoted by permission of Ernest Benn, Ltd., and the Adelphi Company.

concerned to lay the blame for the inflation of the post-war period on his country's enemies, so that the statement quoted cannot be regarded as a purely scientific judgment. But undoubtedly such a situation as it depicts is possible in practice. It seems reasonable to expect that, when a country inflates its currency, imports will be increased and exports diminished, so that the exchange value of the money will decline (this is Cassel's position). But, on the other hand, if, say through the operation of exchange control, a country manages to lower the exchange value of its currency and keep it low, then, because its imports will cost more and its exports bring higher prices, the internal price level will tend to rise (this accords with Helfferich's argument). In other words, internal price level and rate of exchange are inter-connected and either of them may influence the other. As Keynes said in his *Monetary Reform,*

> it is not possible to say in general whether exchange value will move towards purchasing power or the other way around. Sometimes, as recently in Europe, it is the exchanges which are the more sensitive to impending relative price-changes and move first; whilst in other cases the exchanges may not move until after the change in the relation between internal and external price-levels is an accomplished fact.[78]

The Marginal Utility Theory of the Value of Money

Brief mention should be made of the position of certain Austrian writers with regard to money. Some of the outstanding English Neo-Classical economists—W. S. Jevons and Marshall, especially—had devoted considerable attention to money. But their method of treatment was such as to place currency in a separate compartment, as it were, without any close or obvious integration with their main theory of value. On the other hand, Austrian members of the same school endeavored to apply their general value theory to the value of money. The values of all things, they reasoned, went back to utility to the consumer. Thus, von Wieser declared in his *Natural Value:*

> The exchange value of money is the anticipated use value of the things which can be obtained for it.[79]

Ludwig von Mises took what was essentially the same point of view. It cannot be said, however, that the idea of relating the value of money to its utility has been very influential in the English-speaking countries.

The State Theory of Money and the Principle of Authoritarian Regulation of the Currency

More important, in view of the growth of authoritarianism in recent years, are the ideas of those German writers who have stressed the con-

[78] p. 105. Quoted by permission of Harcourt, Brace and Company, Inc., and Macmillan & Co., Ltd.

[79] *Op. cit.*, p. 47.

will perform the remedial functions, with respect to currency and foreign exchange difficulties, that the quantity theorists of England and America have looked for in currency devaluation.

But it is not in Germany alone that money has moved away from the individualistic anchorages of free mining, free issue of bank notes, and optional coining and melting of specie currency. Through the nineteenth century central banking control of the monetary system was developing in England; but, for the most part, the supply of specie (which formed the basis of the whole) seemed to be regarded as being in the category of acts of God, that is, beyond conscious control on the part of man. In this situation, the function of the central bank was confined to preserving the convertibility of its notes, which, in turn, meant that the English price level should move up or down with whatever changes occurred in world price levels. But, increasingly in recent years, this principle has been left behind, not merely by the Bank of England but by the central banks that have been established in other countries. A new principle of authoritative regulation of the monetary basis has been accepted in its place. For some years after the war of 1914–1918, the Federal Reserve Banks of the United States of America virtually controlled the value of gold, through a set of links with the dollar that were maintained by other monetary authorities. Since the currency changes that occurred after 1930, the management of the value of gold has been even more the accepted rule. Hardly anyone now pretends that the value of gold is determined by unregulated supply and demand. It is admitted this value is governed by the decisions of the monetary authorities of the various countries, especially the large gold-holders. The value that has ruled in recent years has been such that large quantities of gold have accumulated in the stores of certain governments and central banks, while the production of the mines has expanded rapidly. It has even been suggested that mining output should be brought under control. Thus is the extension of authoritarianism in other fields paralleled in that of money.

The Problem of Changing Price Levels

The existence of fluctuations in the purchasing power of money raises a problem with respect to contractual obligations. Agreements for future payments of money, that have been entered into at one period, become unexpectedly light if prices rise or unduly heavy if they fall.

The Price Inflation of the Sixteenth and Seventeenth Centuries

As an example of contemporary discussion of this subject in sixteenth century England, when prices were rising rapidly, the *Discourse of the Common Weal of this Realm of England* may be quoted. The author pointed out, very sensibly, that merchants and craftsmen had to recoup themselves in the sale prices of their goods for the enhanced cost of the articles they bought :

I finde everie man greved by it [*i.e.*, the rise in prices] in one thinge or other, yet consideringe that, as manie of theim as have wares to sell, doe enhaunce as muche in the price of all thinges that they sell as was enhaunced before in the price of thinges that they must bie; as the merchante, if he bie dear, he will sell deare agayne. So the artificers, as Cappers, clothiers, showmakers and farriers, have respecte large enoughe, in sellinge theire wares, to the price of victuall, woll and yron, which they bie.[85]

On the other hand, the author said that those whose incomes were fixed lost by reason of the higher price level. This group included laborers, landowners whose properties were leased, and even the government (many of whose taxes were stabilized in terms of money) :

I can not, therefore, understand that theise men have greatest griefe by this common and universall dearthe, but rather suche as have theire Lyvinges and stipendes rated at a certeyntie; as common laborers at vid. [*i.e.*, 6 pence or 0.5 shillings.] the daye, iorney [*i.e.*, journey] men of all occupacions, servinge men (at) xls. [*i.e.*, 40 shillings] the yeare; and gentlemen whose landes ar let by theim or their auncestors either for lives or for terme of yeares, so as they can not enhaunce the rent thereof thoughe they would, and yet have the price enhaunced to theim of everie thinge that they bie. Yea the kinges higheness, whereof we spake nothinge all this while, as he hathe most of yearly revenues and that certeyne, so hathe he most lost by this dearthe, and by the alteracion especially of the coyne.[86]

As a remedy, the author of the *Discourse* proposed that debts be paid in accordance with their original specie value.[87]

In practice, nothing of this kind was done. The monetary payments (for which the occupiers of land commuted the labor dues that had come down from the middle ages) became relatively insignificant, so that copyholders, who held land subject to what had been onerous burdens, became virtually the owners of the property. In connection with wages at this time, it is worth noticing that the English Statute of Apprentices of 1563 gave as one of the reasons for its promulgation the fact that the earlier legal wages had become too small, because of the advance in prices, and could not "without the greatest grief and burden of the poor labourer and hired man be put in due execution." [88] Accordingly, in the new law it was provided that wages should be determined annually, in each locality, by reference to the cost of living.

Government revenue felt the effect of the diminishing purchasing power of money. Some of the most important taxes, which, in earlier times, had been proportioned to produce, had become fixed in money.

[85] *Op. cit.*, p. 33. [86] *Ibid.*, pp. 33-34. [87] See *Ibid.*, pp. 118-119.
[88] A. E. Bland, R. A. Brown, and R. H. Tawney, *English Economic History: Select Documents*, p. 325.

which an outstanding instance was the introduction of the power loom in the textile industry, threw numbers of skilled workers out of employment. At all events, no change was made in monetary policy.

On the theoretical side, two ways of dealing with such a problem of changing prices are apparent. (1) Contracts may be so arranged that they are not affected by price movements, the payments being adjusted by reference to price data in such a manner that their purchasing power remains uniform. (2) Prices may be kept stable. Both these measures were suggested during the period just studied. John Wheatley, in *An Essay on the Theory of Money and Principles of Commerce* (London 1807), proposed the voluntary use of a tabular standard for long-term contracts, based on what were in effect index numbers of commodity prices. Somewhat later Joseph Lowe (flourished 1807–1832), in a work entitled *The Present State of England in regard to Agriculture, Trade, and Finance* (London 1822), supported the same plan, as did G. Poulett Scrope (1797–1876), a member of the English parliament and a prolific pamphleteer on economics and allied subjects. Scrope dealt with the subject in *An Examination of the Bank Charter Question, with an Inquiry into the Nature of a just Standard of Value and Suggestions for the Improvement of our Monetary System* (London 1833) and *Principles of Political Economy* (London 1833).[90] In the latter of these works, he said:

> the next best thing to obtaining a perfect measure of value, is to obtain a means of ascertaining the variations of the imperfect measure we may be compelled to employ for want of a better. Now the variations in value of any commodity might, it would seem, be ascertained approximately, and with quite sufficient accuracy for all practical purposes, by comparing it with the great bulk of other commodities;—by placing gold, for example, on one side, and on the other a large list of the commodities in general use, which may be taken to represent fairly enough the entire mass of goods. Take, for instance, a price-current, containing the prices of one hundred articles in most general request, in quantities determined by the proportionate consumption of each article—and estimated (as they are under the standard of this country) in gold. Any variations from time to time in the sum or mean of these prices will measure, with sufficient accuracy for all practical purposes, the variations which have occurred in the general exchangeable value of gold.[91]

Scrope proposed that such a "price-current" (which would contain information of a similar nature to that summarized in the modern index number of commodity prices) should be published, to

> enable individuals, if they shall think fit, to regulate their pecuniary engagements by reference to this *Tabular Standard of Value*.[92]

[90] Re-published as *Political Economy, for Plain People,* London 1873.
[91] *Political Economy, for Plain People,* pp. 307-308.
[92] *Ibid.*, p. 308.

Lowe and Scrope had in mind something that would do what Lord King had proposed, namely, keep contractual payments at a constant level instead of leaving them at the mercy of fluctuations in the purchasing power of money. But where King sought a constant specie standard, Lowe and Scrope visualized one that was stable in terms of commodities. A case in which something of this kind has been done for many years is in the *fiars prices* of Scotland. These represent grain rents due to feudal superiors (who still exist in Scottish land law) and are calculated yearly, by courts appointed for the purpose, from the average prices of grains grown in the various localities. It is not known exactly how far back this system goes but it was regulated by an act of the Court of Session passed in 1723. Something of a similar nature, but including a wider range of commodities, was what Lowe and Scrope proposed.

John Rooke, co-discoverer with James Anderson, Malthus, and Ricardo of the Ricardian theory of rent and marginal cost, advanced a different plan. In his *An Inquiry into the Principles of National Wealth, illustrated by the Political Economy of the British Empire* (Edinburgh 1824), Rooke advocated that Britain should have a convertible paper currency. This was to be regulated with the object of ensuring that the purchasing power of the monetary unit remained constant, by adjusting the amount of gold that was interchangeable with the notes. Thus the circulating notes would possess a uniform command over commodities but a changing one over gold. Rooke suggested that the average price of farm labor should be taken as the basis of the currency but agreed that other things than farm labor might be taken into account in settling the foundation of the standard. This scheme has considerable resemblance to that put forward in the twentieth century by Irving Fisher.

Less radical proposals were also submitted. Thus, a banker, Thomas Joplin (1790?–1847), in his *Views on the subject of corn and currency* (1826), advocated the suspension of the convertibility of bank notes during crop shortages, to prevent a drain of gold from the country, which would force down the price level. But none of these schemes came to anything and interest in the matter became less intense as prices became more stable towards the end of the 1830's.

1850–1896

Not until after the gold discoveries in Australia and California in 1849 did commodity prices begin to show an upward trend. Then the reversal became so marked that, by 1863, W. S. Jevons was pamphleteering on *A Serious Fall in the Value of Gold Ascertained, and its Social Effects set forth.*[93] In this work, the effects of the current rise in prices upon the economic position of the different groups of people were discussed in

[93] Reprinted in *Investigations in Currency and Finance,* ed. H. S. Foxwell, London 1884.

to exhibit the desired quality of "fixity of value," it becomes necessary that a general rise of wages should take place. Will that rise take place at once? And, if it should, may it not be too slight in some places, too great in others? According to the correct conception of the quality of "fixity of value," things will take an entirely different course from that just described. Prices will decline, and that is all. Money will then acquire increased purchasing power in relation to goods, not to labour. But why should this be deemed objectionable, seeing that it is due to a cause resident not in the money itself but in the goods?

Let us now reverse the hypothesis and suppose that, instead of being reduced, the cost of production (in labour, etc.) is increased for all articles. The simplest thing now is that wages should remain the same but that all prices shall go up. But according to the theory of fixity of purchasing power, prices must remain unaltered and all money wages must fall. Do the supporters of that theory realise what this implies? If the fall in money wages does not take place immediately, depression will ensue in many branches of industry; but no general fall in wages is likely to take place without many strikes and lockouts.

Let us suppose the change in the cost of production to be confined to a certain number of articles. Suppose there are 1,000 different kinds of goods, and that 400 of them are affected by the change. According to the correct conception, the price of these 400 articles will now have to be either raised or reduced. But if money must neither gain nor lose in purchasing power, a difficult practical problem arises. A general movement in prices in two directions will then have to take place. If the 400 articles become cheaper on the average, then the 600 will have to become dearer; otherwise the purchasing power of money must undergo a change. It has been contended that fixity of the purchasing power of money discourages speculation and imparts greater calm and stability to economic conditions. Subject to the reservation stated above, this is true; but if we omit to make that reservation, the proposition is untenable. The examples just given prove this, and at the same time show that, if we insist upon having fixity of purchasing power, we must make a choice. As soon as events like those described take place, money must gain or lose in purchasing power either in relation to goods or in relation to labour. It cannot retain its original value in relation to both. And up to the present nobody has thought fit to explain why fixity of purchasing power in relation to goods is to be preferred to fixity of purchasing power in relation to labour.[95]

In this passage, Pierson made two important points. (1) The general price level is a composite of particular prices, from which it follows that to preserve stability of the general level monetary action may have to be taken where it is uncalled for except for the purpose of counterbalancing an opposite movement elsewhere. (2) It is impossible to stabilize both prices and real incomes in an economy in which the efficiency of production is changing. Keynes re-stated these points in his *Treatise on Money*.

[95] Vol. 1 of the translation (*Principles of Economics*), pp. 587-590. Quoted by permission of Macmillan & Co., Ltd. and The Macmillan Company.

An example of the kind of situation that may arise under the first of these headings was the American agricultural depression of the last quarter of the nineteenth century. To a large extent, what was wrong with agriculture was the rapid expansion of the period after the Civil War. Had sufficient currency been issued, through the adoption of bimetallism or otherwise, to maintain the prices of farm products, or even to keep stable a general index that included these prices, something approaching inflationary conditions might have been caused in the markets for non-agricultural commodities, raising the prices of articles the farmers had to buy.

The validity of Pierson's second point must be conceded. If the sale prices of commodities remain the same, while production becomes more efficient (*i.e.*, a greater quantity is produced per unit of cost in effort and materials), then money incomes must rise in some manner; that is, wages, interest, rent, or profits, must increase. Conversely, if money incomes remain constant, an increase in productive efficiency will lower costs and, therefore, cause prices to decline. In either event real incomes rise. In the first case, money has a constant purchasing power over commodities but money incomes go up. In the second, money incomes remain the same but their purchasing power rises on account of the lower level of commodity prices.

The Period Since 1896

The generation between 1896 and the outbreak of the European war in 1914 was, in the main, one of rising commodity prices, a situation which quantity theorists credited to the output of the South African gold-field. The currency controversy started in the previous period, though no longer of political importance, continued to have repercussions in economic literature. But the inflation of the years to 1920 and the severe deflation that followed gave a new impetus to discussion of monetary stabilization.

Fisher's scheme for stabilizing the dollar was among the best-known projects in this period. According to this plan, periodical adjustments were to take place in the amount of gold represented by the dollar, with a view to keeping the purchasing power of the monetary unit at a constant level. Of the alternatives presented by Pierson, Fisher favored stabilizing commodity prices, using a wholesale index for reasons of convenience. But the English economist, J. M. Keynes, has favored stabilizing commodity prices for a different reason. He has pointed out that, if incomes be stabilized while prices fall, the recipients of fixed incomes (landowners and proprietors of fixed-interest-bearing securities) would receive larger real incomes. Thus, Keynes said in his *Treatise on Money*:

> I think it desirable that obligations arising out of past borrowing, of which National Debts are the most important, should, as time goes on, gradually

command less and less of human effort and of the results of human effort; that progress should loosen the grip of the dead hand; that the dead hand should not be allowed to grasp the fruits of improvements made long after the live body which once directed it has passed away.[96]

From the economic standpoint, however, the "dead hand," in the form of inherited wealth, is not objectionable *per se*. Often legacies serve to maintain widows and orphans whose support, in their absence, would fall on private charity or public relief. The property that is handed down from one generation to another tends to cause inequality, it is true, but it must be remembered that other ways of dealing with this situation are open.[97] A monetary program that falls upon insurance policies and savings bank deposits, while allowing common stocks and landed estates to escape, does not appear to be a very scientific way of dealing with the problem of inheritance.

It is obvious that proposals to stabilize prices by controlling in some way the quantity of money imply an acceptance of the quantity theory of the value of money, but they do not necessarily require a belief that the quantity of money is the only factor of significance. All that is assumed is that the quantity of money has sufficient influence to be able to counteract divergent factors elsewhere. But the mass of contributions to the subject of monetary stabilization in recent years have been concerned less with the problem of long-term stability of value, which has been studied in the present chapter, than with the business cycle and other short-run considerations.

Yet there have been some practical attempts to deal with the former problem. For example, during and after the war of 1914–1918, wage agreements were common that included clauses providing for periodical adjustments according to the variation shown by cost of living index numbers. In the German inflation which came to a head in 1923, obligations were issued whose interest and principal represented constant purchasing power over such commodities as rye and coal. Bonds, giving their owners the option of choosing between two or more currencies at interest and principal repayment dates, have been fairly common. Long-term contracts for the sale of finished articles, containing provisions for price adjustment as raw material prices change, have been employed.

The depression that came after 1929 was remarkable for the manner in which the various governments dealt with contractual obligations that had become unexpectedly burdensome when prices declined. In some countries substantial reductions in wages and interest were decreed. The United States abrogated the protecting gold clause in debt contracts. In some cases laws were enacted for the purpose of re-writing loan agree-

[96] Vol. 2, pp. 393-394. Quoted by permission of Harcourt, Brace and Company, Inc., and Macmillan & Co., Ltd.

[97] Especially taxation. See Chapter IV.

ments. Generally, however, monetary policy was such that substantial reductions in interest were possible through re-funding and in full accord with the original agreements between debtors and creditors. Certain of these measures partake of the nature of the tabular standard, in that they do not represent monetary stabilization but rather furnish means whereby society can conduct its business in the absence of such stabilization. Others, to choose a simile from the field of bodily welfare, resemble surgical operations more than health protection.

Pressure groups have been at work. Industrialists and political representatives of farming areas have campaigned for laws to reduce the value of money or otherwise bring about debt reduction. Insurance companies, in the interests of their policy-holders, have advertised on the opposite side. Taking the period of recorded history as a whole, there has been an impressive tendency for the value of money to fall. Thus, in England in 1300 an ox cost about 10 shillings ($2.50). By 1600 the price had risen to £4 ($20) or so. In the twentieth century it approached £20 ($100). Undoubtedly oxen improved considerably in size and quality over this period, but quite insufficiently to counterbalance the change in price. This general price movement took place throughout western Europe and in some countries the decline in the purchasing power of money was more severe than in England. Ups and downs have been experienced, but as yet there is no indication of a reversal of this broad trend.

Summary of Chapter

Specialized production necessitates exchange and money has acted as a medium in this connection since prehistoric times. Problems like deterioration of the coinage, currency inflation, and devaluation have assumed significance at various periods. Thus, around the close of the middle ages there was a chronic shortage of currency, because increased use of money was taxing the available supply. In the sixteenth century an influx of specie from Central and South America sent prices in Europe upward and led to the formulation of the quantity theory. The Mercantilists argued that accumulation of money served the objectives of the State. Some of them appeared to understand the quantity theory but Hume and Smith had no difficulty in demonstrating that a permanently favorable balance of trade—such as the Mercantilists desired—was impossible of attainment, because prices would rise as the quantity of money within the country increased, and so the favorable trade balance would disappear.

Currency deterioration and later credit inflation led to inquiries on monetary matters about 1700 and still more during the Napoleonic Wars period, when the foundations of some modern doctrines were laid. Ricardo applied his labor theory of value to the value of specie money but saw only quantity as the explanation of the value of inconvertible paper. Thornton and others expounded the principles that governed the distribution of money over the various localities and countries. The growth in importance of bank credit during the nineteenth century made it necessary to modify the earlier theories, so men like Giffen and Sidgwick explained afresh the relationship between specie and prices. The quantity equation of Irving Fisher aroused interest early in the twentieth century, while the war of 1914–1918 brought new problems and renewals of old ones.

In addition, there has been increased interest in the relation of money to the State—a circumstance that calls to mind the ideas of the German, Knapp. Whereas in the monetary theories of the nineteenth century it was commonly assumed that the supply of and demand for currency were determined by factors within the individualistic or business economy, recently there has been a growing recognition of the part played by central banks and governments in regulating the value of money.

Periods of considerable alteration in price levels have attracted attention to the effect of such changes on the distribution of wealth. The price inflations of the sixteenth and seventeenth centuries, of the Napoleonic Wars, and of the war of 1914–1918, were of special importance in this connection, as was the price decline of the last quarter of the nineteenth century. A number of remedies have been suggested, which can be classified into two groups, according as they have aimed at stabilizing prices or adjusting contracts to price movements. Various practical expedients have been tried, especially in recent years. But the historical tendency has been for the value of money to fall and, as yet, there is no sign that this movement has been reversed.

CHAPTER XV

BUSINESS PROSPERITY AND DEPRESSION

One of the foremost economic problems of the past century has been that of business depression. A subsistence economy experiences no trouble on this account. In such an economy, men make the goods that they consume, no exchange with others being necessary. But in a specialized and inter-dependent system, there exists the possibility that for some reason the exchange organization will cease to function properly, so that producers cannot sell their commodities and therefore are unable to procure what they need for their subsistence.

The History of Business Depressions

Today people are familiar with the spectacle of recurring business slumps. History shows that these go back definitely for a century and a half or so but how much farther cannot be said with precision. From the ancient world, as well as the middle ages, there come records of distress from war or famine but nothing definitely identifiable with the modern business cycle. Economic historians mention the appearance of depressions in England during the sixteenth and seventeenth centuries. Thus, there was a pronounced slump in the clothing industry in the south and east of England in 1528. Again, distress was experienced in 1564, 1586, 1607, 1620–1624, 1629–1631, and 1638–1640. Government appeals were made to cloth buyers to continue to make purchases. In 1528, for instance, Cardinal Wolsey is said to have summoned the London merchants before him and addressed them in the following terms :

> Sirs, the King is informed that you use not yourselves like merchants, but like graziers and artificers; for where the clothiers do daily bring cloths to your market for your ease, to their great cost, and there be ready to sell them, you of your wilfulness will not buy them as you have been accustomed to do. What manner of men be you? I tell you that the King straitly commandeth you to buy their cloths as beforetime you have been accustomed to do, upon pain of his high displeasure.[1]

In like manner, during the depression of the 1620's, the clothiers were ordered not to dismiss their operatives.

The dates given in the previous paragraph, respecting the recurrence of trade slumps in the first half of the seventeenth century, are highly suggestive of something in the nature of the business cycle of more mod-

[1] Quoted by E. Lipson, in *The Economic History of England,* vol. 3, p. 303.

ern times, but the paucity of statistical and other evidence makes it impossible to determine with accuracy the characteristics of these early periods of commercial stagnation.

Undoubtedly some of the distress noticed by historians of sixteenth century England resulted from alterations in the type or localization of industry. For example, enclosures of arable land threw cultivators out of work in some areas, while the movement of the woolen manufacturing industry from the corporate towns to the rural districts led to urban unemployment. The depression of 1528 was said to have been caused by a Continental war interfering with the export of British cloth and that of 1586 to the disturbance and uncertainty caused by Spanish preparation for an attack upon England. In 1622 a commission was appointed, believed to have been the first to give special study to unemployment. It listed a number of factors as being responsible. Among them were the growth of Continental competition, the existence of defects in English cloth, the prevalence of monopolistic practices on the part of the merchants, the interruption of trade by foreign wars, and "The scarcity of coin at home and the baseness of foreign coins compared unto ours."[2] The last of these is interesting, as forecasting later ideas concerning the relation between money and trade activity.

Defoe, in *A Plan of the English Commerce*, gave a striking account of a business boom and the succeeding collapse:

1. UPON some sudden Accident in Trade here comes a great unusual Demand for Goods, the Merchants from Abroad have sudden and unusual Commissions, the Call for Goods this Way or that Way encreases, this makes the Factors send large Orders into the Country; and the Price of Goods always rises according to the Demand: The Country Manufacturer looks out sharp, hires more Looms, get more Spinners, gives more Wages, and animated by the advanc'd Price, is not content to answer his new Orders only, but he continues the Excursion he had made into the Country for Spinners, &c. runs on to an Extremity in Quantity, as far, or perhaps farther, than his Stock will allow: and in a Word, gluts the Market with the Goods.

2. THE Accident of Trade, which from Abroad fill'd the Merchants Commissions, and the Factor's Orders being over, those Demands are also over, and the Trade returns to its usual Channel; but the Manufacturer in the Country, who had run out to an unusual Excess in his Business, without Regard to the Circumstances of it, having not stopt his Hand as his Orders stopt, falls into the Mire; his Goods lye on Hand, the Poor which he call'd from the Plow and the Dary [*i.e.,* dairy] to spin and weave, are cast off again, and not finding their Way presently back to their old Drudgery, lye and starve for Want of Work, and then they cry out Trade is decay'd, the Manufactures are lost, Foreigners encroach upon us, the Poor are starv'd, and the like.

[2] *Ibid.,* p. 308.

WHEREAS the Sum of the Matter is, the Manufacturer went mad, his Stream run over into a Flood, he run himself imprudently out of Breath; and upon a little Start of the Trade, willing to furnish the Orders all himself, and loth to let a Neighbour come in with him, run himself out, drag'd the Poor into his Business, nay perhaps robb'd his poorer Neighbour of his Workmen, by giving high Wages; and when the Trade stops a little, he runs a-ground; so the Poor are starving, and ready to mutiny for Want of Work: And this we call a Decay of Trade, whereas the contrary is manifest several Ways.[3]

As an example, Defoe mentioned the "late Accident of a Plague in France" (which probably meant that of the year 1720), as well as another occurring in 1713–1714, after the conclusion of the Treaty of Utrecht, which brought to an end the War of the Spanish Succession. The chief blame, he thought, lay on the manufacturers, who "upon any such hasty Demand from Abroad, shall run rashly out into Extremes in their Business. . ."[4]

Whatever is concluded as to the nature of these earlier crises, there is little difficulty in tracing cyclical depressions of the modern type from about the middle of the eighteenth century. In 1763 a pronounced slump followed the conclusion of the Seven Years War. England experienced another crisis in 1772–1773. Thereafter, 1783, 1793, 1797, 1811, 1815, 1825, 1836–1839, 1847, 1857, 1866, 1873, 1878, 1882, 1890, 1908, 1921, and 1930–1932, signalize the recurrence of depressed conditions.

A period of intense business activity occurs, accompanied by speculation and rising price levels, culminating in monetary stringency, with, perhaps, some spectacular commercial failures. Then follow a collapse of security and commodity prices, slackening of enterprise, and resulting unemployment. After this, a gradual recovery paves the way for a new burst of activity. Such, in brief, is the story of a typical cycle. The dates given by different authorities vary somewhat, as synchronization in the various countries is not complete and one observer regards as a slump or boom something which another inquirer does not put in this class (for instance, the English depression of 1926 or that experienced in America at the end of 1937). It seems that modern industry is afflicted by some kind of chronic disease, whose symptoms manifest themselves periodically. It is only to be expected that economists seek a theoretical explanation of this phenomenon.

MERCANTILIST THEORIES OF TRADE ACTIVITY

Among the welter of Mercantilist ideas, three have special application to business activity. These are considered below.

[3] *Op. cit.*, pp. 192-194.
[4] *Ibid.*, pp. 195-196.

More Money Means More Trade

First may be mentioned the belief that in some manner a plenitude of money is good for business.

In the writings of Petty and Locke there appeared the statement that a certain quantity of currency was required to maintain a country's trade. If there were less than this amount, it was argued that trade would suffer. If there were more, perhaps also it would be injurious to commerce:

there is a certain measure, and proportion of money requisite to drive the trade of a Nation, more or less then which would prejudice the same.[5]

Money is but the Fat of the Body-Politick, whereof too much doth as often hinder its Agility, as too little makes it sick. 'Tis true, that as Fat lubricates the motion of the Muscles, feeds in want of Victuals, fills up uneven Cavities, and beautifies the Body, so doth Money in the State quicken its Action, feeds from abroad in the time of Dearth at Home; even accounts by reason of its divisibility, and beautifies the whole, altho more especially the particular persons that have it in plenty.[6]

there being a certain proportion of money, necessary for driving such a proportion of trade, so much money of this as lies still, lessens so much of the trade.[7]

As to whether an increased quantity of money stimulated business, there was some difference of opinion. Petty, as has been seen, thought that too much money was just as much a hindrance as was an insufficient supply. Mun denied that an augmentation of the quantity would encourage trade, at least as far as foreign purchases were concerned:

If wee were once poor, and now having gained some store of mony by trade with resolution to keep it still in the Realm; shall this cause other Nations to spend more of our commodities than formerly they have done, whereby we might say that our trade is Quickened and Enlarged? no verily, it will produce no such good effect: but rather according to the alteration of times by their true causes wee may expect the contrary. . .[8]

The reason Mun gave for this view was that an increased quantity of money would raise the prices of commodities and so diminish the foreign demand for English products. The industry that was most prominent in economic discussion in England in his time was the manufacture of cloth for export, so it was perhaps reasonable that Mun should hold such an opinion.

On the other hand, some other Mercantilist writers asserted that more

[5] *The Economic Writings of Sir William Petty*, vol. 1, *A Treatise of Taxes & Contributions*, p. 35.

[6] *Ibid.*, *Verbum Sapienti* (written 1665 but not published until 1691), p. 113.

[7] *The Works of John Locke*, vol. 5, *Some Considerations of the Lowering of Interest and Raising the Value of Money*, p. 12.

[8] *England's Treasure by Forraign Trade*, p. 43.

money would give a stimulus to trade. Among these was Edward Misselden, an Englishman who lived during the first half of the seventeenth century. Misselden was an influential member of the Merchant Adventurers Company, whose principal business was the export of English cloth to Continental markets. After agriculture, cloth manufacture was the leading British industry of the time and it suffered a severe depression during 1620–1624. Misselden's important works, *Free Trade, Or, The Meanes To Make Trade Florish. Wherein, The Causes of the Decay of Trade in this Kingdome are discovered: And the Remedies also to remoove the same, are represented* (London 1622) and *The Circle of Commerce. Or the Ballance of Trade, in defence of free Trade...* (London 1623), appeared during this depression. The monopolistic powers and commercial practices of the Merchant Adventurers Company had been criticized and Misselden offered a defense. His concern appeared to be to demonstrate that the company's assailants were mistaken, that its actions were in accordance with the good of the State, and that the real blame for the depression lay elsewhere.

In the work on *Free Trade,* Misselden said that

> Money is the *vitall spirit* of *trade,* and if the *Spirits faile,* needes must the *Body faint.*[9]

Money was necessary if industry were to continue, he declared, and one of his main suggestions for remedying the existing depressed condition was to increase the supply of money by "raising" the currency, that is to say, by depreciating the specie content of the coins. This would have the effect of increasing prices, he admitted, but it would do no harm. Instead, benefit would be conferred, he said:

> And for the dearnesse of things, which the *Raising* of *Money* bringeth with it, that will be abundantly recompensed unto all in the plenty of *Money,* and quickening of Trade in every mans hand. And that which is equall to all, when he that buye's deare shall sell deare, cannot bee said to be injurious to any. And it is much better for the *Kingdome,* to have things deare with plenty of *Money,* whereby men may live in their severall callings: then to have things cheape with want of *Money,* which now makes every man complaine.[10]

So that Misselden's proposal was much the same as that adopted, with respect to the currency, by the government of the United States under similar conditions in 1933. Incidentally, though, the English writer inserted the proviso that payments under such contracts as leases should be made "at the value the *Money* went at" (that is, at the former specie value), a condition the United States Supreme Court refused to countenance, following the devaluation in this country. No doubt Misselden

[9] p. 28.
[10] *Ibid.,* pp. 106-107.

pressed the view that "if the Produce of the Ground were augmented about half, the Wants of the People are great enough to consume it all."[14] But instead of arguing—as he might, and as some of his successors in the twentieth century (notably J. M. Keynes) have done—for increased consumption as such, he went on to propose the elimination of excessive luxury by a greater equality of wealth.

More Money Means Lower Interest

In the chapter dealing with interest theories, it was noticed that some Mercantilists reasoned along a different line. Where Mun accepted that an increase in the quantity of money would raise prices, Petty, Child, and others, said that it would lower interest rates. Locke accepted both possibilities, and even David Hume—ardent quantity theorist as he was—admitted that in some circumstances (*i.e.*, the Spanish example, mentioned in Chapter XI) an augmentation of the supply of money might reduce interest, if only temporarily. None of the writers of this period, however, appears to have gone so far as to argue that more money had the effect of reducing interest and that this, in its turn, stimulated trade.

Lower Interest Means More Trade

John Locke, indeed, was at pains to assert that a diminution of interest did not encourage trade :

High interest is thought by some a prejudice to trade : but if we look back, we shall find, that England never throve so well, nor was there ever brought into England so great an increase of wealth since, as in queen Elizabeth's and king James I. and Charles I. time, when money was at ten and eight per cent. I will not say high interest was the cause of it. For I rather think, that our thriving trade was the cause of high interest, every one craving money to employ in a profitable commerce. But this, I think, I may reasonably infer from it, That lowering of interest is not a sure way to improve either our trade or wealth.[15]

Sir Josiah Child, however, thought that low interest was beneficial :

Low Interest is the Natural Mother of Frugality, Industry, and Arts. . .[16]

There is nothing in the World will engage our Merchants to Spend less and Trade more, than the Abatement of Interest, for the subduing of Interest will bring in multitudes of Traders, as it hath in *Holland,* to such a degree that almost all their People of both Sexes are Traders, and the many Traders will necessitate *Merchants* to Trade for less Profit, and consequently be more frugal in their Expences, which is the true Reason why many considerable *Merchants* are against the lessening of Interest. . .[17]

[14] *Ibid.*, p. 104.

[15] *The Works of John Locke*, vol. 5. *Some Considerations of the Lowering of Interest and Raising the Value of Money*, p. 66.

[16] *A New Discourse of Trade,* Preface (not paged) (iii-iv).

[17] *Ibid.,* Preface (xiv).

Generally; I say, the *Dutch low Interest hath miserably lessened us in all Trades of the World, not secured to us by Laws, or by some natural advantage which over-ballanceth the disproportion of our Interest of Money. .* .[18]

When I think of these things, I cannot but wonder that there should be found *English-men* who want not Bread to eat, or Cloaths to wear, should yet be so unkind and hard hearted to their Country, as strenuously to endeavour (for private Ends) the depriving her of so great a good, as would be the abatement of our Interest to 4 *per cent.* by a Law.[19]

Considering the reasons for the "Prodigious increase of the *Netherlands* in their Domestick and Foreign Trade, Riches, and multitude of Shipping,"[20] Child mentioned a number of factors, of which he thought that low interest was the most important. Holland, it should be said, was the leading commercial country in Europe at the time and it was natural that patriotic Britishers should ask themselves why this was the case. At all events, Child suggested that the legal rate of interest should be lowered in Britain, for the purpose of increasing the prosperity of British trade.

Explaining how low interest was advantageous to business, he remarked:

our greatest disadvantage is, that other Nations, especially our Industrious Neighbours the *Dutch,* are therein Wiser than we; For with them, and so in most Countries with whom we hold Commerce, there is not any Use [*i.e.,* interest] for Money tollerated above the rate of Six in the Hundred: Whereby it must of necessity come to pass, though they have no other Advantages of Industry and Frugality, that they must out Trade us; for if they make return of ten *per cent.* they almost double the Use allowed, and so make a very gainful Trade. But with us, where ten in the Hundred is so current, it is otherwise; for if we make not above ten, we are loosers; and consequently the same Trade, being with them and us equally good for the Publick, is to the private Adventurers lossful with us, with them very gainful.[21]

Here Child presented the essential feature of the theory that later was associated with the names of Thornton and Wicksell. He argued that an enterprise was profitable if it returned a rate of interest above that at which funds could be borrowed in the market. From this the conclusion was reached that, the lower the market rate of interest stood, the greater the number of undertakings that were likely to pay for development. To take the figures of Child's example, ventures capable of returning between 6 and 10 per cent, in Holland (where the market rate of interest was 6 per cent), paid to undertake; in England, however, where interest was 10 per cent on the market, these enterprises were unattractive.

[18] *Ibid.,* Preface (xxiv-xxv).

[19] *Ibid.,* Preface (xxviii-xxix).

[20] *Ibid.,* p. 1.

[21] *Ibid.,* pp. 218-219.

into the Nature and Effects of The Paper Credit of Great Britain, he considered the manner in which credit acted as a stimulus to business activity. Here he forecast the modern doctrine of *forced transfers* of purchasing power from the classes with fixed money properties or incomes to the enterpriser group:

Let us also consider the mode in which the new paper operates through the medium of these individual borrowers, as unquestionably it does, in giving life to fresh industry. The bank notes convey to them the power of obtaining for their own use, or of destining to such purposes as they please, a certain portion of purchaseable commodities. The extraordinary emission of paper causes no immediate difference in the *total* quantity of articles belonging to the kingdom. This is self-evident. But it communicates to the new borrowers at the bank a power of taking to themselves a larger share of the existing goods than they would otherwise have been able to command. If the holders of the new paper thus acquire the power over a larger portion of the existing stock of the kingdom, the possessors of the old paper must have the power over a smaller part. The same paper, therefore, will purchase fewer goods, or, in other words, commodities will rise in their nominal value. The proprietors of the new paper will become greater encouragers of industry than before; the owners of the old paper, being able to command less property, will have less power of employing labour.[23]

It must be also admitted, that, provided we assume an excessive issue of paper to lift up, as it may for a time, the cost of goods though not the price of labour, some augmentation of stock will be the consequence; for the labourer, according to this supposition, may be forced by his necessity to consume fewer articles, though he may exercise the same industry. But this saving, as well as any additional one which may arise from a similar defalcation of the revenue of the unproductive members of the society, will be attended with a disproportionate hardship and injustice.[24]

Thornton criticized Hume for not having noticed this effect. But the idea of forced transfers of purchasing power from those whose real incomes suffered from a rise in prices, to those who received the new money, was not altogether new. It was suggested by the French Physiocratic writer, Guérineau de Saint-Péravy (or Peravi, 1735–1789).[25] At a later date in England, Bentham referred to it incidentally in his *Manual of Political Economy,* which was written about the same time as Thornton's book, though not published until 1843. Bentham was discussing the means of increasing wealth and referred to the effects of a greater quantity of money. The consequence of currency expansion, he said, was "to impose an unprofitable *income tax* upon the incomes of fixed incomists."[26] In Bentham's view, there were two cases, according to

[23] *Op. cit.*, pp. 259-260. [24] *Ibid.*, pp. 263-264.

[25] In *Principes du commerce opposé au trafic,* n.p. 1786 and 1787.

[26] *The Works of Jeremy Bentham,* vol. 3, p. 45.

whether the additional money went first into the hands of men who employed it in unproductive consumption or to persons who used it productively. Thornton had the latter in mind, because he was thinking of the additional money as being in the form of bank loans which, ordinarily, were granted for business enterprise rather than for purposes of consumption.

Thornton examined the effects of this credit creation in some detail. There were two, he said: (1) industry was stimulated and (2) commodity prices were increased. The two were closely connected, because the consequence of "encreased eagerness in the demand," to which greater business activity gave rise, "must, unquestionably, be an enhancement of the price of labour and commodities."[27] Inventory profits emerged as long as prices continued to rise:

> While paper is encreasing, and articles continue rising, mercantile speculations appear more than ordinarily profitable. The trader, for example, who sells his commodity in three months after he purchased it, obtains an extra gain, which is equal to such advance in the general price of things as the new paper has caused during the three months in question: — he confounds this gain with the other profits of his commerce; and is induced, by the apparent success of his undertakings, to pursue them with more than usual spirit. The manufacturer feels the same kind of encouragement to extend his operations; and the enlarged issue of paper supplies both him and the merchant with the means of carrying their plans into effect. As soon, however, as the circulating medium ceases to encrease, the extra profit is at an end; and, if we assume the augmented paper to be brought back to its ordinary quantity, we must suppose industry to languish for a time, through the ill success which will appear to attend mercantile transactions.[28]

The truth of this statement need not be emphasized to those who have had occasion to acquaint themselves with American experience during the period 1916–1922.

Then Thornton went into the subject of the demand for bank advances. The prospective borrower had to bear in mind two factors: (1) the cost of the loan to him and (2) the return he could expect from its employment in commerce or industry:

> In order to ascertain how far the desire of obtaining loans at the bank may be expected at any time to be carried, we must inquire into the subject of the quantum of profit likely to be derived from borrowing there under the existing circumstances. This is to be judged of by considering two points: the amount, first, of interest to be paid on the sum borrowed; and, secondly, of the mercantile or other gain to be obtained by the employment of the borrowed capital.[29]

The "mercantile" gain, he thought, was commonly the highest which was to be had and so it was the influential factor. The point Thornton

[27] *Ibid.*, p. 261. [28] *Ibid.*, pp. 261-262. [29] *Ibid.*, p. 287.

circumstances appeared to have emerged that called for an additional issue, the government was approached to give permission to over-issue. This being authorized, the Bank of England proceeded to break the law that regulated its operations, safely in possession of a government promise of indemnifying legislation. The strength of the government in power, under the British political system, was what made this procedure practicable. Such over-issues were authorized several times during crises, though actual over-issues did not always follow.

When the German Imperial Bank law of 1875 was passed, provision was made for such contingencies. During the discussion that resulted in the British act of 1844, J. H. Palmer (1779–1858), director and for a time governor of the Bank of England, had written to the Prime Minister, mentioning the difficulty. J. W. Bosanquet (1807–1877), director of one of the joint stock banks, recommended a clause permitting additional note issues whenever the bank rate should rise to 8 per cent. Such a plan was incorporated in the German act. The authorized limit of note issue could be exceeded, subject to the payment of a tax of 5 per cent per year on any excess. The expectation was that this would encourage the Imperial Bank (Reichsbank) to issue more notes when the discount rate was above 5 per cent, but lead to the withdrawal of any excess when the rate sank below this percentage. This German scheme has been the model followed by many later central banks, including the Federal Reserve Banks of the United States of America.

The Wicksellian Theory

It was noticed in the last chapter that a number of writers on economics had recognized that changes in the quantity of money had a temporary effect upon the rate of interest. These included Hume (in his Spanish example), Thornton, Sidgwick, Giffen, and others. Sir Josiah Child and, more especially, Thornton, had shown how such a lowering of the interest rate had the effect of stimulating business. The statement of Tooke and Newmarch on the subject is worth quoting. The effect of the increased supply of gold from Australia and California was being discussed and these authors traced the repercussions on the money market of Great Britain:

> The natural and inevitable effect of so sudden and large an addition to the Reserve of the Bank [of England] was (under its present constitution and system of management) to reduce the minimum Rate of Discount from 3 per cent. in January, 1851, to 2 per cent. in April, 1852; and in the general market to reduce the rate still lower, namely, to about 1½ per cent. during the greater part of the year 1852.
>
> It is true, therefore, that the first effect of the Gold Discoveries was to reduce the Rate of Discount, and through the Rate of Discount, to reduce the Rate of Interest on advances made for long periods on Mortgages and

other similar securities. But this effect was in its nature but temporary, and was accompanied by circumstances which tended day by day to counteract its continuance. The most immediate consequence of the extreme reduction of the Rate of Interest was to lessen the cost of producing commodities, and to increase the profits of all persons requiring the accommodation of advances for short or long periods. In other words, the low rates of 1852 set in motion in some important degree the extended trade and enterprise of 1853; and that extended trade and enterprise rapidly raised the requirements for capital beyond the supply; and led, therefore, to those successive elevations of the rate of interest which were the most striking feature, in the early commercial history of 1853.[34]

What happened, therefore, according to Tooke and his collaborator, was that the increased supplies of gold had the effect of lowering interest, but the decline did not last, because it led to a heavy increase in the demand for capital.

J. S. Nicholson examined this point in the first volume of his *Principles of Political Economy,* when studying the factors influencing the volume of capital investment. Low interest, Nicholson thought, encouraged investment:

with a low rate of interest on old investments, there is an encouragement to new undertakings.[1] Suppose, for example, that [investment in] house property which formerly yielded seven per cent now only yields five per cent. The capital value of houses will rise, if we assume that, to begin with, the rents remain the same. But a great stimulus will be given to building new houses, and the ultimate result will be that the country will possess more or better houses at lower rents. A similar argument may be applied to machinery, factories, and all forms of fixed capital.[35]

This point is dealt with below.

The work of Knut Wicksell (1851–1926) has been very influential in molding recent thought on the relation of money to business activity. Wicksell was a Swede, who studied in various European centers before returning to his own country to teach. Theoretically, he was an adherent of the Marginal School but probably he is best known for his ideas concerning the inter-relationships between money, interest, prices, and business activity. The essential features of his theory had been anticipated by earlier writers, notably Thornton, but the theoretical implications of Thornton's contributions had been somewhat neglected and it was left to Wicksell to rediscover and clarify the theory that the English writer had expressed.

Like Thornton, Wicksell distinguished between the interest at which

[34] *Ibid.*, vol. 4 (vol. 6 of the original work), pp. 200-201. Quoted by permission of the Adelphi Company and P. S. King & Son Ltd.

[35] *Op. cit.*, vol. 1, p. 210. Nicholson's footnote reference was to Giffen's *Stock Exchange Securities,* London 1877.

railway companies would be able to offer up to 25 per cent more for wages and raw materials, since 4 per cent on 125 Kroner was the same as 5 per cent on 100 Kroner.[42]

Both Cassel[43] and Keynes[44] have emphasized this. The interest rate, they have argued, determines the value set by the market upon capital goods capable of producing income. If, say, an annual revenue of $10,000 is expected to accrue from the operation of a particular enterprise, over and above all expenses other than the cost of capital, then, capitalized at 5 per cent, the market valuation of the property is $200,000. Capitalized at 4 per cent, it is $250,000. If it should happen that the project under consideration is estimated to cost $220,000, it would be a paying proposition if interest were 4 per cent but not if the rate were 5 per cent. A fall in the interest rate "uncovers," as it were, many such possibilities. It stimulates capital investment, therefore, and increases general business activity. Conversely, a rise in interest rates deters construction and causes business to become depressed. When it is borne in mind that the business cycle is largely a phenomenon of constructional activity, the significance of this factor will be appreciated.

Recent Monetary Theories

Among the more prominent recent writers dealing with business cycles from the monetary angle are F. A. von Hayek (1899–), formerly of Vienna and now of the University of London, R. G. Hawtrey (1879–), of the British Treasury, and J. M. Keynes. The theories of these men have aroused considerable controversy, into which it would be out of place to go in any detail.

Briefly, it can be said that Hayek, whose ideas are set out in *Prices and Production* (London 1931), has continued the Wicksellian assumption of full employment of the productive factors as the basis of his argument, which is even more closely tied up than that of Wicksell with the Austrian theory of roundabout production.[45] According to Hayek, the creation of bank credit in the form of advances to business men permits an increase in the demand for the services of the factors of production to take place, causing the prices of these latter to rise. The shifting of expenditures between the various stages of the roundabout process (*i.e.*, between producers', intermediate, and consumers' goods) affects other prices, on the lines suggested by Wicksell. But the process of expansion is brought to an end by a rise in interest rates, forced on the market by the insufficiency of capital and the decline in bank reserves.

Keynes, in *The Treatise on Money* and *The General Theory of Em-*

[42] *Lectures on Political Economy*, vol. 2, pp. 195-196.
[43] See *The Theory of Social Economy*, pp. 639-640.
[44] *A Treatise on Money*, vol. 1, pp. 202-204.
[45] See Chapter VIII.

ployment Interest and Money, on the other hand, has concentrated on the feature that Wicksell considered incidental, namely the possibility that factors of production hitherto idle may be called into use.

Hawtrey, in his *Currency and Credit* (London 1919) and other works, has dwelt on a different point. He has referred to the connection between interest rates and the cost of carrying traders' stocks, which, of course, affects the willingness of merchants to make purchases. Both Keynes and Hawtrey have devoted attention to such factors as the margin between consumers' money incomes and expenditure and the relationship between money savings and the volume of real capital investment.

All of these writers, and many others, though differing substantially on numerous points of theory, agree that monetary policy is a major influence in the activity of industry and that lowering interest rates is a stimulant, and raising them a deterrent, to business enterprise. This, of course, has been recognized since the time of Thornton, but the neglect with which Thornton's work was attended in recent years is shown by the fact tha' to many Wicksell's theory came as a new discovery. Probably it can be said that the major contribution of the recent writers—especially Keynes—has been the manner in which they have linked together the theories of money, interest, and business activity in an endeavor to furnish an explanation of the business cycle.

The Under-Consumption Theory

The principal competitor of the monetary explanation of the business cycle during the last century has been what is called the *over-production* or *under-consumption theory.*[46]

There was a remarkable separation in British Classical economics between monetary and general theory. Nowhere is this clearer than in the writings of Ricardo. A monetary authority of high standing and very competent to discuss business fluctuations, he limited his book on general economics to long-term or "normal" conditions and by that very fact excluded from consideration the problem of the trade cycle. The same was largely true of Senior and John Stuart Mill. The answer of Classical economics to the problem of commercial depressions was to be found in Say's *law of markets,* which, in effect, denied their possibility altogether, other than as a temporary or frictional condition.

Commodities, argued Say, supplied demands for each other. If every producer brought more goods into existence, he could receive more of other people's products in exchange. True, more of a single article might be produced than was saleable at a profitable price, but—according to Say—general over-production was impossible :[47]

[46] Some writers on business cycle theory make a distinction between "over-production" and "under-consumption" theories.

[47] But see below (p. 713).

the distribution of wealth after it was created, your Reporter could have no difficulty in suggesting the means of beneficial occupation of all who are unemployed, and for a considerable increase to their number.[53]

It is the want of a profitable market that alone checks the successful and otherwise beneficial industry of the working classes. The markets of the world are created solely by the remuneration allowed for the industry of the working classes, and those markets are more or less extended and profitable in proportion as these classes are well or ill remunerated for their labour. But the existing arrangements of society will not permit the labourer to be remunerated for his industry, and in consequence all markets fail.[54]

Owen's remedies, as stated in this *Report,* were the formation of self-contained co-operative villages[55] and the establishment of a new system of exchange based on labor. By these arrangements, he hoped that "*consumption* may be made to keep pace with production."[56]

Even within the camp of economic orthodoxy itself, in his *Principles of Political Economy considered with a view to their Practical Application,* already referred to, Malthus associated himself with the theory propounded by Sismondi. Perhaps it was inevitable that such an explanation of commercial crises should have been forthcoming. The output of industry had expanded by leaps and bounds and, in the end, a time had come when this output could not be sold. It was natural enough to attribute this circumstance to the advances that had occurred in the technique of production in industries catering for a broad demand (as was the case in the then-leading textile industry), unattended by a corresponding expansion of consumer purchasing power.

Rodbertus and Marx

The theory was embraced by many Socialists. Rodbertus gave it a prominent place in his writings, developing what has been called the *law of the diminishing wage share* and explaining the business cycle by the operation of this law:

If every participant in exchange always retained the entire product of his labour; if his purchasing power, therefore, consisted in the market-value of the entire product . . . then no glut could arise from an increase of productiveness, either in respect to any ONE *or to* ALL *commodities, until all the participants had received enough of them for their use, until more of them had been produced than is required by society. . . A like success would attend the increase of productiveness even though the product were divided, as it is to-day, among three sharers, if* THE SHARE OF EACH ONE REMAINED A FIXED, UNALTERABLE QUOTA OF THE PRODUCT. . . *But if neither of these assumptions is realized, if the product is not only divided among three sharers, but the share of the labouring class (i.e. of the great majority of society) is besides, in accordance with the "natural" laws of trade left to itself, not a*

[53] *Ibid.*, p. 248. [54] *Ibid.*, pp. 252-253. [55] See Chapter V.

[56] *A New View of Society and Other Writings*, p. 253.

fixed, unalterable quota of the product BUT, ON THE CONTRARY, BECOMES A SMALLER QUOTA OF THE PRODUCT EXACTLY IN PROPORTION TO THE INCREASE IN PRODUCTIVENESS — *then that fortunate issue of the increase in productiveness cannot occur.* For according to this third supposition, purchasing power and productiveness are no longer in direct proportion to each other. On the contrary, the purchasing power of the greatest part of society diminishes in proportion to increasing productiveness; and society is placed in the position of producing value-in-use which is no longer market value and purchasing power, while yet the need for it is, in the case of most people, unsatisfied.[57]

The idea became an integral part of Marxist doctrine. It was stated in brief form in the *Communist Manifesto.* Engels's work, *Herr Eugen Dühring's Revolution in Science (Anti-Dühring)*, gave the following account:

The enormous expanding power of large-scale industry, compared with which the expanding power of gases is mere child's play, now appears to us as a *necessity* for both qualitative and quantitative expansion that laughs at all counteracting pressure. Such counteracting pressure comes from consumption, demand, markets for the products of large-scale industry. But the capacity of the market to expand, both extensively and intensively, is controlled directly by quite other and far less effective laws. The expansion of the market cannot keep pace with the expansion of production. The collision becomes inevitable, and as it can yield no solution so long as it does not burst the capitalist mode of production itself, it becomes periodic. Capitalist production brings into being a new "vicious circle." And in fact, since 1825, when the first general crisis broke out, the whole industrial and commercial world, the production and exchange of all civilised peoples and of their more or less barbarian dependent people have been dislocated practically once in every ten years. Trade comes to a standstill, the markets are glutted, the products lie in great masses, unsaleable, ready money disappears, credit vanishes, the factories are idle, the working masses go short of food because they have produced too much food, bankruptcy follows upon bankruptcy, forced sale upon forced sale. The stagnation lasts for years, both productive forces and products are squandered and destroyed on a large scale, until the accumulated masses of commodities are at last disposed of at a more or less considerable depreciation, until production and exchange gradually begin to move again. By degrees the pace quickens; it becomes a trot; the industrial trot passes into a gallop, and the gallop in turn passes into the mad onrush of a complete industrial commercial, credit and speculative steeplechase, only to land again in the end, after the most breakneck jumps — in the ditch of a crash. And so on again and again. We have now experienced it five times since 1825, and at this moment (1877) we are experiencing it for the sixth time. And the character of these crises is so clearly marked that Fourier hit them all off when he described the first as *crise pléthorique,* a crisis of superabundance.[58]

[57] *Overproduction and Crises,* pp. 127-131.

[58] *Op. cit.,* pp. 309-310.

booms to waves of innovations, to the theories that depend for their basis on the psychology of the business man.

As long ago as the beginning of the eighteenth century, Daniel Defoe, as has been noted, gave what amounted to a psychological explanation of business cycles. He said that merchants were unduly optimistic in good times and over-reached themselves. Defoe might have added that in bad times merchants became equally pessimistic, in which case his theory would have been a forerunner of the psychological explanation advanced in the twentieth century by A. C. Pigou. Pigou's argument was that business men have a crowd psychology: they are over-optimistic at one time and excessively pessimistic at another.

Another factor that has received attention is the difficulty of making business forecasts. Production takes time. One individual producer decides to expand his output without realizing that others are reaching the same decision, so that when his additional products come to market they meet more competition, and lower prices, than were visualized when their production was decided upon. The French economist, Albert Aftalion (1874–), has emphasized this feature in his *Les crises périodiques de surproduction* (2 vols., Paris 1913) and other writings.

Plainly, such factors as crowd psychology and the magnification of mistakes by reason of the time occupied by the productive process are of considerable influence in the business cycle. In his *magnum opus* on the business cycle (*Industrial Fluctuations*, London 1927), Pigou accepted the position that there are a number of causal factors and even went so far as to estimate their relative significances. But few writers have cared to commit themselves in this way. The majority have either advanced abstract explanations intended to represent the major causal factors, or have been content with description of the theories of others or with realistic studies containing a minimum of theorizing. The well-known book on *Business Cycles, the Problem and Its Setting* (New York 1927) by the American economist W. C. Mitchell (1874–1948), valuable as it is, falls into the last-mentioned category.

If an estimate of the trend of business cycle theory may be hazarded, perhaps it can be said that economists appear to be coming to look upon the cycle as a matter of mechanism. The organization of the modern capitalist economy is thought to be such that, given a suitable impetus, industry is started off on an upward or downward trend, and the familiar features of the business cycle result. If this position be accepted, and especially in view of the diversity of theories that are held concerning causation, it is logical enough to experiment with remedies. When business appears to be on a downward trend, something may be done to start it upwards again. If trade is so brisk that a crisis appears in store, the use of a brake is indicated. This is what the governments of the world appear to be doing. Thus, the American administration that came into power in 1933 depreciated the gold value of the dollar, bought silver, and reduced interest rates, in full accordance with the views of those economists who support the monetary explanation of the business cycle. But the legislators showed that they had an ear for the competing under-consumption theory, for in the National Industrial Recovery Act of 1933 they made certain provisions whose effect was to raise wages and later they levied taxes on the undistributed profits of corporations, so as to favor consumptive spending against further capital investment. Periodically, also, a barrage of propaganda was aimed at the psychology of the business man, and so forth. In other words, the government behaved somewhat like a race-goer who is unable to decide between the "form" of several horses, so backs two or three of the most promising runners and hopes for the best.

Economic theory on this subject has been unsatisfactory. The Classical answer to the problem of the business cycle was Say's "law of markets." Commonly it is charged that this merely denied the possibility of slumps. It is difficult to believe that the Classical economists shut their eyes to the obvious truth of the existence of trade depressions. Rather the explanation is to be found in the Classical propensity to concentrate on long-term tendencies. Matters would right themselves in due course, it was thought, with respect to the business cycle. But as writers from the time of Aristotle have remarked, men tend to emphasize the immediate more than the distant, and to practical people the immediate problem of the cycle has appeared at times to be very serious. Men were interested in the subject, therefore, and, if reputable economists neglected it, it was only to be expected that others would fill the gap — just as quack doctors at country fairs do a thriving trade in mysterious "remedies" for the common complaints for which professional medical men have no cure. This is not to say that all the writings that appeared on the business cycle from the pens of those who had no professional connection with economics can be characterized as quackery. Many of them contain useful thoughts. Indeed, views on the subject are changing, so that Keynes in his *General Theory of Employment Interest and Money* [60] was able to speak in relatively favorable terms of Major Douglas, whom, as a witness before the Macmillan Committee [61] a few years before, he helped to criticize. The matter may be summarized by saying that, in the literature of recent years, the two explanations of the business cycle which have been considered in this chapter have become complementary, rather than competitive.

[60] pp. 370-371.

[61] A British government committee of inquiry into the relationships between finance and industry held in 1930–1931, presided over by Lord Macmillan. Keynes was a member of the committee.

those which are productive ought to be more numerous than the unproductive, and the sources of income ought to be so distributed that they may not run a risk with all their possessions at the same time.[2]

The book is packed with shrewd comments, of which examples were given in Chapter VIII. The second book of *Œconomica* is entirely different, being considered the work of another hand and mainly concerned with the raising of government revenue.

Throughout the Aristotelian *corpus*, economics was subordinated to ethics. This was to be expected in a comprehensive treatment of the whole body of knowledge. Until ends are defined, it does not appear very useful to give attention to the means of achieving the ends. So Aristotle asked what should be the object of human life, and what a State should be like; and it was only in the light of the replies he gave to these questions that he discussed ways of living or of State-building.

The Religious Teachings of the Middle Ages

The writers of the early Christian and medieval periods made economics subsidiary to Christian morals. Like Aristotle, they believed that wealth was not an end in itself but only a means of securing more fundamental objectives. To do God's will and to attain personal salvation were looked upon by Christian teachers as the primary aims of human life. Little attention was paid to economics as the subject is now taught, and this is entirely understandable. People who thought of individual selfishness as a qualification for damnation could not be expected to give much heed to the art of getting rich. What may be regarded as the textbooks of this era, therefore, took the form of guides to practical conduct (including matters connected with wealth), based on religious ethics, such as those of Clement of Alexandria and Thomas Aquinas.

Mercantilism

The Renaissance witnessed an escape from this situation, at least in some degree. But wealth merely changed masters. Not God but the State now assumed the center of the stage. Thus appeared what is known as Mercantilism. Under the new philosophy, wealth was given a more important place than the early Christian teachers had assigned to it. The great leaders of the Church had regarded it as debatable whether wealth served any useful purpose to the Christian man. Some thought that its possession was not unobjectionable, if the wealth were utilized properly, that is, in the service of God, but others considered that believers would be better without it. The Mercantilists, on the other hand, had no doubt whatever that wealth was useful from the standpoint of the State. Hence, there appeared a wide range of writings that gave attention to the subject of wealth, approaching it from the

[2] *Ibid.*, 1344b.

angle of State interest. Men like Hales, Mun, and Child considered wealth, it is true, but did so primarily from the State's point of view. In an earlier chapter, the possibility has been suggested that at times this attitude might have been hypocritical and that what some of the Mercantilist writers had in their minds were the special interests of the trading organizations with which they were associated, if not, indeed, their personal fortunes. But they at least made a pretense that the State's interest would be served by the policies that they advocated, and for this reason their ideas received contemporary attention.

Cameralism

The German *Cameralists* or *Kameralists* are sometimes regarded as a particular school of Mercantilists but their special position in the development of economics justifies separate treatment. Their name comes from the Latin word for chamber (meaning, in this connection, the royal office or treasury) and this indicates to some extent the direction taken by the studies of the Cameralist group.

A longer list of Cameralist writers could be given but perhaps Johann Joachim Becher (1635–1682), Philipp Wilhelm von Hornigk, and J. H. G. von Justi (1720–1771) are most worthy of mention. All three were employed in princely or other public service and interested themselves in State administration and public finance. In general, their outlook was Mercantilist. They accepted the principle that the ends of the individual should be subordinated to those of the State and advocated the policy of economic nationalism which characterized the Mercantilists as a whole.

But Justi, especially, went much farther than the English Mercantilists in surveying the field of economic inquiry. He distinguished between private and public economics, though he made the latter an amplified edition of the former:

> The great management of the state rests virtually upon the same rules which other management must observe. In both establishments the ultimate purposes are to acquire "means," to assure what has been acquired, and to use reasonably the goods possessed. The housekeeping of the state is merely of incomparably greater extent than that of a private person.[3]

According to Justi, the student should endeavor to understand, first, the principles of household economy (*i.e.*, the "economy" of the Aristotelian treatises). Next, there should follow a course on political science, which would be the first part of the "great management of the state" and would include

[3] Quoted by A. W. Small, in *The Cameralists,* Chicago 1909, pp. 306-307. Reproduced by permission of The University of Chicago Press.

All the methods whereby the riches of the state may be increased, in so far as the authority of the government is concerned. . .[4]

The third and concluding study should be that which

deals with the reasonable use of the means of the state, and the entire internal housekeeping. . .[5]

It was with the second and third of these topics that the Cameralists concerned themselves. The Mercantilists of other countries had paid considerable attention to the second, and the Cameralists tended to concentrate on the third, which, in their hands, was very largely what is now called public finance.

In Chapter I it was shown that an outlook that made economics subservient to public policy was a logical product of the times in which the Mercantilists wrote: this is true of the Cameralists also. If princes and kings undertook the regulation of the economic life of the communities over which they ruled, obviously there was both a need and an opportunity for men to elaborate the principles of government economic control. This was what the Mercantilists and the Cameralists were attempting to do. The United States and, indeed, the western world generally have lately been going through a similar experience, as references to publishers' catalogues and lists of college courses will demonstrate.

The Political Arithmeticians

In the meantime, a group of English writers, often called the *Political Arithmeticians,* had worked along another line. John Graunt, Sir William Petty, Gregory King, and Charles Davenant were the most important. Something was said of these writers in Chapter VII but their inquiries covered a wider field than population and vital statistics. They investigated all manner of commercial facts and drew conclusions on the basis of what they found. This is not to say that they possessed no preconceived ideas and made no use of abstract arguments—certainly they did so—but their ideas were based on recorded data to a greater extent than had been usual with their Mercantilist predecessors. Their outlook remained colored by Mercantilist opinions but they showed a willingness to question the older doctrines and mark out a new course for themselves that is not to be found in the writings of the Mercantilists proper. Something much closer to individualistic economics than was Mercantilism itself appears to have represented their point of view.

Economics as a Science of Individual Riches

Hobbes and Hume

The times were changing. The *Leviathan* of Thomas Hobbes had asserted the principle of individual selfishness, and philosophers like

[4] *Ibid.*, p. 307. [5] *Ibid.*

Locke and Hume laid the theoretical basis of modern individualistic thought. Hobbes devoted a chapter of the *Leviathan* to economics, entitling it "Of the Nutrition, and Procreation of a Commonwealth." Hume dealt with the subject in scattered essays, on "Commerce," "Refinement in the Arts," "Money," "Interest," "The Balance of Trade," and certain others. Hume chose his topics and discussed them impartially. In some cases the results were remarkable, as when he utilized the quantity theory of money to overthrow the balance of trade doctrines of the Mercantilists.

What Hume and the writers who came after him—Cantillon, the French Physiocrats, and the British Classical economists—wrote about was the *satisfaction of the wants of individual men,* not the *welfare of States,* to which the Mercantilists had given their attention. For John Locke had denied that there was any such thing as the State or nation, other than a mere association of individuals to satisfy their political needs. According to this view, which Hume and his successors accepted, the wealth of a nation could be nothing more than the wealth of the individuals within the nation, so that Mercantilism was out-moded in the new philosophical environment.

But, though important, Hume's contributions to economics were not organized in a systematic treatise and it was in Cantillon's *Essai sur la nature du commerce en général* that such a work appeared.

Cantillon

Cantillon's *Essai,* therefore, written before Hume's studies but not published until afterwards, is commonly regarded as the first general book on economics in modern times. The verdict of W. S. Jevons is worth quoting:

> The *Essai* is far more than a mere essay or even collection of disconnected essays like those of Hume. It is a systematic and connected treatise, going over in a concise manner nearly the whole field of economics, with the exception of taxation. It is thus, more than any other book I know, *the first treatise on economics.* Sir William Petty's *Political Arithmetic* and his *Treatise of Taxes and Contributions* are wonderful books in their way, and at their time, but, compared with Cantillon's *Essai,* they are mere collections of hints. There were earlier English works of great merit, such as those of Vaughan, Locke, Child, Mun, etc., but these were either occasional essays and pamphlets, or else fragmentary treatises. Cantillon's essay is, more emphatically than any other single work, "the Cradle of Political Economy." [6]

By this Jevons meant that the *Essai* was the first comprehensive book on wealth as such. Production, distribution, population, and exchange had

[6] *Richard Cantillon and the Nationality of Political Economy, Contemporary Review* 1881, reprinted as an appendix to the English translation of the *Essai,* p. 342.

their places in Cantillon's pages. In many respects, as has been noticed in earlier chapters, his treatment was surprisingly modern—more so, indeed, than that of many later writers. Though the book had no wide circulation, indirectly its influence was considerable. The *Essay upon Money and Coins,* published by Joseph Harris, showed clear traces of Cantillon's ideas. The manuscript of the *Essai* was in the possession of the Physiocrat, Mirabeau, for a number of years and was admitted by the latter writer to have helped to mold his views. Adam Smith, whose references to other authorities were not very numerous, mentioned Cantillon's name and, indeed, when discussing wages, used terminology which suggested that he had acquainted himself fully (either directly or through Harris) with the ideas of the earlier economist.

The Physiocrats

The views of the Physiocrats were of greater contemporary significance. Of the works of Quesnay, the acknowledged leader of the group, the articles on *Fermiers* and *Grains,* which were contributed to the great *Encyclopédie* (1751–1780), together with the famous *Tableau économique,* were the most important. Turgot, however, produced a comprehensive book, *Réflexions sur la formation et la distribution des richesses.* Some of the principal features of this treatise have received attention, so only a general comment is needed here. Like Cantillon's *Essai,* the *Réflexions* furnished an integrated treatment of wealth, divorced from ethical or political considerations.

Classical and Neo-Classical Writings

Adam Smith, when he came to write, had before him these various contributions. David Hume was his close friend and Francis Hutcheson, whose work was in many respects similar to that of Hume, had been his teacher. Commercial Glasgow provided his early training and teaching experience. In France he had met the Physiocrats. Except for a short period at the beginning, his teaching field had been moral philosophy or ethics but he devoted a portion of his lecture course to what he called "justice, police, revenue, and arms" and there covered material that today would be included under politics and economics.

The *Wealth of Nations* contained Smith's ideas on economics. It dealt with individual riches and its title is explained by the author's acceptance of the philosophy of Locke and his followers, which made it possible to look upon individual riches as the national wealth. The somewhat puzzling relationship between the views expressed in this book and those contained in the earlier *Theory of Moral Sentiments* has been discussed in Chapter II. All that need be said here is that Smith recognized that wealth-seeking was only one side of human conduct but followed

Cantillon and Turgot in offering a more or less self-contained treatment of this aspect.

From the *Wealth of Nations* grew the impressive tree of British Classical economics, bearing fruit in the writings of Malthus, Ricardo, Senior, and the rest of an illustrious company. In their hands political economy was a science of wealth. Probably Senior best stated this position, though it was not in entire accord with the attitude he took on the occasion of his formal entry into academic economics.[7] In his *Political Economy*, Senior defined political economy as

the Science which treats of the Nature, the Production, and the Distribution of Wealth. . .[8]

The definition of wealth given in this work has been set forth in Chapter II. As an expression of human objectives, it was fairly comprehensive, but the requirements of transferability, exchange, and value at least ruled out such ends as the attainment of God's will on earth and of personal salvation, to which the early Christian teachers had devoted so much attention. Senior criticized some of his predecessors for having adopted a different definition. The Physiocrat, Mercier de la Rivière (1720–1793), proposed to consider all things that were necessary to human happiness, while J. B. Say said that political economy was the economy of society. Even Adam Smith had gone beyond a scientific study to prescribe measures of social improvement. Such matters were important, Senior admitted, but they involved something more than wealth and therefore should not form part of the subject of political economy:

It is impossible to overstate the importance of these inquiries [into measures of social improvement], and it is not easy to state their extent. They involve, as their general premises, the consideration of the whole theory of morals of government, and of civil and criminal legislation; and, for their particular premises, a knowledge of all the facts which affect the social condition of every community whose conduct the Economist proposes to influence. We believe that such inquiries far exceed the bounds of any single Treatise, and indeed the powers of any single mind. We believe that by confining our own and the reader's attention to the Nature, Production, and Distribution of Wealth, we shall produce a more clear, and complete, and instructive work than if we allowed ourselves to wander into the more interesting and more important, but far less definite, fields by which the comparatively narrow path of Political Economy is surrounded. The questions, To what extent and under what circumstances the possession of Wealth is, on the whole, beneficial or injurious to its possessor, or to the society of which he is a member? – What distribution of Wealth is most desirable in

[7] See his *Introductory Lecture on Political Economy*, delivered on taking the Drummond Chair of Political Economy in Oxford University 1826, published 1827.

[8] *Political Economy*, p. 6.

Lionel Robbins, in *An Essay on the Nature and Significance of Economic Science* (London 1932, 2nd edition 1935), said:

Economics . . . is concerned with that aspect of behavior which arises from the scarcity of means to achieve given ends. It follows that Economics is entirely neutral between ends; that, in so far as the achievement of *any* end is dependent on scarce means, it is germane to the preoccupations of the economist. Economics is not concerned with ends as such. It assumes that human beings have ends in the sense that they have tendencies to conduct which can be defined and understood, and it asks how their progress towards their objectives is conditioned by the scarcity of means — how the disposal of scarce means is contingent on these ultimate valuations. It should be clear, therefore, that to speak of any end as being in itself "economic" is entirely misleading.[14]

Superficially, Robbins's position is different from that occupied by Senior. Senior attempted to construct a set of rules for wealth-seeking and, though he gave wealth a broad definition, he did not include *any end* whatever. Robbins purports to do so. In practice, however, the difference is not material, because even Robbins does not appear to make provision, in his writings, for such ends as national glory or personal salvation.

In view of the long series of assertions of scientific purism that have come from the Classical and Neo-Classical economists, it may be in place to inquire how far the writers concerned have in fact refrained from offering advice. Some of them do not appear to have lived up to the standard that has been set. Adam Smith's *Wealth of Nations*, far from being a scientific treatise as Senior defined the latter, was regarded by many contemporaries as a polemic against Mercantilism. Advice was a leading feature of the book — advice to the government to abstain from interference in the economic sphere. Much the same is true of the work of J. B. Say. Ricardo was willing enough to offer counsel on monetary policy, as was Malthus on marriage and the procreation of children. Senior advocated government action to improve the position of the poor, in *A Letter to Lord Howick, on a legal provision for the Irish Poor, etc.*, published in 1831, five years before the work on *Political Economy* (from which his statement on the scope of economics quoted above was taken). The *Report of the Commission on the Condition of Hand-loom Weavers* (1841), which appears to have been Senior's work, also argued in favor of government intervention, while his opposition to the factory acts is well known. Robbins, in *The Great Depression* and *Economic Planning and the International Order* (London 1937), may be criticized in like manner, because both of these books can be interpreted as an attack on government economic planning. It appears difficult for economists to

[14] 2nd ed., p. 24. Quoted by permission of Macmillan & Co., Ltd. and The Macmillan Company.

be coldly scientific. The physicist, having expounded the law of gravity, seems to have no trouble in resisting whatever urge he may feel in the direction of pointing a moral respecting the impropriety of removing one's hand from beneath a watch in mid-air. Not so, however, is it with the economist. Perhaps the reason is that laymen do not apprehend readily the economic principles that are put before them, with the result—at least according to the economists—that the world is full of men who are doing the economic counterparts of allowing their watches to get smashed.

In Chapter II it was pointed out that one of the foremost of the Neo-Classical economists, W. S. Jevons, mentioned a hierarchy of wants: (1) those connected with bodily desires of the ordinary kind, (2) those associated with the welfare of the social group or nation, and (3) moral objectives. Economists, he said, professed only to deal with the first (which Jevons regarded as the lowest) of these. On the other hand, P. H. Wicksteed went some way in developing a marginal theory of valuation which embraced *all* wants:

We may think of Robinson Crusoe withdrawing a little work in one direction and turning it in another, in order to bring the marginal significance of his products into correspondence with the terms in effort on which nature offers the alternatives to him. Or we may think of our indolent young man, when he has fairly begun his day, carefully considering what expenditure of labour will pay best in the examination for which he is preparing, visited at certain moments by compunction as to the sordidness of this view, and genuinely allured (by the fascination of some subject) into the pursuit of knowledge for her own sake; or fraudulently persuading himself, in another mood, that he has a soul above mere utilitarian considerations, that knowledge of the world is better than University distinction, and that his acquaintance with the modern drama or with the points of dogs or horses is in more urgent need of marginal increments than his knowledge of the niceties of the syntax of a dead language. He too is, wisely or foolishly, administering his resources and endeavouring to bring marginal values into a proper balance with the terms on which alternatives are offered.

Thus the same law holds in intellectual, moral, or spiritual as in material matters. Cæsar tells how when surprised by the Nervii he had barely time to harangue his soldiers, obviously implying that the harangue was shorter than usual. He felt that a few moments, even at such a crisis, were well devoted to words of exhortation to his troops; but their value declined at the margin, and the price in delaying the onslaught rapidly rose; so the moment was soon reached when the time could be better spent than in prolonging a moving discourse. In a story of South America, after the war, we are told of a planter who, when warned by his wife in the middle of his prayers that the enemy was at the gate, concluded his devotions with a few brief and earnest petitions, and then set about defending himself. Had he been a formalist those final petitions would never have been uttered at all; but under the circumstances the impulse to prayer, though sincere and urgent, became rapidly less imperative and exacting relative to the urgency of taking steps for defence, as the successive moments passed. The most pious biographers of Alfred the Great praise him for "charging like a boar" at the Battle of Ashdown while his brother was still engaged in prayer; and an entirely devout and sincere person may find himself in the dilemma of having either to curtail (or omit) family prayers or to hurry a guest over his breakfast and perhaps run him uncomfortably close for his train. If he shortens, but does not omit, the prayers, it shews that he attaches declining significance to his devotions as minute is added to minute. And in this we shall see nothing ludicrous, as soon as we give up the cant of the absolute in a world in which all things are relative.[15]

Of course, Cæsar's harangue or the prayers of the South American planter may have been just as much influenced by self-interest as were the actions with which these proceedings competed in the disposal of scarce resources (labor in this case). But evidently Wicksteed's arguments could be extended to cover all the choices that fall to be made by an individual. How much of his salary should be spent on himself, how much on others for whom he has warm feelings, how much given away because he feels that charity is a duty, how much subscribed to a party formed to further certain political ideals, etc.—all these might be worked into the marginal system. True, it can be argued that rational choice, based on the principle of diminishing utility (which Wicksteed employed—speaking of it as the principle of *diminishing psychic returns*), is not applicable to choices between bread, battleships, and charitable gifts—which, presumably, fall into Jevons's three categories. But can one be more certain that it applies to decisions on the relative significance of, say, medical treatment and engagement rings—which are ordinarily brought into the economic calculus? In any event, this is an objection against the marginal theory of value rather than one against the inclusion in economics of all wants that compete with each other for the disposal of scarce resources. After all, men's desires to maintain their culture on the face of the earth by military or naval power, to Christianize the heathen, or to devote themselves to good works at home, conflict with their capacity to satisfy their bodily wants. A science that includes only the last class of desires cannot be described as realistic.

The Methods of the Classical and Neo-Classical Schools

Common to all the Classical and Neo-Classical writings in greater or less degree is the use of what is termed the *abstract, deductive, hypothetical,* or *a priori* method of inquiry. Its characteristic is that principles are arrived at by the logical process of reasoning from premises that are known or assumed beforehand, in contrast with the *concrete, inductive, realistic,* or *a posteriori* method, which is based on a prior examination of facts.

[15] *The Commonsense of Political Economy,* vol. 1, pp. 79-80.

Thus, psychological hedonism was an assumption to men like Smith, Ricardo, and Senior. It was postulated that in their actions men endeavored to promote their own selfish gain. A series of philosophers from Hobbes to Bentham had stated the hedonistic principle of psychology and, at least in England, it seemed to be sufficiently well-established to be used as a basic postulate of economics, without much support being offered in the way of evidence. Another Classical assumption was that men and women reproduced their kind at the maximum rate permitted by the means of subsistence. On the basis of such assumptions, the Classical economic theories were formulated.

Senior, with wonted precision, recognized this characteristic of Classical thought:

the subject treated by the Political Economist . . . is not Happiness, but Wealth; his premises consist of a very few general propositions, the result of observation, or consciousness, and scarcely requiring proof, or even formal statement, which almost every man, as soon as he hears them, admits as familiar to his thoughts, or at least as included in his previous knowledge; and his inferences are nearly as general, and, if he has reasoned correctly, as certain, as his premises.[16]

These premises or assumptions Senior set forth as his "Four Elementary Propositions of the Science of Political Economy." They were as follows:

I. *That every man desires to obtain additional Wealth with as little sacrifice as possible.*
II. *That the Population of the World, or, in other words, the number of persons inhabiting it, is limited only by moral or physical evil, or by fear of a deficiency of those articles of wealth which the habits of the individuals of each class of its inhabitants lead them to require.*
III. *That the powers of Labour, and of other instruments which produce wealth, may be indefinitely increased by using their Products as the means of further Production.*
IV. *That, agricultural skill remaining the same, additional Labour employed on the land within a given district produces in general a less proportionate return, or, in other words, that though with every increase of the labour bestowed, the aggregate return is increased, the increase of the return is not in proportion to the increase of the labour.*[17]

The Classical writers realized that theories based on such assumptions had to conform with observed facts, so, having reached a conclusion by abstract argument, commonly they appealed to the facts to support it. The second edition of the *Essay on the Principle of Population*, published by Malthus, is a good example. The reasoning and conclusions of the second *Essay* were substantially the same as those reached in the first;

[16] *Political Economy*, pp. 2-3.
[17] *Ibid.*, p. 26.

but, whereas in the earlier edition little evidence had been presented, in the second a mass of data drawn from different parts of the world was submitted in support of the author's conclusions.

Both Adam Smith and John Stuart Mill made considerable use of historical material. Smith showed time after time how particular social arrangements affected production and distribution. For example, he said that the high profits that resulted from the Mercantilist restrictions on colonial trade discouraged production, while the "policy of Europe" (*i.e.*, internal regulation) prevented labor from finding its most advantageous employment. Like his contemporary Senior, John Stuart Mill believed that the Classical theories represented the final truths of production :

The laws and conditions of the production of wealth partake of the character of physical truths. There is nothing optional or arbitrary in them. Whatever mankind produce, must be produced in the modes, and under the conditions, imposed by the constitution of external things, and by the inherent properties of their own bodily and mental structure. Whether they like it or not, their productions will be limited by the amount of their previous accumulation, and, that being given, it will be proportional to their energy, their skill, the perfection of their machinery, and their judicious use of the advantages of combined labour. Whether they like it or not, a double quantity of labour will not raise, on the same land, a double quantity of food, unless some improvement takes place in the processes of cultivation. Whether they like it or not, the unproductive expenditure of individuals will *pro tanto* tend to impoverish the community, and only their productive expenditure will enrich it. The opinions, or the wishes, which may exist on these different matters, do not control the things themselves. We cannot, indeed, foresee to what extent the modes of production may be altered, or the productiveness of labour increased, by future extensions of our knowledge of the laws of nature, suggesting new processes of industry of which we have at present no conception. But howsoever we may succeed in making for ourselves more space within the limits set by the constitution of things, we know that there must be limits. We cannot alter the ultimate properties either of matter or mind, but can only employ those properties more or less successfully, to bring about the events in which we are interested.[18]

But Mill said that it was otherwise with distribution. This depended on the laws and customs of men. Mill's book on the subject might have come from a member of the Historical School, discussed below. Starting with two chapters on property and its influence on distribution, Mill considered successively distribution in societies where custom was a ruling factor, slavery, peasant proprietorship, metayage (share tenancy), etc., before dealing with the manner in which wages, profits, and rent were determined in the England of his time.

[18] *Principles of Political Economy*, Bk. 2, Chap. 1, Sect. 1.

J. S. Nicholson, who may be classed broadly as a follower of Mill, showed an outlook even more historical, drawing extensively on the material that was becoming available on English economic history, in the writings of Thorold Rogers and others. But Jevons, Walras, and Menger, with the rank and file of the Neo-Classical school, reverted to the abstractions of Classical economics. The work of Jevons on economic theory, for example, was every bit as abstract and hypothetical as that of Ricardo.[19]

Marshall seemed less sure of his economic laws, partly, no doubt, because of the influence that had been exercised on him by Mill, but also because of the activities of the Historical School in the meantime. At best, according to Marshall, the so-called economic laws were only tendencies:

> For the actions of men are so various and uncertain, that the best statement of tendencies, which we can make in a science of human conduct, must needs be inexact and faulty.[20]
>
> The term "law" means then nothing more than a general proposition or statement of tendencies, more or less certain, more or less definite.[21]

Yet Marshall evidently thought that some general tendencies of human action could be defined:

> The harder the task, the greater the need for steady patient inquiry; for turning to account the experience, that has been reaped by the more advanced physical sciences; and for framing as best we can well thought-out estimates, or provisional laws, of the tendencies of human action.[22]

Marshall admitted that provisional laws might require modification in the light of changes in circumstances:

> Though economic analysis and general reasoning are of wide application, yet every age and every country has its own problems; and every change in social conditions is likely to require a new development of economic doctrines.[23]

The Austrians were more emphatic than Marshall in asserting the permanence of fundamental laws of economics. Thus, Wieser, in his *Natural Value,* made it clear that he believed that his theory was grounded on such laws. The summary given of one of the chapters of this book read as follows:

> The plan of the present work: to find what, among our forms of value, would continue in a perfect or communist state, and so to find the permanent basis of all economic life.[24]

[19] Jevons's treatment of money and prices, however, was much more realistic.
[20] *Principles of Economics,* p. 32.
[21] *Ibid.,* p. 33. [22] *Ibid.,* pp. 32-33. [23] *Ibid.,* p. 37.
[24] *Natural Value,* summary of Bk. 2, Chap. 6, p. xxxix.

The spirit of a people is formed upon a set of received opinions relative to three objects; morals, government, and manners: these once generally adopted by any society, confirmed by long and constant habit, and never called in question, form the basis of all laws, regulate the form of every government, and determine what is commonly called the customs of a country.[30]

In every new step [of government] the spirit of the people should be first examined, and if that be not found ripe for the execution of the plan, it ought to be put off, kept entirely secret, and every method used to prepare the people to relish the innovation.[31]

After Steuart came Adam Smith and the British Classical School, giving economic study an entirely different direction. Not the whole of society, which to Montesquieu had been what mattered, but the economic side alone was the subject of their study. Where Montesquieu had investigated society historically, drawing examples from every stage of human history, the Classical economists inquired into the attributes of men as they were in England at their time. Yet, as has been seen, even the Classical economists were not a uniform group and some of them, notably Smith and John Stuart Mill, gave considerable attention to historical material. But it was left to the German Historical School, the sociologists led by the Frenchman, Auguste Comte (1798–1857), and a few scattered critics in England, to reassert the viewpoint of Montesquieu.

The German School and the Institutionalists

General development. Germany in the early years of the nineteenth century provided a philosophical environment for the development of economic doctrines very different from that which existed in Britain. The dominant British school was that of the hedonists, Hobbes, Locke, Hutcheson, Hume, and Bentham. According to the teachings of these men, individual self-interest was a ruling motive in society. There was no social objective other than the separate ends of the individuals who composed the society. The greatest social good was the maximum individual happiness. In this situation it was entirely logical for British economists to identify the wealth of the nation with the sum of individual riches and to make their professed science an art of wealth-seeking.

This outlook had little influence in Germany. In that country, the development of the leading school was through Kant and Fichte to Hegel and it was marked by a tendency to subordinate individual wants to social and especially national ends. If there were no individual objective other than the social one (and this was the ethical position of Hegel, as was shown in Chapter I), then it must savor of the nonsensical to endeavor to construct an economics based on individual self-seeking. What the German philosophy called for was a broader social or national economics,

[30] *Ibid.*, p. 10.
[31] *Ibid.*, pp. 14-15.

which would assist the nation to achieve *its* ends, that is, something more like Mercantilism or Cameralism than the individualistic economics which the Classical economists had developed in Britain.

Moreover, the Germans had been taught to look upon society as a changing thing—something that evolved as time went by. Hegel had described a process of mental advancement towards an ideal or final state of knowledge and had visualized the altering institutions of society as a reflection of this mental evolution. To a Hegelian, a society whose fundamentals stood still represented a negation of this idea of progress and was, indeed, an impossibility. Admittedly, all Germans did not embrace the theories of Hegel, but the broad social outlook and the concept of historical development, so pronounced in Hegelian thought, had a wide following. This fact influenced German views on law as well as on economics. There arose in Germany a school of legal writers, including Gustav von Hugo (1764–1844), F. K. von Savigny (1779–1861), and K. F. Eichhorn (1781–1854), who followed Montesquieu in relating legal ideas to their general social environment and in emphasizing the concept of evolution. It was this legal group that furnished the economist, Wilhelm Roscher (1817–1894), and his followers, with much of their inspiration.

The Germans delivered a triple challenge to British economics. They attacked its narrow and individualistic *scope,* seeking to substitute for Senior's specialized science of individual wealth a broader study that would bring out the interrelations of the various aspects of the social whole. Secondly, they criticized the *static nature* of the Classical postulates and the "laws" that were based on these assumptions. Thirdly, they objected to the *abstract method* of the Classical economists and endeavored to replace it by more realistic methods of approach.

Already something has been said about the views of Friedrich List, who can be regarded as an early exponent of the historical outlook. List opposed the attitude that identified social good with individual riches and was *cosmopolitan* because it broke down national ties in order that wealth might be maximized. Instead, he set up a *national* political economy. Not the riches of individuals but the welfare of the nation was what he had in mind, much as had been the case with the Mercantilists and Cameralists. The basic features of List's writings have been described in earlier chapters and need no detailed attention here. With respect to scope and method, they had two characteristics. (1) They related economic "laws" and ideas to their environment. Thus, List regarded free trade as reasonable enough for the England of Ricardo's time but unsuitable for contemporary Germany or America. Richard Jones, indeed, writing in the heyday of Classical economics in England, had made the same point with respect to the Ricardian theory of rent. He said that it was based on assumptions that were not universally

The first essay of Ruskin's *Unto this Last,* entitled "The Roots of Honour," brings out this point in a very effective manner:

Among the delusions which at different periods have possessed themselves of the minds of large masses of the human race, perhaps the most curious—certainly the least creditable—is the modern *soi-disant* science of political economy, based on the idea that an advantageous code of social action may be determined irrespective of the influence of social affection.

Of course, as in the instances of alchemy, astrology, witchcraft, and other such popular creeds, political economy has a plausible idea at the root of it. "The social affections," says the economist, "are accidental and disturbing elements in human nature; but avarice and the desire of progress are constant elements. Let us eliminate the inconstants, and, considering the human being merely as a covetous machine, examine by what laws of labour, purchase, and sale, the greatest accumulative result in wealth is obtainable. Those laws once determined, it will be for each individual afterwards to introduce as much of the disturbing affectionate element as he chooses, and to determine for himself the result of the new conditions supposed."

This would be a perfectly logical and successful method of analysis, if the accidentals afterwards to be introduced were of the same nature as the powers first examined. . . Observe, I neither impugn nor doubt the conclusion of the science if its terms are accepted. I am simply uninterested in them, as I should be in those of a science of gymnastics which assumed than men had no skeletons. It might be shown, on that supposition, that it would be advantageous to roll the students up into pellets, flatten them into cakes, or stretch them into cables; and that when these results were effected, the re-insertion of the skeleton would be attended with various inconveniences to their constitution. The reasoning might be admirable, the conclusions true, and the science deficient only in applicability. Modern political economy stands on a precisely similar basis. Assuming, not that the human being has no skeleton, but that it is all skeleton, it founds an ossifiant theory of progress on this negation of a soul; and having shown the utmost that may be made of bones, and constructed a number of interesting geometrical figures with death's head and humeri, successfully proves the inconvenience of the reappearance of a soul among these corpuscular structures. I do not deny the truth of this theory: I simply deny its applicability to the present phase of the world.[40]

In other words, the portion of man that the Classical economists had abstracted for special treatment had no separate existence. The economic man was a meaningless entity, in Ruskin's view. Man as a whole was the only human reality.

The statement that appears on the flyleaf of *The History of Economics,* by the Romanticist, Othmar Spann (1878–) of the University of Vienna, is intended to emphasize the same idea: "Political Economy is not a Science of Business but a Science of Life." The American Institutionalists, also, have followed this line. Not material wealth alone

[40] *The Works of John Ruskin,* vol. 17, pp. 25-26.

but life as a whole—though with special attention to the aspect of wealth—has been the object of their study. Veblen, for instance, in the subject matter of what purported to be economics included psychology (the instinct of workmanship), legal and institutional arrangements (the theory of business enterprise and the effects of absentee ownership), as well as social customs such as women's fashions (the theory of the leisure class), while J. R. Commons (1862–), in his *Legal Foundations of Capitalism* (New York 1924) and *Institutional Economics* (New York 1934) emphasized the relationship between legal ideas and economic affairs.

The evolutionary concept and the existence of laws of social development. Another important feature of the writings of members of the Historical School was the emphasis placed on the concept of social evolution. The idea was older than the school, having been found in the works of Montesquieu and Hegel as well in those of German legal writers.

The views of List and Jones have already been mentioned. Each of these men advanced the idea that economic actions and standards were related to the social environment; that is, they applied to one set of circumstances but not necessarily to another. Roscher made the same point:

> There can no more be an economic ideal adapted to the various wants of every people, than a garment which should fit every individual... Hence, whoever would elaborate the ideal of the best public economy—and the greater number of political economists have really wished to do this—should, if he would be perfectly true, and at the same time practical, place in juxta position as many different ideals as there are different types of people. He would, moreover, have to revise his work every few years; for, in proportion as a people change, and new wants originate, the economic ideal suitable to them must change also.[41]

The criticism of the Ricardian theory of international trade by the Englishman, Walter Bagehot (1826–1877) was along this line. Bagehot was a practical man, representing a West-Country firm of bankers in London as well as editing the London *Economist,* and he had little respect for the Classical abstractions. In a series of essays entitled *The Postulates of English Political Economy,* begun in the *Fortnightly Review* in 1876 and included in the book, *Economic Studies* (London 1880), Bagehot examined two of the chief assumptions of the Classical School, namely the transferability of labor and that of capital. Both were utilized in the Classical theories of value, rent, and international trade. But Bagehot pointed out that the conditions upon which they were based were already passing away. Economic theories were relative, therefore,

[41] *Principles of Political Economy,* vol. I, p. 110.

tionalists have carried their activities in this direction so far that they have come to be looked upon as statisticians rather than as economists or sociologists. There seems no end to the volume of information that is being accumulated in this way. Perhaps the difference between the Classical and the Neo-Classical approach, on the one hand, and that of the Institutionalists, on the other, will be appreciated if a comparison be made between some of the Neo-Classical writings on the subject of the business cycle, such as Hayek's *Prices and Production,* and the Institutionalist W. C. Mitchell's *Business Cycles.* Abstract arguments, aided by diagrams and, in some books, by mathematical formulae, leading to an explanatory theory, are presented in the former case. The latter gives an enormous quantity of statistical data but deals with theories in true Institutionalist manner, by neatly classifying the principal explanations and leaving it at that!

Assessment

What is the ordinary person to conclude with respect of this fundamental conflict? In the first place, it must be conceded that society is complex and that more than economic factors are concerned in its nature and development. From this it follows that the specialized economist—whose knowledge on the non-economic aspects is likely to be meager—cannot hope to do more than offer comments that will enable practical people (who have at their hands the statements of experts in other fields) to reach decisions on policy. However defensible this may be theoretically, it is not very satisfactory in practice. The man-in-the-street or the politician, when faced with a practical problem, such as unemployment, is not interested in a mass of scientific terminology, containing so many qualifications that he cannot make head or tail of it, and which has to be put alongside similar statements from other scientists before it can be of any use at all. He wants advice and he wants it quickly. It need be no matter for surprise, therefore, that Historical economists and Institutionalists—who give a wide scope to their study and claim competence to give advice—have been popular in government circles. Society bristles with problems to be solved, or politicians think that it does, with the result that there is a heavy demand for trained young men who are prepared to help in their solution. Statistical bureaus grow up on all sides and those theorists are at a discount, whose view on their subject is that it leaves them incompetent to furnish advice. Yet in truth it must be asked frequently whether all the work that is being done would be needed if there were somewhat less urge to rush into investigation and a little more willingness to think beforehand.

Against the Historical and Institutional writers, it must be pointed out that the range of social knowledge is so great nowadays that no man can hope to master it in any detail: Senior said this as much as a century ago. There have been outstanding examples of men who have proved themselves capable of achieving distinction in more than one of the social sciences, it is true. Pareto, for instance, one of the most prominent of the Neo-Classical economists, produced an important work on general sociology. But such cases are not general. Names like those of Hume and Adam Smith—to say nothing of Aristotle and Hobbes—call to mind the possibility that knowledge could be broader and more diversified when less information was available on each subject. But the progress of science has been in the direction of intensification and specialization.

Even if the possibility be rejected, of ordinary individuals acquiring a knowledge of the various facets of society sufficiently comprehensive to qualify them to give advice on practical matters, it appears necessary to admit that the specialist must possess at least an elementary acquaintance with thought in fields related to his own. The argument of the Historical School and of Comte, that society can be understood only as a whole, seems to contain a good deal of truth and this belief helps to explain the nature of the present volume.

On the subject of method, it can be said that the Historical criticism has had the effect of stimulating the use of realistic data, so that many economists of recent years can be classified as eclectics, remaining free from formal allegiance and using whatever methods appear appropriate to the problem in hand. In this group may be placed men like J. S. Nicholson, who—though in some respects a close follower of Mill—drew heavily on historical materials, N. G. Pierson, and a long list of other writers. Even Marshall himself—often looked upon as the *doyen* of the Neo-Classical school—went a long way towards assuming this position. It must be borne in mind that the difference between the Classical and the Historical viewpoints on the subject of method is not so marked in reality as may at first appear. The Classical postulates, like selfishness and diminishing returns, purported to be based on observations and experience, if not on measurable data of the kind favored by statisticians. As the quantity of accurate information grew, with the progress of economic history and of statistical inquiry, men like Pierson incorporated it along with the Classical theories in their published treatises. But a fundamental difficulty remained. What historians could recount, and contemporary statisticians could measure, was not an independent economic facet of life but social life as a whole. However complete and accurate were the data available, it was often a serious task—if not indeed an impossibility—to identify the economic components. Mathematicians developed a partial solution in multiple correlation analysis, whereby linkages between quantitative data, on the one hand, and sets of factors, on the other, could be calculated. But it is one matter to bring to light a linkage or correlation and quite another to interpret it. Moreover, often it is clear that the number of factors that are possibly causal is too great for mathematical methods to yield significant results. So practical investigators are driven back on abstract theorizing and the sharp division between the Classical economists and their realistic critics gives place to something that can be likened to the edge of a vignette, where black and white shade into each other by imperceptible gradations.

It may be worth while glancing backwards at Senior's four propositions to see how many of them have stood the test of time. Arguments respecting the reality of non-commercial incentives notwithstanding, it is still true that self-interest is an important factor in human conduct—though, by the time governments have got men thoroughly planned, perhaps what the politicians consider to be the social interest will be accepted by individuals as their own selfish concern. The existence of a tendency towards diminishing returns, when a scarce factor of production is used intensively, is not questioned; and scarce factors are still a phenomenon of social life. Whatever Keynes thinks may occur in the future, it is still the case that the productive powers of labor can be increased by the use of additional capital. Three of Senior's fundamental postulates stand, therefore. But not so the fourth proposition (placed second on Senior's own list). Instead of its being correct to assume that people will multiply as fast as their resources permit, fears are expressed that soon there will be a shortage of population, while agriculture contracts for lack of demand for its produce.

There is nothing sacred about Senior's list, of course. No doubt each of the Classical writers could have prepared a somewhat different one. Adam Smith, for instance, mentioned a natural tendency for men to barter and exchange one thing for another. Some present-day economists feel just as Senior did, that men will always be selfish : others are not certain. Wieser and Cassel have been emphatic in declaring that scarcity is a permanent condition, making this factor, as it were, a "fundamental proposition." But, after all, scarcity as it is known rests on intensity of wants as well as limitation of resources. If population declines, might not a simple economy of the type More's *Utopia* offer the possibility that human desires can be satisfied with only that labor which people undertake for exercise and enjoyment? It must be remembered that even Adam Smith doubted that luxury conferred any real enjoyment. Perhaps, when people get better educated, wants will cease to show their old expansibility.

Recent years have witnessed a powerful resurgence of national economics. Developing gradually, but greatly intensified after the war of 1914–1918 and especially since 1930, what has been called "the new Mercantilism" has arisen. This has been justified partly on individualistic grounds—the individual is said to find it more economic to achieve his ends through government action than by relying on his private resources—but partly there is a Platonic or Hegelian conception that the State is in some way supreme over the individual. National economics—by which is meant the elaboration of means to achieve national ends, as distinct from the individualistic economics of Smith and Jevons—has come to the fore.

From time to time, economists, becoming alarmed at the extent of social change, ask what is to happen to their subject in the future. Obviously, if economics is regarded as a science of means to achieve *any given ends,* and the ends are altered, then new means must be devised to meet the situation. This has been happening with the increased emphasis on nationalism and collective action in recent years. But if productive factors cease to be scarce, then any need for economic study disappears. As has been said, this possibility cannot be excluded altogether but, as far as can be seen at present, it is remote, to say the least. On the other hand, if economics studies the means to satisfy *one given end,* that of individual riches, it faces the possibility of declension should some other end be preferred. This, in a way, is what takes place in war-time. A distinguished economist said in the hearing of the writer of this book that, when war is declared, economic principles are abolished and costs cease to matter. Evidently, what has occurred is that a new objective has assumed significance, namely that of winning the war. In the light of this newly-acquired aim, costs are thought to be worth incurring that were considered unjustifiable when the end was wealth-seeking.

Summary of Chapter

The major shifts of emphasis in economic discussion are largely explained by alterations in men's views respecting ultimate objectives. Ideals like happiness and right living interested the ancient philosophers. The early Christian teachers were concerned with the will of God and the attainment of the soul's salvation. The professed end of the Mercantilists was the good of the State. Classical economists accepted the maximization of individual riches as their aim. The economic writings of the several groups are understandable in the light of these differences. The Germans gave their economics a scope less individualistic and more national than was the case with the British school but, even in those countries where the ideas of the latter have predominated, recent years have witnessed a trend in the direction of social or national economics.

A sharp difference of opinion has appeared in regard to the subject matter of economics. Where the British Classical economists endeavored to study wealth-seeking alone, apart from other angles of life, some other writers have refused to admit the possibility of thus disentangling one facet of life from the whole. Men's motives and actions are too intimately connected with each other to be understood independently, they have said. The German Historical School, the general body of sociologists, and the American Institutionalists, have adopted this attitude.

While the Classical economists built up their science by logical reasoning from stated assumptions, the Historical School and the Institutionalists have employed the realistic method of study, examining historical data and investigating statistics. Obviously, such material represents the process of social life as a whole and it is not always possible to identify the specifically economic ingredient. So the realistic inquirer often falls back on abstract reasoning. On the other hand, the growth of quantitative data makes it possible for Classical assumptions to be reinforced by historical or statistical information, and the dividing line between the two schools becomes less clearly cut.

RETROSPECT

In concluding this study of the development of economic ideas, it may be well to summarize some of the points that have emerged.

In the first place, it is apparent that few beliefs have been widely held without some reason for them, either in the circumstances in which they appeared or the objectives that were sought by the men and women who held them. It might have been sensible enough to justify the payment of interest on loans in the nineteenth century and yet not altogether foolish to prohibit it in the ninth. When Tertullian counseled the early Christians to be content to consume the goods with which Providence had seen fit to endow their home country, rather than import foreign commodities, or when Mun supported a similar policy fourteen hundred years later, the positions they took up were as defensible as was that of Adam Smith on the side of free imports in the eighteenth century. Tertullian subordinated individual riches to the good of the soul, Mun placed them below national self-reliance, and Adam Smith's arguments were irrelevant with respect to the positions occupied by the earlier writers.

Another lesson is the antiquity of many ideas that seem novel to the present generation. State dominance and authoritarian control of social life were characteristic of ancient Egypt and still fondly regarded, though of diminishing significance, in early Greece. These ideas experienced a resurgence in the sixteenth and seventeenth centuries, only to fall into the background again. The "fair return" of modern court decisions had an earlier counterpart in the "just price" of the middle ages. Adam Smith made remarks concerning monopoly similar to those which come from present-day critics of big business. Veblen's biting attack on conspicuous consumption standards was anticipated by Smith and others. As society progresses, men seem to have few important ideas or experiences that are really new, but they have many repetitions and developments of old thoughts and old experiences. Undoubtedly, adventures in thought and practice are often embarked upon, and even executed, without any realization that they are not new. It speaks much for human capacity that problems can be tackled from the beginning and with success, again and again. The first voyage of Columbus across the Atlantic was no less an epic because a few intrepid Norse seamen had gone before his ships. But undoubtedly had the Genoese sailor known what was on the other side of the western ocean his project would have been facilitated. Probably, to most people, this is the chief reason for studying history. A well-known American teacher of economics is said to have remarked, in reply to a criticism that he wrote nothing, that he would publish a new idea when he came across one. He spent his life without doing so. This point of view may represent exaggeration but it has some justification. Yet few tasks can be more serviceable than that of resurrecting a forgotten truth, or of popularizing a useful idea that hitherto has remained obscure.

BIBLIOGRAPHY

In addition to the works referred to on special points in the various chapters, those listed below will be found of value.

Works of Reference

The general encyclopædias and biographical dictionaries contain contributions on many of the individuals and subjects dealt with in the text. The following publications may be consulted also :

Encyclopaedia of the Social Sciences, edited by E. R. A. Seligman, 15 vols., New York 1930–1935. Re-issued, 8 vols., 1937.

Palgrave's Dictionary of Political Economy, edited by H. Higgs, 3 vols., 2nd edition, London 1923–1926.

Palgrave's Dictionary gives more detail on economic topics but the articles in the larger work are useful in relating economics to the general social background. The first edition of Palgrave appeared in 1894–1899 and the material it contained was reprinted without revision in the later issue, more recent matter being added at the end of each of the volumes.

General Works on the History of Economic Thought

Bonar, J., *Philosophy and Political Economy,* 3rd edition, London 1922.

Describes the ideas of the leading philosophers from ancient times onwards, so far as these are of interest to the student of economics. The material is condensed and readers who have made no study of the originals often find it difficult to follow, but it contains much that is not elsewhere available in a concise form.

Cannan, E., *A Review of Economic Theory,* London 1929.

One of the few general books to employ the ideological approach. It is based on the author's lectures in the University of London but is quite inadequate outside English Classical (and to some extent Neo-Classical) thought. Within its limited field, however, it is excellent.

Gide, C. and Rist, C., *A History of Economic Doctrines,* translated by R. Richards, London and Boston 1915.

Begins with the Physiocrats and ends, for all practical purposes, in the late nineteenth century. Written in France, it pays more attention to French thought than is the case with most of the other books mentioned, the treatment of the French socialists being particularly valuable. The writing is clear and interesting.

Gray, A., *The Development of Economic Doctrine,* London 1933.

Though its period stretches from the ancient Greeks to the Neo-Classical School, this book is short and deals only with a small number of writers. Some sections are very useful – those on Lauderdale and Rae, for example – and many students welcome the vein of humor which is introduced.

Haney, L. H., *History of Economic Thought,* 3rd edition, New York 1936.
Carries the history of economic thought from the ancient world into the twentieth century and contains a large amount of information. The treatment of recent writings is sketchy.

Ingram, J. K., *A History of Political Economy,* new edition with supplementary chapter by W. A. Scott, London and New York 1915.
One of the earlier works in the field and, in its original form, did not pass beyond the German Historical School. The supplementary chapter deals with Neo-Classical and other recent writings. Ingram was a British adherent of the Historical School and the book is worth consulting for the views of this school.

Roll, E., *A History of Economic Thought,* London 1938, New York 1939.
A brief survey, containing—among other things—a sympathetic and rather detailed section on the theories of Karl Marx.

Scott, W. A., *The Development of Economics,* New York 1933.
Deals principally with Classical and Neo-Classical economics, especially from the standpoint of the Austrians.

Spann, O., *The History of Economics* (London edition, *Types of Economic Theory*), translated by E. and C. Paul, London and New York 1930.
The author of this book has strong sympathies with the Romanticist position and the section on Adam Müller is of particular interest. Where Spann's enthusiasm is not aroused, however, the treatment is sometimes brief and unsatisfactory.

Suranyi-Unger, T., *Economics in the Twentieth Century,* translated by N. D. Moulton, New York 1931.
Notwithstanding its title, this book reaches back to the nineteenth century and beyond. It pays attention to some of the relations between economic thought and philosophy, and is useful in putting the English-speaking student in touch with Continental ideas. But the author's tendency to appraise briefly a large number of writers—many of whom are unimportant—is a serious defect, as is the arrangements of references.

Specialized Literature

Angell, J. W., *The Theory of International Prices,* Cambridge, Mass. 1926.
Deals at length with the history of theories of money and foreign trade, from the Mercantilists to recent years. Is clear and useful.

Beer, M., *Early British Economics,* London 1938.
Covers the period from the middle ages to 1750 and gives useful information on some writers who have been neglected in the more comprehensive histories on economic thought, for example, Alexander of Hales and John Duns Scotus. Introduces some unusual definitions—Child, for instance, is classified as anti-Mercantilist—but it is very suggestive and may be read with profit.

Beer, M., *A History of British Socialism,* new edition, 2 vols., London 1929.
A detailed study, standard in its field.

Böhm-Bawerk, E. von, *Capital and Interest,* translated by W. Smart, London 1890.

A critique of the theories of capital and interest that had been advanced before its author's own positive contribution was made. Gives information about many Continental writers whose works are not available in English, as well as the interest theories that are better known to English readers.

Böhm-Bawerk, E. von, *Karl Marx and the Close of his System,* translated by A. M. Macdonald, New York 1898.

An attack upon the Marxian theory.

Böhm-Bawerk, E. von, *Recent Literature on Interest (1884–1899),* translated by W. A. Scott and S. Feilbogen, New York 1903.

Deals with some of the theories advanced during Böhm-Bawerk's lifetime.

Bonar, J., *Theories of Population from Raleigh to Arthur Young,* London 1931.

Gives an account of some of the less well-known population theories of the seventeenth and eighteenth centuries, the work of Harrington, Graunt, Petty, Halley, Süssmilch, Hume, and Price being dealt with, besides that of the writers mentioned in the title.

Cannan, E., *A History of the Theories of Production and Distribution in English Political Economy, from 1776 to 1848,* 3rd edition, London 1917.

As its title indicates, this book deals only with the Classical period in England. Within its limits, it is very thorough, though its author is open to the charge of being hypercritical.

Commons, J. R., *Institutional Economics,* New York 1934.

Contains considerable material interpretative of the history of economic thought from the time of John Locke. Special emphasis is placed on law and the book is itself an important representative of Institutional literature. It is not easy reading.

Davenport, H. J., *Value and Distribution,* Chicago 1908.

A critique of Classical and Neo-Classical theories of value and distribution by a writer whose own position has been indicated in the text.

Dickinson, Z. C., *Economic Motives,* Cambridge, Mass. 1922.

The early portion of this book gives an account of psychological theories on the subject of human incentive from the time of Aristotle.

Douglas, P. H., *The Theory of Wages,* New York 1934.

Contains chapters that include material on the history of theories of population, wages, and interest.

Ellis, H. S., *German Monetary Theory, 1905–1933,* Cambridge, Mass. 1934.

Though mainly concerned with writers outside the scope of the foregoing chapters, certain portions of this book are serviceable to the student, notably those dealing with Knapp and Wicksell, and with business cycle theories.

Gierke, O. von, *Political Theories of the Middle Ages,* translated by F. W. Maitland, Cambridge 1900, and *Natural Law and the Theory of Society 1500 to 1800,* translated by E. Barker, 2 vols., Cambridge 1934.

Describe the development of ideas on natural law and natural right from the middle ages, covering many teachers and writers whose works are not available in English. The volumes are detailed and documented but it has to be remembered that Gierke held strong views of his own.

Heckscher, E. F., *Mercantilism*, translated by M. Shapiro, 2 vols., London 1935.

Very informative on Mercantilist thought and practice in Britain and on the continent of Europe, though Heckscher's conclusions can be questioned.

Higgs, H., *The Physiocrats*, London 1897.

Gives a short but good critique of the ideas of the Physiocratic school.

Homan, P. T., *Contemporary Economic Thought*, New York 1928.

Deals with the contributions made by a number of leading modern economists, of the last generation as well as the present one. The sections on J. B. Clark and Alfred Marshall are worth consulting on the Neo-Classical School, those on Thorstein Veblen and W. C. Mitchell on Institutionalism.

Johnson, E. A. J., *Predecessors of Adam Smith: the growth of British economic thought*, New York 1937.

An invaluable source of information on the views of such men as Petty and Steuart, as well as less-known writers.

Keynes, J. N., *The Scope and Method of Political Economy*, 3rd edition, London 1904.

This is still probably the best work on its subject and should be referred to for the controversy between the Classical and Historical Schools, discussed in Chapter XVI of the text.

Laidler, H. W., *A History of Socialist Thought*, New York 1927.

A useful account of some of the more important socialist writers and their theories. Carries the story from the *Republic* of Plato down to the present time and includes portraits of a number of men well known in socialist history.

Laughlin, J. L., *The Principles of Money*, New York 1903.

Contains a chapter on the history and literature of the quantity theory of money, but Laughlin's opposition to this theory has to be borne in mind.

Macfarlane, C. W., *Value and Distribution*, 2nd edition, Philadelphia 1911.

Includes a criticism of theories of value, rent, interest, wages, and profits from Adam Smith to the Austrians. The writing is not detailed, but the book brings out some of the main points and affords a useful introduction to its field.

Menger, A., *The Right to the Whole Produce of Labour*, translated by M. E. Tanner, London 1899.

Foxwell's introduction to the English edition and Menger's own work are valuable in studying socialist thought on this subject.

Mitchell, W. C., *Business Cycles, The Problem and Its Setting*, New York 1927.

Chapter I summarizes and classifies the various theories of the business cycle, though the approach is not historical.

Monroe, A. E., *Monetary Theory before Adam Smith,* Cambridge, Mass. 1923.

A critical study of the monetary literature of western Europe, covering the period from ancient Greece to the eighteenth century. The treatment of writers and ideas is often brief, but the book is worth attention.

O'Brien, G., *An Essay on Medieval Economic Teaching,* London 1920, and *An Essay on the Economic Effects of the Reformation,* London 1923.

Both exceedingly useful but the favorable attitude taken up by the author respecting Catholic thought has to be kept in mind.

Robbins, L., *An Essay on the Nature and Significance of Economic Science,* 2nd edition, London 1935.

A forceful modern statement of the Neo-Classical viewpoint.

Robertson, H. M., *Aspects of the Rise of Economic Individualism,* Cambridge 1933.

Opposes the thesis of Max Weber, respecting the relation of Protestantism to the rise of capitalism.

Schmoller, G. von, *The Mercantile System and Its Historical Significance,* translation, New York 1895.

Brief but expresses an important point of view.

Seligman, E. R. A., *The Economic Interpretation of History,* 2nd edition, New York 1917.

Criticizes the Marxian theory.

Small, A. W., *The Cameralists,* Chicago 1909.

Deals with a group of German writers whose works are not available in English.

Taussig, F. W., *Wages and Capital,* New York 1896.

Gives a detailed account of the development of the wages fund theory as well as Taussig's own contribution.

Tawney, R. H., *Religion and the Rise of Capitalism,* London 1926.

Not unfavorable to the Weber thesis, but cites other factors.

Troeltsch, E., *The Social Teaching of the Christian Churches,* translated by O. Wyon, 2 vols., New York 1931.

A translation of an important German work. The first volume covers the early and medieval Church, the second deals with Protestantism. The portions on subjects of interest to the student of economics can be identified from the list of contents, without much difficulty, and are well worth reading.

Veblen, T., *The Place of Science in Modern Civilization,* New York 1919.

Sharply critical of the central theories of Classical and Neo-Classical economics. The essays on *The Preconceptions of Economic Science* and *The Limitations of Marginal Utility* are especially worth perusal.

Viner, J., *Studies in the Theory of International Trade,* New York 1937.

The first portion of this book gives a very detailed account of theories of money (including banking) and foreign exchange from the mercantile period onwards.

Vinogradoff, Sir P., *Outlines of Historical Jurisprudence,* 2 vols., Oxford 1920–1922.

The second volume deals with law in early Greece and Rome. Though written from the standpoint of the legal historian, some portions are of interest to the student of economic thought.

Weber, M., *The Protestant Ethic and the Spirit of Capitalism,* translated by T. Parsons, London 1930.

Weber's full statement, which has been summarized in the text, is too important to be ignored.

Westermarck, E. A., *The Origin and Development of the Moral Ideas,* 2nd edition, 2 vols., London 1912–1917.

Though its approach is anthropological and it does not take account of recent work, some sections of this book will be found of interest by students of economics.

Whitaker, A. C., *History and Criticism of the Labor Theory of Value in English Political Economy,* New York 1904.

Useful in its limited field.

Selections of Readings

Books containing extracts from the great classics of economic thought are of value in small libraries and where the originals have not been translated in full.

Monroe, A. E., *Early Economic Thought,* Cambridge, Mass. 1924.

In addition to portions of other writings, this book contains selections from some works that have not been translated elsewhere, including that of Dumoulin (Molinæus) on usury, Bodin's statement of the quantity theory of money, and the writings of Hornigk and Justi.

Patterson, S. H., *Readings in the History of Economic Thought,* New York 1922.

Includes a number of extracts from economic classics covering the period from Mandeville and Hutcheson to Böhm-Bawerk.

Books on the Historical Background

Ashley, Sir W. J., *An Introduction to English Economic History and Theory,* 2 vols., 4th edition, London 1906–1909.

A pioneer study of the economic history of England from the eleventh to the sixteenth century. Some chapters are invaluable to the student of the evolution of economic ideas, notably the last section of volume 1, on "Economic Theories and Legislation" and the concluding chapter of volume 2, on "The Canonist Doctrine."

Ashley, Sir W. J., and Allen, G. C., *The Economic Organisation of England,* London 1935.

Shorter than the other general histories mentioned, but useful as a background study to those who possess no previous training in social history, especially where lack of time precludes more extensive reading in the field.

Barnes, H. E., *An Economic History of the Western World,* New York 1937.

Written from the Institutional viewpoint and critical of private capitalism, this book mentions some movements not dealt with in more conventional histories, such as social credit and Technocracy.

Beard, C. A. and M., *Rise of American Civilization,* 3 vols.; vols. 1 and 2, New York 1927 (re-issued in 1 vol., 1933); vol. 3, New York, 1939.

An interesting survey of social development in the United States, reformist in approach.

Birnie, A., *An Economic History of Europe, 1760–1930,* London and New York 1930.

Valuable on labor and social reform.

Condliffe, J. B., *New Zealand in the Making,* London and Chicago 1930.

May be consulted for its accounts of government control of labor relations and land tenure in New Zealand.

Cunningham, W., *The Growth of English Industry and Commerce,* 5th edition, 3 vols., London 1910–1912.

A pioneer work and now in some respects out of date but it contains informative sections on the relationship between economic thought and its practical background, especially in medieval and Mercantile times.

Cunningham, W., *Western Civilisation in Its Economic Aspects,* 2 vols., Cambridge 1898–1900.

Brief and somewhat out of date, but volume 1 is worth reading to gain acquaintance with the environment in which the social ideas of the ancient world were formulated.

Feavearyear, A. E., *The Pound Sterling,* Oxford 1931.

An excellent history of English money, paying attention to some of the matters discussed in Chapter XIV.

Lipson, E., *The Economic History of England,* 3 vols.; vol. 1, 7th edition, London 1937, vols. 2 and 3, London 1931.

Covers the period to about 1700. Is detailed and authoritative, but in the main records events and does not study the interrelations of ideas and practice as did the older works of Ashley and Cunningham. The first chapter of volume 3, however, is a useful aid in studying Mercantilism.

Nussbaum, F. L., *A History of the Economic Institutions of Modern Europe,* New York 1933.

Based on the great German work, Sombart's *Der moderne Kapitalismus,* and centers round the rise of modern capitalistic institutions. Having regard to its scope, it is short, easy to read, and very suggestive.

Pirenne, H., *Economic and Social History of Medieval Europe,* translated by I. E. Clegg, London 1936 and New York 1937.

A stimulating work by a leading French scholar.

Shann, E., *An Economic History of Australia,* Cambridge 1930.

Australian experiences with respect to State intervention in the fields of labor and the tariff are of interest. They are outlined in this book.

Thompson, J. W., *Economic and Social History of the Middle Ages*, New York 1928, and *Economic and Social History of the Later Middle Ages*, New York 1931.

The most comprehensive work in English on the social history of medieval Europe. Some chapters, especially those on the Church, are of service to the student of economic thought.

Weber, M., *General Economic History*, translated by F. H. Knight, New York 1927.

Notwithstanding the special position of its author, as indicated in the text, this is a very useful survey of European social history.

Zimmern, A. E., *The Greek Commonwealth*, 5th edition, Oxford 1924.

An interesting and illuminating description of ancient Greek life.

INDEX

Where an individual is referred to on more than one page in the book, *p* indicates the page or pages on which personal information appears.

C